D1276864

Student's Guide to Congress

Student's Guides to the U.S. Government Series

Volume 1: Student's Guide to **Elections**

Volume 2: Student's Guide to **Congress**

Volume 3: Student's Guide to **the Presidency**

Volume 4: Student's Guide to **the Supreme Court**

Student's Guide to Congress

Advisory Editor

Bruce J. Schulman, Ph.D.

Boston University

CQ Press

A Division of SAGE

Washington, D.C.

Developed, Designed, and Produced by

DWJ BOOKS LLC

CQ Press
2300 N Street, NW, Suite 800
Washington, DC 20037

Phone: 202-729-1900; toll free, 1-866-4CQ-PRESS (1-866-427-7737)

Web: www.cqpress.com

Cover design: Matthew Simmons/www.MyselfIncluded.com

Photo acknowledgments for the Primary Source Library: Library of Congress: pp. 317, 335, 336; Courtesy Harry S. Truman Presidential Library: p. 339; AP Photo, Charlie Neibergall: p. 356.

♾ The paper used in this publication exceeds the requirements of the American National Standard for Information Sciences–Permanence of Paper for Printer Library Materials, ANSI Z39.48-1992.

Printed and bound in the United States of America

12 11 10 09 08 1 2 3 4 5

Library of Congress Cataloging-in-Publication Data

Student's guide to Congress.
p. cm – (Student's guide to U.S. government; v. 2)
Includes bibliographical references and index.
ISBN 978-0-87289-554-6 1. United Sates. Congress.

JK1021.S79 2008
328.73–dc22 2008028980

CONTENTS

Part Three: PRIMARY SOURCE LIBRARY

List of Illustrations

Charts/Graphs

Tables

Maps

Photos

Reader's Guide

The list that follows is provided as an aid to readers in locating articles on related topics. The Reader's Guide arranges all of the A–Z entries in the Guide according to these 9 key concepts of the curriculum in American Government: Congressional Benefits, Congressional Leadership, Congressional Procedures, Elections and Constituents, Constitutional Amendments, Origins of Congress, Powers of Congress, Principles of Government, and Seat of Government. Some articles appear in more than one category.

House of Representatives
How a Bill Becomes a Law
Impeachment Power
Joint Committees
Joint Session
Judicial Review
Legislative Process
Legislative Reorganization Act (1946)
Non-Voting Members of Congress
Mace
Oath of Office, Congressional
Parliamentarian
Powers of Congress
President and Congress
Senate
Senatorial Courtesy
Seniority System
Sergeant at Arms
Sessions of Congress
Spoils System
Two-Thirds Rule
Vetoes and Veto Overrides
Vice President

Elections and Constituents

African Americans in Congress
Amending the Constitution
Asian Americans in Congress
Campaign Finance
Civil Rights Issues and Lobbyists
Classes of Senators
Constituents and Congress
Elections, House of Representatives
Elections, Senate
Electoral College and Electors
Exclusion of Members of Congress
Iraq War Resolution (2002)
Lobbying and Congress
Media and Congress
Midterm Elections
Oath of Office, Congressional
Political Parties and Congress
Public Interest Groups
Women in Congress

Constitutional Amendments

Amending the Constitution
Bill of Rights
Constitution of the United States
Constitutional Amendments Affecting the Presidency
Line-Item Veto
Nineteenth Amendment (1920)
Seventeenth Amendment (1913)

Origins of Congress

Albany Plan of Union
Articles of Confederation
Bicameralism
Classes of Senators
Congress, Constitutional Origins of
Connecticut Compromise
Constitution of the United States
Constitutional Convention
Continental Congresses
Declaration of Independence
Federalism
Federalist, The
House of Representatives
New Jersey Plan
Rules, House and Senate
Senate
Thirteen Colonies, Settling of the
Virginia Plan

Powers of Congress

Ad-hoc Committees
Amending the Constitution
Appropriations Bills
Army-McCarthy Hearings
Bills, Private
Bipartisanship
Calendars, House of Representatives
Calendars, Senate
Campaign Finance
Caucuses
Censure
Checks and Balances
Civil Rights Act (1964)
Cloakroom
Cloture
Commerce Clause
Committees
Conference Committees
Confirmation Power of the Senate
Congress and Commerce
Congressional Immunity
Congressional Investigations

Principles of Government

Seat of Government

About the Advisory Editor

Bruce J. Schulman is The William E. Huntington professor of History at Boston University, a position he has held since 2007. Dr. Schulman has also served as the Director of the American and New England Studies Program at Boston University. Prior to moving to Boston University, Dr. Schulman was associate professor of History at the University of California, Los Angeles. Dr. Schulman received his Ph.D. and M.A. from Stanford University; he received his B.A., Summa Cum Laude with Distinction in history from Yale University.

Since the 1980s, Dr. Schulman has been teaching and writing about the political face of the United States. He has taken an active role in education at the high school level as well as serving as the Principal Investigator for the Teaching American History Grant program with the Boston Public Schools. He also worked with the History Alive program, a curriculum-based interactive instructional program. In addition, Dr. Schulman served as director of The History Project in California, a joint effort of the University of California and the California State Department of Education to improve history education in the public primary and secondary schools.

Dr. Schulman is the author of several award-winning and notable books that combine his interest in history and politics. Among them are: *From Cotton Belt to Sunbelt: Federal Policy, Economic Development, and the Transformation of the South, 1938–1980; Lyndon B. Johnson and American Liberalism; The Seventies: The Great Shift in American Culture, Politics, and Society;* and *Rightward Bound: Making America Conservative in the 1970s* (co-edited with Julian Zelizer). Dr. Schulman's published books and numerous essays have examined and scrutinized the fabric of America's political and socioeconomic life and its direct impact on today's citizens.

PREFACE

As British Prime Minister Winston Churchill once remarked, "It has been said that democracy is the worst form of government except for all those others that have been tried." In CQ Press's new series, *Student's Guides to the U.S. Government,* librarians, educators, students, and other researchers will find essential resources for understanding the strange wonder, alternately inspiring and frustrating, that is American democracy.

In the *Student's Guide to Congress,* the second volume in the *Student's Guides* series, both young and experienced researchers, especially students and teachers, will find all they need to know about America's national legislature–the constitutional provisions and legal procedures, the pivotal campaigns and influential committees, the tactics and strategies, the path-breaking laws, the key players, and the dramatic controversies–the pure pageantry of Congressional politics. The largest and most democratic branch of the federal government, Congress has long drawn critical scrutiny from Americans painfully aware of the institution's weaknesses. "Suppose you are an idiot. And suppose you are a member of Congress," nineteenth-century American author Mark Twain once wryly commented, going on to say, "but I repeat myself." Still, partisans of democracy the world over have also hailed Congress as the world's greatest deliberative body–a place where representatives of a diverse and fractious people can peacefully iron out their differences. The *Student's Guide to Congress* unravels the historical development of American Congress–the ways it has changed over the past two-and-a-half centuries as well as its current status–unlocking the mysteries surrounding such contemporary issues as campaign finance reform, the line item veto, and the powers to make war and conclude treaties.

Each of the three parts of the *Student's Guide to Congress* takes a unique approach to enhancing users' understanding of the national legislature. Part One features three essays, each of which addresses a provocative question about the American Congress: "Members of Congress: Who Gets Elected? Who Elects Them?"; "The Way Congress Works: How Does an Idea Become a Law?"; and "Who Is Running America–Congress Or the President?"

Part Two features 142 A–Z entries covering everything from "Abscam"–the sting operation featuring FBI agents disguised as Arab oil sheiks which brought down several corrupt members of Congress–to "Zone Whips." Entries address the major Congressional committees, leadership positions and institutions, the ways in which members of Congress are elected and what sorts of Americans have held seats, and numerous aspects of the legislative process, including filibusters and cloture, House-Senate conferences, impeachment proceedings, veto overrides, and much more. Special features within Part Two abound: "Point/Counterpoint" highlights opposing views on the same issue using primary evidence and concludes with a thought-provoking "Document-Based Question." "Spotlight" focuses on unique situations and events. "Decision Makers" takes a closer look at notable individuals, and "Justice for All," in this Congress volume, examines important legal and ethical dilemmas.

Part Three contains a "Primary Source Library" of key documents, photos, and political cartoons that are essential to understanding the history of the American Congress. These documents complement the information highlighted in both the essays in Part One and the A–Z entries in Part Two. Part Three also includes guidelines for using the Primary Source Library and for general research. The guidelines offer direction on Researching with Primary and Secondary Sources, Developing Research Questions, Identifying Sources of Information, Planning and Organizing research for use in a paper or report, Documenting Sources for the Bibliography, and Citing Sources.

Other helpful tools include a List of Illustrations, a Reader's Guide that arranges material thematically according to the key concepts of the American Government curriculum, and a timeline of Historical Milestones in U.S. Congress. The *Guide* concludes with a Glossary of political and elections terminology, a Selected Bibliography, and an Index.

An eye-catching, user-friendly design enhances the text. Throughout, numerous charts, graphs, tables, maps, cross-references, sources for further reading, and images illustrate concepts.

The *Student's Guides to the U.S. Government* Series

Additional titles in the *Student's Guides to the U.S. Government* series include the *Student's Guide to Elections,* the *Student's Guide to the Presidency,* and the *Student's Guide to the Supreme Court.* Collectively, these titles will offer indispensable data drawn from CQ Press's collections and presented in a manner accessible to secondary level students of American history and government. The volumes will place at the reader's fingertips essential information about the evolution of American politics from the struggles to create the United States government in the late eighteenth century through the ongoing controversies and dramatic strides of the early twenty-first century.

For study in American history, the *Student's Guides to the U.S. Government* collect a treasury of useful, often hard-to-find facts and present them in the context of the political environment for easy use in research projects, answering document-based questions, and writing essays or reports.

The *Student's Guides* offer valuable tools for civics education and for the study of American politics and government. They introduce young people to the institutions, procedures, and rules that form the foundations of American government. They assemble for students and teachers the essential material for understanding the workings of American politics and the nature of political participation in the United States. The *Guides* explain the roots and development of representative democracy, the system of federalism, the separation of powers, and the specific roles of legislators, executives, and judges in the American system of governance. The *Guides* provide immediate access to the details about the changing nature of political participation by ordinary Americans and the essential role of citizens in a representative democracy.

At the heart of the *Student's Guides to the U.S. Government* is the conviction that the continued success of the American experiment in self-government and the survival of democratic ideals depend on a knowledgeable and engaged citizenry—on educating the next generation of American citizens. Understanding American government and history is essential to that crucial education process, for freedom depends on knowing how our system of governance evolved and how we are governed.

By learning the rudiments of American government—the policies, procedures, and processes that built the modern United States—young people can fulfill the promise of American life. By placing at hand—in comprehensive essays, in easily recovered alphabetical format, and in pivotal primary source documents—the essential information needed by student researchers and all educators, the *Student's Guides to the U.S. Government* offer valuable, authoritative resources for civics and history education.

Bruce J. Schulman, Ph.D., Advisory Editor
The William E. Huntington Professor of History, Boston University

Historical Milestones of the U.S. Congress, 1789–2008: A Timeline

1789: Frederick A. C. Muhlenberg is elected first Speaker of the House (1789–1791). House rules are established and the Committee on Elections is formed. Senate meets with a twenty-two-member quorum.

1790: House amends its rules so the Speaker can appoint all committee members.

1795: Commerce and Manufacturers committee is established. Senate passes treaty with Great Britain. Senate holds first open session.

1798: Senate passes a rule prohibiting absence without leave.

1799: Federalist Theodore Sedgwick is elected Speaker (1799–1801).

1800: Jefferson's Democratic-Republican party wins majority in both houses.

1802: Ways and Means committee is established.

1805: Democratic-Republican Nathaniel Macon is elected Speaker (1801–1807).

1807: Democratic-Republican Joseph B. Varnum elected Speaker (1807–1810) after Macon withdraws from ballot.

1810: Census increases the size of the House to 186 members.

1811: Representative Barent Gardenier speaks for twenty-four hours, prompting the House to resort to the previous question tactic in order to end the debate. Henry Clay leaves the Senate to join the House. Republican Henry Clay is elected Speaker of the House (1812–1813).

1812: Henry Clay appoints fellow war hawks as committee leaders and gains control of the House. Clay radically changes the power of the Speaker.

1813: House Judiciary committee is created.

1814: Henry Clay resigns as Speaker.

1815: Henry Clay is reelected as Speaker (1815–1820).

1816: Senate establishes standing committees for: Foreign Relations, Finance, Commerce and Manufacturers, Military Affairs, the Militia, Naval Affairs, Public Lands, Claims, the Judiciary, the Post Office and Post Roads, and Pensions.

1820: Census increases the size of the House to 213 members. House passes the Missouri Compromise. House passes a rule that a two-thirds vote can suspend any House rule. Antislavery candidate John W. Taylor is elected Speaker (1820–1821), replacing Henry Clay.

1822: Military Affairs, Naval Affairs, and Foreign Affairs committees are created.

1825: The Democratic-Republican party splits. Andrew Jackson forms the new Democratic Party.

1826: The Democratic Party wins both houses.

1827: Daniel Webster is elected to the Senate.

1829: Andrew Jackson is elected president. He exerts considerable control over the House through the veto and the ability to dole out government favors.

1831: Henry Clay returns to the Senate.

1832: John C. Calhoun resigns as vice president and is elected to the Senate.

1833: Census increases the House to 242 members.

1834: Ten ballots are required to arrive at the decision to elect National Republican John Bell as Speaker (1834–1836). Senate censures President Andrew Jackson, starting a bitter battle.

1835: Bell's main competitor, Democrat James K. Polk, is elected Speaker (1835–1839).

1836: John Quincy Adams brings a petition from the citizens of Massachusetts to the floor concerning slavery, breaking a long-standing practice of officially avoiding the slavery issue. As a result, the House passes a resolution that all business dealing with slavery be laid upon the table and forgotten.

1837: A rule is established giving precedence to bills concerning appropriations. Appropriations bills are no longer allowed to contain other legislation. Jacksonian Democrats take over the Senate and expunge the censure of the president.

1839: John Quincy Adams is elected temporary chairman, but it takes nearly two weeks to elect a Speaker of the House because of contested seats in New Jersey, whose votes could not be counted. Robert M. T. Hunter eventually wins the election. The Democrats barely hold a majority.

1840: House passes a rule that it will not receive papers on the subject of abolition under any circumstances.

1841: House majority turns in favor of the Whigs. Senate holds a ten-day filibuster to oppose the removal of the Senate printer and a fourteen-day filibuster concerning the Bank of the United States.

1843: House majority returns to the Democrats.

1844: By a vote of 108–80, the House rescinds the ruling banning the discussion of abolitionist petitions.

1846: A bill in the Senate to grant join occupancy of Oregon to the U.S. and Great Britain is filibustered for two months, broken by the invocation of the unanimous consent agreement. Senate committee members are elected by political parties and based on seniority.

1847: Whigs regain the House majority.

1849: Because five parties are in the House, there is no majority to elect a Speaker. After multiple votes, the House votes to elect by plurality rather than by majority.

1850: Henry Clay attempts to resolve the slavery issue in Mexican territory with the Compromise of 1850.

1851: Lynn Boyd is Speaker of the House (1851–1855), presiding over a proslavery Democratic majority.

1854: New Republican Party succeeds the Whigs.

1855: House membership consists of 108 Republicans, 83 Democrats, and 43 third-party candidates. One hundred and thirty-three ballots are necessary to elect a Speaker. Nathaniel P. Banks (1855–1856) is eventually elected by plurality.

1856: Senator Charles Sumner is beaten by Preston Brooks, a House member from South Carolina over a bill granting Kansas statehood.

1859: House again becomes deadlocked, as pro- and antislavery factions fail to reach a majority. Republican William Pennington (1859–1861) is eventually elected by a slim majority, but he fails to be elected to a second term in the House. Senate moves to its current location in the Capitol, forever changing the nature of senatorial debate.

1860: The House adopts a revised set of rules that still gave minority parties a number of ways to voice their dissent against majority power.

1861: With the secession of eleven states from the Union, sixty-six House seats are left empty. Since most of these are Democratic seats, the Republicans gain and hold a majority through most of the Reconstruction era.

1863: President Abraham Lincoln establishes Reconstruction governments in Louisiana and Arkansas, but the House votes to give Congress control of these governments.

1864: Lincoln pocket-vetoes the House's bill concerning Louisiana and Arkansas, and the House responds with the Wade-Davis Manifesto.

1865: Senator Sumner uses the filibuster to protest readmitting Louisiana to the Union.

1868: House votes to impeach Andrew Johnson for firing his secretary of war without approval from the Senate. Senate comes within one vote of conviction.

1871: Following the massive spending on the Civil War, the House commits itself to reducing government spending. It keeps the budget under $300 million almost every year starting in 1871 and ending in 1890. Senate increases to seventy-four members.

1875: Senate rule enacted allowing that amendments to bills could be voted on separately from the bills themselves.

1876: Filibuster is used to protest the use of federal troops in supervising state elections.

1877: A Democratic majority House battles Rutherford B. Hayes over Reconstruction laws, attempting to add riders to appropriations bills that the president eventually vetoes.

1880: Agricultural appropriations are taken from the Appropriations Committee. Senate adopts a five-minute rule for debate on non-controversial legislation.

1881: Democratic minority uses the filibuster to prevent the Senate from being called to order before two Republican senators resign.

1883: John G. Carlisle is elected Speaker and begins using the power of recognition to keep bills from coming to a vote. This and other delaying tactics bring the House under criticism as a slow and inefficient system.

1890: The Reed Rules, named for Speaker of the House Thomas Reed, are established, giving the Speaker wide-ranging authority. Census numbers increase House membership to 357.

1893: A filibuster against the repeal of the Silver Purchase act lasts for forty-six days in the Senate. William Allen holds the floor for an unprecedented fourteen hours.

1897: James A. Tawney is named first Republican whip, given the job of ensuring that party members attend sessions and vote party line.

1899: Only 30 percent of those elected to the House are newcomers. Senate moves the power of appropriations bills from the Appropriations Committee to other legislative committees.

1900: Census increases House to 391 members. Senate standing committees increase membership to nine members.

1901: Senate increases to ninety.

1903: Joseph G. Cannon (R) is elected Speaker. As Speaker, he uses his powers to thwart the increasingly liberal legislation that he opposes. Senator Tillman threatens to read poetry into the record as part of a filibuster against an appropriations bill.

1908: Senator La Follette holds the Senate floor for eighteen hours. During a break, he finds a lethal dose of poison in his eggnog.

1909: The House adopts the Calendar Wednesday rule.

1910: The Norris resolution is adopted, stripping the Speaker of his authority to appoint committee members.

1911: Champ Clark (D) is elected Speaker, and new House rules are established. The use of the party caucus also comes back into vogue. Senate majority and minority leaders emerge.

1912: Congress approves constitutional amendment changing the system used to elect senators to direct election.

1913: Woodrow Wilson (D) is elected president and issues his State of the Union Address to Congress in person. He helps pass the Underwood Tariff Act, the Federal Reserve Act, and Clayton Antitrust Act, and the Federal Trade Commission Act. Senate whips are added to leadership structure.

1917: Even though a majority supported Wilson's armed neutrality bill, the bill is blocked by a filibuster and the bill fails to pass. Under harsh criticism, the Senate adopts cloture rule.

1918: The Republicans gain control of both houses of Congress.

1919: The Senate makes first use of its cloture rule to bring the Treaty of Versailles to a vote.

1920: The Appropriations Committee regains control of all funding bills.

1921: Arguing that the large numbers of members already hampered proceedings, House votes against increasing the number of representatives to 483.

1922: Spending bills are reassigned to the Appropriations Committee in the Senate.

1923: Senate first votes in favor of the "lame-duck" amendment.

1927: In order to achieve a quorum, several senators are brought to the chamber under arrest warrants.

1929: Creating a permanent system for adjusting the House makeup after each census, the reapportionment bill passes both houses. The Great Depression begins.

1931: Democrats gain control of the House.

1932: Congress passes the "lame-duck" amendment. Franklin Delano Roosevelt (D) is elected president, giving Democrats control of the government.

1935: Senator Huey Long stages a famous filibuster against civil rights legislation, taking the floor for nearly sixteen hours.

1937: A coalition of southern Democrats and Republicans take control of the House Rules Committee in order to oppose Democratic leadership.

1938: Senator Allen Ellender holds a twenty-nine day filibuster against an antilynching law that was accidentally ended when a senator ceded the floor to a compatriot who was not in the room.

1942: Anti-poll tax bill is defeated through a filibuster in the Senate.

1944: President Roosevelt vetoes a revenue bill, sparking resentment in Congress. Anti-poll tax bill is defeated through a filibuster in the Senate.

1946: Legislative Reorganization Act passed, reducing the number of standing committees, altering the handling of the federal budget, designating staff, and regulating salaries and lobbyists. Senate filibuster defeats anti-poll tax and fair employment practices bills.

1947: Republicans gain control of Congress.

1949: Democrats gain control of Congress.

1950: Senator Joseph McCarthy declares that there are hundreds of communists in the State Department.

1953: Republicans gain control of Congress. Dwight D. Eisenhower (R) is elected president. Lyndon B. Johnson (D) becomes Minority Leader in the Senate.

1954: Senate votes to censure Senator McCarthy.

1955: Johnson becomes Majority Leader in the Senate.

1957: The first civil rights bill since Reconstruction is passed.

1958: Democrats gain their largest majority in the House since 1936.

1959: The cloture rule is altered so that it may be invoked by two-thirds of the senators present and could be applied to motions to change Senate rules.

1961: Lyndon B. Johnson resigns from the Senate to join John F. Kennedy's presidential ticket. Kennedy (D) is elected president, and Johnson becomes vice president.

1963: Lyndon B. Johnson assumes presidency after assassination of John F. Kennedy.

1964: The filibuster of a civil rights bill is broken by cloture.

1965: The filibuster on the Voting Rights Act of 1965 is broken by cloture.

1968: Richard M. Nixon (R) is elected president, but both houses of Congress are controlled by the opposition. Congress adopts rules of ethics.

1970: Legislative Reorganization Act passes.

1973: Congress passes the War Powers Act.

1974: Congress passes the Congressional Budget and Impoundment Act.

1975: Senate cloture rule changes to require only a three-fifths vote.

1979: House begins broadcasting its proceedings on television.

1980: Ronald Reagan (R) is elected president. Republicans gain control of the Senate and form close ties with conservative Democrats in the House.

1981: Reagan's economic plan is pushed through the House, despite a slight Democratic majority. Conservative Democrats vie for prominent positions in the House.

1985: Republicans gain fifteen seats, but the election of Richard McIntyre of Indiana's election is contested. A recount costs McIntyre his seat by four votes.

1987: Democrat Jim Wright is elected Speaker (1987–1989), wielding a great deal of power. His tactics win him enemies among Republicans and Democrats alike.

1988: In order to achieve a quorum, a senator is physically carried into the chamber, following his arrest for being absent without leave.

1990: Voters register disapproval with Congress, ousting a number of incumbents.

1991: Congress votes to commit troops to the Gulf War.

1992: Scandal over embezzlement in the House Post Office leads to investigations of congressional misconduct. Republicans gain seats in the House, though it remains a Democratic majority.

1994: Republicans gain majority in the House for the first time in forty years. Newt Gingrich is elected Speaker (1995–1998).

1996: Ways and Means Chairman Dan Rostenkowski pleads guilty to felony mail fraud and Representative Joe Kolter pleads guilty to conspiring to steal taxpayer money.

1997: After returning him to the office of Speaker, House votes to reprimand Newt Gingrich for ethics violations. Senate fails to pass a balanced budget amendment to the Constitution.

1998: The House approves articles of impeachment against Bill Clinton.

1999: The Senate acquits Clinton on both charges.

2000: Republicans retain a majority in the House, though they lose two seats.

2006: Democrats regain a majority in both houses of Congress.

2007: House passes a bill to fund the war in Iraq that requires a time line for withdrawal. President Bush vetoes this bill, and the House passes a second bill with benchmarks instead of a time line. Minority Whip Senator Trent Lott resigns and later forms a lobbying firm before a new law restricting the lobbying efforts of former senators can take effect.

2008: To stimulate the economy, Congress passes a bill authorizing rebate checks of $300 or more to be sent to qualified taxpayers.

PART ONE

Essays

Members of Congress: Who Gets Elected? Who Elects Them?

American voters elect a new Congress on the first Tuesday after the first Monday in November of even-numbered years. Early the following January, the elected representatives and senators begin their first session of that Congress. Who are these representatives and senators? How do they get elected? Who elects them to office? What do we think about their effectiveness in serving us?

Congress As an Institution

Congress has suffered public criticism almost since the nation's beginnings. Alexis de Tocqueville, the astute French visitor to America in the late 1820s, observed the "vulgar demeanor" of the House of Representatives, where often he could not detect even one "distinguished man," as he wrote in his classic *Democracy in America.*

However, de Tocqueville saw a contrast in the Senate.

> [The Senate was] composed of eloquent advocates, distinguished generals, wise magistrates, and statesmen of note, whose arguments would do honor to the most remarkable parliamentary debates of Europe.

Subsequent views of the entire Congress at times seemed no more charitable than de Tocqueville's opinion of the House. Various political polls indicate that as little as 29 percent of the American public approve of how Congress is doing its job.

Strangely, election results often indicate that while Congress as an institution may not be held in high regard, voters are more generous in returning the **incumbents** who represent them. In the modern era, the power of **incumbency** has remained strong, with the turnover rate averaging at about 10 percent or less—historically a very low level. Political scientists suggest that the incumbent's appeal rests on more than his or her record in Congress. In an era of high campaign costs, especially for television advertising, the incumbent has usually achieved greater voter recognition than any challenger and is better positioned to raise campaign funds.

Characteristics of Members

Whether the turnover of representatives is large or small, a certain uniformity pervades Congress. Congress has been dominated since its inception by middle-aged white men with backgrounds in law or business. Their levels of income and education have consistently been above the national average. For many of the lawmakers today, business occupations are past activities. In recent years, ethics rules have limited the income that can be earned outside of Congress. Moreover, serving in Congress has become a full-time job. Since the 1970s, it has attracted career politicians, whose primary earnings have come from government service.

Ever so slowly, other changes also have crept into the makeup of Congress. The numbers of women, African American, and Hispanic American members have increased in recent decades, although still not in proportion to their share of the total population.

Average Age

The average age of members of Congress went up substantially between the post–Civil War period and the 1950s but remained fairly constant until the mid-1970s. In the 41st Congress (1869–1871), the average was 44.6 years; by the 85th Congress (1957–1959), it was 53.8. Over the next eighteen years, the average fluctuated only slightly. When the 110th Congress met in January 2007, the average age was 57 years.

Occupations

The legal profession has been the dominant occupational background of members of Congress since its beginning. In the First Congress, more than one-third of the House members had legal training. The proportion of lawyers in Congress crested at 70 percent in 1840 but remained high. From 1950 to the mid-1970s, it was in the 55–60 percent range.

The first significant decline in members with a law background began with the 96th Congress. Although sixty-five of the one hundred senators were lawyers in 1979, for the first time in at least thirty years, lawyers made up less than a majority of the House. That situation continued through the 1990s and 2000s.

After lawyers, members with a business or banking background make up the second largest group in Congress. Members of the clergy continue to be underrepresented in Congress. Only a handful of Protestant ministers have served in Congress, and no Catholic priest had done so until 1971, when Representative Robert F. Drinan (D-MA), a Jesuit, took a House seat. (Father Gabriel Richard was the nonvoting delegate of the Territory of Michigan from 1823 to 1825.) Drinan served five terms but declined to run again in 1980, the year that Pope John Paul II ordered priests not to hold public office. The pope's directive also prompted Robert J. Cornell, a Catholic priest and former U.S. House member, to halt his political comeback bid in Wisconsin. Cornell, a Democrat elected in 1974, had served two terms before he was defeated in 1978.

A new breed of legislator emerged in the 1970s: the career politician whose primary earnings had always come from political office at the local, state, or federal level. This trend became possible because states and localities had begun to think of political positions as full-time jobs and had raised salaries accordingly. In addition, the demands of modern political campaigns left less time for the pursuit of other careers. Members of the 110th Congress continued this trend.

New members of Congress also tend to lack military experience, continuing a trend that had been prevalent in the 1990s. At the start of the 101st Congress in 1989, 70 senators and 216 House members cited military service. In 2007 at the start of the 110th Congress, only 131 of the 535 members claimed military service (29 in the Senate and 102 in the House).

Religious Affiliations

Among religious groups, Protestants have comprised nearly three-fourths of the membership of both houses in recent years. However, Roman Catholics form the biggest single religious group–a distinction they have held since taking the lead from Methodists in 1965.

In the 110th Congress, Roman Catholics made up the largest religious congregation in both chambers. Among Protestant denominations, Baptists were the most numerous (66), followed by Methodists (61), Presbyterians (44), Episcopalians (37), and Lutherans (17). In all, the members listed affiliations with some nineteen religious groups, including Jewish (43), Mormon (15), Eastern Christian (5), Christian Scientist (5), Unitarian (2), Buddhist (2), and Muslim (1).

Women in Congress

In the 110th Congress, a record 90 women hold seats–74 in the House of Representatives and 16 in the Senate. In 1917, Representative Jeannette Rankin, a Republican from Montana, became the first woman elected to Congress. Her state gave women the right to vote before the Nineteenth Amendment to the Constitution **enfranchising** women was **ratified** in 1920. Several women served out unexpired terms of less than one year. Rebecca L. Felton, the first woman to serve in the Senate, did so for only one day. Felton, a Georgia Democrat, was appointed October 1, 1922, to fill the Senate vacancy created by the death of Thomas E. Watson. She was not sworn in until November 21 and the next day yielded her seat to Walter F. George, who had meanwhile been elected to fill the vacancy.

Gladys Pyle, a South Dakota Republican, was elected November 9, 1938, to fill the unexpired term of Rep. Peter Norbeck, who died in office. His term ended the following January 3 before Congress convened, and thus Pyle never took the oath of office. Margaret Chase Smith, a Republican from Maine, served four full terms in the Senate.

In 1996, Kansas Lt. Governor Sheila Frahm was appointed by Governor Bill Graves to fill the Senate seat of Majority Leader Bob Dole, who had resigned from the Senate to run full time for president. Frahm held the seat

less than five months. A special primary was held in August to fill Dole's seat, and Frahm lost it to a more **conservative** Republican, Sam Brownback, who went on to win the November general election.

California Democrat Nancy Pelosi, who has served in the House since 1987, became the first woman Speaker of the House in January 2007. Pelosi is the daughter of Thomas J. D'Alesandro Jr., a House member from 1939 to 1947 and then mayor of Baltimore.

In 1992, a record number of women ran for and were elected to Congress. The 103rd Congress, which opened in 1993, included forty-seven women in the House, an increase of nineteen, and six in the Senate, an increase of four.

Several factors contributed to the success of women candidates in 1992. Many capitalized on an unusually large number of retirements to run in open seats. They also benefited from reapportionment, which created dozens of opportunities for newcomers in the South and West. Another factor was public dissatisfaction with Congress, which allowed women to portray themselves positively as outsiders. Also, during the 1991 confirmation hearings of Supreme Court Justice Clarence Thomas, the Senate's questioning of law professor Anita F. Hill regarding her accusations of sexual harassment by Thomas, had a profound impact. The televised images of an all-male Senate Judiciary panel sharply questioning Hill brought home dramatically to many women their lack of representation in Congress.

The number of women elected to full Senate terms increased markedly in the 1990s. By 1999, the nine women serving in the Senate were all elected to full Senate terms, and two states—California and Maine—were represented in the Senate solely by women. Democrats Barbara Boxer and Dianne Feinstein were both elected to the Senate from California in 1992, and Republicans Olympia J. Snowe and Susan Collins were elected from Maine in 1994 and 1996, respectively.

In 1992, the first African American woman was elected to the Senate, Democrat Carol Moseley-Braun of Illinois. The daughter of a police officer and a medical technician, Moseley-Braun grew up in Chicago. She served in the state legislature from 1979 to 1988, where she rose to become the first woman assistant majority leader. She also served as the Cook County recorder of deeds (1988–1992). The outrage over the Senate's handling of the confirmation hearings of Supreme Court nominee Clarence Thomas propelled Moseley-Braun into the 1992 Illinois Senate race. She won that election with 53 percent of the vote, but lost in 1998 in her bid for reelection.

Before 1987, only six women had ever won election to full Senate terms. They were Maurine B. Neuberger (D-OR) (1960); Nancy Landon Kassebaum (R-KS) (1978, 1984, 1990); Paula Hawkins (R-FL) (1980); and Barbara A. Mikulski (D-MD) (1986). Kassebaum was the first woman ever elected to the Senate without being preceded in Congress by her husband.

Although women have been entering Congress in record numbers, at the end of the twentieth century, they still found it difficult to move to the top of the committee and party leadership ladders. In 1995, Kassebaum became the first woman to chair a major Senate committee, Labor and Human Resources. She was joined in the House by fellow Kansas Republican, Jan Meyers, who chaired the Small Business Committee. Before Meyers, no woman had chaired a full House committee since 1977, when Merchant Marine Committee Chairwoman Leonor K. Sullivan, a Democrat from Missouri, left Congress.

Mae Ella Nolan, a California Republican who served from 1923 to 1925, was the first woman to chair a congressional committee; she headed the House Committee on Expenditures in the Post Office Department. In 1989, Barbara Mikulski became the first woman to chair a Senate Appropriations subcommittee—the Veterans Administration, Housing and Urban Development and Related Agencies panel.

Congress has been an important starting point, however, for women seeking national office. Shirley Chisholm, a Democratic representative from New York, ran for president in 1972, and Geraldine Ferraro, another New York Democrat who served in the House, was her party's vice presidential nominee in 1984. New York Senator Hillary Rodham Clinton was a major contender for the 2008 Democratic presidential nomination.

African Americans in Congress

Since 1870, more than one hundred African Americans have served in Congress. John W. Menard holds the distinction of being the first black person elected to Congress. His 1868 election in Louisiana was disputed, and the House denied him a seat in the 40th Congress. Hiram R. Revels of Mississippi, who filled an unexpired Senate term from February 1870 to March 1871, thus became the first black person actually to serve in Congress. The first black person to serve in the House, from December 1870 to March 1879, was Joseph H. Rainey of South Carolina.

Menard, Revels, and Rainey were elected during the post-Civil War **Reconstruction** era (1865–1877), when many white voters were **disenfranchised** and Confederate veterans were barred from holding office. During that period, sixteen African American men were sent to Congress from Alabama, Georgia, Florida, Louisiana, Mississippi, North Carolina, and South Carolina. From the end of Reconstruction until the end of the century, only seven black men were elected to Congress, all from the Carolinas and Virginia. They, like their predecessors, were Republicans.

As federal controls were lifted in the South, **literacy tests, poll taxes,** and sometimes threats of violence eroded black voting rights. From the time Blanche K. Bruce of Mississippi left the Senate in 1881, no other black person served in that body until Edward W. Brooke, a Republican from Massachusetts, served from 1967 to 1979. In 1992, Illinois Democrat Carol Moseley-Braun was elected to the Senate, becoming the first black woman to gain a Senate seat. She served one term.

The last black person elected to the House in the nineteenth century was Republican George Henry White of North Carolina; he was elected in 1896 and 1898 but did not seek renomination in 1900. For nearly three decades, there were no black members in Congress—not until Oscar De

Priest, a Republican from Illinois, entered the House in 1929 and served three terms. During the next quarter-century, only three other blacks were elected to Congress: Arthur W. Mitchell in 1934, William L. Dawson in 1942, and Adam Clayton Powell Jr. in 1944. All three represented big-city black constituencies in Chicago (Mitchell and Dawson) and New York (Powell).

The Supreme Court's one-person, one-vote rulings in the early 1960s, **ratification** of the Twenty-fourth Amendment in 1964, and congressional passage of the 1965 Voting Rights Act are credited with opening up the polls to black voters as never before. The Voting Rights Act provided for federal oversight in **jurisdictions** where black registration and voting was exceptionally low. The Twenty-fourth Amendment outlawed poll taxes and similar restrictions on voting. The courts eventually ended a southern practice of diluting black voting power by **gerrymandering** voting districts. As black voter turnouts increased, so did black representation in Congress.

In 1968, Representative Shirley Chisholm, a Democrat from New York, became the first black woman to be elected to Congress. She was joined in the House by Yvonne Brathwaite Burke, a Democrat from California, and Barbara C. Jordan, a Democrat from Texas, who both served from 1973 until 1979. In a 1973 special election, Cardiss Collins won the House seat previously held by her late husband, George W. Collins.

Despite the steady gains of blacks being elected to Congress and the growing power of senior black members, African Americans remained numerically underrepresented in Congress. In 2008, they made up about 12 percent of the population, but only 9 percent of the House and had just one member in the Senate.

Redistricting Battles

Following the 1990 census, many states redrew congressional district lines under the provisions of the 1965 Voting Rights Act, which required that interests of minority voters be protected. Districts in which minorities made up a majority of the voting age population were known as **majority-minority districts.** As state mapmakers pulled districts this way and that to pick up minority voters, many old boundaries were tugged out of shape. In some states, oddly shaped majority-minority districts emerged.

Congressional remapping that went to extreme lengths to elect minorities quickly came under scrutiny by the Supreme Court. In 1993 in *Shaw v. Reno,* the Court ruled against North Carolina's bizarrely shaped majority-minority districts, inviting a new round of lawsuits challenging the constitutionality of districts drawn to ensure the election of minorities. Two years later in *Miller v. Johnson,* the Court struck down a Georgia redistricting plan that created three black-majority districts. The Court cast heavy doubt on any district lines for which race was the "predominant factor." In 1995, a panel of three federal judges imposed a new plan that reduced the black population share to about one-third in two of the districts.

Even though the black-majority 11th District in Georgia was invalidated by the Supreme Court decision, Cynthia A. McKinney, the district's black

representative, scored a comfortable victory in 1996 in the newly drawn white-majority 4th District. Only one-third of the new district's voting age population was black, compared with 64 percent in her old district. In fact, all three of Georgia's black Democrats in the House were reelected to redrawn districts in 1996.

The thrust of the Court's opinions threatened those who defended majority-minority districts as a way to empower minority voters. However, the justices did not make sweeping determinations affecting all such districts. Rather, they seemed inclined to carve out new limits in a sequence of slightly different cases. The following states faced redistricting challenges between 1993–1998: Alabama, Georgia, Florida, Illinois, Louisiana, North Carolina, New York, Ohio, South Carolina, Texas, and Virginia.

Hispanics in Congress

The fast-expanding population of Hispanic Americans has sparked predictions that they would emerge as a powerful voting **bloc.** However, Hispanic voter turnouts traditionally have fallen well below the national average.

By 2007, at the start of the 110th Congress, thirty-three members and one nonvoting delegate from Puerto Rico identified themselves as Hispanics—people of Spanish ancestry. The growth of Hispanic representation in the House was in large part the result of judicial interpretations of the Voting Rights Act, requiring that minorities be given maximum opportunity to elect members of their own group to Congress. After the 1990 census, congressional district maps in states with significant Hispanic populations were redrawn with the aim of sending more Hispanics to Congress, a goal accomplished by the 1992 elections. Before the 1992 elections, there were only thirteen Hispanic members of Congress.

Turnover in Membership

Congress experienced high turnover rates in the nineteenth and early twentieth centuries, principally in the House. The Senate experienced more stability because its members were selected for six-year terms and because state legislatures tended to send the same men to the Senate time after time. The Senate's turnover rate began to increase only after the popular election of senators was instituted by the Seventeenth Amendment in 1913. In the middle decades of the twentieth century, congressional turnover held steady at a relatively low rate. For a quarter-century after World War II, each Congress had an average of about seventy-eight new members. An increase began in the 1970s; more than one hundred new members entered Congress in 1975. Turnover remained fairly high through the early 1980s. Then came a spell of strong incumbency and relatively low turnover, which lasted through the 1990 election.

The 1988 election brought only thirty-three new faces to the House and ten to the Senate, the smallest turnover in history, both numerically and as a share (8 percent) of total membership. Another small turnover followed in 1990; the combined turnover for both chambers, including retirement, amounted to just 10 percent. In the 2006 congressional elections, 61 new

The popularly elected 435 members of the United States House of Representatives meet in the House chamber on the south side of the Capitol. (AP Photo, John Duricka)

members were elected, returning control of both houses of Congress to the Democrats. The Democrats controlled the Senate with 49 members and 1 independent who voted with them. They held a Democratic majority of 233 seats to 202 Republican seats.

The 1996 elections ended up in the record books. Never before had voters reelected a Democratic president and at the same time entrusted both the House and the Senate to the Republican Party. President Clinton, who was almost written off after the disastrous 1994 midterm elections, scored a political comeback by winning handily in November 1996. The Republicans won their first back-to-back majority in the House since the 1920s. The Democrats managed, however, to cut into the GOP's numbers. Democrats gained a net of nine seats, leaving a party breakdown in the House of 227 Republicans and 207 Democrats, and Bernard Sanders of Vermont as the lone independent.

Shifts Between Chambers

From the early days of Congress, members have sometimes shifted from one chamber to the other. Far fewer former senators have gone to the House than vice versa. In the 1790s, nineteen former representatives became senators and three former senators moved to the House. The same pattern continued through the nineteenth century and into the twentieth. By the end of the twentieth century, it was common to find House members

running for the Senate, but senators rarely, if ever, returned to the House. Former senators were more likely to return home to pursue a race for governor, run as their party's vice presidential candidate, or seek the office of president.

Although both chambers are equal under the law, the Senate's six-year terms offer the officeholder greater stability. That body also has larger staffs and more generous perquisites. A senator's opportunity to make a mark is undoubtedly better in a chamber of 100 members than in the 435-member House. The Senate's role in foreign affairs may add to its luster, and senators enjoy the prestige of statewide constituencies.

Perhaps the most notable shift from the Senate to the House was Henry Clay's journey in 1811. Giving up a Senate seat from Kentucky, he entered the House and was promptly elected Speaker, a position he used to prod the country to go to war with Britain in 1812. After five terms in the House, Clay returned to the Senate in 1823. Another prominent transfer was that of John Quincy Adams of Massachusetts; he served in the Senate (1803–1808), as secretary of state (1817–1825), as president (1825–1829), and finally in the House (1831–1848).

Only one other former president, Andrew Johnson, returned to Congress in later years. Like Adams, he had served in both houses of Congress (from Tennessee) before he entered the White House. As vice president in 1865, Johnson was elevated to the presidency upon Abraham Lincoln's assassination. He left office in 1869 a bitter man, having survived **impeachment** charges instigated by his own Republican Party. The Tennessee legislature sent him back to the U.S. Senate in 1875, where he served during the last five months of his life.

The American Voter

Few elements of the American political system have changed so much over the years as the electorate. Since the early days of the nation, when the voting privilege was limited to the upper economic classes, one voting barrier after another has fallen to pressures for wider **suffrage.** First, men who did not own property, then women, next African Americans, and finally young people obtained the **franchise.** By the early 1970s, virtually every adult citizen eighteen and older had won the right to vote.

However, by the end of the 1990s, only about half of those eligible to vote were exercising that right in high-profile presidential elections, and barely one-third of those eligible were bothering to vote in midterm congressional elections. The comparatively low turnout led some observers to speculate that people stayed away from the polls because they were disillusioned with the political process. Others said concern about low turnout was overblown.

Broadening the Franchise

During the nation's first decades, all thirteen of the original states restricted voting to adult male property holders and taxpayers. The Framers of the Constitution apparently were content to continue this time-honored

practice. The Constitutional Convention adopted without dissent the recommendation of its Committee of Detail that qualifications for the electors of the House of Representatives "shall be the same . . . as those of the electors in the several states of the most numerous branch of their own legislatures."

Under this provision, fewer than half of the adult white men in the United States were eligible to vote in federal elections. With women and indentured servants disqualified, fewer than one of every four white adults could cast a ballot. Slaves also were ineligible to vote, although freed slaves could vote in some states if they met whatever other qualifications the state placed on its voters.

Those practices were actually an improvement on the voting restrictions that had prevailed during the colonial period. Roman Catholics had been disenfranchised in almost every colony; Jews, in most colonies; Quakers and Baptists, in some. Not until 1842, for example, did Rhode Island permit Jews to vote.

For half a century before the Civil War (1861–1865), the electorate was steadily broadened. The new western settlements supplied a stimulus for allowing all men to vote, and Jacksonian democracy encouraged its acceptance. Gradually, seven states that had limited voting strictly to men who owned property substituted a taxpaying qualification, and by the middle of the century, most states had removed even that requirement.

The Fourteenth Amendment, ratified in 1868, made everyone born or naturalized in the United States a citizen and directed Congress to reduce the number of representatives from any state that disenfranchised adult male citizens for any reason other than commission of a crime. Although no such reduction was ever made, that amendment–together with the Fifteenth Amendment, which said that the right to vote could not be denied based on "race, color, or previous condition of servitude"–legally prohibited the denial of voting rights on the basis of race alone.

Former slaves did vote in the years immediately following the Civil War, but by the turn of the century, most southern states had in place laws and election practices that effectively barred blacks from voting. Not until passage of the Voting Rights Act of 1965 would the promise held out by the Fifteenth Amendment begin to be fulfilled.

Women fought for nearly ninety years to win their right to vote; success came with ratification of the Nineteenth Amendment in 1920. Residents of the District of Columbia were given the right to vote in presidential elections with ratification of the Twenty-third Amendment in 1961. In 1970, Congress authorized residents of the nation's capital to elect a nonvoting delegate to the House of Representatives.

In 1971, the Twenty-sixth Amendment lowered the voting age to eighteen for federal, state, and local elections. A Supreme Court ruling in 1972 effectively required states to reduce the time citizens had to live there to be eligible to vote; no state now requires more than a thirty-day residency. By the beginning of the 1990s, only insanity, a felony conviction, or failure

to meet a residency requirement barred voting-age citizens from going to the polls.

Turnout Trends

Most significant liberalizations of election law have resulted in a sharp increase in voting. From 1824 to 1856—a period of gradual relaxation in the states' property and taxpaying qualifications for voting—voter participation in presidential elections increased from 3.8 percent to 16.7 percent of the population. In 1920, when the Nineteenth Amendment gave women the franchise, participation rose to 25.1 percent.

Between 1932 and 1976, both the voting-age population and the number of voters in presidential elections roughly doubled. Except for the 1948 presidential election, when barely half the people of voting age went to the polls, the turnout in the postwar years through 1968 was approximately 60 percent, according to Census Bureau surveys. This relatively high figure was attributed to a new sense of civic duty that permeated American society in the immediate postwar years—a population more rooted than it was to be later in the century—and to recent civil rights laws encouraging blacks to vote.

Despite larger numbers of people voting, the rate of voter participation slumped after 1968. In that year's presidential election, 61 percent of the voting-age population went to the polls. Through successive stages, that mark fell below 50 percent in the 1996 election, the lowest level of voter turnout since 1924. By 2004, however, 60.7 percent of the voting-age population voted in the presidential election.

The famous postwar baby boom, together with a lower voting age, had produced by the early 1970s a disproportionate number of young voters—voters who are the least likely to vote. In the 1972 presidential election, the first in which eighteen-year-olds could vote nationwide, some 11 million young voters entered the electorate. The actual number of voting participants was only 4.4 million greater than in 1968, resulting in a five-point drop in the ratio of eligible to actual voters.

One question frequently asked is whether the election results would be different if everyone voted. In a paper that they wrote in 1998, two University of California political scientists, Benjamin Highton and Raymond E. Wolfinger, answered: probably not. "The two most common demographic features of nonvoters are their residential mobility and youth—two characteristics that do not suggest political distinctiveness," they wrote. "To be sure, the poor, less educated, and minorities are overrepresented among nonvoters. But the young and the transient are even more numerous. . . . What our findings have demonstrated is that the 'party of nonvoters' is truly heterogeneous. Taken as a whole, nonvoters appear well represented by those who vote."

Nonetheless, studies by the Census Bureau have shown marked differences in participation among various classes of voters. Older voters tend to vote at a higher rate than younger voters do. Well-educated voters tend

to vote at a higher rate than those less educated. Whites tend to vote at a higher rate than blacks and Hispanics.

Growth of Independents

Although more people identify themselves as Democrats than Republicans, there has been a steady rise over the last half century in voters who do not identify with either party. Polls show the "independent" strain strongest among white, young, northern, and rural voters. Yet when it comes to the act of voter registration, most voters still sign up with one of the two major parties; at least that is the case in the twenty-seven states (and the District of Columbia) where there is such a choice to be made.

The Black Vote: A Long, Painful Struggle

In no period of American history were all black people excluded from the polls. At the time of the Constitutional Convention in 1787, free black men had the right of suffrage in all the original states except Georgia, South Carolina, and Virginia. At the outbreak of the Civil War (1861–1865), black Americans were denied the right to vote solely based on their race, in all except six of the thirty-three states.

President Abraham Lincoln's **Emancipation Proclamation** of 1863 freed the slaves but did not accord them voting rights. To ease the impact of change on the South, Lincoln preferred to move cautiously in expanding the black electorate. After the Civil War, several southern states promptly enacted "Black Codes" barring the newly liberated slaves from voting or holding office. **Radical Republicans** in Congress responded by passing the Reconstruction Act of 1867, which established provisional military governments in the Southern states. The return of civilian control was conditioned on their ratification of the Fourteenth Amendment, which buttressed individual liberty with "due process" and "equal protection" under the law. The amendment's second section threatened to reduce any state's representation in Congress for denying the vote to any male citizen twenty-one years of age or older.

The Reconstruction Act further stated that a **secessionist** state could not be readmitted to the Union unless it extended the franchise to all adult males, white and black. Congress followed in February 1869 by submitting the Fifteenth Amendment, prohibiting racial discrimination in voting, to the states. It was ratified twelve months later.

Congress in 1870 passed an enforcement act to protect black voting rights in the South, but the Supreme Court in 1876 ruled that Congress had exceeded its authority. In the case of *United States v. Reese,* the Court held that the Fifteenth Amendment did not give anyone the right to vote; it simply guaranteed the right to be free from racial discrimination in exercising that right. The extension of the right to vote itself, the Court said, was up to the states, not the federal government. Therefore, the Court said, Congress had overreached its power to enforce the Fifteenth Amendment when it enacted the 1870 law that penalized state officials

who denied blacks the right to vote, or refused to count their votes, or obstructed them from voting.

Mississippi led the way in prohibiting black political activity. A new state constitution drawn up in 1890 required prospective voters to pay a poll tax of two dollars and to demonstrate their ability to read any section of the state constitution or to interpret it when read to them.

Literacy Tests for Voters

In Mississippi and other southern states that adopted voter literacy tests, care was taken not to disfranchise **illiterate** whites. Five states exempted white voters from literacy and some other requirements by "**grandfather clauses**"–regulations allowing prospective voters, if not otherwise qualified, to register if they were descended from persons who had voted–or served in the state's military forces–before 1867. Other provisions allowed illiterates to register if they owned a certain amount of property or could show themselves to be of good moral character–requirements easily twisted to exclude blacks. Still, white voter turnout in the South was lower than in other regions of the country.

At one time or another, twenty-one states imposed literacy requirements as a condition for voting. The first to do so–Connecticut in 1855 and Massachusetts in 1857–sought to disqualify a flood of European immigrants. Between 1890 and 1910, Mississippi, South Carolina, Louisiana, North Carolina, Alabama, Virginia, Georgia, and Oklahoma adopted literacy tests–primarily to restrict the black vote.

Nineteen of the twenty-one states demanded that voters be able to read English, and all but four of them (New York, Washington, Alaska, and Hawaii) required the reading of some legal document or passage from the state or federal Constitution. Either in lieu of, or in addition to, the reading requirements, fourteen states required an ability to write.

Poll-Tax Barrier to Voting

The first poll taxes in America were substitutes for property ownership and were intended to enlarge the voting franchise. Only a few states retained them at the time of the Civil War. They were afterward revived for a far different purpose–to restrict the franchise–in all eleven states of the old Confederacy: Florida (1889), Mississippi and Tennessee (1890), Arkansas (1892), South Carolina (1895), Louisiana (1898), North Carolina (1900), Alabama (1901), Virginia and Texas (1902), and Georgia (1908).

After the **Populist era** reforms, many states voluntarily dropped use of the poll tax, including six southern states–North Carolina (1920), Louisiana (1934), Florida (1937), Georgia (1945), South Carolina (1951), and Tennessee (1953). Proposals to abolish the poll tax were introduced in every Congress from 1939 to 1962. By 1960, only four states still required its payment by voters. In August 1962, the House approved a constitutional **amendment**–already accepted by the Senate–that outlawed poll taxes in federal elections. That amendment, the Twenty-fourth, was ratified in

January 1964. In 1966, the Supreme Court held that the poll tax was an unconstitutional requirement for voting in state and local elections as well.

"Justice William O. Douglas wrote:

Voter qualifications have no relation to wealth nor to paying or not paying this or any other tax. Wealth, like race, creed, or color, is not germane to one's ability to participate intelligently in the electoral process . . .

Women's Vote: A Victory in Stages

The Woman's Rights Convention at Seneca Falls, New York, in July 1848, is generally cited as the beginning of the women's suffrage movement in the United States. The Declaration of Principles, which Elizabeth Cady Stanton read at that meeting, became a sacred text for the movement.

Direct-action tactics first were applied by **suffragists** shortly after the Civil War (1861–1865), when Susan B. Anthony urged women to go to the polls and claim the right to vote under terms of the newly adopted Fourteenth Amendment. In the national elections of 1872, Anthony voted in her home city of Rochester, New York; she subsequently was tried and convicted of the crime of "voting without having a lawful right to vote." For almost a quarter of a century, Anthony and her followers pressed Congress for a constitutional amendment granting women's suffrage. On January 25, 1887, the Senate finally considered the proposal but rejected it by a 16–34 vote.

The suffrage forces had more success in some western states. As a territory, Wyoming extended full suffrage to women in 1869 and retained it upon becoming a state in 1890. Colorado, Utah, and Idaho granted women voting rights before the turn of the century. After that, the advocates of suffrage for women encountered stronger opposition, and it was not until the height of the **Progressive** movement, which called for many governmental reforms, that other states, mostly in the West, gave women full voting rights. Washington granted equal suffrage in 1910; California in 1911; Arizona, Kansas, and Oregon, in 1912; Montana and Nevada, in 1914; and New York, in 1917.

Constitutional Amendment

On the eve of World War I (1914–1918), the advocates of militant tactics took the lead in a national campaign for women's rights. In the congressional elections of 1914, they set out to defeat all Democratic candidates in the nine states (which had increased to eleven by election day) where women had the right to vote. They held the majority Democrats in Congress responsible for not submitting a constitutional amendment to the states for their approval of women's voting rights. Only twenty of the forty-three challenged candidates were elected. However, this showing of electoral strength did not move President Woodrow Wilson to take up their cause.

President Wilson's opposition to a constitutional amendment prompted a series of stormy demonstrations by the suffragists around the White House and other sites in Washington after the United States had entered World War I. The demonstrators insisted that it was unconscionable for

this country to be denying its own female citizens a right to participate in government while at the same time it was fighting a war on the premise of "making the world safe for democracy."

President Wilson changed his mind, however, and announced on January 9, 1918, his support for the proposed suffrage amendment. The House approved it the next day by a 274–136 vote, one vote more than the necessary two-thirds majority. However, the Senate fell short of the two-thirds majority in October 1918 and again in February 1919. After the new Congress (elected in November 1918) met for the first time in May 1919, the two chambers passed the proposed amendment in little more than two weeks to gain the required majorities in both chambers.

On August 18, 1920, Tennessee became the thirty-sixth state to approve the amendment, enough for ratification. On August 26, Secretary of State Bainbridge Colby signed a proclamation formally adding the Nineteenth Amendment to the Constitution.

The Nineteenth Amendment states simply that:

> The right of citizens of the United States to vote shall not be denied or abridged by the United States or any state on account of sex.

In the 1920 presidential election, the first in which women could vote, it was estimated that only about 30 percent of those who were eligible actually voted. Analyses of the 1924 election indicated that scarcely one-third of all eligible women voted while more than two-thirds of the eligible men had done so. The women's electoral performance came as a bitter blow to the suffragists. In more recent national elections, however, surveys by the Census Bureau have found that voting participation by women is about the same as that of men.

The Eighteen-Year-Old Vote

In 1954, President Dwight D. Eisenhower (1953–1961) had proposed a constitutional amendment granting eighteen-year-olds the right to vote nationwide, but the proposal was rejected by the Senate. Eventually Congress was persuaded—perhaps by the demographics of America's fast-expanding youth population, which during the 1960s had begun to capture the nation's attention; perhaps by the separate hopes of Republicans and Democrats to win new voters; perhaps by the Vietnam War in which the young were called on to fight again. In the Voting Rights Act of 1970, Congress added a provision to lower the voting age to eighteen in all federal, state, and local elections, effective January 1, 1971.

On signing the bill into law, President Richard Nixon (1969–1974) restated his belief that the provision was unconstitutional because Congress had no power to extend suffrage by statute, and directed Attorney General John N. Mitchell to ask for a swift court test of the law's validity. The Supreme Court, ruling in *Oregon v. Mitchell* only weeks before the law was due to take effect, sustained the law's application to federal elections but held it unconstitutional in regard to state and local elections.

After the Court ruled, Congress wasted little time in approving and sending to the states a proposed Twenty-sixth Amendment to the Constitution, stating: "The right of citizens of the United States, who are eighteen years of age or older, to vote shall not be denied or abridged by the United States or any State on account of age. The Congress shall have power to enforce this article by appropriate legislation." The proposal received final congressional approval March 23, 1971, and was ratified by the necessary three-fourths of the states by July 1, record time for a constitutional amendment.

More than 25 million Americans became eligible to vote for the first time in the 1972 presidential election. It was the biggest influx of potential voters since women won the right to vote in 1920. However, the younger age group has never fulfilled its potential power at the polls; in election after election, younger voters have had the lowest turnout rate of any age category.

At the beginning of the twenty-first century, American voters–especially young citizens–have the unique opportunity to shape the nation's future. The solutions to the challenges facing our nation–war, poverty, global warming, energy consumption, and more–will be decided in large part by the men and women elected to the United States Congress. Who serves in these crucial roles is up to us.

See also: African Americans in Congress; Civil Rights Act (1964); Elections, House of Representatives; Elections, Senatorial; Hispanic Americans in Congress; Midterm Elections; Political Parties and Congress; Seventeenth Amendment (1913); Voting Rights Act (1965); Women in Congress.

Further Reading

Davidson, Roger H., Walter J. Oleszek, and Frances E. Lee. *Congress and Its Members.* Eleventh edition. Washington, DC: CQ Press, 2007.

Hamilton, Lee H. *How Congress Works and Why You Should Care.* Bloomington: Indiana University Press, 2007.

Smith, Steven S., Jason M. Roberts, and Ryan J. Vander Wielen. *The American Congress.* New York: Cambridge University Press, 2007.

The Way Congress Works: How Does an Idea Become a Law?

The United States Congress is responsible for making the laws of our nation. Because creating a law is extremely complex, it is essential that informed citizens understand the process. Not knowing how Congress works might lead citizens to think that congressional representatives and U.S. senators do not do very much. Actually, the members of Congress have a very heavy workload. In fact, the demands placed upon Congress have increased dramatically as the United States has grown in size and complexity.

The Legislative Process in Action

Through the legislative process, Congress has been able to enact new laws to meet the challenges of our changing society. The process is complicated because of the great variety of rules and procedures, as well as the numerous groups and individuals who determine whether a law is passed and the form in which it will be passed. There are several types of legislative proposals used by the members of the House of Representatives and the Senate.

Types of Bills and Resolutions

Two of the most common types of legislative proposals are public **bills** and private bills. Public bills generally pertain to a large group of citizens, such as farmers, laborers, teachers, or business owners. Some public bills, of course, actually pertain to all citizens. For example, bills involving voting rights concern all groups of citizens except those too young to vote.

Private bills affect only one person or one small group of people. For example, many private bills are passed by Congress to allow individuals to remain in the United States. Such action by Congress is necessary when the immigration quota for a country has already been filled for the year. Other private bills often involve tax liability, veterans' benefits, or armed services recognition.

Three other types of legislative proposals are called **resolutions.** There are joint resolutions, which are used to give guidance to administrative officials or to extend existing laws. A special type of joint resolution, which must be passed by two-thirds of both houses of Congress–the House of Representatives and the Senate–is used for proposing amendments to the United States Constitution. The two other types of resolutions are concurrent resolutions and simple resolutions. Both are used to express congressional opinion or policy. Concurrent resolutions express the attitude or

opinion of both houses; simple resolutions express only the attitude of the chamber by which they are passed.

The Capitol is the seat of the United States Congress, the legislative branch of the nation's government. It is not only a working legislative building, but also one of the most recognizable symbols of democracy in the world. (Scott J. Ferrell, CQ)

Sources of Legislative Proposals

Suggestions for new laws come from a variety of sources. Members of Congress themselves are a major source of legislative proposals. Many senators and representatives campaign on promises to act on an issue or problem and then translate that promise into legislative proposals. Constituents also serve as a source of new ideas. Occasionally an individual will suggest a bill, but generally such proposals come from organized **lobbyists**–pressure groups that represent farmers, teachers, business owners, or similar organizations.

The president and other members of the executive branch form another major source of legislative proposals. Indeed, one of the president's major responsibilities is to suggest legislation. Often, the president carries out this responsibility in the annual State of the Union Address to Congress. In addition, the president works with Congress throughout its sessions to ensure the passage of laws supported by the administration.

Members of the offices and agencies within the executive branch also propose legislation that they believe will help them carry out their specific duties. Indeed, most executive departments have trained staffs that conduct research and draft legislative proposals that are then submitted to Congress.

House Action

Bills may originate in either house of Congress, except for **appropriations** bills, which must originate in the House of Representatives. Any member of the House, and only members of the House, may introduce a bill into the House of Representatives. Members simply writes their names on a bill and place it in the hopper, or box, beside the clerk's desk.

After a bill has been introduced, it is given a number and the title of the bill is recorded. Although this is known as the first reading of a bill, there is really no reading at all. After being printed by the Government Printing Office, copies of the bill are made available to members of the House and to interested citizens.

Each bill is then referred to one of the House standing committees for action. The assignment to a committee is a routine matter based on the subject of the bill and is usually made by the Speaker of the House.

Occasionally, the Speaker assigns the bill to a committee in anticipation of a specific type of action from that committee. Sometimes, for example, the Speaker does not want a bill **reported** by a committee, and at other times, the Speaker wants a bill reported favorably without delay. The assignment of a bill to a particular committee often brings about one of the following results.

Committee Action

Each bill received by a committee is placed on the committee's calendar and the work of Congress begins. Because more than 20,000 bills may be introduced during a session of Congress, committees are needed to screen out all but the most important ones. Only a few hundred bills become law each year.

Sometimes the entire committee handles a proposed bill, but more often, the bill is referred to one or more subcommittees. In either case, one of the first actions may be a series of public hearings to gather information and opinions on the subject of the bill. Members of Congress, officers of the president's cabinet, and other administration officials may appear and testify for or against a bill. Interested citizens may also testify if they desire to do so. In some cases, officials and citizens are summoned to testify if the committee knows they have useful and valuable information on the subject.

Few, if any, bills emerge from the executive sessions in the form in which they were received. Bills that are reported out of a committee for action by the entire House generally contain a number of amendments, and many bills are never reported out of committee for House consideration. The amendments to a bill are the result of committee debate and bargaining. Usually, compromises are made in an effort to report to the House a bill that has a reasonable chance of being passed. These compromises are a part of the democratic process of respecting the rights of the minority as well as the wishes of the majority.

Order of Business

Once a committee favorably reports a bill, it is placed on one of the three regular House calendars. Public bills that do not pertain to appropriating money or raising revenue are placed on the house calendar; bills concerning appropriations or revenue go on the union calendar; private bills are listed on the private calendar.

Bills are placed on the House calendars in the order that the bills are reported from the various committees. Thus, special procedures are needed to get important bills before the House without a long delay. For this reason, some bills are considered privileged business on certain days of the month. The powerful House Rules Committee generally controls the calendars, and it holds the power to decide which bills may be privileged business. In general, bills concerned with the general appropriation of funds or with general revenue are privileged business almost any time. Conference reports and special reports are also considered privileged business in the

House. Any bill may become privileged business if the head of the committee reporting the bill obtains a special rule from the House Rules Committee.

Floor Action

Normally, when the House is considering a bill, each representative may speak for one hour. Thus, there is limited debate in the House. Because a bill before the House may be **amended** from the floor, the bill, if passed, may be very different from what it was when House debate began. Some bills are debated by the House under a special rule that does not permit amendments from the floor. This rule also limits the time for House debate on a particular bill; one-half of this time is allotted to those who favor the bill, and one-half is given to those opposed to the bill.

When House debate has ended, a vote on whether or not to pass the bill finally takes place. This concludes what is called the second reading of the bill. This is a real reading in the sense that most of the bill is read in sections as it is debated. If the vote at the end of the second reading is favorable, the question as to whether the bill should be **engrossed**–reprinted as amended–is raised. A vote to have the bill engrossed brings about the third and final reading. This is a reading of the bill's title; at this point, no further amendments may be made to the bill. The third reading ends with a vote on the final passage of the bill.

Voting Methods

Three methods of voting are used in the House of Representatives. A voice vote is the quickest and most common method. The members simply respond favorably or unfavorably to the questions of whether to pass the bill. A division vote requires the supporters of each side of the issue to stand and be counted when their side of the issue is announced. The third type of vote is the roll-call vote or the record vote. A roll-call vote is held when one-fifth of the members who are present request it. Employing an electronic voting system, House members use one of the many voting stations located on the floor by inserting an identification card into the machine and pushing one of the buttons that then automatically posts their name, their vote, and the vote total. This electronic system makes roll-call votes a relatively simple procedure. In the past, roll-call votes were time-consuming because the clerk of the House was required to call each member's name and then record the votes. A roll-call vote offers the advantage of providing an official record of how each member voted. Often, voters and pressure groups are keen to view the members' voting records. Some citizens object when the House does not take a roll-call vote on certain bills, especially those involving appropriations.

The Committee of the Whole

Sometimes the members sit together as a committee rather than as the House of Representatives. When this occurs, it is known as the Committee of the Whole; during such a meeting, the Speaker of the House appoints another member to chair the meeting. When the House sits as the Committee of the Whole, a **quorum**–the least number of members necessary to do

business–is only 100 members. A quorum for the House in regular session is 218 members–more than one-half the total House membership. The Committee of the Whole operates somewhat informally and has additional rules for restricting debate, thus making it easier to discuss business. For this reason, all bills from the union calendar are considered by the Committee of the Whole before the House itself considers them.

No official record of how members vote is kept by the Committee of the Whole because the committee does not use a roll-call vote. When action by the Committee of the Whole is completed, the members pass a resolution ending their status as the Committee of the Whole and reinstating themselves back into the House of Representatives. Then the chair of the Committee of the Whole reports on the bill and its amendments for final action by the full House.

Senate Action

The process for introducing a bill in the Senate is similar to the process in the House. One key difference, however, is that a senator must be recognized by the presiding officer before the senator can introduce a bill. If any senator objects to the introduction of a bill, the senator must wait until another day to introduce it. Once a bill is introduced in the Senate, it is numbered, and its title is recorded. This is the first reading of a bill in the Senate. The second reading of a bill is supposed to occur before a bill is referred to a committee. However, the reading is not actually done, as the reading of the bill is not a practical necessity because printed copies of all bills are available to the senators and other interested individuals. After a bill is printed, a copy is sent to the Senate committee to which the bill is assigned. Committee treatment of the bill in the Senate is essentially the same as it is in the House. Subcommittees are frequently used, and public hearings are generally held.

Floor Action

Bills that are favorably reported out of committee are placed on the Senate's calendar of business. The Senate uses this calendar for all business except nominations and treaties, which are instead placed on the Senate's executive calendar. Bills are supposed to be taken from the calendar in the order in which they were reported. However, by the unanimous consent of the Senate, bills that are deemed more important are taken from the calendar out of order.

Bills are debated in the Senate without using the Committee of the Whole because the Senate, with 100 members, is a small enough body for spirited debate by the entire membership. (The Committee of the Whole is used in the Senate only for consideration of treaties.) Debate on the Senate floor is practically unlimited. There is no powerful Rules Committee in the Senate to grant rules that limit debate, and there is no Senate rule limiting each member to one hour of debate as there is in the House. Senators believe that unlimited debate is vital to the democratic process; a bill may be, and often is, amended on the floor of the Senate.

After a bill has been debated and amended, it is reprinted. Next, the third reading takes place, which is usually only a reading of the bill's title. The bill is then voted upon and is either defeated or passed. Voting in the Senate is usually by voice vote; however, a roll-call vote may be demanded by a senator and then seconded by one-fifth of the members present.

The Filibuster

The filibuster–a method of purposely delaying the vote on a bill–is a device used only in the Senate. One of the major ways of filibustering is possible in the Senate because of unlimited debate. Thus, a senator may talk for hours to keep a bill from being brought to a vote. Sometimes a senator who filibusters is opposed to a bill either personally or because it appears that the bill will be harmful to some constituents. Over the years, some key legislation has been stopped, or at least delayed, for several years, by the use of the filibuster. Through the 1940s and 1950s, for example, **conservative** senators used the filibuster to prevent the passage of civil rights bills. These tactics were so successful that it was not until 1957 that a major civil rights bill was passed–and this bill had been filibustered by Senator Strom Thurmond for 24 hours and 18 minutes. In the 1960s, as the civil rights movement gained momentum, the filibuster was used again, but this time unsuccessfully, to block civil rights bills in the Senate.

Cloture

According to the Senate rules, filibusters can be ended by invoking cloture. The purpose of the cloture rule is to prevent a minority of senators from blocking the Senate's consideration of a bill that is favored by the majority of senators. The Senate adopted the most recent cloture rule in 1975. According to this rule, 16 senators must submit a motion calling for cloture, and the senate must take up the cloture vote within two days after the motion is submitted. A three-fifths majority of the entire Senate membership must approve the motion; if the cloture motion is accepted, debate is limited to a total of one hour for each senator–on the bill itself and on all motions and amendments concerning the bill.

The Conference Committee

Bills passed by both the House and the Senate are seldom passed in identical form. Before a bill can be sent to the president, however, it must be passed by both houses with exactly the same wording and provisions. Sometimes, one house is willing to accept all the differences in the bill passed by the other house. More often, however, a joint conference committee composed of members from each chamber must settle the differences.

The joint conference committee is supposed to consider only the parts of the bill in which disagreement over wording or provisions exists. In practice, however, committee members may make many important changes in a bill, which are usually justified as compromises necessary to reach agreement on other issues in the bill. Such compromises make possible final passage of the bill by both houses of Congress.

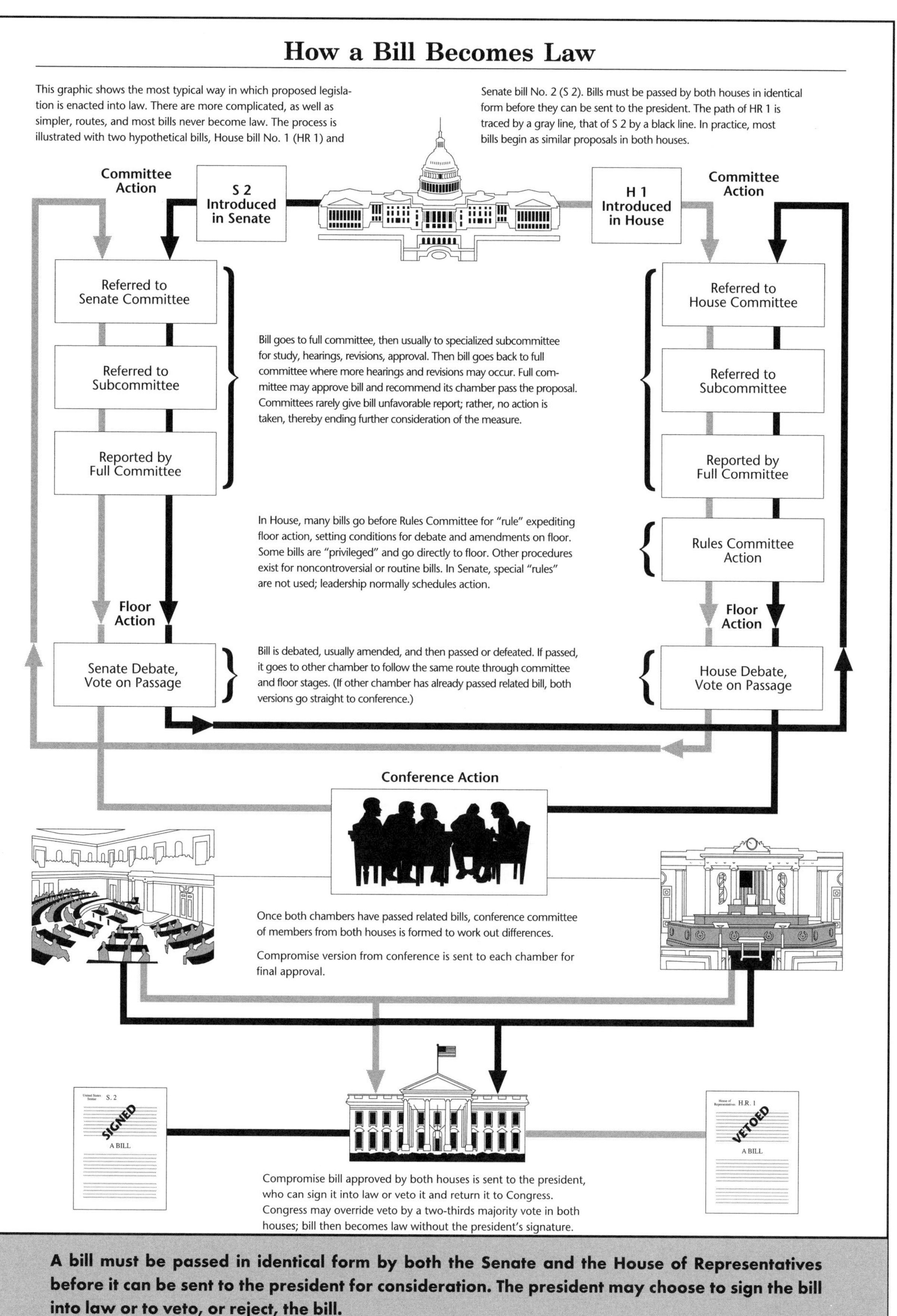

A bill must be passed in identical form by both the Senate and the House of Representatives before it can be sent to the president for consideration. The president may choose to sign the bill into law or to veto, or reject, the bill.

In both the Senate and the House of Representatives, the report of a conference committee is privileged business. The report must be accepted or rejected as it is.

Presidential Action

After a bill has been passed in identical form by both houses of Congress, it is sent to the president. The president may act in one of three ways.

First, the president may sign the bill, which is the action a president normally takes. The president's signature makes the bill the law of the land.

Second, the president may veto the bill, which prevents it from becoming law. In the case of a veto, the president must submit a written statement explaining the reasons for the veto to the house in which the bill originated. Then the bill can become law only if both houses of Congress override the president's veto–pass it again by a two-thirds majority. Most bills vetoed by the president do not become law because Congress usually finds it difficult to achieve a two-thirds vote to override a veto.

The third action the president may take is simply to refuse to act on the bill. At the end of ten days, not counting Sundays, the bill becomes law without the president's signature if Congress is still in session. If Congress has **adjourned,** however, the bill does not become law. This is known as a pocket veto.

See also: Appropriations Bills; Bicameralism; Calendars, House of Representatives; Calendars, Senate; Civil Rights Act (1964); Committees; Congressional Voting Methods; Constitution of the United States; Filibuster; House of Representatives; How a Bill Becomes Law; Joint Committees; Power of the Purse; Senate; Speaker of the House of Representatives; Vetoes and Veto Overrides; Voting Rights Act (1965).

Further Reading

Feinman, Jay M. *Law 101: Everything You Need to Know about the American Legal System.* New York: Oxford University Press, 2006.

Hames, Joanne Banker, and Yvonne Ekern. *Constitutional Law: Principle and Practice.* Clifton Park: NY: Delmar Cengage Learning, 2004.

Waldman, Stephen. *The Bill: How Legislation Really Becomes Law: A Case Study of the National Service Bill.* New York: Penguin, 1996.

Who Is Running America—Congress Or the President?

Of the three branches of government–executive, legislative, and judicial–the Founders envisioned Congress to be the branch closest to the people. In fact, many of the men attending the Constitutional Convention of 1787 were fearful of a powerful executive. Indeed, some Founders proposed a multiple executive to prevent a single executive from gaining too much power. Today, although the president of the United States wields the greatest authority, Congress retains an arsenal of powers to legislate for the nation and investigate perceived wrongdoing by government officials.

The Legislative Powers of Congress

The legislative powers of Congress are by far its most important role. Often referred to as the expressed powers, or enumerated powers, the numerous legislative powers of Congress are listed in the Constitution. In addition to the expressed powers, Congress also has **implied powers**– those powers not specifically stated or listed in the Constitution. Although the powers of Congress are great, they are not unlimited. There are both constitutional and practical limits to the powers that Congress has and the ways in which they may be used.

Financial Powers

The Constitution lists the powers of Congress in Article I, Section 8. Among these are several pertaining to domestic finance, all of which contribute to make Congress a very powerful institution. One of the most important financial powers of Congress is the power to tax. According to the Constitution, which grants Congress broad powers to levy and collect taxes, the expressed purposes for federal taxes are ". . . to pay the debts and provide for the common defense and general welfare of the United States. . . ." The debt of the United States has increased greatly as the federal government has assumed a larger role in the lives of its citizens and in world affairs. A sizeable share of federal tax money goes to pay this debt. Similarly, the cost of "the common defense" has risen significantly as the nation's leadership role in the world has increased. In the twenty-first century, the United States has faced greater costs in its effort to protect the nation from terrorist attacks at home and abroad.

Another financial power of Congress is its power to coin money and regulate the value of money. The value of coins and paper money is fixed by Congress in a variety of standard denominations. All coins and paper money are issued as legal tender, meaning that they must be accepted as payment for all debts, public and private.

One of the most critical powers of Congress is its right to borrow money on the credit of the United States. The Constitution does not place a limit on how much money Congress can borrow, but Congress sets it own limit. To meet changing circumstances, Congress periodically adjusts its borrowing limit.

Today, under its interstate **commerce** powers, Congress also regulates a wide range of activities. Among these are the production of goods; the transmission of radio, television, and other electronic media; and travel by land, water, and air. Congress has continued to broaden its interstate commerce powers through the use of its implied powers. For example, after the September 11, 2001, terrorist attacks, Congress created the Transportation Security Administration (TSA), placing it under federal control, to ensure air safety.

The Court System

Article I, Section 8, grants Congress the power to establish federal courts below the level of the Supreme Court. Congress has used this power to create two types of regular federal courts. Federal courts with original, or initial, **jurisdiction** in most cases concerning the Constitution and the laws passed by Congress are known as federal district courts. These are the federal courts where cases of U. S. citizens involving federal law are tried. The other type of regular federal courts created by Congress are those that exist between the federal district courts and the United States Supreme Court. These courts are known as courts of appeals. As the name implies, judges in the courts of appeal only hear cases that are appeals from the lower courts, namely the district courts. In addition, Congress has established special federal courts, which are responsible for only certain types of cases.

The Constitution also charges Congress with the responsibility of determining certain type of punishments. For example, Congress alone is charged with providing for the punishment of anyone who **counterfeits**–copies–United States money. It is also responsible for defining and punishing acts of piracy or any **felonies**–serious crimes–committed on the high seas.

Governing the Nation

Congress, of course, makes laws for the entire nation. Specifically, however, Article I, Section 8, Clause 17 of the Constitution gives Congress the exclusive right to make laws and rules for federally owned lands and buildings. One of the most important areas over which Congress has direct governing authority is Washington, DC. In addition, Congress has governing responsibilities over military bases, federal administrative buildings, and federal court buildings.

Congress also has the power to admit new states to the Union. Using this power, Congress has increased the size of the nation from the original 13 states to the present 50 states.

The Constitution provides:

The Congress shall have power to dispose of and make all needful rules and regulations respecting the territory or other property belonging to the United States . . .

This provision has enabled Congress to make laws for governing territories such as Guam, the Virgin Islands, and Puerto Rico. Indeed, Puerto Rico has unique **commonwealth** status, meaning it is neither a state nor wholly independent.

Foreign Relations

The Constitution grants Congress several powers dealing with foreign relations. Through its power to regulate commerce with foreign nations, Congress has prohibited the import or export of goods it considers dangerous. For example, importing drugs such as opium, except for medical uses, has been declared illegal by Congress. Congress must also approve laws that establish **free trade** regions, such as the North American Free Trade Agreement (NAFTA) between the United States, Canada, and Mexico. NAFTA is designed to eliminate barriers to trade and increase the exchange of goods among the three partners.

Throughout the nation's history, Congress has also used its foreign commerce powers to pass **embargo** acts–acts that prohibit trade. Such acts have sometimes been used to block American trade with nations that have taken action to which the United States objected.

Probably the most critical power specifically granted to Congress by the Constitution is the power to declare war. Congress has exercised that power only five times in its history–the War of 1812; the Mexican-American War (1846–1848); the Spanish-American War (1898); World War I (1917–1918); and World War II (1941–1945). However, several times in the nation's history, American troops have been sent overseas by order of the president–as commander-in-chief of the armed forces. Because a number of recent wars, such as those in Vietnam and in Iraq, have been fought without any formal declaration of war, Congress has sought to reassert its authority in this area. In 1973, Congress passed the War Powers Resolution, which limits the president's use of troops to 60 days (without a declaration of war by Congress). The resolution also requires that the president inform Congress within 48 hours of the reasons for sending American troops into combat. Furthermore, through its power to **appropriate** funds, Congress retains a great deal of power over the conduct of warfare.

Implied Powers of Congress

Article I, Clause 8, Section 18 provides the constitutional basis for the implied powers of Congress. This clause is sometimes called "the necessary and proper clause" or the "elastic clause." Through the use of the elastic clause, Congress has expanded it powers greatly during the nation's history. For example, under its powers to regulate interstate **commerce,** Congress has used its implied powers to legislate on a wide variety of subjects. Congress has determined that anything indirectly–in other words, not just

directly—related to interstate commerce comes under this power. Thus, Congress legislates on the production, as well as the distribution of goods and services involved in interstate commerce.

The implied powers of Congress cover a wide range of possibilities—and a key requirement is simply that the implied powers be used in conjunction with one of its expressed powers. For example, from the expressed powers of Congress to provide an army and a navy, it is *implied* that Congress also may maintain an air force. From the power of Congress to coin money, it is *implied* that Congress may also establish banks.

Views of the Implied Powers of Congress

From the nation's beginning, the country's leaders have held differences of opinion about the doctrine of implied powers. A very strict, or narrow, interpretation of the doctrine was held by Thomas Jefferson (1800–1809) who insisted that "necessary and proper" meant that Congress had the power to do only those things that became absolutely essential to carry out its other powers. To support their view, Jefferson and his followers cited the Tenth Amendment.

The Tenth Amendment states:

> The powers not delegated to the United States by the Constitution, nor prohibited by it to the states, are reserved to the states respectively, or to the people.

President George W. Bush greets members of Congress before the 2003 State of the Union address to Congress and the nation. The president and the Congress each have authority to check the power of the other. (Scott J. Ferrell, CQ)

The advocates of Jefferson's view thus insisted that not everything that might seem proper was by any means *necessary.* They maintained that all kinds of proper actions might be better left to the states. Thus, Jefferson and his followers became known as *strict* constructionists.

In contrast, Alexander Hamilton and his followers championed the opposite view. Hamilton argued for a broad interpretation of the necessary and proper clause. He maintained that this clause gave Congress the authority to do whatever was appropriate in carrying out its expressed powers. Hamilton and his followers became known as *loose* constructionists. Over time, the views of Hamilton and his followers have generally prevailed. Congress has enacted huge amounts of legislation for which it was granted no specifically expressed powers.

Limits of Congressional Power

Congressional powers are not unlimited. Some of the constitutional limits of congressional powers are included in Article I, Section 8. For example, the clause that grants taxing power states that taxes must be uniform throughout the United States. In addition, the Constitution forbids Congress from imposing any taxes or duties on goods from any state. The clause that gives Congress the power to maintain an army prohibits Congress from appropriating money for this purpose for more than a two-year period.

In addition, Article 1, Section 9, places a number of restrictions upon Congress. Several of these provisions are related to the personal rights of citizens. One provision prohibits Congress from suspending the writ of **habeas corpus**–the right of people to know why they are being arrested–except in cases of rebellion or invasion. Another provision prohibits Congress from passing a **bill of attainder**–a law holding a person guilty for a crime without a trial. Still another provision prohibits Congress from passing an **ex post facto** law–a law that would make illegal something that was committed before the law was passed.

Of course, the Founders built into the Constitution a limit on congressional power through the system of checks and balances. In the federal government, the president may veto laws passed by Congress and the Supreme Court can rule that laws passed by Congress are unconstitutional.

Although the president of the United States is considered the most powerful person in the nation, and perhaps in the world, the president's power is limited by the United States Constitution and by the all-encompassing powers of Congress. The president would be unable to execute the laws passed by Congress without receiving Congress's financial and political support.

President Eisenhower noted:

> All actions of the President, either domestically or in a foreign relations, must be within and pursuant to constitutional authority.

Investigative Functions of Congress

The investigative functions of Congress are designed to assist members of Congress in carrying out their legislative responsibilities. Through

★ ★ ★ ★ ★ ★ ★ ★ ★ ★ ★ ★ ★ ★ ★ ★ ★ ★ ★ ★

investigations, Congress is able to inform its members about many of the issues and problems facing the American people and the nation. Both the House of Representatives and the Senate conduct investigations. Although congressional investigations are as old as Congress, it is only since the 1920s that Congress has utilized its investigative powers on a large scale.

Among the many reasons for congressional investigations, the most important one is to gather information to be used in sponsoring legislation. As our pluralistic society has become more complex, Congress finds it necessary to examine many matters relating to both the national and the public interest. For example, in the early 1970s, rumors and leaks about the burglary at the Democratic headquarters in the Watergate complex led Congress to initiate the Watergate Investigation. The Watergate hearings uncovered the role of White House officials in the burglary and the subsequent cover-up by President Richard M. Nixon (1969–1974). Ultimately, these investigations led to the president's resignation in August 1974.

Congress also conducts investigations to gather information on the conduct of its members in cases where misconduct has been alleged. For example, in 1980, a number of representatives were charged with taking bribes in an undercover operation conducted by the Federal Bureau of Investigation (FBI), known as Abscam. As a result of the House investigation of the matter, one representative was expelled from the House of Representatives—the first expulsion since 1861.

Checking Executive Activities

Congress also uses its investigative authority to check activities of the executive branch. A great deal of congressional legislation has created the independent offices and agencies of the executive branch. A vast number of these bills contain provisions that indicate the general policy and functions that Congress intended to be carried out when it passed such bills. Furthermore, the agencies of the executive branch and the projects that they wish to accomplish receive their appropriation of funds from Congress. Therefore, Congress has a continuing interest in the activities of the executive branch. Thus, through its investigative authority, Congress has a strong tool to check presidential power.

Occasionally, Congress uses its investigative power to embarrass the president politically. This may occur, for example, when the president is a member of one party and a majority from the opposing party dominates Congress. Congressional investigating committees can and do ask embarrassing questions about a particular policy of the president. President Jimmy Carter (1977–1981) suffered such political embarrassment when a Senate subcommittee investigated charges that the president's brother, Billy Carter, used his political connections to obtain loans from Libya. The investigations uncovered no illegal or unethical conduct. The publicity generated by the hearings, however, was detrimental to Carter's reelection campaign.

Investigations and Public Opinion

Sometimes the purpose of a congressional investigation is to make the public aware of a particular problem or issue. By focusing an investigation on such

things as crime, labor problems, or drug abuse, Congress is often able to create a public interest in these issues. For example, between 2005 and 2008, Congress held a series of hearings centered on the use of illegal steroids in sports, especially major league baseball. These hearings led to an increased call for government oversight of professional sports to prevent steroid abuse.

Thus, a major reason for generating public interest in an issue is to create a demand for government action. This is especially true if there is a disagreement with the executive branch over an issue or if an issue is controversial. Congress uses the investigation to demonstrate a need for government action on the issue. In turn, the pressure of public opinion then usually produces some cooperation within the federal government.

The Impact of Non-Legislative Functions

The non-legislative functions of Congress encompass a wide variety of activities. Several of these activities involve the executive or the judicial branches of government. Some functions are the sole responsibility of the House while others are the sole responsibility of the Senate. Still other functions involve both houses of Congress.

Electing a President

The president of the United States is elected by the House of Representatives if no presidential candidate receives a majority of the votes of the electoral college. This function of the House is provided for by Article II, Section 1 of the Constitution and by the Twelfth Amendment.

When electing the president, the members of the House vote by states—one vote per state. Thus, no state has an advantage over other states. To be elected president by the House, a candidate must receive a majority of the votes of all the states.

The House has exercised its electoral function twice in the nation's history. The first time involved the Election of 1800 when two candidates—Thomas Jefferson and Aaron Burr—received the same number of electoral votes. This happened because, in 1800, electors did not vote for president and vice president separately. Thus, although Jefferson and Burr both had the necessary electoral majority, the election had to go to the House to break the tie. The House elected Jefferson president (1801–1809) and Burr became vice president.

The second occasion when the House elected the president occurred during the Election of 1824. In that year, there were four candidates from the same political party—the Democratic-Republicans—and none of the candidates received a majority of the electoral votes. The House then elected John Quincy Adams president (1825–1829).

Although the House has only exercised its electoral function twice, many people would like to see the electoral college changed. As recently as the Election of 1992, people were concerned that the election might have to be decided by the House. This concern was the result of the campaign of H. Ross Perot, the independent candidate who was expected to get enough electoral votes to keep the Republican **incumbent** George H.W.

Bush (1989–1993) or Democratic nominee Bill Clinton (1993–2001) from getting a majority of the electoral votes. In the end, however, Perot did not win any electoral votes. More recently, the closeness of both the controversial Elections of 2000 and 2004 have again raised questions about the democratic nature of the electoral college.

Electing a Vice President

If no vice presidential candidate receives a majority of the electoral votes, the vice president is elected by the Senate. The provisions of the Twelfth Amendment (1804) establish the method of voting the Senate uses when it is necessary to elect the vice president. The senators vote individually, rather than by states. The person receiving a majority of the votes of the total number of senators is elected vice president.

An additional electoral function of Congress was created with the passage of the Twenty-fifth Amendment in 1967. This **amendment** was added to the Constitution to prevent a vacancy in the vice presidency, which most recently occurred when Lyndon B. Johnson (1963–1969) assumed the presidency after the assassination of John F. Kennedy (1961–1963) in November 1963.

“The Twenty-fifth Amendment states:

> Whenever there is a vacancy in the office of vice president, the president shall nominate a vice president who shall take office upon confirmation by a majority vote of both Houses of Congress.

Both Richard M. Nixon (1969–1974) and his successor, Gerald R. Ford (1974–1977), used the Twenty-fifth Amendment in choosing a new vice president.

Proposing and Approving Amendments

The procedure for amending the United States Constitution is contained in Article V. Amendments may be proposed by one of two methods. One method is by a two-thirds vote of both houses of Congress. To date, all amendments to the Constitution have been proposed this way.

A second method for proposing amendments is by a convention called by Congress upon the request of two-thirds of the state legislatures. This method has been attempted on several occasions, but so far, no such convention as ever been called.

Congress plays a role in the **ratification,** or approval, of amendments as well as in their proposal. Article V of the Constitution authorizes Congress to choose one of two means of ratification. One process entails a vote of three-fourths of the states, a means that has been used twenty-six times. The second procedure is ratification by conventions in at least three-fourths of the states. This method has been employed only once—to ratify the Twenty-first Amendment.

Impeachment and Trial

Article II, Section 4, of the Constitution grants Congress the power to charge and to remove from office high government officials of the executive

and judicial branches. The process begins with the power to **impeach,** namely to charge a federal official with wrongdoing. The House has the sole power of **impeachment.** An impeached official is then tried by the Senate; if the Senate finds the official guilty by a two-thirds vote, the person is removed from office and is ineligible to ever hold a federal office again.

In the nation's history, two presidents and several federal judges have been impeached. In several of the cases involving judges, the accused resigned before the case went to trial in the Senate. Of those judges who stood trial, only four were convicted. In 1868, President Andrew Johnson (1865–1869) was impeached but then acquitted in the Senate by one vote. In December 1998, President Bill Clinton (1993–2001) was impeached by the House for perjury and obstruction of justice. In February 1999, the Senate acquitted the president on both charges.

In 1974, the House Judiciary Committee voted three articles of impeachment against President Richard M. Nixon (1969–1974) for his criminal involvement in the Watergate affair and his alleged cover-up of illegal acts by presidential advisers. Faced with impeachment and a likely conviction by the Senate, Nixon resigned on August 9, 1974.

Approving Appointments

Many appointments made by the president require the approval of a majority of the Senate before such persons can take office. The Senate's approval is required by Article II, Section 2 of the Constitution. In the case of the president's cabinet and the heads of most executive offices and agencies, the Senate seldom refuses to give its consent. The president's nominees for justices of the Supreme Court, diplomatic positions, and some executive offices face severe questions from the Senate or are rejected by the Senate. For example, President George W. Bush's (2001–2009) two nominees to the Supreme Court—John G. Roberts Jr. and Samuel A. Alito Jr.—each spent days before the Senate Judiciary Committee, answering a variety of questions before finally being confirmed.

Confirming Treaties

Creating treaties with the governments of other nations is an important duty of the president but one that is shared with the Senate.

Article II, Section 2, of the Constitution states:

> [The president] shall have Power, by and with the Advice and Consent of the Senate, to make Treaties, provided two-thirds of the senators present concur . . .

However, getting two-thirds of the senators to agree to a treaty can be difficult. In the case of very important treaties, the Senate has rarely refused to give its consent. Yet, after World War I (1917–1918), the Senate rejected the Treaty of Versailles, which would have made the nation a member of the League of Nations. In 1926 and again in 1935, the Senate rejected a treaty that would have given the United States membership in

the World Court. In both these instances, a majority, but not two-thirds, of the senators were in favor of confirmation.

Of course, the Founders built into the Constitution a limit on congressional power through the system of checks and balances. In the federal government, the president may veto laws passed by Congress and the Supreme Court, as established by *Marbury v. Madison* (1803), can rule that laws passed by Congress are unconstitutional.

See also: Constitutional Convention; Foreign Policy Powers; Impoundment; Iraq War Resolution (2002); Power of the Purse; Power to Raise an Army; Separation of Powers; Treaty Power; Vetoes and Veto Overrides; War Powers Resolution (1973).

Further Reading

Dodd, Lawrence C., and Bruce I. Oppenheimer (eds.). *Congress Reconsidered.* Eighth edition. Washington, DC: CQ Press, 2004.

Sinclair, Barbara. *Unorthodox Lawmaking.* Washington, DC: CQ Press, 2007.

Wilson, Woodrow. *Congressional Government: A Study in American Politics.* Mineola, New York: Dover, 2006.

Part Two

Congress A–Z

Abscam

In 1980, an FBI undercover operation that implicated seven members of Congress in criminal wrongdoing. By May 1981, juries had convicted the six House members and one senator for their roles in the affair. By March 11, 1982, none of the seven were still in Congress.

The House members involved in the Abscam (a combination of the words Arab and scam) affair were John W. Jenrette, Jr. (D-SC), Richard Kelly (R-FL), Raymond F. Lederer (D-PA), John M. Murphy (D-NY), Michael J. "Ozzie" Myers (D-PA), and Frank Thompson, Jr. (D-NJ). Another House member, John P. Murtha (D-PA), was named an unindicted coconspirator and testified for the government in the trial of Murphy and Thompson. The senator involved in Abscam was Harrison A. Williams, Jr. (D-NJ).

Abscam led to a number of congressional actions with respect to the convicted seven. Myers was expelled from the House of Representatives on October 2, 1980, only the fourth representative expelled and the first since the Civil War (1861–1865). Jenrette, Lederer, and Williams resigned from Congress to avoid almost certain expulsion. Kelly, Murphy, and Thompson were defeated for reelection before being convicted in court. The unindicted coconspirator, Murtha, was cleared by the House Ethics Committee over the objections of the committee counsel.

Two elements made Abscam more than a routine corruption case. One was the FBI's use of videotapes to record the meetings of phony sheiks, members of Congress, and others. The other unusual element of the affair was the prominence of three of those convicted–senior committee chairs, two of whom (Thompson and Williams) were considered party leaders. Published accounts and evidence presented in the court cases that followed the indictments provided a look into the full nature of the scandal. Undercover FBI agents approached

Members of Congress in Abscam

Member	Chamber of Congress	Party	State
John W. Jenrette, Jr.	House	Democrat	South Carolina
Richard Kelly	House	Republican	Florida
Raymond F. Lederer	House	Democrat	Pennsylvania
John M. Murphy	House	Democrat	New York
Michael J. Myers	House	Democrat	Pennsylvania
Frank Thompson, Jr.	House	Democrat	New Jersey
Harrison A. Williams, Jr.	Senate	Democrat	New Jersey

The Abscam scandal affected members of both the United States House of Representatives and the Senate as well as members of both political parties.

a number of members of Congress offering to introduce them to representatives of wealthy Arabs interested in making investments in their districts. Some of the members were asked if they could use their positions to help the Arabs obtain U.S. residency. Others were asked to use their influence in government to obtain federal grants and gambling licenses or to arrange real estate deals. Several of the accused were videotaped accepting cash or stock. Another was tape-recorded saying that he had been given the cash by an associate. The defendants claimed that the government had entrapped them. This claim gained some support in government and in the legal profession, but, in the end, it did not protect those involved.

Ad Hoc Committees

Committees in either the U.S. House of Representatives or the U.S. Senate that meet on a temporary basis to deal with business on behalf of both chambers of Congress. All conference committees created by the House or the Senate to resolve differences in legislation are considered ad hoc committees. The House and Senate also create ad hoc committees for a one-time purpose–such as to investigate a scandal–or to examine a specific subject. Most ad hoc committees are created with a deadline by which they must complete their work. After the deadline, the committees expire.

The Speaker of the House of Representatives has the authority to create ad hoc committees, if approved by a vote of the House, to consider legislation that might be within the **jurisdiction** of several committees. Membership of such ad hoc committees would come from committees that would otherwise have exercised legislative control. The authority to form such committees was created in 1977. Among the most notable uses of this authority was in the 95th Congress, when an ad hoc committee was formed to handle consideration of major energy legislation proposed by President Jimmy Carter's (1977–1981) administration.

In 1995, the new Republican majority in Congress extended this idea to oversight, giving the Speaker of the House the power to propose, subject to a House vote, the creation of ad hoc oversight committees to review specific matters within the jurisdiction of two or more standing committees. The use of oversight to investigate President Bill Clinton's administration (1993–2001) became a Republican priority. This oversight was conducted through standing committees with efforts at coordination by the party leadership. Ultimately, the committee's finding led to President Clinton's impeachment by the House of Representatives. Later, he was acquitted of all charges by the Senate.

Adams, John Quincy (1767–1848)

Government under the sixth president of the United States. John Quincy Adams (1825–1829) was a prominent figure in the early federal government who also served terms in both the Senate and the House of Representatives. Adams gained a reputation as an opponent of slavery and government corruption, and was often outspoken and combative. Both his election as president in 1824 and his later term in the House were marked by controversy.

Adams was the son of the nation's second president, John Adams. His early political career included appointment as minister to several European nations between 1794 and 1801. He ran unsuccessfully for the U.S. House of Representatives in 1802, but the next year he won election to the U.S. Senate. In 1807, he wrote a committee report supporting the Senate's power to expel a member for prior misconduct that came to light after the member had taken his seat. The case concerned John Smith, a senator who allegedly had been connected with an earlier conspiracy to separate several western states from the Union. In the Senate ballot for removal, Smith retained his seat by a single vote.

Adams won the disputed presidential election of 1824. None of the contenders had enough electoral votes to win, so the House chose from among the top three contenders—Adams, Andrew Jackson, and William H. Crawford. When the House met to vote, thirteen of twenty-four state delegations supported Adams—the minimum he needed for election. As president, Adams faced stiff political opposition to his policies and lost his bid for reelection in 1828.

The United States House of Representatives elected John Quincy Adams to the presidency because no candidate received a majority of the electoral votes. The house chose among the top three candidates—Andrew Jackson, John Quincy Adams, and William H. Crawford. (Library of Congress)

Three years later, Adams was elected to the U.S. House of Representatives, where he found himself in the middle of several controversies. In 1836, he challenged the House practice of refusing to receive petitions and memorials on the subject of slavery. Adams offered a petition from citizens of Massachusetts to abolish slavery in the District of Columbia. His action led the House to adopt a resolution stating that any papers dealing with slavery "shall, without being either printed or referred, be laid upon the table and that no further action whatever shall be had thereon."

Adams considered the resolution a violation of the Constitution and of the rules of the House. He reopened the issue in 1837 by asking the Speaker of the House how to dispose of a petition he had received from twenty-two slaves. Southern representatives moved at once to censure, or condemn, Adams for this action. Although the censure resolution failed, the House agreed that "slaves do not possess the right of petition secured to the people of the United States by the Constitution."

Adams faced censure again in 1842 for presenting to the House a petition asking Congress to dissolve the Union and allow the states to go their separate ways. The resolution to censure him was worded so strongly that Adams asserted his Sixth Amendment right to a trial by jury. In the end, his opponents backed down and the resolution never came to a vote.

See also: Censure; Power to Select the President.

Further Reading

Richards, Leonard L. *The Life and Times of Congressman John Quincy Adams.* New York: Oxford University Press, 1988.

Wheelan. Joseph. *Mr. Adams' Last Crusade: The Extraordinary Post-presidential Career of John Quincy Adams.* Washington, DC: PublicAffairs, 2008.

African Americans in Congress

African American membership in the U.S. Congress between 1870 and 2007. One hundred and twenty-one African Americans have served in Congress—five in the Senate and one hundred and sixteen in the House of Representatives, including non-voting delegates. The first African American elected to Congress was John W. Menard. However, his 1868 election in Louisiana was disputed and the House denied him a seat. Hiram R. Revels of Mississippi, who served in the Senate from February 1870 to March 1871, was the first African American actually to serve in Congress. The first African American elected to the House of Representatives was Joseph H. Rainey of South Carolina. Rainey served from December 1870 to March 1879.

The Reconstruction Era and Afterward

Menard, Revels, and Rainey were elected during the period after the Civil War known as **Reconstruction** (1865–1877), when African Americans first gained the right to vote. During that period, sixteen African American men were sent to Congress. From the end of Reconstruction until the late 1800s, however, only seven African American men were elected to Congress. During that period, **literacy tests, poll taxes,** and threats of violence eroded African American voting rights. From the time Blanche K. Bruce of Mississippi left the Senate in 1881, no other African American served in that body until Republican Edward W. Brooke of Massachusetts, who served from 1967 to 1979. In 1992, Illinois Democrat Carol Moseley-Braun was elected to the Senate, becoming the first black woman to gain a Senate seat.

The last African American elected to the House in the nineteenth century was Republican George Henry White of North Carolina, who served from 1896 to 1900. No other African Americans were elected to Congress until

African Americans in Congress, 1945–2009

Congress	Senate	House
79th (1945–1947)	0	2
80th (1947–1949)	0	2
81st (1949–1951)	0	2
82nd (1951–1953)	0	2
83rd (1953–1955)	0	2
84th (1955–1957)	0	3
85th (1957–1959)	0	4
86th (1959–1961)	0	4
87th (1961–1963)	0	4
88th (1963–1965)	0	5
89th (1965–1967)	0	6
90th (1967–1969)	1	5
91st (1969–1971)	1	9
92nd (1971–1973)	1	12
93rd (1973–1975)	1	15
94th (1975–1977)	1	16
95th (1977–1979)	1	16
96th (1979–1981)	0	16
97th (1981–1983)	0	17
98th (1983–1985)	0	20
99th (1985–1987)	0	20
100th (1987–1989)	0	22
101st (1989–1991)	0	24
102nd (1991–1993)	0	26
103rd (1993–1995)	1	39
104th (1995–1997)	1	38
105th (1997–1999)	1	37
106th (1999–2001)	0	37
107th (2001–2003)	0	40
108th (2003–2005)	0	39
109th (2005–2007)	1	42
110th (2007–2009)	1	42

African American membership in the United States House of Representatives has continued to grow since 1945. African American membership in the Senate, however, has not increased over the years.

A–Z

Decision Makers

Barack Obama (1961–)

Senator Barack Obama was born in Honolulu, Hawaii, on August 4, 1961. His father was from Kenya in Africa and his mother was an American from Kansas. Obama received his early education in Indonesia and Hawaii. He later went to New York, where he graduated from Columbia University in 1983.

Although Obama planned to attend law school after Columbia, he decided instead to move to Chicago, where he worked for a church organization that was trying to improve living conditions in poor neighborhoods. That experience made him realize that more than just local efforts were needed to really improve the lives of people. Changes in federal laws and politics were necessary.

Obama later went to Harvard University, earning a law degree in 1991. While at Harvard, he became the first African American president of the *Harvard Law Review.* After receiving his degree from Harvard, he returned to Chicago, worked as a civil rights lawyer, and taught constitutional law at the University of Chicago.

Obama's belief in the need to change laws through political action led him to run for the State Senate in Illinois in 1996. He served there from 1997 to 2004, working to create various programs aimed at helping improve the lives of poor and working families. Among his achievements were tax cuts for low-income families and an expansion of early childhood education programs.

In 2004, Obama decided to run for the U.S. Senate under the Democratic Party banner. He won, and with this victory, Obama became only the third African American since Reconstruction to be elected to the Senate. During his time in the Senate, he has continued to focus his efforts on improving the lives of ordinary Americans and to help them meet the growing challenges of the twenty-first century. He also has worked to increase American security in an increasingly dangerous and competitive world. In 2007, Obama announced that he would run for the U.S presidency in 2008; by early summer, he appeared to have won the nomination.

Republican Oscar De Priest of Illinois entered the House in 1929. During the next quarter-century only three other African Americans were elected to Congress: Arthur W. Mitchell of Illinois in 1934, William L. Dawson of Illinois in 1942, and Adam Clayton Powell Jr. of New York in 1944. All three represented large, **urban** African American populations.

Party Membership

Reflecting a switch in African American voting habits, Mitchell, Dawson, and Powell were all Democrats. Before that time, all African Americans in Congress were Republicans. However, Democratic President Franklin D. Roosevelt (1933–1945) pulled a majority of African American voters away from the Republican Party.

Arthur Mitchell, the first African American Democrat elected to the House, was brought in by a Democratic sweep in the 1934 election. That election also removed African American Republican Oscar De Priest and marked the beginning of a fifty-six-year absence of African American representation among House Republicans. It was not until the election of Gary Franks of Connecticut in 1990 that an African American Republican served again in the House.

House Democrats, in contrast, steadily gained African American members. Only two were added in the 1950s–Charles C. Diggs, Jr. of Michigan and Robert N. C. Nix of Pennsylvania–but the pace quickened after that. Five more were elected in the 1960s, and fourteen each in the 1970s and 1980s. The number of African Americans elected to Congress more than doubled during the 1990s.

Growth In African American Membership

Supreme Court rulings in the early 1960s, **ratification** of the Twenty-fourth Amendment in 1964, and passage of the 1965 Voting Rights Act all increased rights for African American voters. The Voting Rights Act helped increase voter registration among African Americans. The Twenty-fourth Amendment outlawed poll taxes and other restrictions on voting. The courts eventually ended a southern practice of diluting African American voting power by **gerrymandering** voting districts. As African American voter turnouts increased, so did African American representation in Congress.

House Ways and Means Committee chairman Charles B. Rangel, D-N.Y. (left), talks to reporters on the escalator at the Longworth House Office Building. They spoke after the committee's hearing with Treasury Secretary Henry M. Paulson, Jr., in early 2007. (Scott J. Ferrell, CQ, C-SPAN)

In 1968 Representative Shirley Chisholm, a Democrat from New York, became the first African American woman elected to Congress. In 1973 she was joined in the House by Democrats Yvonne Brathwaite Burke of California, Barbara C. Jordan of Texas, and Cardiss Collins of Illinois. Next came Democrat Katie Hall of Indiana, elected in 1982. The 1990 election brought Democrats Maxine Waters of California and Barbara-Rose Collins of Michigan into the House. Barbara Jordan, along with Democrat Andrew Young of Georgia, also elected in 1972, were the first African Americans in the twentieth century to go to Congress from states of the Old Confederacy.

The 103rd Congress (1993–1995) included several firsts for African Americans. Carol Moseley-Braun of Illinois became the first African American woman elected to the Senate. Also, for the first time since Reconstruction, Alabama, Florida, North Carolina, South Carolina, and Virginia elected African Americans to the House. Georgia elected its first African American woman representative, Cynthia McKinney. Dramatic gains for African Americans in the 1992 elections were largely a result of redistricting aimed at increasing minority strength in Congress. However, redistricting efforts came under attack later in the 1990s. By 1999, a number of Supreme Court decisions had set new standards that limited this method of increasing African American representation in Congress.

Despite the steady gains of African Americans being elected to Congress, they remained underrepresented there. In 1999, African Americans made up about 12 percent of the population of the United States, but only 9 percent of the House was African American and they had only one representative in the Senate.

The new generation of African Americans elected to Congress in the 1990s reflected the changes begun during the civil rights era of the 1960s. Many came to Congress with considerable experience in state and local government. Bobby L. Rush of Illinois had served for a decade on the Chicago City Council. Earl F. Hilliard, Alabama's first African American representative since Reconstruction, served in the Alabama legislature for 18 years.

See also: Civil Rights Act (1964); Congressional Black Caucus; House of Representatives; Political Parties and Congress; Redistricting; Senate; Voting Rights Act (1965); Women in Congress.

Further Reading

Tate, Katherine. *Black Faces in the Mirror: African Americans and Their Representatives in the U.S. Congress.* Princeton, NJ: Princeton University Press, 2002.

The Albany Plan of Union

Created at a meeting in Albany, New York, an early attempt to form a union of the British colonies. Attended by representatives of seven of Britain's thirteen North American colonies, the Albany Congress of 1754 was initiated by the British in an effort to secure the wavering friendship of their longtime allies, the six Indian nations of the Iroquois Confederacy. The Iroquois had come under increasing pressure from the French along the western frontier of their territory. The Americans who represented the seven colonies that took part–Massachusetts, New Hampshire, Connecticut, Rhode Island, New York, Pennsylvania, and Maryland–were more ambitious. They not only concluded a treaty with the Iroquois, but they also adopted a plan of union drafted largely by Benjamin Franklin.

The Albany plan called on the British Parliament to create "one general government" in America. This government was to be administered by a president-general appointed by the Crown and a grand council of representatives from all of the colonies (in proportion to their financial contributions) elected by the colonial assemblies. This government was to have the sole authority to regulate Indian affairs. It also was to have the power to purchase and sell new lands, raise troops for the common defense, and levy "such general duties, imposts, or taxes . . . as may be collected with the least inconvenience to the people."

Benjamin Franklin was one of the primary leaders in the move to create a union of colonies. He was also a major force in the development of the Albany Plan of Union. (Library of Congress)

Both the British Crown and the colonial assemblies opposed the Albany Plan because it granted too much power to the proposed central government. Britain was not prepared to give the colonies that much **autonomy,** while the colonial assemblies were not ready to share their power to tax. "The different and contrary reasons of dislike to my plan made me suspect that it was really the true medium," Franklin later wrote, "and I am still of the opinion it would have been happy for both sides of the water if it had been adopted."

As it was, the Albany Plan reflected a growing awareness of the need for a common approach to administration of the expanding American colonies. Rejection of the plan was a major landmark along the path to the Declaration of Independence in 1776 and the Constitutional Convention of 1787, which created the U.S. Constitution.

Major Points of the Albany Plan

- The government will be administered by a President-General appointed by the Crown.
- The government will consist of a Grand Council.
- Members of the Grand Council will be elected every three years.
- The number of members on the Grand Council for each state will be determined by the revenues that each state pays to the government treasury.
- The Grand Council will meet at least once a year.
- All acts of the Grand Council must be approved by the President-General.
- The Grand Council and President-General will make laws for regulating and governing new settlements.

The Albany Plan of Union was the first attempt to unite the Thirteen Colonies. Under the proposal, a president-general would be appointed by the British Crown.

Amending the Constitution

The individuals who drafted the Constitution wanted it to be flexible enough to deal with changing social and political realities. For this reason, they provided a mechanism for proposing **amendments,** or formal changes, to the document. Congress and the state legislatures play the central roles in this process. The president has no formal authority over constitutional amendments.

The Amendment Process

Article V of the Constitution provides two separate procedures for amendment. Under the first method, Congress may propose an amendment that it then submits to the states for **ratification,** or approval. Under the second method, the state legislatures may request that Congress call a general convention to propose a Constitutional amendment. This requires two-thirds of the state legislatures to submit petitions to Congress. Congress, however, determines what form such a convention takes.

Regardless of which method is used, Congress determines the process by which the states vote on a proposed amendment. Congress may specify that the state legislatures must vote on the amendment, or it may call for the states to hold conventions to vote on the amendment. In either case, if three-fourths of the states vote to ratify, or approve, the amendment, it becomes a part of the Constitution. The amendment comes into effect on the day when the required number of state ratifications is reached.

In every case except one, Congress has specified that the state legislatures must vote on ratification. The sole exception was the Twenty-first Amendment, **ratified** in December 1933. The amendment called for **repeal,** or reversal, of the Eighteenth Amendment, passed fourteen years earlier. The Eighteenth Amendment enacted **Prohibition,** which outlawed the manufacture and sale of alcohol in the United States. Congress chose to call state conventions for ratification in this case for several reasons. First, it wanted speedy ratification of the proposed amendment, and it considered conventions a quicker process than voting by state legislatures. Second, backers of the Twenty-first Amendment argued that the state legislatures ratified the Eighteenth Amendment under pressure from Prohibition supporters. They claimed that the vote in favor of Prohibition did not represent the views of the majority of the people. Finally, Congress wanted to end the political divisions between states, regions, and parties caused by Prohibition.

The Role of Congress

Although the Constitutional Convention envisioned a substantial role for the states in the amendment process, Congress has dominated that procedure. The states never have successfully petitioned Congress to call a convention to amend the Constitution. During the first hundred years of its existence, Congress received only ten such petitions from state legislatures, but between 1893 and 1974, it received more than three hundred. By contrast, Congress has proposed 33 Constitutional amendments. The states have approved twenty-seven of these amendments and refused to ratify only six.

The need to obtain the approval of three-fourths of the states often has deterred Congress from proposing amendments. On at least one occasion, however, Congress took the lead in order to prevent the states from petitioning for a Constitutional convention. For years, the Senate had repeatedly blocked efforts to allow for the direct election of senators by voters (the Constitution called for state legislatures to choose the senators for each state). By the early 1900s, the state legislatures were under great public pressure to call for a convention to change the process. Congress responded by proposing the Seventeenth Amendment, which provided for direct election of senators. The states ratified the amendment in 1913.

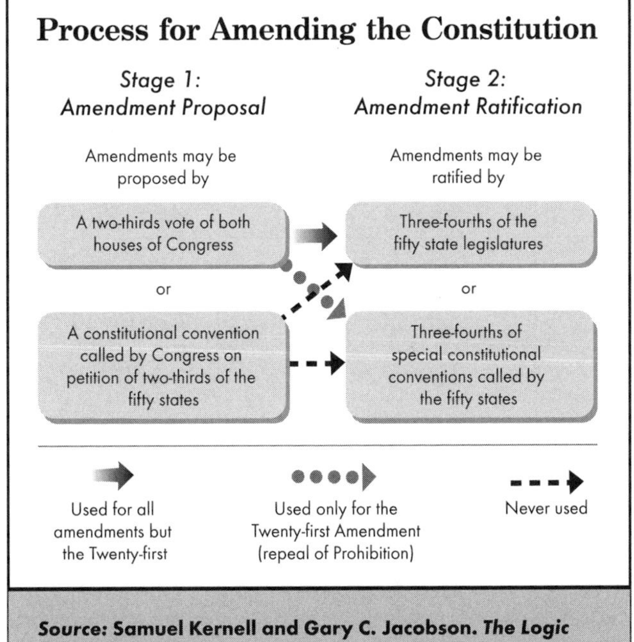

Source: Samuel Kernell and Gary C. Jacobson. *The Logic of American Politics*. Third Edition. Washington, D.C.: CQ Press, 2005.

The Founders outlined several procedures for amending the United States Constitution. To date, all amendments have been proposed by Congress.

The Supreme Court has said little about the amending power of Congress. Most of the Court's decisions came in the wake of the controversial Prohibition amendments. The Court ruled at that time that liquor was a proper subject for a constitutional amendment. It also stated that two-thirds of the members of the House or Senate present must approve a proposed amendment, not two-thirds of the entire membership. The Court also ruled that Congress has the power to set a time limit for ratification.

Questions still exist regarding several aspects of the amendment process. These questions arise because the wording of the Constitution often leaves room for different interpretations. Areas of debate include the procedures for a Constitutional convention, the process of ratification itself, and time limits on ratification.

Constitutional Conventions

Because the states have never successfully petitioned Congress to call a constitutional convention, important questions about the procedures for holding such a convention have never been answered. In 1971 and 1973, the Senate passed **bills** establishing convention procedures, but the House never considered either bill. The Senate Judiciary Committee approved similar bills in 1982, 1984, and 1985, but the full Senate refused to consider them. The major concerns about a constitutional convention center on a number of questions:

Valid Convention Call

What constitutes a valid call of two-thirds of the legislatures? Must each state's **resolutions** to Congress be identical in all details, or must they simply relate to one general subject? Is it a valid convention call if thirty-four states wish to consider different amendment proposals?

Length of Time to Call

In what time span must the required two-thirds of the states submit their resolutions? The Constitution is silent on this point. Throughout most of the twentieth century, Congress specified a seven-year maximum period for ratification.

A – Z

Length of Ratification Time

Amendment	Passed Congress	Ratified	Time elapsed Years	Days
1–10 (Bill of Rights)	Sept. 25, 1789	Dec. 15, 1791	2	81
11 (Suits against states)	March 4, 1794	Feb. 7, 1795		340
12 (Presidential electors)	Dec. 9, 1803	June 15, 1804		189
13 (Abolition of slavery)	Jan. 31, 1865	Dec. 6, 1865		309
14 (Civil rights: due process)	June 13, 1866	July 9, 1868	2[a]	26
15 (Black suffrage)	Feb. 26, 1869	Feb. 3, 1870		342
16 (Income tax)	July 12, 1909	Feb. 3, 1913	3[a]	206
17 (Direct election of senators)	May 13, 1912	April 8, 1913		330
18 (Prohibition)	Dec. 18, 1917	Jan. 16, 1919	1	29
19 (Women's suffrage)	June 4, 1919	Aug. 18, 1920	1[a]	75
20 ("Lame-duck")	March 2, 1932	Jan. 23, 1933		327
21 (Prohibition repealed)	Feb. 20, 1933	Dec. 5, 1933		288
22 (Presidential tenure)	March 24, 1947	Feb. 27, 1951	3[a]	340
23 (D.C. vote)	June 16, 1960	March 29, 1961		286
24 (Poll tax)	Sept. 14, 1962	Jan. 23, 1964	1	131
25 (Presidential disability)	July 6, 1965	Feb. 10, 1967	1	219
26 (18-year-old vote)	March 23, 1971	July 1, 1971		100
27 (Congressional pay raise)	Sept. 25, 1789	May 7, 1992	202[a]	225

Note: a. Includes leap year(s).

Sources: Congressional Research Service, Library of Congress, *The Constitution of the United States of America: Analysis and Interpretation* (Washington, D.C., Government Printing Office, 1973); and *Congressional Quarterly Almanac: 102nd Congress, 2nd Session, 1992*, vol. 48 (Washington, D.C.: Congressional Quarterly, 1993), 58–59.

The length of time for the ratification of proposed amendments to the Constitution varies greatly. The first ten amendments were proposed and ratified as a group. The Twenty-sixth Amendment was ratified after 100 days, while the Twenty-seventh Amendment took more than 202 years.

Rescinding a Call

Can a state rescind, or take back, a previous call for a convention? The Constitution says nothing about the legality of such an action. When New Jersey and Ohio attempted to withdraw their ratifications of the Fourteenth Amendment in 1868, Congress refused to accept the withdrawals.

Forcing Congress to Act

If the required two-thirds of the legislatures issue a convention call, is Congress obligated to call the convention? According to the Constitution, it would appear to have no choice. Congress, however, might find an excuse to invalidate individual state petitions, and the Supreme Court might consider Congress the final judge of those petitions.

Procedures for a Call

How would Congress act to call a convention? The Senate and House Judiciary committees probably would pass resolutions that the two houses would approve. What would happen, however, if one of the Judiciary committees refused to pass such a resolution? Even if the resolution passed, what if Senate opponents blocked the resolution with a filibuster?

Restricting a Convention

How should a congressional resolution calling a convention be worded? A convention might decide to consider a whole range of changes that could threaten the very foundations of the Constitution. Should, or could, Congress limit the convention to the subject named in the states' petitions? Could it narrowly define that subject? The convention that wrote the U.S.

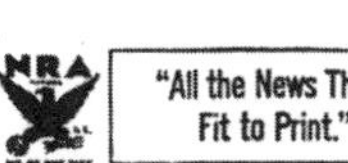

"All the News That's Fit to Print."

The New York Times.

LATE CITY EDITION

WEATHER—Rain and warmer today; tomorrow fair and colder.

VOL. LXXXIII....No. 27,710. NEW YORK, WEDNESDAY, DECEMBER 6, 1933. TWO CENTS

LINDBERGHS AT SEA ON BRAZIL FLIGHT; 'O.K.' SHE REPORTS

630 MILES FROM AFRICA

Breeze Starts Fliers After Twenty Attempts in Dead Calm.

MOON LIGHTS THEIR WAY

10,000 Natives See Take-Off as Motor's Roar Stirs Them From Slumber.

RIDE THROUGH SQUALLS

Wife Radios Every Fifteen Minutes of Progress on 1,800-Mile Flight.

Lindbergh Flight to Fame Twice as Long as New Hop

PWA READY TO BAR CITY SUBWAY LOAN

Security for $25,000,000 Advance to Finish System Is Held Inadequate.

BANKERS' PACTS A FACTOR

Officials Here Say Attitude of Washington Is Based on a Misunderstanding.

TAX PLAN OFFERED TO CURB EVASIONS, RAISE $237,000,000

House Subcommittee Urges a Check on Personal Holding Concerns by 35% Levy.

WOULD INCREASE SURTAX

Normal Income Tax of 4% and Revision of Capital Gains Are Also Proposed.

PROHIBITION REPEAL IS RATIFIED AT 5:32 P. M.; ROOSEVELT ASKS NATION TO BAR THE SALOON; NEW YORK CELEBRATES WITH QUIET RESTRAINT

State House Bootlegger Is Barred in Maryland

RATIFYING BY UTAH ENDS PROHIBITION

With Impressive Ceremony, the 36th State Follows Ohio and Pennsylvania in Day.

CONVENTIONS ALL SOLEMN

Moderation Pleas Are Made at Columbus—Hush Greets Vote at Harrisburg.

CITY TOASTS NEW ERA

Crowds Swamp Licensed Resorts, but the Legal Liquor Is Scarce.

CELEBRATION IN STREETS

Marked by Absence of Undue Hilarity and Only Normal Number of Arrests.

MANY SPEAKEASIES CLOSE

Machine Guns Guard Some Liquor Trucks—Supplies to Be Rushed Out Today.

The Repeal Proclamation

WASHINGTON, Dec. 5.—The text of the proclamation by William Phillips, Acting Secretary of State, certifying to the adoption of the Twenty-first Amendment repealing prohibition, follows:

WILLIAM PHILLIPS,
Acting Secretary of State of the United States of America.

JOINT RESOLUTION.

ARTICLE.

WILLIAM PHILLIPS.

Roosevelt Proclaims Repeal; Urges Temperance in Nation

FINAL ACTION AT CAPITAL

President Proclaims the Nation's New Policy as Utah Ratifies.

PHILLIPS SIGNS DECREE

Orders 21st Amendment in Effect on Receiving Votes of Three Final States.

RECOVERY TAXES TO END

$227,000,000 a Year Automatically Dropped—Canadian Whisky Quota Is Raised.

The *New York Times* announced the passage of the Twenty-first Amendment, repealing the Eighteenth Amendment and ending Prohibition, on December 6, 1933. The Twenty-first Amendment is the only amendment that repeals an earlier amendment. (The Granger Collection, New York)

JUSTICE FOR ALL

The Equal Rights Amendment

The proposed Equal Rights Amendment (ERA) to the Constitution, approved by Congress in March 1972, after a forty-nine-year campaign by ERA proponents, died June 30, 1982. In all, thirty-five states voted for ratification, three short of the required three-fourths majority.

The proposed amendment originally required ratification within seven years, but Congress in 1978 extended the deadline by thirty-nine months. Despite a massive **lobbying** campaign by women's groups and other supporters, not a single additional state voted to ratify the amendment during the extension. The amendment's fate was sealed in June 1982, when the legislatures of North Carolina, Florida, and Illinois voted against ratification. They were among fifteen states that rejected the amendment during the ten-year ratification period. The proposal was brief and to the point, stating that:

> Equality of rights under the law shall not be denied or abridged by the United States or by any state on account of sex.

The amendment authorized Congress to enforce the provision by "appropriate legislation." The amendment would take effect two years after ratification.

A resolution proposing such an amendment had been introduced in every Congress since 1923. In 1950 and 1953, the Senate had approved the proposed amendment but the House took no action.

Less than two hours after the Senate acted on March 22, 1972,

A – Z

Constitution originally was charged merely with amending the Articles of Confederation. Instead, it created an entirely new governing document.

Apportionment of Delegates

How many representatives would each state have at a constitutional convention? Here again, the Constitution is silent. The Constitutional Convention of 1787 had different numbers of delegates representing their states, but each state received only one vote. Congress presumably could require that each state have the same number of representatives at a constitutional convention as it does in the U.S. House, or the House and Senate combined.

Selecting Delegates

How would delegates be chosen? Congress could leave that question to the state legislatures, or it might try to lay down ground rules for election.

Ratification Procedures

Unresolved questions also exist about ratification of amendments. Constitutional scholars disagree about whether Congress or the state legislatures should determine the procedures for ratification by state conventions. Bills have been introduced in Congress to spell out procedures, but none has passed. State legislatures have been divided on this question. At least twenty-one legislatures require state officials to follow procedures specified in a federal law if Congress

Hawaii became the first state to ratify the measure. In the six months following congressional passage, twenty other states followed suit. Nine states endorsed the amendment in 1973, three in 1974, and only one—North Dakota—in 1975.

By early 1978, thirty-five states had ratified the amendment, but several state legislatures had either shelved or flatly rejected it. Moreover, several states that had ratified it tried to rescind their approval. The validity of this action was challenged in the federal courts, but the Supreme Court never made a definitive ruling.

Despite official endorsements from a wide spectrum of women's groups, labor unions, and political and civic organizations of every stripe, the drive for passage of the Equal Rights Amendment encountered vigorous opposition. It was argued that passage would subject women to the draft, abolish protections women had from dangerous and unpleasant jobs, wipe out women's rights to privacy in public facilities (hospital facilities, rest rooms, and so forth), and adversely affect marriage laws and property and divorce rights. Supporters responded that the ERA would not have affected constitutional privacy rights but would have ended unlawful discrimination, ensuring equal treatment for men as well as women in areas such as employment, pay, benefits, and criminal trials and sentences.

Identical constitutional amendments were introduced in the mid-1980s, but by then support for the ERA had waned and none was approved by Congress. The House in November 1983 came close to approving another ERA attempt, voting 278–147 for a new constitutional amendment, but it was six votes short of the necessary two-thirds majority.

should enact one. Sixteen legislatures passed their own laws for determining procedures for ratification. New Mexico has claimed exclusive authority to decide on ratification procedures. It has ordered state officials to resist congressional attempts to challenge that authority.

Another question in this area is whether a state can change its mind and rescind its ratification of a proposed amendment. The Supreme Court has ruled that a state can ratify an amendment that it initially opposed, but it has never addressed the opposite situation.

Time for Ratification

Another uncertainty concerns the definition of a "reasonable" time period for ratification. The Supreme Court has left that definition to Congress. In 1921, the Court ruled that Congress had the power to fix a definite ratification period "within reasonable limits." In 1939, the Court said that the definition of a "reasonable" period was essentially political and should be answered by Congress, rather than by the Court.

Congress got an opportunity to address the issue in 1992, when three-quarters of the states ratified the Twenty-seventh Amendment. The amendment, first proposed by James Madison in 1789, states that changes in the salary of Congress members can only take place after the next general election. The amendment was intended to restrain Congress's power to set its own salary. The final ratification was

Amendments Not Ratified by the States

As of 2007, more than 9,000 proposed amendments to the Constitution had been introduced in Congress. Of these, about one-third had been introduced since 1960. Many were identical or similar in content, and some were introduced repeatedly. The unsuccessful Equal Rights Amendment (ERA), for example, was introduced in every Congress between 1923 and 1972.

Congress has acted on proposals to amend the Constitution only when there was persistent and widespread public support. Only thirty-three proposals have been approved and sent to the states for ratification. Of these, twenty-seven were ratified and only six did not win the required three-fourths majority of the states—an indication of how well Congress usually reflects public sentiment.

Of the six congressionally approved amendments that were not ratified by the states, one was proposed in September 1789, along with the Bill of Rights. Concerned with the **apportionment** of representatives, it was ratified by ten states, one fewer than the number then required.

In 1810, an amendment providing for revocation of the citizenship of any American accepting a gift or title of nobility from any foreign power, without the consent of Congress, was submitted to the states for ratification. The amendment was ratified by twelve states and by the senate of the South Carolina Legislature; had it been approved by that legislature's other chamber, it would have become a part of the Constitution. The impression prevailed for nearly a generation that the amendment had been adopted.

A proposed amendment to prohibit interference by Congress with the institution of slavery in the states, offered in 1861 as a last attempt to ward off the impen-

A – Z

controversial. Scholars considered the amendment dead because it had been around for more than 200 years. Supporters, however, noted that the measure had been sent to the states without a deadline. In the end, lawmakers were unwilling to oppose such a popular measure and embraced the new amendment.

A related question was whether Congress has the power to extend the period for ratification of an amendment beyond the original deadline. The issue arose after Congress in 1978 extended the ratification period for the Equal Rights Amendment for thirty-nine months, to June 30, 1982. A federal district court ruled that Congress had exceeded its power when it extended the ERA ratification period. However, the Supreme Court overturned the lower court's decision. The issue thus remains unresolved.

See also: Articles of Confederation; Balanced Budget Amendment; Bill of Rights; Constitution of the United States; Constitutional Amendments Affecting the Presidency; Constitutional Convention; Nineteenth Amendment 1920, in the **Primary Source Library;** Seventeenth Amendment, 1913; Twelfth Amendment, 1804 in the **Primary Source Library;** Twentieth Amendment, 1933, in the **Primary Source Library;** Twenty-fifth Amendment, 1967, in the **Primary Source Library.**

Further Reading

Katz, William L. *Constitutional Amendments.* New York: Franklin Watts, 1974.

Kelly, Alfred H., Winfred A. Harbison, and Herman Belz. *The American Constitution: Its Origins and Development.* Seventh edition. New York: Norton, 1991.

SPOTLIGHT

ding conflict between North and South, was ratified by the legislatures of only two states—Ohio and Maryland. A convention called in Illinois in 1862 to revise the state constitution also ratified the amendment, but because Congress had designated state legislatures as the ratifying bodies, this ratification was invalid.

The Child Labor Amendment would have empowered Congress to "limit, regulate, and prohibit the labor of persons less than 18 years of age." The amendment sought to reverse rulings by the Supreme Court in 1918 in *Hammer v. Dagenhart* and in 1922 in *Bailey v. Drexel Furniture Co.* that had struck down child labor laws enacted by Congress. Submitted to the states June 4, 1924, without any deadline, the amendment had been ratified by twenty-eight of the forty-eight states by 1938. In that year, Congress enacted a child labor law by exercising its constitutional power to regulate interstate **commerce.** In 1941, the Supreme Court in *United States v. Darby Lumber Co.* upheld the law, specifically reversing its 1918 decision. No further ratifications of the proposed amendment have been made since the 1930s.

The Equal Rights Amendment, approved by Congress in 1972, failed to win ratification by the deadline of June 30, 1982. Only thirty-five states approved it, three short of the necessary thirty-eight.

The proposed constitutional amendment providing for voting representation in Congress for Washington, DC, was approved by Congress in 1978. It won ratification from only sixteen states by the August 22, 1985, deadline and thus did not become a part of the Constitution. It was the most recent proposed amendment to be approved by Congress.

Newman, Roger K., ed. *The Constitution and Its Amendments.* New York: Macmillan, 1999.
Onuf, Peter S., ed. *Ratifying, Amending, and Interpreting the Constitution.* New York: Garland, 1991.
Orfield, Lester B. *Amending the Federal Constitution.* New York: Da Capo, 1971.
Pritchett, C. Herman. *The American Constitution.* Third edition. New York: McGraw-Hill, 1977.
Vose, Clement E. *Constitutional Change: Amendment Politics and Supreme Court Litigation Since 1900.* Lexington, MA: Lexington Books, 1972.

Appropriations Bills

Bills that **appropriate,** or spend, money to fund government programs and agencies. Congress's appropriation of funds is part of a two-step process that must take place in most cases before money from the U.S. Treasury can be spent. Authorization bills set up or continue a federal program or agency; appropriations bills then permit federal agencies to assume financial obligations and make payments out of the Treasury.

The Constitution gives the House power to originate tax bills, but no specific authority concerning appropriations bills. Delegates to the Constitutional Convention at first phrased the provision for raising money as follows: "All bills for raising or appropriating money, and for fixing the salaries of the officers of Government, shall originate in the House of Representatives, and shall not be altered or amended by the Senate." After a good deal of debate, the phrase was changed to: "All bills for raising revenue

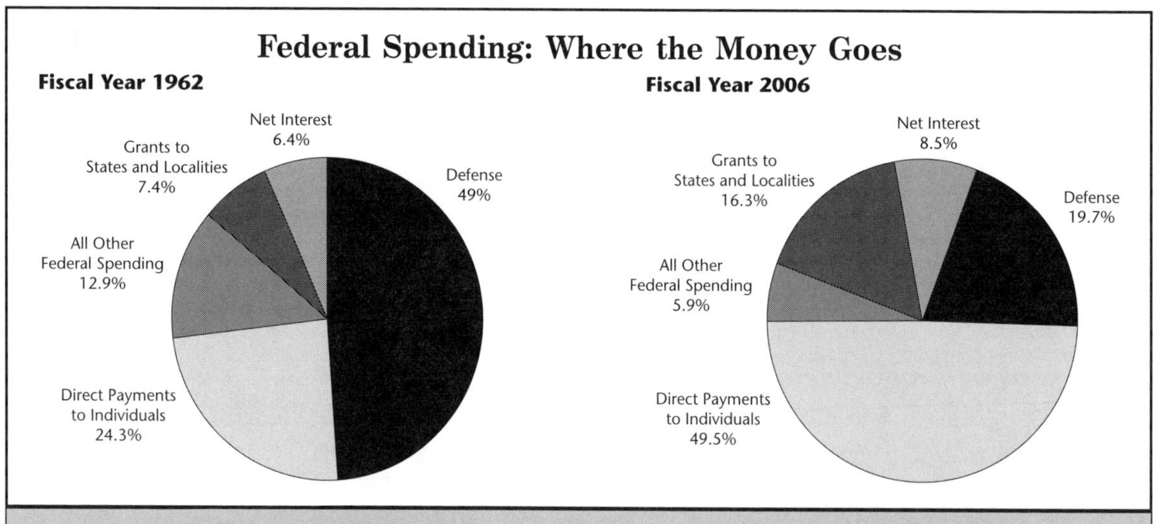

Since the 1960s, defense spending as a percent of total federal spending has decreased, while direct payments to individuals, such as Social Security and Medicare, have increased significantly.

shall originate in the House of Representatives, and shall be subject to alterations and **amendments** by the Senate; no money shall be drawn from the Treasury but in consequence of appropriations made by law." The House nevertheless assumed the authority to originate spending as well as revenue bills.

Authorizations

By its own rules, Congress cannot consider appropriations for a federal program until the president has signed legislation authorizing the program during a specific year. There are some exceptions. For example, a portion of the annual appropriations for the military is authorized by the Constitution. Generally, however, appropriations must await congressional action on the authorizations.

An authorization may be for a single year (annual authorizations), a specified period of years (multiyear authorizations), or an indefinite number of years (permanent authorizations). Since the 1950s, Congress increasingly has required annual authorizations of programs that previously had permanent or multiyear authorizations. The trend toward annual authorizations represented a victory for the legislative committees—such as Agriculture, Armed Services, and Education and Labor—which felt that they had lost control over their programs to the Appropriations committees. The Appropriations committees, particularly in the House, took a dim view of annual authorizations, in part, because they felt the procedure tended to diminish their power.

Annual authorizations also have added one more roadblock to the funding process. With government programs growing in number and becoming more complex, congressional committees need more time to review agency operations and financing needs. In its 1974 budget law, Congress set a deadline of May 15 for legislative committees to report authorization bills. The deadline was eliminated in the mid-1980s when Congress consistently missed the target date.

Appropriations

Congress funds federal programs through thirteen annual appropriations bills and often one or two additional appropriations measures. In recent years, a continuing appropriations resolution has been used to fund programs that have not received their annual appropriation by the beginning of the fiscal year on October 1.

The appropriations process begins in the House Appropriations Committee. The committee is composed of thirteen subcommittees that share authority for determining how to divide up the money approved for the federal budget. Each subcommittee deals with a separate area—such as agriculture, defense, or energy—and has responsibility for one of the thirteen annual appropriations bills. The full Appropriations Committee determines how much money to give to each of the subcommittees, which then shape their individual bills. Generally, members of the subcommittees become expert in their assigned areas. The subcommittees, and particularly their chairpersons, thus have substantial power over spending.

The House procedure used for appropriations bills permits amendments from the floor (the entire chamber) when the full House debates the bill. However, the Appropriations Committee enjoys such prestige that relatively few major changes are made.

Appropriations bills that have been passed by the House are sent to the Senate. There, the Senate Appropriations Committee sends the bills to subcommittees, just as in the House. Senate subcommittees review the work of the House at hearings that are open to the public. The Senate usually does not attempt to perform the same amount of work on a bill that the House already has gone over thoroughly. The time required and the heavy workload of most senators prevent the same detailed consideration that is given in the House.

Despite the great effort that goes into the appropriations process, only about one quarter of the money the government spends each year goes through the annual appropriations process. Congress deliberately authorized some so-called uncontrollable, or "backdoor," spending simply because the government must shield certain programs from political controversy. An example is the permanent appropriation to pay interest on the national debt. The government must meet that obligation to retain its ability to borrowing money when necessary. For many other programs, Congress set up backdoor financing arrangements to shield their budgets from annual scrutiny by the Appropriations committees.

See also: How a Bill Becomes Law; Line-Item Veto; Power of the Purse.

Army-McCarthy Hearings

In the early 1950s, a series of wide-ranging and controversial congressional hearings that were headed by Senator Joseph R. McCarthy, a Republican senator from Wisconsin. The Army-McCarthy hearings in 1954 were the highpoint of the so-called "McCarthy era." Under the chairmanship of McCarthy, the Permanent Investigations Subcommittee of the Senate Government Operations Committee investigated a variety of subjects, including Korean War atrocities. However, the main focus of McCarthy's investigations was the alleged Communist subversion of the U.S. government, including the armed forces, and the United Nations (UN).

McCarthy had an abrasive and aggressive character, and he often tangled with the press, and other senators. The three Democratic members of the subcommittee–senators Henry M. Jackson of Washington, John L. McClellan of Arkansas, and Stuart Symington of Missouri–resigned from the subcommittee on July 10, 1953, in protest against the chairman's handling of the staff. The following January, McCarthy announced changes in subcommittee procedure, and the three Democrats returned.

A Controversial Figure

Long before the stormy McCarthy hearings got under way, the senator had become a controversial public figure. In February 1950, he delivered

During the so-called McCarthy era, Senator Joseph McCarthy used the power of his position in Congress to investigate suspicions of Communist sympathizers in government. (Library of Congress)

a speech before a Women's Republican Club in West Virginia, in which he claimed that a number of people in the U.S. State Department were members of the Communist Party and part of a spy ring. A special subcommittee of the Senate Foreign Relations Committee was set up to investigate McCarthy's charges. The subcommittee, in one of the most bitterly controversial investigations in the history of Congress, held thirty-one days of hearings between March 8 and June 28, 1950. During the course of the hearings, McCarthy charged ten individuals by name with varying degrees of communist activity.

The investigation was a major issue in the 1950 congressional elections. Charges of "softness" toward communism on the part of committee chair Millard Tydings, Democrat from Maryland, were widely credited with his defeat in the Maryland senatorial contest that year. In August 1951, after the release of a Senate committee report criticizing McCarthy's part in the Maryland election, Senator William Benton, Democrat from Connecticut, demanded McCarthy's expulsion from the Senate. The following April, McCarthy demanded an investigation of Benton, which resulted in a Senate investigation of both men. A report released in January 1953 asserted that McCarthy had "deliberately set out to thwart" the investigation, although it did not accuse him of any specific wrongdoing; Benton was criticized for accepting a campaign contribution from a former director of the Reconstruction Finance Corporation, a government agency.

Subcommittee Activities

With the 1952 election, Republicans gained a majority in both chambers of the 83rd Congress. McCarthy became chair of the Senate Government Operations Committee and its Permanent Investigations Subcommittee. After the first year of McCarthy's chairmanship, the subcommittee claimed in its annual report that it had exposed a number of communists, caused the removal of incompetent and undesirable persons from federal employment, and brought about the indictment of several witnesses.

The subcommittee's work continued in 1953 with an investigation of the armed forces. McCarthy became involved during the first half of 1954 in a controversy with high officials of the army and with the Eisenhower administration itself. At

VIEWPOINTS

A 1947 political cartoon points to the Committee on Un-American Activities' disregard for citizens' rights in the name of searching for communists. (A 1947 Herb Block cartoon, copyright The Herb Block Foundation)

issue was the question of whether McCarthy and his staff had used improper means to secure preferential treatment for a former subcommittee consultant, G. David Schine, who had been drafted into the army. Also involved was a charge that the army had tried to pressure McCarthy into calling off his investigation of alleged communists in the army.

In April 1954, the army filed charges against McCarthy, his subcommittee chief counsel Roy M. Cohn, and subcommittee staff director Francis P. Carr. The subcommittee responded in April by filing charges against Secretary of the Army Robert T. Stevens, army counsel John G. Adams, and Assistant Secretary of Defense H. Struve Hensel. Meanwhile, the subcommittee held hearings to investigate the charges. In effect, the subcommittee began an investigation of its own activities.

The Hearings

The thirty-five days of hearings, from April 22 to June 17, 1954, attracted millions of viewers during hours of television coverage. In addition to the principals charged in the case and the subcommittee members, the drama featured army counsel Joseph N. Welch and subcommittee counsel Ray H. Jenkins as the main **interrogators.** In a report issued on August 31, the Republican majority on the subcommittee concluded that the charge of "improper influence" by McCarthy on behalf of Schine was not established. However, it concluded that Roy Cohn had been "unduly aggressive and persistent" on Schine's behalf.

The Republicans also said that Stevens and Adams had tried "to terminate or influence" investigations of the army. The Democratic minority on the subcommittee said that McCarthy had consented to and condoned the "improper actions" of Cohn. They also said that Cohn had "misused and abused the powers of his office and brought disrepute to the committee." The Democrats noted that Stevens deserved severe criticism for "an inexcusable indecisiveness and lack of sound administrative judgment."

Censure of McCarthy

On June 11, 1954, while the Army-McCarthy hearings were in progress, Republican Senator Ralph E. Flanders of Vermont initiated a six-month controversy over the Senate's official attitude toward McCarthy's actions. Flanders introduced a resolution to remove McCarthy from his committee chairmanships and prohibit him from reassuming such posts unless he answered questions about his activities.

Senate Majority Leader William F. Knowland, Republican of California, voiced opposition to the **resolution.** So on July 30, Flanders introduced a new resolution, charging McCarthy with "personal contempt" of the Senate. Both resolutions were referred to a Senate Committee formed to study charges of censure. After nearly two weeks of hearings, the committee on September 27 unanimously recommended that the Senate censure McCarthy for his conduct in the investigations of 1952 and for his conduct toward Army Brigadier General Ralph W. Zwicker, whom McCarthy had criticized as "not fit to wear that uniform." The Senate did not accept that recommendation. Instead, on December 1, 1954, a majority in the Senate adopted a substitute resolution that "condemned" McCarthy's abuse of power and a number of his statements. McCarthy lost his committee and subcommittee chairmanships when control of Congress passed to the Democrats in January 1955. His activities no longer attracted any notable attention, and he died on May 2, 1957.

McCarthy's Main Accusations

- McCarthy claimed that as many as 205 members of the Communist Party were working in the government at the U.S. State Department.
- McCarthy accused a number of prominent private citizens of participating in Communist activities or of being Communist sympathizers.

During televised hearings in the early 1950s, Senator McCarthy's claims of Communist infiltration in the U.S. government were found to be baseless.

Further Reading

Cohen, Daniel. *Joseph McCarthy: The Misuse of Political Power.* Brookfield, CT: Millbrook Press, 1996.

A–Z

Sherrow, Victoria. *Joseph McCarthy and the Cold War.* Farmington Hills, Blackbirch Press, 2001.

Wicker, Tom. *Shooting Star: The Brief Arc of Joe McCarthy.* Orlando: Harcourt, 2006.

Articles of Confederation

The first governing document, or constitution, of the United States of America, which was later replaced by the U.S. Constitution. On June 7, 1776, Richard Henry Lee of Virginia, one of the nation's Founders, called for a declaration of independence from Great Britain. At the same time, he proposed that a plan of confederation be prepared and sent to the Colonies for their consideration. On June 11, the Continental Congress agreed to his proposal and named a committee of thirteen representatives–one from each colony–to prepare this document. The plan that was recommended, based on a draft written by John Dickinson of Delaware, was presented to Congress on July 12. However, it was not until November 15, 1777, that the Congress–after much debate and some revision–adopted the Articles of Confederation and Perpetual Union.

The Articles of Confederation reflected the most important desire of Americans who were rebelling against British rule. They wanted to preserve their freedoms from a strong centralized government. At the same time, few of the delegates or other American leaders were prepared to entrust a national government with any power that would lessen the **sovereignty** and independence of the states. Thus, the extent of federal authority was not a central concern in the design of the confederation.

What was more important was the relative standing of thirteen rival and jealous states. Would they be represented equally in the national legislature, as the smaller states desired, or in proportion to their population, as the larger states wished? The cost of a national government would have to be shared, but on what basis–wealth, the total population of each state, or, as southerners insisted, on the white population only? States without claims to land west of the Appalachian Mountains thought Congress should control that area; those with claims were unwilling to give them up.

As finally adopted, the Articles of Confederation gave less authority to the national government than had been proposed in the Albany

Weaknesses of the Articles of Confederation

- The Articles of Confederation did nothing to relieve the chaotic state of the federal government's finances, and the nation's foreign debt grew.
- It was difficult to change the Articles because amendments required unanimous agreement by the states.
- There was no separation of powers.
- Passing major legislation required approval by 9 of the 13 states, which often proved to be difficult.
- The majority of power rested with the states, which could pass laws that might be contrary to federal law.
- Congress had no power to levy taxes to pay for the federal government.
- Congress had no authority or ability to make states comply with federal laws.
- Congress had no power to help states deal with problems within their borders.
- Congress did not have the power to regulate commerce between the states.
- Congress did not have the power to regulate diplomatic issues that might arise within a state.

The Articles of Confederation, the nation's government from 1781 until 1789, was a weak government that did not provide for the separation of powers between the branches of the government. Under the Articles, the states were sovereign countries, with the unicameral Congress having little power.

Plan of Union of 1754. Congress remained the sole branch of government. The states kept their equality, each having one vote in the Congress. And of the specific powers given to Congress, the most important could only be used by agreement of nine of the thirteen states. These powers included the power to declare war, enter treaties and alliances, raise an army and a navy, regulate coinage, and borrow money. Congress could also regulate Indian affairs, establish a postal service, and oversee disputes between the states. However, it had no power to tax; instead, the amount each state would pay to support the government would be in proportion to the value of its land. The states also were assigned quotas for troops in proportion to the number of white inhabitants.

Under the Articles, each state would send from two to seven representatives to Congress. The delegates would be selected annually and paid by the states, but they could serve for no more than three years in any six. Members of Congress could not hold any federal post for pay and they were immune from arrest while attending Congress and from legal action for anything said in a congressional debate. A Committee of the States (with one delegate from each) was authorized to act for Congress during a recess on matters that did not require the agreement of nine states.

Congress was authorized to appoint committees and officials needed to manage the affairs of the United States. The Articles made no provision for a federal executive or judiciary, and they gave Congress no means to enforce any of its decisions. Control of taxation and **tariffs** was left to the states, and unanimous consent of the states was required for the adoption of amendments to the Articles. The Articles of Confederation were finally adopted and took effect on March 1, 1781, after **ratification** by the states.

See also: The Albany Plan of Union; Constitution of the United States.

Further Reading

Feinberg, Barbara. *Articles of Confederation.* Minneapolis, MN: 21st Century, 2002.

Rebman, Renee C. *The Articles of Confederation.* Mankato, MN: Compass Point, 2006.

Asian Americans in Congress

Prior to the 1950s, the nation's Asian American population was not large enough to elect members to Congress. In addition, American laws restricted Asian immigration to the United States until 1965. Since that time, however, Asians have immigrated to the United States

In 1959, Daniel K. Inouye was elected to represent Hawaii, the fiftieth state, in the House of Representatives. Since 1963, he has represented Hawaii in the Senate. (Scott J. Ferrell, CQ)

Decision Makers

Patsy Mink (1927–2002)

The first Asian American female elected to Congress, Patsy Mink also played a major role in advancing civil rights. Her most notable achievement was authoring the 1972 Title IX Amendment of the Higher Education Act, which bans discrimination on the basis of sex at any educational institution that receives government funding.

Mink became active in fighting discrimination long before her election to Congress. As a student at the University of Nebraska, she organized a coalition to protest the university's policy of racially segregated housing. As a result of her efforts, the university ended the policy. When she later sought to attend medical school, Mink found that none of the schools she applied to accepted women. She went to law school instead and decided to use her legal training to fight discrimination.

First elected to Congress in 1965, Mink served in the House until 1977, resigning her seat to run for the Senate. Although she failed in that bid, President Jimmy Carter (1977–1981) named her an assistant secretary of state. She returned to the House in 1991 and served until her death in 2002.

in significant numbers, and Asian Americans have won election to both the House of Representatives and the Senate.

The first Asian American member of Congress was Dalip Singh Saund, a Democrat from California. Saund, a native of India, won a House seat in 1956 and served three terms. In 1959, Republican Hiram Fong of Hawaii became the nation's first Asian American senator. That same year, Democrat Daniel Inouye entered the House as the nation's first Japanese American Congress member, also representing Hawaii. In 1962, Inouye joined Fong in the Senate. Fong and Inouye were the first of several Asian Americans from Hawaii elected to Congress.

Hawaiians chose Democrat Patsy Mink as the first female Asian American member of the House in 1964. Daniel Akaka, another Democrat from Hawaii, became the first Polynesian-American member of the House in 1977. He won election to the Senate in 1990.

After Hawaii, California has sent the most Asian Americans to Congress. They include Democrat Norman Mineta, who won a House seat in 1974, and Republican S. I. Hayakawa, who went to the Senate in 1976. In 1992, Californians elected Republican Jay Kim as the first Korean-American to serve in Congress.

See also: Women in Congress.

★ ★ ★ B ★ ★ ★

Balanced Budget Amendment

Constitutional **amendment** aimed at reducing government spending by requiring Congress to balance the federal budget. As with any proposed amendment to the U.S. Constitution, passage of a balanced budget amendment would require passage in both the House of Representatives and the Senate by at least two-thirds of the members. The proposed amendment would then need to be **ratified** by three-fourths of the state legislatures before it could be added to the Constitution. If adopted someday, a balanced budget amendment would require that federal revenues each year equal or exceed federal expenditures.

During the last three decades, Congress has shown periodic support for the type of budget restraint that would be required by a balanced budget amendment. The drive to adopt a balanced budget amendment first gained popularity in the states in the mid-1970s. By 1984, the legislatures of thirty-two states–just two short of the two-thirds needed to force a constitutional convention–had adopted **resolutions** calling for a constitutional convention to draft a balanced budget amendment. Shortly thereafter, however, a number of states began rescinding the resolutions they had passed previously. As a result, the balanced budget movement lost momentum in the states.

Congress came close to adopting a resolution calling for a balanced budget amendment to the U.S. Constitution in 1982. That year, the Senate passed a balanced budget amendment by slightly more than the two-thirds majority needed for passage. However, the measure failed to gain enough votes in the House. In 1986, the Senate rejected a balanced budget proposal by just one vote. Further efforts in the House to pass such an amendment were defeated in 1990 and 1992. Both houses of Congress rejected a balanced budget amendment in 1994.

When the Republicans took control of Congress in 1995, the centerpiece of the House Republicans' ambitious agenda was passage of a balanced budget amendment. As part of their Contract With America, the Republicans promised to send to the states a constitutional amendment requiring a balanced budget. The House passed such a measure in 1995, but the Senate rejected it that year and the next. During the 105th Congress, in 1997, the Senate again rejected an amendment to balance the budget. The House declined to push for a floor vote that year, expecting certain defeat. In the years since, some representatives in Congress have continued to push for a balanced budget amendment. Despite such efforts, the desire to adopt such an amendment remains unfulfilled. See the "Point/Counterpoint" discussion on pages 58–59.

Bicameralism

The division of the legislative branch of government into two houses, or chambers. The Congress is a **bicameral** legislature consisting of the House of Representatives and the Senate.

American colonists had a long experience of bicameralism. The English Parliament was bicameral, as were most of the colonial legislatures. After the American Revolution (1775–1783), ten of the thirteen states retained bicameral governments. Nevertheless, the national Congress was **unicameral** under the republic's first governing document, the Articles of Confederation. When the first Constitutional

POINT/COUNTERPOINT

FOR AND AGAINST A BALANCED BUDGET AMENDMENT

The explosion of the federal deficit in the last several decades has led many observers to call for a constitutional amendment that would require Congress to balance the annual budget. Advocates for such an amendment, including Republican Senator Jeff Sessions of Alabama, argue that an amendment is the only way to maintain **fiscal discipline.** Some opponents, such as Robert Kuttner, a member of the Economic Policy Institute, fear unforeseen costs in such an action.

Senator Jeff Sessions

The arguments in favor of a balanced budget amendment are not new. In fact, the concerns Americans raise today were advocated by our Founding Fathers, and none more vocal than Thomas Jefferson. Where today's families worry about the crushing debt that is being passed onto their children, Jefferson warned, and I quote, "Each successive generation ought to be guaranteed against dissipations and corruptions of those preceding."

And corruption it is. It is irresponsibility. It is a corruption of the highest duties and responsibilities of office in this Government that we fail to make the hard choices when confronted with competing priorities and simply adopt both priorities and pass that debt to our children.

A balanced budget amendment would also afford protection against another evil Jefferson foresaw: the inability of Congress to restrain its spending with any degree of self-discipline . . . Our $5.2 trillion national debt is a sad testament to that fact. Our inability to live within our means on the national level is unacceptable and adds to the increasing lack of confidence the American public—who must live within its budgets—feels for its Federal Government.

A balanced budget amendment is needed to regain the people's trust, because the people know that there has not been a balanced budget since 1969, and they know that we are continuing to run budget deficit after

Convention met in 1787 to revise the Articles, however, they decided that the new Congress should be bicameral. The new Constitution thus called for a popularly elected House of Representatives and a Senate whose members would be chosen by the state legislatures.

Almost since it was created, some people have questioned whether the Senate was a good idea. The chamber's very nature conflicts with the basic democratic principle that each citizen has an equal voice in government. While each state receives a number of House seats based on its population, every state has the same number of senators (two), regardless of its size. Some scholars claim that that the Senate clearly violates the one person, one vote principle. They argue that that it would certainly be struck down by the Supreme Court as unconstitutional were it not already written into the founding document itself.

The Framers of the Constitution, however, had specific goals in mind when they created budget deficit. They are skeptical of our ability to keep our promises, because they do not believe that we have the political will to keep them without a law requiring it. And they are right.

Robert Kuttner

The proposed constitutional amendment requiring a balanced federal budget, now facing an early vote in the new year, is fiscal overkill . . . A balanced budget requirement, especially one locked into the Constitution, would deepen recessions . . . In recessions, the federal government, like the states, would have to reduce its own spending to match reduced revenues . . .

Moreover, if government could not borrow, it would have to finance capital outlays out of current expenditures. No state or city government and few businesses or households do that. If families had to pay for homes and cars out of current income, far fewer people would own them.

Public discourse about the deficit is now out of sync with fiscal reality. With Congress and the White House moving toward balancing the budget via the appropriations process, the great deficit crisis is ending. It was a product of the fiscal imbalance of the '80s and early '90s. That, in turn, was a monument to the failure of supply-side economics. But thanks to the deficit reduction of the Clinton years, the budget is now on a sustainable path. We are nearly back to where government can again use fiscal as well as monetary policy as tools of economic management.

The (high) deficits . . . typical of the 1980s, reflected the excess of one brand of **conservative** zealotry. As a remedy, a constitutional amendment requiring absolute budget balance would yield a different brand of conservative excess—with even longer and more destructive consequences.

Document-Based Question

Why does Senator Sessions believe a balanced budget amendment is needed? What possible dangers does Robert Kuttner foresee?

the Senate. Some of the Framers intended it to act as an **aristocratic** check against the potential excesses of popular rule as expressed by the House. The Senate was also meant to express the "federal principle," in contrast to the "national principle" embodied by the House of Representatives. The Framers saw election of senators by state legislatures as a way to make the states part of the national governing system. The federal government paid senators' salaries, and the state legislatures that elected senators had no power to recall them. As a result, most senators refused to consider themselves merely the agents of the state governments. **Ratification** of the Seventeenth Amendment to the Constitution in 1913, however, took the election of senators out of state legislators' hands. Popular election meant that senators had to become more responsive to the needs of local voters, and greater champions of their states' interests.

See also: Articles of Confederation; House of Representatives; Senate; Seventeenth Amendment, 1913; United States Constitution, Article 1, Sections 1–7, 1789, in the **Primary Source Library.**

Further Reading

Bickford, Charlene Bangs, and Kenneth R. Bowling. *Birth of the Nation: The First Federal Congress, 1789–1791.* Washington, DC: First Federal Congress Project, George Washington University; New York: Second Circuit Committee on the Bicentennial of the United States Constitution, 1989.

Dodd, Lawrence C., and Bruce I. Oppenheimer, eds. *Congress Reconsidered.* Eighth edition. Washington, DC: CQ Press, 2004.

A–Z

Bill Becomes a Law, How a

See How a Bill Becomes Law.

Bill of Rights

The first ten **amendment**s to the United States Constitution, added in 1791. These amendments, which guarantee the basic civil liberties of American citizens, are considered by many scholars the most significant part of the Constitution.

Background

Few delegates to the first Constitutional Convention argued for the inclusion of a bill of rights. Most were satisfied that fundamental liberties would be safe because the Constitution limited the federal government to specific powers. They felt that these limits were enough to prevent the government from denying citizens their rights. South Carolina's Charles Pinckney and others did propose adding a number of provisions similar to those contained in the **bills** of rights of the various states. The delegates appointed a committee to draft a bill of rights, but ten states voted "no." Anxious to complete their work and return home, the delegates were in no mood to spend more time on something most of them believed to be unnecessary.

During the campaign for **ratification,** however, it became clear that many citizens felt the Constitution did not go far enough to safeguard basic rights from government power. Omission of a bill of rights was the principal source of dissatisfaction with the new Constitution in the state ratifying conventions held in 1788. When Massachusetts **ratified** the new Constitution, its convention recommended amending the document to protect basic rights. The Virginia ratifying convention chose a committee to report on amendments to submit in the First Congress. New York attached a bill of rights to its ratification. There was little doubt that quick action was required to add explicit guarantees of fundamental liberties.

Virginia's James Madison, a powerful early opponent of a bill of rights, eventually yielded and proposed amendments to be fitted into the Constitution. Congress approved twelve of the proposed amendments and submitted them to the states. The first two, which dealt with **apportionment** of representatives and compensation for members of Congress, were not ratified. The remainder were made part of the Constitution when Virginia became the eleventh state to ratify the document on December 15, 1791.

In 1833, the Supreme Court ruled in *Barron v. Baltimore* that the Bill of Rights protected individuals against action by the federal government only–it did not apply to actions taken by state governments. The Fourteenth Amendment, ratified in 1868, took steps to address this issue. It required the states to provide equal protection under the law to all persons in their jurisdiction, or area of legal authority. In a series of rulings beginning in 1925, the Court held that the Fourteenth Amendment requires the states to uphold most of the guarantees in the Bill of Rights.

Text of the Amendments

The First Amendment protects the freedom of thought and belief. It forbids Congress to restrict the freedom of religion, speech, the press, peaceable assembly, or petition. The Second Amendment ensures the right of the states to maintain a militia. In connection with that state right, it also protects the right of the people to keep and bear arms. The Third Amendment restricts government power to quarter soldiers in private homes. The Fourth Amendment forbids the government to conduct unreasonable searches of an individual's person, house, papers, or effects.

The Fifth Amendment requires indictment of all persons charged with serious crimes in civilian proceedings. It also forbids trying a person twice for the same offense or forcing a person to testify against himself. It protects individuals against being deprived of life, liberty, or property without due process of law. It also protects private property against being taken for public use without just compensation to the owner.

The Sixth Amendment guarantees a speedy and public trial by jury for all persons accused of a crime. It also assures the defendant the right to be notified of the charge against him, to confront those who testify against him, to compel witnesses to appear to testify for him, and to have the aid of a lawyer in his defense. The Seventh Amendment provides for a jury trial in all lawsuits involving more than $20. The Eighth Amendment forbids excessive bail, excessive fines, and cruel and unusual punishment.

The Ninth Amendment states that the Constitution's explicit mention of certain rights does not deny or impede other rights not mentioned. The Tenth Amendment declares that all powers that the Constitution does not give to the federal government–or does not deny to the states–are reserved to the states or the people.

See also: Amending the Constitution; Constitution of the United States; Expressed Powers; Implied Powers.

Further Reading

Amar, Akhil R. *The Bill of Rights: Creation and Reconstruction.* New Haven: Yale University Press, 1998.

Kelly, Alfred H., Winfred A. Harbison, and Herman Belz. *The American Constitution: Its Origins and Development.* Seventh edition. New York: Norton, 1991.

Newman, Roger K., ed. *The Constitution and Its Amendments.* New York: Macmillan, 1999.

Patrick, John J. *The Bill of Rights: A History in Documents.* New York: Oxford University Press, 2003.

Bills, Private

Legislation in Congress intended for the benefit of a specific individual or entity rather than the general public. At one time, hundreds, even thousands, of such **bills** would be enacted into law during a Congress, but in recent decades, the number has dropped dramatically.

Private legislation is used essentially as a court of last resort because those seeking relief must have exhausted all reasonable administrative and judicial procedures before asking Congress to intercede on their behalf. Courts and federal administrative agencies can make decisions based only on interpretations of public laws; Congress reserves to itself the privilege of aiding some parties who, for various reasons, are seen as deserving of special treatment. Most private bills deal with claims against the federal government and immigration and naturalization matters. Their titles usually begin with the words: "For the relief of. . . ."

A fine line sometimes separates public and private bills. House parliamentarian Asher C. Hinds offered the following explanation in his 1907 *Precedents of the House of Representatives:* "A private bill is a bill for the relief of one or several specified persons, corporations, institutions, etc., and is distinguished from a public bill, which relates to public matters and deals with individuals only by classes." As an example, Hinds cited bills benefiting soldiers' widows: A bill that granted pensions to soldiers' widows as a class would be a public bill. A bill that granted a pension to a particular soldier's widow would be a private bill.

The history of private bills dates at least from Roman times when they were called *constitutionis privilegia,* privileges accorded to specified individuals. Private bills were also passed by the English Parliament. The first private bill was passed by Congress September 24, 1789, and signed by President George Washington (1789–1797) five days later. The bill gave seventeen months' back pay at the rank of captain to the Baron de Glaubeck, a foreign officer in the service of the United States.

Changing Usage

Private bill usage has fluctuated over the years, largely because changes in federal law have made exceptions for individuals more necessary sometimes and less necessary other times. For example, if Congress passed legislation giving people other ways to pursue their claims against the government, the numbers would decline. If Congress enacted a stricter immigration law, the numbers would jump.

Ten private bills were enacted into law in the First Congress (1789–1791), the same number enacted in the 105th Congress (1997–1999). Over those more than two hundred years, the numbers varied substantially. For example, there were 6,248 private laws enacted in the 59th Congress (1905–1907), but only 234 enacted in the very next Congress. There were 457 enacted in the 80th Congress (1947–1948), and 1,103 in the 81st Congress. In modern times, there has been a sharp decline in the use of private bills. Since the early 1980s, the totals have dropped to double—sometimes single—digits.

Reasons for Decline

There have been several reasons for the decline in the use of private bills. The most important of these is that Congress has taken steps over the years to limit the need for private bills. These steps have included the establishment of the U.S. Court of Claims (now the U.S. Court of Federal Claims) with the authority to decide certain claims cases and to issue advisory reports on private bills when requested by the House or Senate. Congress also has approved a series of public laws authorizing executive agencies to act on other cases previously handled by Congress. Title IV of the 1946 Legislative Reorganization Act, known as the Federal Tort Claims Act, provided for settlement of certain claims by executive agencies and U.S. district courts. Another title of the 1946 act provided for the correction of military records by civilian review boards. When passage of the Immigration and Nationality Act of 1952 resulted in a marked increase in requests for relief from immigration restrictions, Congress adopted **amendments** easing some of the restrictions or authorizing the attorney general to do so.

Scandals involving private bills have resulted in tighter procedures for their consideration and have contributed to the drop-off. Members are reluctant to assign staff to handle private bills because they can be so time-consuming, and the claims can sometimes be incorrect or fraudulent. Budget deficits in the 1980s and much of the 1990s also made it more difficult for members to focus on the needs of just one individual or entity, while they were cutting back on programs for the general public.

Types of Bills

The two kinds of private legislation that Congress deals with most often are claims and immigration cases. Before 1950, private bills dealing with land claims, military justice, and pensions were more common.

The Constitution provides in Article I, Section 8, clause 1, that "the Congress shall have Power . . . to pay the Debts . . . of the United States." This provision has been interpreted broadly to include not only legal but also moral obligations. Bills introduced in Congress for payment of private claims against the government include refund cases that aim to wipe out individuals' obligations to give back money the government paid them in error; waiver cases that allow the government to honor a claim after the government's obligation has expired; and tort (wrongful act, injury, or damage) claims not covered by the Federal Tort Claims Act of 1946.

Private laws are also used to provide relief to **aliens** because public immigration and naturalization laws do not cover all hardship cases. Private laws permit them to come to the United States, to remain here, or to become citizens, even though they technically may not be eligible.

Enactment Process

The general course of a private bill, from introduction to presidential approval, is much the same as that of a public bill. There are, however, some important differences. A private bill generally is initiated at the request of the individual, company, group, or locality that stands to benefit from its enactment. By contrast, public laws usually originate in the executive branch or in Congress itself. The intended beneficiary of a private bill may get in touch with a member directly or use an intermediary, such as a lawyer or **lobbyist,** to present the facts and considerations believed to justify the introduction of a bill.

Virtually all private bills are referred to the House or Senate Judiciary committees. Once a private bill is **reported** out of committee, it is placed on the Private Calendar in the House and on the Calendar of Business in the Senate.

In the House, the Private Calendar, also known as the Calendar of the Committee of the Whole House, must be called on the first Tuesday of the month (unless dispensed with by a two-thirds vote or moved to another day by unanimous consent) and may be called on the third Tuesday at the Speaker's discretion. In the Senate, private bills may be taken up on any day after the conclusion of the morning hour.

The House uses a formal system of objectors to monitor private bills. The majority and minority leaders each select three party members to serve as objectors who will screen the bills for controversial provisions. They also answer questions that arise during floor consideration.

A bill must be on the Private Calendar for at least seven days before it can be called up for floor consideration. If one House member objects to a bill's consideration, the bill is passed over for later consideration. If two or more object, the bill is recommitted, a procedure that usually kills the bill.

Bills passed over for later consideration may be pulled together into an omnibus bill, which is given preference over other bills when the Private Calendar is called on the third Tuesday. When such an omnibus bill is passed, the bills within it are considered to have been passed separately. This type of omnibus bill, however, has rarely been used in recent decades.

When a private bill is taken up on the floor, it is considered in "the House as in Committee of the Whole," which means the House is operating under a combination of procedures from the general rules of the House and rules of the Committee of the Whole. No time is allotted for general debate and amendments are considered under expedited procedures.

As with public bills, once a private bill has been passed in identical form by both chambers, it is sent to the president. If the president signs it into law, the measure is given a private law number. Vetoes of private bills are handled in the same manner as vetoes of public bills. There may be an immediate vote to override or sustain the veto, the vote may be postponed to a fixed date, or the veto message may be referred to a committee. Committee referral, in effect, kills the bill in most cases.

Abuses of the System

Private bills occasionally have given rise to impropriety, or at least the appearance of it. A newspaper investigation in 1969, for example, produced accusations of wrongdoing in the introduction of hundreds of private immigration bills to help Chinese seamen stay in the United States. Knight Newspapers reported evidence that New York lawyers and Washington **lobbyists** had been getting $500 to $2,500 for each Chinese immigration bill involved. The disclosures resulted in a preliminary investigation by the Senate ethics panel into allegations that some senators—or their aides—received gifts and campaign contributions for introducing bills to help Chinese ship-jumpers escape deportation. Senate leaders moved to put an end to the practice of allowing staff aides to introduce private bills.

Representative Henry Helstoski, a Democrat from New Jersey, was indicted by a federal grand jury in 1976 on charges that he solicited and accepted bribes in return for introducing bills to delay deportation of Chilean and Argentinian aliens living illegally in the United States. The indictment alleged that Helstoski received "at least" $8,735 for his sponsorship of the immigration bills. The charges were thrown out after the Supreme Court ruled in *United States v. Helstoski* that, because of the Constitution's grant of immunity to members of Congress under the speech and debate clause, federal prosecutors could not use any evidence relating to Helstoski's legislative acts against him.

The power to introduce private immigration legislation proved ruinous to the members of Congress caught in the FBI's Abscam operation in 1980. Agents of the FBI, posing as Arab sheiks or their representatives, asked the members to introduce private bills to permit wealthy "Arabs" to enter the United States in exchange for money. Although the investigation turned up no evidence of bills actually introduced on behalf of the fictitious Arabs, the videotapes and recorded conversations of the members and the government agents were enough to end seven congressional careers.

See also: Abscam; How a Bill Becomes Law.

Bipartisanship

Cooperation between the two major parties to pass legislation or achieve political objectives. By its nature, congressional politics is a **partisan** affair, with each party attempting to pass **bills** that reflect its particular **ideology.** In some cases, however, members of each party find common ground on an issue, or come to realize that they need the support of members of the other party to advance their political interests.

The daily workings of Congress often demonstrate bipartisanship in action. For example, scheduling which bills will be debated in the Senate is primarily the responsibility of the majority party. Because of the need to secure unanimous consent to bring up a bill, however, the majority leader also works closely with the minority leader and his or her staff in working out the schedule. This **bipartisan** cooperation is in sharp contrast to the House, where scheduling is solely a responsibility of a majority party, which has the ability to enforce its decisions by majority vote.

At one time, presiding over the House and Senate was also largely a bipartisan effort. Until 1977, members of each party took turns presiding in the Senate. The bipartisan practice was ended abruptly when the presiding officer, Republican Jesse Helms of North Carolina a member of the minority, broke with Senate custom and refused to recognize the majority leader, Democratic Senator Mike Mansfield of Montana. The Democratic leadership then decided that the majority should retain control of the chair at all times, unless the vice president, who might be a member of the opposite party, decided to occupy it. Republicans continued this practice when they controlled the Senate.

The postwar period spanning the late 1940s and early 1950s is usually cited as the high-water mark for bipartisanship in foreign policy. While President Harry S. Truman (1945–1953) often found himself in a struggle with congressional Republicans over domestic legislation, he was able to craft a bipartisan foreign policy in cooperation with Republican lawmakers. In the 1950s, President Dwight Eisenhower (1953–1961) often received more support from Democrats than from members of his own party, particularly in the early years of his administration on foreign policy issues. Partisanship increased as the 1960 elections approached, however, and many domestic bills were not enacted.

Many observers feel that bipartisanship has declined significantly in recent years. The 1998 **impeachment** of President Bill Clinton (1993–2001) highlighted this divide, with the votes for impeachment splitting along definite partisan lines. This trend continued during the administration of George W. Bush (2001–2009), with Republicans and Democrats consistently lining up on different sides of proposed legislation.

Byrd, Robert C.

See Congress, Constitutional Origins of.

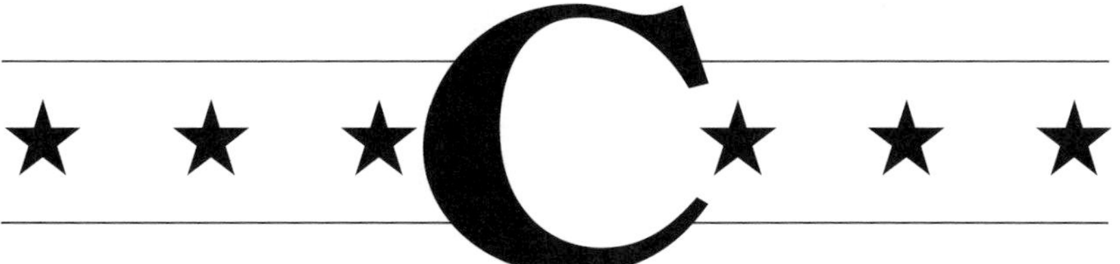

Calendars, House of Representatives

Use of various House calendars to schedule the consideration of legislation. House calendars provide a structure that allows the House to act efficiently. After a bill is considered by a House committee, it is introduced into the full House. However, before it is scheduled for debate and a vote, it is placed on one of three legislative calendars: the Union Calendar, the House Calendar, or the Private Calendar. **Bills** already on the Union or House calendars may also be placed on a Corrections Calendar. Another calendar, the Discharge Calendar, is used only for motions to discharge committees from consideration of a measure after a majority of the members of the committees have signed the motions. Each day while the House is in session, it also publishes a Calendar of the House. This document lists all matters on each of the other calendars, and it provides a history of all actions on those matters.

All bills that have any impact on the Treasury go on the Union Calendar, which is the most important calendar. The bills listed on it are first considered in the Committee of the Whole and reported back to the House for a final vote on passage. Other types of matters, such as investigative reports, may also appear on the Union Calendar. Legislation on the Union Calendar may be considered on the House floor, debated, and amended in a wide variety of different ways under the rules of the House.

Matters that have no direct effect on the Treasury are placed on the House Calendar. These bills or **resolutions** generally deal with administrative and procedural matters and are usually taken up directly by the full House rather than in committee. However, some legislation of great significance, such as constitutional amendments, appear on the House Calendar. Simple and concurrent resolutions also go on the House Calendar, including the concurrent resolution that starts off yearly action on the budget process and special rules reported from the Rules Committee allowing consideration of other legislation. On the floor, matters from this calendar may also be considered in several different ways.

The Corrections Calendar is under the control of the Speaker of the House. It was created as a way to promote a specific political agenda. Bills may be placed there by the Speaker if they are considered noncontroversial and deal with correcting "mistakes" in previously enacted legislation or in government actions or regulations. The Corrections Calendar may be called only on the second and fourth Tuesdays of each month. Passage of all measures on the Corrections Calendar requires a 60 percent vote, which effectively prevents the Speaker from using it for consideration of controversial matters.

Private immigration bills and bills for the relief of individuals with claims against the United States are placed on the Private Calendar. This calendar must be called on the first Tuesday of each month, unless called for by a two-thirds vote or by unanimous consent. The Private Calendar may also be called on the third Tuesday of each month by the Speaker of the House. Most private bills are called up from the Private Calendar and simply passed by unanimous consent without debate, although debate sometimes occurs.

The House also has a Discharge Calendar that is used to list motions to discharge committees from further consideration of bills or resolutions. Discharge motions are rarely attempted, so the Discharge Calendar usually consists of a

House Calendars and Their Purposes

Union Calendar
This calendar is the most important calendar. The bills listed on this calendar are considered first. Included are all bills affecting the Treasury, including authorization bills, and certain legislative matters such as investigative reports.

House Calendar
This calendar includes legislative matters that have no direct effect on the Treasury. It may include bills, or more commonly, resolutions, which generally deal with administrative matters or matters concerning procedures within the House. Some important legislative matters, such as constitutional amendments or the approval of compacts among states, may also appear on the House Calendar.

Private Calendar
This calendar includes private immigration bills and bills for the relief of individuals with claims against the United States. Bills on this calendar may be passed over by unanimous consent in the House.

Corrections Calendar
This calendar is completely under the control of the Speaker of the House. The Speaker may place bills here if they are considered noncontroversial and deal with correcting "mistakes" in legislation already enacted by the House. The calendar may also include matters concerning government actions or regulations that need correcting.

Discharge Calendar
This calendar is used to list motions for discharging committees from further consideration of bills or resolutions. In effect, the items on this calendar are meant to stop the work of committees on certain matters.

restatement of the discharge rule followed by a blank page.

The five House calendars–Union, House, Private, Corrections, and Discharge–are printed in one document called "Calendars of the United States House of Representatives and History of Legislation." This calendar is printed daily when the House is in session. The first issue of the week lists in numerical order all House and most Senate measures that have been **reported** by committees, with a history of congressional action on each. Bills are placed on the calendars in the order in which they are reported. However, they do not come to the floor in chronological order. In fact, some never come to the floor at all. The Speaker of the House, working with the Majority Leader, committee chairs, and the Rules Committee, determines which bills will come to the floor and when.

See also: Calendars, Senate.

Calendars, Senate

Use of different Senate calendars to schedule the consideration of legislation by the full Senate. In the House of Representatives, calendars provide a structure that allows the House to act efficiently. However, the Senate has an elaborate framework of procedures that guide its actions, and these procedures are far more flexible than those of the House. Almost anything can be done by unanimous consent. That very flexibility also means that a single member can delay or threaten to delay action on a bill until his or her wishes are accommodated or a compromise is reached. Thus, every individual senator has a great deal of power over Senate action and schedule.

From time to time the Senate reviews its procedures in an attempt to pick up the pace and predictability of action in the chamber. However, the Senate is rarely receptive to proposals for change because such proposals almost always curb the rights of the individual member. In a chamber devoted to preserving individual members' rights, the challenge of scheduling floor action can thus sometimes be difficult. Senators can–and do–insist that the legislation in which they are interested be scheduled for floor action at a time convenient to them. At the same time, senators faced with ever-increasing political, constituent, and legislative demands on their time have sought greater predictability in the Senate schedule.

Scheduling in the Senate is mainly the responsibility of the Senate majority leader, who works closely with the majority party's policy committee, committee chairs, and other colleagues to develop a legislative program acceptable to a majority of the party. Because of the need to get unanimous consent to bring up a bill, the majority leader also works closely with the minority leader and his staff in working out a schedule for considering legislation. This **bipartisan** cooperation is in sharp contrast to the House, where scheduling is solely the responsibility of the majority party, which has the ability to enforce its decisions by majority vote.

A system based largely on unanimous consent also requires that the membership be kept informed about the status of legislation. The majority leader regularly begins each session with an announcement of the day's anticipated schedule and concludes it with the likely schedule for the next session. Notices from party leaders, televised floor proceedings, and an automatic telephone connection to each member's office also help the Senate leadership keep the members informed.

As much as possible, the Senate leadership tries to accommodate the schedules of individual senators. This can be very difficult since no matter when something is scheduled it is usually an inconvenient time for some senator. Nevertheless, the Senate has two primary calendars for scheduling the consideration of legislation. The first is the Calendar of General Orders. All legislation reported from Senate committees is placed on this calendar. All treaties and nominations that require the Senate's advice and consent are placed on the Executive Calendar. To consider treaties or nominations, the Senate resolves into an "executive session." There are no restrictions on when the Senate may enter executive session. Although the term "executive session" sounds as if it involves only a few select individuals, it is an open session of the Senate just like any other.

Senate rules require that bills and reports on certain matters be placed on a calendar for one legislative day before they are brought to the full Senate. This rule is usually waived by unanimous consent. Moreover, the Senate often stays in the "same legislative day" for a considerable period of time. The Senate normally recesses from day to day, rather than **adjourns.** The effect is the same–an end to the day's session. A recess, rather than an adjournment, avoids creating a new legislative day. It is thus not uncommon for the Senate to remain in the same legislative day for weeks or even months at a time. These types of Senate rules complicate scheduling and the use of calendars.

See also: Calendars, House of Representatives.

A–Z

Campaign Finance

The various ways in which money is raised to pay for election campaigns. Candidates today typically spend millions of dollars to win election to Congress. This has raised concerns that money has become too important in the election process, and has led to a series of laws intended to regulate campaign financing.

Financing Campaigns

The modern congressional election is a complex financial affair. Fund-raisers, accountants, lawyers, and a variety of consultants play crucial roles in today's campaigns. Decisions on how to raise money and how to spend a campaign's resources can be key to a candidate's success.

Money pours in from a vast array of sources, including individuals, party committees, candidates themselves and their families, and private organizations called political action committees, or PACs. Money flows out for rent, computers, salaries, polls, consulting fees, printing, postage, and radio, television, and newspaper advertising. In 2002, the average congressional election

POINT/COUNTERPOINT

Should Congressional Elections Be Publicly Financed?

The powerful influence of money on the political system in the United States has led some observers to call for public financing of political campaigns. Supporters of such an idea, including political scientist and author David Sirota, feel that public financing is the best way to level the playing field so the average person has more say in the electoral process. Opponents, such as John Samples of the libertarian Cato Institute, which has often been associated with conservative positions, argue that eliminating private money from election campaigns violates the Constitution's free speech protections.

David Sirota

[T]he campaign financing system really is at the root of corruption. We have a system that is legalized bribery—legal campaign contributions go in, and legal legislative favors go out. But just because it is legal, doesn't mean it isn't unethical and isn't one of the major reasons why our government can no longer solve problems. It is. A government cannot solve problems if members of Congress making decisions are forced by virtue of their campaign finances to appease the Big Money interests that are often at the root of those problems.

Well-respected lawmakers have been pushing public financing for some time, including top Democrats who authored bills in the last Congress. Meanwhile, polls show the public has long supported the concept. As recently as 2000, the *Washington Post* reported that national polling on the issue showed "respondents did show enthusiasm for [public financing systems] that have already been endorsed by voters in Maine, Arizona, Vermont and Massachusetts." Even "when pollsters offered criticism of public financing, suggesting for instance that it would be 'welfare for politicians'

campaign cost just over $1 million; the average Senate campaign cost more than $3 million.

Individual Contributions

Individual donors traditionally have financed political campaigns. The biggest difference today is that many more contributors are now involved in the process. This is due to laws that limit the amount of money an individual can contribute to a single candidate. A few large donors have been mostly replaced by many smaller donors, who either give directly to a candidate or contribute through a PAC. By law, individuals are limited to giving $1,000 per candidate per election.

Political Action Committees (PACs)

Organizations such as labor unions and corporations may not use money from their general treasuries to make campaign contributions or pay campaign costs. Instead, they often form separate organizations called political action committees to raise money for candidates. Most PACs are permitted to contribute $5,000 per candidate per election, with no overall limit. They also may give $15,000 per year to a national party committee. By 2000, nearly 4,000 registered PACs were operating in Washington, DC, contributing over $200 million to congressional campaigns that year.

and would encourage more fringe candidates to run, support for full public funding remained at 67 percent."

John Samples

Campaign-finance laws often raise questions about restricting freedom of speech. Public financing seems to foster more speech by giving candidates money. But such laws restrict liberty in other ways. Government does not fund public financing; taxpayers do. These programs force taxpayers to support candidates they oppose.

Taxpayer financing often involves further limiting private contributions and restricting independent spending by anyone other than the candidates and the two major political parties. Such restrictions are inherent in public funding; without them, candidates would reject public funding for fear of being outspent by their opponents. Advocates say public financing brings more electoral competition, giving voters more choices, but most studies indicate such programs have not increased competition in state elections . . .

There is a larger issue here: Few Americans believe the government should control the financing of newspapers and television because public funding of the media would enable public officials to restrict or even eliminate spending on ideas that challenged the political status quo. Complete public financing of campaigns would pose the same danger to candidates and causes—the very sources of change and choice. Private funding of private political activity is thus vital to our limited and democratic government.

DOCUMENT-BASED QUESTION

Why does David Sirota believe public financing of election campaigns is needed, and in what way does John Samples counter Sirota's argument?

Political Parties

Political parties traditionally have provided direct assistance to candidates in two ways: through contributions, and by paying a candidate's campaign expenses. This can include paying for a wide range of services such as polling, research, direct mailing, advertising, or buying TV time. Party committees also persuade PACs, individuals, and **incumbents**–current officeholders–to support the party's most competitive candidates. A party's national committee, as well as its House and Senate campaign committees, are each permitted to make contributions of $5,000 per candidate per election. State and local party committees may give a combined total of $5,000 per election.

Parties can raise unlimited amounts of so-called "**soft money**" from unions, corporations, trade associations, and individuals for state and local party activities. The party may not use this money for congressional candidates. However, they may use it for activities such as voter registration, education, and turnout, which benefits candidates at all levels. It may also be used to pay a portion of the expenses of party committees, which frees up more funds for direct contributions to candidates. Soft money also funds "issue ads" that promote a party's

Twelve Most Expensive 2006 Congressional Races

Race	Winner	Winner Spent (in millions)	Loser	Loser Spent (in millions)	Total Spent
New York Senate	Hillary Clinton – D	$36	John Spencer – R	$5	$41
Pennsylvania Senate	Bob Casey – D	$14	Rick Santorum – R	$24	$38
Missouri Senate	Claire McCaskill – D	$8	Jim Talent – R	$19	$27
Connecticut Senate	Joseph Lieberman – I	$13	Ned Lamont – D	$13	$26
Tennessee Senate	Bob Corker – R	$14	Harold E. Ford, Jr. – D	$11	$25
Arizona Senate	Jon Kyle – R	$12	Jim Pederson – D	$12	$24
Washington Senate	Maria Cantwell – D	$14	Mike McGavick – R	$9	$23
Ohio Senate	Sherrod Brown – D	$9	Mike DeWine – R	$12	$21
Florida Senate	Bill Nelson – D	$11	Katherine Harris – R	$8	$19
Nebraska Senate	Ben Nelson – D	$7	Pete Ricketts – R	$11	$18
Florida 13th District	Vern Buchanan – R	$6	Christine Jennings – D	$2	$8
Illinois 8th District	Melissa L. Bean – D	$4	David McSweeney – R	$4	$8

Note: Total dollars spent may not add up because of rounding.

Spending for the 2006 congressional races reached all-time highs. Outspending an opponent, however, did not always result in an election victory.

positions but do not specifically target candidates for election or defeat.

Candidate's Own Money

There are no limits on how much candidates may contribute or lend to their own campaigns. Personal wealth makes a greater difference early in the election campaign as candidates seek to establish name recognition. As the campaign progresses, the advantage of personal wealth diminishes. At that time, candidates without a personal fortune have greater access to other sources of money, such as parties and public funding. In addition, more free publicity is available as the general election draws nearer.

Regulating Campaign Finances

Campaign finance is hardly a new issue. In the early years of the twentieth century, Congress attempted to limit the influence of money in politics. Then, as now, the public demanded reforms to curb the ability of special interests and wealthy individuals to dominate the flow of campaign money. Congress enacted the first law regulating campaigns in 1907. The next major new law in this area was the 1925 Federal Corrupt Practices Act, which limited campaign expenditures. The limits were unrealistically low, however, and the law proved ineffectual.

The next serious attempt to regulate campaign finances occurred during the 1970s. In 1971 Congress passed the Federal Election Campaign Act (FECA), which put a cap on the amount of money federal candidates could spend on media advertising. It also required candidates to make available a public record of the contributions they received, and how they spent that money. Congress amended FECA in 1974, setting limits on contributions and expenditures for congressional elections.

In 2002, Congress passed the Bipartisan Campaign Reform Act. It is also known as the McCain-Feingold act after its sponsors, Senators John McCain of Arizona and Russell Feingold of Wisconsin. The act prohibits national political party committees from raising or spending any "soft money" funds not subject to federal limits. It also prohibits corporations, unions, and non-profit issue organizations from paying for "issue ads" within 30 days of a **primary election** or 60 days of a general election.

See also: Teapot Dome Scandal.

Further Reading

Drew, Elizabeth. *The Corruption of American Politics: What Went Wrong and Why.* New York: Birch Lane, 1999.

Fritz, Sara, and Dwight Morris. *Gold-Plated Politics: Running for Congress in the 1990s.* Washington, DC: CQ Press, 1992.

Herrnson, Paul S. *Congressional Elections: Campaigning at Home and in Washington.* Fifth edition. Washington, DC: CQ Press, 2007.

Nugent, Margaret L., and John R. Johannes. *Money, Elections, and Democracy: Reforming Congressional Campaign Finance.* Boulder, CO: Westview, 1990.

Cannon, Joe

See Speaker of the House of Representatives.

Capitol

The building that houses Congress and serves as the nation's seat of government. The U.S. Capitol was built in the late 1700s and early 1800s and has been remodeled and expanded several times since then. In addition to its practical role in housing Congress, the Capitol stands as a public symbol of the United States government.

Design and Construction

The Capitol has undergone four major periods of construction. The first, which included the original design work, stretched from 1792 to about 1811. The second, from 1815 to 1829, saw the completion of the original building. The third period, from 1851 to 1892, included erection of the present wings used by the House and Senate and landscaping of the grounds. The fourth period began in 1949 with repairs to the roofs of the House and Senate wings and included extension of the East Front in 1962. The most recent work was the restoration of the West Front from 1983 to 1987.

Early Construction, 1792–1811

In 1790, Congress passed an act setting aside the land for a national capital to house the federal government. The following year, President George Washington (1789–1797) appointed architect Pierre Charles L'Enfant, to prepare a plan for the new city. L'Enfant recommended a site for the Capitol that has been known ever since as Capitol Hill. Washington also named three commissioners to oversee development of the city and the public buildings. In 1792, the commissioners conducted a public competition to design the new Capitol. They offered a prize of five hundred dollars and a plot of land in the city for the winning entry.

Dr. William Thornton, a physician and inventor, submitted the winning design. It called for a stately, three-story building, capped by a low dome. Thornton, however, was an amateur architect and his design was merely a sketch. The commissioners thus hired Stephen M. Hallet, a professional French architect, to prepare working drawings. Although Hallet modified some of Thornton's designs, Thomas Jefferson remarked that Hallet had "preserved the most valuable ideas of the original and rendered them acceptable of execution, so that it is considered Dr. Thornton's plan rendered into practical form."

George Washington laid the first cornerstone in a ceremony on September 18, 1793. By March 1796, the foundations had been laid, and the north wing was rising above ground level. When Congress arrived from Philadelphia

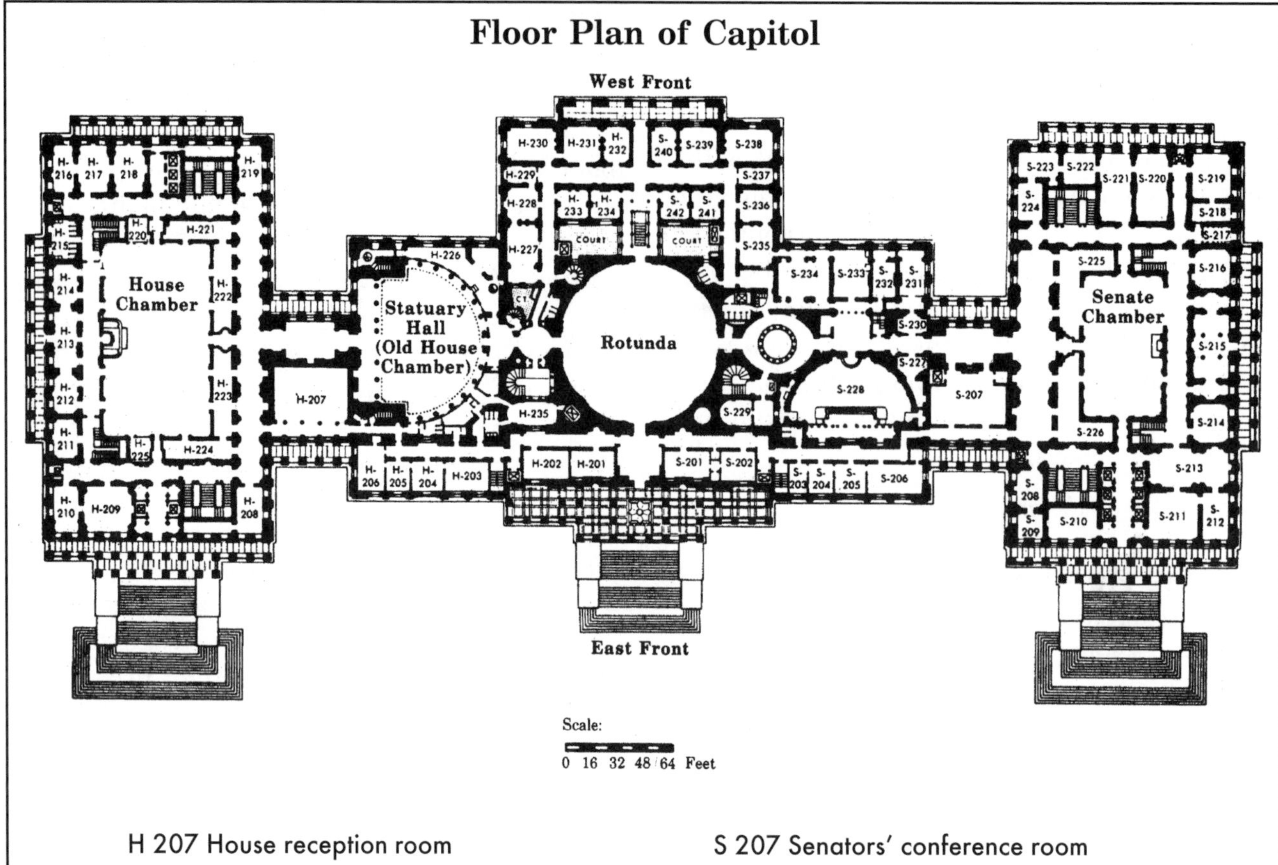

H 207 House reception room
H 208 Ways and Means Committee
H 209–210 Speaker
H 216–218 Appropriations Committee
H 220 Speaker's floor office
H 221–224 Cloakrooms (lobbies)
H 227–233, 236 Speaker

S 207 Senators' conference room
S 213 Senate reception room
S 214 Vice President's formal office
S 216 President's room
S 225–226 Cloakrooms (lobbies)
S 228 Old Senate chamber, 1810–1859

The United States Capitol is an expansive building and the seat of the nation's legislature. It includes not only the Senate and House chambers but also the Statuary Hall, offices, and several meeting rooms.

in the autumn of 1800, the foundations of the south wing had been completed. It took slave labor to build the home of a free government. The Capitol workforce was composed in large part of black slaves hired out by their masters in the District of Columbia and nearby Maryland and Virginia, a common custom at the time.

The first session of Congress in the new Capitol met on November 17, 1800. At that time, both the House and the Senate were housed in the north wing because it was the only part of the building that had been completed. It would be seven years before the House would move into chambers in a completed south wing.

In 1803, President Thomas Jefferson (1801–1809) placed Benjamin Henry Latrobe, an English architect, in charge of finishing the Capitol. Upon completing the south wing, Latrobe turned to repairing and remodeling the north wing. The threat of an approaching war with Britain, however, began to cut into funding for the Capitol. Work slowed, then halted. The north and south wings stood apart, separated by an unfinished center section.

Reconstruction and Expansion, 1815–1829

During the War of 1812, British forces under Robert Ross and Sir George Cockburn landed in Maryland and entered Washington unopposed. On August 24, 1814, British troops set the Capitol, the White House, and the Treasury building afire. A violent rainstorm later drowned the flames, preventing complete destruction of the buildings.

In 1815, Congress authorized President James Madison (1809–1817) to accept a $500,000 loan to pay for rebuilding the Capitol. Madison recalled Latrobe to oversee the work, but Latrobe resigned from the position two years later. Madison's successor, James Monroe (1817–1825), then appointed Boston's Charles Bulfinch as the first American-born architect of the Capitol. Laying the cornerstone on August 24, 1818, Bulfinch completed the reconstruction of the north and south wings and supervised work on the central section. The original Capitol dome was completed in 1827. It was much lower than the present dome and made of wood sheathed in copper. Construction of the original Capitol was finally completed two years later.

SPOTLIGHT

The Capitol Police

This special police force is charged with protecting the United States Congress. The force was organized in 1828, after an assault on one of John Quincy Adams' sons, also named John Adams, in the Capitol Rotunda. The group's original mission was to protect the building itself. Over time, the force's authority expanded to provide Congress, as well as visitors, with a variety of police services.

Among the force's responsibilities are protecting life and property; detecting, preventing, and investigating criminal acts; and enforcing traffic laws throughout the Capitol complex of buildings and parks. The force has exclusive **jurisdiction** with the Capitol grounds and concurrent, or shared, jurisdiction with other police agencies, such as the District of Columbia Police, throughout an area of about 200 blocks around the Capitol. In addition to protecting the Capitol itself, the force is responsible for protecting members of Congress and their families throughout the District of Columbia, the United States, and its territories.

Today, the force numbers about 1,700 and uses the most advanced technologies available to carry out its duties. Among its chief sections are a Community Emergency Response team, a K-9 unit, a Hazardous Devices and Hazardous Materials section, and a Patrol/Mobile Response division. Members of the force receive twelve weeks of initial training at the Federal Law Enforcement Training Center (FLETC) in Glynco, Georgia. Members are then sent to another FLETC site in Cheltenham, Maryland, for an additional twelve weeks of training.

Expansion, 1851–1892

The finished Capitol was plagued with problems. The House and Senate chambers were difficult to heat in winter and ventilate in summer. In addition, by the mid-1800s, the two chambers were becoming overcrowded by the increase in the number of members of Congress representing newly admitted states. It was clear that the Capitol would have to be expanded.

In September 1850, Congress approved a design competition to "provide for the extension of the Capitol, either by additional wings, to be placed on the north and south of the present building, or by the erection of a separate and distinct building" to the east of the existing Capitol. On June 10, 1851, President Millard Fillmore (1850–1853) approved a plan submitted by Philadelphia architect Thomas Ustick Walter. Charges of fraud and poor construction led ultimately to Walter's dismissal as architect. His plan, however, was retained. By December 1857, the new House chamber was completed, but the Senate was unable to meet in its new chamber until January 1859.

It soon became clear that the greatly enlarged building dwarfed the old dome. The dome Walter designed as a replacement became the most distinguishing feature of the Capitol. The entire dome, including the thirty-six columns in its lower section, is made of cast iron painted to match the Capitol's stonework. It consists of inner and outer shells girded and bolted together. The dome is more than 135 feet wide at its base, and the Rotunda inside is ninety-six feet in diameter. Work on the dome began in 1856 and was completed in 1865. On December 20, 1863, the last section of the Statue of Freedom atop the dome was bolted into place, crowning the Capitol.

During the Civil War (1861–1865), Union troops were temporarily quartered in the Capitol. In 1862, the building was used as a hospital for wounded soldiers from the battles of Second Bull Run and Antietam. About 1,500 cots were set up in the corridors, the Rotunda, and the House and Senate chambers. The patients were transferred to other hospitals before Congress returned in December.

Twentieth-Century Alterations

For seventy-five years after the completion of the dome, little important architectural work was done on the Capitol. In 1940, Congress authorized remodeling of the House and Senate chambers and replacement of their cast-iron and glass ceilings with new ceilings of stainless steel and plaster. Work was delayed by World War II (1941–1945), and the actual remodeling was carried out from July 1949 to January 1951.

The most controversial recent alteration of the Capitol was the 1958–1962 extension of the East Front. Although such an extension had been discussed for years, in 1956, it became a major dispute. Opponents of the extension said the existing East Front should be repaired and preserved. Despite these objections, work began in 1958 and was completed in 1962. The East Front extension added 100,000 square feet of space to the Capitol and provided 102 new rooms, additional elevators, and a private corridor for members between the Senate and House wings. The extension also added a subway terminal under the Senate wing steps.

As work on the East Front drew to a close in 1962, the question of whether to restore or extend the West Front began developing into perhaps the most controversial construction issue in the Capitol's long history. A structural weakness had developed in the west wall of the Capitol's central section, leading to a proposal for a 285-room extension in 1966. Various groups objected to the extension on economic, historical, and architectural grounds. After years of debate, the advocates of restoration won out, and in 1983, Congress appropriated $49 million to stabilize the wall. The work was completed in 1987.

The Capitol Today

In addition to the House and Senate chambers, the Capitol today includes office space for members of Congress and rooms used for a wide variety other purposes. Both chambers have galleries to hold the press. The House side of the Capitol includes a member's dining room and a carryout. Senators have two dining rooms: one private and one that permits guests. The House and Senate also provide three barber and beauty shops in the Capitol and office buildings.

In June 2000, construction began on the Capitol Visitors Center on the East Front. The center is designed to provide a more orderly entrance for visitors. Prior to the center being built, visitors waited in the parking lot and entered the building through a small and cramped security checkpoint. The new facility will feature a grand entrance hall, a visitors' theater, an exhibit room, and dining and restroom facilities.

See also: Capitol, Architect of the; Capitol Subways; District of Columbia.

Further Reading

Aikman, Lonnelle. *We, the People: The Story of the United States Capitol.* Fifteenth edition. Washington, DC: United States Capitol Historical Society, 2002.

Brown, Glenn. *Glenn Brown's History of the United States Capitol.* Washington, DC: United States Congress, 2007.

U.S. Congress. *The Capitol: A Pictorial History.* Ninth edition. Washington, DC: Government Printing Office, 1988.

Capitol, Architect of the

Formal position given to certain individuals who are appointed by the president to serve as the official architects of the Capitol and other government structures. The post of Architect of the Capitol has existed as a permanent position since 1876. At that time, Congress transferred to the Architect of the Capitol the functions performed previously by the commissioner for public buildings and grounds. However, beginning with William Thornton, who was appointed Architect of the Capitol in 1793, nine presidential appointees have had the responsibility for construction and maintenance of the Capitol.

Architects of the Capitol, 1800–2007

Following is a list of persons who have been appointed by the president to serve as Architect of the Capitol, although under other titles in the early years:	
William Thornton	1793–1794
Benjamin Henry Latrobe	1803–1811 1815–1817
Charles Bulfinch	1818–1829
Thomas Ustick Walter	1851–1865
Edward Clark	1865–1902
Elliott Woods	1902–1923
David Lynn	1923–1954
J. George Stewart	1954–1970
George M. White	1971–1997
Alan M. Hantman	1997–2007
Stephen T. Ayers	2007–Serving as Acting Architect of the Capitol until a new Architect is appointed by the President

The Architects of the Capitol are responsible for the upkeep of the building itself as well as the surrounding landscape. Benjamin Latrobe, the second Architect of the Capitol, was responsible for its rebuilding after the British burned it in 1814, during the War of 1812.

Interestingly, the person appointed to be the Architect of the Capitol does not have to be a professional architect. As the position exists today, the role is largely an administrative one. The Architect of the Capitol is charged with the structural and mechanical care of the following buildings: the Capitol and two hundred acres of grounds, the Senate and House office buildings, the Library of Congress buildings and grounds, the U.S. Supreme Court buildings and grounds, the Senate garage, the Robert A. Taft Memorial, and the Capitol Power Plant, which heats and cools some buildings in addition to the Capitol complex. The Architect of the

SPOTLIGHT

Frederick Law Olmsted (1822–1903)

Frederick Law Olmsted was an American landscape architect who, beginning in the 1870s, created the look and the landscape of the United States Capitol. Olmsted is also renowned for designing Central Park in New York City and the Biltmore Estate in Asheville, North Carolina, as well as the park systems of several cities throughout the United States.

In 1873, Vermont Senator Justin Morrill wrote to Olmsted, asking him if he would plan the design of the renovation of the U.S. Capitol and its grounds. Olmsted threw himself into the task, developing a plan that took nearly twenty years to complete. Initially, however, Congress was hesitant to fund Olmsted's lavish project.

In 1874, Congress funded the project and awarded Olmsted the commission. His plan called for grand marble terraces to be constructed on the north, west, and south sides of the building—resulting in the building to "gain greatly in the supreme qualities of stability, endurance, and repose." He also developed the plan for the Summer House, an open hexagonal building designed to give visitors a place to rest and enjoy the view of the Capitol. Olmsted's plan called for the planning of more than 7,000 trees and shrubs, along with other landscape plants and for curved footpaths and roads across the grounds. He also included ornamental iron trellises, low stone walls, and lights in his plan.

By the 1890s, Olmsted had turned the Capitol into a showplace. The Capitol and its grounds were stunningly landscaped. Visitors to the Capitol might stroll the walkways to admire the landscaping or stand on the west terrace and admire the view. Alternatively, they could linger in the Summer House, completed in 1880 or 1881. It was built into a sloping hillside on the west front lawn, under the shade of the massive trees, which in years past, had been part of two separate barbecue areas—one for the Democrats and one for the Whigs.

Capitol also is charged with the operation of the U.S. Botanic Garden and the Senate restaurants.

The Architect of the Capitol performs these tasks under the direction of the Speaker of the House of Representatives, the Senate Committee on Rules and Administration, the House Office Building Commission, and the Joint Committee on the Library. Among the many employees working for the Architect of the Capitol are tree surgeons, stone inspectors, nurses, subway car operators, elevator operators, garage workers, and flag clerks. The Architect of the Capitol's office also provides various services for congressional committees and members of Congress. These services include designing workspaces, purchasing and delivering furniture, housekeeping, painting, and catering meals and various events.

Capitol Subways

Underground trains that link various federal office buildings in Washington, DC. The office buildings for the U.S. Senate and the House of Representatives are linked to the U.S. Capitol by a series of underground tunnels. Subway cars have shuttled members of Congress through these tunnels for more than a century. A subway line has run from the Senate wing of the Capitol to the Russell Building since 1909, to the Dirksen Building since 1960, and to the Hart Building since 1982. The only subway service for the House of Representatives operates from the Rayburn Building. There are tunnels linking the Capitol with the Cannon and Longworth buildings, which are used by members of the house, but they are restricted to pedestrian traffic only.

In 1909, two Studebaker battery-operated vehicles with solid rubber tires provided the first subway transportation between the Capitol and the Russell Building. Faster service came in 1912 with the addition of two monorail cars powered by overhead electrical wires. Two redesigned monorail cars, produced at the Washington Navy Yard and put into service in 1920, remained in use until 1961. A new subway system connecting the Senate office buildings with the Capitol began service in 1960. It consists of four eighteen-passenger electric cars on two-rail tracks. The trains run at approximately twenty miles an hour, which means that the running time to the Capitol is forty-five seconds from the Russell Building, sixty seconds from the Dirksen Building, and sixty-five seconds from the Hart Building. A similar system for the House of Representatives was installed between the Rayburn Building and the Capitol in 1966. The running time on this subway line is forty seconds.

All Capitol subways operate during working hours when Congress is in session. Although built primarily to shuttle members or Congress to and from the Capitol and their office buildings, the public may ride free if space is available. When the cars are not running, all the tunnels in this subway system remain open to pedestrian traffic, both for members of Congress and the general public.

Caucuses

Groups of individuals who share a common political identification or interest. The term *caucus* may refer to all the members of a particular party in one house of Congress, as well as to smaller groups of members who work together to advance a common legislative program. Examples of the latter type of caucus include the Congressional Black Caucus, the Congressional Children's Caucus, and the Congressional **Urban** Caucus.

Major party groupings in Congress call themselves either caucuses or conferences. The full membership of the Democratic Party in the House of Representatives, for example, is known as the Democratic House Caucus. Its counterpart in the Senate calls itself the Democratic Senate Conference. The Republicans use the term *conference* to refer to their party caucuses in both the House and Senate.

More narrow caucuses are often based on shared characteristics of members such as race, ethnicity, or gender. The Congressional Black Caucus, the Congressional Hispanic Caucus, and the Congressional Women's Caucus are examples of caucuses organized along such lines. Many of these caucuses are partisan in nature, with separate caucuses for each party addressing issues important to the same group. For example, the Congressional Hispanic Caucus is composed solely of Democrats, while the corresponding Congressional Hispanic Conference includes only Republicans.

Other more narrowly focused caucuses are bipartisan in nature, containing members of both parties. The Congressional Internet Caucus, for example, which advocates the growth and advancement of the Internet, contains both Republican and Democratic members.

Caucuses organized to pursue common legislative goals are officially known as Congressional

Member Organizations, or CMOs. A CMO must register with the Committee on House Administration at the beginning of each Congress. Each CMO must declare its purpose and the names of its officers, and submit a list of employees authorized to work with the CMO. Congressional rules require at least one person on each CMO to be a member of the House; otherwise, a CMO may contain both Senate and House members. As of 2008, nearly 200 CMOs were registered with the Committee on House Administration.

Caucuses operate under certain restrictions that do not apply to their individual members. For example, CMOs may not use the franking privilege, which allows Congress members to send mail free of charge to their constituents. Nor may individual members use their frank to send materials on behalf of a CMO. A CMO also may not establish its own web page on the Internet, although its members may devote part of their individual web sites to promote the work of the CMO.

See also: Congressional Black Caucus; Congressional Hispanic Caucus; Franking.

Censure

Public reprimand of a member of Congress for inappropriate behavior. Censure usually occurs when a member of the House or Senate commits an offense that is serious but not so serious that it demands expulsion. Censure is a way for the other members of the chamber to express their disapproval of the action without removing the offender from office. It is usually reserved for punishing actions a member takes while serving in Congress. Both houses have sparingly used their power to penalize a member for prior offenses or misdeeds committed during a previous Congress.

Procedure

The Constitution does not mention censure nor do the formal rules of the House or Senate. Instead, the procedure is based on informal customs and Congress's tradition of imposing self-discipline. For minor transgressions of the rules, the presiding officer of either chamber may call a member to order, without a formal move to censure. If a formal motion to censure is called for, a simple majority of the chamber must vote to impose the censure. By contrast, a two-thirds majority vote is required to expel a member.

In the Senate, censure proceedings are carried out with a degree of moderation typical of that chamber's proceedings. Alleged offenders, for example, are allowed to speak in their own defenses. The House treats offenders more harshly, often denying them the privilege of defending themselves. In most cases, a censured member is treated like a felon. The Speaker calls the person to the bar of the House and makes a solemn pronouncement of censure.

Censure by the House

A House rule adopted in 1789, reads: "If any member, in speaking or otherwise, transgress the rules of the House, the Speaker shall, or any member may, call him to order; . . . and if the case require it, he shall be liable to censure or such punishment as the House may deem proper." The censure clause of this rule has been invoked thirty-six times, and censure has been voted twenty-two times.

The first censure motion in the House was introduced after Virginia's Matthew Lyon physically attacked Connecticut's Roger Griswold on the House floor in January 1798. Griswold had taunted Lyon on his allegedly poor military record. The censure motion failed. The following month, Lyon and Griswold fought again on the House floor. Again a motion was introduced to censure both members, and again the motion failed. In 1832, William Stanbery of Ohio became the first House member to be formally censured for insulting the Speaker of the House during a debate in the House floor.

Including Stanbury, the House has censured members for unacceptable language or offensive publications in seven other cases. Corruption has been the basis for censure or proposed censure in five cases. Other House members have been censured for physically assaulting colleagues, financial misconduct, and sexual misconduct.

Censure Proceedings in Congress

1798	Matthew Lyon, Anti-Fed-Vt.	Assault on representative	Not censured
1798	Roger Griswold, Fed-Conn.	Assault on representative	Not censured
1832	William Stanbery, JD-Ohio	Insult to Speaker	Censured
1836	Sherrod Williams, Whig-Ky.	Insult to Speaker	Not censured
1838	Henry A. Wise, Tyler Dem.-Va.	Service as second in duel	Not censured
1839	Alexander Duncan, Whig-Ohio	Offensive publication	Not censured
1842	John Q. Adams, Whig-Mass.	Treasonable petition	Not censured
1842	Joshua R. Giddings, Whig-Ohio	Offensive paper	Censured
1856	Henry A. Edmundson, D-Va.	Complicity in assault on senator	Not censured
1856	Laurence M. Keitt, D-S.C.	Complicity in assault on senator	Censured
1860	George S. Houston, D-Ala.	Insult to representative	Not censured
1864	Alexander Long, D-Ohio	Treasonable utterance	Censured
1864	Benjamin G.Harris, D-Md.	Treasonable utterance	Censured
1866	John W. Chanler, D-N.Y.	Insult to House	Censured
1866	Lovell H. Rousseau, R-Ky.	Assault on representative	Censured
1867	John W. Hunter, Ind-N.Y.	Insult to representative	Censured
1868	Fernando Wood, D-N.Y.	Offensive utterance	Censured
1868	E. D. Holbrook, D-Idaho[a]	Offensive utterance	Censured
1870	Benjamin F. Whittemore, R-S.C.	Corruption	Censured
1870	Roderick R. Butler, R-Tenn.	Corruption	Censured
1870	John T. Deweese, R-N.C.	Corruption	Censured
1873	Oakes Ames, R-Mass.	Corruption	Censured
1873	James Brooks, D-N.Y.	Corruption	Censured
1875	John Y. Brown, D-Ky.	Insult to representative	Censured[b]
1876	James G. Blaine, R-Maine	Corruption	Not censured
1882	William D. Kelley, R-Pa.	Offensive utterance	Not censured
1882	John D. White, R-Ky.	Offensive utterance	Not censured
1883	John Van Voorhis, R-N.Y.	Offensive utterance	Not censured
1890	William D. Bynum, D-Ind.	Offensive utterance	Censured
1921	Thomas L. Blanton, D-Texas	Abuse of leave to print	Censured

(continued on next page)

Censure Proceedings in Congress, *continued*

1978	Edward R. Roybal, D-Calif.	Lying to House committee	Not censured[c]
1979	Charles C. Diggs Jr., D-Mich.	Misuse of clerk-hire funds	Censured
1980	Charles H. Wilson, D-Calif.	Financial misconduct	Censured
1983	Gerry E. Studds, D-Mass.	Sexual misconduct	Censured
1983	Daniel B. Crane, R-Ill.	Sexual misconduct	Censured
1990	Barney Frank, D-Mass.	Discrediting House	Not censured[c]

Notes: **a. Holbrook was a territorial delegate, not a representative. b. The House later rescinded part of the censure resolution against Brown. c. Reprimanded after censure resolution failed or was withdrawn.**
Sources: **Hinds and Cannon, *Precedents of the House of Representatives of the United States,* 11 vols. (1935–1941); Joint Committee on Congressional Operations, *House of Representatives Exclusion, Censure, and Expulsion Cases from 1789 to 1973,* 93rd Cong., 1st sess., 1973, committee print; *Congress and the Nation 1977–1980, 1981–1984, 1985–1988, 1992–1996,* vols. 5, 6, 7, 9, (Washington, D.C.: Congressional Quarterly); *Congressional Quarterly Almanac 1990.***

The United States House of Representatives, like the Senate, is responsible for disciplining its members if they behave in an inappropriate manner. Over the years, both houses have used their power to censure members sparingly.

Censure by the Senate

Six members of the Senate have been censured, starting with Timothy Pickering of Massachusetts. Pickering was punished for reading aloud in the chamber secret documents relating to the 1803 purchase of Louisiana from France. In 1844, Ohio's Benjamin Tappan received a similar censure for releasing to the press confidential material relating to a treaty to **annex** Texas.

Threatened violence was involved in the next two censure cases in the Senate. On February 22, 1902, Republican Benjamin R. Tillman and Democrat John L. McLaurin, both from South Carolina, engaged in a fistfight after Tillman questioned McLaurin's integrity. The Committee on Privileges and Elections recommended censure for both men, and the Senate adopted the resolution.

Perhaps the most famous case of censure in the Senate involved Wisconsin's Joseph McCarthy. McCarthy accused several political opponents of Communist sympathies in the 1950s and claimed that Communists had even infiltrated the U.S. Army. McCarthy's aggressive tactics and explosive charges led some members to call for censure. In the spring of 1954, the Senate Permanent Investigations Subcommittee conducted hearings on mutual accusations of misconduct by McCarthy and U.S. Army officials. The Committee on Rules and Administration also held hearings, but McCarthy refused to testify before the committee.

Vermont's Ralph Flanders introduced a resolution to censure McCarthy for his refusal to testify before the Rules subcommittee, as well as for questionable actions by McCarthy's staff and McCarthy's "habitual contempt for people." A committee formed to consider the charges against McCarthy recommended censure, but later substituted the word "condemned" for "censured." The motion passed 67–22. Despite the wording of the charge, historians count the Senate's rebuke of McCarthy as a censure.

See also: Army-McCarthy Hearings; Ethics, Congressional.

Further Reading

Butler, Anne M., and Wendy Wolff. *United States Senate: Election, Expulsion and Censure Cases, 1973–1990.* Collingdale, PA: Diane, 1998.

Watkins, Arthur V. *Enough Rope: The Story of the Censure of Senator Joe McCarthy.* Englewood Cliffs, NJ: Prentice-Hall, 1969.

Census

A count of the national population used to determine representation in the House of Representatives. Article I, Section 2, of the Constitution calls for a census to be conducted every ten years of the "whole number of free persons." The delegates to the first Constitutional Convention decided that the each state should have one representative for every 30,000 persons counted by the census. This figure changed as the nation grew. Today, each member of the House represents about 650,000 people.

Counting the number of people in the United States has never been easy due to the political importance of the census. The census not only affects the reapportioning of House seats among the states; it also determines how district boundaries for state and local public officials are drawn and how billions of dollars in federal spending is distributed.

Questions about the accuracy of the census are as old as the Republic, but they have intensified since 1911, when Congress fixed the number of representatives at 435. Since then, a gain of representation in any one state can come only at the loss of representation in another. After the 1920 census showed for the first time that the majority of Americans lived in cities, rural interests objected that the farm population had been undercounted. In 1941, concerns about the accuracy of the census arose when the number of men turning out for the wartime draft was considerably higher than expectations based on the 1940 census.

In the latter years of the twentieth century, there was intense controversy about the census' undercounting of certain groups, especially minorities. The undercount issue became a particular concern for major cities and for the Democrats who tended to represent them. They led an effort to persuade the Census Bureau to use a statistical method to adjust the census for the undercount. Several states and cities pursued the matter in court, but a 1996 Supreme Court ruling went against them. The Court has also rejected more recent attempts to use statistical sampling methods to increase the accuracy of the census.

Members of Congress and other public officials also have taken a strong interest in the practice of including illegal **aliens** in the census. The Census Bureau has never attempted to exclude illegal aliens from the census. This policy is troubling to states that fear losing House seats to states with large numbers of illegal aliens.

For the 1990 census, the Commerce Department reversed a long-standing policy and counted military personnel and dependents stationed overseas. "Historically we have not included them because the census is based on the concept of usual residence," said Charles Jones, associate director of the Census Bureau. "People overseas have a 'usual residence' overseas." For the purposes of reapportionment, overseas personnel were assigned to the state each individual considered home.

See also: Reapportionment; Redistricting.

Further Reading

Monmonier, Mark. *Bushmanders and Bullwinkles: How Politicians Manipulate Electronic Maps and Census Data to Win Elections.* Chicago: University of Chicago Press, 2001.

Checks and Balances

A system of safeguards built into the Constitution which allows each branch of government to prevent abuse of power by other branches. The Framers of the Constitution were concerned about the possibility that one branch of the government might amass enough power to impose its will on the others. To ensure against this happening, they gave each branch certain tools to restrain the activities of the others.

Perhaps the most significant check that Congress exercises over the other branches is the power to **impeach,** or accuse government officials for misconduct committed while in office.

The House of Representatives may impeach government officials and judges appointed by the executive branch. The Senate tries officers and judges impeached by the House.

The advice and consent power is another important check that Congress has over the executive. The president must seek Senate approval to appoint cabinet members, ambassadors, and federal judges. The Senate must also vote to approve any treaty negotiated by the president. When the Senate is in recess, the president may make temporary appointments, called recess appointments, without any confirmation process. These appointments, however, are only valid until Congress comes back into session. At that point, the president must seek congressional approval for any recess appointments. Other powers that Congress has to check the actions of the other branches include the ability to establish courts, to regulate the size of courts, and to determine compensation for judges and executive branch officials.

The main presidential check on Congress is the power to **veto,** or refuse to sign into law, **bills** passed by Congress. Congress, however, may override a veto if two-thirds of the members in each house vote to do so. The president may also call emergency sessions of either or both houses of Congress. The president exercises a considerable check over the judicial branch though the power to appoint judges. Without the consent of Congress, the president may also pardon individuals found guilty of crime or misconduct by the courts.

Judicial review serves as the judiciary's most importance check on the other branches. This concept states that federal courts have the power to strike down any law they consider unconstitutional. This power does not appear in the Constitution; rather the Supreme Court established it in the 1803 case of *Marbury v. Madison.* Congress exercises some control over judicial review through its power to set the jurisdiction, or area of legal authority, of the courts.

See also: Confirmation Power of the Senate; Impeachment Power; Judicial Review; Separation of Powers; Treaty Power.

Citizenship and Naturalization

Citizenship refers to membership in a political community. A citizen is a person who enjoys the right to participate in the political process. Naturalization is the legal process by which a person who is not born a citizen obtains citizenship. Although the Constitution refers to "citizens" several times, nowhere does it define who is a citizen. As a result, the definition of citizenship has been a matter of dispute throughout the nation's history.

Who is a Citizen?

At the time of the nation's founding, it was assumed that a citizen was a person born in the country and who remained under its **jurisdiction** and protection. This definition was accepted in England, while in the rest of Europe, citizenship was determined by the nationality of one's parents. The definition, however, did not apply to every resident of the United States. Until the **ratification** of the Fourteenth Amendment in 1868, slaves were not considered citizens, even those who were born in the United States. The first sentence of that amendment states: "All persons born or naturalized in the United States and subject to the jurisdiction thereof, are citizens of the United States and of the State wherein they reside." The Supreme Court upheld this definition in the 1898 case of *United States v. Wong Kim Ark.* The Court declared that, under the Fourteenth Amendment, children born in the United States to resident alien parents were citizens, even if their parents were barred from becoming citizens themselves.

Congress, however, may establish whatever condition it deems necessary for citizenship through the process of naturalization. "Naturalization is a privilege, to be given, qualified, or withheld as Congress may determine and which the alien may claim as of right only upon compliance with the terms which Congress imposes," the Supreme Court said in 1931. The Court has also held that Congress may exclude an entire class or race of people from eligibility for citizenship. In 1893, the Court upheld a statute expelling Chinese laborers from the country if they did not obtain a residence certificate within a specified time. The Court wrote:

> The right of a nation to expel or deport foreigners, who have not been naturalized or taken any steps towards becoming citizens . . . is as absolute and unqualified as the right to prohibit and prevent their entrance into the country. . . . The power to exclude or expel aliens, being a power affecting international relations, is vested in the political departments of the government, and it is to be regulated by treaty or by act of Congress, and to be executed by the executive authority according to the regulations so established.

After ratification of the Fourteenth Amendment, Congress enacted laws limiting naturalized citizenship to whites and to blacks of African descent. It also extended citizenship to the residents of some, but not all, of the U.S. territories. The residents of Hawaii became citizens in 1900, those of Puerto Rico in 1917, and those of the Virgin Islands in 1927. The residents of the Philippines, however, were denied citizenship throughout the period the United States held the islands as a trust territory. Other Asians did not fare any better in winning citizenship through naturalization. The final barriers to their naturalization did not fall until passage in 1952 of the Immigration and Nationality Act, which barred the use of race as a reason for denying citizenship.

Immigrants from about 42 different countries were sworn in as new American citizens in this ceremony held on May 22, 2006 at Mount Vernon, Virginia—the site of George Washington's home. Congress has the power to establish the requirements for citizenship. (Alex Wong, Getty Images)

Congress has set other conditions for naturalization that have excluded **anarchists,** members of the U.S. Communist Party, and others who advocate the violent overthrow of the government. To qualify for naturalization, an alien must have been a resident of the country for five years and be of good moral character. This latter phrase has been applied at various times to exclude drunks, adulterers, gamblers, convicted felons, and homosexuals.

As early as 1824, the Supreme Court declared that there was no difference between a naturalized citizen and one who was native-born. A naturalized citizen, wrote Chief Justice John Marshall, "becomes a member of the society, possessing all rights of the native citizen, and standing, in the view of the Constitution, on the footing of a native. The Constitution does not authorize Congress to enlarge or abridge those rights. The simple power of the national Legislature is to prescribe a uniform rule of naturalization, and the exercise of its power exhausts it, so far as respects the individual."

With two major exceptions, this statement remains true. Naturalized citizens do enjoy the same rights, privileges, and responsibilities as do native-born citizens. One exception is that naturalized citizens may be denaturalized. The other exception is that they are not eligible to run for President.

Loss of Citizenship

The Supreme Court has repeatedly held that a naturalized citizen may lose citizenship that was obtained fraudulently. In 1981, the Court ruled that a Russian native naturalized in 1970 should be stripped of his U.S. citizenship for hiding the fact that he had served as a concentration camp guard in World War II (1941–1945). Concealing

VIEWPOINTS

An 1880 political cartoon by Joseph Keppler shows the United States, symbolized by Uncle Sam, welcoming an unlimited number of immigrants. Over the years, Congress has passed laws regulating, and in some instances, limiting, immigration. (The Granger Collection, New York)

his wartime activities made his admission to the United States unlawful and invalidated his naturalization.

Naturalization also may be lost if it is obtained in bad faith. In the 1913 case of *Luria v. United States,* the Court upheld the denaturalization of a man who apparently never intended to become a permanent resident of the United States at the time he was naturalized. The decision upheld an act of Congress that made residence in a foreign country within five years of naturalization evidence of bad faith.

Expatriation

The question whether Congress may expatriate citizens, or revoke their citizenship, has troubled the Supreme Court for a number of years. People may voluntarily give up their citizenship, and Congress may declare that a person who voluntarily performs certain acts automatically loses citizenship. In 1915, for example, the Court upheld part of the Citizenship Act of 1907 that stated any female citizen who married an alien surrendered her citizenship in the United States. Congress repealed that part of the act in 1922, but in 1950, the Court ruled that a woman who had voluntarily sworn allegiance to Italy in order to marry an Italian citizen had effectively renounced her U.S. citizenship.

The Immigration and Nationality Act of 1952 contained a long list of circumstances under which an American would lose citizenship. These included voting in a foreign election, being convicted and discharged from the armed services for desertion during wartime, and leaving or remaining outside the country to avoid military service. In 1958 the Supreme Court upheld the provision revoking citizenship of a person who voted in a foreign election. On the same day, however, it struck down the provision

Requirements for Becoming a Naturalized Citizen of the United States

1. You have resided in the United States as a permanent resident continuously for five years. (You can qualify after only three years of permanent residence if you received your green card through marriage to a U.S. Citizen and you have lived together for the last three years.)
2. You have been physically present in the United States for half of the five years (or half of the three, if you are married to a U.S. Citizen).
3. You are a person of good moral character.
4. You have a basic knowledge of U.S. government and history.
5. You are able to read, write, and speak simple English (with exceptions for some older and long-time permanent residents, and for disabled permanent residents).
6. You are at least 18 years of age and legally competent to take an oath of allegiance to the United States.
7. You express your allegiance to the United States.

Throughout the years, Congress has altered the residency requirement for immigrants to become American citizens. Presently, an immigrant married to a citizen has a shorter residency requirement than someone who is single or married to an immigrant.

of the immigration law that revoked the citizenship of persons convicted and discharged from the armed services for desertion. Five years later, it also struck down the provisions of the act that revoked the citizenship of anyone who left or remained outside the country in order to evade military service.

In 1967, the Supreme Court again divided over the question of Congress's power to revoke citizenship. Five justices argued that Congress did not have that power. "In our country the people are sovereign, and the government cannot sever its relationship to the people by taking away their citizenship," the majority said. The four justices who disagreed insisted there was nothing in the citizenship clause of the Fourteenth Amendment that denied Congress the power to revoke citizenship under certain conditions. Because of the narrow 5–4 vote, this decision did not settle the issue. The question of congressional power to revoke a person's citizenship remains undecided.

Citizenship and Officeholding

One very important aspect of citizenship is its role as a qualification for holding office. The delegates to the Constitutional Convention specified that members of Congress must meet minimum requirements for citizenship. Originally, House members were required to be U.S. citizens for at least three years, while senators must be citizens for four years. Fearful of making it too easy for foreigners to be elected, the convention lengthened the citizenship requirement to seven years for representatives and nine years for senators. The Constitution specifies even stricter requirements for serving as president of the United States. Presidents must be natural-born citizens of the United States; although naturalized aliens may serve as members of Congress, they are forbidden from holding the office of president.

See also: Congress, Constitutional Origins of; House of Representatives; Senate.

Further Reading

Green, Nancy L., and Francois Weil, eds. *Citizenship and Those Who Leave: The Politics of Emigration and Expatriation.* Eagan, MN: Thomson West, 2007.

Kimmel, Barbara, and Alan M. Lubiner. *Citizenship Made Simple: An Easy-to-Read Guide to the U.S. Citizenship Process.* Dallas, TX: Next Decade, 2006.

Newman, John J. *American Naturalization Processes and Procedures: 1790–1985.* Indianapolis: Indiana Historical Society, 1985.

SPOTLIGHT

Who Is a Citizen?

The definition of a U.S. citizen has undergone considerable change since the founding of the **republic.** In general, people born in the United States, regardless of their parents' nationality, historically have been considered citizens. The U.S. Supreme Court upheld this definition as a settled legal principle in 1898.

There have been exceptions to this rule, however. African American slaves and their descendants were denied citizenship until the states **ratified,** or formally approved, the Fourteenth Amendment to the Constitution in 1868. In addition, children born to foreign diplomats living in the United States are not considered U.S. citizens.

A person need not be born in the United States to receive U.S. citizenship. Children born abroad to parents who are both U.S. citizens are themselves citizens. This is true even if only one of the child's parents lived in the United States prior to the birth of the child. In fact, a child born overseas may receive citizenship if only one of the parents is a U.S. citizen. That parent must have lived in the United States for at least five years before the child's birth, and at least two of those years must have been after the parent's fourteenth birthday.

A person not born with U.S. citizenship may acquire it through a process called *naturalization.* Only people who are eighteen years old or older and permanent residents of the United States are eligible for naturalization. (Young people under the age of eighteen who are permanent residents may become citizens at the time when a parent applies for citizenship.) People seeking naturalization must have lived in the country for a period of five years before applying. Applicants are ineligible if, during that five-year period, they spent six months or more continuously living outside the U.S. Besides these residency requirements, people applying for naturalization must be of "good moral character."

All applicants for naturalization must take a brief written exam testing a basic knowledge of U.S. history and government. It includes such questions as "Who elects the president of the United States?" "How many voting members are in the House of Representatives?" "In what year was the Constitution written?" An applicant must correctly answer six of ten questions to pass. Most applicants also must demonstrate a basic ability to read, write, and speak English. Congress, however, has created exemptions from this requirement for older applicants or those with physical or mental disabilities.

Naturalized citizens enjoy all of the rights of U.S. citizenship except the ability to serve as president or vice president. All other elective and appointed offices are open to naturalized American citizens. Perhaps one of the best-known naturalized citizens to hold high public office is California governor Arnold Schwarzenegger, who was born in Austria.

Justice for All

Congressional Authority Over Aliens

The congressional power held over aliens is absolute and derives from the fact that the United States is a sovereign nation. That power was recognized by the Supreme Court in 1889 when the Court upheld an act of Congress barring entry of Chinese aliens into the country. The Court wrote in *Chae Chan Ping v. United States* (1889):

> That the government of the United States through the action of the legislative department, can exclude aliens from its territory is a proposition which we do not think open to controversy. Jurisdiction over its own territory to that extent is an incident of every independent nation. It is a part of its independence. If it could not exclude aliens, it would be to that extent subject to the control of another power. . . . The United States, in their relation to foreign countries and their subjects or citizens, are one nation, invested with powers which belong to independent nations, the exercise of which can be invoked for the maintenance of its absolute independence and security throughout its entire territory,

Under this authority, Congress has barred from entry convicts, prostitutes, epileptics, **anarchists,** and professional beggars. It has excluded people because of their race, and it has established national origin quotas. This absolute authority also empowers Congress to regulate to a large extent the conduct of aliens in the country and to provide that aliens convicted of certain crimes may be deported.

The Supreme Court has held that aliens involved in deportation proceedings are entitled to certain constitutional rights, including protections against self-incrimination, unreasonable searches and seizures, cruel and unusual punishment, **ex post facto** laws and **bills of attainder,** and the rights to bail and procedural due process.

However, the Court upheld a provision of the 1950 Internal Security Act that authorized the attorney general to keep in jail without bail aliens who were members of the Communist Party pending a decision on whether they would be deported (*Carlson v. Landon,* 1952).

In addition, although the Court has ruled that the Fourteenth Amendment protects aliens as well as citizens from discrimination, the Court has upheld federal laws that treat aliens and citizens differently. Because the Constitution gives Congress absolute authority over admission and naturalization, the Court has required Congress only to present some rational basis for making a distinction between citizen and alien or between some aliens and other aliens (*Mathews v. Diaz,* 1976).

Civil Rights Act (1964)

Legislation that outlawed segregation in U.S. schools and public facilities and forbade racial or sex discrimination in hiring. President John F. Kennedy (1961–1963) introduced the bill in 1963, asking Congress to give "all Americans the right to be served in facilities which are open to the public–hotels, restaurants, theaters, retail stores, and similar establishments," as well as "greater protection for the right to vote."

The **bill** was unpopular with many members of Congress, especially representatives of Southern states, where so-called "Jim Crow laws" legalized racial segregation. Howard Smith, a representative from Virginia, declared that he would use his position as chair of the House Rules Committee to hold up the bill and refuse to allow the House to vote on it. After President Kennedy was assassinated in November 1963, his successor, Lyndon Johnson (1963–1969), publicly announced his support for the bill. This helped turn public opinion against Smith and other Congress members who wanted to deny a vote on the bill. On February 10, 1964, the House passed the bill, followed shortly after by the Senate, but only after a cloture motion to end a filibuster. President Johnson signed the bill into law on July 2, 1964.

The act addresses inequalities in voting, segregation of public facilities, discrimination by government agencies, and discrimination in employment. It requires states and localities to establish the same registration requirements for all voters. It forbids discrimination in public accommodations, but makes exceptions for "private" clubs. The act also prohibits state and municipal governments from denying access to public facilities based on race, religion, or ethnicity. In addition, it prohibits discrimination by government agencies that receive federal funding. It calls for the desegregation of public schools and authorizes the U.S. Attorney General to file lawsuits to enforce the act, if necessary.

Title VII of the act prohibits discrimination by employers on the basis of race, color, religion, sex, or national origin. It also prohibits discrimination against an individual who associates with someone of a particular race, color, religion, sex, or national origin. The laws does

African Americans at a "whites only" lunch counter in Nashville, Tennessee, protest discrimination by staging a sit-in in 1960. The Civil Rights Act of 1964 put an end to such discrimination. (The Granger Collection, New York)

make some exceptions to these rules. Employers may discriminate on the basis of religion, sex, or national origin if they can show that one or more of those characteristics is a qualification for a particular job. Employers may never, however, legally discriminate on the basis of race. Native American tribes. religious groups doing work connected to the group's activities, and private nonprofit organizations are also exempt from the act's hiring requirements. Title VII of the act also established the Equal Employment Opportunity Commission to enforce laws prohibiting discrimination in workplace hiring and promotions.

The Supreme Court has ruled that the act also prohibits sexual harassment by employers. In the 1986 case of *Meritor Savings Bank v. Vinson,* the Court declared sexual harassment a form of discrimination prohibited by Title VII. Since that time, Congress has added amendments to the act that prohibit discrimination based on age, pregnancy, and disability.

See also: Voting Rights Act (1965).

Further Reading

Hasday, Judy L. *The Civil Rights Act of 1964: An End to Racial Segregation.* London: Chelsea House, 2007.

Civil Rights Issues and Lobbyists

A number of groups **lobby,** or try to persuade, Congress to support legislation protecting the civil rights of their members. Civil rights lobbyists represent a range of interests–those of African Americans, Hispanics, women, and free speech advocates, among many others.

African Americans

One of the first organizations formed specifically to fight for civil rights is the National Association for the Advancement of Colored People (NAACP). Founded in 1909, the NAACP was created, in part, to resolve disputes among black intellectuals. The most important of these issues at first was the question of whether or not African Americans should use violent tactics to secure black civil rights. Over time, the NAACP transformed from a small group of intellectuals into a national policy-making body with thousands of members. The NAACP's strategy for combating racism relied on two principal tactics: the use of marches and nonviolent protests to appeal to the conscience of white America, and prosecution of civil rights cases in the courts. By the height of the Civil Rights Movement in the 1950s and 1960s, the NAACP enjoyed a great deal of prestige and influence in Washington. The organization was key to the Supreme Court's decision to hear the landmark case of *Brown v. Board of Education* (1954).

As the oldest and best-known civil rights organization, the NAACP was long seen as the leader in the fight for equality. By the mid-1990s, however, it was burdened with debt and had been badly crippled by a fight over leadership of the group. Despite these problems, by 1999, the NAACP had reemerged as a major force under new leaders, including Kweisi Mfume, a former House member. It confronted businesses over minority hiring, led a legal attack against gun dealers, and loudly criticized the major television networks for the lack of black characters in primetime programs. Observers felt that this represented a return of the NAACP to the major role it had held for decades in promoting the interests and rights of African Americans.

Other highly visible civil rights groups included the Congress of Racial Equality (CORE) and the Student Nonviolent Coordinating Committee (SNCC). Another influential organization, the National Urban League, was founded just one year after the NAACP. It was originally known as a social welfare organization that appealed primarily to middle-class blacks. The league eventually became an important voice for impoverished citizens of America's large cities. Although militant "black power" groups including the Black Panthers and the Black Muslims gained significant media attention, for the most part these groups rejected traditional means of achieving power in Washington.

Other Groups

Hispanic Americans adopted the organizing and lobbying tactics of groups such as the NAACP through a number of similar organizations. These include the League of United Latin American Citizens (LULAC), the National Council of La Raza, and the Mexican American Legal Defense and Educational Fund. LULAC was founded in 1929, while the others arose during the Civil Rights Movement in the 1960s. Founded in 1968, the Mexican American Legal Defense and Education Fund) (MALDEF) was modeled on the NAACP. Women's rights groups also gained significant influence on Capitol Hill in the 1970s and 1980s. Groups such as the National Organization for Women, formed in 1966, continue to be important voices on abortion and employment issues.

In dealing with Congress, civil rights groups present a united front through the Leadership Conference on Civil Rights. Formed in 1950, the conference includes representatives from labor groups, women's rights organizations, organizations for disabled people, senior citizens' organizations, and faith-based groups. Its representatives often have the ability to influence the wording of major legislation and influence government actions. In 1987, for example, the conference led the fight that defeated the nomination of Robert H. Bork to the Supreme Court.

See also: Civil Rights Act (1964); Lobbying and Congress; Voting Rights Act (1965).

Further Reading

Chong, Dennis. *Collective Action and the Civil Rights Movement.* Chicago: University of Chicago Press, 1991.

Levy, Peter B. *The Civil Rights Movement.* Westport, CT: Greenwood, 1998.

Powledge, Fred. *Free at Last? The Civil Rights Movement and the People Who Made It.* Boston: Little, Brown, 1991.

Classes of Senators

Term referring to the fact that one-third of the members of the Senate are up for election every two years. Senators elected in the same year form part of the same class. This practice stands in contrast to the House of Representatives, whose entire membership must stand for election every two years.

Article I, Section 3, of the Constitution assigns the initial members of a state's Senate delegation to one of three classes: Class I, Class II, or Class III. Senators in Class I serve either a two-year term or a six-year term. Those in Class II serve either a four-year term or a six-year term. Those in Class III serve either a two-year term or a four-year term. When the terms of these first senators expire, the individuals who replace them serve a full six-year term. The Framers came up with this plan in order to avoid complete turnover in the Senate every six years. By establishing three separate classes, the Framers ensured that only a third of Senate seats changed hands during each election.

When a new state is admitted to the union, its initial senators are assigned to two of the three classes. The assignments are made so as to ensure that the classes are as equal in size as possible. There are currently 33 senators each is Classes I and II, and 34 senators in Class III. Thus, the senators representing the next new state added to the Union would be assigned to Classes I and II.

Class I currently consists of the 33 senators who are up for re-election in November 2012, and whose terms end in January 2013. Class II consists of the 33 senators who are up for re-election in November 2008, and whose terms end in January 2009. Class III consists of the 34 senators who are up for re-election in November 2010, and whose terms end in January 2011.

See also: Elections, Senatorial; Midterm Elections.

Clay, Henry

See Elections, House of Representatives.

Clinton, Hillary Rodham

See Women in Congress.

Clinton, William Jefferson

See Impeachment Power.

Cloakroom

Chambers located in the Capitol which members of Congress use for a variety of purposes. Cloakrooms serve as a refuge where members can escape for privacy, a convenient place to wait between votes, and a place to conduct personal or political business with other members. They even offer a place where members can simply rest or sleep. The cloakrooms lead directly into the House and Senate chambers, and they typically are the first place that congressional staffers go to search for missing members.

The Senate and House cloakrooms originally were just places to store members' coats and personal belongings. After senators and representatives were assigned private offices in the early 1900s, the cloakrooms became private

SPOTLIGHT

Smoking in Congress

In Washington, DC, smoking was banned in restaurants, dining rooms, and other indoor public places in January 2006. Congress exempted itself from the ban. In January 2007, however, after becoming the first woman Speaker of the House, Nancy Pelosi (D-CA) banned all smoking from the Speaker's **lobby,** a well-known smokers' haven. The Speaker's lobby is a comfortable space dotted with fireplaces, leather armchairs, and chandeliers. Lawmakers often relax there between votes and debates, meeting with staff members, reporters, or the public. The Speaker's lobby also provides representatives with an informal place to meet. During 2006, visitors could find Representative John A. Boehner (R-OH) smoking cigarettes between votes or Representative Barney Frank (D-MA) enjoying a cigar.

No more. According to Pelosi, she banned smoking to protect the health of staff, reporters, and the public who visit the lobby. "Medical science has unquestionably established the dangerous effects of secondhand smoke, including an increased risk of cancer and respiratory diseases. I am a firm believer that Congress should lead by example," said Pelosi. "The days of smoke-filled rooms in the United States Capitol are over."

In the Senate wing of the Capitol, smoking was banned in the Senate chamber in 1914. Not until 1995, however, was smoking banned throughout the Senate wing.

There are still a few places left for smokers—two designated smoking rooms on the House floor and a small room in the Capitol basement. These spaces, however, may soon be history. The American Lung Association is working to make the entire Capitol complex a smoke-free area.

lounges for the members. Over time, they gained a reputation as places where members conducted private negotiations over legislation before Congress. As a result, the cloakrooms became associated with secrecy and backroom political bargaining.

Although the cloakrooms are reserved for members' use, staff assigned to the House and Senate leaders may enter at any time, as may House and Senate **pages.** Other staffers may enter only when summoned by a member. Each cloakroom has its own staff that answers phones, delivers messages to members on the floor, and answers questions about the daily schedule of the chamber. Journalists often call the cloakrooms to get the latest information about the schedules of the House and Senate. Each cloakroom also has its own phone booths for members' use. The booths are numbered, and cloakroom staff tell members which booths they may use.

The cloakrooms contain a few other facilities for members. Both House cloakrooms, for example, have snack bars where members can purchase a quick bite to eat. The Senate cloakrooms lack snack bars, but leftover food from receptions is often sent to the cloakrooms for the senators there. The rooms are modestly furnished with lounge chairs, sofas, and televisions mounted on the walls. The cloakrooms once had many ashtrays because members of Congress who smoked congregated there. This contributed to their reputation as the proverbial "smoke-filled rooms" in which politicians struck deals with one another.

See also: Congressional Staff.

Cloture

Procedure by which the Senate can vote to place a time limit on consideration of a **bill** or other matter, and thereby overcome a filibuster. This procedure is outlined under the cloture rule, which is Rule XXII of the Senate's Standing Rules. According to the cloture rule, the Senate may limit consideration of a pending matter to 30 additional hours, but only by a vote of three-fifths of the full Senate, which is normally 60 votes. Cloture is the Senate's ultimate check on the filibuster.

The original Rule XXII was adopted in 1917. Its adoption followed a furor over the "talking to death" of a proposal by President Woodrow Wilson (1913–1921) for arming American merchant ships before the United States entered World War I (1917–1918). The rule required the votes of two-thirds of all of the senators present and voting to invoke cloture. In 1949, during a skirmish preceding the consideration of a Fair Employment Practices Commission bill, the voting requirement was raised to two-thirds of the entire Senate membership.

Another revision of the rule in 1959 provided for limitation of debate by a vote of two-thirds of the senators present and voting, two days after a cloture petition was submitted by sixteen senators. If the Senate adopted cloture, further debate was limited to one hour for each senator on the bill itself and on all **amendments** affecting it. No new amendments could be offered except by unanimous consent. Amendments that were not relevant to the pending business could not be submitted for debate. The rule applied both to regular legislation and to motions to change the Standing Rules of the Senate.

Rule XXII was revised significantly in 1975 by lowering the vote needed for cloture to three-fifths of the Senate membership. That revision applied to any matter except proposed rules changes. For changes in Senate rule, the required vote for cloture remained a two-thirds majority of the senators present.

The 1975 revision made it easier for a Senate majority to vote for cloture and thus cut off an extended debate mounted by a minority. Much of the revision's success relied on the willingness of senators to abide by the spirit as well as the letter of the Senate's rules. When cloture was invoked on a particular measure, senators generally admitted defeat and proceeded to a vote without further delay. However, some senators began violating this unwritten rule of conduct, using a variety of loopholes in the rule. They often succeeded in greatly extending debate even after a vote of cloture.

A–Z

The Senate closed such loopholes in 1979 when it agreed to an absolute limit on delaying tactics used after a vote of cloture. The rule provided that once the required number of senators voted for cloture, a final vote had to be taken after no more than one hundred hours of debate. All other tactics used to try to extend debate had to be included in that time limit. In 1986, the Senate reduced the time allowed for additional debate after a vote of cloture from one hundred to thirty hours.

Commerce Clause

Statement in the U.S. Constitution that gives Congress the power to regulate **commerce.** Article I, Section 8, Clause 3, of the U.S. Constitution states that "The Congress shall have Power . . . To regulate Commerce with foreign Nations, and among the several States, and with the Indian Tribes." With this grant of authority, the Founders attempted to fix one of the basic weaknesses of the federal government under the Articles of Confederation. Under the Articles of Confederation, each state had the right to regulate its own trade. That power prevented the national government from settling trade disputes between states or with other nations.

To fix that situation, the drafters of the Constitution wrote a broad and general commerce clause that did not list the powers reserved to the states or define terms. Only a few limitations could be applied from other parts of the Constitution, and only one of those limitations–a provision forbidding Congress to place a tax or duty on articles exported from any state–has had much practical significance.

Because the commerce clause is so broad and general, the courts have played an important role in determining the full scope of the clause over the years. The evolution of the commerce clause has not been an easy one. Chief Justice John Marshall gave the commerce power broad interpretation in the landmark case *Gibbons v. Ogden* in 1824. In that decision, the Court strongly asserted the supremacy of federal control over commerce with foreign countries and between the states. That Supreme Court decision gave Congress virtually unrestricted authority to regulate all commerce crossing state lines (interstate commerce) and any commerce within a state (intrastate commerce) that in any way affects interstate commerce.

For several decades after *Gibbons v. Ogden,* most cases before the Supreme Court involved the question of state power to regulate commerce in the absence of federal controls. Only in the last decades of the nineteenth century did Congress begin actively to regulate interstate commerce with the passage of such laws as the Interstate Commerce Act of 1887 and the Sherman Antitrust Act of 1890.

Court rulings in the 1900s repeatedly reaffirmed Congress's control over commerce. In addition to its use for more detailed supervision of the commercial life of the nation by Congress and the executive branch, the power was extended further to accomplish such goals as establishing a minimum wage, controlling child labor, prohibiting racial discrimination in public accommodations, and regulating environmental pollutants. For decades, Congress seemed to have unlimited commerce power. However, that era seemed to be coming to a close in the 1990s. In a 1996 decision striking down a federal law that prohibited people from carrying guns near local schools, the Court held that lawmakers had overstepped their authority to intervene in local affairs. This was one of the few times that the Court had found unconstitutional a congressional exercise of the commerce power.

Committees

Groups of members in Congress that perform specific duties, as opposed to the general business of the chamber. Committees are where most of the work of Congress is done. They hold hearings, conduct investigations, and oversee government programs. They initiate **bills,** approve legislation, and control most of the time for debate on the floor. They can kill a bill by refusing to allow the chamber to vote on it or by simply taking no action on it. In addition, committee membership enables members to develop specialized knowledge of the matters under their **jurisdiction,** or area of authority.

Types of Committees

There are four principal classes of committees in Congress:

- Standing committees, the most important and numerous, have permanent staff and deal with broad areas of responsibility.
- Select or special committees have a limited jurisdiction and may be restricted to an investigative rather than a legislative role. These committees operate for a specific period of time or until the project for which they are created has been completed.
- Joint committees have members drawn from both houses of Congress and usually perform investigations or housekeeping duties.
- Ad hoc committees, which appear mainly in the House, deal with complex legislation that falls within the normal jurisdiction of several committees.

Standing Committees

The standing committees are at the center of the legislative process. Legislation usually must be considered and approved in some form at the committee level before it can be sent to the House or Senate for further action. These committees also oversee agencies, programs, and activities within their jurisdictions, as well as some matters that cut across committee jurisdictions. Most standing committees decide upon funding for government programs, but several have other duties.

Standing committees typically have a number of subcommittees that further divide responsibilities of committee members. In the House, subcommittees usually review and make initial changes to a bill before sending it to the full committee. In the Senate, subcommittees may hold hearings but the full committee generally does the writing of legislation. Subcommittees vary in importance from committee to committee. Some, especially the Appropriations subcommittees, have well-defined jurisdictions and a good deal of independence. The full committee often accepts their work without significant changes. In recent years, however, full committee members have been more willing to intervene in the work of subcommittees.

Select and Special Committees

Select and special committees are established from time to time in both chambers to study special problems or concerns, such as population, crime, hunger, or drug abuse. On other occasions, they deal with a specific event or investigation. Special panels are created by **resolutions,** or formal declarations, of the House or Senate, which fix their term of operation. In most cases, these committees remain in existence for only a short time. Some of these committees, however, such as the Special Aging Committee in the Senate, have gone on continuously and are, for all intents and purposes, permanent. Ordinarily, select committees are not permitted to send

The House Rules Committee has considerable power in controlling the flow of legislation from committees to the House floor. Thus, hearings by the Rules Committee are very important to the successful passage of a bill. (Scott J. Ferrell, CQ)

Date Committees Were Established

Only committees in existence at the outset of the 110th Congress (2007–2009) are listed. Where major committees have been consolidated, the date cited is when the component committee was established first. Names in parentheses are those of current committees when they differ from the committees' original names.

HOUSE

1789—Rules (originally as select committee; became permanent in 1880)
1789—Enrolled Bills (House Administration)
1795—Commerce and Manufactures (Energy and Commerce)
1802—Ways and Means
1805—Public Lands (Natural Resources)
1808—Post Office and Post Roads (Oversight and Government Reform)
1808—District of Columbia (Oversight and Government Reform)
1813—Judiciary
1813—Pensions and Revolutionary Claims (Veterans' Affairs)
1816—Expenditures in Executive Departments (Oversight and Government Reform)
1820—Agriculture
1822—Foreign Affairs
1822—Military Affairs (Armed Services)
1822—Naval Affairs (Armed Services)
1837—Public Buildings and Grounds (Transportation and Infrastructure)
1865—Appropriations
1865—Banking and Currency (Financial Services)
1867—Education and Labor
1941—Select Small Business (Small Business)
1958—Science and Astronautics (Science and Technology)
1967—Standards of Official Conduct
1974—Budget
1977—Select Intelligence
2005—Homeland Security

SENATE

1789—Enrolled Bills (Rules and Administration)
1816—Commerce and Manufactures (Commerce, Science, and Transportation)
1816—District of Columbia (Homeland Security and Governmental Affairs)
1816—Finance
1816—Foreign Relations
1816—Judiciary
1816—Military Affairs (Armed Services)
1816—Naval Affairs (Armed Services)
1816—Post Office and Post Roads (Homeland Security and Governmental Affairs)
1816—Public Lands (Energy and Natural Resources)
1825—Agriculture (Agriculture, Nutrition, and Forestry)
1837—Public Buildings and Grounds (Environment and Public Works)
1842—Expenditures in Executive Departments (Homeland Security and Governmental Affairs)
1867—Appropriations
1869—Education and Labor (Health, Education, Labor, and Pensions)
1913—Banking and Currency (Banking, Housing, and Urban Affairs)
1950—Select Small Business (Small Business and Entrepreneurship)
1958—Aeronautical and Space Sciences (Commerce, Science, and Transportation)
1970—Veterans' Affairs
1975—Budget
1976—Select Intelligence
1977—Indian Affairs

NOTE: Both the House and Senate Select Intelligence committees are permanent committees, but for reasons relating to congressional rules on committee organization they are called select committees.

SOURCES: *Constitution, Jefferson's Manual and Rules of the House of Representatives* (110th Congress); *House Practice;* and George Goodwin Jr., *The Little Legislatures: Committees of Congress* (Amherst: University of Massachusetts Press, 1970).

Committees have been used to guide legislation through Congress since the nation's founding. Although committees may lack the clout they held in the past, they are still essential to the legislation process.

legislation to the full chamber, although there are exceptions, such as the Intelligence committees in both chambers. This is a special case, however, since the Intelligence committees are effectively permanent.

Joint Committees

Joint committees are permanent panels created by a law or resolution that also fixes their size. Chairmanships of joint committees generally rotate from one chamber to another at the beginning of each Congress. When a senator serves as chairman, the vice chairman usually is a member of the House, and vice versa. The last joint committee to have legislative responsibilities was the Joint Committee on Atomic Energy, which was abolished in 1977. Conference committees, a special variety of joint committee, are created on a temporary basis to resolve differences in Senate and House versions of the same legislation.

Loss of Committee Positions

Stripping members of their positions on committees as a punishment for political heresy, the going against of one's party's ideals, has been resorted to occasionally on Capitol Hill. In 1859, for example, the Senate Democratic Caucus removed Stephen A. Douglas, a Democrat from Illinois, from the chairmanship of the Committee on Territories because he refused to go along with President James Buchanan (1857–1861) and the southern wing of the party on the question of slavery in the territories. In 1866, three Senate Republican committee chairs were dropped to the bottom of their committees for failing to vote with the **Radical Republicans** on overriding a presidential veto of a civil rights bill.

Members of the Progressive wing of the Republican Party in the House also were denied the fruits of seniority in this period after they put up their own candidate for Speaker in 1925. Two of their leaders were ousted from their committee chairs for having campaigned as La Follette Progressives, and nine GOP members from the Wisconsin delegation who voted with the insurgents' candidate for Speaker were either dropped to the bottom rank on their committees or moved to less prestigious committees. La Follette had been the Progressive Party's candidate for president in 1924.

In 1983, House Democrats stripped **conservative** Representative Phil Gramm of Texas of his seat on the Budget Committee because of his two-year collaboration with the White House in supporting President Ronald Reagan's budget. Gramm's behavior was especially aggravating to the

Ad Hoc Committees

The Speaker of the House has the authority to create ad hoc committees, if approved by a vote of the House. Ad hoc committees consider legislation that might be within the jurisdiction of several committees. Members of ad hoc committees come from committees that would otherwise have dealt with these matters. The authority to create such committees has been used twice, most notably to handle consideration of major energy legislation proposed by the administration of President Jimmy Carter (1977–1981).

In 1995, the new Republican majority gave the Speaker the power to propose the creation of ad hoc oversight committees to review specific matters within the jurisdiction of two or more standing committees. Aggressive use of oversight to investigate the Clinton administration became one of the new majority's priorities. However, it was conducted through the standing committees.

Committee Assignments

The rules of the House and Senate state that the membership of each house shall elect its members to standing committees. In the House all rules, committees, and assignments from the previous Congress effectively expire on January 3 of each odd-numbered year. Committees cannot function until they are re-created on the opening day of the new Congress and their members are reappointed. Sometimes the committees try to get around this by inviting witnesses for "forums" that allow the returning committee members to gather and discuss issues or informally question witnesses as "guests." Senate committees retain their members from the previous Congress while they await appointment of

SPOTLIGHT

Democratic leadership because he had been placed on the committee with the strong support of Majority Leader Jim Wright, a Democrat from Texas, after Gramm had given assurances that he would be a team player.

In 1995, some conservative Senate Republicans advocated stripping Senator Mark O. Hatfield, a Republican from Oregon, of his chairmanship of the Appropriations Committee because he had cast the lone Republican—and deciding—vote which defeated a balanced budget amendment to the Constitution. The amendment was a major element in the new Republican majority's legislative agenda and had earlier passed the House for the first time. After debate in the Republican Conference, no action was taken against Hatfield. He retained the chairmanship, but announced shortly thereafter that he would not seek reelection.

On January 3, 2001, James A. Traficant, Jr., a Democrat from Ohio, voted with House Republicans to reelect Speaker J. Dennis Hastert, a Republican from Illinois. In response, the Democratic Caucus stripped Traficant of his committee assignments from the previous Congress and then ejected him from the caucus itself. In January 2005, the Republican Steering Committee refused to renominate Christopher H. Smith of New Jersey as Chair of the Veterans' Affairs Committee. Smith had repeatedly opposed his party's position on the funding of veterans' programs. In that same month, Republican leaders removed Joel Hefley of Colorado from the chairmanship of the House Ethics Committee because the committee had admonished Majority Leader Tom DeLay, a Republican from Texas.

new members. The committees retain full power to act during this time.

The Assignment Process

The committee assignment procedure takes place at the beginning of every Congress and throughout the next two years as vacancies occur. **Incumbents** are nearly always permitted to retain their existing committee assignments unless their party lost a large number of seats in the preceding election, or control of the chamber shifted from one party to the other. Representatives of the two parties negotiate on committee assignments in advance and then submit the committee rosters for approval by their party caucuses and finally the full chambers. Each party maintains a committee on committees that makes key appointment decisions. There are always some adjustments in each new Congress in both chambers to take into account recent election results, member preferences, and the shifting demands placed on committee workloads.

In the House, nothing in the rules guarantees members any committee assignments. In practice, however, each member who wants to serve on a committee has at least one assignment. Because committee assignments originate from political parties, members who switch parties automatically lose their seats under House rules. The Republicans have made a point of allowing new party members to retain their old posts or have given them even more desirable assignments to help them win reelection.

Until 1995, the number and types of committees and subcommittees on which any member might serve were left almost entirely to the Republican Conference and the Democratic

Caucus. In that year, the Republican majority changed the rules to limit each member to a maximum of two committee and four subcommittee assignments. However, almost immediately exceptions started to be made. The party realized that having rules and formulas for organizing committees was less important than retaining party control of committees and satisfying individual members' political needs.

Both parties in each chamber generally follow **seniority** in positioning members on committees and in filling vacancies. Longer-serving members have first shot at the best committee assignments and committee leadership positions; new members are ranked at the bottom of their committees. Starting in 1974, however, the House Democratic Caucus began the practice of occasionally bypassing seniority if a chairman did not show enough support for party policies.

Committee Chairs

Each committee is headed by a chairperson, who is a member of the majority party of a chamber. A chair's power once resulted from the rigid operation of the seniority system. By the end of the 1990s, most chairs were still usually the most senior member of the committee in terms of consecutive service. However, in 1995, the House adopted a new rule limiting committee and subcommittee chairs to a maximum of three terms. That same year, Senate Republicans adopted a party rule to limit committee chairs to three terms.

Even with these changes, committee chairs remain powerful figures on Capitol Hill, especially in the Senate. At the full committee level, the chair calls meetings and establishes agendas, schedules hearings, coordinates work by subcommittees, oversees sessions to **amend** bills, files committee reports, acts as floor manager, controls the committee budget, supervises the hiring and firing of staff, and serves as spokesperson for the committee and the chair's party in the committee's area of expertise. Committees can also establish rules that permit committee chairs to call witnesses to testify in a congressional investigation.

Committees in Transition

Committees today lack the clout they once held. At one time, committees dominated the presentation of legislation to Congress and set the agenda, from floor action through presidential action. However, changes in membership, shifts in power in relation to the leadership, the evolution of new rules and procedures, demands of **partisan** political agendas, extensive media coverage, and the availability of new sources of information and technology have all served to alter the **balance of power** within Congress.

During the 1970s, a new generation of younger, activist Democrats enacted reforms that weakened committee chairs, dispersed power to subcommittees, strengthened the leadership, and fostered the growth of staff in both chambers. Many lawmakers no longer simply allowed committees to determine the details of legislation. Challenges to committees became more common once members had gained the expertise and staff needed to make independent judgments.

Unchallenged in previous Congresses, committee leaders became accountable for their actions and could be removed by a vote of their parties. This happened to Democratic committee chairs six times in the House between 1975 and 1990, though never in the Senate. Indeed, House reformers struggled repeatedly to find better ways to control, restrict, discipline, or challenge chairs, and to remind them that they were always under scrutiny.

Today, committees are much less the independent power centers than they were thirty years earlier. Committees now serve many political masters who are no longer reluctant to try to influence the committees' work. Party leaders are also more willing to go around committees to attain important political goals. Some observers wonder if Congress–and the House in particular–has entered a period marked by a more informal style of legislating that relies less on the work of committees.

See also: Ad Hoc Committees; Caucuses; Conference Committees; Congressional

Investigations; Joint Committees; Seniority System.

Further Reading

Deering, Christopher J., and Steven S. Smith. *Committees in Congress.* Third edition. Washington, DC: CQ Press, 1997.
Duvall, Jill. *Congressional Committees.* London: Franklin Watts, 1997.
Sandak, Cass R. *Congressional Committees.* Minneapolis, MN: Lerner, 1997.

Committee System

See Committees.

Conference Committees

An ad hoc joint committee appointed by members of Congress to work out differences between Senate and House versions of legislation that is being considered. This method of resolving differences, used by Congress since 1789, had developed into the modern conference committee by the mid-1800s.

Before a **bill** can be sent to the president, it must be passed in identical form by both chambers of Congress. Often, different versions of the same bill are passed, and neither the House nor Senate is willing to accept the version passed by the other chamber or to make changes by sending the bill back-and-forth. In this situation, a conference committee becomes necessary to determine the final form of the legislation. It is unusual for the Senate or House to reject the work of a conference committee.

In the past, conference committees were composed of senior members of the committees that handled the bill. This is still largely true, but there are also opportunities for junior members and non-committee members to be appointed to a conference committee. Members of the committee are appointed by the Speaker of the House and the presiding officer of the Senate. Appointment is usually based on the recommendations of the committee chairs and ranking minority members.

It is not necessary to have an equal number of conferees from each chamber of Congress. Each chamber has a single vote on the committee, which is determined by a majority vote of its conferees. Therefore, a majority of committee members from both the Senate and the House must agree before a provision emerges from conference as part of the final bill. Both political parties are represented on conference committees, with the majority party in the House and Senate having a larger number. Members of either house can preside over the committee, though the role is largely honorary. For certain legislation considered on an annual basis, such as appropriations bills and the congressional budget resolution, the chair alternates between the chambers.

Most conference committees met in secret until late 1975 when both chambers amended their rules to require open meetings unless a majority of either chamber's conferees vote in open session to close the meeting for that day. Despite this rule, committees have found various ways to avoid negotiating in public, including the use of informal sessions, separate meetings of each delegation with congressional aides serving as go-betweens, and meeting rooms too small to accommodate all who wish to attend.

After conferees reach agreement, they sign and submit to each chamber a conference report along with a detailed explanation of their actions. When conferees are unable to agree, the bill may die in conference if they take no further action. Sometimes conferees file a report incorporating only matters on which they have agreed, leaving out other matters on which they disagree to await further negotiation or additional votes on the floor of each house. On rare occasions conferees formally report "in disagreement" and await further amendments by both houses.

Once the conference committee report is approved by the first chamber to consider it, the conference committee automatically is dissolved and the report goes to the remaining chamber for a vote. If either chamber rejects the conference report, the legislation remains in the form it existed in before it went to conference, to await additional amendments or a new conference. The first chamber to consider the report may also send the bill back to conference, usually with instructions, to make further changes. This action has the effect of rejecting the initial conference report, but does not require the appointment of a new conference. The conferees may simply resume meeting and try to reach an agreement that is suitable to both chambers.

Confirmation Power of the Senate

Authority that the Senate shares with the president to fill various high-level government positions. According to Article II, Section 2, of the U.S. Constitution, the president "shall nominate, and by and with the Advice and Consent of the Senate, shall appoint" various government officials. The constitutional language governing the appointment power, drafted and agreed to in the final weeks of the Constitutional Convention of 1787, represented a compromise between delegates who favored giving the Senate the sole authority for appointing principal officers of the government and delegates who believed that the president alone should control appointments.

It is this power of "advice and consent" that allows the Senate to participate in the selection of Supreme Court justices, cabinet and subcabinet officials, members of independent boards and commissions, ambassadors, and other top government officials. The Senate also uses its confirmation power as a tool to help shape public policy. Although under the Constitution, only the president has the formal right to nominate individuals to top-level positions in government, the Senate may use its confirmation power to turn down presidential nominees or pressure the president into selecting people more acceptable to a majority of the senators. In some cases, such as certain federal judgeships, senators traditionally have exerted great pressure on the president regarding the selection of nominees.

The Senate approves most presidential nominations with little debate or objection. The effect of the Senate's confirmation power is seen most clearly in the small number of cases in which a presidential nominee encounters substantial opposition. Often such nominations are rejected or kept in committee and never reach a Senate floor vote. A single senator may also delay action on a nomination by placing a "hold" on it. In many instances presidents, or the nominees themselves, will withdraw an appointment when it becomes clear that a large

The Senate confirmed John G. Roberts, President George W. Bush's nominee for Chief Justice of the United States, in September 2005. The Senate's confirmation power is an important check on the power of the executive branch. (Scott J. Ferrell, CQ)

Supreme Court Nominations Not Confirmed by the Senate

Nominee	President	Date of nomination	Senate action
William Paterson	Washington	February 27, 1793	Withdrawn
John Rutledge	Washington	December 10, 1795	Rejected
Alexander Wolcott	Madison	February 4, 1811	Rejected
John J. Crittenden	John Quincy Adams	December 17, 1828	Postponed
Roger Brooke Taney	Jackson	January 15, 1835	Postponed
John C. Spencer	Tyler	January 9, 1844	Rejected
Reuben H. Walworth	Tyler	March 13, 1844	Withdrawn
Edward King	Tyler	June 5, 1844	Postponed
Edward King	Tyler	December 4, 1844	Withdrawn
John M. Read	Tyler	February 7, 1845	Not acted upon
George W. Woodward	Polk	December 23, 1845	Rejected
Edward A. Bradford	Fillmore	August 16, 1852	Not acted upon
George E. Badger	Fillmore	January 10, 1853	Postponed
William C. Micou	Fillmore	February 24, 1853	Not acted upon
Jeremiah S. Black	Buchanan	February 5, 1861	Rejected
Henry Stanbery	Andrew Johnson	April 16, 1866	Not acted upon
Ebenezer R. Hoar	Grant	December 15, 1869	Rejected
George H. Williams	Grant	December 1, 1873	Withdrawn
Caleb Cushing	Grant	January 9, 1874	Withdrawn
Stanley Matthews	Hayes	January 26, 1881	Not acted upon
William B. Hornblower	Cleveland	September 19, 1893	Rejected
Wheeler H. Peckham	Cleveland	January 22, 1894	Rejected
John J. Parker	Hoover	March 21, 1930	Rejected
Abe Fortas	Lyndon Johnson	June 26, 1968	Withdrawn
Homer Thornberry	Lyndon Johnson	June 26, 1968	Not acted upon
Clement F. Haynsworth Jr.	Nixon	August 18, 1969	Rejected
G. Harrold Carswell	Nixon	January 19, 1970	Rejected
Robert H. Bork	Reagan	July 1, 1987	Rejected
Harriet E. Miers	George W. Bush	October 7, 2005	Withdrawn
John G. Roberts Jr.	George W. Bush	July 29, 2005	Withdrawn

Of all of the appointments confirmed by the United States Senate, perhaps nominees to the United States Supreme Court receive the most careful consideration because the justices serve for life.

A – Z

number of senators are prepared to vote against it. Less often, presidents will continue to press for approval of an appointment even though it clearly faces possible defeat on the Senate floor. Outright rejection of an important nomination represents a major political setback for a president.

The Senate's use of its confirmation power has evolved into more than simply accepting or rejecting a presidential nominee. It has become a tool that the Senate can use to increase its influence on public policy decisions. In effect, nominations become bargaining chips in a contest between the president and the Senate. Instead of simply rejecting a nomination, the Senate more commonly will use its power of rejection as a threat. It may withhold action until either the nominee or the White House agrees to pursue certain courses of action or policies. Or the Senate may use its power to negotiate a policy issue completely unrelated to the nomination. The confirmation power is thus an effective weapon in the give-and-take relationship between the executive and legislative branches of the government.

Virtually every president has faced difficult confirmation battles with the Senate. Presidents with solid political support have generally fared better than those who had to contend with a hostile Senate. Even strong chief executives sometimes have been subjected to embarrassing defeats of their nominees. Such battles can dominate newspaper headlines and broadcast news, generate great activity among interest groups, and strain relations between the political parties and the branches of government.

Such cases are the exception, however. Most of the time, the Senate's power over presidential appointments is little more than a bureaucratic chore. In 1993, for example, during the first year of Bill Clinton's presidency, the Senate received more than 42,000 nominations from the president. Only about 700 involved high-level positions that might invite greater Senate scrutiny. There was little that was controversial over most of the remaining nominations. The vast majority of these–nearly 39,500–consisted of routine military commissions and promotions or civilian nominations to the Foreign Service, Public Health Service, and other government positions.

See also: Senatorial Courtesy; Spoils System.

Congress and Commerce

From the beginning of the nation's history, the congressional power to regulate foreign **commerce** has been complete. The constitutional grant encompasses "every species of commercial intercourse between the United States and foreign nations. No sort of trade can be carried on between this country and any other, to which this power does not extend," wrote Chief Justice John Marshall in *Gibbons v. Ogden* (1824), in the classic interpretation of the commerce clause.

Commerce Power

The power to regulate commerce is inextricably tied to the powers over foreign relations and fiscal policies. Using these powers, Congress may pass legislation to set **tariffs;** regulate international shipping, aviation, and communications; and establish **embargoes** against unfriendly countries. In conjunction with its powers to coin money, regulate its value, and borrow funds for government activities, Congress may authorize U.S. participation in and **appropriate** contributions for international financing, banking, and monetary systems such as the International Development Association and the World Bank.

The commerce power may be used to promote, inhibit, or simply make rules for trade with other nations. It may be implemented by treaty or executive agreement as well as by acts of Congress.

Policies to encourage trade may take the form of opening up new markets for U.S. goods in other countries or securing favorable conditions for American traders abroad. The earliest actions in this field were efforts to replace markets lost when the nation won its independence from Great Britain. Modern laws have ranged from antitrust exemptions for exporters to the use of tariff reductions to stimulate trade.

Efforts to encourage American shipping have ranged from legislation providing preferential duties for goods imported in U.S. vessels (first enacted in 1789) to federal subsidies (since 1936) for merchant ships that sailed under the U.S. flag.

Tariffs

Historically, the predominant mechanism to restrict foreign trade has been the protective tariff. The first major business of the House of Representatives in 1789 was to devise a tariff schedule. Unlike many later tariff laws, this one had as its chief objective the raising of revenue to finance the new government.

The Franklin D. Roosevelt (1933–1944) administration's economic recovery program in 1934 included expansion of American exports, and the president proposed that Congress delegate some of its constitutional powers by authorizing him to negotiate U.S. trade greements with other nations. The administration asked authority to cut tariffs by as much as 50 percent in return for equivalent concessions from other nations. Prodded by Secretary of State Cordell Hull, the Democratic-controlled 73rd Congress, over nearly unanimous Republican opposition, made this grant of authority in the Trade Agreements Act of 1934. Since then, no serious efforts have been made to restore congressional tariff making in place of executive branch negotiation of bilateral and, after World War II, multilateral trade agreements.

Nontariff Barriers and Embargoes

Nontariff barriers to the free flow of trade range from import quotas to embargoes. Although export taxes are forbidden under the Constitution, Congress can control export trade through licensing or other means. Thus, it may bar shipment of strategic materials to hostile countries or restrict exports that would deplete essential domestic supplies. Congress has curbed imports that would interfere with domestic regulatory programs (such as agricultural commodities under production-control and price-support programs). It also has enacted "Antidumping," "Buy American," and "Ship American" legislation.

The ultimate restraint on foreign commerce is the embargo, which suspends commerce completely with specified countries. Examples include the embargo President Jimmy Carter (1977–1981) imposed on the Soviet Union in 1980 after that country invaded Afghanistan, and the one President George H.W. Bush (1989–1993) imposed on Iraq in 1990 after it invaded Kuwait. President Bill Clinton (1993-2001) in 1995 tightened sanctions against Iran that had originally been imposed by President Ronald Reagan (1981–1989) in response to Iran's involvement in the 1983 bombing of a U.S. Marine barracks in Beirut, Lebanon.

See also: *Gibbons v. Ogden,* 1824, in the **Primary Source Library.**

Congress, Constitutional Origins of

Decisions made during the drafting of the Constitution that determined the overall structure of Congress, including its size, basis of representation, elections, terms of office, and basic rules of each house. These decisions were the result of many compromises among competing visions of the proposed national legislature.

Basic Structure

The Continental Congress and the Congress under the Articles of Confederation were **unicameral,** consisting of a single house. Once the convention decided to abandon the Articles, however, there was little question that the new Congress should be **bicameral,** featuring two houses. Only Pennsylvania dissented with the call for two houses, and the delegates adopted a bicameral structure by a vote of seven to three.

Elections

The method of electing members of Congress was the subject of considerable debate among the delegates to the Constitutional Convention. Some insisted that the new government be elected directly by the people, while others felt that the state legislatures should choose members of Congress.

Election to the House

James Madison argued that "the first branch," the House, be elected "by the people immediately." The government "ought to possess . . . the mind or sense of the people at large," said James Wilson. The House "was to be the grand depository of the democratic principles of the government," said George Mason.

Those who were suspicious of a national government preferred election of the House by the state legislatures. "The people immediately should have as little to do" with electing the government as possible, said Roger Sherman, because "they want information and are constantly liable to be misled." Elbridge Gerry was convinced that "the evils we experience flow from the excess of democracy," while Charles Pinckney thought "the people were less fit judges" than the legislatures to choose members of the House. The proposal for election by state legislatures twice was defeated, however, and popular election of the House was confirmed June 21 by a vote of nine states to one.

Election to the Senate

The Virginia Plan proposed that the House elect the Senate from persons nominated by the state legislatures. This plan received little support because it would have made the Senate subservient to the House. Neither was there any support for the view of Madison and Wilson that the people should elect the Senate as well as the House. In the end, election of senators by the state legislatures was approved by a vote of nine states to two. In 1913, the states **ratified** the Seventeenth Amendment, which provided for direct popular election of senators.

Basis of Representation

The Virginia Plan also called for representation of the states in both the House and Senate in proportion to their wealth or free population. Smaller states vigorously opposed this idea, and the delegates eventually agreed to equal representation of the states in the Senate. The principle of proportional representation in the House was never seriously challenged, but debate arose about whether it should be based on a state's wealth or free population.

To retain southern support for proportional representation in the Senate, Wilson proposed that the House be **apportioned** according to a count of the whole number of free citizens and three-fifths of all others (meaning slaves), excluding Indians not paying taxes. The convention then decided that the new Congress should have the power "to regulate the number of representatives upon the principles of wealth and number of inhabitants." Because southerners regarded slaves as property, this led northerners who wanted representation in the House to be based on population alone to ask why slaves should be counted at all.

Gouverneur Morris then proposed that each state should be taxed based on its representation in Congress. This seemed to mean that the South would have to pay additional taxes for any increases in representation it gained by counting slaves. As a result, northerners dropped their opposition to the three-fifths count demanded by the southerners. Because it was

First State Constitutions

STATE	DATE ADOPTED
New Hampshire (1st)	January 6, 1776
South Carolina (1st)	March 26, 1776
Virginia	June 29, 1776
New Jersey	July 2, 1776
Delaware	August 22, 1776
Pennsylvania	September 28, 1776
Maryland	November 11, 1776
North Carolina	December 18, 1776
Georgia	February 5, 1777
New York	April 20, 1777
Vermont[1]	July 8, 1777
South Carolina (2nd)	March 19, 1778
Massachusetts	June 15, 1780
New Hampshire (2nd)	June 13, 1784

1. Vermont became a state in 1791.

The Thirteen original states and Vermont all adopted state constitutions in the 1770s and 1780s. In general, the legislature was the most powerful branch of state government.

agreed that representation was to be based solely on population, the word "wealth" was deleted from the final draft of the Constitution.

Size of Congress

The committee that recommended equal representation in the Senate also proposed that each state have one vote in the House for every forty thousand inhabitants. This proposal led to a debate on representation, during which it was decided to let Congress regulate the future size of the House so as to allow for population changes and the admission of new states. Some delegates, however, feared that under such an arrangement, a majority in Congress would be able to block a reapportionment plan or change the basis of representation for slaves. Thus, northerners and southerners now agreed that the periods between reapportionments, and the rules for revising representation in the House, ought to be fixed by the Constitution.

Edmund Randolph proposed holding a regular census, linking the **apportionment** of representatives to an "enumeration" every ten years of the "whole number of free persons . . . and three fifths of all others." It was further decided that the number of representatives "shall not exceed one for every 40,000," a figure that was lowered to 30,000 on the last day of the convention. Until the first census was taken, the size of the House was fixed at sixty-five representatives.

The size of the Senate was fixed when the Convention adopted a proposal that the body should consist of two members from each state. A proposal to allow each state three senators had been turned down on the ground that it would penalize poorer and more distant states and that "a small number was most convenient for deciding on peace and war," as Nathaniel Gorham put it.

Terms of Office

Many delegates had a strong attachment to the tradition of annual elections, but James Madison argued that representatives would need more than one year to become informed about the office and the national interests. The convention adopted his proposal of a three-year term for the House, but many delegates continued to press for more frequent elections. The convention reconsidered the question and compromised on a two-year term for representatives, with the entire House standing for election every two years.

The delegates also changed their minds about the Senate, agreeing first to a term of seven years. This decision was reviewed, and alternatives of four, six, and nine years were considered. Charles Pinckney opposed six years, arguing that senators would be "too long separated from their constituents, and will imbibe attachments different from that of the state." The convention voted for a six-year term in the Senate, with one-third of the membership to be elected every two years.

Qualifications of Members

The convention decided in June on a minimum age of twenty-five for representatives and thirty for senators. It later added two more qualifications: United States citizenship (three years for the House, four for the Senate) and residence within the state to be represented. Fearful of making it too easy for foreigners to be elected, the convention lengthened the citizenship requirement to seven years for representatives and nine years for senators, after voting down fourteen years as likely to discourage "meritorious aliens from emigrating to this country." Some delegates wanted to require residence in a state for a minimum time—from one to seven years. These proposals were voted down, and the Constitution simply required that a member of Congress should be "an inhabitant of that state in which he shall be chosen."

Most of the state constitutions required members of their legislatures to own certain amounts of property, and the delegates initially agreed to a property qualification. The provision was rejected during debate, and no further efforts were made to include a property qualification. Every state except New York and Virginia imposed a religious qualification on state representatives. However, the delegates unanimously adopted the idea that "no religious test shall ever be required as a qualification to any office

Decision Makers

Robert C. Byrd (1917–)

Robert C. Byrd is the senior United States Senator from West Virginia and, as of 2008, the longest-serving member in the history of the United States Senate. Byrd began his legislative career by winning election to the House of Representatives in 1952. He was twice reelected to the house before successfully challenging **incumbent** Republican W. Chapman Revercomb for a Senate seat in 1958. Since that time, Byrd has been reelected to the Senate eight times. A controversial figure because of his early opposition to civil rights legislation, Byrd is also known as one of the most influential members of Congress and a leading expert on the history of the Senate.

Prior to his election in 1952, Byrd was an active member of the Ku Klux Klan, a white supremacist group that was particularly active throughout the American South in the early-to-mid twentieth century. During World War II (1941–1945), he wrote several letters to acquaintances expressing his opposition to integrating the military. During his first campaign for Congress, however, Byrd claimed that he had lost interest in the Klan and dropped his membership and support for the organization.

Although he publicly renounced the Klan and its racist ideas, Byrd spearheaded Senate opposition to the 1964 Civil Rights Act. He was one of several Democratic senators from Southern states who led a filibuster against the bill. This is a type of delaying tactic that allows

or public trust under the United States." Thus, the only qualifications established by the Constitution for election to Congress were those of age, citizenship, and residence.

Rules and Regulation of Congress

Article I of the Constitution included four provisions for regulation of the House and Senate. These included a provision that "Each House shall be the Judge of the Elections, Returns and Qualifications of its own Members." This language was found in the constitutions of eight of the states and was agreed to without debate. Article I also states that, "Each House may determine the Rules of its Proceedings, punish its Members for disorderly Behaviour, and, with the Concurrence of two-thirds, expel a Member." Originally, expulsion required only a majority vote, but Madison argued that "the right of expulsion was too important to be exercised by a bare majority." His proposal was approved unanimously.

The delegates also decided that "Each House shall keep a Journal, and from time to time publish the same." When Madison proposed giving the Senate some discretion in the matter, Wilson objected that "the people have a right to know what their agents are doing or have done, and it should not be in the option of the legislature to conceal their proceedings." The convention voted to require publication of the journals of each house, "excepting such parts as may in their judgment require secrecy." The clause also provided for recording the "yea" and "nay" votes of members. Finally, the delegates prohibited either house from **adjourning,** or suspending its meetings, for more than three days, a minority of senators to prevent the entire chamber from voting on a bill. The filibuster failed after 83 days, and the Senate passed the bill by a vote of 73 to 27. Byrd voted against the 1965 Voting Rights Act as well, but later supported the Civil Rights Act of 1968. In later writing, Byrd apologized to voters for his earlier views on race and admitted he had been wrong.

Byrd has held a variety of leadership positions in the Senate, twice serving as Majority Leader. His leadership positions and **seniority** in the Senate have given him immense influence, which he has used to benefit his home state. The watchdog group Citizens Against Public Waste dubbed Byrd "King of Pork" for the massive amounts of federal spending he has secured for West Virginia, one of the nation's smallest and poorest states. Since Byrd has been in the Senate, West Virginia has been the recipient of more than $1 billion of public spending from the federal government.

Byrd is noted for his interest and expertise in the legislative process and history of the Senate. In the 1980s, he delivered a hundred speeches on the floor of the Senate dealing with the Senate's history. These were later published as *The Senate, 1789–1989: Addresses on the History of the Senate.* The book earned him the American Historical Association's Theodore Roosevelt-Woodrow Wilson Award for Civil Service in 2004. Byrd also has extended his interests to promote the teaching of history in public schools. In 2002, he sponsored legislation to award grants of $50 to $120 million a year to school districts for strengthening the teaching of "traditional American history."

or from meeting at a different location from the other house, without the consent of the other house.

See also: Bicameralism; Census; Constitution of the United States; Constitutional Convention; Elections, House of Representatives; Elections, Senatorial; House of Representatives; New Jersey Plan; Reapportionment; Senate; Seventeenth Amendment (1913); Virginia Plan.

Further Reading

Barbash, Fred. *The Founding: A Dramatic Account of the Writing of the Constitution.* New York: Linden/Simon and Schuster, 1987.

Collier, Christopher, and James Lincoln Collier. *Decision in Philadelphia: The Constitutional Convention of 1787.* New York: Ballantine, 1986.

Kelly, Alfred H., and Winifred A. Harbison. *The American Constitution: Its Origins and Development.* Seventh edition. New York: Norton, 1991.

Congressional Black Caucus

In Congress, African American legislators who have joined together to work on common interests and policies. Ethnic and minority groups have often banded together when Congress has considered issues of particular importance to them. These minorities have formed organized groups in Congress called caucuses.

The Congressional Black Caucus, which includes nearly every black legislator, is one of the most effective of all caucuses in Congress. When it was formed in 1969, the caucus had only nine members, who had little role in the congressional power structure. By 2008, forty-two House members and one senator belonged to the Congressional Black Caucus. At times, the mostly Democratic caucus has drawn support from black legislators across the aisle, although the only black Republican in the House in the late 1990s, J. S. Watts of Oklahoma, refused to join the caucus.

In the 1980s, pressure from the Congressional Black Caucus led the Democratic leadership in Congress to appoint black legislators to the most powerful House committees. A measure of the caucus's success was the election, in 1985, of William H. Gray III, a black Pennsylvania Democrat, as chairman of the Budget Committee, an important and highly visible post. Gray went on to win election as Democratic **whip** in 1989, the third-highest leadership post in the House, before retiring from Congress in 1991 to become president of the United Negro College Fund. In the 110th Congress, which began in 2007, the Caucus appointed Congresswoman Carolyn Cheeks Kilpatrick of Michigan to the powerful House Appropriations Committee, which authorizes spending for all levels of the federal government. She was also elected as Chair for the Congressional Black Caucus. Other African American committee chairs in the 110th Congress are John Conyers on the Judiciary Committee, Charles Rangel on the Ways and Means Committee, and Bennie Thompson of the Homeland Security Committee.

In 1968, Shirley Chisholm became the first African American woman elected to the United States House of Representatives. In 1972, she announced her candidacy for the Democratic presidential nomination. (Library of Congress)

Founders of the Black Caucus

Founder	State	Years in Congress
Charles Diggs, Jr.	Michigan	1955–1980
Robert Nix, Sr.	Pennsylvania	1958–1979
Augustus Hawkins	California	1963–1991
John Conyers, Jr.	Michigan	1965–present
Shirley Chisholm	New York	1968–1992
William Clay, Sr.	Missouri	1969–2000
Louis Stokes	Ohio	1969–1999
Ronald Dellums	California	1970–1998
George Collins	Illinois	1970–1972
Charles Rangel	New York	1971–present
Walter Fauntroy	Washington, DC	1971–1991
Parren Mitchell	Maryland	1971–1987
Ralph Metcalfe	Illinois	1971–1978

Representative Shirley Chisholm of New York was the only female founder of the Congressional Black Caucus. The Caucus tends to be heavily Democratic.

Legislatively, the Congressional Black Caucus has lobbied for an economic agenda that would help the poor, who are disproportionately black, and for legislation that would strengthen and enforce civil rights laws. A major victory was the passage, in 1986, of legislation imposing economic sanctions on South Africa. Members of the Congressional Black Caucus, who are among the House's most **liberal** lawmakers, denounced GOP cuts to poverty programs in the 1990s and emerged as some of President Clinton's most passionate defenders during the **impeachment** proceedings in 1998. More recently,

Decision Makers

Shirley Chisholm (1924–2005)

Shirley Chisholm, a member of the House of Representatives from New York, became the first African American woman elected to Congress in 1968. The daughter of immigrants from British Guiana and Barbados, Chisholm later became the first African American to compete for the presidential nomination of a major political party.

Born in Brooklyn, New York, Chisholm spent much of her early childhood in Barbados, where she lived with her grandmother. When she was ten years old, Chisholm returned to the United States. She eventually earned a degree in elementary education from Columbia University. In 1964, she successfully ran for a seat in the New York State Legislature. Four years later, she won her first term as a U.S. Representative on behalf of New York's Twelfth Congressional District. Her election marked the first of seven consecutive terms Chisholm would spend in the House.

During her first term, Chisholm joined with several other African American members of Congress to found the Congressional Black Caucus. Although initially appointed to the House Agricultural Committee, she raised some eyebrows by requesting to be reassigned, a bold move for a first-term member. However, Chisholm argued that since she represented an urban district in New York City, it seemed pointless to assign her to a committee dealing with agricultural policy. She won reassignment to the Veteran's Affairs Committee and later served on the Education and Labor Committee. During her time in office, Chisholm earned a reputation for her integrity and determination to accomplish her objectives despite any obstacle.

In 1972, Chisholm announced her candidacy for the Democratic Party's presidential nomination. She eventually lost the nomination to South Dakota Senator George McGovern. Chisholm's run for president as a major party candidate was the first for an African American. It would not be repeated until 1984, when civil rights activist Jesse Jackson campaigned as a Democratic presidential candidate. Chisholm's campaign was the subject of an award-winning 2005 documentary film, *Shirley Chisholm '72: Unbought and Unbossed.*

After retiring from Congress after the end of her seventh term in 1983, Chisholm took a teaching position at Mount Holyoke College in Massachusetts. She later settled in Florida, where she died in 2005.

members of the Congressional Black Caucus have been outspoken critics of the war in Iraq.

See also: African Americans in Congress; Committees.

Congressional Hispanic Caucus

In the United States Congress, a body comprised of Democratic members of Hispanic descent. The members of the Congressional Hispanic Caucus use their positions as lawmakers to advance issues that are important in the lives of Hispanic Americans. The caucus serves as a forum in which Hispanic members of Congress can plan and develop policies that have a direct impact on the Hispanic community. The Congressional Hispanic Caucus also monitors activities of the executive and judicial branches of the government that affect Hispanic Americans.

The caucus, which was founded in December 1976, does most of its work through a series of task forces that address specific areas of legislation. These include task forces on Economic Development; Civil Rights; Corporate America, Technology, Communications, and the Arts; Education; Health and Environment; Immigration; International Relations; Labor; and Veterans' Affairs. Immigration issues are a major focus of the caucus. Its members support comprehensive immigration reform, equal access to higher education and student financial aid, reunification of families divided as a result of visa restrictions, protecting the rights of guest workers, and reform of immigration enforcement procedures.

As of 2007, the Congressional Hispanic Caucus was composed of twenty-one members, all of whom were Democrats. Despite its all-Democratic makeup, however, the members range from **liberal** to **conservative** in their political views and thus rarely take a unanimous position on issues. In 2003, six Republican members of Congress founded a similar group called the Congressional Hispanic Conference. This body is dedicated to promoting legislation important to Hispanic and Portuguese Americans.

Founders of the Congressional Hispanic Caucus

Founders
Herman Badillo (NY)
Baltasar Corrada (PR)
E. "Kika" de la Garza (TX)
Henry B. Gonzalez (TX)
Edward Roybal (CA)

In 1976, five members of Congress founded the Congressional Hispanic Caucus (CHC) to monitor all legislative and government activity that affects Hispanics and Latinos. Today, most Hispanic members of Congress belong to the caucus.

See also: Caucuses; Congressional Black Caucus.

Further Reading

Enciso, Carmen E., and Tracy North. *Hispanic Americans in Congress, 1822–1995.* Darby, PA: Diane, 1996.

Vigil, Maurilio E. *Hispanics in Congress.* Lanham, MD: University Press of America, 1996.

Congressional Immunity

Policy by which Congress promises to free witnesses in congressional hearings from legal obligations or charges against them in return for testimony. Congressional grants of immunity from prosecution allow Congress to obtain testimony from individuals who otherwise would claim a constitutional right to remain silent to avoid incriminating themselves.

In 1857, Congress approved a federal statute that provided for the punishment of reluctant witnesses before congressional committees. At the same time, Congress added a section to the statute that contained an automatic and sweeping grant of immunity to witnesses testifying before Congress. As enacted, the law provided that

Decision Makers

Baltasar Corrada (1935–) and Herman Badillo (1929–)

The Congressional Hispanic Caucus was organized in 1976 by five Hispanic Democratic Congressmen: Herman Badillo, Baltasar Corrada, Eligio "Kika" de la Garza, Henry B. Gonzalez, and Edward Roybal. Two of the founding members of the caucus—Corrada and Badillo—were natives of Puerto Rico.

Corrada grew up in Puerto Rico and set his sights on becoming mayor of the capital, San Juan. In 1976, however, he was elected Resident Commissioner, a non-voting seat in the U.S House representing Puerto Rico. There, he met the other members of Congress with whom he co-founded the Congressional Hispanic Caucus. After leaving Congress in 1985, Corrada fulfilled his goal of becoming San Juan's mayor, serving in that post from 1985 to 1989. He later served as secretary of state for Puerto Rico and was named to its Supreme Court. In 2005, he retired upon reaching age 70, as required by Puerto Rico's constitution.

Although born in Puerto Rico, Herman Badillo moved to New York City at age 11 after his parents died of tuberculosis. He excelled in school and eventually earned a law degree from Brooklyn Law School in 1954. In 1970, he became the first native Puerto Rican to serve as a voting member of the U.S. Congress, representing New York in the House. Prior to this time, Puerto Rican service in Congress had been limited to the position of Resident Commissioner.

Badillo resigned from a Congress the year after he co-founded the Congressional Hispanic Caucus to become deputy mayor of New York City. He unsuccessfully sought the Democratic nomination as New York's mayor on five occasions and later switched party affiliations, becoming a Republican in 2001. That year, he ran for mayor of New York City, but lost in the Republican primary to Michael Bloomberg.

"no person examined and testifying before either House of Congress or any committee of either House, shall be held to answer criminally in any court of justice, or subject to any penalty or forfeiture, for any fact or act touching which he shall be required to testify before either House of Congress, or any committee of either House, as to which he shall have testified, whether before or after this act. . . . Provided, that nothing in this act shall be construed to exempt any witness from prosecution and punishment for perjury committed by him in testifying as aforesaid."

The disadvantages of this sort of immunity first became evident in 1862 when it was revealed that embezzlers of millions in Indian trust bonds would escape prosecution because they had testified about their crime to a congressional committee and so, under the 1857 law, could not be prosecuted for it.

In 1862, Congress replaced the 1857 law with one that narrowed the basis for immunity. It stated that "No testimony given by a witness before either House, or before any committee of either House . . . shall be used as evidence in any criminal proceedings against him in any court, except in a prosecution for perjury committed in giving such testimony." Thus, a witness's own testimony could not be used as evidence to convict him, but nothing could prevent that testimony from being used as a lead in discovering other evidence of a crime.

An 1892 Supreme Court ruling raised questions about the adequacy of the 1862 immunity law. Nevertheless, the law remained unchanged until Congress passed the Immunity Act of 1954. That law permitted either chamber of Congress, by majority vote, or a congressional committee by two-thirds vote, to grant immunity to witnesses in national security investigations, provided that an order was first obtained from a U.S. district court judge and the attorney general was given an opportunity to offer objections in advance. The law also permitted the U.S. district courts to grant immunity to witnesses before the courts and before grand juries. The act granted immunity from prosecution for criminal activity revealed during testimony.

In 1970, Congress wrote a new immunity law as a part of the Organized Crime Control Act. It set out the rules for granting immunity to witnesses before congressional committees, courts, grand juries, and administrative agencies. Under the new law, witnesses who received immunity to waive their Fifth Amendment rights and testify were guaranteed that their testimony and the information it contained would not be used against them in any criminal prosecution unless they lied in their testimony. Witnesses under oath may be prosecuted for perjury if they do not tell the truth in their testimony.

Congressional Investigations

Procedures by which Congress examines a person, issue, or event of importance to the nation. Investigations serve as the eyes and ears of the legislative branch. They test the effectiveness of existing laws and gather information on the need for further legislation. They inquire into the performance of government officials, including members of Congress. They expose waste and corruption in government. They educate the public on great issues of the day. The ability of Congress to investigate is one of its most controversial and highly publicized powers.

Sources of Investigative Power

The authors of the Constitution were familiar with two centuries of British **precedents** for legislative investigations. The House of Commons had asserted its investigative power as early as the sixteenth century. That practice had been adopted in America by colonial legislative bodies, the Continental Congress, and the new state legislatures.

Although the delegates to the Constitutional Convention of 1787 generally accepted Congress's power to investigate, they disagreed about its scope. Some argued that Congress's authority was limited to powers specifically granted it by the Constitution. Thus, they insisted that its investigations be confined to clearly defined areas such as election disputes, impeachments, and cases involving congressional privileges. Others argued that Congress's investigative power was much broader. This group prevailed and, since that time, the basic authority of Congress to investigate has not been seriously challenged.

The Investigative Process

Congressional investigations must be approved in advance by the House or Senate, or by both in case of a joint inquiry. A sponsor first introduces a resolution setting out the need for the inquiry and its scope. In the Senate such a resolution is considered by the Rules and Administration Committee and by the standing (permanent) committee with **jurisdiction** over the subject to be studied. The House Oversight Committee considers the funding of investigations in that chamber. After being **reported** by the committees, a resolution is voted on by the full chamber.

In both the House and Senate, the sponsor presides over the inquiry. When the study is made by a standing committee, the committee chair appoints a subcommittee to handle the investigation. When a select (temporary) committee makes the study, the members are chosen by the vice president or the Speaker of the House, along with the majority and minority leaders of that chamber.

The first step in an investigation is the gathering of information by staff members. Following the staff inquiry, the committee holds formal hearings, at which witnesses appear. Congress has the power to **subpoena** witnesses, or compel them to testify, in an investigation. Those who refuse may be cited for contempt of Congress, which is punishable by jail time. Witnesses may be accompanied by counsel and they may testify in a secret session if the testimony might "tend to defame, degrade, or incriminate any person." They may also refuse to answer questions if they feel the answers would tend to incriminate them, or cause them to appear to be guilty. To obtain testimony in such cases, Congress may grant witnesses immunity from prosecution based on their testimony.

Senator Harry S. Truman of Missouri (second from left) led the Special Committee Investigating National Defense during World War II (1941–1945). The committee, known as the Truman Committee, oversaw defense plant spending and management. (U.S. Navy, Courtesy of Harry S. Truman Library)

At the conclusion of the investigation, the committee issues a report summarizing its findings and offering recommendations for future action. Many investigations have **partisan** overtones, and votes on the final committee recommendation may divide along party lines. Partisanship may be the reason that an investigation is undertaken in the first place, and this can influence how it is conducted.

Executive Privilege

Congressional investigations have often sparked conflict with the executive branch, most frequently when a president refuses to comply with congressional demands for information. Practically every presidential administration has clashed with Congress over the question of "executive privilege" to withhold information, and the issue has yet to be resolved. An argument can be made that executive departments, established by Congress and maintained by its **appropriations,** are created by the legislature and cannot deny it information regarding their activities. However, presidents have defied congressional demands for information on many occasions. Those precedents tend to support arguments that the constitutional separation of powers permits the president to withhold information sought by Congress.

SPOTLIGHT

Politics and Congressional Investigations

The three most intensive periods of congressional investigative activities—the last years of the Ulysses S. Grant administration (1869–1877) and the periods immediately following World Wars I and II—coincided with shifts of congressional majorities that transferred power to a party long in the minority.

Grant was a Republican. When the Democrats in the 1874 election recaptured control of the House for the first time since 1859, the number of investigations soared. In the 1918 election, Republicans gained control of the House and set off on a series of studies of World War I mobilization under President Woodrow Wilson (1913–1921), a Democrat. In similar fashion, World War II mobilization and reported infiltration of the government by communists during the administrations of Democratic Presidents Franklin D. Roosevelt (1933–1945) and Harry S. Truman (1945–1953) were studied closely by committees of the Republican 80th Congress, elected in 1946.

A subtler form of investigation politics takes place in the maneuvering for control of a particular inquiry. The conduct of investigations depends substantially on the attitude of the investigating committees and their chairs. Thus **Radical Republicans,** gaining control of the joint committee investigating the conduct of the Civil War, used the committee as a forum for criticizing the moderate policies of President Abraham Lincoln and to force more vigorous prosecution of the war.

Another example, after World War II, had different results. President Truman's release in August 1945 of army and navy reports on the attack on Pearl Harbor brought numerous Republican demands for a congressional investigation. Through quick maneuvering, the Democrats initiated action, establishing a joint House-Senate committee, which, with the Democrats in control of Congress, would have a Democratic majority. The resolution was adopted by both chambers without opposition.

The committee's final report, filed July 20, 1946, absolved President Roosevelt of blame for the Pearl Harbor disaster but held the chief of naval operations and the army commander in Hawaii primarily responsible. A Republican minority report laid the primary blame on Roosevelt, suggesting what might have been the majority view if Republicans had been in command of the inquiry.

Presidents have used a variety of reasons to justify denying information to Congress. Perhaps the most common has been the need for secrecy in military and diplomatic activities. Presidents have also sought to avoid needlessly exposing individuals to unfavorable publicity. The need for confidential exchange of ideas between members of an administration has been cited as justifying refusal to provide records or describe conversations in the executive branch. Fears that disclosures would interfere with criminal or security investigations sometimes have prompted administrative secrecy. Critics however, have frequently charged that an administration's real motive for refusing to divulge information was to escape criticism or scandal.

See also: Army-McCarthy Hearings; Checks and Balances; Congressional Immunity; Contempt of Congress; President and Congress; Watergate Hearings; Whitewater Investigations.

Further Reading

Hamilton, James. *The Power to Probe: A Study of Congressional Investigations.* New York: Vintage, 1977.

Mayhew, David R. *Divided We Govern: Party Control, Lawmaking, and Investigations, 1946–2002.* New Haven, CT: Yale University Press, 2005.

Congressional Office Buildings

Buildings constructed specifically to house members of Congress and their staffs. Most committees of Congress have space in separate office buildings, although a handful of House and Senate committees have rooms in the Capitol. The buildings also house a number of noncongressional organizations.

Pressure for Space

The construction of separate office buildings for senators and representatives occurred relatively recently in the history of Congress. The first congressional office building, for House members, opened in 1908. Until then, a member's office consisted of a desk in the House or Senate chamber and a residence in Washington. This was because congressional service was at most a part-time occupation for the first hundred years of the Republic. A member who was not on the floor of a chamber had virtually no sanctuary, although the lobbies just off the chambers provided some relaxation. These were open to the public, and favor-seekers took advantage of the chance to meet with legislators there, hence the term **lobbying.**

As standing committees increased in number in the second half of the nineteenth century, they quickly overflowed the rooms allocated to them in the unfinished Capitol. Expansions of the Capitol provided more committee rooms, but committees devoured the new space almost as fast as it was provided. As the committees outgrew the space provided, they rented additional space in nearby privately owned buildings.

The Capitol Complex

Today, the Capitol complex contains six official congressional office buildings–three for the House of Representatives and three for the Senate–plus an additional office annex for the House. Completed in 1908, the oldest congressional office building is the Cannon House Office Building. Located southeast of the Capitol, the land for the building was acquired in 1903, and construction began in 1904. Originally, the building contained 397 offices and 14 committee rooms. By 1913, the House had outgrown the building and a fifth floor, with 51 additional rooms, was added. A 1932 renovation resulted in 85 two- and three-room suites, 10 single rooms, and 23 committee rooms. It is connected to the Capitol by an underground passage. In 1962, the building was named after former House Speaker Joseph G. Cannon (1903–1911) from Illinois.

The Senate's oldest office building is the Russell Senate Office Building, which was built between 1904 and 1908, at about the same time as what is today the Cannon House Office Building. Originally, there were 98 offices and 8 committee rooms in the building; in 1933, the First

The Hart Senate Office Building is one of three Senate office buildings in which some of the business of Congress takes place. (Scott J. Ferrell, CQ)

A–Z

Street Wing was added to the building, resulting in 28 suites and 2 more committee rooms. The Russell Caucus Room still houses its original benches from 1910. This room has been the site of hearings of national significance, from the hearings on the sinking of the *Titanic* (1912), to the Watergate Hearings (1974), to the sexual harassment hearings against Justice Clarence Thomas (1991). In 1972, the building was named for former Senator Richard B. Russell, Jr. (1933–1971) from Georgia.

The Longworth House Office Building, completed in 1933, is the second-oldest office for the House of Representatives. It is also the smallest of the office buildings. When first built, it included 251 congressional suites, 12 conference rooms, and a large assembly room, which seats 450 people. Today, the House Ways and Means Committee meets in the assembly room. In 1949 and 1950, the House met in this assembly room while its chamber was undergoing renovation. The building was named in honor of Speaker of the House Nicholas Longworth (1925–1931) in 1962. Longworth, who was from Ohio, served as speaker when the building was approved.

By the 1940s, the Senate, too, had outgrown is office space. In 1949, Congress authorized the construction of a second Senate office building, which, in 1972, was named the Dirksen Senate Office Building in honor of Minority Leader Senator Everett McKinley Dirksen (1951–1969) from Illinois. Although approved in 1949, construction was delayed until 1954 and the building was finally completed in 1958. The new building was fitted with all the modern conveniences of the time—television and broadcast studios, a cafeteria seating a few hundred people, and a parking garage for 200 cars.

Completed in 1965, the Rayburn House Office Building is the third office for the members of the House. Located southeast of the Capitol, the four-story building accommodates 169 House members in three-room suites. Nine House committees also moved into the building. State-of-the art amenities of the time included toilets and kitchens in each suite, as well as an underground parking garage, a gymnasium, a recording studio, a post office, and facilities for the television and the press. The building was named in 1962 in honor of House Speaker Sam Rayburn from Texas, who served several terms as speaker between 1940 and 1961.

Located northeast of the Capitol, the Hart Senate Office Building is the newest of the congressional office structures. Planned as an extension to the Dirksen Senate Office Building, the Hart Senate Office Building was authorized in 1974, and excavation started in 1975. The structure was named in honor of Democratic Senator Philip A. Hart (1959–1976) of Michigan. Completed in 1982, Senate Majority Leader Howard Baker was the first occupant.

In addition, the House acquired another office building in 1975. Originally built for the Federal Bureau of Investigation (FBI), it was named in honor of Gerald R. Ford, who served as House Minority Leader (1965–1973).

See also: Capitol, Architect of the.

Congressional Pay and Benefits

Article I, Section 6, of the Constitution states that “Senators and Representatives shall receive

Congressional Pay

Year	Salary	Year	Salary
1789–1795	$6 per diem	December 1982–1983	$69,800 per year (House)
1795–1796	$6 per diem (House) $7 per diem (Senate)	July 1983	$69,800 per year (Senate)
1796–1815	$6 per diem	1984	$72,600 per year
1815–1817	$1, 500 per year	1985–1986	$75,100 per year
1817–1855	$8 per diem	January 1987	$77,400 per year
1855–1865	$3,000 per year	February 1987–1989	$89,500 per year
1865–1871	$5,000 per year	1990	$96,600 per year (House)
1871–1873	$7,500 per year	1990	$98,400 per year (Senate)
1873–1907	$5,000 per year	January 1991	$125,100 per year (House) $101,900 per year (Senate)
1907–1925	$7,500 per year	August 1991	$125,100 per year (Senate)
1925–1932	$10,000 per year	1992	$129,500 per year
1932–1933	$9,000 per year	1993–1997	$133,600 per year
1933–1935	$8,500 per year	1998–1999	$136,700 per year
1935–1947	$10,000 per year	2000	$141,300 per year
1947–1955	$12,500 per year	2002	$150,000 per year
1955–1965	$22,500 per year	2003	$154,700 per year
1965–1969	$30,000 per year	2004	$158,100 per year
1969–1975	$42,500 per year	2005	$162,100 per year
1975–1977	$44,600 per year	2006	$165,200 per year
1977–1979	$57,500 per year	2007	$168,000 per year
1979–1982	$60,662.50 per year	2008	$169,300 per year

Note: The top six leaders of Congress—the Speaker of the House, the Senate president pro tempore, and the majority and minority leaders of both chambers—receive additional pay. Highest paid is the House Speaker, who earned $175,400 in 1999. The Speaker's pay was scheduled to rise to $181,400 in 2000 as the result of a 3.4 percent pay increase for all members of Congress under the annual adjustment procedures of law.
***Source:* Congressional Research Service; House Sergeant at Arms; Senate Disbursing Office.**

The salaries of representatives and senators have increased significantly since the beginning of the Republic.

a Compensation for their Services, to be ascertained by Law, and paid out of the Treasury of the United States." The document also leaves it to Congress to decide what that salary should be. Members of Congress also receive certain perquisites, or benefits, such as expense allowances and retirement plans.

History

The first bill proposal for congressional pay in 1789 called for members to receive $6 a day. After much debate, Congress agreed to increase senators' pay to $7 a day in 1795. This bill also provided the first congressional perquisite: a travel allowance of $6 for every twenty miles.

SPOTLIGHT

The Madison Amendment

Proposed by James Madison (1809–1817) and approved by Congress in 1789, the Madison Amendment states that any pay raise that Congress votes itself cannot take effect until after the next House election. It was intended to prevent sitting members of Congress from voting themselves a pay raise during the current session. First proposed in September 1789, it did not gather the minimum number of state approvals to win **ratification** until 1992, more than two hundred years after gaining congressional approval. The long delay between proposal and ratification raised a question of timeliness: Can an **amendment** remain valid after such a long period of time?

On May 13, 1992, the congressional archivist announced that he found the amendment constitutional. A week later, the Senate unanimously approved two proposals to recognize the measure as the Twenty-seventh Amendment. On the same day, the House voted overwhelmingly for a resolution supporting the amendment.

It also doubled the salary of the House Speaker and increased compensation for some lesser House and Senate officials.

In 1816, Congress voted to give itself a pay increase and a change from daily compensation to an annual salary of $1,500. The public widely condemned the pay raise and voted out of office several members who had approved the bill. The following year, Congress repealed the $1,500 salary and restored daily compensation at the rate at $8 for all members. Congress did not attempt to raise its pay until 1856, when it voted members a yearly salary of $3,000. This time the move met little public opposition.

Congressional pay rose gradually until the Great Depression of the 1930s, when Congress members took pay cuts that reduced their annual salaries by 15 percent. Following World War II (1941–1945), congressional pay once again increased. It has risen steadily since. In 1955, Congress approved an increase that nearly doubled members' salaries to $22,500. Congressional salaries continued to increase during the 1960s and 1970s, reaching almost $61,000 a year by 1979. After making comparatively small gains in the 1980s, Congress voted itself a nearly 40 percent pay raise in 1989. As of 2006, the base pay for members was $165,200. The Speaker of the House of Representatives earned $212,100, while other congressional leaders received $183,500.

Allowances and Other Benefits

Lawmakers enjoy an array of allowances and benefits that help to ease the pressures of congressional life. Members of Congress have free mailing privileges for official business and use of free office space in federal buildings in their home states or districts. Each member receives an expense allowance for home office space rental, travel, telecommunications services, stationery, printing, computer services, postage for mass mailings, office equipment, and other expenses.

Members are allowed free storage of files and records, the use of office decorations and furniture, use of recording and photographic studios, authority to make a limited number of appointments, and free publications. They also can receive various health protection plans and emergency care while at work, life insurance, and a generous retirement pension.

Senators and representatives have access to elaborate computerized mailing and legislative analysis systems and gym facilities, including swimming pools, saunas, and masseurs. Legislative counsels, legal counsels, chaplains, and photographers stand by at the Capitol to assist members. Attractive dining rooms, barber and beauty shops, and convenient rail and airline ticket offices are available in the Capitol and congressional office buildings.

Totalling the Cost

Trying to calculate the total amount of money Congress spends on itself can be very difficult. Most information is available in reports published by the secretary of the Senate and the clerk of the House of Representatives. These publications list the salaries for all congressional employees and all expenditures made by members in their official duties. The annual legislative branch appropriations, which include funding for Congress itself and for several related agencies such as the Library of Congress, came to $3.85 billion in 2006. However, it is hard to attach a dollar value to many fringe benefits offered to Congressional members.

Perhaps the biggest current benefit is the official office expense allowance. This covers domestic travel, telecommunications, stationery, computer services, postage, printing, office expenses in Washington, DC, and in the member's congressional district or state, and other expenses. As of 2004, each House member was allowed $187,236 for such expenses, plus an additional per mile allowance for travel between Washington, DC, and the member's home district. Each House member also received an annual allowance of $748,312 per year for hiring staff.

Each senator's office allowance varies due to several factors, primarily the distance between Washington, DC, and the member's home state, the population of the state, and the senator's official mail allocation. Allowances range from $128,567 to $467,800 annually. Senate staff allowance is based on the population of a senator's state. It ranges from $1,685,301 for a senator representing a state with a population under 5,000,000 to $2,833,718 for a senator representing a state with a population of 28,000,000 or more. In addition, the allowance provides each senator $450,477 to appoint three legislative assistants.

See also: Congressional Staff; Congressional Travel Allowances; Franking.

Further Reading

Congressional Quarterly. *Congressional Pay and Perquisites: History, Facts, and Controversy.* Washington, DC: Congressional Quarterly, 1992.

Davidson, Roger H., and Walter J. Oleszek. *Congress and Its Members.* Eleventh edition. Washington, DC: CQ Press, 2007.

Dodd, Lawrence C., and Bruce I. Oppenheimer. *Congress Reconsidered.* Eighth edition. Washington, DC: CQ Press, 2004.

Congressional Record

The primary source of information about what happens on the floors of the Senate and House of Representatives. Published daily when Congress is in session, the *Record* provides an account of each chamber's debate and shows how individual members voted on all recorded votes. The *Record* is not the official account of congressional proceedings. That is provided in each chamber's Journal, which reports actions taken but not the accompanying debate. Courts, however, often use the *Record* to determine what Congress intended when it passed a law.

By law, the *Record* is supposed to provide "substantially a verbatim (word-for-word) report of the proceedings." Until recent years, however, the *Record* was edited to fix grammatical errors and even to delete some words spoken in the heat of floor debate. The *Record* often included speeches not given on the floor, but both the House and Senate have tightened rules about "inserting remarks," as this process is known. The full texts of **bills,** conference reports, and other documents, rarely read in full on the floor, often appear in the *Record.*

When Republicans took control of the House in 1995, they limited changes in the *Record* "only to technical, grammatical and typographical corrections," which prohibited removing remarks actually made. Members can still insert written statements in the *Record,* as long as they appear in a different typeface. The Speaker of the House often inserts written material into the *Record,* especially at the beginning of a Congress, to clarify certain practices to be followed in such matters as recognizing members or referring bills.

History

Before 1825, reports of congressional debates were infrequent. Some of the better newspapers reported haphazardly on House debate between 1790 and 1825, but Senate debates scarcely were reported at all. In 1834, Gales and Seaton published the first of forty-two volumes of *Annals of Congress.* This record brought together material from newspapers, magazines, and other sources on congressional proceedings from 1789 to 1824. From 1824 through 1837 Gales and Seaton published a *Register of Debate,* which directly reported congressional proceedings. In 1833, Blair and Rives began to publish *The Congressional Globe,* but debates were still not reported systematically until 1865. In that year, the *Globe* took on a form and style that later became standard. When the government contract for publication of the *Globe* expired in 1873, Congress ruled that the Government Printing Office would produce the *Congressional Record.*

Contents, Cost, and Availability

The *Record* contains four sections: the proceedings of the Senate and the House, extensions of remarks, and the Daily Digest. The proceedings are edited accounts of floor debate and other action taken in each chamber. A member may request "unanimous consent to extend my remarks at this point in the *Record*" to include a statement, newspaper article, or speech, which will appear in the *Record* where the member requested. Even if a member reads only a few words from a speech or article, it appears in the *Record* as if the member had delivered it in its entirety. The records of House floor debates show roughly when particular discussions occurred; records of Senate proceedings have no indication of time.

In addition to inserting material, senators and representatives are given further space to extend their remarks. By unanimous consent, they may add material such as speeches given outside Congress, selected editorials, or letters. Such material may also be included in the body of the *Record* by unanimous consent if a member prefers.

The Daily Digest summarizes House and Senate floor action for the day as well as Senate and House committee meetings and conferences. It also notes committee reports filed, the time and date of the next House and Senate sessions, and all committee meetings. The last issue of the Digest in the week lists the program for the coming week. At the beginning of each month the Digest publishes a summary of congressional activity in the previous month. An index to the *Record* is published semimonthly.

About 6,000 copies of each day's issue of the *Record* are printed. In 2006, the total cost came to an estimated $22.2 million. The *Record* is also available on microfiche. In addition, the public can gain free access to the daily *Congressional Record* through Internet websites run by the U.S. Government Printing Office (http://www.access.gpo.gov) and the "Thomas" service provided by the Library of Congress (http://thomas.loc.gov).

See also: Library of Congress.

Congressional Research Service

A department of the Library of Congress which provides Congress with various types of information and also acts as a policy consultant. The Congressional Research Service (CRS) provides much of the research and reference work on public policy issues prepared for members of Congress, congressional committees, and congressional staff.

Congress depends heavily on support from the Congressional Research Service. The 700-member CRS staff annually responds to more than a half-million requests for information and analysis from Capitol Hill. The Congressional Research Service maintains several research and information centers throughout the Capitol complex to deal with these matters. The CRS is noted for its efficiency in providing information.

There are six research divisions that deal with policy analysis and long-term research projects: American law; domestic social policy; foreign affairs, defense, and trade; government and finance; information research; and resources, science, and industry. In addition, CRS employs a number of senior specialists–nationally recognized experts, many of whom have published widely and have had extensive careers outside CRS.

Members of Congress may request any kind of public policy research from the Congressional Research Service. CRS reports are prized for their objectivity and nonpartisanship. The Service tries to anticipate congressional needs for information and some of its studies look far into the future, but it can respond very quickly in times of crisis or if circumstances require.

In addition to in-depth analyses prepared for congressional committees and individual members, CRS products and services include the following:

- Issue briefs, which are fifteen-page analyses of major policy issues. At the beginning of each session of Congress the CRS identifies major issues most likely to result in hearings or legislation. The list provides a focus for CRS activity.
- *Major Legislation of the Congress,* a report which is issued two to three times a year, and *Major Legislation,* which provides a summary of **bills** in Congress and their status in the legislative process. The CRS also maintains four automated databases: legislation (Bill Digest) for the current and two preceding Congresses, major issues (issue briefs), bibliography (public policy literature), and an index to the daily *Congressional Record.*
- CRS Web site (http://www.loc.gov/crs), which provides House and Senate offices and legislative branch agencies with round-the-clock access to such material as the full text of issue briefs, reports, and analyses of appropriations bills.
- *Legislative Alert,* a weekly collection of CRS material relevant to expected floor action. The service is distributed by fax and e-mail to all members of Congress as well as to congressional committees and subcommittees.

The Congressional Research Service has more than 700 employees, including lawyers, economists, engineers, information scientists, librarians, defense and foreign affairs analysts, political scientists, public administrators, and physical and behavioral scientists. The service is housed in the Madison Memorial Building of the Library of Congress.

Congressional Staff

Term applied to men and women who work for congressional committees or for individual members of Congress. Capitol Hill staffers may be policy and legal experts or they may excel at running an efficient office for a member, helping constituents, and doing whatever they can to get their **bosses** reelected.

Members rely heavily on staff during all stages of the legislative process. Some staffers draft legislation, negotiate with **lobbyists,** and plot legislative strategy. These so-called "entrepreneurial staffers" are given considerable responsibility for legislative decision making. Faced with more complex issues, more technical legislation, and more demanding constituents, members apparently have encouraged the growth of entrepreneurial staff.

For the public, congressional staff are the voices at the other end of phone calls to members' offices, or the blurred faces behind members at televised congressional committee meetings. Staffers are drawn to Capitol Hill by the exciting prospect of being at the center of important political, social, and economic issues;

by the hope of making a difference in public service; and—often—by raw ambition. Although staff members cannot vote, their imprint is everywhere—on legislation, politics, and public policy. Some critics believe that congressional staff wield excessive power and cost too much tax money. Legislators reply that staffs provide the expertise on complex issues that members could never master alone.

Staff is roughly divided into two types: those who work for a committee and those who work in a member's office serving that person's requirements. Staff that work for committees usually serve either the majority or minority party on the panel. Staffers in a member's office also may be assigned to work on the issues addressed by the committee on which the member serves. Even without this close link, all members have someone on staff to handle legislative issues.

Committee Staffs

Committee staff members are responsible for the day-to-day running of congressional committees. They also assist the committee members and other staff who concentrate on issues under the committee's **jurisdiction,** or area of authority. Routine staff tasks include keeping the committee calendar up to date; processing committee publications; sending pending bills to the executive branch for comment; preparing the list of bills to be considered; maintaining files; announcing committee hearings and contacting witnesses; opening and sorting mail; and—increasingly—preparing or updating electronic data, including committee websites. Other staff members handle committee policy and legislative matters, including legal and other types of research, public relations, statistical and other technical work, and drafting and redrafting bills and amendments.

All of these staffers are a committee's statutory, or permanent, staff. Their positions are established by rules of the House or Senate or by law. Their activities are funded each year in the legislative branch **appropriations** (spending) bill. Permanent House committees are entitled to thirty staffers paid out of statutory funds.

Committees also hire additional personnel for special work. These so-called "investigative" employees are considered temporary, but they often remain with the committees for extended periods. These staffers are paid from a separate investigative budget, which is reviewed yearly by the House Administration Committee. Over the years, investigative employees have accounted for much of the increase in committee staff costs, as the budgets for these aides are flexible.

Functions of Committee Staff

While committee responsibilities vary, most staff perform these basic functions:

Planning Agendas: This includes helping chairs select issues to consider, scheduling hearings and bill amendments, and planning floor action.

Organizing Hearings: Staffers set up hearings on legislation and issues under the committee's jurisdiction; select witnesses; prepare questions; inform the press; brief committee members; and occasionally substitute for members who cannot attend hearings, often asking questions prepared by the absent legislator.

Oversight and Investigations: Staff members conduct original research on existing legislation, court decisions, and current practices relating to matters under the committee's jurisdiction. Sometimes staffers hold regional hearings outside Washington, DC.

Bill Markup and Amendment Drafting: Staff aides assist members in marking up (amending) bills by analyzing and explaining technical aspects of legislation. They also often work with committee members, government agencies, and **special interest groups** during the drafting of legislation.

Preparing Reports: Committee reports that accompany bills sent to the full chamber are written almost entirely by staff. Staff aides consult with the chair or the majority party members about information and emphasis in the report.

Preparing for Floor Action: Top aides most familiar with the legislation often accompany the committee chair or another sponsor of the bill when the legislation is debated in the Senate or House. They advise the bill's supporters and sometimes help prepare amendments. They also may draft a script for the bill's managers to follow during the floor debate, including opening and closing remarks.

Conference Committee Work: The staffs of corresponding committees in each chamber work together to resolve differences in legislation initially considered by those committees and subsequently passed by the House and Senate.

Committee Liaison: Staff aides communicate frequently with executive branch officials and lobbyists on proposals before the committee. Some members regard this activity as the most important of all staff work. Representatives of special interest groups often provide staff aides with detailed information and answers to questions.

Press Relations: Committee staffers alert reporters to upcoming hearings, markup sessions, and floor action on committee-reported measures. Aides answer questions from the press and public, and they write press releases. Also, they provide background information on legislation before the committee and on recent committee decisions on legislation. In addition, they make committee members accessible to the media and generally work to obtain favorable publicity for the committee.

Recruitment and Tenure

The chair or top-ranking minority party member of a committee selects most committee employees, subject to approval by the full committee. Staffers as a group are relatively young, and most are male. The majority of them have advanced degrees, particularly in law, and many have previous experience in the executive branch. While committee staff tend to retain their positions over time, experienced staffers often are replaced when control of a chamber shifts from one party to another. The same phenomenon occurs when committee leadership posts change frequently, which may occur when a senior member retires or is defeated. Congressional aides accept positions knowing there is no job security. Their tenure is subject to the whims of the chair or member who hired them, and aides can be fired with or without cause.

Personal Staff

In the modern Congress no senators or representatives try to manage their activities entirely unassisted. Members generally depend on staff to handle the routine work of a congressional office.

Functions of Personal Staff

Like committee staff, personal staff handle a variety of tasks for their members:

Constituent Service: Personal staffs, especially in the House, respond to requests from constituents. This includes solving bureaucratic problems; answering constituents' questions; helping local organizations obtain federal funding; and producing newsletters and other mailings to keep constituents informed of their boss's activities.

Legislation: Members of Congress rely on their legislative assistants for guidance through the daily maze of complex issues they face. Members depend heavily on staff to draft bills and amendments and recommend policy initiatives and alternatives. Staffers also monitor committee sessions that members cannot attend and may prepare lawmakers' speeches and position papers.

Other Duties: Casework and legislation are only some of the chores handled by personal staffers. The press secretary serves as the congressional member's chief spokesperson to the news media. Press aides compose news releases about legislative issues, write newsletters, and organize press conferences. Because they deal almost exclusively with hometown media outlets, some House press aides are based in the district offices rather than in Washington. Where there is no press secretary, press relations are handled by an administrative assistant or a legislative assistant. Senators, who receive more national publicity and represent larger areas than members of the House, often have several deputy press secretaries or assistant press staff.

Recruitment and Tenure

Representatives and senators hire their own personal aides. Although House and Senate employment offices are available, most hiring is based on informal contacts, but word of mouth and just plain luck are important as well. Potential staffers may seek out members who are involved in particular issue areas, who are known to pay well, who are from a certain area of the country, or who have a particular **ideology,** or political outlook. In recent years members with private business backgrounds have used the congressional employment offices and even newspaper ads to solicit job applications. Members of the House are entitled to withdraw funds from the chamber's clerk-hire allowance to run and staff their offices. These funds are divided equally among representatives. For senators, the money is divided according to their state's population.

In seeking knowledge and experience, members must decide whether to hire from the state or district, or from Washington circles. This is an especially delicate problem for first-term congressional members who may have limited Washington contacts and who feel indebted to their campaign staff.

The characteristics of personal staff vary greatly from those of committee staff. A former House legislative assistant summarized them as "commonly in their twenties; theirs can be an entry-level professional position requiring no previous Hill experience. (Committee staffers, in contrast, tend to be more specialized, and therefore older and of greater experience.)" Like committee staff, personal staffers have little job security. Their tenure is up to the member who hired them.

See also: Congressional Pay and Benefits; Interns, Congressional.

Further Reading

Bisnow, Mark. *In the Shadow of the Dome: Chronicles of a Capitol Hill Aide.* New York: Morrow, 1990.

Fox, Harrison W., Jr., and Susan Webb Hammond. *Congressional Staffs: The Invisible Force in American Lawmaking.* New York: Free Press, 1979.

Congressional Travel Allowances

Public funds provided to members of Congress to pay for certain travel expenses. Congressional Travel Allowances cover both foreign and domestic travel. All travel, however, is subject to various limits and restrictions according to law.

Members of Congress sometimes travel to foreign countries at government expense to learn about world problems, especially those that are being debated in Congress. According to current law, lawmakers using public funds may go on fact-finding trips abroad for up to seven days if the trips are connected with official duties and are disclosed within thirty days of their completion. Because of criticism about using public funds for foreign trips, lawmakers are increasingly accepting privately funded trips. In terms of private funding, current law allows members and their staffs to accept free trips for meetings, speeches, and fact-finding tours related to their official duties. Foreign travel using private funds is limited to seven days excluding travel time. Lawmakers have thirty days to report to the clerk of the House the purpose of the trip, who paid for it, the destination, and the cost.

Members of Congress generally undertake foreign travel on congressional committee business, in delegations appointed by the Speaker of the House or by the president pro tempore of the Senate, or by request of the executive branch. Members must regularly submit travel reports that detail the costs of such trips. Although travel reports do not have to be filed for foreign travel funded by the executive branch or by private organizations, members must report privately funded travel in regular financial reports regarding their total expenses.

Domestic travel for members of Congress has more clearly defined limits. In the early 1960s, senators and representatives were allowed three government-paid trips home each year. The number was raised repeatedly during the following decades so that by the late 1970s senators could take more than forty trips home and representatives were allowed thirty-three. By 1980, there were no limits on the number of domestic trips that a member of Congress could take each year.

In the House of Representatives, domestic travel allowances are calculated based on how far the member's district is from Washington, DC. The House calculates a domestic travel allowance for each member and uses that figure in determining the official expense allowances. Members are reimbursed for the actual cost of travel, including rail and airfare, food, and lodging. When a member travels in a privately owned or leased vehicle, he or she is reimbursed at a standard rate per mile. Members also may be reimbursed for travel on official business that is in addition to visits to their home district or state. The Defense Department also provides members of Congress with free transportation in the line of official business. However, department officials do not release figures on the cost of such special shuttle service.

In the Senate, travel is one of several items authorized as part of senators' official expense accounts. Reimbursable travel expenses include actual transportation costs as well as funds to cover food, lodging, tips, laundry, and other miscellaneous charges. Members are not reimbursed for entertainment, and they do not receive reimbursement for transportation costs (airfare and rail fare) that are greater than actual expenses.

There is another travel allowance for a senator-elect and up to two employees. This allowance covers one round trip between a senator-elect's home and Washington, DC. The travel allowance for each senator used to be based on the cost of forty to forty-four round trips a year to their state of residence. However, the travel allowance for senators no longer sets limits on the number of trips that can be taken each year. Unlike the House, which permits travel outside the district only for educational seminars or authorized meetings, the Senate will reimburse for travel expenses that include official travel anywhere within the United States.

Congressional Voting Methods

Procedures developed by the House and Senate for voting on matters before the chamber. Each chamber has its own set of rules, the requirements for which are spelled out in the Constitution.

House Voting Methods

The House has developed a complex set of rules governing how members' votes on the House floor are recorded. The House regularly uses three types of votes: voice votes, division votes, and votes recorded by the name of the member, also called "yeas and nays" or "recorded vote." Often, the House takes several votes on the same proposition, using the simplest method first and then increasingly more complex voting methods, before reaching a decision. In the House, a roll-call vote may come only after debate on a matter has been concluded.

A voice vote is the quickest method of voting and the type nearly always used first. The officer in charge calls for all members supporting the proposition to shout "aye"; all members opposed then shout "no." The chair then decides which side commands more votes. If the result of a voice vote is in doubt, or if any member requests it, a division, or standing vote, may occur. Those in favor of the proposal stand up while the chair takes a head count; those against it then stand and are counted. Only vote totals are announced; there is no record of how individual members voted.

Few issues are decided by division vote. After a voice vote, members will usually skip it and ask for a vote in which members are recorded by name. This kind of vote, which is nearly always taken using an electronic voting system, draws many more members to the chamber. It is called "the yeas and nays" or a

In 1973, the House began using an electronic voting system. Members insert plastic cards in the voting boxes at forty-four stations throughout the chamber and vote "YEA," "NAY," or "PRESENT." Their votes are displayed on the wall above the House gallery. (Scott J. Ferrell, CQ)

"recorded vote" depending on the circumstances in which it is taken, but the result is identical.

The House uses an electronic voting system for recording members' votes. Members insert plastic cards into one of forty-four voting stations mounted on the backs of chairs along the aisles of the House chamber. The member punches a button and a giant electronic board behind the Speaker's desk flashes green for "yes" and red for "no" next to the legislator's name. Members may also vote "present," which shows up as a yellow light. Members may change their votes at any time until the result is announced.

Once electronic voting begins, members have fifteen minutes to record their votes, although an additional two minutes is usually allowed to accommodate latecomers. The voting time is often shortened to five minutes for each vote after the first one cast. Regardless of the time limit, any member who is in the chamber at the time the result is to be announced has the right to record a vote, or to change one already cast.

Senate Voting Methods

Only two types of votes are in everyday use in the Senate–voice votes and roll-call votes, or "yeas and nays." Standing votes are seldom employed. The Senate does not use an electronic voting system.

As in the House, the most common method of deciding issues is by voice vote. The officer in charge determines the outcome. Under the Constitution, one-fifth of the senators present must support a demand for a roll call. Unlike the House, the Senate assumes that an actual **quorum,** or majority of the members, is present when this demand is being made. Thus, a minimum of eleven senators must rise in support (Since the Senate has 100 members, a quorum consists of 51; one-fifth of that total, rounded up, is eleven). In some situations however, the number needed is one-fifth of the senators who actually show up to vote, up to a maximum of twenty. Informal practices have also evolved in which a vote may be ordered if only a few senators are present and the two parties' floor managers agree.

Unlike the House, senators may demand the yeas and nays on pending business long in advance of the actual vote. The Senate usually allows fifteen minutes for a roll-call vote, although members may agree to shorten the voting time in specific situations. The fifteen-minute period also may be extended to accommodate late-arriving senators. Senators who miss a vote cannot be recorded after the result has been announced. Unlike the House, if a senator's vote was not recorded or was incorrectly recorded, the senator may have the proper vote recorded if it would not change the result.

See also: How a Bill Becomes Law.

Connecticut Compromise

Also known as the Great Compromise, an agreement reached by delegates of the Constitutional Convention of 1787 regarding the organization of Congress and state representation within it.

Decision Makers

Roger Sherman (1721–1793)

One of the Founders of the United States, Roger Sherman, was born on April 19, 1721, in Newton, Massachusetts, and died on July 23, 1793, in New Haven, Connecticut. A signer of the Declaration of Independence, he also played an important role at the Constitutional Convention of 1787, which led to the creation of the U.S. Constitution.

Largely self-taught, Sherman became a distinguished lawyer and went on to serve in the colonial legislature of Connecticut. He eventually gave up a career in law, however, and became a successful and prosperous businessman. During the Revolutionary period, Sherman held a number of colonial and state offices. Early on, he became involved in the Revolutionary cause and became an active and influential member of the Continental Congress as a delegate from Connecticut. A member of the committee that drafted the Declaration of Independence, he also was one of the signers of that document. He also served on a number of congressional committees.

Named a delegate to the Constitutional Convention of 1787, Sherman played an active role in that as well. He originally favored merely strengthening the Articles of Confederation. He soon realized, however, that the young nation needed a completely new constitution to resolve the problems it faced. He was one of the delegates who drafted the New Jersey Plan, which was favored by small states like Connecticut because it gave equal representation to the states. When the convention became deadlocked over the proposed Congress, Sherman became the prime mover toward a compromise. He thus helped draft the Connecticut Compromise, which solved the problem of representation in the new Congress and saved the Convention from failure.

After the Constitutional Convention, Sherman worked to ensure that the new Constitution would be **ratified** in Connecticut. He wrote a number of letters to the New Haven *Gazette* in support of **ratification.** When the new government was established, Sherman served as a representative in the House of Representatives of the first Congress, which sat from 1789 to 1791. As a member of Congress, he supported measures favorable to the New England states. In 1791, he became a member of the U.S. Senate, where he served until his death in 1793.

The Connecticut Compromise created the basic structure of the Congress under the U.S. Constitution. It created a **bicameral** legislature with both equal and proportional representation for the states.

During the course of the Constitutional Convention of 1787, a serious disagreement arose between the delegates from the smaller states and those from the larger states. The delegates from the smaller states wanted representation in both houses of Congress to be equal to the representation from the larger states. Delegates from the larger states wanted representation based on the size of a state's population, which would give them more power in Congress.

Early in the Convention, Edmund Randolph of Virginia had proposed what became known as the Virginia Plan. It called for creating a bicameral legislature in which representation of both houses would be based on population. Smaller states did not like this plan because it would give the larger states more power in Congress. After much debate, William Paterson of New Jersey proposed the so-called New Jersey Plan. This plan called for a legislature consisting of just one house, with equal representation from each state. Both plans were debated, and neither side could reach agreement. The deadlock between the small states and large states nearly ended the Convention as well as all hopes of creating a new constitution for the nation to replace the Articles of Confederation, which was not working.

It became evident that a compromise was needed if the convention was to achieve its goal. Early in July 1787, the convention named a special committee to work on a compromise that would be acceptable to both small and large states. Roger Sherman, a delegate from Connecticut, proposed a compromise that became known as the Connecticut Compromise or the Great Compromise. The committee presented this plan to the full convention on July 5. According to the Connecticut Compromise, Congress would consist of two houses–a Senate and House of Representatives. Each state would have equal representation in the Senate, but representation in the House would be proportional to the population of a state. In return for equality of state representation in the Senate, the House would be given sole power to originate money **bills,** which the Senate could accept or reject but not modify. This plan for the new government was finally approved by the delegates to the Constitutional Convention of July 16, 1787.

See also Constitutional Convention; New Jersey Plan; Virginia Plan.

Constituents and Congress

Constituents are the voters who elect members to Congress. Even though Congress is charged with looking out for the interests of the nation, individual members cannot ignore the voters who elect them. Constituents thus hold the ultimate power over legislators, who must take into account voters' wishes when making decisions.

Representation: Members and Constituents

Eighteenth-century British statesman Edmund Burke identified two styles of representation. The first is the trustee, who follows his or her own personal convictions, principles, judgments, and conscience. The second type is the delegate, who consults with constituents and follows their wishes. Few members of Congress follow only one style or the other. Most are what political scientists refer to as "politicos," who assume a particular style of representation depending on the circumstances.

Members of Congress and their constituents agree on issues more often than they disagree. Where they disagree, legislators often have considerable freedom to exercise their own judgment. For one thing, the large number of decisions that senators and representatives make means they do not depend heavily on public support for any one vote. Members also have much more information and expertise about complex legislation than most of their constituents. This gives them leeway to explain their decisions to voters.

Perhaps most important, however, few constituents have extensive knowledge of or care deeply about many issues. People are more likely to judge a legislator on personality rather than on his or her stance on issues.

Serving Constituents: Communications and Casework

Legislators try to present themselves in a way that encourages the voters' trust. This presentation, which varies from lawmaker to lawmaker, is what political scientist Richard F. Fenno, Jr. has called "home style." Two essential elements in the development of this sense of trust are (1) casework and (2) communications with constituents.

Casework

Casework involves a member of Congress assisting constituents in dealing with government agencies. Virtually all members acknowledge that prompt and effective casework pays off at election time. As one member put it, "A near idiot who has competent casework can stay in Congress as long as he wants, while a genius who flubs it can be bounced very quickly."

The variety of casework is almost unlimited. Typical requests from constituents concern questions about military service, Social Security benefits, veterans' affairs, immigration, passports, unemployment claims, and problems arising from federal aid programs. The nature of the requests may also vary from one region to another. Agricultural areas, for example, might generate casework related to crop **subsidies**—government payments made to producers that allow them to sell goods at a profit.

Staff members handle most casework. At both the Washington and home offices, at least one member of a senator's or representative's staff specializes in casework. A telephone call by a staffer to the appropriate agency is often all that is needed, especially if a constituent is merely seeking information. Matters that are more complex are usually addressed through a letter to the agency. A legislator's help increases the chances of a prompt and favorable response of the constituent's case. However, members usually get personally involved only in particularly difficult cases or those involving a friend, an important supporter, an influential political figure, or large numbers of constituents.

Constituent Communications

Although most members of Congress see casework as their key function, they also understand the importance of staying in touch with their constituents. As one member has stated, "Staying in contact with the people . . . Answering the mail. That's my first priority, because it may well be their only contact with the office."

Each year, Americans send members of Congress tens of millions of letters and postcards

U.S. Representative John Dingell (D-MI, right) speaks with Iraqi Fadil Jassem on September 30, 2002, at the University of Michigan Dearborn campus. Dingell held a forum to seek input from his constituents regarding the possibility of war with Iraq. (AP Photo, John F. Martin)

requesting assistance or urging support for particular positions on issues before the House and Senate. Even so, the mail does not always accurately reflect constituents' feelings. Well educated, wealthy, and politically active individuals are much more likely to write to their representatives. Constituents are also more likely to write to members with whom they agree than to those with whom they disagree. Nevertheless, mail provides at least some measure of an issue's importance to certain constituents.

Members of Congress can reach out to constituents by mail as well, using their franking privilege. This allows legislators to send mail to their constituents free of postage charges. Members use this privilege to send newsletters and other mailings to voters in their districts, as well as to respond to constituents' correspondence.

Home Visits

Legislators receive a travel allowance that enables members to return frequently to their states or districts. While there, lawmakers often attend fund-raising and other political events and travel about the state or district, meeting with groups of constituents about their particular concerns. In addition, nearly all senators and representatives have state or district offices; some even have mobile offices that travel from town to town. Some members handle substantial amounts of casework out of their home offices, especially if regional offices of federal agencies are located nearby. Others prefer to deal with all casework in Washington and to use the district or state office primarily for public relations work or to keep track of events back home.

See also: Congressional Pay and Benefits; Congressional Travel Allowances; Franking.

Further Reading

Davidson, Roger H., and Walter J. Oleszek. *Congress and Its Members.* Eleventh edition. Washington, DC: CQ Press, 2007.

Fenno, Richard F. Jr. *Home Style: House Members in Their Districts.* Boston: Little, Brown, 2002.

Wright, James. *You and Your Congressman.* Revised edition. New York: Capricorn, 1976.

Constitution of the United States

The governing document of the United States since 1788. The Constitution not only defines the basic form of national government but also the political relationship between the federal government and the states. The Constitution established the three branches of the government—executive, legislative, and judicial—as well as a **bicameral,** or two-house, Congress.

Prior to **ratification,** or approval, of the Constitution by the states, the country operated under the Articles of Confederation. The Articles created a weak central government that had little power to compel the states to follow its orders. Many early leaders such as George Washington and Thomas Jefferson feared that the country could not survive without a stronger central authority. As a result, in 1787, national leaders met in Philadelphia to revise the Articles. The delegates to that meeting, known as the Constitutional Convention, ended up abandoning the Articles and creating an entirely new governmental structure as set forth in the Constitution. The states finally **ratified** the Constitution in 1789.

One significant difference between the Articles and the Constitution was the structure of Congress outlined by each. The Articles featured a single-house legislature in which each state had a number of seats based on its population. The Constitution, by contrast, established a bicameral legislature. In the lower house, or House of Representatives, each state received seats based on its population. Every state had two seats in the upper house, or Senate, regardless of population.

The Constitution gave equal power to both houses of Congress and established procedures that ensured that neither would dominate the other. No **bill,** for example, can become law unless both houses pass identical versions of it. If the two houses pass different versions of the same bill, they must hold a joint meeting called a Conference Committee to resolve the difference before the law can pass. In addition, the Constitution gives each house certain powers that it denies to the other. Only the House, for example, can propose revenue bills that allow the government to raise money. The Senate may accept or reject revenue bills passed by the House, but it cannot change them in any way. For its part, the Senate has the sole power to approve or reject treaties signed by the president. The Senate may also approve or reject the president's nominees to fill federal judgeships or other government positions.

Another important power divided between the houses of Congress is the power to **impeach** federal officials, or charge them with crimes or misconduct while in office. The Constitution gives the House the power to begin **impeachment** proceedings. Trials for impeached officials are held in the Senate, however, which ultimately decides whether the accused is guilty or innocent.

See also: Articles of Confederation; Bicameralism; Bill of Rights; Checks and Balances; Commerce Clause; Confirmation Power of the Senate; Constitutional Convention; Expressed Powers; House of Representatives; Impeachment Power; Implied Powers; New Jersey Plan; Power of the Purse; Senate; Separation of Powers; Treaty Power; United States Constitution, Sections 1–7, 1789, in the **Primary Source Library;** Virginia Plan; War Powers.

Constitutional Amendments Affecting the Presidency

Changes to those parts of the Constitution that deal with the election, terms of office, and powers of the President. Five **amendments**–the twelfth, twentieth, twenty-second, twenty-third, and twenty-fifth–deal with matters affecting the presidency.

Elections and Terms of Office

Under the Constitution, federal officials called electors cast the votes that determine the winners in presidential elections. At one time, their votes also determined who would be vice president. The Constitution originally provided that the candidate receiving the most electoral votes would be named president, and the candidate with the next highest number of votes would be named vice president. In 1800, however, Republican candidates Thomas Jefferson and Aaron Burr tied, with the most electoral votes. In such a case, the House of Representatives decides which candidate is the winner.

Although the Republicans had intended that Jefferson would be president and Burr vice president, there was no way of determining which one should be named president. On the thirty-sixth ballot, the House finally chose Jefferson as president. However, the confusion led Congress to propose an amendment requiring electors to cast separate votes for president and vice president. In 1803, both houses approved the proposed amendment. The states **ratified,** or voted to accept, the Twelfth Amendment in 1804.

The Twentieth Amendment, which was ratified in 1933, moved the date of the inauguration of the president and vice president from March 4 to January 20. It also required Congress to meet annually at noon on January 3. Before this change, the terms of representatives and outgoing senators did not end until March 4, four months after the election of a new Congress. In addition, the first session of the new Congress did not start until the first Monday of the following December, thirteen months after the election. The Twentieth Amendment also gives Congress power to act if a president-elect or a vice president-elect dies or fails to qualify for office by the date their terms are to begin.

The Twenty-second Amendment states that no one may be elected president more than twice. In addition, no one who has served as president for more than two years of a term for which someone else was elected president may be elected more than once. Republican members of Congress proposed the amendment soon after Democrat Franklin D. Roosevelt (1933–1945) won his fourth consecutive term as president. During House debate, Republicans insisted that the proposal had nothing to do with politics. The purpose, they said, was merely to incorporate in

Constitutional Amendments Affecting the Presidency

Amendment	Affect on the Presidency
Twelfth Amendment (1804)	Provides for electors to cast separate ballots for president and vice president
Twentieth Amendment (1933)	Moved presidential inauguration from March 4 to January 20; clarifies presidential succession
Twenty-second Amendment (1951)	Limits a president to two terms
Twenty-third Amendment (1961)	Provides the District of Columbia with electors for presidential elections
Twenty-fifth Amendment (1967)	Provides for the president to nominate a vice president if that office becomes vacant; sets up procedure in case of presidential disability; further clarifies presidential succession

Five amendments to the United States Constitution have modified some aspect of the presidency—from determining how electors cast their ballots to procedures for succession.

the Constitution the two-term tradition set by George Washington (1789–1797). That tradition had held until 1940, when Roosevelt was elected to a third term. Republicans argued that term limits would check any tendency toward dictatorship. Democrats contended that the amendment would impose "a limitation upon the people," who had a right to make their own choice of president.

The Twenty-second Amendment was submitted to the states March 24, 1947, but not ratified until February 27, 1951. In 1959, a Senate subcommittee approved a proposal to **repeal** the amendment but took no further action.

Presidential Disability and Succession

The Twenty-fifth Amendment deals with two separate but related matters: presidential disability and vice presidential succession. Before **ratification** of the Twenty-fifth Amendment, no formal procedures existed for dealing with these issues.

Section 1 of the amendment affirms that the vice president becomes president–not just acting president–upon the president's death, resignation, or removal from office. Section 2 provides that whenever a vacancy in the office of vice president exists, the president shall nominate a replacement. A majority of the House and the Senate must vote to confirm the nominee.

Sections 3 and 4 specify that the vice president assumes the president's powers and responsibilities if the president is unable, either temporarily or permanently, to perform them. The disability provisions apply in two situations. First, if the president informs Congress that he or she is unable to perform the duties of the office, the vice president becomes acting president. Second, if the vice president and a majority of the "principal officers" of executive departments determine that the president is unable to perform the duties of office, the vice president becomes acting president. In both cases, the vice president remains in that role until the president informs Congress that he or she is resuming presidential responsibilities. If the president remains incapacitated for four days, the vice president continues as acting president. Congress then has twenty-one days to determine the president's fitness for office.

See also: Amending the Constitution; President and Congress; Twelfth Amendment; Twelfth Amendment, 1804, in the **Primary Source Library;** Twentieth Amendment; Twentieth Amendment, 1933, in the **Primary Source Library;** Twenty-fifth Amendment; Twenty-fifth Amendment, 1967, in the **Primary Source Library;** Vice President.

Constitutional Convention

Meeting of representatives from 12 of the 13 original states in Philadelphia in 1787 to consider revising the Articles of Confederation. Rhode Island did not send any representatives to the convention. Nonetheless, the convention created a new government under the U.S. Constitution.

At the time of the Constitutional Convention in 1787, the reasons for seeking a more effective form of national government for the newly independent United States of America seemed clear. The state of the Union under the Articles of Confederation had become a source of growing concern to leading Americans. Many feared that the Union could not survive the strains of internal dissension and external weakness without some strengthening of central authority. However, the exact form that new government should take was by no means clear. What finally emerged from the Constitutional Convention was a document that largely reflected the shared experience of the Founders, who had grown up in a colonial America that was predominantly English in origin and who expected certain basic rights and freedoms as a part of that heritage.

Revising the Articles

In 1782, Alexander Hamilton urged the New York Assembly to ask the Continental Congress to call a general convention of the states for the purpose of revising the Articles of Confederation. The Massachusetts Legislature seconded the request in 1785. The Continental Congress studied the proposal but was unable to reach any agreement. Then, in 1785, Virginia and Maryland worked out a plan to resolve conflicts between the two states over **commerce** and navigation. This gave James Madison the idea of calling a general meeting on commercial problems. In January 1786, the Virginia Assembly issued the call for a meeting in Annapolis, Maryland, in September.

Nine states named delegates to the Annapolis convention, but the dozen persons who finally assembled in September represented only five states–New York, New Jersey, Pennsylvania, Delaware, and Virginia. Instead of seeking a commercial agreement from so small a group, Madison and Hamilton persuaded the delegates to adopt a report that described the state of the Union as "delicate and critical." The report recommended that the states appoint commissioners to meet the next May in Philadelphia to devise provisions that would make the constitution adequate for the needs of the new nation.

A New Convention Meets

Soon after the Philadelphia convention opened on May 25, 1787, the delegates were asked to decide whether to try to patch up the Articles of Confederation or to ignore them and draw up a new plan of government. The Continental Congress, the state legislatures, and many of the delegates expected the session in Philadelphia to do no more than draft proposals to revise the Articles of Confederation in a way that would somehow strengthen the Union without altering the system of state **sovereignty.** Madison and others, however, who had worked to bring about the convention, were convinced of the need for fundamental reform.

Madison and these others had come prepared, and on May 29, they seized the initiative. Edmund Randolph of Virginia introduced fifteen **resolutions** that would create a new national government of broad powers. The so-called Virginia Plan called for a national legislature of two houses, one to be elected by the people and the other by members of the other house. It also called for a national executive to be chosen by the legislature and a national judiciary. The states would be represented in both houses in proportion to their wealth or their white population.

The convention moved to form a committee to consider the resolutions. The proposals clearly planned for a central government that, unlike that of the Articles of Confederation, would operate directly upon the people and independently of the states. What the Virginia plan would create was a system in which national and state governments would exercise dual sovereignty over the people within separate areas.

To many delegates the term *national government* implied single government of potentially unlimited powers that would extinguish the independence of the states. Nevertheless, on May 30, with only Connecticut opposed and New York divided, the delegates adopted Randolph's proposal that "a National Government ought to be established consisting of a supreme Legislative, Executive, and Judiciary."

The next step was to debate and approve several of the specific proposals of the Virginia Plan. As the debate proceeded, some members from smaller states became alarmed by the insistence of the larger states on proportional representation in both houses of the proposed legislature. They believed that this would allow larger states to dominate the smaller ones. Many delegates spoke out strongly against this idea.

On June 11, the convention voted six states to five to create a Senate on the same proportional basis as the House. That decision led some delegates to draft an alternative to the Virginia Plan. The New Jersey Plan, presented on June 15, proposed amending the Articles of Confederation to give Congress authority to levy import duties and to regulate trade. It also would provide for an executive by Congress and a federal judiciary. The plan would have left each state with an equal voice in Congress

Several delegates spoke out against the New Jersey Plan, arguing that it failed to solve various serious problems of the Articles of Confederation. On June 19, the delegates were asked to decide whether there should be a full or partial reform of the Articles of Confederation. A clear majority of the delegates were committed to abandoning the Articles of Confederation and to drafting a new constitution.

A New Constitution

The task of drafting a new constitution was to take three months. Few points of agreement existed among the fifty-five delegates to the Convention. Even delegates from the same state often were divided. The Constitution could not have been written without some degree of willingness on all sides to compromise in the interests of designing a workable and acceptable plan for a new government.

The need for compromise became evident soon after defeat of the New Jersey Plan when the small states continued to demand, and the large states to oppose, equal representation in the Senate. Faced with a deadlock on this issue, the convention named a committee to seek a compromise. It proposed on July 5 that, in return for equality of state representation in the Senate, the House be given sole power to originate money **bills,** which the Senate could accept or reject but not modify. This formula was finally approved by a majority on July 16. On July 24, a committee was appointed to draft the Constitution according to the **resolutions** adopted by the convention. Without the so-called Great Compromise–sometimes called the Connecticut Compromise–the convention would have collapsed.

What finally emerged on September 17, 1787, as the Constitution of the United States, was a unique blend of national and federal systems based on republican principles of representative and limited government. It met the basic objective of the nationalists by providing for a central government of broad powers that could function independently of the states. It also met the concerns of states' rights supporters by surrounding that government with checks and balances to prevent any one branch of the government from becoming too powerful.

See also: Appropriations Bills; Connecticut Compromise; Constitution of the United States; House of Representatives; New Jersey Plan; Senate; Virginia Plan.

Further Reading

Patrick, John J. *The Bill of Rights: A History in Documents.* New York: Oxford University Press, 2003.

Contempt of Congress

Obstructing or impeding the functioning of Congress or the work of its committees. Contempt of Congress is a misdemeanor, or minor crime, punishable by a fine between $100 and $1,000 and a jail sentence of one to twelve months.

The use of the contempt power falls into two general classes. The first class involves positive acts, such as bribery, which directly or indirectly obstruct the legislature from carrying out its function. The second class involves refusal to perform acts that the legislature claims authority to compel, such as testifying or producing documents. Few cases of the first type have occurred in recent years, and the courts have had little opportunity to define positive acts of contempt. The second type, which is far more common, continues to raise many legal questions because of its greater complexity.

In 1821, the Supreme Court upheld the congressional use of the contempt power in the case, of *Anderson v. Dunn.* A man named John Anderson tried to bribe a member of the House of Representatives to help push a land claim through Congress. Anderson was tried by the House and reprimanded. He then sued Thomas Dunn, the House sergeant at arms, for assault and battery and for false arrest.

The Supreme Court rejected Anderson's complaint, arguing that Congress required the power of contempt. Without it, the Court said, Congress could be "exposed to every indignity and interruption that rudeness, caprice, and even conspiracy may meditate against it." However, the Court ruled that the contempt power was limited "to the least power adequate to the ends proposed," and imprisonment for contempt could not extend beyond the term of the current Congress.

In 1857, Congress made it a criminal offense to refuse information demanded by either chamber. The law enabled Congress to turn over contempt citations to federal prosecutors for court action. However, for a long time afterward, Congress still preferred to deal out its own punishment. The lawmakers reasoned that, by retaining control of the punishment, they might convince a reluctant witness to cooperate by agreeing to reduce the time of his confinement. Neither chamber, however, has imposed its own punishment since 1932. Since that time, all contempt of Congress citations have been prosecuted by the Justice Department in the courts.

See also: Congressional Investigations.

Continental Congresses

Meetings of representatives from the British colonies in America called to discuss colonial grievances against British rule. These meetings brought together the individuals who would lead the American Revolution and serve as the nation's government during the rebellion against Great Britain.

During the 1760s and 1770s, the British Parliament passed a number of acts aimed at raising additional revenue from the colonies by taxing a wide variety of common items including paper, glass, paint, and tea. They were dubbed the Intolerable Acts by resentful American colonists. Then, in 1774, Parliament passed an act giving the Canadian province of Quebec all of the land west of the Appalachians lying north of the Ohio River and east of the Mississippi. This further angered the colonists and created broad support for a "general congress of all the colonies" to discuss potential responses to Parliament's actions.

First Continental Congress

Every colony except Georgia, whose governor blocked the selection of delegates, was represented at the First Continental Congress in Philadelphia on September 5, 1774. While some delegates hoped to come to an agreement with the English, others wanted to defy all British controls. As the session continued, more and more delegates joined in the movement to protest and reject British policies toward the colonies.

The turning point came when Paul Revere arrived with a declaration called the Suffolk Resolves. Adopted by a convention of towns around Boston, the declaration called on Massachusetts to arm itself against efforts to "enslave America" and urged the Congress to adopt economic sanctions against England. By a vote of

An etching depicts John Hancock showing other Constitutional Convention delegates his large and prominent signature on the Declaration of Independence. Hancock, the first delegate to sign the declaration, supposedly commented, "There, I guess King George will be able to read that!" (Library of Congress)

six colonies to five, the delegates endorsed the Suffolk Resolves. The Congress then adopted a Declaration of Rights and Grievances against all British acts to which "Americans cannot submit." It agreed to ban the import and consumption of British goods, as well as the export of goods to Britain. Locally elected committees were directed to enforce the boycott by publicizing violations so that "all such foes to the rights of British-America may be publicly known and universally condemned as the enemies of American liberty." The Congress **adjourned** October 22, 1774, after agreeing to meet again the following May if necessary.

Britain's King George III (r. 1760–1820) immediately declared the colonies to be in a state of rebellion and stated that, "blows must decide whether they are to be subject to this country or independent." In the colonies, patriot forces began to gather arms and supplies and to train militia. In Massachusetts, rebels soon controlled all of the colony except Boston, where the governor, General Thomas Gage, was based with five thousand English troops.

On April 19, 1775, Gage sent 1,000 of his soldiers to destroy the patriots' supplies in Lexington and Concord. The soldiers were met by armed colonists, and shooting broke out. British casualties included 247 dead and wounded before Gage's forces could retreat to Boston. This encounter turned out to be the opening shots of the Revolutionary War, although more than a year would pass before the Americans were sufficiently united to declare their independence.

Second Continental Congress

On May 10, 1775, delegates again met in Philadelphia, still hoping to avoid war with England. Faced with pleas for help from Massachusetts, the delegates agreed to raise an army of 20,000 men, to ask the colonies for $2 million for the army's support, and to make Virginia's George Washington the army's commander in chief.

The Congress, however, also approved a petition asking George III for "a happy and permanent reconciliation" between the colonies and England. The delegates also adopted a Declaration of the Causes of Necessity of Taking up Arms, in which they denied any desire for independence from Britain, but resolved "to die free men rather than live slaves." King George responded by proclaiming a state of rebellion in America, hiring German soldiers to fight the colonists, and to encouraging Native Americans to take up arms against the colonials. The American Revolution had begun.

VIEWPOINTS

In 1754, Benjamin Franklin drew what is considered the first American editorial cartoon. In his *Pennsylvania Gazette*, Franklin published the drawing of a snake divided into separate parts, each representing one of the colonies. (Library of Congress)

The Second Continental Congress would continue to meet throughout the revolution and served as the functioning national government during that time. In 1776, delegates drafted the Declaration of Independence, formally proclaiming the country's freedom from British rule. The Second Continental Congress adjourned March 1, 1781, after drafting the Articles of Confederation, the first document under which the new nation was governed.

See also: Articles of Confederation; Constitution of the United States.

Further Reading

Cogliano, Frank. *Revolutionary America, 1763–1815: A Political History.* London: Routledge, 1999.

Gammon, C.L. *The Continental Congress: America's Forgotten Government.* Frederick, MD: PublishAmerica, 2005.

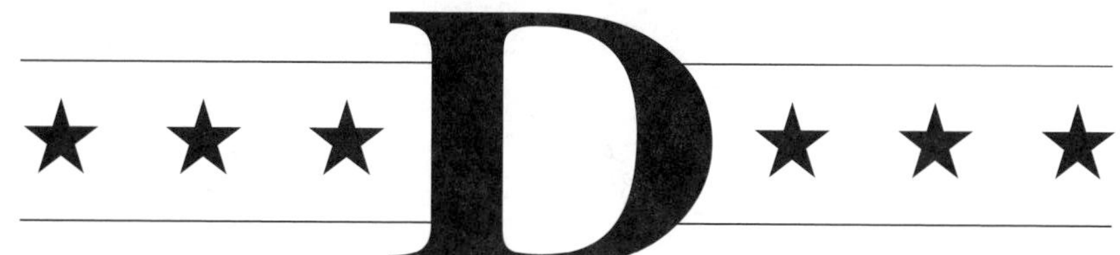

Declaration of Independence

Written by the nations' Founders in 1776, document in which the 13 English colonies declared their independence from Great Britain. Faced with increasing opposition to royal policies in 1775 and 1776, King George III (r. 1760–1820) of England proclaimed a state of rebellion in America. The British also began hiring mercenaries and encouraged the Iroquois to attack colonials. Meanwhile, in the colonies there was increasing demand for complete independence from Great Britain.

Pressure on the Continental Congress to act reached a climax on June 7, 1776, when Richard Henry Lee of Virginia introduced a resolution in Congress. This resolution stated, "these United Colonies are, and of right ought to be, free and independent States." Thomas Jefferson (1801–1809), John Adams (1797–1801), Benjamin Franklin, Roger Sherman, and Robert Livingston were named to draw up a declaration of independence. However, the draft presented to the Continental Congress on June 28, 1776, was largely Jefferson's work. Lee's resolution was adopted a few days later on July 2. Jefferson's Declaration of Independence then was debated and changed slightly before it was approved on July 4, 1776, by all of the delegates to the Continental Congress except those from New York, although they later voted for it after receiving new instructions from the state leaders.

The greater part of the Declaration of Independence—and the most important to Americans at that time—consisted of a list of every grievance against English colonial policy that had emerged since 1763. The grievances were presented as facts to prove that King George III was seeking "the establishment of an absolute Tyranny over these States" and to justify the colonists' decision to dissolve "all political connection" with Britain. However, the preamble to the Declaration was to exert the greatest influence on others as a statement of political philosophy with universal appeal. Rooted in the concept of natural rights as developed by such English philosophers as John Locke, the preamble made these assertions:

> We hold these truths to be self-evident, that all men are created equal, that they are endowed by

> their Creator with certain unalienable Rights, that among these are Life, Liberty, and the pursuit of Happiness. That to secure these rights, Governments are instituted among Men, deriving their just powers from the consent of the governed. That whenever any Form of Government becomes destructive of these ends it is the Right of the People to alter or to abolish it, and to institute new Government, laying its foundation on such principles and organizing its powers in such form, as to them shall seem most likely to effect their Safety and Happiness.

John Trumball's painting of the Declaration of Independence shows John Adams, Roger Sherman, Robert Livingston, Thomas Jefferson, and Benjamin Franklin presenting the document to Congress for signatures on July 4, 1776. (Library of Congress)

In conclusion, the signers of the Declaration, declared that "these United Colonies are, and of Right ought to be Free and Independent States," that as such "they have full Power to levy War, conclude Peace, contract Alliances, establish Commerce, and to do all other Acts and Things which Independent States may of right do," and that in support of this stand "we mutually pledge to each other our Lives, our Fortunes, and our Sacred Honor." With the signing of the Declaration of Independence the Founders declared a full break from Great Britain and announced the formation of a new nation–the United States of America.

District of Columbia

City that serves as the seat of the federal government. Because it was specifically created to house the government, the District is quite different from other cities. Congress exercises a great deal of control over city operations, and District residents do not enjoy some basic rights granted to other American citizens. The question of whether the city's affairs should be handled by Congress or a locally elected government has never been fully answered and remains a source of controversy.

Founding and Government

The first Congress favored a location for the national capital in Pennsylvania, but it failed to name a site before adjourning in 1789. The states of Virginia and Maryland then stepped in to offer to donate land along their common border on the Potomac River to house the District. A 1790 act of Congress established the federal district on the Potomac, and the government moved in by April 1800.

In 1802, Congress set up a government for the city of Washington consisting of a mayor appointed by the president and a twelve-member council elected by the people. In 1812, it permitted the council to select the mayor, and in 1820 to let the voters elect him. That form of government continued until debt and race issues led Congress to take control over the District in 1871.

After the Civil War (1861–1865), the city's mayor, Sayles Bowen, launched a series of projects that put the District into financial trouble. When Bowen's successor fared no better at solving the city's fiscal ills, Congress looked to another form of government for the District. In 1871, Congress adopted a modified territorial form of government for the District. The law provided for a governor appointed by the president, an elected nonvoting delegate in the

House of Representatives, an assembly partly appointed by the president and partly elected by the people, and a board of public works appointed by the president. In 1878, this government was replaced by a three-member commission appointed by Congress.

The commission form of government prevailed in the District of Columbia until 1967. In that year, President Lyndon B. Johnson sent Congress a plan to replace the three-member commission with a single commissioner, an assistant commissioner, and a nine-member city council, all to be appointed by the president and confirmed by the Senate.

In 1973, Congress passed a more complete home rule law that called for election of a mayor and a thirteen-member city council. Congress, however, continues to make annual budget decisions for the District. In addition, the council cannot impose taxes on federal property, amend or repeal any act of Congress affecting the District, or raise the height limitation on buildings. To ensure its continued control over the District, Congress reserved the right to legislate for the District at any time and to veto any action taken by the city council.

Voting and Representation in Congress

Residents for the District were not eligible to cast votes in presidential elections until 1961. The previous year, Congress authorized a proposed constitutional amendment allowing District of Columbia voters to elect three electors for president and vice president. The Twenty-third Amendment quickly won ratification, or approval by the states, in early 1961.

Although originally ineligible to elect the president, District residents had nonvoting representation in Congress briefly in the nineteenth century. An 1871 law let them elect a nonvoting delegate to the House for service on the District of Columbia Committee. The post was later abolished when Congress voted to adopt a commission form of government for the District. Bills to reestablish nonvoting representation were introduced repeatedly to Congress, but they made little significant progress until 1969. In that year, President Richard M. Nixon (1969–1974)

An engraving shows the White House shortly after it was completed in the early 1800s. (The Granger Collection, New York)

Governing the District

1802–1871	Mayor-Council Government
1871–1874	Territorial Government
1874–1967	Commission Government
1967–1974	Commissioner-Council Government
1974–	Limited Home Rule

Over the years, Congress has established various forms of government for the District of Columbia, the nation's capital.

endorsed the idea of a constitutional amendment giving the District voting representation in Congress. He also advocated a nonvoting delegate in the House until the states ratified such an amendment. This proposal won approval of both houses in 1970, and the following year the District regained its nonvoting delegate.

In 1978, Congress approved a constitutional amendment to treat the District as a state for purposes of congressional and electoral college representation. The state legislatures, however, were reluctant to ratify an amendment that would give another political entity equality with the states in Congress. The amendment died at the end of the seven-year ratification period.

See also: Non-Voting Members of Congress.

Further Reading

Melder, Keith E. *City of Magnificent Intentions: A History of Washington, District of Columbia.* Silver Spring, MD: Intac, 1997.

Eastland, James O.

See Seniority System.

Elections, House of Representatives

Every two years, voters elect members to the lower house of Congress, the House of Representatives. The Constitution specified two-year terms so that voters would have a chance to pass judgment frequently on their representatives.

Constitutional Foundation

Early American leaders who preferred a strong central government believed that the lower house should be elected "by the people immediately," as James Madison put it. The House "was to be the grand depository of the democratic principles of the government," said Virginia's George Mason. Those who were suspicious of a national government preferred election of the House by the state legislatures. "The people immediately should have as little to do" with electing the government as possible, said Connecticut's Roger Sherman. The final draft of the Constitution, however, called for popular election of the House.

The Constitution largely left the qualification of voters to the states. At first, most states enacted property qualifications for voting. A democratic trend early in the nineteenth century, however, swept away most property qualifications. By the 1830s, virtually all adult white males were eligible to vote. Nevertheless, the system of local elections, held under rules that varied from state to state, would lead to a number of problems over time.

Many delegates to the Constitutional Convention preferred annual elections for the House, believing that the body should reflect as closely as possible the wishes of the people. James Madison, however, argued for a three-year term, to let the representatives gain knowledge and experience in national and local affairs. The result was a compromise on a two-year term.

Article I, Section 2, of the Constitution established the size of the original House of Representatives. It also required Congress to apportion the House, or divide its seats between the states, according to population as determined by a national census. The first census was scheduled to occur in 1790, with a new census to take place every ten years.

Changing Election Practices

Over time, Congress has amended some House election practices originally written into the Constitution. For example, in 1792 it determined that the House should have one representative for every 33,000 inhabitants, 105 members in all, and fixed the number of members for each state. Nevertheless, Congress has devised new apportionment schemes every ten years, constantly revising them to keep up with the country's growing population. As new states were added, and established states grew in population, the House added many new seats. In 1911, Congress passed a law limiting the number of seats in the House to 435. From that point on, each state that added House members because of population growth took seats from states that were not growing as rapidly.

Perhaps the most dramatic changes came following the Civil War (1861–1865). Article I, Section 2, of the Constitution contained a formula that counted slaves as three-fifths of a person for apportionment purposes. Thus, the total population of a state to be used in determining its congressional representation would be the free population plus three-fifths of the slave population. After the Civil War, blacks were fully counted for the purposes of apportionment. The Fourteenth Amendment, ratified, or approved, in 1868, required that apportionment be based on "the whole number of persons in each State. . . . " On this basis, several southern states tried to claim immediate additional representation on their readmission to the Union. Tennessee, Virginia, and South Carolina, for example, each chose an extra U.S. representative between 1868 and 1870. The House declined to seat the additional representatives, however, ruling that the states would have to await the 1870 census for any changes in their representation.

The Fourteenth Amendment also provided for reducing the House representation of any state that denied the vote to any male citizen over twenty-one. However, it never enforced this effort to prevent the southern states from denying the vote to newly freed slaves. Congress instead frequently filed challenges against members elected from the South. Between 1881 and 1897, the House unseated eighteen Democrats from the former Confederate states, often on charges that black voting rights were abused in their districts.

Contested Elections

Contested House elections have been relatively common occurrences. Many times a losing candidate feels that he or she actually received more votes than the official count showed. Most scholars agree that the number of contested congressional elections since 1789 probably is in the hundreds. Congress passed a series of laws in the eighteenth and nineteenth centuries that established procedures for settling contested elections. The Federal Contested Election Act of 1969 replaced these earlier laws. The new law prescribed procedures for challenging election results and presenting testimony, but did not establish criteria to make final decisions.

See also: Elections, Senatorial; Reapportionment.

Further Reading

Krasno, Johnathan S. *Challengers, Competition, and Reelection: Comparing Senate and House Elections.* New Haven, CT: Yale University Press, 1997.

Welborn, Angie. *House Contested Election Cases: 1933–2000.* New York: Novinka, 2003.

Decision Makers

Henry Clay (1777–1852)

Known as the "Great Compromiser," Henry Clay represented Kentucky in both the United States House of Representatives and Senate. Clay was born in 1777 in Hanover County, Virginia. In 1797, he moved to Lexington, Kentucky, to set up a law practice, and quickly got involved in local politics.

In the summer of 1811, Clay was elected to the United States House of Representatives. He was chosen as Speaker of the House on the first day of his first session, a unique and surprising event, in that the House Speaker is traditionally a senior member with years of experience.

Tensions over the slavery issue flared in 1820 when Missouri sought admission to the Union as a slave state. Missouri's admission would upset the **balance of power** in the Senate, where eleven free states and eleven slave states were represented. To resolve the crisis, Clay proposed what has become know as the Missouri Compromise. Under the terms of this agreement, Missouri would be admitted to the Union as a slave state. Slavery would be banned north of 36'30° latitude, except in Missouri. To maintain balance in the Senate, Maine, which had been part of Massachusetts, would be admitted as a free state.

In 1824, Henry Clay ran for the presidency, but won only 37 electoral votes—behind Andrew Jackson (99 votes), John Quincy Adams (84 votes), and William H. Crawford (41 votes). Because no candidate re-

Elections, Senatorial

Every two years, elections are held to fill one-third of the seats in the Senate. Senators serve six-year terms that are staggered to ensure that only one of a state's two Senate seats is contested at a time. This is one of several differences between Senate and House election procedures outlined in the Constitution

Constitutional Foundations

The Senate resulted from the so-called "Great Compromise" at the Constitutional Convention in 1787. Smaller states wanted equal representation in Congress, fearing that representation by population would lead to domination by the large states. Larger states naturally wanted a legislature based on population, where their strength would prevail. In the end, the delegates agreed to apportion, or divide, House seats by population while giving each state two Senate seats.

Delegates also disagreed on how senators should be chosen. Some wanted state legislatures to nominate candidates that the House would then vote on. Others argued that the people should directly elect the Senate as well as the House. Eventually, delegates decided that each state's legislature would elect the senators for that state. They reasoned that legislatures were more able than the electorate to give proper thought to the selection. This also gave the individual states a greater interest in supporting the new national government.

ceived a majority of the electoral vote, the House of Representatives was required to select the president from among the top three candidates. Clay gave his support to Adams, and the House awarded Adams the presidency. Soon after, Adams appointed Clay as secretary of state. Outraged, Jackson and his followers claimed that Clay and Adams had made a "corrupt bargain."

In 1849, Clay was again elected to the U.S. Senate from Kentucky, and soon another sectional crisis loomed. After the United States acquired vast new western lands after the Mexican-American War (1846–1848), the question arose of whether slavery should be allowed to extend into the new territories.

In 1850, California applied for admission to the Union as a free state. Members of Congress from slave states strongly opposed the request. Once again, Clay developed a solution, which has become known as the Compromise of 1850. Under the terms of this agreement, California would be admitted to the Union as a free state, but slavery was not specifically prohibited in the other western territories. The state of Texas gave up its claims to other western lands in return for financial compensation. Finally, a strict Fugitive Slave Law was passed.

Henry Clay died in 1852, in Washington, DC, at the age of 75. He was the first person to lie in state in the U.S. Capitol before his burial in Lexington Cemetery in Kentucky. A 1957 commission chaired by John F. Kennedy called Clay one of the five greatest senators in American history.

Changing Procedures and Disputes

At first, the legislatures made their own arrangements for electing senators. Many states required the two houses of the legislature, sitting separately, to agree on the same candidate. Others required a ballot of the two houses in a joint session. These procedures resulted in frequent deadlocks and delays in choosing senators. As a result, in 1866 Congress used its constitutional authority to establish procedures for the legislatures to follow that streamlined the process of electing senators. The new system, however, did not have the desired effect. The requirement for a majority vote continued to result in voting deadlocks.

The system had other faults as well. Members of the state legislatures who chose senators

A poll worker (left) oversees a voter as she casts her ballot in a senatorial election. (AP Photo, Mark Humphrey)

SPOTLIGHT

Disputed Senate Elections

The closest Senate election since popular voting for the Senate was instituted in 1913 occurred on November 5, 1974, in New Hampshire. Republican Louis C. Wyman led Democrat John A. Durkin by only two votes after the ballots were counted and recounted. The election spawned a long, bitter, and embarrassing dispute in the Senate covering seven months and forty-one roll-call votes. It ended when the Senate for the first time declared a seat vacant because of its inability to decide the outcome of an election.

The final unofficial returns gave Wyman a 355-vote margin over Durkin, but a recount found Durkin the winner by ten votes. The state ballot commission examined the recount and declared Wyman the winner by two votes. Durkin filed a petition of contest with the Senate on December 27, challenging Wyman's right to the seat and defending the validity of his own recount victory. On January 5, 1975, Wyman filed his own petition in the Senate urging that Durkin's petition be dismissed. He also asked that the disputed seat be declared vacant, to open the way for a new election in New Hampshire.

On January 28, the Senate turned aside Republican attempts to seat Wyman temporarily and to declare the seat vacant. It then voted to send the dispute to the Senate Rules and Administration Committee. The Rules Committee agreed to examine and recount the ballots in dispute. The committee, however, failed to agree on twenty-seven of the ballots, and the matter went to the Senate floor to be resolved.

Floor consideration of the disputed election began June 12 but dragged on with no resolution. The Senate began to spend less and less time each day on the dispute, but neither side appeared ready to compromise. Public pressure mounted for the Senate to declare the seat vacant and hold a new election. Durkin ultimately agreed to a new election, which he won with 53.6 percent of the vote. Durkin finally took his seat on September 18, 1975, more than ten months after the original election.

were subject to intense and unethical lobbying, or political persuasion, by supporters of various candidates. Because of the frequent charges of illegal election tactics, the Senate found itself involved in many election disputes.

The main criticism of legislative elections was that they distorted, or even blocked, the will of the people. Throughout the nineteenth century, a movement for popular elections in several states had given voters the right to choose governors and presidential electors. Now attention focused on the Senate. Popular pressure, especially in several western states, led the Senate to approve a constitutional amendment for the popular election of senators in 1911. Congress passed the amendment in 1912, and the states ratified, or approved it, the following year.

Popular election did not result in a dramatic change in the Senate's membership. In the first election after passage of the amendment, voters returned all but two of the twenty-five incumbents, or previous office holders, to their Senate seats. Even today, incumbents win reelection more than 90 percent of the time.

Senate Classes

The Framers of the Constitution envisioned the Senate as a more deliberative body than the House–one that would take more time and care in making decisions. They also felt that senators needed time to gain experience in their positions so they could better serve the nation. This led the Framers to settle on longer terms for senators–six years as opposed to two years for House members–and to design a system to slow down the turnover of membership in the Senate.

While the Constitution called for the entire House to stand for election every two years, the Framers intended the Senate to change membership much more gradually. To achieve this goal, the Constitution divided senators into three separate classes, or groups, of senators. Each class of senators stands for election every two years, so only one-third of the Senate is subject to change at a time.

In order to stagger the election years for each class, at least one senator from each of the original thirteen states served a term of less than six years. A third of the original senators served two-year terms, a third served four-year terms, and a third served six-year terms. All individuals subsequently elected to those Senate seats served six-year terms. As each new state was admitted to the Union, its initial senators were also assigned to different classes, with some serving terms shorter than six years. Congress assigns new senators in such a way as to balance the number of senators in each class.

See also: Classes of Senators; Elections, House of Representatives.

Further Reading

Krasno, Johnathan S. *Challengers, Competition, and Reelection: Comparing Senate and House Elections.* New Haven, CT: Yale University Press, 1997.

Electoral College and Electors

Institution established by the Constitution to choose the president; the members of that institution who cast presidential ballots. Although the United States holds a popular election for president, the winner is not actually determined by the outcome of the popular vote. Instead, electors from each state cast votes that are intended to reflect the will of the voters.

Early History

The Framers of the Constitution, wary of popular opinion, were unwilling to accept direct popular election of the president. They intended to leave selection of the president to the country's most learned and distinguished citizens. These presidential electors–the electoral college–were to be chosen by the states in any manner each state determined. Until 1832, there were three basic methods for choosing electors: popular vote in statewide contests, popular vote in district contests, and selection by state legislatures.

This changed with the growth of party politics. Political parties began to back statewide popular elections, which would allow the winning party to control all of the state's electors. By 1836, all states except South Carolina were choosing electors by statewide popular vote (South Carolina adopted popular voting for presidential electors after the Civil War). Since that time, winner-take-all popular vote for electors has been the almost universal practice, except for a few isolated cases. In 1969, the Maine Legislature enacted a district system for choosing presidential electors. Two of the state's four electors are selected by statewide vote, while the other two are awarded to the party that wins each of the state's two congressional districts. The system is still in force, and has also been adopted by Nebraska.

The number of a state's electors is determined by its number of representatives in Congress.

How Electors Vote

When voters go to the polls on general election day, they see the names of presidential candidates on the ballot. However, they are actually casting their votes for electors who have pledged to vote for the candidate who wins the state's popular vote. The electors usually are chosen at state party meetings called caucuses, at party conventions, or in primary elections.

Disputed Electoral Votes

The Constitution offers no guidelines for handling disputed electoral ballots. This has led several times to controversy. The electoral bargain that settled the presidential election of 1876, for example, created one of the country's greatest electoral crises.

Early election night returns indicated that Democrat Samuel Tilden had been elected over Republican Rutherford B. Hayes. Tilden led the popular vote by more than a quarter of a million votes. However, by the following morning it was clear that if the Republicans could hold on to win South Carolina, Florida, and Louisiana, Hayes would win 185 electoral votes to 184 for Tilden. If a single elector in any of those states voted for Tilden, it would throw the election to the Democrats. To complicate matters, several states filed two sets of electoral vote counts, and in Oregon a question arose over whether a Republican elector was legally eligible for the position.

To solve the dilemma, Congress established a fifteen-member Electoral Commission that had final authority over disputed electoral votes. In every disputed case, the commission voted 8–7 for Hayes, with all eight Republican members backing Hayes. Angry Democrats in the House threatened to launch a filibuster so that the vote count could not be completed before inauguration day. Hayes' backers, however, reached a compromise with southern Democrats. In return for their support, Hayes agreed to withdraw federal troops that had occupied the South since the end of the Civil War and to make other concessions. On March 2, 1877, Congress declared Hayes the winner.

Not until 1887 did Congress enact permanent legislation to handle disputed electoral votes. The Electoral Count Act of that year gave each state final authority in determining whether its choice of electors was legal. Challenged electoral votes could be sustained by Congress only upon majority vote of both the House and Senate. The act also established procedures to guide Congress in counting the electoral votes.

The election of 1876 also pointed out another controversial aspect of the electoral college system; the fact that a candidate can win the popular vote, yet lose the electoral vote. This has happened three other times in U.S. history: in 1824, 1888, and 2000.

Faithless Electors

Nothing in the Constitution requires electors to vote in any particular way. Regardless of his or her party affiliation, an elector cannot be forced to vote for the party's candidate for president. In practice, almost all electors do vote for their party's candidate, but legally they are free to vote for whomever they choose. This faithless-elector phenomenon has been a long-standing controversy. On at least nine occasions, presidential electors voted for a candidate other than their own party's choice. In none of these instances, however, did the switch alter the election result.

See also: Power to Select the President; 📖 Twentieth Amendment, 1804, in the **Primary Source Library.**

Further Reading

Hewson, Martha S. *The Electoral College.* New York: Chelsea House, 2002.

Ethics, Congressional

Rules or standards governing the conduct of members of Congress. Concern for the ethical conduct of members of Congress is reflected in the Constitution, federal statutes, and Senate and House rules. Congress has several ways of dealing with ethical violations of its members, up to and including expulsion.

Constitutional and Legal Basis

Article I, Section 5, of the Constitution states "Each House may determine the Rules of its Proceedings, punish its Members for disorderly Behavior, and, with the Concurrence of two thirds, expel a Member." The Constitution goes on to list a number of cases in which members of Congress may be disciplined. For example, Article I, Section 6, forbids members from holding any other "civil Office under the Authority of the United States" while serving in Congress. Section 9 prohibits members from accepting an "Office, or Title, of any kind whatever, from any King, Prince, or foreign State."

A series of U.S. laws also make it a federal crime for members of Congress to engage in certain actions. Prohibited acts, excluding those relating to campaign spending, include:

- Soliciting or receiving a bribe for the performance of any official act.
- Soliciting or receiving anything of value for any official act performed or to be performed by the member.
- Soliciting or receiving any compensation for services in relation to any matter in which the United States is a party or has a direct and substantial interest.
- Practicing law in the Court of Claims.
- Receiving anything of value in return for using or promising to use influence to obtain an appointive government office for anyone.
- Buying a vote, promising employment, soliciting political contributions from federal employees, or threatening the job of a federal employee who fails to give a campaign contribution.

A-Z

Members convicted of any of the above violations are subject to fines ranging from $1,000 to $10,000 and prison terms from one to fifteen years.

Codes of Conduct

In addition to the laws mentioned above, members must also abide by codes of conduct adopted by the Senate and House of Representatives in 1958. According to this code, which applies to all federal government employees, any person in government service should:

1. Put loyalty to the highest moral principles and to country above loyalty to persons, party, or Government department.
2. Uphold the Constitution, laws, and legal regulations of the United States and of all governments therein and never be a party to their evasion.
3. Give a full day's labor for a full day's pay; giving to the performance of his duties his earnest effort and best thought.
4. Seek to find and employ more efficient and economical ways of getting tasks accomplished.
5. Never discriminate unfairly by the dispensing of special favors or privileges to anyone, whether for remuneration or not; and never accept, for himself or his family, favors or benefits under circumstances which might be construed by reasonable persons as influencing the performance of his governmental duties.
6. Make no private promises of any kind binding upon the duties of office, since a Government employee has no private word which can be binding on public duty.
7. Engage in no business with the Government, either directly or indirectly, which is inconsistent with the conscientious performance of his governmental duties.
8. Never use any information coming to him confidentially in the performance of government duties as a means for making private profit.
9. Expose corruption wherever discovered.
10. Uphold these principles, ever conscious that public office is a public trust.

Revising the Code

While binding on members, the code had no legal force. Ten years after adopting it, the House and Senate separately formulated new rules intended to help prevent conflicts of interest in Congress. At the time, both chambers also established special committees on ethics. In 1964, the Senate voted to set up a strictly bipartisan committee to investigate charges of improper conduct by senators and Senate employees.

Following the Watergate scandal in the 1970s, Congress strengthened its ethical standards, which led to a major congressional reform movement. Like most waves of reform, this one was followed by counter-movements and some backsliding, but its major achievements remained historic. For the first time, the law required members of Congress to disclose the source and amount of major campaign contributions. Congressional members and top officers of the executive and judicial branches were also required to disclose their financial holdings.

Reluctance to Punish

Despite the toughened ethics rules, Congress has shown little determination to punish ethical indiscretions by its own members. Congress has expelled few of its own members, and tends to shy away from taking harsh measures against those found guilty of ethics violations. For example, members found guilty of influence peddling in the 1977–1978 "Koreagate" scandal received little more than a slap on the wrist.

Senators and representatives have even less enthusiasm for serving on the ethics committees. Most members avoid those committees, which must deal with all the behavior problems of their colleagues, and thus require every member to take a stand. The two relatively unpopular panels are the Senate Ethics Committee and the House Committee on Standards of Official Conduct.

In addition, committee members must continue to work with colleagues they have censured. William L. Armstrong of Colorado, who participated in the unanimous denouncement of his Republican colleague, Minnesota's Dave Durenberger, in 1990, put it this way: "When this is all over and after we have voted to denounce him, we will still want him to be our friend. We will still want to go down to the dining room and have lunch with him."

Enforcement

The most common form of discipline in response to an ethics violation is censure, or a public reprimand. In the House, censure is always public; the lesser punishment of a simple reprimand occurs in private. In the Senate, both censures and reprimands are administered privately. The House has censured twenty-two members in its history; the Senate has done so nine times.

Congress has expelled a total of nineteen members—fifteen from the Senate and four from the House. The first was Tennessee Senator William Blount, expelled in 1797 for treason. Blount was convicted of urging Native American tribes to help Great Britain invade Florida. Most of the remaining expulsions involved members from Southern states who supported the Confederacy during the Civil War (1861–1865). The Senate expelled eleven Southern members immediately following the secession of the Southern states in 1861. The House expelled three of its members at the same time for the same reason. The following year the Senate expelled three more members for supporting the rebellion.

Recent Cases in the Senate

Aside from the extraordinary case of the Civil War actions, the Senate has shied away from both expulsion and censure. As of early 2008, no senator had been expelled since 1862 or censured since 1967. Two senators, Democrat Harrison Williams of New Jersey and Republican Bob Packwood of Oregon, resigned in the face of certain expulsion in 1982 and 1995, respectively.

During House testimony, two former associates of Jack Abramoff, a lobbyist and businessman, invoked their Fifth Amendment right not to answer questions. Because of his involvement in various scandals, Abramoff was sentenced to five years and ten months in federal prison. (AP Photo, Gerald Herbert, File)

The Senate has censured just seven members since 1861 and only three since 1954. In 1967, Democrat Thomas Dodd of Connecticut was censured for using campaign funds for personal benefit and for "conduct unbecoming a Senator." In 1979, Democrat Herman Talmadge of Georgia was censured for financial misconduct and improper reporting of campaign receipts and expenditures. The most recent censure was handed out in 1990 to Republican David Durenberger of Minnesota for unethical conduct relating to reimbursement of Senate expenses and acceptance of payments and gifts.

Recent Cases in the House

The House has expelled just two members in its history. In 1980, Democrat Michael Myers of Pennsylvania was expelled after being convicted of bribery in connection with the Abscam investigation. In 2002, Ohio Democrat James Traficant was expelled after he was convicted of bribery, obstruction of justice, defrauding the government, racketeering, and tax evasion.

Several other House members have resigned rather than face expulsion. The House Ethics Committee recommended expelling New York Democrat Mario Biaggi in 1988 after his conviction for accepting illegal gifts. Biaggi resigned before the House acted on the motion. In 1995, the House filed an expulsion resolution against Democrat Walter Tucker of California, who was convicted of extortion and tax evasion. Tucker resigned on the day the resolution was filed. In 2006, Republican Bob Ney of Ohio resigned his seat after being convicted in a bribery scandal involving high-powered Washington lobbyist Jack Abramoff. Florida Republican Mark Foley resigned the same year after it was revealed that he sent sexually suggestive emails to current and former House pages.

The full House has censured only five members since 1900. The most recent involved Illinois Republican Daniel Crane and Massachusetts Democrat Gerry Studds. In 1983, each was discovered to have been involved in a sexual relationship with a House page. The House Ethics Committee recommended privately reprimanding both members, but the full House voted to publicly censure them instead.

See also: Abscam; Censure of Senator Joseph McCarthy, 1954, in the **Primary Source Library;** Pages, Congressional; Teapot Dome Scandal; Watergate Hearings.

Further Reading

Hilton, Stanley G., and Anne-Renee Testa. *Glass Houses: Shocking Profiles of Congressional Sex Scandals and Other Unofficial Misconduct.* New York: St. Martin's, 1998.

Stern, Philip M. *The Best Congress Money Can Buy.* New York: Pantheon, 1988.

Tolchin, Susan J., and Martin Tolchin. *Glass Houses: Congressional Ethics and the Politics of Venom.* Boulder, CO: Westview, 2004.

Exclusion of Members of Congress

The practice of refusing to admit an individual to Congress because he or she does not meet the qualifications for office set forth in the Constitution. Exclusion is a very rare practice; only three senators-elect and ten representatives-elect have been denied seats because of a lack of qualifications.

Consitutional Grounds for Exclusion

Article I of the Constitution outlines the qualifications for membership in the House and Senate. Representatives must be at least twenty-five years old, must have been citizens of the United States for the past seven years, and must live in the state they represent. Senators must be at least 30 years old, must have been citizens for at least the past nine years, and must also live in the state they seek to represent. Congress may refuse to seat a person who fails to meet any of these requirements.

The Fourteenth Amendment, passed in 1868, added another grounds for exclusion. Any federal official who swears an oath to uphold the Constitution, but later rebels against the U.S. or aids its enemies, may not serve in Congress. This condition was added to exclude former U.S. officials who backed the Confederacy during the Civil War (1861–1865).

All three of the senators-elect denied seats were excluded under these rules. Pennsylvania's Albert Gallatin had not been a citizen nine years when the Pennsylvania Legislature elected him to the Senate in 1793. James Shields of Illinois was denied a seat in 1848 because he would not be a citizen until October 20, 1849. Congress declared his election void, but then elected Shields to fill the vacant seat beginning October 27, 1849. In 1866, Phillip F. Thomas of Maryland was excluded on grounds of disloyalty because he had given $100 to his son when his son had entered Confederate military service.

Other Exclusions

In addition to the qualifications set forth in the Constitution, Congress may exclude members for behavior considered immoral or unethical. Several of the exclusions from the House occurred on these grounds. Benjamin F. Whittemore, a Republican from South Carolina, was censured, or reprimanded, by the House in 1870 for selling appointments to the U.S. Military Academy. He resigned in February of that year, but was reelected to the same Congress. The House, however, voted to exclude Whittemore.

Adam Clayton Powell (1908–1972) was excluded from the House of Representatives in 1967 because of allegations of misuse of congressional funds and corruption. (AP Photo, Charles Gorry)

The House based two exclusions on polygamy, or having several wives. George Q. Cannon from the Utah Territory was accused of polygamy after he was first elected in 1872. He survived that challenge, but in 1882 the issue arose again. The House, considering both of Cannon's polygamy and doubts about the validity of his election, declared his seat vacant. In 1900, members of the House questioned the right of Utah's Brigham H. Roberts to take his seat. The House refused to seat Roberts, who had been found guilty of polygamy some years earlier.

Exclusion Cases Rejected

Exclusion proceedings have not always blocked a member from taking a seat. Severe illness prevented Democrat John M. Niles from taking the Senate seat to which the Connecticut Legislature had elected him in 1843. Because Niles showed signs of mental strain when he arrived in Washington in April 1844, the Senate appointed a committee to consider his case. The committee reported that Niles was "laboring under mental and physical debility, but is not of unsound mind." It said there was "no sufficient reason why he be not qualified and permitted to take his seat," which he did within a month.

Mississippi's Hiram R. Revels, a Republican elected to the Senate in 1870, was challenged on the basis of length of citizenship. As a former slave, he had not become a citizen until the Fourteenth Amendment was ratified, or approved, by the states, in 1868. The Senate ruled that, since the amendment made all former slaves citizens, Revels was eligible to serve and seated him.

In 1903, Utah citizens challenged Republican senator-elect Reed Smoot, claiming that he favored polygamy and opposed the separation of church and state. Smoot took the oath of office on a temporary basis, but the Committee on Privileges and Elections concluded that he was not entitled to his seat. However, the Senate did not vote on the issue until years later, in 1907. By that time, Smoot had been in office four years. Senator Philander C. Knox of Pennsylvania argued that a two-thirds vote was required because the action involved expelling a sitting senator, not exclusion. Senators approved the two-thirds requirement, but it never mattered. The Senate rejected both the motions to expel and to exclude Smoot.

See also: Ethics, Congressional; House of Representatives; Senate.

Excluded Members of Congress

Senate

Congress	Session	Year	Member-elect	Grounds	Disposition
3rd	1st	1793	Albert Gallatin, D-Pa.	Citizenship	*Excluded*
11th	1st	1809	Stanley Griswold, D-Ohio	Residence	Admitted
28th	1st	1844	John M. Niles, D-Conn.	Sanity	Admitted
31st	Special	1849	James Shields, D-Ill.	Citizenship	*Excluded*
37th	2nd	1861	Benjamin Stark, D-Ore.	Loyalty	Admitted
40th	1st	1867	Phillip F. Thomas, D-Md.	Loyalty	*Excluded*
41st	2nd	1870	Hiram R. Revels, R-Miss.	Citizenship	Admitted
41st	2nd	1870	Adelbert Ames, R-Miss.	Residence	Admitted
59th	2nd	1907	Reed Smoot, R-Utah	Mormonism	Admitted[a]
69th	2nd	1926	Arthur R. Gould, R-Maine	Character	Admitted
74th	1st	1935	Rush D. Holt, D-W.Va.	Age	Admitted
75th	1st	1937	George L. Berry, D-Tenn.	Character	Admitted
77th	2nd	1942	William Langer, R-N.D.	Character	Admitted[a]
80th	1st	1947	Theodore G. Bilbo, D-Miss.	Character	Died before Senate Acted
83rd	2nd	1964	Pierre Salinger, D-Calif.	Residence	Admitted

House

Congress	Session	Year	Member-elect	Grounds	Disposition
1st	1st	1789	William L. Smith, Fed-S.C.	Citizenship	Admitted
10th	1st	1807	Philip B. Key, Fed.-Md.	Residence	Admitted
10th	1st	1807	William McCreery,–Md.	Residence	Admitted
18th	1st	1823	Gabriel Richard, Ind-Mich. Terr	Citizenship	Admitted
18th	1st	1823	John Bailey, Ind-Mass.	Residence	*Excluded*
18th	1st	1823	John Forsyth, D-Ga.	Residence	Admitted
27th	1st	1841	David Levy, R-Fla. Terr.	Citizenship	Admitted
36th	1st	1859	John Y. Brown, D-Ky.	Age	Admitted
40th	1st	1867	William H. Hooper, D-Utah Terr.	Mormonism	Admitted
40th	1st	1867	Lawrence S. Trimble, D-Ky.	Loyalty	Admitted
40th	1st	1867	John Y. Brown, D-Ky.	Loyalty	*Excluded*

Excluded Members of Congress, *continued*

House					
Congress	Session	Year	Member-elect	Grounds	Disposition
40th	1st	1867	John D. Young, D-Ky.	Loyalty	*Excluded*
40th	1st	1867	Roderick R. Butler, R-Tenn.	Loyalty	Admitted
40th	1st	1867	John A. Wimpy, Ind-Ga.	Loyalty	*Excluded*
40th	1st	1867	W.D. Simpson, Ind-S.C.	Loyalty	*Excluded*
41st	1st	1869	John M. Rice, D-Ky.	Loyalty	Admitted
41st	2nd	1870	Lewis McKenzie, Unionist-Va.	Loyalty	Admitted
41st	2nd	1870	George W. Booker, Conservative-Va.	Loyalty	Admitted
41st	2nd	1870	Benjamin F. Whittemore, R-S.C.	Malfeasance	*Excluded*
41st	2nd	1870	John C. Conner, D-Texas	Misconduct	Admitted
43rd	1st	1873	George Q. Cannon, R-Utah Terr.	Mormonism	Admitted
43rd	2nd	1874	George Q. Cannon, R-Utah Terr.	Polygamy	Admitted
47th	1st	1881	John S. Barbour, D-Va.	Residence	Admitted
47th	1st	1882	George Q. Cannon, R-Utah Terr.	Polygamy	Seat Vacated[b]
50th	1st	1887	James B. White, R-Ind.	Citizenship	Admitted
56th	1st	1899	Robert W. Wilcox, Ind-Hawaii Terr.	Bigamy, Treason	Admitted
56th	1st	1900	Brigham H. Roberts, D-Utah	Polygamy	*Excluded*
59th	1st	1905	Anthony Michalek, R-Ill.	Citizenship	Admitted
66th	1st	1919	Victor L. Berger, Socialist-Wis.	Sedition	*Excluded*
66th	2nd	1920	Victor L. Berger, Socialist-Wis.	Sedition	*Excluded*
69th	1st	1926	John W. Langley, R-Ky.	Criminal Misconduct	Resigned
70th	1st	1927	James M. Beck, R-Pa.	Residence	Admitted
71st	1st	1929	Ruth B. Owen, D-Fla.	Citizenship	Admitted
90th	1st	1967	Adam C. Powell Jr., D-N.Y.	Misconduct	*Excluded*[c]
96th	1st	1979	Richard A. Tonry, D-La.	Vote fraud	Resigned

***Notes:* a. The Senate decided that a two-thirds majority, as in expulsion cases, would be required for exclusion. The resolution proposing exclusion did not receive a two-thirds majority. b. Discussions of polygamy and an election contest led to a declaration that the seat was vacant. c. The Supreme Court June 16, 1969, ruled that the House had improperly excluded Powell.**
***Sources:* Senate Committee on Rules and Administration, Subcommittee on Privileges and Elections, *Senate Election, Expulsion, and Censure Cases from 1793 to 1972*, compiled by Richard D. Hupman, 92nd Cong. 1st sess., 1972, S Doc 92–7.**
Hinds and Cannons, *Precedents of the House of Representatives of the United States*, 11 vols. (1935–1941); Joint Committee on Congressional Operations, *Exclusion, Censure, and Expulsion Cases from 1789 to 1973*, 93rd Cong., 1st sess., 1973, committee print.

Members of both houses of Congress have been prevented form taking their seats for a variety of reasons, including citizenship, residence, loyalty, and misconduct.

Expressed Powers

Powers specifically granted to Congress in Article I, Section 8, of the Constitution; also called enumerated powers. While some of these powers are specific, others are subject to interpretation. Congress historically has expanded its authority by interpreting some of these powers very broadly.

The Constitution gives Congress the power:

- To lay and collect taxes and duties, and to pay the debts and provide for the common defense and general welfare of the United States;
- To borrow money on the credit of the United States;
- To regulate **commerce** with foreign nations, among the states, and with the Indian tribes;
- To establish uniform rules for naturalization and bankruptcy throughout the United States;
- To print money, control its value, and fix a standard for weights and measures;
- To punish counterfeiters;
- To establish post offices and post roads;
- To assign patents and copyrights to protect the rights of authors and inventors to their creations;
- To establish courts below the U.S. Supreme Court;
- To define and punish piracy and felonies on the high seas, and offenses against international law;
- To declare war, authorize the seizure of enemy property, and make rules concerning captures on land and water;
- To raise and support armies;
- To provide and maintain a navy;
- To make rules for the government and regulation of the land and naval forces;
- To provide for calling forth the militia to execute the law, suppress uprisings, and repel invasions;

Expressed Powers of Congress
• Regulate foreign and Interstate Commerce
• Make treaties
• Establish naturalization laws
• Coin money
• Establish post offices
• Issue patents and copyrights
• Declare War
• Provide and maintain the armed services
• Fix standards of weights and measures
• Admit new states
• Establish a court system

The expressed, or enumerated, powers of Congress are listed in Article I, Section 8, of the United States Constitution.

- To provide for organizing, arming, and disciplining the militia, and to govern militia employed by the United States;
- To choose a place as the seat of the government of the United States, and to exercise authority over it and all places purchased by Congress for national purposes, and;
- To make all laws necessary and proper to carry out powers granted Congress by the Constitution.

The "necessary and proper" clause has been the subject of much Constitutional debate. Some observers argue that it means Congress should be able to pass a law only if failing to do so prevents it from exercising its expressed powers. Others counter that the clause allows Congress to take whatever steps it deems necessary to achieve its goals, as long as it does not deprive the other branches of government of their Constitutional powers.

Congress has often cited the necessary and proper clause and the commerce clause to uphold its authority in matters not specifically addressed by the Constitution. For example,

Congress used the commerce clause to prohibit segregation in private businesses such as hotels and restaurants. It outlawed segregation on the basis that it had the potential to impede commerce between the states.

See also: Federalism; Implied Powers; United States Constitution, Article I, Section 8, 1789, in the **Primary Source Library.**

Federalism

System of government in which power is shared between a central government and individual state or provincial governments. The United States is a federal republic, consisting of a national government and fifty separate state governments. Under the U.S. Constitution, states have authority over matters within their own borders, but they are bound to uphold all laws passed by the national government.

The Constitution grants specific powers to Congress, known as expressed powers. It also imposes certain limitations on the powers of Congress, such as forbidding it from passing certain types of taxes, granting titles of nobility, or suspending habeas corpus. It also cedes to the states any powers not specifically granted to the national government. This gives the states great leeway to act within their own boundaries.

Article VI of the Constitution, however, provides that the laws and treaties of the United States "shall be the supreme law of the land . . . and that the Judges of the several States shall be bound thereby in their decisions, anything in the respective Constitutions or laws of the individual States to the contrary notwithstanding." This so-called "supremacy clause" means that state judges and officials are bound to uphold the Constitution over any local or state laws. The "supremacy" clause was reinforced by a provision stating that all members of Congress and of the state legislatures, as well as all executive and judicial officers of the national and state governments, "shall be bound by Oath or Affirmation to support this Constitution."

The "supremacy" clause was designed to prevent the states from passing laws contrary to the Constitution. To eliminate any doubt of their intention to put an end to irresponsible acts of the individual states, the delegates decided to specify what the states could not do as well as what the states were required to do. Acts prohibited to the states were placed in Section 10 of Article I, while those required of them were placed in Sections 1 and 2 of Article IV.

Most of these provisions were uncontroversial. For example, states were required to use gold or silver as legal tender unless Congress agreed to another form of currency. Article IV also required each state to give "full faith and credit" to the acts of other states, to respect "all Privileges and Immunities" of all citizens, and to deliver up fugitives from justice. As with the rest of the Constitution, the enforcement of these provisions was assigned, by the "supremacy" clause, to the courts.

See also: Expressed Powers; Implied Powers.

Federalist, The

Also known as The Federalist Papers, a collection of eighty-five letters to the public that argued in favor of the ratification of the Constitution. The articles, written by Alexander Hamilton, James

Madison (1809–1817), and John Jay, appeared at short intervals in the newspapers of New York City beginning in October 1787. The essays probably had only a small impact on the ratification of the Constitution, but they gained importance later as a classic statement of the philosophy underlying the Constitution.

Background

The idea for *The Federalist* letters came from Alexander Hamilton, who wanted to wage a literary campaign to explain the proposed Constitution and build support for it. Two of his fellow delegates to the Constitutional Convention of 1787, James Madison and John Jay, agreed to work with him. The first letter appeared simultaneously in *The Independent Journal, The New York Packet,* and *The Daily Advertiser* on October 27, 1787. In all, the newspapers published a series of eighty-five letters between October 1787 and August 1788. Of these, Hamilton wrote fifty-six; Madison, twenty-one; and Jay, five. Hamilton and Madison collaborated on three. Jay's low productivity was attributed to a serious illness in the fall of 1787.

All of the letters bore the signature "Publius," a pseudonym–false name–adopted by the three authors. The name was chosen in honor of the ancient Roman statesman Publius Valerius Publicola. Publius, whose last name translates as "friend of the people," played a key role in deposing Rome's last king and helping to establish the Roman Republic.

John Jay was the author of five of The Federalist Papers, which was originally published as a series of newspaper articles in 1787 and 1788. Jay later was appointed as the first Chief Justice of the United States. (AP Photo, Robert Fridenberg)

Topics Covered

Federalist No. 1 listed six main topics as the subjects of the subsequent articles. These included the advantages of political union for the states, the weaknesses of the Articles of Confederation, the necessity for a strong federal government, how the proposed Constitution expressed the true principles of republican government, similarities between the proposed Constitution and existing state constitutions, and how adopting the Constitution would preserve republican government, liberty, and prosperity. In the end, the last two topics were discussed only briefly.

Two of the most noted of the letters are *Federalist No. 10* and *Federalist No. 84. Federalist No. 10* warns of the dangers of "factions," or interest groups. James Madison, the author of the essay, cautioned that factions would pursue their own interests, regardless of the rights of others or the will of the majority of the people. He argued that factions would exercise much more political power in smaller republics, such as the individual states, than they would in a larger republic. According to Madison, adopting a Constitution that bound the states together in a larger union would thus reduce the influence of factions.

Federalist No. 84, authored by Hamilton, is best known for outlining arguments against including a Bill of Rights in the proposed Constitution. He claimed that a Bill of Rights was not only unnecessary, but also potentially dangerous to individual liberties. Hamilton suggested that later governments might consider liberties listed in a Bill of Rights to be the only rights enjoyed by the people. As he put it:

Decision Makers

James Madison (1751–1836)

James Madison is often called "The Father of the Constitution" because of the extensive work he did in crafting that document. Madison played a part in virtually all of the major decisions made during the Constitutional Convention of 1787, and he authored the first ten amendments to the Constitution, known as the Bill of Rights. He later served as secretary of state under President Thomas Jefferson and was elected as the fourth president of the United States in 1808.

Madison was a passionate defender of both the individual liberties of citizens and the authority of state governments against the power of the federal government. Despite these beliefs, however, he realized that the new nation could not survive with a weak central government. As a result, he joined with Alexander Hamilton and John Jay to author The Federalist Papers that urged **ratification** of the Constitution, which proposed a much stronger federal government than the existing Articles of Confederation.

Ironically, like Hamilton, Madison initially opposed including a Bill of Rights in the Constitution. Both men argued that it was unnecessary and that naming some rights might imply that citizens did not enjoy other, unnamed rights. In the end, however, it was Madison who drew up the proposed amendments that became the Bill of Rights. He originally submitted twelve proposals, but the states **ratified** only ten. More than 200 years later, in 1992, his eleventh proposal was adopted as the Twenty-seventh Amendment.

A – Z

I go further, and affirm that bills of rights . . . are not only unnecessary in the proposed constitution, but would even be dangerous. They would contain various exceptions to powers which are not granted; and on this very account, would afford a colorable pretext to claim more than were granted. For why declare that things shall not be done which there is no power to do? Why for instance, should it be said, that the liberty of the press shall not be restrained, when no power is given by which restrictions may be imposed? . . . (S)uch a provision . . . would furnish, to men disposed to usurp, a plausible pretense for claiming that power."

Historian Clinton Rossiter wrote in a 1961 introduction to the papers: "*The Federalist* is the most important work in political science that has ever been written, or is likely ever to be written, in the United States. It is, indeed, the one product of the American mind that is rightly counted among the classics of political theory. . . . *The Federalist* stands third only to the Declaration of Independence and the Constitution itself among all the sacred writing of American political history."

See also: Federalism.

Further Reading

Hamilton, Alexander, James Madison, and John Jay (authors), and Clinton Rossiter (ed.). *The Federalist Papers.* New York: Signet Classics, 2003.

Filibuster

In the Senate, an extreme form of unlimited debate that is sometimes used to try to stop voting on legislation or some other action. A filibuster is the deliberate use of extended debate or procedural delays to block action on a measure supported by a majority of senators. Filibusters once provided the Senate's best political theater. Those who used the tactic had to be ready for days or weeks of freewheeling debate, and all other business was blocked until one side conceded. In the modern era, such political drama is rare in filibusters. Visitors to the Senate gallery are likely to look down on an empty floor and hear only the drone of a clerk reading absent senators' names in a mind-numbing succession of quorum calls. Often, today's filibusters do not even have to take place on the Senate floor.

Despite the lack of political drama, filibusters are still effective weapons. Any controversial legislation that comes to the Senate floor without a prearranged time agreement is vulnerable to a filibuster. The success of a filibuster is most likely near the end of the Senate session, when a filibuster on one bill may imperil action on other, more urgent and important legislation. Filibusters may be intended to kill a measure outright, by forcing the Senate leadership to pull the measure off the floor so that the full Senate can move on to other business. However, filibusters also are often mounted to force a compromise on a measure that is being considered. Time is such a precious commodity in the Senate that individual members who even threaten to hold a bill hostage to the lengthy debate of a filibuster can usually force compromises on a measure, either in a Senate committee or on the floor of the full Senate.

Filibusters have always generated intense controversy. Supporters of the tactic view filibusters as a defense against hasty or ill-advised legislation and as a guarantee that minority views will be heard. Those who oppose the use of filibusters argue that filibusters allow a minority of senators to thwart the will of a majority and prevent the orderly consideration of other important issues before the Senate.

A filibuster can be ended by negotiating a compromise on the disputed matter or by gathering a pre-determined supermajority of senators to cut off the extended debate. Since 1917, the Senate has also been able to vote to invoke cloture to cut off a filibuster, though the number of senators required to do so has changed over the years.

The procedure to end a filibuster is contained in Senate Rule XXII. This procedure requires sixteen senators to sign a cloture petition and file it with the presiding officer of the Senate. Two days later, and one hour after the Senate meets, the presiding officer establishes the presence of a quorum and then poses the question: "Is it the sense of the Senate that the debate shall be brought to a close?" If three-fifths of the senators (sixty senators) vote in favor of the motion, cloture is invoked. (A two-thirds majority of those present and voting, which would be sixty-seven senators if all were present, is needed to invoke cloture on proposals to amend the Senate's rules, including Rule XXII. This means that an even larger majority would be needed to change the rule. In practice, this makes it almost impossible to end the cloture rule entirely and create a situation of simple majority rule in the Senate.)

There is no limit on how long a filibuster must go on before a cloture petition can be filed. The late Senator Strom Thurmond, a Republican from South Carolina, set the record for the longest filibuster by a single individual—twenty-four hours and eighteen minutes on a 1957 civil rights bill (which became law despite his efforts). This record is likely to stand in the modern era. Nor are there any limitations on the number of times the Senate can try to in-

Famous Filibusters

Length of Filibuster	Year	Senator	Filibuster opposed to:
24 hours, 18 minutes	1957	Strom Thurmond, R. South Carolina	Civil Rights Bill
22 hours, 26 minutes	1953	Wayne Morse, Ind. Oregon	Tideland Oil Bill
18 hours, 23 minutes	1908	Robert M. LaFollette, Sr., R. Wisconsin	Aldrich-Vreeland Currency Bill
16 hours, 12 minutes	1981	William Proxmire, D. Wisconsin	Raising the Public Debt to more than a Trillion Dollars
15 hours, 30 minutes	1935	Huey P. Long, D. Louisiana	Extension of the National Industrial Recovery Act
11 hours, 35 minutes	1915	Reed Smoot, R. Utah	Woodrow Wilson's Ship Purchase Bill

The techniques of filibustering go back to the time of colonial legislatures. Today, the Senate can limit debate by invoking cloture. Since 1975, a vote of three-fifths of the Senate membership (sixty, if there are no vacancies), is needed for cloture.

voke cloture on the same filibuster. There used to be an unwritten rule that three cloture votes were enough, but in 1987–1988, the Senate took eight cloture votes to shut off a Republican filibuster over of a campaign spending bill before conceding defeat and shelving the measure.

For most of the Senate's history, the filibuster was used sparingly and for the most part only on legislative battles of historical importance, such as peace treaties and civil rights matters. Since the mid-1970s, however, the Senate has seen a significant increase in the use of filibusters. At the same time, however, a change in Senate rules made it easier to invoke cloture to cut off a filibuster. In 1975, after years of trying, Senate liberals succeeded in pushing through a change in the Senate's cloture rule. Instead of two-thirds of those voting (sixty-seven if all senators are present), three-fifths of the membership, or sixty senators, could invoke cloture on a filibuster.

Several factors account for the increase in the use of filibusters. More issues come before the Senate these days, making time an even scarcer commodity than in the past. In addition, constituents and special-interest groups put more pressure on senators, and senators are more apt to pursue their political goals even if it means inconveniencing their colleagues. In the 1990s, filibusters and threats of filibuster were common weapons of senators hoping merely to spotlight or to change legislation, as well as to delay or to kill it.

See also: Committees; Senate.

Foreign Policy Powers

Constitutional authority to determine national policy for dealing with foreign affairs. The Constitution grants certain powers in this area exclusively to the executive branch, and others to the legislative branch. In some areas, however, either the Constitution was not clear about which branch was foremost, or it gave the two branches overlapping authority.

The Constitution: Division of Powers

Article I, Section 8, of the Constitution assigned to Congress the powers

> to . . . Provide for the common Defence and general Welfare of the United States; . . . To regulate Commerce with foreign Nations, and among the several States, and with the Indian Tribes; . . . To define and punish Piracies and Felonies committed on the high Seas, and Offences against the Law of Nations; To declare War, grant Letters Of Marque and Reprisal, and make Rules concerning Captures on Land and Water; To raise and support Armies . . . ; To provide and maintain a Navy; . . . And To make all Laws which shall be necessary and proper for carrying into Execution the foregoing Powers, and all other Powers vested by this Constitution in the Government of the United States, or in any Department or Officer thereof.

The Constitution also provided that

> the President shall be Commander in Chief of the Army and Navy. . . . He shall have Power, by and with the Advice and Consent of the Senate, to make Treaties, provided two-thirds of the Senators present concur; and he shall nominate, and by and with the Advice and Consent of the Senate, shall appoint Ambassadors, other public Ministers, and Consuls. . . . He shall receive Ambassadors and other public Ministers; he shall take Care that the Laws be faithfully executed.

President's Authority

Whatever the Founders' intent, the president historically has held the initiative in formulating foreign policy. In a series of articles published in a Philadelphia newspaper, Alexander Hamilton argued that the conduct of foreign relations was by nature an executive function. Except where the Constitution provided otherwise, he claimed that it belonged to the president, upon whom was bestowed "the executive power." The fact that Congress possessed the power to declare war, as well as other powers affecting foreign relations, did not diminish the ability of the president to exercise the president's constitutional powers. Over time, Hamilton's view has prevailed.

Congressional Powers

Despite the widely recognized powers of the president in foreign relations, Congress also has enormous powers that are indispensable to the support of any administration's foreign policy. Congress's specific foreign policy powers include the power to declare war and the Senate's powers to give advice and consent to treaties and to the appointment of ambassadors, public ministers, and other diplomatic officers.

Beyond those, Congress has general powers it can use to influence foreign policy. The most potent, but least utilized, of these has been the power to raise revenues and authorize and appropriate funds for national defense, war, foreign aid, and the general execution of foreign policy. Congress can also use its regular legislative powers to express its view about, set limits on, or promote foreign policies it favors.

The power to regulate commerce has given Congress authority in a number of areas of foreign policy, including international trade, shipping, aviation, and communications. Other powers with international applications include Congress's powers over U.S. territory; maritime law; the postal system; regulation of patents and copyrights; and the District of Columbia, the center of U.S. diplomatic activity.

Struggle for Control

The struggle over roles and prerogatives began in George Washington's presidency and contin-

A – Z

Speaker of the House Nancy Pelosi (left) met with Syrian President Bashir al-Assad in Damascus in April 2007. The meeting was controversial because the Bush administration believed Syria was a state sponsor of terrorism. (AP Photo, Hussein Malla, File)

ues today. From the beginning, it was apparent that the presidency had decided advantages over Congress, including its unity of office, capacity for secrecy and speed, and superior sources of information. Moreover, the president was readily available for decision making, at a time when Congress was often not in session.

Congress itself contributed to the steady growth of presidential power. It generally did not oppose the president's deployment of forces and negotiation of executive agreements. It was willing to accept informal consultations with the executive branch, instead of demanding formal participation in decision making. It quickly ratified, or confirmed, actions the president had already taken and delegated its own huge powers in broad terms so that the president could later claim to have acted under Congress's authority as well as the president's own. In addition, Congress formally contributed to the growth of presidential power in foreign policy, by passing laws such as the Atomic Energy Act of 1946 and the National Security Act of 1947.

When Congress does choose to assert itself, however, it has an impressive array of powers to use, including its war, treaty, and foreign commerce powers, as well as general legislative powers. The effect is such, in the words of scholars Roger H. Davidson and Walter J. Oleszek, that "[e]ven the most decisive chief executives can find themselves constrained by active, informed, and determined policy makers on Capitol Hill."

See also: Power of the Purse; Power to Raise an Army; President and Congress; Treaty Power; War Powers; War Powers Resolution (1973).

Further Reading

Crabb, Cecil V., Jr., and Pat M. Holt. *Invitation to Struggle: Congress, the President, and Foreign Policy.* Fourth edition. Washington, DC: CQ Press, 1992.

Peterson, Paul E., ed. *The President, the Congress, and the Making of Foreign Policy.* Norman: University of Oklahoma Press, 1994.

Point/Counterpoint

Should Congressional Leaders Conduct Foreign Policy?

Presidents and members of their administrations often express displeasure when members of Congress deal directly with representatives of foreign nations. The executive branch typically sees this as encroaching on the president's authority to conduct foreign policy. The debate becomes even more heated when Congress and the administration differ on their foreign policy views.

In April 2007, Democratic Speaker of the House Nancy Pelosi drew fire from the Republican administration of President George W. Bush for undertaking a diplomatic trip to Syria. The Bush administration was opposed to holding talks with Syria, a country it accused of sponsoring terrorism. Vice President Dick Cheney was particularly critical of Pelosi's trip. New York Senator Hillary Rodham Clinton, however, defended Pelosi's initiative and her right to deal with foreign leaders.

Vice President Dick Cheney

She's not entitled to make policy. In this particular case, by going to Damascus at this stage, it serves to reinforce, if you will, and reward Bashir al-Assad for his bad behavior. He's done all kinds of things that are not in the interest of the United States, including allowing Syria to be an area from which attacks are launched against our people inside Iraq. He, obviously, is heavily involved right now in supporting an effort by Hezbollah to try to topple the government of Lebanon. This is a bad actor, and until he changes his behavior, he should not be rewarded with visits by the Speaker of the House of Representatives.

I've been around a long time. I'm obviously disappointed. I think it is, in fact, bad behavior on her part. I wish she hadn't done it. But she is the

A-Z

Franking

One of the most valuable and controversial privileges of Congress in which members can send out mail at public expense. Every year, millions of American households receive pieces of mail that bear a facsimile of the signature of a member of Congress, known as the *frank,* in place of a stamp. Mailing letters and packages under one's signature at taxpayers' expense is one of the nation's oldest privileges. The Continental Congress adopted the practice of franking in 1775.

Through newsletters and other mailings, sent at government expense, legislators can communicate directly with constituents, informing them about congressional decisions and passing on useful news about the federal government. The franked envelope might contain a legislator's response to a constituent question or request, a copy of the legislator's newsletter, a survey, a press release, a packet of voting information, government publications or reports, or other printed matter that in some way relates to the legislator's official duties as a member of Congress. Mailings related to political campaigns or political parties, personal business,

Speaker of the House. And, fortunately, I think the various parties involved recognize she doesn't speak for the United States in those circumstances, she doesn't represent the administration. The President is the one who conducts foreign policy, not the Speaker of the House.

Senator Hillary Rodham Clinton

I think that both her delegation, which was primarily Democrats, and a Republican delegation that was there approximately at the same time are doing the right thing. We have got to engage these countries. Obviously we have serious differences with a country like Syria, but we're sure not making progress towards our goals in the region by isolating and ignoring them. So I wish the President were engaged in the region, in the way that I would think a President should be.

You know we were always engaged, whether it was a Republican or Democratic President. With the former Soviet Union, we had a Communist Empire with thousands of missiles pointed at us, with Presidents who said that they wanted to bury us, running proxy wars against us. We never stopped engaging and talking and we never gave up on our values. In fact I think we learned a lot about our adversaries which helped us eventually bring about their decline and defeat in the Cold War. Well I think that's the much smarter way. I don't agree with the President's view that we don't talk to bad people because clearly that's not a smart way to figure out how you can bring leverage on them and that's what I'm interested in.

DOCUMENT-BASED QUESTION

What is the key difference in the way that Vice President Dick Cheney and Senator Hillary Rodham Clinton view members of Congress's ability to meet with foreign leaders?

or friendships may not be franked. A lawmaker cannot use the frank on an invitation to a party fund-raiser or a request for political support. Yet opponents of the frank argue that it gives incumbents running for reelection a boost over challengers who do not have the same cheap access to voters.

Although no stamp is needed, a franked letter is not actually mailed free of charge. Each year, Congress budgets a certain amount of money to cover the cost of members' franking privileges. The U.S. Postal Service keeps records on the franked mail it handles and periodically sends Congress what amounts to a bill. If Congress has not appropriated enough money to cover the costs of franked mail, it appropriates more money in a supplemental bill. The Postal Service, however, is obligated to send all franked mail whether or not Congress appropriates enough money to cover the costs.

One aspect of the franking privilege that has often been criticized is its cost to the taxpayer. Recent regulations, however, have lowered the cost considerably. An even more controversial issue has been the advantage that the franking privilege gives incumbents. Despite restrictions on political content and self-promotion, members can and do take advantage of loopholes and lax regulations. For example, members' newsletters often report awards presented to the lawmaker as well as favorable ratings of his or her voting record by various interest groups. They also send mass mailings to selected groups of people and avoid sending materials to groups of people thought to be unsympathetic to their ideas.

Persons authorized to use the frank include the vice president, members and members-elect of Congress, and officers of the House and Senate. Members and others given the franking privilege are entitled, on a restricted basis, to use the frank during the ninety days immediately following the date on which they leave office. During this period, use of the frank is limited to matters directly related to the closing of the member's congressional office. Former members may not send newsletters, questionnaires, or other mass-mailed material.

Franking regulations prohibit a person entitled to use the frank from lending it to any nonmember, private committee, organization, or association. Use of the frank for the benefit of charitable organizations, political action committees, trade organizations, and other groups is expressly forbidden. Nor may the frank be used for mail delivered to a foreign country. Despite these restrictions, a wide range of material may be sent out under the frank. Among the major categories of mail eligible for the franking privilege are newsletters and news releases, questionnaires, and other materials regarding government programs and proposed legislation.

See also: Congressional Pay and Benefits; Constituents and Congress.

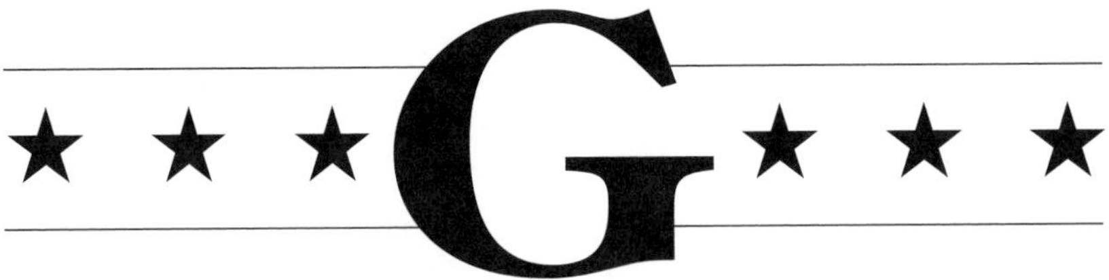

Gavel

A small mallet, or hammer, used by the presiding officer of the Senate to call the members to attention during sessions. The first Senate gavel, made of ivory and tipped with silver, was replaced in 1954, when it began to disintegrate from years of repeated use. An exact replica has been used since that time.

According to the U.S. Senate website, Vice President John Adams (1789–1797) used the original gavel to call the first Senate to order in spring 1789. The first recorded instance of its use, however, dates to 1831. In the late 1940s, silver tips were added to each end of the gavel to strengthen and preserve it. During a 1954 debate over atomic energy, the original gavel fell apart. Senate officials wanted to create an exact replica of the original gavel, but could find no source of ivory of sufficient size to replace it. The Indian embassy then donated a new hand-carved ivory gavel with exactly the same dimensions as the old one. This gavel is still in use today.

Each day the Senate is in session, a case carrying both the old and new gavels is carried into the Senate chamber and placed on the vice president's desk just before the opening of the session. The new gavel is removed from the case for use by the presiding officer. The old gavel remains in its case, a symbol of the continuity of the Senate. At the end of each day, the gavel is placed in a box beside the mended original gavel.

Gibbons v. Ogden (1824)

Landmark Supreme Court case that helped determine the scope of the federal government's power over commerce under the Commerce Clause of the Constitution. At the Constitutional Convention in 1787, the Founders recognized the importance of uniform regulations concerning interstate and foreign commerce. The Commerce Clause that they inserted into the Constitution gave Congress broad powers to regulate commerce. Over time, the federal government's power over interstate commerce became one of its most important powers. However, in the first years of the nation's history that power was used so rarely that there was no need to define precisely what was meant by commerce "among the several States." Not until thirty-five years after the adoption of the Constitution did a case involving the scope of this power come before the Supreme Court.

The circumstances leading to the Supreme Court's decision in the case of *Gibbons v. Ogden* involved a dispute over a monopoly over steamboat operations in New York and New Jersey. Other states fought this monopoly by closing their waters to ships operating under the monopoly and by granting steamship monopolies of their own. The result was navigational chaos.

The case that broke the monopoly involved Aaron Ogden, a former New Jersey governor (1812–1813), and his partner Thomas Gibbons, who ran a steam-driven ferry between New Jersey and New York City. In 1815, Ogden had acquired a license from the New York monopoly, and Gibbons held a permit under a federal coastal licensing act for his two boats. Despite their partnership, Gibbons ran his boats to New York in defiance of the monopoly rights that Ogden held, and in 1819, Ogden sued for an injunction to stop Gibbons's infringement of his rights under the monopoly. New York courts ordered Gibbons to halt his ferry service. Gibbons appealed to the Supreme Court, arguing that his federal license took precedence over the state-granted monopoly license and that he should be allowed to continue his ferrying in New York waters.

The Supreme Court considered two basic questions. Did Congress have power under the commerce clause to regulate navigation? If so, did Congress have exclusive power to regulate it, or did the states also have power to regulate commerce? Delivering the Court's opinion on March 2, 1824, Chief Justice John Marshall answered the first question by refusing to interpret the federal commerce power narrowly or to omit navigation from its scope. Concerning the second question, Marshall said that the commerce power of Congress applied to commerce with foreign nations as well as to commerce among the states. However, Marshall did not find that the commerce power prohibited all state regulation.

Marshall did not address the question of whether states could regulate areas of commerce that Congress had not regulated. Nor did he answer the question of whether the states could regulate commerce simultaneously with Congress. His opinion settled only two points–first, that navigation was commerce and, second, that where state exercise of its power conflicts with federal exercise of the commerce power, the state must give way. In making the second point, Marshall laid the groundwork for extending the commerce power to other forms of transportation and communications. By leaving the power to regulate wholly internal commerce to the states only so long as that commerce did not "extend to or affect" other states, he planted the seeds that eventually would allow Congress to regulate the manufacture of goods and matters that themselves were not in commerce, but would affect interstate commerce.

Congress did not make much use of the power claimed for it by *Gibbons v. Ogden* until later in the century. Between 1824, when *Gibbons v. Ogden* was decided, and the 1880s, when a need arose for federal regulation of the nation's railroads and interstate corporations, the Court's rulings on the commerce power focused primarily on determining when state actions on commerce were unconstitutional.

See also: Commerce Clause; Constitution of the United States; *Gibbons v. Ogden,* 1824, in the **Primary Source Library.**

Great Compromise

See Connecticut Compromise.

Gulf of Tonkin Resolution (1964)

Resolution adopted by Congress in 1964, during the Vietnam War (1964–1975), which gave the president greater power to use U.S. armed forces in foreign conflicts. The Gulf of Tonkin Resolution was one of the most controversial resolutions passed by Congress in the post-World War II era. Signed into law on August 10, 1964, the resolution authorized the president to use U.S. armed forces to repel attacks against U.S. forces and affirmed U.S. determination to defend any member of the Southeast Asia Treaty Organization (SEATO) or nation allied to it (including Vietnam) that requested assistance.

The Gulf of Tonkin Resolution was approved overwhelmingly by Congress on the basis of what later emerged as a distorted account of a minor naval engagement. Reports from Vietnam in August 1964 indicated that the North Vietnamese had attacked American ships patrolling the Gulf of Tonkin on August 2 and August 4 of that year. In response to these attacks, President Lyndon B. Johnson (1963–1969) ordered a retaliatory air strike on the North Vietnamese naval base at the capital city of Hanoi that destroyed or damaged twenty-five boats. On August 5, President Johnson asked Congress to adopt a resolution to "give convincing evidence to the aggressive Communist nations, and to the world as a whole, that our policy in Southeast Asia will be carried forward, and that the peace and security of the area will be preserved."

Congress adopted the Gulf of Tonkin Resolution by an 88–2 vote in the Senate and 414–0 in the House of Representatives. The resolution authorized the president to "take all necessary measures" to stop aggression in Southeast Asia. When Congress adopted the Gulf of Tonkin Resolution, it virtually gave up its power to declare war in Vietnam. Moreover, the resolution became the main legal justification for the continued war efforts by the Johnson administration. The president also considered the resolution adequate authority for expanding U.S. involvement in the Vietnam War. Years later, the Gulf of Tonkin Resolution came to represent one of the most vivid examples of congressional willingness to give the president unchecked authority in foreign policy, even in the area of war making and U.S. military commitments abroad. As public support for the Vietnam War deteriorated, Congress had second thoughts about its 1964 decision. Congress eventually voted to repeal the Gulf of Tonkin resolution in January 1971.

See also: Iraq War Resolution (2002); President and Congress; War Powers.

Hispanic Americans in Congress

The rapid expansion of the Hispanic American population since the 1960s sparked predictions that the group would emerge as a powerful voting bloc and elect a significant number of its members to Congress. Nevertheless, Hispanics remain underrepresented in proportion to their share of the total population.

Hispanics in the House

The first Hispanic American elected to Congress was Joseph Marion Hernandez, a member of the Whig party, who represented the territory of Florida in the House of Representatives from 1822 to 1823. Most of the early Hispanic members of the House, in fact, represented territories that only later gained admission as states. Eleven of the House's first thirteen Hispanics were territorial delegates, ten of them from New Mexico. The first Hispanic House member to represent an established state was Romualdo Pacheco, elected as a representative from California in 1877.

For many years, Hispanic members held few House seats and represented a very limited number of states, primarily New Mexico. Prior to its admission as a state in 1912, New Mexico elected ten Hispanic territorial delegates to the House. Between 1912 and 1960, the state of New Mexico sent six Hispanics representatives to the House. Louisiana (two members) and California (one member) were the only states besides New Mexico to send Hispanic Americans to the House prior to 1960. During this time, the only other Hispanic members of Congress were the resident commissioners of Puerto Rico, an unincorporated territory of the United States. Resident commissioners may speak in the House, but are ineligible to cast votes.

Representative José E. Serrano (D-NY) serves on the powerful House Appropriations Committee and the Subcommittee on Financial Service and General Government. (AP Photo, Charles Dharpaka)

The growth of Hispanic representation in the House was in large part the result of judicial interpretations of the Voting Rights Act of 1965. The courts ruled that minorities should be given maximum opportunity to elect members of their own group to Congress. As a result, the number of Hispanic Americans in the House increased significantly after 1965. Prior to that date, a total of 32 Hispanics had held House seats. Between 1965 and 2006, 50 Hispanics were elected to the House.

After the 1990 census, congressional district maps in states with significant Hispanic populations were redrawn with the aim of sending more Hispanics to Congress. This goal was accomplished by the 1992 elections. Nine Hispanics won first-time House seats in 1992; in no previous election year had more than three non-incumbent Hispanic candidates been elected to the House.

Hispanics in the Senate

Only six Hispanic Americans have been elected to the United States Senate. The first was Octavio Ambrosio Larrazolo, who served as a Republican senator from New Mexico from 1928–1929. New Mexico subsequently sent two Democrats to the Senate: Dennis Chavez (1935–1962) and Joseph Manuel Montoya (1964–1977).

The 2005 House elections marked the first time that more that one Hispanic American was elected to the Senate in the same year. In that year, Colorado voters chose Ken Salazar to represent their state in the Senate, while Floridians elected Republican Mel Martinez. In 2006, Democrat Robert Menendez of New Jersey joined Salazar and Martinez in the upper house. John Corzine held the seat prior to being elected governor of New Jersey that year. As governor, Corzine appointed Menendez to fill his vacant seat.

Current Representation

As of early 2008, a total of twenty-six Hispanic Americans held seats in Congress—twenty-three in the House and three in the Senate. Although this represents an increase by historical standards, Hispanics are still underrepresented in Congress. According to the U.S. Census Bureau, Hispanics comprised about one-seventh of the nation's population in 2004. That would translate into 62 house seats and 14 Senate seats if Hispanics were represented in proportion to their total population. One of the main reasons for the relatively small number of Hispanic Congress members is the fact that Hispanic voter turnouts traditionally have fallen well below the national average. This has limited their ability to elect Hispanic senators and representatives.

See also: Congressional Hispanic Caucus.

Further Reading

Vigil, Maurilio E. *Hispanics in Congress.* Washington, DC: University Press of America, 1996.

Hispanic Americans in Congress 1947–2009

Congress	Senate	House
80th (1947–1949)	1	1
81st (1949–1951)	1	1
82nd (1951–1953)	1	1
83rd (1953–1955)	1	1
84th (1955–1957)	1	1
85th (1957–1959)	2	0
86th (1959–1961)	2	0
87th (1961–1963)	2	1
88th (1963–1965)	1	3
89th (1965–1967)	0	4
90th (1967–1969)	0	4
91st (1969–1971)	0	5
92nd (1971–1973)	0	6
93rd (1973–1975)	0	6
94th (1975–1977)	0	6
95th (1977–1979)	0	5
96th (1979–1981)	0	6
97th (1981–1983)	0	7
98th (1983–1985)	0	10
99th (1985–1987)	0	11
100th (1987–1989)	0	11
101st (1989–1991)	0	11
102nd (1991–1993)	0	11
103rd (1993–1995)	0	17
104th (1995–1997)	0	17
105th (1997–1999)	0	18
106th (1999–2001)	0	18
107th (2001–2003)	0	19
108th (2003–2005)	2	24
109th (2005–2007)	3	23
110th (2007–2009)	3	23

Note: House totals exclude non-voting delegates.

The number of Hispanic Americans serving in Congress has increased since 1947.

Decision Makers

Romualdo Pacheco (1831–1899)

Romualdo Pacheco, a Republican representative from California, was the first Hispanic to represent an established state in Congress and the only Hispanic to serve in Congress during the nineteenth century. The Mexican-born Pacheco served as governor of California in 1875 and ran for Congress the following year. Although he won a disputed election, the House leadership named his opponent the winner. Pacheco returned home and ran again—successfully—twice more. Upon leaving Congress he became ambassador to Honduras and then Guatemala. No other Hispanic American was elected to Congress until 1912.

House of Representatives

The lower house of the national legislature of the United States. The House is often referred to as the "people's chamber" because its members are considered to be in closer touch with the voters who elect them than are members of the Senate. This perception is generally accurate; House members represent voters who live in a single city or locality, while senators represent an entire state.

Basic Organization

Perhaps the most basic distinction between the House and Senate lies in the number of seats each state controls in the two chambers. In the House, each state has a number of representatives proportional to its population. The more people in a state, the more seats it controls in the House. In the Senate, by contrast, each state has two seats, regardless of population.

Apportionment

The formula for apportionment, or determining the number of House seats each state should receive–has changed over time and has been the subject of considerable debate. The Constitutional Convention of 1787 linked the apportionment of representatives to a census every ten years of the "whole number of free persons . . . and three fifths of all others." In this case "all others" referred to slaves, who were counted as three-fifths of a person for purposes of determining a state's population. The delegates decided that the number of representatives "shall not exceed one for every 30,000" and fixed the size of the original House at 65 members.

The very first Congress changed the formula for apportionment, and later Congresses continued to do so as the national population increased and new states were added. Congress also repeatedly modified the maximum size of the House. A 1929 bill fixed the House at its current size of 435 members, and established the current formula for apportionment. Every ten years the new census totals determine any changes in the number of House seats each state controls. Because the number of House seats cannot increase until new states are added, any time a state gains seats as a result of population growth, at least one other, slower-growing state must lose seats.

Congressional Districts

Each member of the House represents the people in a specific geographical area, known as a congressional district. District boundaries are drawn so that each district in a state contains approximately the same number of inhabitants.

Increase in House Membership Since 1789

Year	House Membership
1789	65
1803	105
1813	142
1823	182
1833	213
1843	240
1853	223
1863	234
1873	238
1883	292
1893	325
1903	356
1913	386
1923	435
1933	435
1943	435
1953	435
1963	435
1973	435
1983	435
1993	435
2003	435

The number of representatives in the House of Representatives has increased greatly since the Constitution established 65 as the number of members of the first House. Between 1790 and 1920—after each decennial census—the number of members of the House usually increased because of the growing national population and the addition of new states. At the beginning of the twentieth century, legislators established the size of the House at 435 seats.

In fact, though, the Constitution does not require congressional districts to be equal or nearly equal in population. Nor does it require that a state create districts at all. However, most scholars agree that that it was the Framers' intention to create congressional districts with populations that were roughly equal. Today, the population of each district within a state is roughly equal, but the average size of a district varies from state to state.

Term of Office, Elections, and Qualifications

House members serve two-year terms, and all House seats are up for election in every even-numbered year. Congressional elections—for both the House and Senate—are held on the Tuesday following the first Monday in November. Each congressional district holds a separate election in which voters choose a candidate to represent their interests. By contrast, senators are elected by a statewide ballot.

The Constitution requires that a representative be at least twenty-five years old, a citizen of the United States for the seven years prior to being elected, and must be an inhabitant of the state he or she represents at the time of election. It does not require members to live in the districts they represent, but many state laws do have this requirement for their representatives.

Leadership and Procedures

At its most basic level, the House is organized along party lines. The majority party—the one that controls the most seats—assumes leadership of the House and elects its members to leadership positions. The majority party usually plays the lead role in the House through its control of leadership positions and committees, groups of members responsible for drawing up legislation.

The amount of influence the minority party exercises depends upon its numbers. If the majority party controls only a few more seats than the minority, its members may be forced to deal with the minority to pass important legislation. If the majority party enjoys a substantial numerical advantage, however, it can usually pass legislation it supports without the cooperation of the minority.

Leadership Positions

The Speaker of the House of Representatives is considered the most powerful figure in Congress. The Speaker serves as presiding officer of the House and is second in line, after the vice president, to succeed the president. The Speaker must recognize members before they may speak in the chamber and may call on any members he or she pleases. As a result, the speaker exerts significant control over floor debate. The Speaker also has great influence over House committees. The Speaker appoints members to fill a large number of committee seats and determines which committee will consider each bill.

The Majority Leader manages the legislative affairs of the House. This involves planning, promoting, and defending legislation favored by the majority party. The Majority Leader works to convince members to support the party's position in order to get enough votes to pass or defeat bills. Majority leaders also have considerable influence over the scheduling of debate and the selection of members to speak on bills.

The Majority Leader is assisted by one or more whips, who serve as the party's acting floor leaders in the absence of the regular leaders. Whips gather information from members that the Majority Leader uses to determine whether and when to bring a bill to the floor. The whips are also responsible for ensuring that members are present for important votes.

The minority party elects its own floor leader, but the Minority Leader exerts little influence. The Speaker and Majority Leader will often consult with the Minority Leader on important legislation, but the Minority Leader has no control over floor debate or committee appointments. Like the Majority Leader, the Minority Leader has several whips who help maintain party discipline.

Committees

Committees are where most of the work of Congress is done. Each committee is composed of a group of members who are responsible for drawing up legislation in a specific area of expertise. The Agriculture Committee, for example, draws up bills affecting farmers and ranchers. Serving on a committee enables members to develop specialized knowledge of the matters under the committee's jurisdiction, or area of authority. Committees exert great power over which bills the House considers. A committee can stop a bill by refusing to allow the chamber to vote it, or by simply taking no action on it.

The most powerful committees in the House are probably Appropriations, Rules, and Ways and Means. The Appropriations Committee exercises enormous control over the budget by deciding how federal money will be divided among various government programs. The Rules Committee decides how long the House will debate a bill and determines the rules of debate. This gives it great power to decide when and under what conditions the House can consider a bill. The Committee on Ways and Means controls the writing of all tax laws and any other laws used to raise money. It decides how and from what sources Congress funds the government.

Each party typically receives a number of committee seats roughly in proportion to its total membership in the House. One exception is the Rules Committee, where the majority party usually controls at least twice as many seats as the minority. All committees are led by a chairperson, who is always a member of the majority party. Committees frequently divide themselves into smaller subcommittees to consider specific issues. Chairpersons of these subcommittees also come from the majority party.

Until 1975, control of committee and subcommittee chairs was determined by seniority, or length of service. Members who had served in the House longest were given first consideration for filling committee chairs. A rules change in 1975 ended the seniority system and gave party leaders the power to select committee chairs. This change was a reaction to dissatisfaction among party leaders with senior chairpersons who refused to go along with their party's program. Party leaders could now threaten to withhold powerful committee appointments to senior members who went their own way.

Floor Procedures

In order for the House to do business, a quorum, or minimum number of members, must be present. A quorum is always assumed to be

Decision Makers

Jeanette Rankin (1880–1973)

Elected to the House of Representatives in 1916, Jeanette Rankin was the first woman to serve in the United States Congress. Born in 1880 on a Montana ranch, Rankin moved to Missoula as a child. She eventually enrolled at Montana State University, where she earned a degree in biology. She then worked as a teacher, a seamstress, and later studied furniture design. In 1902, her father died, leaving her enough money for the rest of her life.

Rankin later enrolled in the University of Washington in Seattle and became involved in the women's **suffrage** movement. During a visit to Montana, she became the first woman to address the state legislature, speaking for the Equal Franchise Society, a women's suffrage group that she had organized.

She moved to New York where she continued her fight for women's suffrage. She worked for the New York Suffrage Party, and in 1912, became field secretary for the National American Woman Suffrage Association. In 1914, she returned to Montana where she helped win a successful campaign for women's suffrage in that state. With World War I (1917–1918) looming, Rankin turned to working for peace. In 1916, after running for Congress as a Republican and winning the election, she became the first woman to serve in the House of Representatives and the first woman elected to a national legislature in any western democracy.

present unless an actual count of the members shows otherwise. Before a bill reaches the floor, the Rules Committee passes a rule to govern debate on that measure. An "open rule," for example allows members to offer relevant amendments to a bill. A "closed rule," by contrast, prohibits some or all amendments.

A member may only speak if called upon by the presiding officer. As noted earlier, the presiding officer decides whom to recognize, thus controlling the debate. Debate on a bill usually is limited to one hour, equally divided between the majority and minority parties. The majority and minority leaders determine which members of their party will speak and for how long. After the debate ends, the members traditionally have fifteen minutes to vote. They may receive more time if the leadership needs time to convince members to vote in a particular way. Most legislation must pass the House by a simple majority vote; a tie defeats the measure being voted on.

A Typical Schedule in the House

The House conducts different types of business on different days, so its daily routine varies. However, from week to week, a pattern is usually followed.

- The House convenes early for morning hour debate for five-minute speeches on Mondays and Tuesdays, sixty to ninety minutes before the formal opening of the day's session, even if that is in the afternoon. No votes or legislative business can occur. The House then recesses until the formal convening of the day's session.

Rankin again made history when she voted against the United States's entry into World War I, noting, "I want to stand by my country, but I cannot vote for war." Later, however, she voted in favor of several acts that supported the war. In 1917, Rankin introduced the so-called "Susan B. Anthony Amendment," granting women the right to vote. The amendment passed in the House in 1917 and in the Senate in 1918 and was sent to the states for approval. It was **ratified** as the Nineteenth Amendment in 1920.

In 1918, Rankin ran for the Senate from Montana, but lost. During the 1920s and 1930s, speaking across the nation, she continued to work for peace. She returned to Montana and, in 1940, again ran for Congress as a Republican. Rankin won the election. After the Japanese attack on Pearl Harbor in December 1941, she again voted against Congress's declaration of war, the only member of Congress to do so. With her vote, she announced, "As a woman I can't go to war, and I refuse to send anyone else." Believing she was unpatriotic, many colleagues and the press criticized Rankin's vote. She ran again for Congress in 1942 and lost the election.

Rankin then moved to her Georgia farm, but she continued to be active in the peace movement. In 1968, demanding the withdrawal of United States troops, she led more than 5,000 women in a peace march against the Vietnam War. Often speaking at peace rallies, she remained an active anti-war activist. Rankin died in 1973 in California.

- The chaplain delivers the opening prayer, and a House member leads the chamber in the Pledge of Allegiance.
- The Speaker approves the Journal, the record of the previous day's proceedings. Often a member demands a roll-call vote on the approval of the Journal, which can be used to determine who is present and to allow the leadership to "whip" them on other matters. The Journal vote can also be postponed by the Speaker until later in the day and clustered with other votes that may be occurring.
- After the House receives messages from the Senate and the president, receives privileged reports from committees, and conducts other similar procedural activities, members are recognized by unanimous consent for one-minute speeches on any topic.
- The House then turns to its legislative business. On Mondays and Tuesdays only, the House usually considers less controversial bills, sometimes dozens at a time, under the suspension of the rules process requiring a two-thirds majority for passage. Recorded votes are postponed until late in the day, or until the next day. Measures that are even less controversial are frequently passed by unanimous consent. A "Corrections Calendar" for the consideration of bills that the Speaker determines would change erroneous actions or regulations by the federal government may be called on the second and fourth Tuesdays of each month. A 60 percent majority of members present and voting is

required for passage. The House must call the Private Calendar on the first Tuesday of each month, and the Speaker may direct it to be called on the third Tuesday.

- Virtually every bill of any significance is considered under a special rule, **reported** from the Rules Committee, which sets guidelines for floor action. The rule may be approved with little opposition but the vote can also be a first test of a bill's popularity. If the rule restricts the amendments that may be offered, those members barred from offering amendments may work with opponents of the bill itself to defeat the rule or to defeat the previous question so that amendments to the rule can be offered.
- After the rule is adopted, the House resolves into the Committee of the Whole to consider the bill. The Speaker relinquishes the gavel to another member, who serves as chair of this "committee" and presides over the activities. Debate time is controlled by the managers of the bill, usually the chair and ranking minority member of the standing committee with jurisdiction over the measure.

After time for general debate has expired, amendments that are permitted under the rule may be offered and debated. Debate on an amendment may be for a fixed time. If none is specified in the rule, it is conducted under the "five-minute rule," which limits each side to five minutes. However, members may obtain additional speaking time by offering amendments to "strike the last word," a pro forma action that allows additional time for discussion and debate.

Voting may be conducted in three different ways plus variations depending on whether the House or the Committee of the Whole is sitting: by voice, the usual procedure; by division (members stand to be counted but no record of names is kept); or by electronic device (referred to as "the yeas and nays" or a "recorded vote," depending on the parliamentary circumstances). Certain matters in the House require a roll-call vote under the Constitution (for example, to reconsider a vetoed bill) or the rules of the House (for example, passing a general appropriations bill or closing a conference committee meeting to the public). Most electronic votes last fifteen minutes. If several votes in sequence are conducted, the second and any subsequent votes are usually reduced to a minimum of five minutes.

- After the amending process is complete, the Committee of the Whole "rises," and the chair reports to the Speaker on the actions taken. The House votes on whether to accept the amendments adopted in the Committee, usually a pro forma action. The House then votes on final passage of the bill, sometimes after voting on a motion by opponents to recommit the bill to its committee of origin, which would kill it, or to recommit the bill with instructions to report it back "forthwith" with additional amendments that would be adopted prior to final passage. After final passage, a motion to reconsider is in order but is usually announced as "laid on the table" by the Speaker to save time.
- After the House completes its legislative business, members may speak for up to 60 minutes each under "special orders," with hour speeches limited to four hours evenly divided between the parties (except on Tuesdays). Members must reserve the time in advance but can speak on any topic—often to an almost deserted chamber. Members seeking recognition for short periods of time, such as five or ten minutes, are recognized first, alternating between the parties. In 1994, the House limited the total time available for special orders to prevent sessions from extending too long, and special orders cannot extend beyond midnight.

See also: Committees; Elections, House of Representatives; How a Bill Becomes Law; Mace; Majority Leader; Midterm Elections; Minority Leader; Party Whips; Political Parties and Congress; Reapportionment; Redistricting; Senate; Seniority System; Speaker of the House of Representatives.

Further Reading

Koestler-Grack, Rachel A. *The House of Representatives.* London: Chelsea House, 2007.

Remini, Robert V. *The House: The History of the House of Representatives.* New York: HarperCollins, 2007.

How a Bill Becomes Law

The process by which legislation moves through Congress and is enacted into law. Passing a law is not as simple as introducing a measure and taking a vote. All proposed legislation passes through several stages of review and revision in Congress before it is presented to the president for approval or rejection.

Introducing Legislation

Thousands of pieces of legislation are introduced in Congress each year. Only a small percentage, however, are ever debated, much less passed into law.

Developing and Sponsoring Legislation

Proposed legislation can come from a variety of sources. One or more members of Congress may develop ideas for legislation, or they may get ideas from their constituents, the voters who elect them. Ideas often come from a special interest group or lobbyist, a person paid by an organization to persuade politicians to support the organization's goals.

The president is a major source of new legislative proposals, especially when the president's party controls Congress. Every year, the president draws up a list of political goals to achieve. Executive branch agencies and departments then draw up legislation to help achieve these goals and send it to Congress.

Regardless of where legislation originates, only a member can introduce it in Congress. There is no limit to the number of bills and resolutions members may introduce, nor any restrictions on the time during a Congress when they may do so. However, all bills for raising or spending money originate in the House; all other bills may originate in either chamber. For most major legislation, identical bills are introduced to the House and Senate to speed up the legislative process.

Referral to Committee

After introduction, most bills are sent to the appropriate committee, a group of members responsible for drawing up legislation in a specific area of expertise. The Speaker of the House and the presiding officer in the Senate are responsible for referring bills introduced in their respective chambers to the appropriate committees. If a bill is uncontroversial or very urgent, a member might ask unanimous consent to consider it immediately without referral to committee. This is a relatively rare occurrence.

The jurisdictions, or areas of authority, of the standing committees are pretty clear—tax bills go to House Ways and Means and Senate Finance Committees, banking bills to the banking committees in both chambers, and so on. However, bills may cover a variety of subjects that have little or no relationship to each other, which complicates the referral process. Many issues cut across the jurisdictions of several committees. The International Relations, Commerce, and Ways and Means Committees, for example, might all claim jurisdiction over a trade measure. In such a case, the Speaker might refer it to all of them for consideration.

The Committee Process

The standing, or permanent, committees of Congress determine the fate of most proposals. Any major revisions in legislation usually occur at the committee or subcommittee level, rather than during floor debate. Committees usually start with hearings to gather opinions and information. Further revision occurs at meetings where a bill is "marked up" when amendments, or formal changes, are offered, debated, and voted on.

Several things may happen to a bill after referral:

- It may be ignored if the chairman never puts it on the agenda. This is the fate of most legislation.
- It may be approved, or "reported favorably" with or without amendments.

- It may be reported "negatively" or "without recommendation," which might still allow the full House or Senate to consider it.
- It might be killed outright through a tabling motion, which happens only rarely.

Subcommittee Proceedings

If the committee feels that the legislation is worthy of further consideration, it typically refers it to smaller groups within the committee called subcommittees. Few bills reach the House or Senate floor without first being the subject of subcommittee hearings. Hearings are used to gather information, to attract media attention, and to test initial reaction to a legislative idea. They may also be used to gauge the degree of support or opposition to a particular bill.

Following hearings, the subcommittee may take no action, in effect, killing a bill. It may also "mark up" the bill, changing some of its provisions, discarding others, or perhaps rewriting the measure altogether. When the markup is finished, the subcommittee reports its version of the legislation to the full committee. In some instances, the full committee may review the bill directly, bypassing the subcommittee markup stage.

Full Committee Action

The full committee may repeat the subcommittee procedures, sometimes even holding additional hearings. It may mark up a bill, especially if it did not refer the bill to subcommittee, or it may simply approve the action of the subcommittee. Frequently the full committee will propose additional amendments. If these are relatively minor, the original bill is "reported with amendments." If the changes are substantial and the legislation is complicated, the committee chairman or another committee member may introduce a "clean bill" including the proposed amendments.

When a committee votes to approve a measure, it is said to "order the bill reported." House rules and Senate custom require that a written report accompany each bill reported from a committee to the floor. The report, written by the committee staff, typically describes the purpose and scope of the bill, explains committee amendments, indicates proposed changes in existing law, estimates additional costs to the government of the recommended program changes, and often includes any input the committee received from interested parties.

Scheduling

Before a bill is scheduled for floor action, it is placed on a legislative calendar. Bills are placed on the calendars in the order in which they are reported, but they do not come to the floor in that order. Some never come to the floor at all. The leadership in each chamber usually works with members to determine which bills will come to the floor and when. In the House, the majority party controls the calendars and thus decides which bills come to the floor. The Senate process is more bipartisan, with the leadership working to accommodate individual members.

In the House, major legislation must receive a rule from the Rules Committee before being brought up for action. A rule describes the conditions under which the chamber will debate a matter. It also determines whether members may amend a bill and what types of amendments they may propose. The Senate, by contrast, does not use special rules. Amendments of any type are typically permitted during Senate floor action.

Floor Action

After adopting a rule, the entire House membership meets as the Committee of the Whole House on the State of the Union to debate and amend the legislation. The Committee of the Whole is a parliamentary device to speed up House action. It allows the House to do business when only 100 members are present, rather than the 218 members required when it meets as the full House. The Committee of the Whole has no counterpart in the Senate.

The Committee of the Whole debates amendments, on which members then vote. The Committee of the Whole cannot pass a bill. Instead, it reports the measure back to the full House with whatever changes it makes. The House then may adopt or reject the proposed amendments, amend a bill further, send it back to the committee where it originated, or vote on it. Amendments adopted in the Committee of the Whole are always put to a second vote in the full House. The Committee of the Whole itself may not send a bill back to committee.

The first order of business in the Committee of the Whole is general debate on the bill. The rules on most bills allot an hour for general debate, although more time may be granted for particularly controversial measures. The allotted time is divided equally between the two parties. Debate on any amendment is theoretically limited to five minutes for supporters and five minutes for opponents. Members regularly obtain more time, however.

Debate in the senate is unlimited, which sometimes results in a tactic called the filibuster. In a filibuster, a senator opposed to a piece of legislation engages in delaying tactics such as making a very long speech, or even reading out of the phone book. The goal is to bring debate to a halt, often to frustrate the will of the majority. Opponents can end a filibuster if three-fifths of the senators present vote for cloture.

Amendment and Voting

Once general debate is completed, the measure is read for amendment. In the House, each part of a bill must be considered in order. Members offer amendments to the appropriate part as it is read. Once a part is completed, amendments to it can be made only by unanimous consent of the members. House rules require amendments to be germane, or relevant, to the bill itself. The rule adopted by the Rules Committee may, however, permit nongermane amendments. Amendments made by committees are considered before amendments offered from the floor.

In the Senate, any part of the measure is open immediately to amendment. Moreover, amendments need not be germane, except in the case of general appropriations, or spending bills. The Senate is not bound by a five-minute rule governing debate on amendments. Unless limited by a unanimous consent agreement or cloture, debate on amendments may continue until no senator seeks to offer further amendments.

Following debate and amendment, members vote on the final legislation. In the House, the Committee of the Whole dissolves itself and the membership meets as the full House. In both chambers, voting occurs at this point. Most bills require a simple majority to pass, although some measures require a two-thirds vote. A tie defeats the measure in question. If the vote in the Senate is tied, however, the vice president may cast a tie-breaking vote. A measure passed in one chamber is then sent to the other chamber where it must go through the same legislative process.

Both chambers must pass identical forms of the bill before sending it to the president for signature. In many instances, the two chambers pass different versions of a bill. In this case, a conference committee, consisting of members from both chambers, is assembled to work out the differences.

Signing and Vetoes

After both chambers have given final approval to a bill, a final copy of the bill, known as the enrolled bill, is sent to the White House. The president has ten days (not counting Sundays) from the day of receipt to act on it. If the president approves the measure, he or she signs it, dates it, and usually writes "approved" on the document. A bill also may become law if the president does not sign a bill within the ten-day limit.

The president may veto a bill, returning it to the chamber in which it originated without signing it. If no further action is taken, the bill dies. However, Congress can override a presidential veto if two-thirds of those present and voting in both chambers vote to do so. There must be a quorum present for the vote and only "yea" and "nay" votes are counted; those who vote "present" are not considered.

The president may avoid a veto override by exercising a pocket veto. This occurs if the president refuses to sign a bill and the ten-day limit expires after Congress has adjourned, or suspended its activities. With Congress out of session, it cannot act to override a pocket veto. This tactic can only be used to veto legislation passed very close to the end of a session.

Legislative Irregularities

Peculiar situations have arisen occasionally when Congress searches for an appropriate manner to achieve a new or unique result. Even if Congress cannot find a method, it may do what it wants to anyway. Here are several examples.

In 1978, for example, Congress attempted a new form of legislative enactment to extend the time permitted for ratification of a constitutional amendment. The so-called Equal Rights Amendment (ERA), passed by Congress in 1972 and intended to enhance women's rights, carried within it a seven-year time limit for ratification by the necessary three-fourths of the states. It would die on March 22, 1979, unless ratified by thirty-eight states. Congress had first set time limits on amendment ratifications beginning in 1917 to ensure that the initial proposal of an amendment and its ultimate ratification were roughly at the same time.

With the deadline nearing, Congress wanted to keep the amendment alive to see if additional states might ratify the amendment. A joint resolution was passed extending the life of the amendment by thirty-nine additional months, until June 30, 1982. Congress first had determined, by simple majority, that a two-thirds vote was not required for passage of the time-extension. (It also would have been more difficult to obtain a two-thirds vote in 1978 than in 1972 because the amendment had become far more controversial after its passage.)

Once passed by both houses, the joint resolution was sent to President Jimmy Carter (1977–1981), who proceeded to sign it even while raising doubt that he had any role in the process and questioning whether the joint resolution was really a law. The Archivist of the United States, who received the joint resolution next, did not give it a public law number, but instead notified the states of its existence. A federal judge ruled in 1981 that Congress had acted improperly, but the question became moot when additional states failed to ratify the amendment even under the extended timetable. The Supreme Court dismissed the case as moot in 1982 and vacated the lower court's decision, leaving the ultimate validity of the congressional action in constitutional limbo.

Other examples of unusual legislative actions have involved constitutional amendments. Congress does not need to take any formal action once an amendment has been ratified. In 1868, however, Congress passed a concurrent resolution to declare that the Fourteenth Amendment to the Constitution had been ratified by the requisite number of states. In 1992, reeling from scandals and low public approval ratings, members rushed to identify themselves with the so-called Madison Amendment to the Constitution, which required that an election intervene before any congressional pay raise could take effect. The amendment, originally proposed by Congress in 1789, suddenly reemerged in 1978, more than a century since the last time a state legislature had approved it, to begin a flurry of new ratifications. Previous historical concerns by Congress about contemporaneous enactment of constitutional amendments were thrown to the winds as members rushed to embrace what was still one of the most popular forms of Congress-bashing—denying themselves pay raises.

Each house passed a concurrent resolution stating that the new Twenty-Seventh Amendment was properly ratified, but neither house passed the concurrent resolution adopted by the other. Not satisfied with that, the Senate also adopted a simple resolution declaring ratification of the amendment. Adding to the confusion, the Archivist of the United States had already declared the amendment ratified on May 18, 1992, before Congress acted.

In 1998, as Congress awaited the results of an investigation by Special Prosecutor Kenneth Starr into scandals involving the Clinton administration, rumors of possible impeachment proceedings waxed and waned on Capitol Hill with each passing news cycle. Under the Constitution, the House, by majority vote, can initiate articles of impeachment that would result in a trial by the Senate, where a two-thirds majority is required for conviction and removal from office. Until 1998 only one president, Andrew Johnson (1865–1869) had ever been impeached, but he was acquitted by a single vote in the

Senate. Richard M. Nixon (1969–1974) was believed to have faced certain impeachment, conviction, and removal from office had he not resigned first.

That changed late in 1998 when the Republican-led House, following elections in which the GOP lost seats, approved articles of impeachment against President Bill Clinton (1993–2001), which forced the issue to the Senate. In 1999, the Senate took up the articles but voted not to convict the president.

In the course of this, members in both chambers–but particularly the Senate–looked for ways to express strong disapproval of Clinton's actions involving a female White House intern and his response to legal proceedings that grew out of the matter. Senate Majority Leader Trent Lott, a Republican from Mississippi, suggested a censure of the president by Congress if the charges against Clinton were insufficient for impeachment conviction. The Senate had done this before, to President Andrew Jackson (1829–1837), in 1834, in a political dispute over the Bank of the United States, whose reauthorization Jackson had vetoed. He later directed U.S. funds be removed from the bank and deposited in state banks. Bank supporters in Congress and Jackson's bitter enemies then arranged a presidential censure, but the action carried no legal weight and was never repeated by any future Congress. The Constitution does not recognize any punishment other than impeachment and removal from office. Jackson's allies later expunged the censure from the Senate Journal. In 1999, once conviction of Clinton was defeated, the idea of censure was not raised again.

Presumably, if Senator Lott's suggestion were to be followed, either House could initiate a concurrent resolution to censure the president or act separately by simple resolution. However, such measures would not be privileged for consideration in either chamber and would be subject to a filibuster in the Senate.

In 1997, the Senate reached back to rewrite history again. In 1996, the House had passed a conference report containing continuing appropriations funding government agencies. However, to deal with possible Senate opposition, the House also passed the funding as a separate bill that the Senate might amend if it chose to do so. Ultimately, the Senate passed both bills; the conference report was sent to the president and signed into law. However, instead of simply killing the unnecessary separate bill, it was passed without amendment by a roll-call vote and the Daily Digest of the *Congressional Record* noted that it was cleared for the president. However, this did not happen. The Senate never sent a message to the House formally notifying it of the bill's passage, which prevented the House from enrolling it for presentation to the president, as required. Presumably, had this been done, the president could simply have disposed of the bill with a quiet pocket veto. With the bill in limbo, the 104th Congress expired, preventing any enrollment.

Nevertheless, Representative David Skaggs, a Democrat from Colorado, was concerned with setting a precedent that a bill passed in identical form by both houses of Congress could be kept from the president by direction of the majority leadership of one chamber. He called Majority Leader Lott demanding an explanation. He also inserted a letter to Lott and a history of the incident into the *Congressional Record.* In response, in February 1997, Senate Majority Whip Don Nickles, Republican from Oklahoma, rose on the floor to ask unanimous consent to amend the Senate Journal of the preceding Congress to state that the bill had been indefinitely postponed.

See also: Calendars, House of Representatives; Calendars, Senate; Committees; Cloture; Congressional Voting Methods; Filibuster; House of Representatives; Majority Leader; Minority Leader; President and Congress; Senate; Sessions of Congress; Speaker of the House of Representatives; Two-Thirds Rule; Vetoes and Veto Overrides; Vice President.

Further Reading

Donovan, Sandy. *Making Laws: A Look at How a Bill Becomes Law.* Minneapolis, MN: Lerner, 2003.

Waldman, Stephen. *The Bill: How Legislation Really Becomes Law.* New York: Penguin, 1996.

A–Z

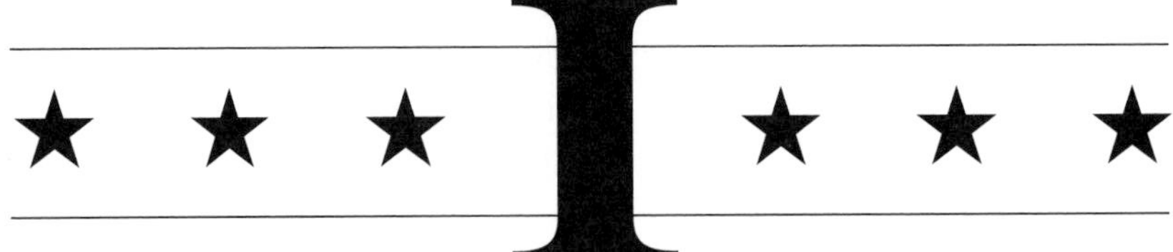

Impeachment Power

Congressional authority to charge a government official with crimes or misconduct while in office. Most impeachment proceedings have been directed against federal judges, who cannot be removed by any other method. Congress has also initiated impeachment proceedings against presidents, cabinet members, diplomats, customs collectors, a senator, and a U.S. district attorney.

Constitutional Basis

The provisions on impeachment are scattered through the first three articles of the Constitution. Impeachments may be brought against "the President, Vice President and all civil officers of the United States" for "treason, bribery or other high crimes or misdemeanors." The House of Representatives has the power to bring charges against an official. If a majority of the members agree to impeachment, the accused official is tried by the Senate. Convicted officials are removed from office and may be disqualified to hold further public office.

There is no appeal of a conviction. The Constitution states that the presidential power to grant reprieves and pardons does not include cases of impeachment. Officials convicted and removed from office remain subject to prosecution in the regular courts.

Treason and bribery are fairly straightforward charges, but "High Crimes and Misdemeanors" can be almost anything that the prosecution wants to make them. In 1970, Representative Gerald R. Ford of Michigan declared, "An impeachable offense is whatever a majority of the House of Representatives considers it to be at a given moment in history." Ironically, Ford ascended to the presidency four years later when Richard Nixon resigned to avoid impeachment proceedings.

House Proceedings

The House has no standing rules dealing with its role in the impeachment process. Impeachment proceedings have started in a variety of ways. The eight cases to reach the Senate between 1900 and 1991 were based initially on Judiciary Committee resolutions. When Bill Clinton (1993–2001) was impeached in 1998, a court-appointed independent counsel initiated impeachment proceedings.

After bringing charges against an official, the House creates a committee to investigate the matter. The committee decides whether the subject of the inquiry has the right to be present at committee proceedings, to be represented by an attorney, and to present and question witnesses. If the investigation seems to support the charges, the committee issues an impeachment resolution.

If a majority of the House votes to adopt a resolution of impeachment, the case goes to the Senate for a trial. House members are selected to present the case, acting as prosecutors in the Senate trial. An odd number–from five to eleven–traditionally has been selected, including members from both parties who voted in favor of impeachment.

Senate Trial

An impeachment trial is conducted in a fashion similar to a criminal trial. Both sides may present witnesses and evidence, and the defendant is allowed counsel, the right to testify, and the right of cross-examination. If the president or the vice president is on trial, the Constitution requires the Chief Justice of the United States to preside. The Constitution does not specify a presiding officer for lesser defendants. By Senate custom, the vice president or the president pro tempore of the Senate presides.

Impeached Officials, 1798–2008

Year	Official	Position	Outcome
1798–1799	William Blount	U.S. senator	charges dismissed
1804	John Pickering	district court judge	removed from office
1805	Samuel Chase	Supreme Court justice	acquitted
1830–1831	James H. Peck	district court judge	acquitted
1862	West H. Humphreys	district court judge	removed from office
1868	Andrew Johnson	president	acquitted
1876	William Belknap	secretary of war	acquitted
1905	Charles Swayne	district court judge	acquitted
1912–1913	Robert W. Archbald	commerce court judge	removed from office
1926	George W. English	district court judge	charges dismissed
1933	Harold Louderback	district court judge	acquitted
1936	Halsted L. Ritter	district court judge	removed from office
1986	Harry E. Claiborne	district court judge	removed from office
1989	Alcee L. Hastings	district court judge	removed from office
1989	Walter L. Nixon Jr.	district court judge	removed from office
1999	Bill Clinton	president	acquitted

***Note:* The House in 1873 adopted a resolution of impeachment against District Judge Mark H. Delahay, but Delahay resigned before articles of impeachment were prepared, so the Senate took no action.**

Between 1789 and 1999 the Senate sat as a court of impeachment sixteen times. Most impeachment trials have involved members of the judicial branch. Two presidents, however, have been impeached—Andrew Johnson in 1868 and Bill Clinton in 1999.

The presiding officer can compel witnesses to appear and enforce obedience to Senate orders. He or she makes final rules on all questions of evidence, although senators may request a vote on such matters. The presiding officer questions witnesses and asks questions submitted in writing by senators, who do not directly question witnesses themselves.

If the defendant faces several articles or charges, the Senate votes separately on each article. A two-thirds vote is required for conviction. If no article is approved by two-thirds of the senators present, the impeached official is acquitted. If any article receives two-thirds approval, the person is convicted. The Senate may vote separately to remove the person from office, but this is not required.

The Senate also may vote to disqualify the person from holding future federal office. Disqualification is not mandatory. Only two of the seven officials convicted in an impeachment trial have been disqualified. Disqualification requires only a majority vote instead of the two-thirds needed for conviction.

History

By far the largest category of government officials impeached has been federal judges. Through 1999, the House impeached seventeen federal officials, thirteen of whom were judges. The

Senate subsequently tried twelve impeached judges, but only seven were convicted and removed from office. The other impeached officials—none of whom were convicted by the Senate—were President Andrew Johnson (1868), Senator William Blount (1797), Secretary of War William Belknap (1876), and President Bill Clinton (1999). The cases of Chase, Johnson, and Clinton stand out from all the rest.

Samuel Chase

On January 7, 1804, the House voted to authorize an investigation of Associate Supreme Court Justice Samuel Chase, and also of Richard Peters, a U.S. district judge from Pennsylvania. The investigation supposedly was intended to study their conduct during a recent treason trial. Many observers, however, considered it a partisan political attack against Chase. On March 12, the House dropped the probe of Peters but voted for a resolution calling for Chase's impeachment.

The House approved eight articles of impeachment, charging Chase with harsh and partisan conduct on the bench and with unfairness to litigants. A majority of senators voted for three of the counts. However, Chase was acquitted when the Senate failed to reach the required two-thirds vote on any article.

Andrew Johnson

The first presidential impeachment occurred in 1868. President Andrew Johnson (1865–1869) was charged with violating a federal statute, the Tenure of Office Act. The impeachment, however, was part of a larger political struggle dealing with larger questions, such as control of the Republican Party and the chaos in the South following the Civil War.

This ticket allowed spectators to the Senate galleries to observe the impeachment trial of President Andrew Johnson in 1868. (Library of Congress)

Johnson had been the only member of the U.S. Senate from a seceding southern state (Tennessee) to remain loyal to the Union in 1861. Johnson was a lifelong Democrat, but he and Lincoln ran on the Union Ticket in 1864 in an attempt to bridge the divisions within the war-torn nation. When Lincoln died in 1865, Johnson succeeded to the presidency. His ideas on rebuilding and readmitting the southern states to the Union clashed with those of Congress, which was overwhelmingly controlled by the Republicans.

In March 1867, Congress passed the Tenure of Office Act, overriding Johnson's attempt to veto, or reject, the bill. The act forbade the president from removing civil officers without the approval of the Senate. In December, however, Johnson suspended Secretary of War Edwin Stanton without consulting the Senate. The Senate refused to accept this action and returned Stanton to his post. On February 21, 1868, citing the power and authority vested in him by the Constitution, Johnson fired Stanton.

This action enraged Congress, who impeached Johnson three days later. There were eleven articles of impeachment, the main one directed at Johnson's removal of Stanton in violation of the Tenure of Office Act. The Senate, however, fell one vote shy of convicting Johnson on any of the articles.

Bill Clinton

When impeachment proceedings began against President Bill Clinton (1993–2001) in 1998, he had been under scrutiny in two legal investigations for four years. One focused on his involvement in a failed Arkansas land deal called Whitewater. Clinton also was the defendant in a sexual harassment suit brought against him in February 1994 by Paula Corbin Jones, a former Arkansas state employee.

Jones' attorneys hoped to show that Clinton's alleged conduct with Jones was part of

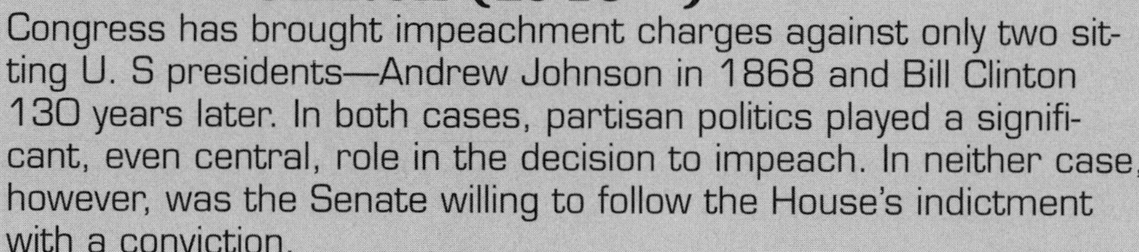

SPOTLIGHT

Andrew Johnson (1808–1875) and Bill Clinton (1946–)

Congress has brought impeachment charges against only two sitting U. S presidents—Andrew Johnson in 1868 and Bill Clinton 130 years later. In both cases, partisan politics played a significant, even central, role in the decision to impeach. In neither case, however, was the Senate willing to follow the House's indictment with a conviction.

Johnson, who ascended to the presidency after the assassination of Abraham Lincoln in 1865, soon found himself politically at odds with the Republican-controlled Congress. Most Republicans wished to punish the former Confederate states by imposing martial law in the South and denying former rebel soldiers the right to vote. Johnson favored a less punitive plan for "**Reconstruction**" of the South originally championed by Lincoln.

Tension between Johnson and the Republicans in Congress reached a peak after Congress passed the Tenure of Office Act in 1867. Johnson considered the law, which forbade the president from dismissing cabinet officers without Senate approval, a direct challenge to his authority. When Johnson fired Secretary of War Edwin Stanton without consulting Congress, the House filed impeachment charges.

Clinton also suffered from often-bitter disagreements with political opponents in Congress. His efforts at healthcare reform, his "don't ask, don't tell" policy toward gays in the military, and his policy of raising taxes on wealthier citizens made him extremely unpopular with congressional Republicans.

In 1998, it came to light that Clinton had had an extramarital affair with a White House intern named Monica Lewinsky. In the meantime, claiming that Clinton made improper advances to her while he was governor of Arkansas, a woman named Paula Jones had filed a charge of sexual harassment against him. In a sworn statement related to that charge, Clinton denied that he had had sexual relations with Lewinsky. When that claim later proved untrue, the House impeached Clinton on charges of perjury and obstructing justice in the sexual assault case.

As with Johnson, the Senate declined to convict Clinton. However, while Johnson won acquittal by only a single vote, Clinton's opponents fell far short of the two-thirds majority needed to convict. The primary difference was that Clinton retained the support of his party's members in Congress. While most Republican senators voted to convict Johnson, no Democratic senators voted against Clinton, who—also unlike Johnson—remained a very popular president with the public after the impeachment.

a broader pattern of sexual harassment. They compiled a list of women whose names had been linked with Clinton's. The list included Monica S. Lewinsky, a Pentagon employee who had been a White House intern. Lewinsky argued that she had no information relevant to the Jones case and filed a sworn statement in which she denied ever having sexual relations with Clinton. She had, however, told several friends about having an involvement with Clinton. One friend, Linda R. Tripp, taped conversations in which Lewinsky described her intimate relationship with Clinton and said that Clinton had urged her to lie about it.

Clinton told Jones' attorneys that he had never had sexual relations with Lewinsky. However, Lewinsky admitted to a grand jury that she and Clinton had had an affair but insisted that he never told her to lie about it. President Clinton then admitted to an "inappropriate" relationship with Lewinsky and to making "misleading" statements under oath, but he denied that he had done anything illegal. On September 9, special prosecutor Kenneth Starr delivered a report to the House charging that Clinton had committed impeachable offenses. The House approved two articles of impeachment against Clinton. The first accused him of lying in his grand jury testimony about Monica Lewinsky. The second charged Clinton with obstruction of justice for "using the powers of his high office" to "delay, impede, cover up and conceal" his involvement with Lewinsky.

On February 12, 1999, the article accusing Clinton of committing perjury before a federal grand jury, was defeated, 45–55, with ten Republicans joining all forty-five Democrats. Article II, which charged the president with obstructing justice, was also defeated 50–50.

In the aftermath of the trial, bitterness over the impeachment remained in Congress. Republicans blamed it on the president himself, saying that his character flaws brought about the national ordeal. Democrats, with some admitting that the president had committed moral misdeeds, saw the whole affair as an attempt to embarrass President Clinton.

See also: Article of Impeachment Against Andrew Johnson, 1868, in the **Primary Source Library;** Articles of Impeachment Against William Jefferson Clinton, 1998, in the **Primary Source Library;** President and Congress; Two-Thirds Rule; Watergate Hearings; Whitewater Investigations.

Further Reading

Aaseng, Nathan. *Famous Trials–The Impeachment of Bill Clinton.* Farmington Hills, MI: Lucent, 1999.

Benedict, Michael Les. *The Impeachment and Trial of Andrew Johnson.* New York: W.W. Norton, 1999.

Impeachment Rules, Senate

Rules first written for the trial of President Andrew Johnson (1865–1869) in 1868. Rule XI was adopted on May 28, 1935. The rules were modified slightly in 1986. Following are the major provisions of rules used by the Senate during impeachment trials.

> I. Whensoever the Senate shall receive notice from the House of Representatives that managers are appointed on their part to conduct an impeachment against any person and are directed to carry articles of impeachment to the Senate, the Secretary of the Senate shall immediately inform the House of Representatives that the Senate is ready to receive the managers, for purpose of exhibiting such articles of impeachment, agreeably to such notice.
>
> II. When the managers of an impeachment shall be introduced at the bar of the Senate and shall signify that they are ready to exhibit articles of impeachment against any person,

the Presiding Officer of the Senate shall direct the Sergeant at Arms to make proclamation, who shall, after making proclamation, repeat the following words, viz: 'All persons are commanded to keep silence, on pain of imprisonment, while the House of Representatives is exhibiting to the Senate articles of impeachment' . . . after which articles shall be exhibited, and then the Presiding Officer of the Senate shall inform the managers that the Senate will take proper order on the subject of the impeachment, of which due notice shall be given to the House of Representatives.

III. Upon such articles being presented to the Senate, the Senate shall, at 1 o'clock afternoon of the day (Sunday excepted) following such presentation, or sooner if ordered by the Senate, proceed to the consideration of such articles and shall continue in session from day to day (Sundays excepted) after the trial shall commence (unless otherwise ordered by the Senate) until final judgment shall be rendered . . .

IV. When the President of the United States or the Vice President of the United States . . . shall be impeached, the Chief Justice of the United States shall preside; and in a case requiring the said Chief Justice to preside notice shall be given to him by the Presiding Officer of the Senate of the time and place fixed for the consideration of articles of impeachment, as aforesaid, with a request to attend. . . .

V. The Presiding Officer shall have power to make and issue, by himself or by the Secretary of the Senate, all orders, mandates, writs, and precepts authorized by these rules or by the Senate, and to make and enforce such other regulations and orders in the premises as the Senate may authorize or provide.

VI. The Senate shall have power to compel the attendance of witnesses, to enforce obedience to its orders, mandates, writs, precepts, and judgments, to preserve order, and to punish in a summary way contempts of, and disobedience to, its authority. . . .

VII. The Presiding Officer of the Senate shall direct all necessary preparations in the Senate Chamber, and the Presiding Officer on the trial shall direct all the forms of proceedings while the Senate is sitting for the purpose of trying an impeachment . . . And the Presiding Officer on the trial may rule on all questions of evidence including, but not limited to, questions of relevancy, materiality, and redundancy of evidence and incidental questions, which ruling shall stand as the judgment of the Senate, unless some Member of the Senate shall ask that a formal vote be taken thereon. . . .

VIII. Upon presentation of articles of impeachment and the organization of the Senate as hereinbefore provided, a writ of summons shall issue to the person impeached, reciting said articles, and notifying him to appear before the Senate upon a day and at a place to be fixed by the Senate and named in such writ, and file his answer to said articles of impeachment and to stand to and abide the orders and judgments of the Senate thereon. . . .

IX. At 12:30 o'clock afternoon of the day appointed for the return of the summons against the person impeached, the legislative and executive business of the Senate shall be suspended, and the Secretary of the

Senate shall administer an oath to the returning officer. . . .

X. The person impeached shall then be called to appear and answer the articles of impeachment against him. If he appears, or any person for him, the appearance shall be recorded. . . .

XI. That in the trial of any impeachment the Presiding Officer of the Senate, if the Senate so orders, shall appoint a committee of senators to receive evidence and take testimony at such times as the committee may determine . . .

XII. At 12:30 o'clock afternoon, or at such other hour as the Senate may order, of the day appointed for the trial of an impeachment, the legislative and executive business of the Senate shall be suspended, and the Secretary shall give notice to the House of Representatives that the Senate is ready to proceed to the impeachment of [the president] in the Senate chamber.

XIII. The hour of the day at which the Senate shall sit upon the trial of an impeachment shall be (unless otherwise ordered) 12 o'clock [noon]; and when the hour shall arrive, the Presiding Officer upon such trial shall cause proclamation to be made, and the business of the trial shall proceed. The adjournment of the Senate sitting in said trial shall not operate as an adjournment of the Senate; but on such adjournment the Senate shall resume the consideration of its legislative and executive business.

XIV. The Secretary of the Senate shall record the proceedings in cases of impeachment as in the case of legislative proceedings, and the same shall be reported in the same manner as the legislative proceedings of the Senate.

XV. Counsel for the parties shall be admitted to appear and be heard upon an impeachment.

XVI. All motions, objections, requests, or applications whether relating to the procedure of the Senate or relating immediately to the trial (including questions with respect to admission of evidence or other questions arising during the trial) made by the parties or their counsel shall be addressed to the Presiding Officer only, and if he, or any Senator, require it, they shall be committed to writing and read at the Secretary's table.

XVII. Witnesses shall be examined by one person on behalf of the party producing them, and then cross-examined by one person on the other side.

XVIII. If a Senator is called as a witness, he shall be sworn, and give his testimony standing in his place.

XIX. If a Senator wishes a question to be put to a witness, or a manager, or to counsel of the person impeached, or to offer a motion or order (except a motion to adjourn), it shall be reduced to writing, and put to the Presiding Officer. The parties or their counsel may interpose objections to witnesses answering questions propounded at the request of any Senator and the merits of any such objection may be argued by the parties or their counsel. Ruling on any such objection shall be made as provided in Rule VII. It shall not be in order for any Senator to engage in a colloquy.

XX. At all times while the Senate is sitting upon the trial of an impeachment the doors of the Senate shall be kept open, unless the Senate shall direct the doors to be closed while deliberating upon its decisions. A motion to close the doors may be acted upon without objection, or, if objection is heard, the motion shall be voted on without debate by the yeas and nays, which shall be entered on the record.

XXI. All preliminary and interlocutory questions, and all motions, shall be argued for not exceeding one hour (unless the Senate otherwise orders) on each side.

XXII. The case, on each side, shall be opened by one person. The final argument on the merits may be made by two persons on each side (unless otherwise ordered by the Senate upon application for that purpose), and the argument shall be opened and closed on the part of the House of Representatives.

XXIII. An article of impeachment shall not be divisible for the purpose of voting thereon at any time during the trial. Once voting has commenced on an article of impeachment, voting shall be continued until voting has been completed on all articles of impeachment unless the Senate adjourns for a period not to exceed one day or adjourns sine die. On the final question whether the impeachment is sustained, the yeas and nays shall be taken on each article of impeachment separately; and if the impeachment shall not, upon any of the articles presented, be sustained by the votes of two-thirds of the Members present, a judgment of acquittal shall be entered; but if the person impeached shall be convicted upon any such article by the votes of two-thirds of the Members present, the Senate shall proceed to the consideration of such other matters as may be determined to be appropriate prior to pronouncing judgment . . . the Presiding Officer shall first state the question; thereafter each Senator, as his name is called, shall rise in his place and answer: guilty or not guilty.

XXIV. All the orders and decisions may be acted upon without objection, or, if objection is heard, the orders and decisions shall be voted on without debate by yeas and nays, which shall be entered on the record, subject, however, to the operation of Rule VII, except that when the doors shall be closed for deliberation, and in that case no member shall speak more than once on one question, and for not more than 10 minutes on an interlocutory question, and for not more than 15 minutes on the final question, unless by consent of the Senate, to be had without debate. . . .

XXV. Witnesses shall be sworn. . . . Which oath shall be administered by the Secretary, or any other duly authorized person. . . .

XXVI. If the Senate shall at any time fail to sit for the consideration of articles of impeachment on the day or hour fixed therefor, the Senate may, by an order to be adopted without debate, fix a day and hour for resuming such consideration.

Implied Powers

Authority not specifically granted to Congress in the Constitution but which is assumed to be necessary to carry out its functions. While the Constitution is very specific about some of the powers granted to Congress, others are subject to interpretation. Congress historically has expanded its authority by interpreting some of these powers very broadly.

Article I, Section 8, of the Constitution contains a list of powers specifically granted to Congress, known as expressed powers. The last clause of that section, the so-called "necessary and proper" clause, gives Congress the power "[t]o make all Laws which shall be necessary and proper for carrying into Execution the foregoing Powers, and all other Powers vested by this Constitution in the Government of the United States, or in any Department or Officer thereof."

The intent of this clause was simply to enable Congress to enact legislation that would enable it to exercise the specific powers listed earlier in Section 8. None of the delegates to the Constitutional Convention suggested that it was meant to confer powers in addition to those previously specified. However, the meaning of the clause and of the words "necessary and proper" was to become the focus of a continuing battle between two different views of the Constitution: broad and strict construction.

Strict constructionists argue that the federal government should exercise only those powers specifically granted in the Constitution. They claim that Congress can exercise implied powers under the "necessary and proper" clause only if failing to do so would prevent it from carrying out its expressed powers. Broad constructionists, on the other hand, claim that the clause allows Congress to take whatever steps it deems necessary to achieve its goals, as long as it does not infringe upon the powers granted to the other branches of government.

Alexander Hamilton's proposal to establish a national bank offered an early test of the limits of implied powers. Opponents of the bank claimed that the Constitution did not grant Congress the specific authority to establish a bank. Hamilton countered that it was impossible for the Constitution to specify all the powers the government could use, because it was impossible to know what kinds of needs it might face in the future. He argued that the bank was "necessary and proper" to serve the general welfare, a task assigned to Congress by the Constitution. Hamilton won the argument, and President George Washington (1789–1797) signed into law the bill establishing the bank.

See also: Expressed Powers; Federalism; United States Constitution, Article I, Section 8, 1789, in the **Primary Source Library.**

Impoundment

The refusal by the president to spend money appropriated by Congress. Many presidents have withheld funds set aside by Congress for certain government programs, but the issue remained largely uncontroversial until the 1970s.

In the early 1970s, President Richard Nixon impounded billions of dollars Congress had provided—despite the president's objections—for certain government programs. By withholding the funds, Nixon set off a legal and political struggle over the issue of whether the executive or the legislature held final authority over how the government spent its money. Nixon argued that he was withholding funds only as a financial management technique, primarily to slow inflation through temporary reductions in federal spending. House and Senate Democratic leaders contended that Nixon used impoundments to impose his own priorities in defiance of laws passed by Congress. In 1974, Congress passed a budget law that set up procedures whereby presidents could delay or cancel the expenditure of congressionally appropriated funds. The law provided that, if the president felt that money should not be spent at all, the president must

President Richard M. Nixon (1969–1974) set off a legal and political struggle in the 1970s by refusing to spend all the money Congress appropriated. (Richard Nixon Library)

propose that Congress rescind, or cancel, the appropriation making the funds available. In that case, both the House and Senate must approve the decision within forty-five days. If the two houses did not act, the president must release the funds at the end of the forty-five-day period. To simply delay spending temporarily, the law provided a way for the president to defer outlays. Under the budget act, the deferral stood unless either the House or Senate passed a resolution directing that the money be spent. Congress could act on a deferral at any time.

By law, the president must keep Congress informed of impoundments by sending deferral and rescission requests to Capitol Hill. The General Accounting Office may review deferral and rescission messages for accuracy, and the comptroller general has authority to report to Congress any executive branch action that impounds funds without proper notification of Congress. Such a report triggers rescission or deferral proceedings as though the president had made a request to Congress. The comptroller general also may reclassify deferrals as rescissions, or vice versa, and may go to federal court to enforce the law's impoundment requirements.

See also: Appropriations Bills.

Interns, Congressional

Temporary employees, including young men and women, who assist members of Congress with various tasks and activities. Little is known about the origins of the use of interns in Congress. It probably began when members of Congress hired college students studying American government or the sons and daughters of constituents in their districts to work in their offices during the summer. This diverse and informal method of employment expanded greatly during the 1960s.

Today, interns work in Congress throughout the year, although most student interns just work there during the summer. Congressional interns vary widely in their experience and their office responsibilities. Less experienced interns may undertake clerical tasks such as sending faxes, filing papers, or copying reports and other papers. They may help to answer mail or escort visitors around the Capitol. Those with more experience may be assigned to help with work related to constituents, draft speeches and reports, or aid the permanent staff of congressional committees. These more experienced interns sometimes get to do research for members of Congress and attend congressional hearings.

Interns may be paid from a congressperson's annual staff allowance or from other funds available to the office. Many interns are not paid at all. They work merely for the experience of working in Congress. Some interns are under private internships and their expenses are paid by their sponsors. The Congressional Fellowship program of the American Political Science Association, for example, brings each year a few dozen experienced journalists, teachers, and government officials to Congress to serve as interns. Employees of federal agencies also may be assigned to Congress as interns for a time if necessary. Many student interns receive academic credit for their work from their colleges and universities.

Iran-Contra Hearings

Congressional hearings held in 1987 to investigate possible wrongdoing concerning sales of arms to Iran by the administration of President Ronald Reagan (1981–1989). In November 1986, the administration of President Reagan was shaken by disclosures of secret U.S. arms sales to Iran and by reports of the illegal diversion of some of the profits from these sales to U.S.-backed rebels in Nicaragua. Those profits went to a rebel group in Nicaragua known as the Contras, who were fighting the Cuban-backed government in Nicaragua, known as the Sandinistas. The revelations of these possible illegal activities by the Reagan administration triggered multiple investigations in Congress and curtailed the political effectiveness of an otherwise popular president. Several participants in the affair, including key White House aides, were indicted by a federal grand jury and two of them were given prison sentences.

When the Iran-Contra story broke, investigators scrambled to find out what happened. Their job was complicated by such problems as conflicting recollections, contradictory statements from the White House, sloppy record keeping, a misleading chronology prepared by key participants, and destruction and alteration of documents. Attorney General Edwin Meese III conducted the first inquiry into the affair, on behalf of the Reagan administration. Although Meese's inquiry was much criticized for its investigative techniques, the inquiry did uncover a memo from Lieutenant Colonel Oliver North, a member of the National Security Council staff based in the White House. The memo mentioned the diversion of funds to the Contras. In the aftermath of that disclosure, North was fired and his boss, Vice Admiral John M. Poindexter, resigned.

President Reagan then appointed a special board of inquiry, headed by former Senator John Tower, a Texas Republican. The group also included Edmund S. Muskie, a Maine Democrat who had served as both a senator and secretary of state, and former national security adviser Brent Scowcroft.

Meanwhile, Congress began its own investigations of the affair. The House and Senate Intelligence Committees and the House Foreign Affairs Committee held hearings. Each chamber also appointed a special investigating committee. In January 1987, the Senate Intelligence Committee released a report chronicling the affair. A much more complete picture of the affair was provided the next month when the Tower Commission released its report. While cautiously worded, the Tower report presented a harsh picture of failures by Reagan and his aides. The commission criticized the president's inattention to detail and the failure of White House staff to act appropriately.

After the Tower report, Reagan fired his White House chief of staff, Donald T. Regan, and in a televised speech, accepted responsibility for any failures of his administration. For the first time, he also acknowledged that the United States had traded arms to Iran, a bitter enemy, in the hope of gaining the release of Americans being held hostage in Lebanon. The House and Senate intelligence committees filled in many details of what had happened during a series of televised hearings. For the American public, the focal point of the hearings was the combative testimony of Oliver North, who portrayed himself as a loyal military man who had done only what he had been told to do.

Marine Lt. Col. Oliver North is sworn in before giving testimony to a 1987 Senate-House Committee hearing concerning the Iran-Contra affair, which involved funding money to the Nicaraguan rebels, or Contras, in Central America. (AP Photo, J. Scott Applewhite)

In other testimony, Admiral Poindexter testified that he had never told the president about the diversion of funds to the Contras. Congress had cut off U.S. support for the Contras over Reagan's objections. To fill the void, North apparently worked closely with the Central Intelligence Agency (CIA) to provide the Contras with intelligence information and advice on military tactics. In addition, the Reagan administration obtained money for the Contras from wealthy conservative Americans. Then through private agents, North secretly arranged to supply the Contras with what they needed. By early 1986, the Contra operation crossed paths with another covert operation, the arms sales to Iran. Profits from these sales were funneled into the various aid given to the Contras.

In a strongly worded report released in November 1987, the bipartisan majority of the congressional select committees harshly criticized the White House for "secrecy, deception, and disdain for the rule of law." Reagan himself was held responsible for setting loose a group of zealots and for failing to instill a respect for the law among members of his administration. One chapter in the report proposed that Congress and the executive branch have shared power over foreign policy. However, North and Poindexter bluntly told Congress that it should stay out of foreign policy. A Republican minority on the joint committees agreed that Reagan had made mistakes, but said most of the fault had lain with Congress for interfering with the president's policies.

In March 1988, a federal grand jury indicted Oliver North, John Poindexter, and two other participants in the affair on various charges related to Iran-Contra. Robert C. McFarlane, Poindexter's predecessor as national security adviser, had already pleaded guilty to misdemeanor charges arising from the same investigations. North and Poindexter were tried and convicted on felony charges, but they appealed their sentences. The charges against North were dropped in 1991. Poindexter's conviction was reversed upon appeal the same year.

See also: Congressional Investigations.

Iraq War Resolution (2002)

Name popularly used for the Authorization for Use of Military Force Against Iraq Resolution of 2002. The resolution became the basis for the subsequent U.S. invasion of Iraq in March 2003. It has been the subject of significant controversy, especially since the arguments used to justify its passage were later found to be based on faulty information.

In 2002, President George W. Bush (2001–2009) asserted that Iraq posed a threat to U.S. national security and asked Congress to pass a resolution that authorized the administration to use military action against that nation. The administration cited a number of factors that it claimed justified the use of force. The most prominent among these were its claims that Iraq was developing weapons of mass destruction and was interfering with the work of United Nations (UN) weapons inspectors. It also asserted that Iraq was cooperating with and aiding international terrorist organizations including al-Qaeda.

Although these claims were challenged by members of the U.S. intelligence community, the administration relied heavily upon them to make its case for war. The National Intelligence Estimate (NIE), a comprehensive security report prepared by the nation's intelligence agencies, included many of these reservations about the administration's claims. However, few members of Congress read the NIE, instead relying on administration briefings that downplayed or omitted contradictory views. Several senators later admitted that they voted on the resolution without reading the NIE.

The House approved the resolution on October 11, 2002, by a vote of 296–133, with three members abstaining, or not voting. The next day the Senate also passed the resolution, by a vote of 77–23. The resolution authorized the use of force to "defend the national security of the United States against the continuing threat posed by Iraq; and enforce all relevant United Nations Security Council Resolutions regarding Iraq." An amendment that would have required the administration to seek United Nations authorization for an invasion failed in the House, 270–155. Five months later, acting without UN approval, U.S. and British forces invaded Iraq and toppled its ruler, Saddam Hussein.

Questions arose almost at once about whether the invasion violated international law. The U.S. and Britain claimed that Iraq had broken the terms of the cease-fire it signed after

SPOTLIGHT

No Unlimited Force

Some observers have compared the Iraq War Resolution to the 1964 Gulf of Tonkin Resolution that led to the escalation of U.S. military involvement in Vietnam. In August 1964, responding to reports of North Vietnamese attacks on the U.S. destroyer *Maddox,* President Lyndon B. Johnson (1963–1969) requested a congressional resolution "expressing the unity and determination of the United States in supporting freedom and in protecting peace in southeast Asia." The resolution, passed unanimously by the House and with only two nay votes in the Senate, authorized the president "to take all necessary steps, including the use of armed force, to assist any member or protocol state of the Southeast Asia Collective Defense Treaty requesting assistance in defense of its freedom."

Unlike the Iraq War Resolution, the Gulf of Tonkin Resolution granted the president unlimited authority to use force. Like the 2002 measure, however, the events that gave rise to it were later called into question. A Senate investigation found that the *Maddox* was a spy ship gathering intelligence off the coast of North Vietnam, contrary to administration claims. It also questioned whether the *Maddox* suffered a second attack, as its commander had asserted. In 1971, President Richard Nixon signed a bill repealing the Gulf of Tonkin Resolution.

the 1991 Gulf War by hindering the work of weapons inspectors. They argued that the threat posed by Iraq was sufficient to allow them to act to defend themselves. Opponents of the invasion argued that Iraq did not pose an immediate threat to U.S. national security, and characterized the invasion as a war of aggression, not self-defense.

Controversy over the resolution increased after the invasion, when U.S. and British inspection teams failed to discover any evidence of active Iraqi programs to produce weapons of mass destruction. The U.S. government's Duelfer Report concluded that Iraq had no such weapons, but maintained the pretense of having them to appear more formidable to its enemies. Accusations that Iraq's leadership had ties to al Qaeda also proved to be inaccurate, according to a 2007 report by the Inspector General of the U.S. Department of Defense. Critics have claimed that the Bush administration deliberately distorted intelligence reports and ignored information that contradicted their assessment of the threat Iraq posed in order to justify the invasion.

See also: Gulf of Tonkin Resolution (1964); War Powers.

Further Reading

Knights, Michael. *Operation Iraqi: Freedom and the New Iraq: Insights and Forecasts.* Washington, DC: Washington Institute for Near East Policy, 2004.

Lowry, Richard. *U.S. Marine in Iraq: Operation Iraqi Freedom.* Westminster, MD: Osprey, 2003.

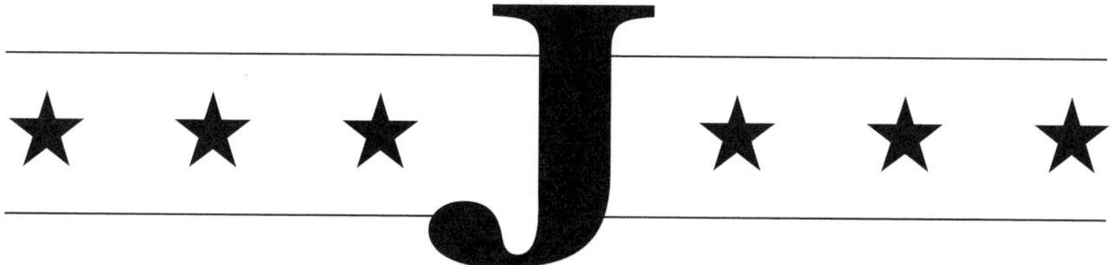

A–Z

Johnson, Andrew

See Impeachment Power.

Joint Committees

Committees that have a membership drawn from both houses of Congress and usually are investigative or housekeeping in nature. Joint committees may be either permanent or temporary panels created by law, or by a resolution passed by both houses of Congress, which also fixes their size.

Permanent Joint Committees

As of 2007, there were four standing, or permanent, joint committees in Congress. The Joint Economic Committee examines national economic problems and reviews the execution of fiscal and budgetary programs. The Joint Committee on Taxation, made up of senior members of both parties from the House Ways and Means and Senate Finance committees, serves chiefly to provide a professional staff that long enjoyed a nonpartisan reputation on tax issues. When the Republicans assumed control of both houses in 1995, the new majority used it as a resource to develop its agenda for enacting major tax cuts. The other two joint committees deal with administrative matters. The Joint Committee on Printing oversees the Government Printing Office, and the Joint Committee on the Library oversees the Library of Congress and works of art in the Capitol.

Chairs of joint committees generally rotate from one chamber to another at the beginning of each Congress. When a senator serves as chair, the vice chair usually is a representative and vice versa.

Temporary Joint Committees

Congress occasionally creates temporary joint committees to address specific issues that it wishes to address. In 1861, for example, Congress formed the Joint Committee on the Conduct of the War to "inquire into the conduct" of the Civil War (1861–1865). In 1947, a Joint Committee on the Legislative Budget attempted to set limits on federal appropriations and expenditures much lower than the amounts requested in President Harry S. Truman's (1945–1953) budget request but failed to reach a working agreement. The last joint committee to have legislative responsibilities was the Joint Committee on Atomic Energy, which was abolished in 1977.

Three times in its history Congress has formed a Joint Committee on the Organization of Congress to consider changes to review and revise procedures in the House and Senate. The most recent such body, which existed in 1993 to propose reforms in the operations of the House and Senate, adopted a report that was never formally acted upon in either house.

A conference committee is a special type of temporary joint committee formed to resolve differences between competing House and Senate versions of a measure. Conference committees propose compromises between different versions of a bill passed by each chamber. These proposals are then submitted to the full House and Senate for approval.

See also: Committees; Conference Committees.

Joint Session

A meeting of the combined Senate and House of Representatives. Joint sessions occur only on

Congress meets in joint session for the president's annual State of the Union address on January 23, 2007. (AP Photo, Susan Walsh)

special occasions, including presidential inaugurations and presidential addresses, such as the State of the Union address. Both houses of Congress must pass a resolution to meet in joint session.

A joint meeting of Congress is a gathering similar to a joint session but which does not require a resolution by both houses. Instead, Congress may call a joint meeting by passing a unanimous agreement consenting to do so. Joint meetings often are called to hear addresses by military leaders or foreign dignitaries, to hold memorial services for deceased presidents or outstanding public servants, or to mark the anniversary of a significant historical event or the birth of a president.

Congress first met in joint session on April 6, 1789, to count the electoral votes from the nation's first presidential election. The first joint meeting of Congress took place on December 18, 1874, to hear a speech by King Kalakaua of Hawaii.

Judicial Review

Principle that allows the courts to determine the constitutionality of acts of Congress. Although the Constitution does not explicitly authorize the courts to pass judgment on the constitutionality of acts of Congress, some of the delegates to the Constitutional Convention clearly saw that power as one of the acknowledged functions of the courts.

The courts' role in determining the constitutionality of the laws of the land also was implied by a provision in Article VI of the Constitution. It states that the Constitution, the laws, and the treaties of the United States "shall be the supreme law of the

As Chief Justice of the United States, John Marshall established the principle of judicial review in the landmark case of *Marbury v. Madison* (1803). (Library of Congress)

Decision Makers

Marbury v. Madison

The principle of judicial review received its first major test in the Supreme Court case of *Marbury v. Madison* (1803). The case involved President John Adams' (1797–1801) appointment of several judges two days before he was to leave office in 1801. By law, the new appointees could not take office until the secretary of state delivered their commissions, or written appointments. The outgoing secretary of state, however, was unable to deliver all of the commissions before his term of office expired. President Thomas Jefferson (1801–1809), who succeeded Adams ordered the new secretary of state, James Madison, not to deliver the commissions, thus denying judgeships to some of Adams' appointees.

Three of those appointees, including a man named William Marbury, sent a petition to the Supreme Court asking that it force Madison to deliver the commissions. Because Marbury filed his petition directly in the Supreme Court, the Court needed to be able to exercise original **jurisdiction,** or legal authority, over the case in order to have the power to hear it. Marbury claimed that the Judiciary Act of 1789, under which he had been appointed, granted the Supreme Court original jurisdiction for such petitions. The Court disagreed, ruling that the section of the Judiciary Act of 1789 that authorized the Court to issue such a writ was unconstitutional and thus invalid.

respective States, or their citizens and inhabitants–and that the Judges of the several States shall be bound thereby in their decisions, anything in the respective laws of the individual States to the contrary notwithstanding." The wording of this clause underwent several changes in order to make it clear that all judges, state and federal, were bound to uphold the supremacy of the Constitution over all other acts.

The so-called "supremacy" clause was reinforced by a further provision in Article VI stating that all members of Congress and of the state legislatures, as well as all executive and judicial officers of the national and state governments, "shall be bound by Oath or Affirmation to support this Constitution."

See also: Checks and Balances; Separation of Powers.

Legislative Process

See How a Bill Becomes Law.

Legislative Reorganization Act (1946)

Legislation enacted by Congress in 1946 which reorganized Congress and created the modern Congress we know today, including its procedures, organization, structure, and staffing. As early as 1941, senators and representatives realized that congressional operations–including staffing procedures and the committee structure–required modernization to deal with new challenges facing the national government. Members of Congress pointed out that the growing congressional workload placed too heavy a burden on them and their staffs. In addition, improved communications and transportation permitted voters to ask more of elected officials, thereby increasing the amount of time needed to deal with constituent concerns. In addition, issues and legislation had become more complex as the federal government expanded.

Faced with more complex legislation, Congress realized that it lacked staff with technical knowledge and skills. It had to rely instead on the executive branch and private groups for specialized assistance and help with drafting bills. Members thus began to fear that their excessive dependence on the executive branch would make Congress a secondary, rather than a coequal, institution in the federal government. This fear increased after a warning issued in 1942 by President Franklin D. Roosevelt (1933–1945). Frustrated with congressional delays in enacting key proposals of his administration, Roosevelt warned that "In the event that Congress fails to act, and act adequately, I shall accept the responsibility, and I shall act." At the time, however, Congress did not have money to expand its staff because the United States was entering World War II (1941–1945).

The lack of professional congressional staff was to an extent self-inflicted. Members were reluctant to increase their own funding for fear that the public would view them as unable to carry out their traditional tasks. Nevertheless, as frustrations rose, Congress passed legislation in 1944 creating the Joint Committee on the Organization of Congress to study the organization, operation, and staffing of the House and Senate; House, Senate, and committee interactions; and relations between the legislative and executive branches of the government. Two years later Congress incorporated most of the committee's recommendations into the Legislative Reorganization Act of 1946.

The central elements of the Legislative Reorganization Act of 1946 reduced the number of standing committees in the Senate from thirty-three to fifteen and in the House from forty-eight to nineteen. The act also authorized the hiring of professional committee staff. Senators were assigned two committees instead of as many as nine. Representatives served on one committee instead of five. In addition, each committee's jurisdiction was more strictly defined. Congress also tried to separate the roles of committee staff from personal staff by specifying that the committee staff would work only on committee business and would not have any other duties.

The House and Senate Appropriations Committees and the Joint Committee on

Key Provisions of the Legislative Reorganization Act of 1946

Standing Committees • Reduced number of Senate committees from 33 to 15 • Reduced number of House committees from 48 to 19
Federal Budget • Directed the House Ways and Means Committee and Senate Finance Committee, as well as both houses' Appropriations Committees, acting as a Joint Committee, to prepare an annual government budget
Congressional Workload • Prohibited private bills from being used for certain types of payments
Committee Staff • Authorized each standing committee to hire four professional and six clerical staff members • Made the Legislative Reference Service (now the Congressional Research Service) a separate department of the Library of Congress
Salaries and Benefits • Increased the salaries of senators and representatives from $10,000 to $12,500 • Increased the salaries of the vice president and the speaker of the house to $20,000 • Included members of Congress under the Civil Service Retirement Act and made them eligible at age sixty-two after at least six years of service
Regulation of Lobbying • Required lobbyists to register and report their expenses to the clerk of the House

Although a sweeping reform act designed to streamline the workings of Congress, the Legislative Act of 1946 proved inadequate in many ways. The provisions for budget control became unworkable and were dropped, and the regulations on lobbyists proved too weak to monitor their actions and spending.

Taxation had already begun building nonpartisan professional staffs in the 1920s. The success of those staffs led Congress in 1946 to institutionalize the practice by allowing each standing committee to hire a total of ten staff members–four professional and six clerical–based solely on their ability to perform the duties of office. The professional staff provided expert knowledge on a subject while the clerical staff supplied administrative and secretarial support. Although the terminology has changed some, and other names–such as investigative, associate, or temporary–have come into use, this broad distinction remains today.

The Joint Committee on the Reorganization of Congress also recommended that each member of Congress be allowed to hire an administrative assistant for his or her personal staff. This recommendation was dropped from the final Legislative Reorganization Act because of resistance in the House of Representatives. It was, however, adopted separately by the Senate shortly after the act's passage.

Under the Legislative Reorganization Act of 1946, majority party members were responsible for hiring and firing committee staff. In practice, however, committees usually delegated that power to committee chairs, who often consulted with the senior minority party member. Normally, the chairperson obtained most staff funding from the House Administration and the Senate Rules and Administration committees.

In two other important reforms, the Legislative Reorganization Act of 1946 expanded the Legislative Reference Service (now the Congressional Research Service) and created senior specialist positions in subject areas roughly equivalent to those of the standing committees. The specialists received salaries comparable to those of their counterparts in the executive branch. In addition, the act expanded the bill-drafting service available through the Office of the Legislative Counsel.

See also: Committees; Congressional Research Service; Congressional Staff; Constituents and Congress.

Library of Congress

An extensive collection of books and other documents owned by Congress and accessible to the public. The library contains more than 115 million items, housed in three sprawling buildings on Capitol Hill. The Library of Congress contains such treasures as Thomas Jefferson's rough draft of the Declaration of Independence, James Madison's notes from the Constitutional Convention, one of three known perfect copies of the Gutenberg Bible, a nearly complete set of Mathew Brady's photographs of the Civil War, and the personal papers of twenty-three presidents, from George Washington to Calvin Coolidge.

Role of the Library

The library has the dual role of assisting Congress and serving as the nation's library. The librarian of Congress oversees both functions, which are carried out by a staff of more than 4,000. The librarian is a presidential appointee, confirmed by the Senate, and reports to Congress and its ten-member Joint Committee on the Library.

As a national library, it maintains its huge collections and provides central services to authors, scholars, government agencies, and the public. It also provides services to other libraries throughout the United States in book preservation, interlibrary loans, sales of cataloging cards, and computer linkups.

Congress, however, established the library for its own use, and senators and representatives are its most privileged users. A 1975 library pamphlet stated the relationship clearly: "The primary role of the Library of Congress is to perform research work for members and committees of Congress." The Law Library provides reference and research services for all known legal systems, present and past. The library's attorneys consult with individual members of Congress and may testify as expert witnesses

Renovations on the Library of Congress's circular main reading room were completed in 1990. (Library of Congress)

SPOTLIGHT

Thomas Jefferson's Library

During the fall and winter of 1814–1815, Thomas Jefferson offered to sell his private library to the government to make up for the losses the library sustained when invading British troops burned Washington, DC, during the War of 1812. Anti-Jeffersonian members of Congress opposed the offer because Jefferson's library included books by Voltaire and other unorthodox thinkers. After considerable debate, the House **appropriated** $23,950 for the purchase. Jefferson's library became the nucleus of the Library of Congress as it exists today, even though most of his books have been lost.

The 6,487 volumes Jefferson contributed contained 4,931 works in forty-four categories. Jefferson's classification system served as the basis for the library's entire catalog until 1897. Whereas the library's previous collection had been very narrow in its focus, Jefferson's library featured knowledge from many different fields. The acquisition of Jefferson's library, wrote author Lucy Salamanca, "proved to be the life-stream that restored energy and enterprise to the expiring . . . Library of Congress."

In 2008, a group of rare-book dealers completed a decade-long task of recreating Jefferson's original library, much of which had been lost in a fire in 1851. Specialists combed bookstores throughout Europe and North America to uncover the more than 6,000 volumes. Jefferson's recreated library—some originals and some replacements—is now on display at the Library of Congress.

before congressional committees. Located within the Madison Memorial Building is the Congressional Reading Room, which provides members with individual reference service. Congressional requests for books or background information are handled by a separate division, the Congressional Research Service. Senators and representatives, their families, and specific members of their staffs are among the few who may borrow books from the Library of Congress.

Library Services

The Library of Congress provides a wide range of services to the public. One of the most important is the cataloging of books. The library assigns to every book published in the United States, and many published abroad, a catalog number that indicates the book's subject matter. It also registers copyright claims. Many of the books and other works deposited for copyright protection are kept, adding to the permanent collection.

Any person over high school age may use the Library of Congress's two general reading rooms. The library also contains specialized reading rooms for the blind and physically handicapped, and in subject areas including geography and maps, local history and genealogy, manuscripts, microfilms, music, newspaper and current periodicals, prints and photographs, rare books, and science. Admission to the reading rooms is free, but materials may not be removed from the library. Books requested by readers are delivered to them in the reading rooms, and readers may use the reference books available on the open shelves without filling in a request slip. Hundreds of publications and recordings produced by the library are also available to the public. The library also publishes facsimiles of historic documents, manuscripts, and posters, and a variety of greeting cards and gift items. In addition, the library sells compact discs produced from its vast collection of folk music and other recordings.

The Library of Congress provides special services to users who are blind, partially sighted, or otherwise physically unable to read conventional printed materials. The library and 140 cooperating regional libraries throughout the nation have books in raised characters (Braille) and in large type, "talking books" on discs and tapes, and other recorded aids for the physically handicapped.

See also: Congressional Research Service.

Further Reading

Cole, John Y. *Jefferson's Legacy: A Brief History of the Library of Congress.* Washington, DC: U.S. Government Printing Office, 1993.

Goodrum, Charles A., and Helen W. Dalrymple. *Treasures of the Library of Congress.* New York: Abrams, 1991.

Limited Government

Government that intervenes as little as possible in the daily activities and personal freedoms of its citizens. The Constitution includes many safeguards that limit the reach of government of the United States. Many of the principles of limited government that are enshrined in the Constitution have roots in the British system of government from which the U.S. evolved.

Until the time of the American Revolution (1775–1783), rulers in the vast majority of countries exercised absolute power over their subjects. With relatively rare exceptions such as ancient Athens, the people had little or no say in how they were governed. Rulers and their agents had the authority to do virtually whatever they pleased. In Western Europe, the doctrine of the "divine right of kings" declared that rulers received their authority from God, and only God could take it away.

One of the earliest and most significant attempts in Europe to limit the power of government occurred in England in 1215. Angered by a series of actions taken by King John, English barons forced the king to sign a document called the Magna Carta, or "great Charter." The document required John to give up some of his powers and agree to follow established legal procedures. Perhaps its most important requirement was called the writ of habeas corpus, which prevents the government from arresting someone without formally charging the individual with a crime. It also requires the government to produce the prisoner in court. The writ of habeas corpus was meant to end the practice of rulers seizing their enemies without cause and imprisoning them indefinitely.

Although King John ignored certain aspects of the Magna Carta, the document did check his worst abuses of power and placed real limits on the king's power. Over time, the English legislature, or Parliament, assumed more of the king's powers. By the 1700s, England was moving toward a more limited form of government while still hanging on to remnants of an absolute monarchy.

It was in this political environment that the individuals who led the American Revolution came of age. This was also an age in which European philosophers began to champion human dignity and the right of individuals to be free of outside interference in their lives. Early supporters of American independence complained of intrusive English policies such as taxes on virtually all necessities and forcing colonists to shelter and feed British soldiers. After the colonists won their independence, they were determined to give the new government only as much power as it needed to perform its basic duties.

The first step toward a limited government was drafting a written constitution. This ensured that government officials had to follow specific laws and could not simply make up laws as they chose. The second step was dividing the government into three equal branches, to ensure that no one person or group could easily seize power. The third step was creating a series of checks and balances, which gave each branch the power to limit the authority or reach of other branches. The final step was incorporating a Bill of Rights that spelled out the basic freedoms to which all citizens are entitled.

See also: Bill of Rights; Checks and Balances; Constitution of the United States; Separation of Powers.

Line-Item Veto

An executive power that would give the president the ability to reject individual items within federal spending bills. For decades, presidents had sought a line-item veto as a way to curb government spending and to have more say on how much the government spends. In 1996, the Republican-led 104th Congress finally passed a bill giving the president the equivalent of a line-item veto. The new law took effect on January 1, 1997. However, the Supreme Court in 1998 declared the law unconstitutional, stating that such a power would be in violation of the constitutional structure that creates a separation of powers.

Technically, the legislation that Congress passed in 1996 did not provide for a true line-item veto, which would allow the president to strike individual lines from an appropriations bill before signing it. A constitutional amendment would have been required to give the president a true line-item veto power. Instead, lawmakers gave the president what was termed a legislative line-item veto. It significantly strengthened the president's existing power to reject, or cancel, individual items within already signed bills.

The new law created a complex process under which the president could send Congress a message proposing to cancel specific items in any appropriations bill, new spending on certain entitlement programs, or targeted tax benefit that met certain criteria. The proposed cuts would take effect automatically unless blocked by a special bill passed in identical form by both chambers of Congress. The president could then veto that bill, requiring a two-thirds vote in each chamber of Congress to override the presidential veto.

Proponents of the line-item veto, generally political conservatives opposed to government spending and programs, argued that the overwhelming majority of state governors possessed the line-item veto in some form and that it had proved to be a useful tool in controlling expenditures. They believed that such a veto would help curb the practice of putting pork-barrel spending into appropriations bills. Supporters responded to constitutional concerns by arguing that there was a long history of presidential action declining to carry out spending passed by Congress, and that Congress could properly delegate authority to the president to cancel certain spending authority.

Opponents of the line-item veto have argued that the Constitution clearly requires that bills be approved or rejected by the president in their entirety, not in pieces. They said that the new procedure gave the president the power to change laws after their enactment—in effect, to make laws, a power that is reserved exclusively to Congress according to the Constitution. Another basic argument against the line-item veto concerned the balance of power between Congress and the executive branch. Opponents warned that a line-item veto would upset this balance of power among the branches of government by giving too much political power to the president. They believed that the executive branch would have a powerful weapon to use against Congress not only on spending issues but on other issues as well.

On June 25, 1998, the Supreme Court, in a 6–3 decision, struck down the law. The Court declared the law unconstitutional because it permitted the president to rewrite bills that had already been signed into law. Under the Constitution, the president must accept or reject bills in their entirety. Thus, Congress's historic enactment of the 1996 law was only a short-lived experiment.

See also: President and Congress.

Lobbying and Congress

Applying political persuasion to convince a member of Congress to support or oppose a proposal. Lobbying activities range from individual citizens talking to their representatives at public events to large interest groups, such as the American Association of Retired Persons (AARP), conducting major media campaigns. Through lobbying, citizens make their wishes known to their legislators, call attention to their problems, bring the issues of the day to public attention, and discover potentially damaging consequences of legislation before they cause harm.

Purpose and Importance

Lobbying has become crucial to governing a democracy as vast and complex as the United States. As government has grown in size and complexity, it has become more difficult for individuals to make their voices heard. Lobbyists help communicate people's needs and desires to those in positions of power. It is in large part through lobbying that government gets the information it needs to govern.

The idea that lobbying performs a vital function in a democracy fits in with the theory of political science known as *pluralism.* According to this theory, much of the strength of American democracy comes from the interaction of different forces that compete with and balance each other. In this view, the compromises and complexity of the U.S. government's decision making lead to diversity, flexibility, and stability in governance. Those who take a more negative view of lobbying argue that interests with the most power or money usually get what they want. Others claim that even a healthy competition among interests that are roughly equal in influence cannot take account of all viewpoints.

Historical Development

Columnist William Safire traces the political use of the term *lobbying* to the mid-seventeenth century. At that time, citizens would use a large anteroom, or lobby, near the English House of Commons to plead their causes to members of Parliament. By 1829, the phrase *lobby-agents* was being applied to special favor-seekers who hovered in the lobby of the New York Capitol in Albany. By 1832, the term had been shortened to *lobbyist* and was widely used in the U.S. Capitol.

The Constitution makes no direct reference to lobbying. However, the First Amendment protects the essence of lobbying by guaranteeing freedom of speech and allowing citizens "to petition the Government for redress of grievances." In the early years of the Republic, the ties between legislators and private interests were quite direct. While Congress forbade bribery of judges in 1790, bribing a legislator was not illegal until 1853. In addition to making direct payments, outside interests could hire members to do their legal work. The excesses of the era led to a series of reforms that began in 1907 by banning campaign contributions from banks and corporations. These efforts were hampered by the Constitutional guarantee of the right to seek help from Congress. As a result, reformers had to settle for laws that required lobbyists to register with Congress and to make basic information about their activities available to the public. In recent years, political scandals and the soaring costs of political campaigning have raised public expectations that legislators would behave with integrity. Lobbyists themselves banded together into an organization, the American League of Lobbyists, which promotes its own code of conduct.

Who Lobbies?

Professional lobbyists most often come from backgrounds in law, public relations, business, and industry. Still, others have experience as former legislators, government officials, or congressional staff aides. Some lobbyists have the added advantage of being related to members of Congress.

Others are simply people who had a problem and set out to solve it. In the early 1970s, David Saks was a retired furniture salesman who had never finished high school. When his wife discovered that public telephones would not work with her hearing aid, David set out to do something about it. He flooded Capitol Hill with telephone calls, organized a group of hearing-aid users, and patiently explained the problem to staff aides and members. After fifteen years, he finally won passage of legislation that outlawed the sale of telephones that were not equipped for use by callers with hearing aids.

At the other extreme are "superlobbyists" such as Jack Abramoff, who was perhaps the most powerful lobbyist in Washington before being convicted on fraud and corruption charges in January 2006. At the height of his influence, Abramoff's employer, Greenberg Traurig, described him as "directly involved in the Republican party and conservative movement leadership structures" and "one of the leading fund raisers for the party and its congressional candidates." Abramoff's clients included several foreign governments and various Indian tribes with gambling interests in the southern and southwestern United States.

Other lobbyists get their clout from the numbers of people they represent. The American Association of Retired Persons (AARP), which represents the interests of Americans over age 50, boasted some 38 million members in 2008. AARP has its own zip code and in 2006 reported spending $23 million on lobbying efforts.

Lobbying Techniques

At one time, lobbying involved a persuasive individual pleading a case to a senator or representative. Most of today's lobbyists, however, depend far less on personal contacts and individual style than on highly coordinated lobbying techniques made possible by modern means of communication.

Direct Lobbying

Lobbyists using the direct approach continue to meet with members of Congress and their staffs, provide in-depth information, and give testimony at congressional hearings. Their methods have grown more sophisticated, relying more on information than on personal connections. Despite changes in lobbying techniques since the early 1970s, however, most legislators, staff, and lobbyists agree that effective, face-to-face presentation of the facts remains the basis of the lobbying profession.

A differently-abled lobbyist brings his message to members of Congress. Lobbyists have become an important factor in the legislative process. (AP Photo, Susan Walsh)

To communicate with legislators, a lobbyist needs access to them. Whether lobbyists are partners in a Washington law firm or employees of unions, they will more often than not already have close ties to Congress. Many lobbying firms believe that hiring staff with insider credentials is a good investment. Personal ties count for a great deal in the small world of the House and perhaps even more in the Senate. According to Charles Black, a one-time campaigner for presidential candidate Ronald Reagan and a member of a political consulting firm, "Number one is the access–to get them in the door and get a hearing for the case."

Access is essential, but the skillful presentation of knowledge is also crucial. Congressional staffs rarely have the resources to gather their own data and examples. An outside group that can offer reliable data to a committee or legislator can frame the issue, a critical step in formulating a solution. However, successful lobbyists are cautious not only to be accurate and complete, but also to alert legislators to any negative aspects of the policy they advocate. "The greatest mistake a lobbyist can make is to mislead a member of Congress," said Charles O. Whitley, a North Carolina Democrat who became a lobbyist after leaving Congress.

Indirect Lobbying

Many organizations use indirect lobbying techniques such as grassroots mobilization, media campaigns, and financial contributions to influence legislators. Nearly every large company, trade association, or public interest group of any stature has developed its own grassroots network. These networks ensure that a lobbyist's message is reinforced by the voices of voters who elect members of Congress. Traditional grassroots lobbying methods include maintaining a steady stream of written and oral communication with a lawmaker; inviting legislators to visit local establishments when Congress is not in session; and maintaining frequent contact with local newspapers and television stations.

Mass media campaigns–through radio, television, newspapers, or magazines–are another popular indirect lobbying technique. The campaigns may be designed either to stir up grassroots support or to influence legislators directly. In the late 1980s, for example, business lobbyists met regularly with newspaper editors from across the country. Resulting newspaper editorials that favored the lobbyists' point of view were arranged by state, gathered into two thick volumes, and sent to every member of Congress. Legislators have often protested that such media campaigns can mislead voters and members of Congress alike.

Another form of indirect lobbying is campaign contributions to members of Congress. Such support can encourage a senator or representative to back a group's legislative interests and help ensure that legislators friendly to the group's goals remain in office. Although corporations and labor unions are barred from making direct contributions to campaigns for federal office-seekers, contributors have found numerous ways to get around the restrictions. Labor unions pioneered the practice of creating separate political wings that collect voluntary contributions from union members and their families. They use the money to help elect candidates favorable to the labor cause. Unions can also legally endorse candidates.

Similarly, corporations can organize political action committees (PACs) to seek contributions from stockholders, executives and their families. In recent years, corporate PACs have accounted for more than one-fourth of all the money raised in federal elections. These contributions overwhelmingly go to Republican candidates. By 1998, for example, Democrats received only one-third of the total corporate PAC contributions to House and Senate races.

Lobbying Regulations

The principal approach of lobbying regulation has been to require disclosure rather than control. Thus, several laws require lobbyists to identify themselves, their employers, and their legislative interests, and to report how much they and their employers spend on lobbying. The definitions, however, are unclear, the enforcement minimal, and the impact questionable.

One reason for the relative absence of limitations on lobbying is the difficulty of imposing effective restrictions without infringing on the constitutional rights to free speech, press, assembly, and petition. Other reasons include (1) the concern that restrictions would hamper legitimate lobbying without curbing serious abuses and (2) the lobbies' consolidated and highly effective opposition to more regulation. Another possible factor is the desire on the part of some members of Congress to keep the doors open to future lobbying careers.

Congress has tried on several occasions to limit campaign contributions from corporations, organizations, and individuals in connection with federal elections. Although some limits on gifts to congressional campaigns were passed, they were struck down by the courts as unconstitutional.

See also: Abscam; Ethics, Congressional; Public Interest Groups.

Further Reading

deKieffer, Donald E. *The Citizen's Guide to Lobbying Congress.* Chicago: Chicago Review, 2007.

Levine, Bertram J. *Lobbying Congress: How the System Works.* Washington, DC: CQ Press, 1996.

Rosenthal, Alan. *The Third House: Lobbyists and Lobbying in the States.* Washington, DC: CQ Press, 2001.

Mace

A large, ceremonial staff that serves as a traditional symbol of legislative authority in the House of Representatives. The sergeant at arms of the House occasionally wields the mace to call for order from an unruly member or when House debate becomes too disorderly.

The House adopted the mace in its first session in 1789 as a symbol of office for the sergeant at arms, who is charged with preserving order on the House floor. The first mace was destroyed when the British burned the Capitol in 1814. A mace of painted wood was used until 1841. In that year, a New York silversmith named William Adams made a replica of the original mace of 1789 for the sum of $400. That mace consists of a bundle of thirteen ebony rods bound in silver, terminating in a silver globe topped by a silver eagle with outstretched wings. It is forty-six inches long.

The concept of the mace originated in the ancient Roman republic as the fasces, an ax bound in a bundle of rods. The fasces symbolized the power of Roman officials. The British House of Commons later adopted the mace as a symbol of authority, and the House borrowed the concept of the mace from the British.

On a number of occasions in the history of the House, the sergeant at arms, on order of the Speaker, has lifted the mace from its pedestal and "presented" it before an unruly member. On each of these occasions, order is said to have been promptly restored. At other times the sergeant at arms, bearing the mace, has passed up and down the aisles to quell unruly behavior in the chamber.

In recent years, the mace more often has served as a signal. When the House is in regular session, the staff rests on a tall pedestal at the right of the Speaker's desk, but when the House is sitting as the Committee of the Whole, the mace is moved to a low pedestal nearby. The Committee of the Whole is a forum in which the entire membership of the House meets as a single large committee, usually for purposes of debating a proposal. Members entering the chamber can thus tell at a glance whether the House is meeting in regular session or as the Committee of the Whole.

See also: Gavel.

Madison, James

See Federalist, The.

Majority Leader

Leadership position in both the House and the Senate which wields considerable influence over the affairs of the chamber. In the Senate, the Majority Leader is the most powerful officer. The House Majority Leader ranks just below the Speaker of the House in importance.

In the modern House, the Majority Leader's primary responsibility is to manage the legislative affairs of the chamber. To that end, the Majority Leader helps formulate, promote, negotiate, and defend the party's program, particularly on the House floor. The Speaker's duties, which spring from the Constitution and from the rules and traditions of the House, include presiding over House sessions, recognizing members to address the House, deciding points of order, referring bills and reports to the appropriate committees and House calendars, appointing the House members for House-Senate

South Dakota Democrat Thomas A. Daschle served as Senate Majority Leader from January 3, 2001, until January 20, 2001, and again from June 6, 2001, until January 3, 2003. (Scott J. Ferrell, CQ)

conferences on legislation, and appointing members of select committees.

In practice, the Majority Leader's job has been to formulate the party's legislative program in cooperation with the Speaker and other party leaders, to steer the program through the House, to persuade committee chairmen to report bills deemed of importance to the party, and to arrange the House legislative schedule. The Majority Leader is also the party's field general on the floor, coordinating with the bill's manager and others to anticipate problems before they develop. The Majority Leaders in both the House and Senate appoint officials to shape and direct party strategy on the floor. They devote their efforts to building voting majorities to pass or defeat bills. Majority floor leaders have considerable influence over the scheduling of debate and the selection of members to speak on bills.

Like the Speaker, the Majority Leader is in a position to do many favors for colleagues. These include scheduling floor action at a convenient time, speaking on behalf of a member's bill (or refraining from opposing it), meeting with a member's important constituents, or campaigning for a member in the member's home district. Such favors clearly help the leadership build coalitions and maintain party unity; indeed, the opportunity to campaign for colleagues has become, in recent years, an opportunity eagerly sought after by leaders of both parties.

A Majority Leader was not officially designated in the House until 1899, when Sereno E. Payne, a Republican from New York, was named to the post. From the earliest days, however, the Speaker has appointed someone to help him guide his party's legislative program through the House. Members of the Senate did not use the term *Majority Leader* to designate the head of the majority party until the 1920s. Republican Charles Curtis became the first senator to hold the title of Majority Leader in 1925.

VIEWPOINTS

A political cartoon demonstrates the power of Senate Majority Leader Alben W. Barkley, who served in that position from 1939 to 1947. (U.S. Senate Historical Office)

House Majority Leaders, 1899–2008

Congress		Majority
56th	(1899–1901)	Sereno E. Payne, R-N.Y.
57th	(1901–1903)	Payne
58th	(1903–1905)	Payne
59th	(1905–1907)	Payne
60th	(1907–1909)	Payne
61st	(1909–1911)	Payne
62nd	(1911–1913)	Oscar W. Underwood, D-Ala.
63rd	(1913–1915)	Underwood
64th	(1915–1917)	Claude Kitchin, D-N.C.
65th	(1917–1919)	Kitchin
66th	(1919–1921)	Franklin W. Mondell, R-Wyo.
67th	(1921–1923)	Mondell
68th	(1923–1925)	Nicholas Longworth, R-Ohio
69th	(1925–1927)	John Q. Tilson, R-Conn.
70th	(1927–1929)	Tilson
71st	(1929–1931)	Tilson
72nd	(1931–1933)	Henry T. Rainey, D-Ill.
73rd	(1933–1935)	Joseph W. Byrns, D-Tenn.
74th	(1935–1937)	William B. Bankhead, D-Ala.[a]
75th	(1937–1939)	Sam Rayburn, D-Texas
76th	(1939–1941)	Rayburn/John W. McCormack, D-Mass.[b]
77th	(1941–1943)	McCormack
78th	(1943–1945)	McCormack
79th	(1945–1947)	McCormack
80th	(1947–1949)	Charles A. Halleck, R-Ind.
81st	(1949–1951)	McCormack
82nd	(1951–1953)	McCormack
83rd	(1953–1955)	Halleck
84th	(1955–1957)	McCormack

(continued on next page)

House Majority Leaders, 1899–2008, *continued*

Congress		Majority
85th	(1957–1959)	McCormack
86th	(1959–1961)	McCormack
87th	(1961–1963)	McCormack/ Carl Albert, D-Okla.[c]
88th	(1963–1965)	Albert
89th	(1965–1967)	Albert
90th	(1967–1969)	Albert
91st	(1969–1971)	Albert
92nd	(1971–1973)	Hale Boggs, D-La.
93rd	(1973–1975)	Thomas P. O'Neill Jr., D-Mass.
94th	(1975–1977)	O'Neill
95th	(1977–1979)	Jim Wright, D-Texas
96th	(1979–1981)	Wright
97th	(1981–1983)	Wright
98th	(1983–1985)	Wright
99th	(1985–1987)	Wright
100th	(1987–1989)	Thomas S. Foley, D-Wash
101st	(1989–1991)	Foley/Richard A. Gephardt, D-Mo.[d]
102nd	(1991–1993)	Gephardt
103rd	(1993–1995)	Gephardt
104th	(1995–1997)	Dick Armey, R-Texas
105th	(1997–1999)	Armey
106th	(1999–2001)	Armey
107th	(2001–2003)	Armey
108th	(2003–2005)	Tom Delay, R-Texas
109th	(2005–2007)	Roy Blunt (acting) R-Mo./John Boehner, R-Oh.
110th	(2007–2009)	Steny Hoyer, D-Md.

Notes: **a. Bankhead became Speaker of the House on June 4, 1936. The post of majority leader remained vacant until the next Congress. b. McCormack became majority leader on Sept. 26, 1940, filling the vacancy caused by the elevation of Rayburn to the post of Speaker of the House on Sept. 16, 1940. c. Albert became majority leader on Jan. 10 1962, filling the vacancy caused by the elevation of McCormack to the post of Speaker of the House on Jan. 10, 1962. d. Gephardt became majority leader on June 14, 1989, filling the vacancy created when Foley succeeded Wright as Speaker of the House on June 6, 1989.**
Sources: **Randall B. Ripley, *Party Leaders in the House of Representatives* (Washington, D.C.: Brookings Institution, 1967); *Biographical Directory of the American Congress, 1774–1996* (Alexandria, VA: CQ Staff Directories, 1997); *CQ Weekly*, selected issues.**

In the twentieth and twenty-first centuries, House Majority Leaders have come from across the country.

A – Z

See also: House of Representatives; Minority Leader; Party Whips; Senate.

Media and Congress

News outlets including newspapers, magazines, radio, and television, and the impact of their coverage of Congress. Legislators have something of a love-hate relationship with the media. On one hand, constant and sometimes critical media scrutiny can call negative attention to members of Congress. On the other hand, members of Congress depend on the media to advance their own political ambitions and to inform their constituents, the voters who elect them to office.

History of Media Relations

Working behind closed doors and windows nailed shut to ensure secrecy, the Constitutional Convention of 1787 deliberately excluded the press and public. The Constitution itself omitted any guarantee of freedom of speech for the press. Thomas Jefferson criticized this omission, writing,

> The basis of our government being the opinion of the people, the very first object should be to keep that right (of a free press); and were it left to me to decide whether we should have a government without newspapers or newspapers without a government, I should not hesitate for a moment to prefer the latter.

The states, however, refused to ratify, or approve a Constitution without a bill of rights that included a guarantee of freedom of the press. By 1791, eleven states ratified ten amendments, or changes known as the Bill of Rights. Among other provisions, the First Amendment prohibits Congress from making any law that limits freedom of the press.

Early Press Coverage

The House of Representatives opened its doors to the public and the press in its second session on April 8, 1789. The Senate conducted its business behind closed doors until December 1795. Both chambers had galleries to accommodate the press and public.

The early congressional reporters focused on recording floor proceedings and paraphrasing floor speeches for their readers. Newspapers of the era were openly associated with political parties, which often financed the press. The *National Intelligencer,* for example, was the official newspaper of the Democratic-Republican party from 1801 to 1825. Under the presidencies of Andrew Jackson (1829–1837) and Martin Van Buren, (1837–1841), the *Globe* was the administration news organ. These papers received generous government printing contracts, a practice that ended in 1860 with the establishment of the Government Printing Office.

By the end of nineteenth century, newspapers—or at least their reporters—were less closely identified with political parties. Political journalism became more independent and objective. Interviews of legislators became standard procedure. Newspapers no longer reported full floor proceedings as they had in the early years of the Republic. A Washington reporter noted as early as 1903, "Washington has become so fruitful in gossip and scandal, and intrigue, political and otherwise, that in contrast the ordinary debates can prove exceedingly dry reading."

Growth of the Modern Media

The Washington press corps grew steadily in the first decades of the twentieth century. In response to the Great Depression of the 1930s, the federal government took on much larger responsibilities, requiring coverage by a larger press corps. As government increased in complexity and size, the number of specialized publications covering particular areas of policy rose. The advent of radio and television helped changed how news was covered and brought a new group of reporters to Washington.

Since the early 1970s, four factors have intensified the pressure of media coverage on members of Congress. First, reforms in the 1970s opened many more congressional activities to the press and the public. Second, since the Watergate scandal of the early 1970s, the

Washington press corps has remained on the alert for official misconduct by public officials. Third, since the 1980s, satellite transmissions have enabled local television stations to cover daily events in Washington. The have also allowed the political parties to set up their own television studios and broadcast their points of view to constituents. Fourth, new technologies, such as the World Wide Web, created new channels to distribute information widely and rapidly.

The combination of these four factors has made it possible for the press, constituents, and political opponents to watch lawmakers' actions more closely than ever before. Today, more than seven thousand journalists, photographers, and technicians are permitted in the House and Senate press galleries. Many of them work for specialized publications that focus on particular issues.

Getting Media Coverage

Members of Congress use a variety of methods to attract favorable media coverage. They distribute press releases and videotapes, issue weekly news columns, appear on television interview shows, create their own cable television programs, grant personal interviews to reporters, give floor speeches on major issues, and hold press conferences and briefings for journalists. Occasionally, a member may draw widespread attention by conducting a highly publicized hearing or investigation.

Nearly all lawmakers employ press officers, often former journalists, to handle relations with reporters. Congressional committees also hire press secretaries and may even set up separate press information offices. Press secretaries steer journalists to knowledgeable staff members, set up interviews with members of Congress, and provide much of the background information that reporters use to write Capitol Hill stories. They also create printed press releases and videotaped "interviews" with their bosses.

Most of this effort is directed at getting members media coverage in their own states or districts. The local audience is likely to consist of constituents, and the coverage is more extensive and more favorable than in the national media. Even so, more and more legislators look for opportunities to attract national, as well as local, press coverage. A veteran Senate press secretary explained, "As a general rule, the home-state press has got to be any smart member's priority." He added, "the national press can be very effective in getting your views across to people you work with."

Aggressive Investigations

As long as they are quoted accurately and shown in a positive light, most legislators welcome national media attention, no matter how brief. National coverage can turn members of Congress into celebrities almost overnight, or end political careers just as abruptly. Since Watergate, Washington investigative journalists have sought more aggressively to uncover misconduct on the part of legislators. Their investigations have led to House and Senate ethics investigations, criminal proceedings, and in some cases, resignations from Congress.

Since the 1980s, reporters have focused increasing attention on the personal lives of legislators. This trend accelerated with the emergence of on-line journalism in the late 1990s and the extensive coverage of the sex-related scandals involving President Bill Clinton. Gossipy Web sites run by cyberjournalists, such as Matt Drudge, reached millions of people, spreading rumors of sexual misconduct and compelling reporters in other media to follow up on them.

A 1990 survey by the Pew Research Center found that growing numbers of journalists were concerned that the lines had blurred between reporting and commentary. It reported that the media were driving news about scandals rather than merely reacting to events. Some news experts believe that the need for instant, twenty-four hour news updates on the World Wide Web will make journalism increasingly aggressive.

Assessing Media Influence on Congress

The media exerts a powerful impact on Congress both directly, through editorials, and indirectly, by helping to shape public opinion. In the late 1890s, newspaper reports by New York City's sensationalist press helped push the

In 1998, reporters press Republican Speaker of the House to comment on budget issues as the Speaker makes his way to his office. (Scott J. Ferrell, CQ)

United States into the Spanish-American War (1898). For months, the city's two leading newspapers tried to outdo each other with reports of Spanish atrocities in Cuba.

Seventy-five years later, media coverage helped to bring an end to the Vietnam War (1964–1975). Daily press coverage of the war, the antiwar movement, and the Senate Foreign Relations Committee's hearings on the war significantly influenced public opinion against continued U.S. involvement in Vietnam. It also eventually turned congressional opinion against the war.

In addition to affecting the issues that legislators take up, media coverage has changed the way that legislators do business. Perhaps the most obvious change is the expanding role of television advertising in political campaigns. With today's expensive media campaigns, lawmakers must spend ever-increasing amounts of time raising money. Savvy legislators can also sometimes harness the media to help whip up support for their initiatives.

Television coverage has had other effects as well. Because of the immediacy and power of television images, members cannot easily take stands on national issues that differ greatly from those of their constituents. Television coverage is typically so brief that members may oversimplify issues or focus only on problems and solutions that are easy to understand. The political process has become increasingly geared toward "sound bites," very brief statements that attempt to make an emotional impression on the audience rather than convey detailed information.

Some members feel that the extensive coverage of Congress provided by outlets such as C-SPAN, which allows millions of Americans to watch lawmakers in action, are causing Americans to become more cynical about government. According to Stephen Frantzich, co-author of *The C-SPAN Revolution,* "Congress started [televising its proceedings] under the premise that to know us is to love us," but "The data shows that familiarity breeds contempt."

See also: Bill of Rights; Campaign Finance; *Congressional Record;* Television Coverage of Congress; Watergate Hearings; Whitewater Investigations.

Further Reading

Graber, Doris A. *Mass Media and American Politics.* Seventh edition. Washington, DC: CQ Press, 2007.

Graber, Doris A.. *Media Power in Politics.* Fifth edition. Washington, DC: CQ Press, 2006.

Midterm Elections

Elections held two years after each presidential election, during which time voters select members of Congress. The entire membership of the House of Representatives must face the voters in each midterm election. By contrast, only one-third of the members of the Senate are elected during the midterms.

The Constitution calls for congressional elections to be held on the Tuesday following the first Monday in every even-numbered year. Every four years, the voters also cast ballots in presidential elections. Congressional elections that do not coincide with presidential races are called midterm elections, because they occur midway through a president's term of office. In addition to members of Congress, voters also elect members of their state legislatures during midterm elections, as well as some state governors.

Historically, the president's party loses seats in Congress during the midterm elections,

Congressional Seats Lost/Gained in Mid-term Elections, 1950–2006

Year	President	Party	Gaines/Losses	
			House Seats	Senate Seats
1950	Harry S. Truman	D	-29	-6
1954	Dwight D. Eisenhower	R	-18	-1
1958	Dwight D. Eisenhower	R	-48	-13
1962	John F. Kennedy	D	-4	+3
1966	Lyndon B. Johnson	D	-47	-4
1970	Richard Nixon	R	-12	+2
1974	Gerald R. Ford *(Nixon)*	R	-48	-5
1978	Jimmy Carter	D	-15	-3
1982	Ronald Reagan	R	-26	+1
1986	Ronald Reagan	R	-5	-8
1990	George Bush	R	-8	-1
1994	William J. Clinton	D	-52	-8
1998	William J. Clinton	D	+5	0
2002	George W. Bush	R	+8	+2
2006	George W. Bush	R	-30	-6

Most often in midterm elections, the president's party loses seats in Congress. However, in the 2002 congressional election, Republicans gained seats in both the House and Senate.

typically by large margins. Ten times since 1940, for example, the party controlling the presidency has lost twenty or more seats in the House. Over that same time period, only a handful of times has the party controlling the presidency gained seats in the House or Senate during midterm elections. In 1962, the Democrats picked up four seats in the Senate while controlling the presidency; however, they lost 45 seats in the House that year. In 1998, Democrats held the presidency and gained five House seats, while the balance of power in the Senate remained the same. In 2002, Republicans gained six House seats and two Senate seats while they controlled the presidency.

Observers offer a variety of reasons for the loss of seats during midterm elections. Some suggest that it is a natural consequence of being in power. After two years in office, they claim, presidents make mistakes that undermine their popularity with voters, who take out their frustrations on the president's party in Congress. Others believe that it occurs because vulnerable first-term incumbents attract strong challengers during midterm elections. Political scientist Kevin Phillips cites what he calls the "six-year itch," arguing that the loss of seats is much greater during a president's second term, after six years in office. According to Phillips, voters grow tired of the party in power during the president's second term and tend to throw their support behind the opposition. While the trend of losing congressional seats during the midterm elections is well documented, none of the theories to explain it is embraced by all political scientists.

See also: Elections, House of Representatives; Elections, Senatorial.

Further Reading

Busch, Andrew E. *Horses in Midstream: U.S. Midterm Elections and Their Consequences.* Pittsburgh: University of Pittsburgh Press, 1999.

Mink, Patsy

See Asian Americans in Congress.

Minority Leader

Title given to the leader of the minority party in both the House and the Senate. Because the majority party controls the legislative agenda in both houses of Congress, the Minority Leader enjoys much less power and prestige than the leader of the majority party. The Minority Leader's main role is to defend his or her party's interests in the chamber.

In the House of Representatives, the Minority Leader is the spokesperson for his or her party. The Minority Leader also is typically the party's leading candidate for Speaker of the House in case the party regains control of the chamber. For this reason, the Minority Leader is sometimes called the "shadow Speaker." In fact, every Speaker between 1900 and 1989 advanced to that post from either the majority or minority leadership position. Although the House Minority Leader exercises no direct control over legislation, he or she often meets with the Majority Leader or Speaker of the House to discuss compromises and agreements on important or controversial legislation.

The basic duties of the Minority Leader were described by Bertrand Snell, a former Republican House member who held the post from 1931 to 1939: "He is spokesman for his party and enunciates its policies. He is required to be alert and vigilant in defense of the minority's rights. It is his function and duty to criticize constructively the policies and program of the majority, and to this end employ parliamentary tactics and give close attention to all proposed legislation." Snell might also have added that if the Minority Leader's party occupies the White House, the Minority Leader is likely to become the president's chief spokesperson in the House.

Although individual members occasionally stepped forward to lead the opposition against the majority position on specific bills or issues, the position of House Minority Leader first

Senate Minority Leader Everett Dirksen (R-IL) (left) confers with President Lyndon B. Johnson (1963–1969). Dirksen served as Senate Minority Leader from 1959 until his death in 1969. (Frank Wolfe, LBJ Library)

A–Z

House Minority Leaders, 1899–2008

Congress		Minority
56th	(1899–1901)	James D. Richardson, D-Tenn.
57th	(1901–1903)	Richardson
58th	(1903–1905)	John Sharp Williams, D-Miss.
59th	(1905–1907)	Williams
60th	(1907–1909)	Williams/Champ Clark, D-Mo.[a]
61st	(1909–1911)	Clark
62nd	(1911–1913)	James R. Mann, R-Ill.
63rd	(1913–1915)	Mann
64th	(1915–1917)	Mann
65th	(1917–1919)	Mann
66th	(1919–1921)	Clark
67th	(1921–1923)	Claude Kitchin, D-N.C.
68th	(1923–1925)	Finis J. Garrett, D-Tenn.
69th	(1925–1927)	Garrett
70th	(1927–1929)	Garrett
71st	(1929–1931)	John N. Garner, D-Texas
72nd	(1931–1933)	Bertrand H. Snell, R-N.Y.
73rd	(1933–1935)	Snell
74th	(1935–1937)	Snell
75th	(1937–1939)	Snell
76th	(1939–1941)	Joseph W. Martin Jr., R-Mass.
77th	(1941–1943)	Martin
78th	(1943–1945)	Martin
79th	(1945–1947)	Martin
80th	(1947–1949)	Sam Rayburn, D-Texas
81st	(1949–1951)	Martin
82nd	(1951–1953)	Martin
83rd	(1953–1955)	Rayburn
84th	(1955–1957)	Martin
85th	(1957–1959)	Martin

House Minority Leaders, 1899–2008, *continued*

Congress		Minority
86th	(1959–1961)	Charles A. Halleck, R-Ind.
87th	(1961–1963)	Halleck
88th	(1963–1965)	Halleck
89th	(1965–1967)	Gerald R. Ford, R-Mich.
90th	(1967–1969)	Ford
91st	(1969–1971)	Ford
92nd	(1971–1973)	Ford
93rd	(1973–1975)	Ford/John J. Rhodes, R-Ariz.[b]
94th	(1975–1977)	Rhodes
95th	(1977–1979)	Rhodes
96th	(1979–1981)	Rhodes
97th	(1981–1983)	Robert H. Michel, R-Ill.
98th	(1983–1985)	Michel
99th	(1985–1987)	Michel
100th	(1987–1989)	Michel
101st	(1989–1991)	Michel
102nd	(1991–1993)	Michel
103rd	(1993–1995)	Michel
104th	(1995–1997)	Richard A. Gephardt, D-Mo.
105th	(1997–1999)	Gephardt
106th	(1999–2001)	Gephardt
107th	(2001–2003)	Nancy Pelosi, D-Ca.
108th	(2003–2005)	Pelosi
109th	(2005–2007)	Pelosi
110th	(2007–2009)	John Boehner, R-Oh.

***Notes:* a. Clark became minority leader in 1908. b. Rhodes became minority leader on Dec. 7, 1973, filling the vacancy caused by the resignation of Ford on Dec. 6, 1973, to become vice president.**

***Sources:* Randall B. Ripley, *Party Leaders in the House of Representatives* (Washington, D.C.: Brookings Institution, 1967); *Biographical Directory of the American Congress, 1774–1996* (Alexandria, VA: CQ Staff Directories, 1997); *CQ Weekly*, selected issues.**

The House Minority Leader serves as the chief opposition to the majority party.

A – Z

became identifiable in the 1880s. However, the post was not formally recognized as a leadership position until the 1920s.

See also: House of Representatives; Majority Leader; Party Whips; Senate.

Missouri Compromise

Congressional agreement reached in 1820 that regulated slavery in the western territories of the United States. While the agreement settled for a time the difficult question of the expansion of slavery to the western United States, it failed to end the debate.

In the early decades of the nineteenth century, the issue of slavery became an increasingly difficult point of disagreement between northern and southern states. By the end of 1819, the Union was evenly divided with eleven free and eleven slave states. Most northerners opposed the spread of slavery into the country's western territories, while most southerners opposed any restrictions on the spread of slavery.

At this time, Missouri sought admission to the Union as a slave state, which would tip the balance in favor of the slave states. In the House, representatives of northern states introduced a bill to admit Maine as a free state, with an amendment that would admit Missouri as a slave state. Specifically, the amendment allowed the citizens of Missouri to draw up a state constitution without any restrictions on slavery. The bill also prohibited the expansion of slavery into the former Louisiana Territory north of what is now the Arkansas-Missouri border, except for the state of Missouri.

The original agreement almost fell apart over a clause in the Missouri constitution that excluded "free negroes and mulattoes" from living in the state. In other words, the state constitution allowed only enslaved blacks to live in Missouri. Kentucky Congressman Henry Clay arranged a compromise that accepted the clause but also stated that the Missouri constitution should "never be construed to authorize the passage of any law" that infringed upon the rights of any U.S. citizen. Both sides accepted the compromise, and President James Monroe signed the measures into law on March 5 and 6, 1820.

Key Provisions of the Missouri Compromise, 1820

- Missouri admitted to the Union as a slave state
- Maine admitted to the Union as a free state
- Slavery would be permitted south of the 36°30′ line of latitude, the southern border of the state of Missouri

Most members of Congress believe that the Missouri Compromise of 1820 solved the question of slavery in the nation's western territories.

The Missouri Compromise ended the legislative debate about slavery in the territories only temporarily. The Kansas-Nebraska Act of 1854 would later repeal, or overturn, the portion of the compromise that prohibited slavery north of the Arkansas-Missouri border. Three years later, in the case of *Dred Scott v. Sandford,* the Supreme Court ruled that such provisions were unconstitutional. The collapse of the Missouri Compromise led to violent clashes between pro- and anti-slavery forces in Missouri and Kansas that foreshadowed the coming Civil War (1861–1865).

See also: House of Representatives; Senate.

Money Bills

See Appropriations Bills.

New Jersey Plan

Proposed at the Constitutional Convention of 1787, plan of government that would have given all states equal representation in a newly formed Congress. During the Constitutional Convention of 1787, among the issues being debated concerning the creation of a new government was the type of representation each state would have in the new Congress. As the debate proceeded, some members from smaller states became alarmed by the firmness of the larger states on proportional representation in both houses of the proposed Legislature. Under one formula, this would have given Virginia, Pennsylvania, and Massachusetts–the three most populous states–thirteen of twenty-eight seats in the Senate, as well as a similar share of seats in the House. The smaller states, accustomed to the equality that prevailed in the Congress under the Articles of Confederation, feared that, under this plan, the larger states would dominate the country.

Luther Martin of Maryland argued that such a plan meant "a system of slavery which bound hand and foot ten states of the Union and placed them at the mercy of the other three." John Dickinson of New Jersey declared, "we would rather submit to a foreign power than submit to be deprived of . . . equality . . . in both branches of the Legislature, and thereby be thrown under the domination of the large states."

On June 11, 1787, the convention voted six states to five to create a Senate on the same proportional basis as the House of Representatives. That decision led William Paterson of New Jersey and others to draft an alternative to the Virginia Plan. The New Jersey Plan, presented on June 15, proposed amending the Articles of Confederation to give Congress authority to levy import duties and to regulate trade. It also would have provided for a plural executive, to be chosen by Congress, and a federal judiciary. It proposed that treaties and acts of Congress "shall be the supreme law" and that the executive be authorized to call on the states to enforce the laws, if necessary. Significantly, the plan also would have left each state with an equal voice in Congress and most of the attributes of **sovereignty.**

The need for a compromise became clear when the New Jersey Plan was defeated, and the small states continued to demand, and the large states to oppose, equal representation in the Senate. Faced with a deadlock, the convention named a committee to seek a compromise. The result, called the Great Compromise or Connecticut Compromise, created a **bicameral**

The New Jersey Plan

- **Three Branches: Legislative, Executive, and Judicial:**
  - A one-house legislature with equal representation for all states
  - The legislature appoints members of the Executive Branch
  - The Executive Branch appoints members of the Supreme Court
- **Powers of the federal government:**
  - Levy taxes
  - Impose import duties
  - Regulate trade
  - State laws secondary to federal laws

William Paterson's plan of government favored the small states by retaining equal representation in the one-house legislature. The plan did little to correct the weaknesses of the Articles of Confederation.

Decision Makers

William Paterson (1745–1806)

Born in County Antrim, Ireland, in 1745, William Paterson moved with his family to what is today New Jersey when he was two years old. Paterson was reared in the village of Princeton, where his father, a shopkeeper and tinsmith, settled when William was five years old.

By 1769, Paterson was practicing law. At age 30, he began his outstanding career as a public servant. During his public life, he served first as secretary of the New Jersey Provincial Congress and then as a member of the convention that wrote the state constitution. In the new state government, he served as the first attorney general and later he was appointed to lead the New Jersey delegation to the Constitutional Convention. Paterson was then elected as one of the first two United States senators from New Jersey, after which he served as New Jersey governor. In 1793, George Washington appointed him an associate justice of the United States, a position he held for thirteen years.

While at the Constitutional Convention, Paterson offered delegates the New Jersey Plan, which favored the small states, but later accepted the Connecticut Compromise, which provided for equal representation in the Senate and proportional representation in the House of Representatives. As a senator, he helped draft the Judiciary Act of 1789. He died in 1806 in Albany, New York.

legislature with both equal and proportional representation for the states.

See also: Articles of Confederation; Connecticut Compromise; Constitutional Convention; Virginia Plan.

New States, Admission of

Process by which new states are admitted to the United States of America and the history of their admission. Article IV, Section 3, of the U.S. Constitution gives Congress the power to admit new states to the Union so long as the process does not result in the formation a new state by dividing an existing state or by joining parts or all of two or more states without their consent. It also authorizes Congress "to dispose of and make all needful Rules and Regulations respecting the Territory or other Property belonging to the United States."

In the decades after the adoption of the U.S. Constitution, five new states were formed from land that was claimed by one of the original thirteen states. With four of these new state admissions–Vermont (1791), Maine (1820), Kentucky (1792), and Tennessee (1796)–the original states had agreed to allow parts of their claims to be organized into new states. The fifth state, West Virginia (1863), was formed when the western counties of Virginia that wanted to remain in the Union during the Civil War era (1861–1865) split away from the rest of the state, which had joined the Confederacy. A special legislature comprised of people from the western counties met to give its approval to the split. However, Virginia did not formally agree to the division of its territory until after the Civil War ended. Texas was an independent nation before its admission to the Union in 1845, and California was carved from a region **ceded** to the United States by Mexico in 1848. The remaining thirty states were all territories before being granted statehood.

Under procedures commonly used to gain statehood, the people of a territory submitted a petition asking for admission as a new state.

Admission of States to the Union, 1787–1959

Delaware	December 7, 1787	Michigan	January 26, 1837
Pennsylvania	December 12, 1787	Florida	March 3, 1845
New Jersey	December 18, 1787	Texas	December 29, 1845
Georgia	January 2, 1788	Iowa	December 28, 1846
Connecticut	January 9, 1788	Wisconsin	May 29, 1848
Massachusetts	February 6, 1788	California	September 9, 1850
Maryland	April 28, 1788	Minnesota	May 11, 1858
South Carolina	May 23, 1788	Oregon	February 14, 1859
New Hampshire	June 21, 1788	Kansas	January 29, 1861
Virginia	June 25, 1788	West Virginia	June 20, 1863
New York	July 26, 1788	Nevada	October 31, 1864
North Carolina	November 21, 1789	Nebraska	March 1, 1867
Rhode Island	May 29, 1790	Colorado	August 1, 1876
Vermont	March 4, 1791	North Dakota	November 2, 1889
Kentucky	June 1, 1792	South Dakota	November 2, 1889
Tennessee	June 1, 1796	Montana	November 8, 1889
Ohio	March 1, 1803	Washington	November 11, 1889
Louisiana	April 30, 1812	Idaho	July 3, 1890
Indiana	December 11, 1816	Wyoming	July 10, 1890
Mississippi	December 10, 1817	Utah	January 4, 1896
Illinois	December 3, 1818	Oklahoma	November 16, 1907
Alabama	December 14, 1819	New Mexico	January 6, 1912
Maine	March 15, 1820	Arizona	February 14, 1912
Missouri	August 10, 1821	Alaska	January 3, 1959
Arkansas	June 15, 1836	Hawaii	August 21, 1959

Beginning in 1791 with the admission of Vermont, new states have been admitted to the Union with status equal to that of the original 13 states.

Congress then authorized a convention for the territory to draft a state constitution. The constitution was then submitted to Congress and the president for approval. Once it had been approved, Congress passed a joint resolution granting statehood, and the president issued a proclamation announcing the admission of a new state into the Union.

Although Congress generally has the power to **repeal** any statute or law that it passes, it cannot repeal statehood once a new state has been admitted to the Union. The Supreme Court confirmed this, ruling that once a state has joined the Union, its admission cannot be revoked.

No state has been admitted to the Union since Alaska and Hawaii became states in 1959. Both had to overcome obstacles that led to lengthy delays in gaining statehood. Southern lawmakers were unwilling to allow four new seats in the Senate from areas unsympathetic to racial segregation. Democrats opposed Hawaii statehood because the territory traditionally voted Republican. Republican lawmakers opposed Alaska statehood because the territory traditionally voted Democratic. The legislative deadlock was finally broken, however, and Alaska became the forty-ninth state in 1959, followed by Hawaii as the fiftieth state later that year.

The people of Puerto Rico have been debating their relationship with the United States almost from the time Congress made the island a **commonwealth** in 1952. However, a clear majority of islanders have never demonstrated that they want to exchange their commonwealth status for statehood or independence.

Statehood proposals for the District of Columbia have been clouded not only by politics and state interests but also by the intent of the Constitution. Crafters of the Constitution did not want to place the capital of the nation in any state, so the District of Columbia was carved out of portions of Virginia and Maryland.

See also: Resolution Annexing Texas to the United States, 1845, in the **Primary Source Library.**

Further Reading

Stein, Mark. *How the States Got Their Shapes.* New York: Collins, 2008.

Nineteenth Amendment (1920)

Adopted in 1920, **amendment** to the U.S. Constitution that gave women the right to vote in elections in the United States. When the United States was founded, only men could vote in elections. The idea of women's **suffrage** was not considered because of traditional attitudes about the roles of women and men in society and about their participation in politics. Because the Constitution left it to the states to set the qualifications for voting in federal elections, early attempts to grant women's suffrage focused on the state legislatures. When the Fourteenth (1868) and Fifteenth (1870) amendments were considered, efforts were made to extend their guarantees of voting rights for blacks to women as well. After these efforts proved unsuccessful, a resolution proposing a constitutional amendment granting the vote to women was introduced in the Senate in 1878. The resolution was reintroduced regularly thereafter until it was finally adopted more than forty years later.

Meanwhile, some of the states gave the vote to women within their own **jurisdictions.** Wyoming, which became a state in 1890, had begun blazing the trail toward women's suffrage by giving women the right to vote for territorial officials in 1869. By 1914, equal suffrage had been granted in eleven states; New York, considered a center of opposition to women's suffrage, granted women equal suffrage in 1917.

World War I (1917–1918) added impetus to the women's suffrage movement because it was viewed as a crusade for democracy. President Woodrow Wilson (1913–1921), who had previously favored allowing women's suffrage through state action, decided to support a movement toward adopting an amendment to the Constitution because of women's contributions to the war effort. The House of Representatives adopted a resolution proposing the Women's Suffrage Amendment in 1918 by a vote of 174 to 136, a bare two-thirds majority. President Wilson, in a surprise visit to the Senate on

A–Z

September 30 of that year, urged approval of the amendment as "vitally essential to the successful prosecution of the great war of humanity in which we are engaged." The next day, however, Senate supporters failed, in a 62–34 vote, to obtain the necessary margin for passage.

When the Republicans won the November election of 1918, President Wilson pleaded for approval by the **lame-duck** Democratic Congress. However, a Senate vote of 55–29 in February 1919 again fell short of the required two-thirds majority. Within three weeks, however, the proposed Nineteenth Amendment was approved at a special session of the new Congress. Submitted to the states in June 1919, it was **ratified** in August 1920 and added to the Constitution. With the adoption of the Nineteenth Amendment, women were finally equal to men in terms of the right to vote.

See also: Amending the Constitution.

Non-Voting Members of Congress

Members of the House of Representatives who may perform most of the duties of regular members but are not allowed to cast votes. These members represent the District of Columbia and the U.S. territories of American Samoa, Guam, Puerto Rico, and the U.S. Virgin Islands. They may vote in committee, give floor speeches, and even hold chairs, but they are not allowed to vote on the House floor.

In 1871, Congress established a territorial form of government over the entire District of Columbia. The new city administration included an elected nonvoting delegate to the House of Representatives. However, financial mismanagement by city leaders led Congress to replace the District territorial government with three commissioners appointed by the president and to abolish the position of House delegate in 1875.

In 1970, Congress restored the non-voting delegate from the District of Columbia. The delegate was given all House privileges except that of voting on the floor; the delegate could, however, vote in committee. This caused city residents to complain of taxation without full representation, because DC residents pay federal income taxes.

Non-Voting Members of Congress

American Samoa–1978
District of Columbia–1970
Guam–1972
Puerto Rico–1901
U.S. Virgin Islands–1972

As of 2008, there are five non-voting members of Congress: delegates from American Samoa, the District of Columbia, Guam, and the U.S. Virgin Islands, as well as the resident commissioner from Puerto Rico. The dates in the chart indicate the year in which their representation began.

Congress considered proposals for representation of Guam and the Virgin Islands as early as the mid-1950s. In 1972, it authorized one non-voting House delegate each from Guam and the Virgin Islands. American Samoa sent its first delegate to the House in 1979. While most non-voting delegates serve two-year terms, Puerto Rico sends a "resident commissioner" who serves a four-year term. The first resident commissioner from Puerto Rico, Federico Degetau, went to the House in 1900.

In December 1992, Democrats approved a proposal to give the non-voting delegates the right to vote on the floor when the House considered legislation in the Committee of the Whole, that is, when House members meet to debate and **amend** legislation. The full House accepted the proposal as part of a package of rule changes in January 1993. Some Democrats had reservations about giving the delegates the right to floor votes and they eventually approved a compromise measure. It required that, whenever a question was decided on the strength of delegate votes, the committee would dissolve and the House would immediately vote on the issue again without the delegates.

Republicans were not happy with the rules change, perhaps because at the time all five delegates were Democrats. On January 7, 1993, a dozen Republican members and three citizens filed suit in U.S. District Court challenging the delegates' new voting rights. Although District Judge Harold H. Greene ruled that the delegate voting procedure was constitutional, the Republicans stripped away the delegates' limited floor-voting privileges when they gained the House majority in 1994.

See also: District of Columbia.

Oath of Office, Congressional

Made by a member of Congress prior to taking office, sworn statement in which the member promises to assume certain responsibilities and tasks. Article VI of the Constitution states that senators and representatives "shall be bound by Oath or Affirmation, to support this Constitution."

The original congressional oath of office was created by an act of June 1, 1789. It stated "I, (name of the member), do solemnly swear (or affirm) that I will support the Constitution of the United States." The oath was amended several times during the Civil War due to fears of disloyalty by civilian employees of the federal government. In 1862, the so-called "Ironclad Test Oath" required "every person elected or appointed to any office . . . under the Government of the United States . . . excepting the President" to swear that they had not previously engaged in criminal or disloyal conduct. The Senate later required its members to sign a written statement of the oath as well as simply speaking it.

In 1868, three years after the end of the war, the oath was again changed to read:

> I, (name of member), do solemnly swear (or affirm) that I will support and defend the Constitution of the United States against all enemies, foreign and domestic; that I will bear true faith and allegiance to the same; that I take this obligation freely, without any mental reservation or purpose of evasion; and that I will well and faithfully discharge the duties of the office on which I am about to enter. So help me God.

At the first meeting of each chamber in a new Congress, the presiding officer–the Speaker in the House and the vice president in the Senate–administers the oath orally in the form of a question beginning, "Do you solemnly swear (or affirm) . . . ?" and the answer by each new member is, "I do." New members chosen between regular elections are sworn in the same way.

One of the issues touching on the oath concerns challenges to seating members elected to Congress. Specifically, the question has arisen as to whether a challenged member-elect should take the oath before Congress decides whether the member can be seated. A member's right to take the oath and be seated may be challenged by an already seated member or by a private individual or group. A member-elect whose right to a seat is questioned appears in the usual way to take the oath. The presiding officer may then ask the individual to stand aside while the oath is administered to other members-elect. Sometimes, a member-elect takes the oath and a resolution to investigate the person's right to the seat is introduced later.

Obama, Barack

See African Americans in Congress.

Olmsted, Frederick Law

See Capitol, Architect of the.

Pages, Congressional

Young House and Senate employees who serve as messengers and perform other errands for members of Congress on Capitol Hill. Congressional **pages** must be at least juniors in high school and at least sixteen years of age. They serve for one or two semesters, or for a summer session. Pages attend school early in the morning and then go to work in the Capitol, where they answer phones, run errands, deliver messages, or distribute information until early evening or later if there is a night session of Congress. There are approximately seventy-two page positions in the House of Representatives and thirty in the Senate.

The demands on a page's time are high. Nevertheless, hundreds of young men and women apply for the positions each year. Those who are nominated by more senior members of Congress have the best chance of being selected. Being a page gives a young person a tremendous opportunity to observe the workings of Congress. In addition, the pay is good for young people. As of 2006, House pages earned $18,817 a year, and Senate pages earned $20,491. House pages live in the House Page Dormitory near the Capitol. Senate pages are housed in the Daniel Webster Page Residence near the Senate.

The House and Senate have always used messengers, usually men. However, they began to use boys to fill these positions in 1827, when three youngsters were employed as "runners," or pages, in the House. Many of the runners were orphans or children of poor families, whose plight had come to the attention of a representative. Although there was no law authorizing the use of young boys for these jobs, hundreds were employed over the years. Members of Congress often paid the boys a bonus if they performed their duties well. However, this practice was discontinued in 1843 after a special review of financial allocations in the House.

Congressional pages must conform to a dress code while they are working in the Capitol. House pages wear dark blue jackets and dark gray slacks (girls wear dark gray skirts), navy blue ties, black shoes and socks, and long-sleeved white shirts. They must wear their jackets at all times. Senate pages wear navy blue suits and ties; the dress code is the same for both males and females. The Senate does not require its pages to wear jackets in the summer months. All congressional pages were boys until 1971, when the first girl page served after the Senate passed a resolution permitting the appointment of female pages in the Senate.

Pages are under the direction of the House Clerk or the Senate sergeant at arms. Pages assigned to the House and Senate floors distribute documents to each legislator's seat in preparation for the day's business. When the House is called to order, the pages retire to a bench in the rear of the chamber to await a representative's call. A button next to a member's seat triggers a light on a board in the rear of the chamber signaling that a page is wanted. Senate pages sit on a platform at the front of the chamber and are called to run errands by the snapping of a senator's fingers or the wave of a hand. Other pages in both chambers may answer phones in the minority or majority cloakroom, deliver messages, and distribute documents.

Pages are required to attend school. Until 1946, they had to rely on private tutors if they wanted to continue their education. In 1946, however, Congress set up the Capitol Page School in the Library of Congress. This is a public school operated by the District of Columbia. Presently, House pages attend the House Page School in the Library; Senate pages attend the Senate Page School in their residence hall.

Parliamentarian

A non-partisan employee of Congress who advises members and staff on questions of procedures, rules, and **precedents**–decisions that serve as examples for similar cases that arise in the future. The parliamentarian is also responsible for preparing, compiling, and publishing the precedents of the House.

Both the House and Senate employ parliamentarians that advise members of both parties. The House parliamentarian is appointed by the Speaker of the House, while the Secretary of the Senate appoints that chamber's parliamentarian. Parliamentarians serve at the pleasure of these officers, who may replace them at any time.

The main duty of parliamentarians in both chambers is to advise the member presiding over floor debate, also known as the Chair. The parliamentarian helps the Chair prepare responses to questions about procedure and rulings on points of order. The Chair is not required to take the advice of the parliamentarian, but most members follow his or her guidance because they lack full knowledge of the chamber's procedures. The Senate Parliamentarian also keeps track of the time granted to members to address the chamber. In the House, this task falls to the Parliamentarian's clerk.

Parliamentarians also answer a wide range of questions from members and staff. For example, parliamentarians may be asked to review drafts of **bills** or amendments to make sure they do not violate to the rules of the chamber. Parliamentarians review all proposed bills and refer them to the appropriate committees for consideration. They also assist committees to prepare for and conduct hearings and to amend, or "mark-up," proposed legislation. The Office of the Parliamentarian is responsible for compiling and publishing any changes to the rules of the chamber at the start of each new Congress.

The job of the Parliamentarian is very complex and typically requires years of apprenticeship. Gaining the necessary expertise for the job takes a great deal of time and effort. This includes earning a law degree and spending years observing parliamentary maneuvers in the House or Senate. Parliamentarians hire their own assistants, who typically take over as Parliamentarian when a vacancy occurs. Many Parliamentarians serve for extended periods of time. One House Parliamentarian, Lewis Deschler, held the position for 46 years.

Party Whips

Leadership positions in both the House and Senate charged with keeping track of the whereabouts of party members and **lobbying** them for their votes. The term **whip** comes from British fox hunting lore, where the "whipper-in" was responsible for keeping the foxhounds from leaving the pack.

Whips serve as the party's acting floor leaders in the absence of the regular leaders. They poll members about their views on issues and positions on specific votes, information that the majority leader uses to determine whether and when to bring a bill to the floor. Through weekly whip notices, whips inform members about upcoming floor action, including key amendments.

The whips are also responsible for ensuring that members are present for tight votes. Sometimes, House whips and their assistants stand at the door of the House chamber, signaling the leadership's position on a vote by holding their thumbs up or down. They also put out information sheets to members describing the vote. During recorded votes, a computer on the floor prints out how members have voted. If the vote is close, the whips can use that list as a guide to seek out members who may switch their votes before the result of the voting is announced. Occasionally the whip organization goes to extremes. In 1984, for example, deputy whip Marty Russo actually carried Daniel K. Akaka, a Democratic representative from Hawaii, onto the House floor in an effort to persuade him to change his vote.

Parties in both houses of Congress choose whips, known as the majority whip and the minority whip. In the Senate, the majority whip is the third or fourth highest-ranking member of the majority party behind the Majority Leader, the President Pro Tempore, and the President of the Senate. The House majority whip ranks behind the Majority Leader and the Speaker of the House. In both the House and the Senate, the minority whip ranks behind only the Minority Leader in terms of power.

The U.S. Congress adopted the position of whip from the British Parliament, but the influence of the whip in the U.S. is weaker than its counterpart in the British system. For example, unlike in Britain, a whip in the United States cannot bargain with a congressman by denying him or her promotion to a leadership position. Whips in the United States are also less menacing in their techniques than in the United Kingdom. Even so, taking stances on issues that differ too much from the party's position can limit a member's political ambitions or ability to pass legislation.

Party whips (in background) assist Senate Majority Leader Harry Reid and Speaker of the House Nancy Pelosi with proposed legislation. (Scott J. Ferrell, CQ)

In the British system, where political parties are well disciplined, a whip's major concern is good party attendance. Whips in the U.S., by contrast, try to line up votes, determine which way members are likely to vote, and gather information as well as distribute it. "We try to keep our people . . . informed of the leadership's position on things–what they'd like, what we're seeking, what we're trying to do," a member of the Democratic whip organization said. "Not only on policy, but also on scheduling and programming. . . . We pick up static from our people and relay it to the leadership, so that they know what's going on, but we also pick up information from the leadership and convey it back. It's a two-way conduit."

House Republicans have always elected their whip, but until 1986, the Democratic whip was appointed by the Speaker and Majority Leader. In recent decades, the Democratic whip position has frequently been a first step toward the speakership. The Democrats changed to an election process in response to demands by party members who did not want an appointed member to gain the advantage of such an important post with the potential for advancement on the leadership ladder. Members also wanted the whip to act as a liaison, or mediator, between the leadership

Decision Makers

Joe Cannon (1836–1926)

Joseph Gurney Cannon, a Republican Congressman from Illinois, is widely considered by historians to have been the most powerful Speaker of the House of Representatives. Cannon, who served in Congress for over 40 years, dominated debate in the House during his term as Speaker from 1903 to 1911. It took a revolt by his fellow legislators to break Cannon's hold on power.

Cannon was the son of a North Carolina doctor who died when Joe was just ten years old. Cannon eventually developed an interest in the law and left home at age 19 to attend the University of Cincinnati's law school. He opened his first legal practice in the city of Terre Haute, Indiana, in 1858, but later moved to Illinois. In 1861, he was chosen as a state attorney for Illinois' twenty-seventh judicial district, his first experience with public office.

Cannon began his career in Congress by winning election to the House of Representatives in 1873. He then served nine consecutive terms until 1890. That year, he lost his bid for a tenth straight term. In 1892, however, he returned to the House, where he would remain until 1913. In 1903, after four previously unsuccessful attempts, Cannon won election to the speakership of the House.

In addition to his position as Speaker of the House, Cannon was chair of several key committees, including the Committee on Appropriations and the Committee on Rules. As both Speaker and chair of the Rules Committee, Cannon exercised great authority over which **bills** would come to the floor for debate, as well the conditions under which debate on bills would be conducted. This combination gave him enormous power to shape legislation and decide which bills would pass and which would never be given a hearing.

Cannon eventually angered not only members of the opposition Democratic Party, but many Republican lawmakers as well. Members of both parties in Congress felt that Cannon was abusing his authority. In response, they passed new House rules that prohibited the Speaker from also serving as chair of the Rules Committee. They also stripped the Speaker of his power to appoint members to other committees. These changes greatly reduced the power of the Speaker in general, and Cannon in particular.

After losing this power struggle, Cannon failed to win reelection to the House in 1912. As before, however, he was absent from Congress for just a single term, winning back his seat in 1914. He served in the House for four more terms, retiring in 1922. On his last day in office, his picture appeared on the cover of the first issue of *Time* magazine. He died three years later. Although it opened in 1908, the Cannon House Office Building was not named for the powerful House speaker until 1962.

and the other party members, and not simply as an enforcer and intelligence gatherer.

The whip system of both parties has expanded over time to involve more members in the process and to gather greater amounts of political intelligence. For example, in mid-1999 Republican House majority whip Tom DeLay of Texas had one chief deputy whip, eight deputy whips, and thirty-one assistant whips. The whip's responsibilities as formally defined by the Republican leadership included floor strategy, counting votes, identifying member concerns, providing information on floor activities, an automatic system to call Republican members to the floor for voting, a job bank for Republican politicians, and acting as an ombudsman to investigate and deal with complaints from party members.

Further Reading

Mackaman, Frank H., editor. *Understanding Congressional Leadership.* Washington, DC: CQ Press, 1981.

Paterson, William

See New Jersey Plan.

Patronage

The practice of granting favors, such as providing government jobs, to political supporters. Senators and representatives once controlled thousands of federal jobs such as local postmaster, health inspector, or tax collector. Congressional patronage provided members with a long list of jobs with which to pay off political supporters.

Today on Capitol Hill, the only jobs remaining under patronage are those that do not require specialized skills or technical knowledge, such as elevator operators and doorkeepers. Members now find the available patronage jobs of little help in strengthening their political positions or rewarding campaign supporters back home. Once one of the major advantages of holding public office, political patronage has declined to virtually nothing.

The practice of considering political loyalty when filling jobs began with President George Washington (1789–1797), but Andrew Jackson (1829–1837) was the first president to openly back political patronage. During Jackson's time, however, the number of government jobs requiring technical skills was not large. Patronage appointments seemed to do little damage to the general efficiency of the government.

As the business of government expanded and grew more complex, the problems with the patronage system became clear. Criticism of patronage increased sharply after the assassination of President James A. Garfield (1881) by a disappointed job seeker in 1881. In response, Congress passed the 1883 Pendleton Act that established the Civil Service Commission. Congress gave the commission authority to certify applicants for federal employment after they took competitive examinations.

The 1883 act covered only about 10 percent of federal employees in the executive branch, but it gave the president power to expand the civil service classifications by executive order. A series of such orders, and additional legislation in the years that followed, removed from politics nearly all nonpolicy-making jobs in the federal government.

The last blow to the patronage system was dealt in 1969, when the Nixon administration decided to remove 63,000 postmaster and rural carrier appointments from politics. Instead, special boards were set up to select candidates for these positions. The Postal Reorganization Act of 1970, which established the U.S. Postal Service, put an end to patronage in the post office.

One remnant of the patronage system that continues to flourish is congressional appointments to the major military service academies. These appointments account for about three-fourths of these academies' combined enrollment. Although occasional efforts have been made to remove all academy appointments from the patronage system, members of Congress have been reluctant to let the last sizable group

JUSTICE FOR ALL

Rise and Fall of the Spoils System

The term *spoils system* refers to a practice in which the political party that wins an election rewards its supporters by appointing them to political offices or awarding them government contracts. The spoils system arose in the United States in the early nineteenth century and endured until the passage and enforcement of federal civil service laws in the late 1800s.

Due to the lack of powerful political parties in the early days of the Republic, the first several presidents tended to appoint officeholders who expressed a wide range of political views. In fact, even the president and vice president were sometimes from different parties. This was because the original electoral system awarded the presidency to the candidate who received the most popular votes, while the person who received the second-highest total became vice president. This changed when the states **ratified,** or formally approved, the Twelfth Amendment in 1804.

In the early 1800s, political parties grew and assumed a great deal of power over the control of political appointments. By the 1820s, the party that won the national election began to fill vacant government posts with its supporters, regardless of their qualifications. President Andrew Jackson (1829–1837) formalized the spoils system after his election in 1828. Under his Second Party System, Jackson publicly proclaimed the victorious party's right to appoint its own officers. By the 1880s, the spoils system was firmly rooted in national politics.

It took the assassination of President James A. Garfield to put an end to the spoils system. On July 2, 1881, a frustrated office-seeker named Charles Guiteau shot Garfield while the president was walking through a Baltimore railroad station with his sons and two members of his cabinet. Garfield did not die immediately of his wounds; he lingered for eighty days after the shooting. During this time, doctors made repeated attempts to locate a bullet lodged within Garfield's body, to no avail. Indeed, their efforts may have done more harm than good, and one doctor punctured the president's liver while attempting to find the bullet. Alexander Graham Bell, the man credited with inventing the telephone, even created a metal detector to try to find the bullet, also without success. Garfield eventually died on September 19, 1881.

For many years prior to Garfield's death, proposals to replace the spoils system with a professional civil service based on merit had made no progress in Congress. The assassination, however, brought about dramatic changes in many lawmakers' attitudes. In January 1883, Congress passed the Pendleton **Civil Service Reform** Act, which required all applicants for federal jobs to pass a standard civil service examination to prove their fitness for the position. By the end of the nineteenth century, only a handful of federal jobs were still filled by patronage; the vast majority were awarded based on merit.

in the congressional patronage system slip away from them.

See also: Spoils System.

Pelosi, Nancy

See Speaker of the House of Representatives.

Political Parties and Congress

Groups of people who join together to seek governmental power by winning elections. Members of a party typically share a loosely defined set of common beliefs, although members of the same party often hold extremely different opinions and outlooks. Citizens rely on political parties to define issues, to support or oppose candidates on the basis of those issues, and then to carry out the agreed-upon policies when the party is in power.

Functions of Parties

The chief functions of the parties in Congress are to help select and elect candidates for Congress, and to organize and distribute power within the institution. The party that holds a majority of seats in each chamber controls all key positions of authority.

Choosing Candidates

One essential function of the parties is to provide a mechanism for choosing and supporting congressional candidates. In the early decades of the Republic, party caucuses–groups composed of all the members of one party in the legislature–nominated the party's candidates for office. This practice gave members of state and federal legislatures control over distributing offices.

In 1824, supporters of presidential candidate Andrew Jackson rebelled against their party caucus. Jackson was unpopular with many of the party's members in Congress and would never win nomination by the party caucus. Jackson's backers instead began to organize party conventions, in which large groups of party members who were not members of the legislature selected the party's candidates. Members of the state and federal legislatures soon realized that they could not successfully defy the majority of party members. By 1828, most states had abandoned the caucus for the more democratic process of the convention.

In the early 1900s, conventions gradually gave way to direct **primary elections,** in which local voters cast ballots for candidates. Supporters of the primary argued that powerful organizations had seized control of the nominating conventions, often ignoring the preferences of local party members. Wisconsin enacted the first mandatory primary law in 1903, and by 1917, almost every state had adopted the direct primary. The convention survived only for the selection of presidential candidates and candidates for a few state offices. The Republican Party also continued to use conventions to nominate its party's candidates in Southern states controlled by the Democratic Party.

In 1913, the states **ratified,** or formally approved, the Seventeenth Amendment, which called for the direct popular election of senators. Up until that time, members of each state's legislature chose the senators for that state. Beginning with the congressional election of 1914, senators were not only elected by popular vote but also nominated in most states through party primaries.

Organizing Congress

Parties also play an essential role in the internal organization of Congress. All formal authority in Congress is arranged according to party. The party that holds the majority in each chamber has the votes to select leaders such as Speaker of the House and the Majority Leader in the Senate. All committee and subcommittee chairs are members of the majority party and majority party leaders control the legislative agenda. Within each party, subordinate leaders called whips enable party leaders to pressure party members to support the party position on key issues.

Party Control of House/Senate and the Presidency, 1901–2009

		House		Senate		
Year	Congress	Majority Party	Principal minority party	Majority Party	Principal minority party	President
1901-1903	57th	R-197	D-151	R-55	D-31	R (McKinley) R (T. Roosevelt)
1903-1905	58th	R-208	D-178	R-57	D-33	R(T. Roosevelt)
1905-1907	59th	R-250	D-136	R-57	D-33	R (T. Roosevelt)
1907-1909	60th	R-222	D-164	R-61	D-31	R (T. Roosevelt)
1909-1911	61st	R-219	D-172	R-61	D-32	R (Taft)
1911-1913	62nd	D-228	R-161	R-51	D-41	R (Taft)
1913-1915	63rd	D-291	R-127	D-51	R-44	D (Wilson)
1915-1917	64th	D-230	R-196	D-56	R-40	D (Wilson)
1917-1919	65th	D-216	R-210	D-53	R-42	D (Wilson)
1919-1921	66th	R-240	D-190	R-49	D-47	D (Wilson)
1921-1923	67th	R-301	D-131	R-59	D-37	R (Harding)
1923-1925	68th	R-225	D-205	R-51	D-43	R (Coolidge)
1925-1927	69th	R-247	D-183	R-56	D-39	R (Coolidge)
1927-1929	70th	R-237	D-195	R-49	D-46	R (Coolidge)
1929-1931	71st	R-267	D-167	R-56	D-39	R (Hoover)
1931-1933	72nd	D-220	R-214	R-48	D-47	R (Hoover)
1933-1935	73rd	D-310	R-117	D-60	R-35	D (F. Roosevelt)
1935-1937	74th	D-319	R-103	D-69	R-25	D (F. Roosevelt)
1937-1939	75th	D-331	R-89	D-76	R-16	D (F. Roosevelt)
1939-1941	76th	D-261	R-164	D-69	R-23	D (F. Roosevelt)
1941-1943	77th	D-268	R-162	D-66	R-28	D (F. Roosevelt)
1943-1945	78th	D-218	R-208	D-58	R-37	D (F. Roosevelt)
1945-1947	79th	D-242	R-190	D-56	R-38	D (F. Roosevelt) D (Truman)
1947-1949	80th	R-245	D-188	R-51	D-45	D (Truman)
1949-1951	81st	D-263	R-171	D-54	R-42	D (Truman)
1951-1953	82nd	D-234	R-199	D-49	R-47	D (Truman)
1953-1955	83rd	R-221	D-211	R-48	D-47	R (Eisenhower)
1955-1957	84th	D-232	R-203	D-48	R-47	R (Eisenhower)

Party Control of House/Senate and the Presidency, 1901–2009, *continued*

		House		Senate		
Year	Congress	Majority Party	Principal minority party	Majority Party	Principal minority party	President
1957–1959	85th	D-233	R-200	D-49	R-47	R (Eisenhower)
1959–1961	86th	D-283	R-153	D-64	R-34	R (Eisenhower)
1961–1963	87th	D-263	R-174	D-65	R-35	D (Kennedy)
1963–1965	88th	D-258	R-177	D-67	R-33	D (Kennedy) D (L. Johnson)
1965–1967	89th	D-295	R-140	D-68	R-32	D (L. Johnson)
1967–1969	90th	D-247	R-187	D-64	R-36	D (L. Johnson)
1969–1971	91st	D-243	R-192	D-57	R-43	R (Nixon)
1971–1973	92nd	D-254	R-180	D-54	R-44	R (Nixon)
1973–1975	93rd	D-239	R-192	D-56	R-42	R (Nixon) R (Ford)
1975–1977	94th	D-291	R-144	D-60	R-37	R (Ford)
1977–1979	95th	D-292	R-143	D-61	R-38	D (Carter)
1979–1981	96th	D-276	R-157	D-58	R-41	D (Carter)
1981–1983	97th	D-243	R-192	R-53	D-46	R (Reagan)
1983–1985	98th	D-269	R-165	R-54	D-46	R (Reagan)
1985–1987	99th	D-252	R-182	R-53	D-47	R (Reagan)
1987–1989	100th	D-258	R-177	D-55	R-45	R (Reagan)
1989–1991	101st	D-259	R-174	D-55	R-45	R (Bush)
1991–1993	102nd	D-267	R-167	D-56	R-44	R (Bush)
1993–1995	103rd	D-258	R-176	D-57	R-43	D (Clinton)
1995–1997	104th	R-230	D-204	R-53	D-47	D (Clinton)
1997–1999	105th	R-227	D-207	R-55	D-45	D (Clinton)
1999–2001	106th	R-222	D-211	R-55	D-45	D (Clinton)
2001–2003	107th	R-221	D-212	R-50	D-48	R (G. W. Bush)
2003–2005	108th	R-229	D-204	R-51	D-48	R (G. W. Bush)
2005–2007	109th	R-232	D-202	R-55	D-44	R (G. W. Bush)
2007–2009	110th	D-233	R-202	D-51	R-49	R (G. W. Bush)

Note: **Figures are for the beginning of the first session of each Congress. Key to abbreviations: D—Democratic; R—Republican.**
Sources: **U.S. Bureau of the Census, *Historical Statistics of the United States, Colonial Times to 1970* (Washington, D.C.: Government Printing Office, 1975); and U.S. Congress, Joint Committee on Printing, *Official Congressional Directory* (Washington, D.C.: Government Printing Office, 1967-); *CQ Weekly*, selected issues.**

Since the beginning of the twentieth century, political control of Congress has shifted between Republicans and Democrats.

A–Z

Without structures for bringing together like-minded members for common action, Congress might find itself in constant chaos as each member fought to advance a personal agenda. Instead, the parties help to create a system in which leaders and followers can work together in pursuit of a common program. Members, however, are under no obligation to support party positions or obey party leaders. In recent decades, individual legislators have relied less on party labels to attract voters.

Since the Republican takeover of Congress in 1995, however, partisanship has been on the rise. During that time, the number of party-line votes in Congress—those in which all members of one party vote one way and all members of the opposing party vote the other way—have been at some of their highest levels in the past 50 years.

History of Parties

The Founders never envisioned the importance that political parties would develop in Congress and the nation. The authors of the Constitution had little understanding of the functions of political parties. They were indifferent, if not hostile, to the new party system that developed in the early years of the Republic. "If I could not go to heaven but with a party, I would not go there at all," Thomas Jefferson said in 1789.

The Constitution did not mention parties, either to authorize or prohibit them. It made possible a permanent role for parties, however, by giving citizens civil liberties and the right to organize. At the same time, it erected safeguards against **partisan** excesses by creating a system of checks and balances within the government. The "great object" of the new government, wrote James Madison in *Federalist No. 10,* was "to secure the public good and private rights against the danger of such a **faction** [party], and at the same time to preserve the spirit and the form of popular government."

Early Parties

Parties emerged soon after the adoption of the Constitution. Federalists generally held the upper hand in these early years, controlling the Senate and contending equally for power with the Democratic-Republicans in the House. Following the election of Thomas Jefferson as president in 1800, Democratic-Republicans took control of the White House and Congress until 1829. After the 1816 elections, the Federalist Party dropped off to a small minority.

With no effective opposition party, regional groups struggled for influence within the Democratic-Republican organization. By the mid-1820s, two groups emerged: the National Republicans and the Democrats. The Democrats captured control of Congress in 1826 and the White House in 1828. They were the dominant party in Congress for the next three decades.

In 1834, the National Republicans changed their name to Whigs, an English political term expressing opposition to the overuse of royal power. The Whigs always held a substantial number of seats in Congress, but were able to capture a majority of either chamber on only a few occasions.

Rise of the Two-Party System

The issue of slavery split the Democratic Party into northern and southern factions in the mid-1800s. It also paved the way for the emergence of the Republican Party, which opposed the spread of slavery. Republicans won majorities in the House and Senate in 1861 and controlled both chambers until 1875.

Since 1857, almost all members of Congress have belonged either to the Democratic or to the Republican Party. Members of other parties occasionally win election, such as several candidates from the Progressive Party in the early 1900s. Sometimes, a member is elected as an independent, with no ties to any political party. Both of these cases have been relatively rare.

During the years from 1875 to 1900, neither party dominated Congress. The Democrats typically controlled one chamber with the Republicans holding the other. By the early decades of the twentieth century, however, the Republicans gained majorities in both the House and the Senate. The great Depression of the 1930s ended Republican dominance in Congress and the Democrats controlled both chambers for fifty-two of the sixty-two years from 1932 to 1994. Between 1995 to 2007, the Republicans enjoyed a majority in the House and control of the Senate for ten of the twelve years. In 2007, Democrats retook both chambers for the first time in a dozen years.

Decline of Party Influence

Following the end of World War II in 1945, the parties suffered a noticeable decline in their influence on Congress. Parties and party leaders had much less power than they did at the beginning of the century. Members of Congress increasingly functioned as individuals rather than loyal party members, both in their campaigns and in the way they voted in Congress.

In many respects, the increasing individualism was a natural outgrowth of divided government. While the voters in many congressional districts were voting Republican for president, they were electing a Democrat to Congress. This created a situation where many members of Congress felt they had to buck their party in order to stay in favor with their constituents.

At the same time, the growth of party primaries as a means for selecting congressional candidates added to the decline of party importance. Originally introduced to reduce the power of corrupt party **bosses,** primaries have had the unintended effect of undermining the parties as institutions. Congressional candidates today often bypass the established party leadership in their area and appeal directly to the voters.

Other factors have contributed to the decline of the parties within Congress. In the 1950s and 1960s, a **conservative** alliance of Republicans and southern Democrats effectively controlled both the House and Senate. For many years, it was able to frustrate efforts by the Democratic leadership to push through civil rights and other legislation. Then, in the 1970s, a congressional reform movement stripped away much of the power of the old-line party leaders. That made it possible for members to ignore the party leadership and vote according to their own interests, without fear of much punishment.

Reemergence of Parties

Republicans and Democrats in Congress have made strong efforts in recent years to restore some of their influence in electoral politics. Each party has a House and Senate campaign committee, and all four committees play key roles in recruiting, training, organizing, and funding campaigns.

Nothing has revived the parties in Congress as much as the Republican takeover in 1995. By the end of 1995, the proportion of party-line votes reached a forty-year high in both the House and Senate. The highly partisan 1998 House vote to impeach President Bill Clinton demonstrated the bitter party divisions within Congress. The parties remained sharply opposed throughout the administration of George W. Bush (2001–2009). After Democrats recaptured both chambers in 2007, Senate Republicans repeatedly used a delaying tactic called the filibuster to prevent votes on Democratic legislation they opposed.

See also: Bipartisanship; Caucuses; Filibuster; House of Representatives; Party Whips; Senate.

Further Reading

Bibby, John F., and L. Sandy Maisel. *Two Parties, or More? The American Party System.* Boulder, CO.: Westview, 1998.

Blevins, David. *American Party Politics in the Twenty-First Century.* Jefferson, NC: McFarland, 2006.

Cox, Gary W., and Samuel Kernell, ed. *The Politics of Divided Government.* Boulder: Westview, 1991.

Hershey, Majorie J. *Party Politics in America.* New York: Longman, 2008.

Reichley, James. *The Life of the Parties: A History of American Political Parties.* New York: Free Press, 1992.

Popular Sovereignty

The belief that government is subject to the will of the people, who are the source of political power. The notion of popular sovereignty is built into the language of the U.S. Constitution, which begins, "We the people of the United States . . . do ordain and establish this Constitution for the

United States of America." It is also built into the constitutional provisions for popular election of the legislative and executive branches of government.

European philosophers of the seventeenth and eighteenth centuries including Thomas Hobbes, John Locke, and Jean-Jacques Rousseau, were among the first to discuss the doctrine of popular sovereignty. In his book *The Social Contract,* Rousseau set forth the central principle of popular sovereignty–that government springs from the consent of the governed. He argued that individuals in a society choose to enter into a "social contract" in which they willingly surrender some freedoms in exchange for the protection that government can provide. Legitimate government, therefore, springs from the wishes and needs of the people.

Popular sovereignty is directly opposed to monarchy, which was the prevailing form of government during Rousseau's time. The underlying assumption of monarchy was that kings and queens ruled by "divine right." That is, monarchs received their authority directly from God, and only God could strip them of it. The English Civil War of the 1640s challenged this assumption, as the English Parliament overthrew King Charles I and established a **republican** government. Although this experiment was short-lived, and Charles II restored the English monarchy in 1660, the idea of popular sovereignty refused to die.

The British subjects who settled in America embraced the idea of popular sovereignty, creating colonial governments with broad powers of self-governance. One of their main grievances against the English government was that the colonies had no representation in Parliament. Thus, acts that affected the colonies were passed without their consent. This basic principle appears in the Declaration of Independence, which states that "governments are instituted among Men, deriving their just powers from the consent of the governed, That whenever any Form of Government becomes destructive of these ends, it is the Right of the People to alter or abolish it, and to institute new Government." Popular sovereignty thus fueled the movement for independence that led directly to the founding of the United States.

See also: Constitution of the United States; Limited Government.

Pork-Barrel Spending

The spending of money on projects in the home district of a member of Congress to win support from constituents. Public works projects–and their value as a means of winning support from voters–are nearly as old as Congress itself. In the earliest years of the nation, legislators supported spending on various projects that would help the people at home. From then until the present, virtually all legislators have tried to protect their electoral bases through the time-honored use of "pork-barrel" politics.

The term *pork-barrel spending* refers to the means by which Congress distributes federal public works, funds, and other government benefits across the American landscape. A legislator who secures the construction of a dam in a home state or district or obtains a defense contract for a local weapons manufacturer contributes directly to the livelihood of both business and labor. A lawmaker with a reputation for "bringing home the bacon" is hard to beat in an election.

To voters, the benefits of pork-barrel spending are often more obvious than most campaign issues, which are usually about ideas. Pork-barrel spending provides jobs, programs, and other things that voters can benefit from directly. Those who benefit from federal projects attributed to the efforts of their legislators may feel that contributing time and money toward members' reelection is merely a practical investment in their own well-being. Similarly, constituents may put heavy pressure on their senators and representatives to bring home some federal projects or risk being ousted from office.

Traditionally, "pork" has been identified with public works projects such as roads, bridges, dams, and harbors. As the economy and the country have grown, the variety of public works projects has expanded. Today, they may include sewer projects, waste site cleanups, the construction of parks, funding for solar energy laboratories, money for fish hatcheries, and many other types of projects.

Spending on defense projects is a particularly popular form of pork-barrel spending. Because of the billions of dollars and thousands of jobs involved, members of Congress take great interest in Department of Defense decisions on the location of military bases and the assignment of weapons contracts. Influential legislators–indeed entire state delegations–have often cooperated to win military installations and defense contracts for their state–or, in times of economic difficulties, to prevent base closings in their districts or the cancellation of defense contracts.

Appropriations bills have long been a favorite vehicle for pork-barrel projects. When the federal budget is tight, there is intense competition among legislators to get their pet projects into spending **bills.** Some members believe that the increased competition provides a benefit by improving the quality of the projects that received approval. Others, however, argue that tighter competition simply eliminates projects sponsored by less well-connected members of Congress. In general, critics of pork-barrel spending say that the money is spent on many unnecessary projects and that the practice of pork-barrel spending just increases greatly the amount of money spent by the government. Nevertheless, most legislators view their efforts to distribute federal funds back home as a legitimate aspect of their jobs.

See also: Appropriations Bills; Constituents and Congress; Power of the Purse.

Power of the Purse

Constitutional authority of Congress to tax, spend, and borrow money. No other congressional power confers so much control over the policies and goals of government or has such an impact on the nation's well-being.

The Power to Tax

The Constitution, along with the Sixteenth Amendment, grants Congress the right to enact virtually any tax, within certain limits. It forbids Congress from collecting export taxes and from direct taxation unless each state paid a share in proportion to its population. It also requires that taxes be imposed uniformly throughout the nation. The Sixteenth Amendment, however, removed the limitation on direct taxation by providing for an income tax. The Constitution exempts state and local governments, as well as income from most state and local bonds, from federal taxes.

In the course of the nation's history, the primary source of revenue has shifted from **tariffs,** taxes on imported goods, to individual and corporate income taxes. Today, the main sources of revenue are individual income taxes, corporate income taxes, and social insurance taxes and contributions. Estate and gift taxes, customs duties and fees, and excise taxes on domestically produced goods, such as alcohol and tobacco, make up the remainder.

The Power to Spend

The Constitution directs the government to perform certain functions–establish post offices, roads, armed forces, and courts, pay debts, and conduct a census–that can be accomplished only by spending money. Congress's duty to "provide for the common defense and general welfare of the United States," also gives it broad authority to spend. The Constitution gives Congress the basic authority to decide how the government should spend the money it collects, and sets few limits on the spending power.

Before the Great Depression of the 1930s, government spending was limited by the principle that expenses should not exceed revenues except in times of war. Furthermore, the federal government's role in the economic affairs of the country was minimal. Between the end of the Civil War and the 1920s, however, the nation experienced rapid change. Its population soared, and its economy grew vastly larger and more complex. People crowded into fast-sprawling metropolitan regions and moved from place to place more frequently. Life expectancies lengthened, while families grew apart.

During the Great Depression of the 1930s, the government first took on responsibility for managing the economy. At this time, President Franklin D. Roosevelt's (1933–1945) New Deal produced a host of programs that redistributed the nation's wealth from one group to another and from some regions to others. Those programs grew gradually from the late 1930s to the mid-1960s. In the 1960s, President Lyndon B. Johnson's (1963–1969) administration enacted many new programs that extended the government's role in providing medical care, education assistance, regional development, nutrition, urban renewal, job training, and other services for people and localities. During the 1970s, Congress kept enlarging most of these programs and adding a few new ones.

Recent presidents have made efforts to curb federal spending. In 1996, President Bill Clinton (1993–2001) signed into law a bill ending the federal government's sixty-one-year-old program of direct cash aid to poor women and children. Federal funding would instead be provided to states, which would determine eligibility. In addition, the new law cut the federal food stamp program and made it more difficult for certain classes of individuals to receive federal aid.

The Power to Borrow

The Constitution gives Congress the authority to borrow funds in any amounts for any purposes. In recent years the federal debt has grown dramatically; the government incurs debt when it becomes necessary to spend more than the Treasury collects in taxes and other forms of revenue. When expenditures outstrip revenues, the deficit must be made up by borrowing. Through the first 150 years of the nation's history, a surplus resulting from an excess of revenues over expenditures was used, at least in part, to reduce outstanding debt. In the long string of federal budget deficits that began in fiscal 1931 and ended in fiscal 1998, there were budget surpluses in only eight years.

Budget Timetable

First Monday in February: President submits budget request and the executive branch's economic forecast to Congress for the fiscal year beginning October 1.
February 15: Congressional Budget Office (CBO) submits its budget and economic outlook for the next ten years to Congress (usually occurs in January).
Six weeks after president submits budget: All legislative committees submit their "views and estimates" of spending under their jurisdiction for the coming fiscal year to the Budget committees.
April 1: Senate Budget Committee reports its budget resolution to the Senate floor (no comparable deadline for the House Budget Committee).
April 15: Congress completes action on its budget resolution.
May 15: Annual appropriations may be considered on the House floor, even if there is no adopted budget resolution.
June 10: House Appropriations Committee reports the last annual appropriations bill to the floor.
June 15: Congress completes action on reconciliation bill, if it is required by the budget resolution (unless the budget resolution sets a different deadline).
June 30: House completes action on last annual appropriations bill.
July 15: President submits executive branch's midsession review of the budget to Congress.
Mid-August: CBO submits an updated version of its budget and economic outlook to Congress.
October 1: Fiscal year begins.

The annual budget process begins in January of each year and lasts until September 30, the end of the government's fiscal year.

During the 1980s, Congress attempted to slow the growth of the federal debt by holding down annual budget deficits. In 1985, Congress passed legislation designed to automatically cut the budget to meet specified deficit targets each year, with the goal of completely eliminating deficits over a five-year period. In the 1990s, deficit control agreements between Congress and the White House, plus a booming economy, were pouring revenues into the Treasury. The government actually had a surplus of cash when George W. Bush (2001–2009) first took office as president. However, a costly war in Iraq, coupled with massive tax cuts that reduced federal revenues, quickly eliminated the surplus and caused deficits to soar again.

Control of the Nation's Currency

The Constitution, in Article II, Section 8, gave Congress express power to "coin Money, regulate the Value thereof, and of foreign Coin, and fix the Standard of Weights and Measures." This power has been construed, with one brief but significant exception, to give Congress complete control over the nation's currency.

A national currency did not exist until the Civil War (1861–1865). Then, in 1862 and 1863, Congress passed the legal tender acts, which authorized the printing of paper money or "greenbacks" and made them legal tender for the payment of debts. In 1869, the Supreme Court upheld a federal tax that was intended to drive state bank notes out of circulation and leave a single uniform national currency.

In 1870, however, the Court ruled in the *First Legal Tender Case* that Congress had exceeded its authority by making paper money legal tender for the payment of debts incurred before the passage of the laws. The outcry from debtors and the potential economic repercussions from this decision were so great that in the *Second Legal Tender Cases* of 1871 the Court–with two new members–reconsidered and overturned its earlier decision, thus upholding Congress's authority to establish paper money as a legal currency.

Despite its ruling in the *Second Legal Tender Cases,* the Supreme Court in 1872 reaffirmed its 1869 decision that creditors holding contracts specifically calling for payment in gold did not have to accept paper money in payment. As a result, more and more creditors insisted on gold clauses, and eventually they were contained in almost every private contract.

Devaluation

In 1933, to counter gold hoarding and exporting, as well as speculation in foreign exchanges, Congress required all holders to surrender their gold and gold certificates to the Treasury in return for an equivalent amount of paper currency. In an effort to raise prices, Congress next devalued the dollar by lowering its value to one thirty-fifth of an ounce of gold.

Congress, in a third act, then **nullified** all gold clauses in contracts. The clauses could not be enforced because gold was no longer in circulation, and the statute also prohibited creditors from requiring a higher payment in the devalued currency to make up the value of the gold stipulated in the contract. The nullification statute was challenged on a number of grounds, but in a series of rulings known as the *Gold Clause Cases,* the Supreme Court in 1935 upheld the absolute power of Congress to regulate the value of currency.

The value of the dollar remained fixed at the 1933 level until December 1971, when an international monetary crisis forced President Richard M. Nixon (1969–1974) to devalue the dollar as part of a general realignment of many national currencies. The new exchange rates took effect immediately, even before Congress officially changed the gold value of the dollar. Lawmakers approved a 10 percent devaluation early in their 1972 session, setting the new par value of the dollar at one thirty-eighth of an ounce of gold. As international financial difficulties continued to grow, Congress authorized a further 10 percent devaluation in 1973.

The link between gold and the dollar finally was severed in 1976, when Congress approved changes in the international monetary system that eliminated gold as the standard of international value and permitted currency exchange rates to "float" according to market forces.

Dollars and Cents

Congress also exercises its control over the currency in more direct ways. In 1985, for example, it authorized the minting of four gold coins in various denominations. The measure gave Americans their first chance to buy new noncommemorative gold coins in more than half a century.

At the other end of the scale, legislation approved in 1974 permitted the secretary of the Treasury to lower the amount of copper contained in the penny whenever the price of copper threatened to make the penny more valuable for its copper content than for its use as a coin. That bill was inspired by rumors of a potential penny shortage as the price of copper climbed. In the late 1990s, lawmakers authorized the minting of a one-dollar coin, but did not end the printing of one-dollar bills.

See also: Appropriations Bills; Balanced Budget Amendment; Impoundment; Pork-Barrel Spending.

Further Reading

Bittle, Scott, and Jean Johnson. *Where Does the Money Go: Your Guided Tour to the Federal Budget Crisis.* New York: HarperCollins, 2008.

Keith, Robert, and Allen Schick. *The Federal Budget Process.* New York: Nova Science, 2003.

Power to Raise an Army

Article I, Section 8 of the Constitution grants Congress the power to "raise and support Armies." This clause of the Constitution has served as a basis for the enactment of laws to draft men into the armed forces.

Conscription was first used in the United States during the Civil War (1861–1865). The 1863 Enrollment Act set up a draft system run by the War Department and administered by military officers. The draft was instituted again in World War I (1917–1918), when Congress passed the Selective Service Act of 1917 setting up a system for registering and drafting men. The draft was conducted by local and state draft boards composed entirely of civilians.

The 1917 act was challenged in the courts, but the Supreme Court in 1918 unanimously upheld the law in a series of cases known collectively as the *Selective Draft Law Cases.* The Court held that Congress had the authority to institute the draft under its express war powers, as well as through its mandate to make laws "necessary and proper" to carry out its constitutional powers. Moreover, the Court held that military service was one of a citizen's duties in a "just government."

The threat of World War II (1941–1945) prompted Congress to reinstate conscription in 1940, before the United States had entered the war. This was the first peacetime draft law in U.S. history. The Selective Training and Service Act took administration of the draft out of the War Department and established an independent Selective Service System, headed by a presidential appointee. The law required one year of military service. As with the 1917 law, the 1940 act created civilian-run local and district draft boards.

American troops meet up with Iraqi children in the city of Kirkuk. The U.S. Constitution gives Congress the power to raise and maintain armies. (Photo courtesy of U.S. Army, Air Force Master Sgt. Steve Cline)

JUSTICE FOR ALL

The Draft Or a Professional Military?

Many observers have questioned whether having an all-volunteer professional military is consistent with the basic principles on which the nation was founded. Those who oppose a professional military argue that it removes most citizens from the immediate consequences of going to war. They point out that the vast majority of Americans not only will never serve, but also, that very few of their relatives, friends, or acquaintances will serve, either. They claim that this leads to widespread indifference to military actions performed in the name of the American public, which makes political leaders less reluctant to seek military solutions to international problems. Some also assert that the current system places the burden of military service on the poor and less educated members of society, who have fewer career options than wealthier and more educated individuals.

Supporters of a professional military counter that voluntary service is part of the American tradition, dating back to the widespread participation of citizen militias in the Revolutionary War. They argue that the nation should only resort to a draft in times of extreme national emergency, such as the Civil War or World War II. Others suggest that the highly technological nature of modern warfare requires trained professional soldiers who are familiar with the use of today's sophisticated weaponry and other military hardware. Draftees, they assert, will require too much training to be effective soldiers in the modern battlefield environment. Another argument in favor of a professional military is that it provides soldiers who are eager to serve, rather than soldiers who are forced into serving. Supporters suggest that morale and unit cohesion are much stronger in a professional force composed of willing soldiers.

Congress amended the draft law in 1941 to lower the minimum draft age to eighteen from twenty and extend required service to eighteen months. The draft law was extended again in 1945 and 1946 before Congress allowed it to expire in 1947. The following year, however, Congress voted to reinstate the Selective Service Act, which was still in effect at the beginning of the Korean War (1950–1953). Draft eligibility was broadened somewhat by 1951 amendments to include eighteen-and-a-half-year-olds, once all men nineteen and older had been called. The draft law then was amended five times between 1955 and 1971.

The 1971 extension of the draft was allowed to expire July 1, 1973. This paved the way for the establishment of all-volunteer armed services. Peacetime draft registration resumed in 1980, at the urging of President Jimmy Carter (1977–1981), with the enactment in June of that year of legislation requiring nineteen- and twenty-year-old men to register. Registration of eighteen-year-olds began in 1981. The House in 1993 attempted to end the Selective Service System by

Military Spending 1980–2009

1980	303.4	1995	321.6
1981	317.4	1996	307.4
1982	339.4	1997	305.3
1983	366.7	1998	296.7
1984	381.7	1999	298.4
1985	405.4	2000	311.7
1986	426.6	2001	307.8
1987	427.9	2002	328.7
1988	426.4	2003	404.9[1]
1989	427.7	2004	455.9[1]
1990	409.7	2005	495.3[1,2]
1991	358.1	2006	535.9[1,2]
1992	379.5	2007	527.4[1,2]
1993	358.6	2008	494.4[1,2]
1994	338.6	2009	494.3[1,2]

1. Figures do not include expenses for the Iraq and Afghanistan wars.
2. Figures based on requested defense budget or projections, not actual spending.
***Source:* Center for Defense Information.**

Congress has the authority and the responsibility to appropriate funds for the United States military.

slashing its funding, but the proposal was killed during a conference with the Senate. All nineteen year-old men must still register, even though the nation retains an all-volunteer military.

See also: War Powers.

Power to Select the President

Constitutional power granted to Congress to determine the winner of a presidential election in which no candidate receives a majority of the electoral vote. Congress has twice played a role in selecting the president, but only once has it done so in the way prescribed by the Constitution.

Constitutional Basis

Delegates to the Constitutional Convention in 1787 originally envisioned Congress choosing the president. Some delegates, however, thought this would not leave the president sufficiently independent. Delegate Edmund Wilson proposed election by officials called electors, who would be chosen by the people. Other delegates, however, did not trust the people to choose electors wisely, and the proposal was rejected. A proposal was made to have state legislatures choose electors but failed over concern that it put too much power in their hands. Delegate Elbridge Gerry then proposed that the governors of the states pick the president to avoid the corruption he foresaw in having Congress choose, but this plan also was rejected.

In the end, the delegates settled on using electors to choose the president. They left it to each state to determine how to choose its own electors. Each state would choose a number of electors equal to the number of seats it controlled in Congress. It was assumed that the electors were pledged to vote for the candidate who won the popular vote in that state. The candidate who captured the most electoral votes would become president. In case of ties, or when no single candidate collected a majority of the electoral votes, the Senate would choose the president. The delegates later transferred this power to the House, fearing that the Senate was becoming too powerful.

Disputed Elections

One peculiarity of the electoral system is that a candidate can win the popular vote and still lose the election. In 1888, for example, Democrat Grover Cleveland collected almost 1 million more popular votes than Republican Benjamin Harrison, but Harrison easily won the electoral vote, 233–168. In 2000, George W. Bush also won the electoral vote even though his opponent, Al Gore, Jr., collected more popular votes.

The elections of 1824 and 1876, however, produced no clear electoral vote winner. In both cases, Congress was called upon to choose a winner. Both elections were tainted with charges that the outcomes were products of political corruption and secret deal making.

Presidents Elected by the House of Representatives and Close Calls

1800	A tied electoral college vote causes the presidential election to be thrown into the House, which takes 36 ballots to pick Thomas Jefferson over Aaron Burr,
1824–1825	John Quincy Adams trails in popular vote and electoral votes to Andrew Jackson, but is elected president on first ballot.
1876–1877	Rutherford B. Hayes is elected with a one-vote electoral college majority, 185–184, after a 15-member commission splits along party lines in awarding him the disputed vote from four states.
1888	Incumbent Grover Cleveland wins a majority of the popular vote but loses 233 to 168 in the electoral college; Benjamin Harrison becomes president.
1960	John F. Kennedy wins an electoral college majority over Richard M. Nixon, 303–219. Kennedy's popular vote margin is the closest in the twentieth century. Fourteen unpledged electors and one faithless Republican elector vote for Senator Harry F. Byrd, a Virginia Democrat.
1968	Many people believe the election will be settled in the House of Representatives because of a strong third-party candidacy of Alabama governor George C. Wallace. Republican Richard M. Nixon wins an electoral majority over Democrat Hubert H. Humphrey and Wallace. Both Nixon and Humphrey had vowed not to negotiate with Wallace if the election were thrown into the House.
1992	Strong third-party bid by H. Ross Perot stirs fears of throwing the election into the House, but Bill Clinton wins an electoral college majority. Perot fails to carry any states.
2000–2001	Democrat Al Gore surpasses Republican George W. Bush in popular vote, but electoral college outcome turns on close count in Florida. Gore and Bush vie in state and federal courts over recount of Florida votes. U.S. Supreme Court halts count, settling the election in Bush's favor.

The United States House of Representatives is responsible for electing the president if no candidate receives a majority of the electoral vote. The House has selected two presidents—Thomas Jefferson in 1801 and John Quincy Adams in 1825. Since the founding of the Republic, there have been several elections in which it was thought the House would have to choose the president.

Election of 1824

In the 1824 presidential election, four candidates earned electoral votes, but none captured the majority needed for victory. The two top vote-getters were Andrew Jackson, with 99 electoral votes and John Quincy Adams, with 84. The remaining 77 electors were split between William H. Crawford and Henry Clay. Because no one controlled a majority, the Constitution called for the election to go to the House. Each state would cast a single vote to break the tie.

According to the Twelfth Amendment, only the top-three vote-getters were allowed to participate in an election decided by the House. Clay was thus left out of the running. A bitter opponent of Jackson, Clay threw his support to Adams, who was elected on the first ballot by a vote of thirteen votes, to seven for Jackson, and four for Crawford. Jackson and his supporters were furious, because Jackson had won the most electoral votes and popular votes in the general election. When Adams appointed Clay as his secretary of state, Jackson accused the two of striking a "corrupt bargain" for the presidency.

Election of 1876

In 1876, disputed vote counts in several states delayed reporting of the popular vote and forced Congress to strike a compromise to decide a winner. The first election returns showed Democrat Samuel Tilden leading Republican Rutherford B. Hayes by nineteen electoral votes, with twenty votes remaining uncounted. In Florida, Louisiana, and South Carolina, both parties claimed victory. In Oregon, an elector who voted for Tilden was declared illegal and replaced with a

POINT/COUNTERPOINT

SHOULD THE ELECTORAL COLLEGE BE ABOLISHED?

The United States is the only modern democracy in which a presidential candidate can win the popular vote but lose the election. Many politicians and political observers, such as California's Democratic Senator Diane Feinstein, feel that it is time to change this by abolishing the electoral college. Others, including Texas Republican Representative Ron Paul, claim that the Founders had solid reasons for establishing an electoral system and caution against abandoning it lightly.

Senator Diane Feinstein

Under the current system, it is possible for a Presidential candidate to lose the popular vote, but to be elected by the Electoral College. This has happened four times in the nation's history, most recently in 2000. And the current system enables a handful of states to become battleground states, and disenfranchises tens of millions of American voters in the most important election in the nation. By amending the Constitution to abolish the Electoral College, and replacing it with a system in which the winner is the candidate with the most votes nationwide, we will ensure that the method of electing the President and Vice President is fair and uniform . . . .

I am mindful that amending one of our nation's most sacred documents requires careful thought, study and debate. I do not take such a proposal lightly. But the current law is archaic and denies Americans the full measure of this most fundamental right. The day of the Electoral College has come and gone, and that's why I will be introducing legislation in the 110th Congress to abolish it. Past attempts to abolish the Electoral College by amending the Constitution have run into difficulty. But I deeply believe that every vote should be treated equally regardless of the state in which it is cast.

substitute who voted for Hayes. Neither side accepted the claims of victory put forth by the other.

Congress quickly formed an Electoral Commission composed of five senators, five House members, and five Supreme Court justices. Eight of the members of the commission were Republicans; seven were Democrats. In every disputed state, the commission voted to accept the Republican election results. Each time, the vote was eight to seven along strict party lines. The commission awarded Hayes all twenty disputed electoral votes, giving him a 185–184 victory over Tilden.

Many historians believe that the Republicans struck a deal with Democrats from the Southern states to elect Hayes. In the so-called Compromise of 1877, Hayes agreed to remove federal troops from most of the former Confederate states and to appoint a Southern Democrat to his cabinet.

See also: Constitution of the United States; Constitutional Amendments Affecting the

Representative Ron Paul

The Founding Fathers sought to protect certain fundamental freedoms, such as freedom of speech, against the changing whims of popular opinion. Similarly, they created the Electoral College to guard against majority tyranny in federal elections. The president was to be elected by the fifty states rather than the American people directly, to ensure that less populated states had a voice in national elections. This is why they blended Electoral College votes between U.S. House seats, which are based on population, and U.S. Senate seats, which are accorded equally to each state. The goal was to balance the inherent tension between majority will and majority tyranny. Those who wish to abolish the Electoral College because it's not purely democratic should also argue that less populated states like Rhode Island or Wyoming don't deserve two senators.

A presidential campaign in a purely democratic system would look very strange indeed, as any rational candidate would focus only on a few big population centers. A candidate receiving a large percentage of the popular vote in California, Texas, Florida, and New York, for example, could win the presidency with very little support in dozens of other states. Moreover, a popular vote system would only intensify political pandering, as national candidates would face even greater pressure than today to take empty, middle-of-the-road, poll-tested, mainstream positions. Direct democracy in national politics would further dilute regional differences of opinion on issues, further narrow voter choices, and further emasculate political courage.

DOCUMENT-BASED QUESTION

What shortcomings does Senator Feinstein see in the electoral college, and what strengths in the present system does Representative Paul identify?

Presidency; Electoral College and Electors; House Procedure for the Election of John Quincy Adams, 1825, in the **Primary Source Library;** President and Congress; Separation of Powers; Twelfth Amendment, 1804, in the **Primary Source Library.**

President and Congress

The chief officer of the United States and the relationship of the executive branch with Congress. The Constitution established a government composed of three separate branches and gave each branch distinct powers.

Separation of Powers

Article I of the Constitution lays out the specific, or expressed, powers granted to Congress. These include the power to raise and spend money, to declare war, to regulate **commerce,** and to "make all Laws which shall be necessary and proper for carrying into Execution the foregoing Powers." This gives the Congress wide scope for action.

Article II outlines the expressed powers of the executive branch, which are much narrower than those of Congress. The president has the power to appoint a large number of important government officials, including the heads of cabinet departments, ambassadors, and Supreme Court justices. The president may make treaties with foreign powers and is commander in chief of the armed forces. In that role, the president has the power to commission military officers. He or she also has the power to grant pardons for crimes, except in cases where a government official is **impeached,** or charged with crimes or misconduct while in office.

President George W. Bush (2001–2009) delivers his last State of the Union address to Congress and the nation in January 2008. The Constitution requires the president "from time to time to give to the Congress Information of the State of the Union, and to recommend to their Consideration such Measures as he shall judge necessary and expedient." (Scott J. Ferrell, CQ)

The president can perform many of these functions only with "the Advice and Consent" of Congress. That is, the president must seek approval from the legislature to carry out many of the duties of office. The Senate must approve all presidential nominees for federal offices, except those that Congress grants the president authority to appoint without consent. The Senate must also approve all treaties signed by the president. In each of these cases, approval requires the support of two-thirds of the senators present and voting.

The president also exercises a check over Congress with the power to **veto,** or reject, any bill passed by Congress. The Congress can override a presidential veto if two-thirds of the members of both chambers vote to do so. In this case, the bill becomes law even though the president refuses to sign it. The president has ten days after receiving a bill to veto it; otherwise it automatically becomes law. However, if that ten-day period expires after Congress **adjourns,** or suspends its activities, the bill is automatically vetoed. This type of veto, called a pocket veto, cannot be overridden by Congress.

Appointments and Treaties

Virtually every president has faced difficult confirmation battles with the Senate. Presidents with solid political support have generally fared better than those who had to contend with a hostile Senate. Even strong chief executives sometimes have been subjected to embarrassing defeats of their nominees. While such battles dominate the news, they are the exception.

Appointments

In the vast majority of cases, the Senate's power over appointments is little more than a bureaucratic formality. In 1993, the first year of Bill Clinton's presidency, the Senate received more than 42,000 nominations. Over 39,000 of those were routine military commissions and promotions; only about 700 involved high-level positions that might require Senate scrutiny. Some appointments, however, generate considerable controversy and friction between Congress and the president.

In the past few decades, much of this controversy has centered on appointments to the U.S. Supreme Court. President Ronald Reagan (1981–1989) had the opportunity to fill three vacancies on the Court during his two terms of office. His most divisive nominee was Robert Bork, whom Reagan named to replace retiring Associate Justice Lewis Powell in 1987. Civil rights groups strongly opposed Bork, who was critical of major civil rights legislation that Powell had championed while on the Court. In the end, the Senate rejected the nomination. Reagan's successor, George H. W. Bush (1989–1993), also ran into stiff opposition to his nomination of Clarence Thomas to the Court. After a bitter confirmation hearing, the Senate narrowly approved Bush's choice.

Treaties

The clause that clearly gives the president the power to make treaties is unclear on some points. For example, the Constitution never spelled out the Senate procedure for advising the president, nor did it specify at what stage in the treaty-making process the Senate was to advise the president.

In the early years of the nation, the executive branch sought to incorporate Senate advice into the treaty process. It held presidential meetings with senators, allowed the Senate to confirm negotiators, and sent the chamber special presidential messages about treaties. As international relations became more complicated, however, presidents abandoned these various devices to obtain the Senate's advice.

The Senate responded by attaching drastic **amendments,** or formal changes to some treaties, and rejecting others outright. The classic display of senatorial dissatisfaction came in 1919 and 1920. After prolonged debate, the Senate ultimately rejected the Treaty of Versailles, which ended World War I (1917–1918). The treaty also created the League of Nations, an international body that was the predecessor to today's United Nations (UN). Many senators were opposed to the structure of the proposed League of Nations. They tried to amend the treaty to alter the League's structure, but, dooming the treaty to Senate rejection, President Woodrow Wilson refused to accept their changes.

War Powers

The wording of the Constitution also makes it unclear which branch has the final authority to commit U.S. forces to combat. Article I gives Congress the power "to declare war," while Article II makes the president commander in chief of the armed forces. This distinction has produced a number of conflicts between the branches, and called into question the relevance of Congress's power to declare war.

Congress has declared war only five times in more than 200 years. The last congressional

VIEWPOINTS

A 1957 political cartoon shows President Dwight D. Eisenhower (1953–1961) in a helicopter flying over angry citizens who represent various concerns, such as aid to education, immigration, and civil rights. President Eisenhower looked to Congress for leadership on these and other issues. (A 1957 Herb Block cartoon, copyright by The Herb Block Foundation)

JUSTICE FOR ALL

Congress and Executive Privileges

In the course of Independent Counsel Kenneth W. Starr's investigation into President Bill Clinton's extramarital affair, courts ruled on questions of "executive privilege," attorney-client privilege, and the "protective function" privilege involving the president's Secret Service detail. The loser in almost all the rulings was the White House. Legal scholars speculated that the effect might be a shifting of power from the presidency to Congress.

U.S. District Court Judge Norma Holloway Johnson ruled on May 4, 1998, that Clinton could not invoke executive privilege to keep his aides from testifying before Starr's grand jury. While Johnson recognized claims of executive privilege, she found that the needs of the prosecutors outweighed the privilege in this case.

A federal appeals panel July 7, 1998, upheld Johnson's May 22 ruling that the Secret Service agents were obligated to testify about what they witnessed while protecting the president. The Justice Department sought to create a protective function privilege because it feared that a president would not trust having Secret Service agents close enough to protect him. Johnson had written that such a privilege would have to be established by Congress, not the courts.

On July 27, 1998, a three-judge panel of the U.S. Circuit Court of Appeals for the District of Columbia also upheld Johnson's May 4 ruling rejecting the administration's claim of attorney-client privilege in Clinton's effort to keep White House deputy counsel Bruce Lindsay from testifying before

declaration of war occurred shortly after the Japanese Attack on Pearl Harbor in December 1941 that brought the U.S. into World War II (1941–1945). Since that time, the U.S. has fought two major wars and dozens of smaller conflicts and multinational military operations. In almost every instance, the president cited national security interests to commit U.S. troops without prior congressional approval. In each case, Congress–often reluctantly–agreed to support the president's action.

In 1973, Congress passed the War Powers Resolution to try to reclaim its role in the deployment of U.S. troops. The resolution required the president to notify Congress before sending troops into battle and to seek congressional approval within forty-eight hours of doing so. It also prevented the president from committing troops for more than ninety days without congressional approval. In practice, the resolution has done little to limit the president's power to deploy the nations' armed forces.

Impeachment

The last section in Article II states simply, "The President, Vice President and all civil Officers of the United States, shall be removed from Office on Impeachment for, and Conviction of, Treason, Bribery, or other high Crimes and Misdemeanors." Article I gives Congress the power both to start **impeachment** proceedings and to determine the guilt or innocence of the accused. Congress has exercised its impeachment power only rarely against the president, but each time it has been accused of using the power for purely political purposes.

One source of controversy concerning the impeachment power is the meaning of the term

Starr's grand jury. White House attorneys were not seen by the panel as any different from other government lawyers who were called on to give evidence about possible criminal wrongdoing.

Although legal scholars found the Clinton rulings persuasive, they noted that, if presidents could not count on candid advice from their advisers, they likely would have a difficult time asserting control over the vast executive branch. Presidents routinely use their most trusted White House aides to imbue the federal bureaucracy with their policy objectives. They do this through centralization of the decision-making process and control of the flow of information, among other things. A hamstrung White House would presumably mean more decisions being made further down the chain of command, sometimes by bureaucrats or officers less sympathetic to the goals of the administration. If presidential advisers know they could be forced to testify—either as a result of a court order or because a president does not have the power to stand up to a congressional subpoena—they might be more inhibited in what they say.

The question arises as to whether the country is better off with such court rulings. Most legal experts argue that presidential privileges are a separation-of-powers issue. As such, it is best if they are left undefined and constantly argued over by the legislative and executive branches as they try to advance their policy and political agendas. In hindsight, President Clinton could have avoided the legal downside of the court rulings on future presidential privileges by not challenging Starr's subpoenas.

"high crimes and misdemeanors." The phrase is so vague that it could include any number of charges. When the House impeached President Andrew Johnson (1865–1869) in 1868, the stated reason was Johnson's refusal to follow the Tenure of Office Act. The act prohibited the president from dismissing certain appointed officials without congressional approval. Most historians, however, agree that Johnson's unpopularity with members of his own party in Congress was the driving force behind his impeachment.

Bill Clinton (1993–2001) was also the subject of what many observers considered a politically motivated impeachment attempt. This time, however, it was members of the opposing party who launched the effort. House Republicans impeached Clinton in 1998 after the president lied under oath about a sexual relationship with a White House intern. As with Johnson, the Senate failed to convict Clinton. Unlike Johnson, Clinton remained popular with the American public despite the impeachment attempt.

Divided Government

Tensions between the legislative and executive branches tend to flourish in times of divided government, when one party controls Congress and the other holds the presidency. The impeachment of President Clinton, for example, was the climax of a long and bitter **partisan** battle between the Republican-controlled Congress and the Democratic Clinton administration.

In the first half of the twentieth century, divided government was rare. From 1900 to 1955, there were only eight years in which the same party failed to hold the presidency and both chambers of Congress simultaneously. Since that time, however, divided government has been the rule rather than the exception. Between 1956 and 2009, the same party has controlled the executive and legislature just one-third of the time. It has been during this time that most of the struggles over war powers and many of the most contentious appointment battles have been waged.

However, single party dominance of both the executive and legislative branch is no guarantee of friendly relations between the two. Such conflicts have often come at times of strong presidential leadership. Abraham Lincoln (1861–1865), Woodrow Wilson (1913–1921), and the two Roosevelts–Theodore (1901–1909) and Franklin Delano (1933–1945)–had difficulties with their parties' congressional leaders, although all four men were largely successful in enacting their legislative programs.

Congress has also clashed with less aggressive presidents of their own party, usually when attempting to force through their own legislative program. One of the earliest examples came when House Speaker Henry Clay used his political influence to pressure President James Madison to pass a series of anti-British measures. The move led to war with Britain, a development that Clay favored and Madison opposed. The impeachment of Andrew Johnson offers perhaps the most extreme example of congressional opposition to a president of the same party.

See also: Checks and Balances; Expressed Powers; Separation of Powers; Impeachment Power; Iran-Contra Hearings; Power to Select the President; Supreme Court and Congress; Treaty Power; Vetoes and Veto Overrides; War Powers; War Powers Resolution (1973); Watergate Hearings; Whitewater Investigations.

Further Reading

Sollenberger, Mitchel A. *The President Shall Nominate: How Congress Trumps Executive Power.* Lawrence: University of Kansas Press, 2008.

Thurber, James A. *Divided Democracy: Cooperation and Conflict Between the President and Congress.* Washington, DC: CQ Press, 1991.

Wright, Jim. *Balance of Power: Presidents and Congress from the Era of McCarthy to the Age of Gingrich.* Nashville, TN: Turner, 1996.

President Pro Tempore

Official who presides over the Senate in the absence of the vice president. The Constitution specifies that the vice president "shall be President of the Senate, but shall have no vote, unless they (the senators) be equally divided." It also provides that the "Senate shall choose . . . a President pro tempore, in the absence of the Vice President, or when he (the Vice President) shall exercise the office of President of the United States."

Duties

As presiding officer, the principal function of the president pro tempore–a term which means "for the time being"–is to recognize senators. The presiding officer also decides points of order, subject to appeal to the full Senate; appoints senators to House-Senate conference committees; enforces decorum; administers oaths; and appoints members to special committees. The president pro tempore may appoint a substitute to replace him in the chair. As a senator, the president pro tempore may also vote on all matters. By law, the president pro tempore is third in line, behind the vice president and the speaker of the House of Representatives, to succeed to the presidency.

By custom, the senior member of the majority party in the Senate holds the position of president pro tempore, but the Senate usually puts a freshman member in the chair. That relieves more senior members of a time-consuming task and gives newcomers firsthand lessons in Senate rules and procedures. New senators are heavily dependent on an officer known as the parliamentarian, who provides advice on rules and procedures. In the Senate, the rules require the presiding officer to recognize "the Senator who shall first address him" if several senators are seeking to speak. However, by custom, the Majority and Minority Leaders are always recognized first if they seek recognition

A – Z

Presidents Pro Tempore of the Senate, 1979–2009

96th Congress (1979–1981)
Warren G. Magnuson (WA)
January 15, 1979–December 4, 1980
Milton R. Young (ND)
December 5, 1980–December 5, 1980
Warren G. Magnuson (WA)
December 6, 1980–January 4, 1981

97th Congress (1981–1983)
Strom Thurmond (SC)
January 5, 1981–January 2, 1983

98th Congress (1983–1985)
Strom Thurmond (SC)
January 3, 1983–January 2, 1985

99th Congress (1985–1987)
Strom Thurmond (SC)
January 3, 1985–January 5, 1987

100th Congress (1987–1989)
John C. Stennis (MS)
January 6, 1987–January 2, 1989

101st Congress (1989–1991)
Robert C. Byrd (WV)
January 3, 1989–January 2, 1991

102nd Congress (1991–1993)
Robert C. Byrd (WV)
January 3, 1991–January 4, 1993

103rd Congress (1993–1995)
Robert C. Byrd (WV)
January 5, 1993–January 3, 1995

104th Congress (1995–1997)
Strom Thurmond (SC)
January 4, 1995–January 6, 1997

105th Congress (1997–1999)
Strom Thurmond (SC)
January 7, 1997–January 6, 1999

106th Congress (1999–2001)
Strom Thurmond (SC)
January 7, 1999–January 3, 2001

107th Congress (2001–2003)
Robert C. Byrd (WV)
January 3, 2001–January 20, 2001
Strom Thurmond (SC)
January 20, 2001–June 6, 2001
Robert C. Byrd (WV)
June 6, 2001–January 3, 2003

108th Congress (2003–2005)
Theodore (Ted) Stevens (AK)
January 3, 2003–January 3, 2005

109th Congress (2005–2007)
Theodore (Ted) Stevens (AK)
January 4, 2005–January 4, 2007

110th Congress (2007–2009)
Robert C. Byrd (WV)
January 4, 2007–January 4, 2009

Note: **From January 3 to January 20, 2001, the Democrats held the majority, due to the deciding vote of outgoing Democratic Vice President Al Gore. Senator Robert C. Byrd became president pro tempore at that time. Starting January 20, 2001, the incoming Republican Vice President Richard Cheney held the deciding vote, giving the majority to the Republicans. Senator Strom Thurmond resumed his role as president pro tempore. On May 24, 2001, Senator James Jeffords of Vermont announced his switch from Republican to Independent status, effective June 6, 2001. Jeffords announced that he would caucus with the Democrats, changing control of the evenly divided Senate from the Republicans to the Democrats. On June 6, 2001, Robert C. Byrd once again became president pro tempore. On that day, the Senate adopted S. Res. 103, designating Senator Thurmond as President Pro Tempore Emeritus.**

The President Pro Tempore of the Senate may preside over the Senate in the vice president's absence. The President Pro Tempore is third in line of succession to the presidency, after the vice president and the Speaker of the House.

Senate President Pro Tempore Strom Thurmond, R-SC (right) and Speaker of the House Newt Gingrich, R-GA (left) applaud before South Korean President Kim Young-sam addresses a joint session of Congress in 1995. (AP Photo, Doug Mills)

when no one else holds the floor. Many senators tend to view presiding as drudge work to be avoided, because the job frequently involves presiding over **quorum calls**–the summoning of absent members to the chamber for a vote.

History

The first president pro tempore, John Langdon of New Hampshire, was elected on April 6, 1789, before Vice President John Adams (1789–1797) appeared in the Senate to assume his duties as presiding officer. When the first vice president took his seat on April 21, Langdon's service as president pro tempore ended. For the next 100 years, the Senate acted on the theory that a president pro tempore could be elected only in the vice president's absence and that his term expired when the vice president returned. By 1890, the Senate had elected presidents pro tempore on 153 occasions. In 1890, the Senate passed a resolution that allowed the sitting president pro tempore to hold that post until another person was elected to take his place. That removed the need to elect a new president pro-tempore every time the vice president failed to attend Senate sessions.

Until 1977, members of each party took turns presiding in the Senate. This practice ended abruptly following an incident the previous year. The presiding officer at the time was Republican Senator Jesse Helms of North Carolina, a member of the minority. Helms broke with Senate custom by denying recognition to the Majority Leader, Democratic Senator Mike Mansfield of Montana. Instead, Helms recognized **conservative** Democratic Senator James B. Allen of Alabama. The Democratic leadership then decided that the majority should retain control of the chair at all times, unless the vice president, who might be a member of the opposite party, decided to occupy it. Republicans continued this practice when they controlled the Senate.

By custom, the most senior member of the majority party in terms of Senate service is elected president pro tempore. Since 1945, only one person elected to the post did not follow this pattern: Republican Arthur H. Vandenberg of Michigan was the second-ranking Republican when elected in 1947. Before 1945, there were several notable exceptions to the custom.

Few presidents pro tempore in the twentieth century have had much influence on the Senate. One who did was Vandenberg, who was also chairman of the Foreign Relations Committee. One observer noted that Vandenberg "no doubt exerted as much influence in what was done and not done as the Speaker of the House." Robert C. Byrd of West Virginia also wielded considerable authority as president pro tempore between 1989 and 1995. As chairman of the Appropriations Committee and a former majority and minority leader, Byrd brought far more stature to the position than it would normally enjoy simply through seniority.

See also: Parliamentarian; Party Whips; Vice President.

Further Reading

Sachs, Richard C. *The President Pro Tempore of the Senate: History and Authority of the Office.* New York: Nova Science, 2003.

Public Interest Groups

Organizations that seek to achieve goals that benefit the public as a whole and not just the members or supporters of the organization. A large number of public interest groups exist, dedicated to addressing a wide range of issues including civil rights, consumer and environmental protection, citizens' participation in government, and government ethics. Several thousand organizations calling themselves public interest groups collect billions of dollars annually in contributions.

Several established groups set the pattern for the more recent explosion of public interest groups. The nonpartisan League of Women Voters, for example, was founded in 1920 to educate women on the use of their newly won voting rights. It soon extended the scope of its activities to include the political education of the general public. The league sponsored debates between candidates during several presidential elections, and it engaged in **lobbying** during the 1970s for the passage of the Equal Rights Amendment and the Clean Air Act.

A broad-based group with a more distinct political agenda is the Americans for Democratic Action (ADA), founded in 1947 to "formulate **liberal** domestic and foreign policies." It is best known for its annual ratings of legislators' votes on issues of concern to the group. Its conservative counterpart, the American Conservative Union, was founded in 1964 and began rating lawmakers in 1971.

Two of the most well-known public interest groups are Public Citizen, established in 1971 by lawyer-activist Ralph Nader, and Common Cause, founded in 1970 by John Gardner, a former cabinet secretary. Both groups share the general goal of increasing citizens' influence over political, economic, and social concerns. Each, however, has its own areas of specialty. Public Citizen addresses a wide range of concerns that reflect Nader's interests: auto safety, consumer protection, insurance, medicine, nuclear power, aviation, pension rights, drug and food safety, product liability, occupational health and safety, and pesticide control. Common Cause focuses on issues of political structure and procedures. In the early 1980s, it took up the cause of arms control before returning to "good government" issues such as campaign finance and ethics laws. Since the 1990s, Common Cause has focused increasingly on the reform of campaign financing laws.

Both groups undertake direct lobbying in Washington and maintain sophisticated local lobbying operations. Unlike many other **special-interest groups,** neither organization endorses candidates or makes campaign contributions. Gardner viewed Common Cause as a way to offer interested private citizens an opportunity to influence decisions in Washington, just as business organizations and labor unions do. It uses an insider-outsider strategy, with experienced Washington **lobbyists** working the halls of Congress while state and local chapters pressure legislators from their home bases. Congress Watch, a Public Citizen organization devoted to legislative affairs, employs policy specialists who register to **lobby** on specific issues, such as freedom of information, consumer protection, and health and safety.

Both groups are characterized by a grassroots emphasis. Common Cause developed an indirect lobbying operation that could mobilize its members–some 300,000 in 2008–to write or call their senators or representatives when significant issues arose. During congressional elections, the organization took out advertisements in the local media that attacked individual legislators for their stands on issues such as campaign finance. Those tactics–and the fact that Common Cause initiated the ethics complaint that led to the resignation of House Speaker Jim Wright in 1989–angered some of the group's traditional allies in the Democratic Party. Its vigorous and repeated attacks on the current campaign financing system further damaged its relations with members of both parties.

The primary objective of the Nader organization's efforts is to spark local action on local problems, and the group is often more effective at the state than the national level. Nader often urges the audiences at his speeches to become more directly involved in public affairs; he himself has taken a high-profile role in state ballot initiatives, including a successful 1988 California drive to reduce auto insurance rates. Public Citizen has also been willing to make political alliances, uniting with trial lawyers in the 1980s to combat industry's efforts to weaken product liability laws.

The largest of the activist groups is Citizen Action, which was founded in Cleveland in 1979. A decade later, the organization changed its name to The Citizen Action Foundation and relocated its headquarters to Washington, DC. The group's priorities include environmental conservation, campaign finance, health care, and legal reforms.

See also: Lobbying and Congress.

Further Reading

Browne, William P. *Groups, Interests, and U.S. Public Policy.* Washington, DC: Georgetown University Press, 1998.

Cigler, Allan J, and Burdett A. Loomis (editors). *Interest Group Politics.* Seventh edition. Washington, DC: CQ Press, 2006.

Randolph, Edmund

See Virginia Plan.

Rankin, Jeanette

See House of Representatives.

Reapportionment

The redistribution of the 435 House seats among the states to reflect shifts in population. Reapportionment occurs every ten years based on the census. States where populations grew quickly during the previous ten years typically gain congressional seats, while those that lost population or grew much more slowly than the national average may lose seats.

The Constitution made the first **apportionment** before the first census was taken, at a time when no reliable figures on the population were available. This apportionment yielded a sixty-five member House. The First Congress submitted to the states a proposed constitutional amendment that would give each state one representative for every 30,000 people until the House membership reached 100. Once that level was reached, there would be one representative for every 40,000 people until the House reached 200, when there would be one representative for every 50,000 people. The states, however, refused to **ratify,** or approve the **amendment.**

A major problem with the bill was that the population of each state was not a simple multiple of 30,000; significant fractions were left over. For example, Vermont was found to be entitled to 2.85 representatives, New Jersey to 5.98, and Virginia to 21.02. A new bill, approved in April 1792, provided one member for every 33,000 inhabitants, disregarding all fractions, and fixed the exact number of representatives to which each state was entitled. The total membership of the House was to be 105.

As the country's population grew, so did the total number of House seats, even though Congress continually increased the ratio, from one seat per 33,000 inhabitants to one per 47,700 by 1832. At that time, the House had 240 members. Following the 1840 census Congress fixed the size of the House at 223 seats and divided that figure into the total population, yielding a result

House Seats, 2000 Reapportionment

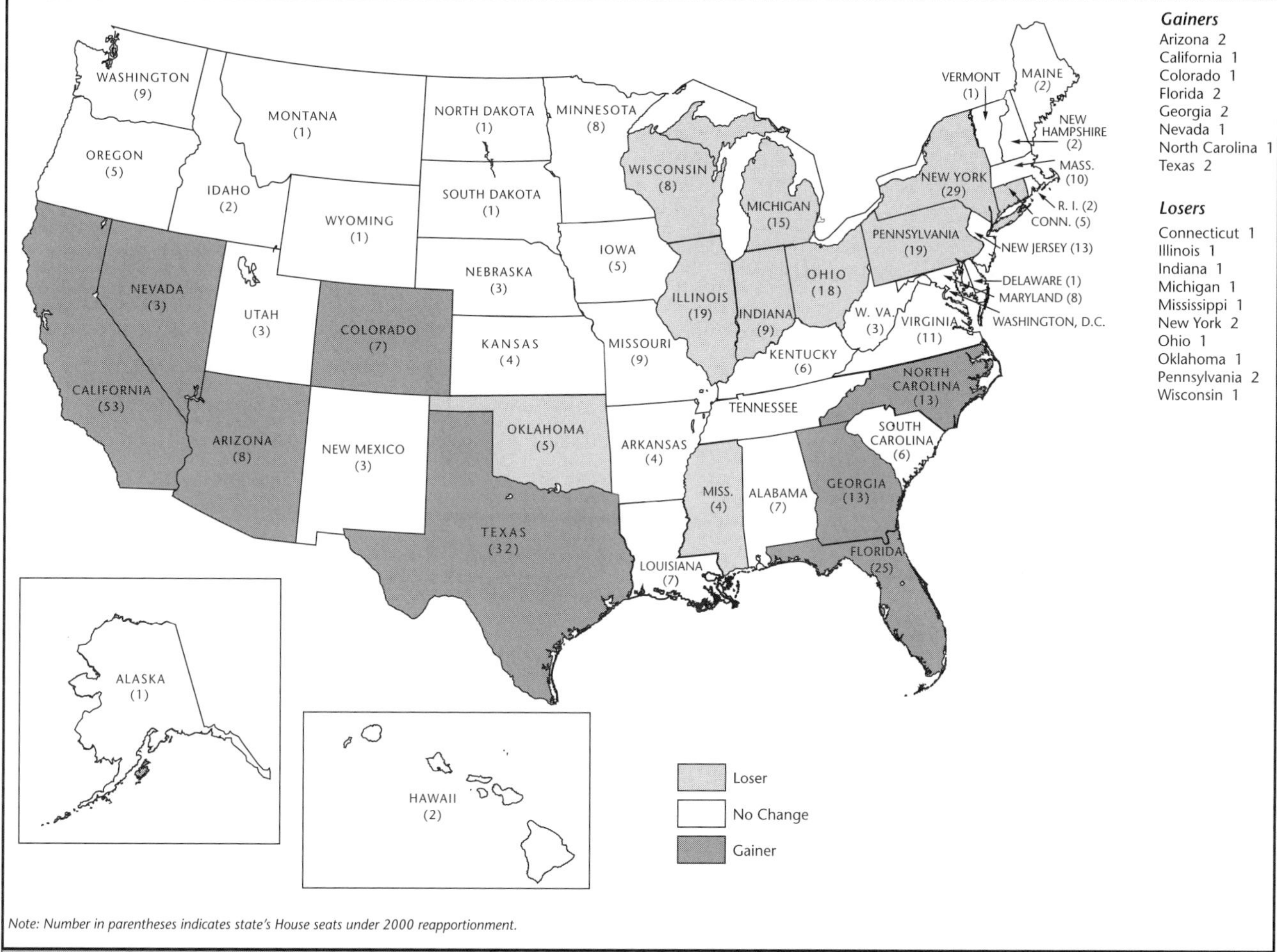

Note: Number in parentheses indicates state's House seats under 2000 reapportionment.

The membership of the United States House of Representatives is reapportioned every ten years after the decennial, or ten-year, census.

of 70,680. The population of each state was then divided by this number to find the number of its representatives. States were then assigned an additional representative for each fraction more than one-half.

Congress made another change following the census of 1850. The total population of the country was divided by the set number of representatives, and the resulting number became the ratio of population to each representative. The population of each state was divided by this ratio, eliminating fractions, to determine its number of representatives. Congress then added additional representatives based on the remaining fractions, beginning with the state having the largest fraction. Under this formula, however, an increase in the total size of the House actually caused some states to lose seats even without a corresponding change in population.

In 1911, the membership of the House was fixed at 433, with one representative each to be added for Arizona and New Mexico, which were expected to become states in the near future. Thus, the size of the House reached 435, where it has remained with the exception of a brief period from 1959 to 1963, when the admission of Alaska and Hawaii raised the total temporarily to 437.

In 1929, a new law established a permanent system of reapportioning the 435 House seats called the method of equal proportions. Each of the fifty states is first assigned the one seat to which it is entitled by the Constitution. Congress then uses a complex mathematical equation to calculate "priority numbers" for states to receive second seats, third seats, and so on. The priority numbers are then lined up in order and the seats given to the states with priority numbers until 435 are awarded. This method is still in use today.

See also: Census; House of Representatives; Redistricting.

Further Reading

Schwab, Larry M. *The Impact of Congressional Reapportionment and Redistricting.* Lanham, MD: University Press of America, 1988.

Redistricting

The redrawing of congressional district boundaries within the states. For purposes of assigning seats in the House, each state is divided into one or more geographical areas, called districts. Every ten years, the boundaries of these districts may be redrawn based on changes in the state's population as shown by the latest census.

Although the Constitution contains provisions for the **apportionment,** or division, of House seats among the states, it is silent about how the members should be elected. From the beginning, most states divided their territory into geographic districts, permitting only one member of Congress to be elected from each district. Some states, however, allowed would-be House members to be chosen in statewide elections, with each voter able to cast as many votes as there were seats to be filled. These are called "at large" elections. Still other states created what were known as multimember districts, in which a single geographic unit would elect two or more members of the House. At various times, some states used combinations of these methods. For example, a state might elect ten representatives from ten individual districts and two at large.

Congress has made repeated efforts to lay down national rules for congressional districting. A law passed in 1842 required representatives to be "elected by districts composed of contiguous (physically touching) territory equal in number to the representatives to which said state may be entitled, no one district electing more than one Representative." An 1872 act added that districts should contain "as nearly as practicable an equal number of inhabitants." Despite these laws, some states continued to elect House members at large, and those states that used districts did not always draw them equally.

Finally, in a series of decisions beginning in 1962 with *Baker v. Carr,* the Supreme Court exerted great influence over the redistricting process. It ordered that congressional districts as well as state and local legislative districts be drawn so that their populations would be as nearly equal as possible. Two years later, in *Wesberry v. Sanders,* the Court ruled that congressional districts must be substantially equal in population. The Court stated that "as nearly as is practicable, one man's vote in a congressional election is to be worth as much as another's." As a result of these and other Court decisions, nearly every state was forced to redraw its congressional district lines.

In most states, the state legislatures are responsible for redrawing new congressional district maps. Today, states must follow several guidelines when drawing district boundaries. These include:

- The districts must be relatively equal in population,
- The redistricting plan must not dilute the strength of minority voters,
- Districts created under the plan must be compact and contiguous,
- The plan must respect political subdivision lines and must not divide "communities of interest,"
- The plan must not be a "racial gerrymander."

The term *gerrymander* refers to the practice of drawing district lines so as to maximize the advantage of a political party or interest group. The name originated from a salamander-shaped

Decision Makers

The Census: Who Should Be Counted?

Counting the number of people in the United States has never been easy. When it comes to the census, the political stakes are huge, and so is the interest in how the count is conducted and just who should be counted.

Some complain that the Census Bureau's effort to count all people living in the United States is politically unfair. For example, members of Congress and other public officials have taken a strong interest in the traditional inclusion of illegal **aliens** in the census. The Census Bureau has never attempted to exclude illegal aliens from the census, a policy troubling to states that fear losing House seats and clout to states with large numbers of illegal aliens.

Another issue is the counting of overseas military personnel. The 1990 census was the first to count military personnel and dependents stationed overseas. "Historically we have not included them because the census is based on the concept of usual residence," said Charles Jones, associate director of the Census Bureau. "People overseas have a 'usual residence' overseas." An exception was made once in 1970 during the Vietnam War. For the purposes of reapportionment, overseas personnel were assigned to the state each individual considered home.

A – Z

congressional district created by the Massachusetts Legislature in 1812 when Elbridge Gerry was governor.

The majority party in each state legislature is often in a position to draw a district map that enhances the fortunes of its **incumbents,** or current officeholders, and candidates at the expense of the opposing party. As a result, redistricting is often the subject of intense political debate and disagreement. In 2003, for example, the Republican-controlled Texas state legislature broke with precedent and redrew district boundaries between censuses. Democrats challenged the plan, arguing that redistricting could only be done after every census, but the Supreme Court upheld the new boundaries.

See also: Census, House of Representatives; Reapportionment.

Further Reading

Schwab, Larry M. *The Impact of Congressional Reapportionment and Redistricting.* Lanham, MD: University Press of America, 1988.

Regulation of Commerce

See Commerce Clause.

Reed, Thomas

See Speaker of the House of Representatives.

Rules, House and Senate

Article I, Section 5, of the Constitution stipulates that, "Each House may determine the Rules of its Proceedings." In addition to the standing rules adopted under this authority, the House and Senate each have a separate set of precedents, practices, and customs that guide their conduct of business.

House Rules

The standing rules of the House are set forth in the *Constitution, Jefferson's Manual, and Rules of the House of Representatives,* or the House Manual as it is commonly called, which is published with revisions during the first session of each Congress. The House Manual is also available on Congress's web site.

This is the most important single source of authority on the rules and contains great numbers of annotations. In addition to the written chamber rules, the document contains the text of the Constitution, portions of the manual on parliamentary procedure that Thomas Jefferson wrote when he was vice president, and the principal rulings and precedents of the House. The formal rules of the Senate are found in the *Senate Manual Containing the Standing Rules, Orders, Laws, and Resolutions Affecting the Business of the United States Senate.*

In the House, on the day when a new Congress convenes, the chamber has no formal rules and thus, no committees, which are created in the rules. It operates under what is called "general parliamentary law," which relies on *Jefferson's Manual* and many House precedents. Before opening day, the rules have been drafted by the majority party's conference or caucus; amendments suggested by individual majority members are considered at such party meetings.

Following the election of the Speaker and the administration of the oath of office to members, the proposed rules of the House are offered directly from the floor as a resolution, usually by the Majority Leader. After one hour of debate, the minority has an opportunity to offer a substitute. After it is defeated, the majority's rules package is then formally adopted, usually on a party-line vote, and becomes effective immediately. Once adopted, House rules continue in force through the Congress, unless further amended, and expire at its end.

Amendments to the rules package on the House floor are not permitted unless opponents can "defeat the previous question," the motion offered by the majority party that has the effect of cutting off debate and forcing a vote on final passage. This has not occurred since 1971, when a **conservative** coalition of Republicans and southern Democrats defeated the previous question and forced the Democratic leadership to drop a provision for a "twenty-one-day rule," a procedure that would have allowed legislation to reach the floor without action by the Rules Committee.

When Republicans took over the House in 1995 after forty years in the minority, they deviated from the traditional practice by splitting their rules proposal into numerous pieces to highlight what they considered major reforms in the rules. All passed, some by votes largely along party lines; others, with substantial **bipartisan** support. However, in the 105th Congress that began in 1997, Republicans returned to a single rules package. In the 106th Congress, for the first time since 1880, the House recodified its rules, reducing them in number, reorganizing provisions without making substantive changes, and eliminating archaic language.

Senate Rules

The Senate, on the other hand, does not readopt its rules at the beginning of a Congress. Because only one-third of the chamber turns over every two years, the Senate considers itself a continuing body. Any proposed changes in existing rules are adopted subject to provisions already in the rules, such as Rule XXII, the cloture rule requiring a supermajority to cut off debate. This interpretation of the Senate's continuing nature was challenged by **liberals** for years as conflicting with Article I, Section 5, of the Constitution, but their contention that the Senate could cut off debate on proposed rules changes by majority vote at the beginning of a Congress was unsuccessful.

In the controversy leading to the most recent important change in the cloture rule, the Senate did cast a series of votes in 1975 that appeared to support the right of a simple majority to avoid a filibuster and change Senate rules. Agreement was subsequently reached to change Rule XXII, however, by invoking cloture first by a two-thirds vote. Before doing so the Senate cast procedural votes which, it was argued, reversed this "majority" precedent.

Rulemaking Statutes

House precedents, based on past rulings of the chair, are contained in three multivolume series: *Hinds' Precedents of the House of Representatives* covers the years 1789 through 1907; *Cannon's Precedents of the House of Representatives* covers 1908 through 1935; and *Deschler's Precedents of the United States House of Representatives,* volumes one to nine, and *Deschler-Brown Precedents of the United States House of Representatives,* volumes ten to fifteen, cover 1936 through 1999. In addition, *Procedure in the U.S. House of Representatives* is a summary of all important rulings of the chair through 1984. *House Practice: A Guide to the Rules, Precedents and Procedures of the House,* published in 1996, is a single volume by retired House Parliamentarian William Holmes Brown that discusses selected precedents and the operation of current House rules in a less intimidating format and includes material on rules changes following the shift in party control in the 104th Congress.

Riddick's Senate Procedure: Precedents and Practices, by retired parliamentarian Floyd M. Riddick and Alan S. Frumin, who was parliamentarian when the book was last revised in 1992, contains current precedents and related standing rules and statutory provisions through the end of the 101st Congress.

In addition to precedents, each chamber has particular traditions and customs that it follows—recognition of the Senate majority leader ahead of other senators seeking recognition from the chair is an example of such a practice. Moreover, each party in each chamber has its own set of party rules that can affect the chamber's proceedings.

Many public laws also contain provisions that affect House and Senate procedures. Prominent examples are the Congressional Budget and Impoundment Control Act of 1974; the Balanced Budget and Emergency Deficit Control Act of 1985, better known as Gramm-Rudman-Hollings, after its sponsors; and so-called "fast track" legislation, enacted in previous Congresses but blocked from a House vote on renewal in 1997, which would have forced each chamber to vote on the president's proposed international trade agreements without amendments.

Such rulemaking statutes obviate the need for each chamber to create special procedures on an ad hoc basis whenever it takes some action on the subject matter dealt with in these laws. Without "fast track," for example, it would be extremely difficult for the president to negotiate credibly with foreign nations without the advance assurance that each chamber would not **amend** the agreements in potentially unpredictable ways, ultimately rendering them unacceptable to these nations. The existence of procedures set out by law is particularly significant in the Senate, where they serve to limit debate and prevent filibusters. However, such statutes, even though they are laws passed by both chambers and signed by the president, remain subservient to each chamber's constitutional power to amend its rules at any time. For example, the House could always adopt a special rule allowing amendments to a "fast track" trade agreement. In the Senate, however, where there is no equivalent of the House's Rules Committee, any alterations in process would be far more difficult.

A - Z

Senate

The upper house of the national legislature of the United States. The Senate always has been viewed as a more deliberate and less **partisan** body than the lower chamber, the House of Representatives. The Framers of the Constitution intentionally aimed to achieve that goal when they designed the structure of Congress.

Constitutional Basis

Prior to **ratification,** or formal passage, of the Constitution, the United States had a **unicameral,** or one-house legislature, whose members were chosen by popular vote. Nevertheless, many of the delegates to the Constitutional Convention of 1787 were suspicious of popular rule—or "mob" rule as some called it. They decided to add a Senate, chosen by members of the legislature in each state, to provide a check to the possible excesses of popular rule.

The Senate also was meant to take a broader, national view of issues before Congress. The Framers felt that House members would tend to put the interests of their states ahead of national interest when considering legislation. The fact that senators did not face popular election meant they should be less influenced by local interests. To further promote their independence, senators' salaries were paid by the federal government instead of by the states. And although a state's legislature had the power to elect its senators, it had no power to recall them. As a result, most senators, even in the early years, refused to consider themselves merely agents of the state governments.

By the late nineteenth century, popular pressure for more democratic representation led to a change in senatorial elections. In 1913, the states ratified the Seventeenth Amendment to the Constitution, which provided for the direct popular election of senators.

Leadership

The only two Senate leaders mentioned by the Constitution have little effective power. The vice president serves as President of the Senate, but can only vote to break ties. In the absence of the vice president, the Senate can choose a president pro tempore ("for the time being") to fill the role. The presiding officer's main function is to recognize senators, but this is rarely significant since Senate rules usually require the presiding officer to recognize the senator who first seeks recognition.

The Senate has no counterpart to the powerful Speaker of the House, who exercises great influence over which **bills** the House considers. By contrast, leaders of the two parties in the Senate typically work together to determine what legislation to consider and the rules under which it will be debated. As in the House, a Majority Leader plans strategy for the party in control of the Senate and a Minority Leader performs the same function for the opposition party.

Committee and Floor Procedures

The initial legislative process in the Senate is very similar to that in the House. After a member introduces a bill, it is assigned to a committee, groups of members responsible for drawing up legislation. Committees may appoint subgroups called subcommittees to study details of the bill. Committees and subcommittees may **amend** the bill, or make formal changes to it. This process is called "marking up" a bill. At some point, the committee either lets the bill die or reports it to the full Senate for debate.

Procedures for floor debate are much more informal than those in the House. The sheer size of the House requires it to adopt strict rules and procedures to maintain order during floor debate. By contrast, the smaller size of the Senate allows it much more freedom. For example, debate in the House is limited to one hour, with each speaker being allotted no more than five minutes. The Senate, on the other hand, imposes no time limits on debate. In addition, a senator may offer any type of amendment to a bill during floor debate. In the House, the Rules Committee decides whether and what type of amendments members may offer.

In the Senate, legislation can only come to the floor as the result of a unanimous consent agreement. These complicated agreements determine which amendments may be offered, how long they will be debated, and when they will be voted on. Because a single senator can block a unanimous consent agreement, the majority party must work with the minority to get broad agreement on what matters to consider. The House procedure, by contrast, allows the majority party to have much greater control over which bills are debated and under what conditions. The overall effect of the Senate's leadership structure and floor procedure is to force senators to work more closely across party lines and to give greater consideration to the national impact of their actions.

A Typical Day in the Senate

A typical day in the Senate might go like this:

- The Senate is called to order by the presiding officer. The constitutional presiding officer, the vice president, is seldom in attendance. Sometimes the president pro tempore presides over the opening minutes of the Senate session. During the course of the day, other members of the majority party take turns presiding.
- The Senate chaplain delivers the opening prayer and pledge.
- The Pledge of Allegiance is recited.
- The Majority and Minority Leaders are recognized for opening remarks. The majority leader usually announces plans for the day's business, which are developed in consultation with the minority leadership.
- The Senate usually conducts morning business (which need not be in the morning and should not be confused with the "morning hour," so if morning business is put off, other business will necessarily precede it). During morning business senators may introduce bills and the Senate will receive reports from committees and messages from the president, and conduct other routine chores. Senators who have requested time in advance are recognized for speeches on any subject.
- The Senate may turn to consider legislative or executive matters. To begin work on a piece of legislation, the Majority Leader normally asks for unanimous consent to call up the measure. If any member objects, the leader may make a debatable motion that the Senate take up the bill. The motion gives opponents the opportunity to launch a filibuster, or extended debate, even before the Senate officially begins to consider the bill. Certain types of measures, such as budget **resolutions,** omnibus budget reconciliation bills, and reports from House-Senate conference committees, are privileged, and a motion to consider them is not debatable.

Floor debate on a bill is generally handled by managers, usually the chair and ranking minority member of the committee with **jurisdiction** over the measure. Most measures are considered under a unanimous consent, or time, agreement in which the Senate unanimously agrees to limit debate and to divide the time in some prearranged fashion. In the absence of a time agreement, any senator may seek recognition from the chair and, once recognized, may talk for as long as the senator wishes. Unless the Senate has unanimously agreed to limit amendments, senators may offer as many as they wish. In most cases, amendments need not be germane, or directly related, to the bill.

Most bills are passed by voice vote with only a handful of senators present. Any member can request a roll-call vote on an amendment or motion or on final passage of a measure. Senate roll calls are casual affairs. Senators stroll in from the cloakrooms or their offices

DECISION MAKERS

Stephen A. Douglas (1813–1861)

Stephen A. Douglas of Illinois, known as the "Little Giant," was the dominant figure in the United States Senate in the decades prior to the Civil War (1861–1865). Douglas, who was short (5' 4") and had a large head and shoulders, did not cut an impressive figure. However, his keen political skills made him one of the most effective leaders in the history of the Senate.

Douglas was born in Vermont but moved to Illinois at the age of 20. After teaching for a short time, he studied law and later set up a legal practice in the town of Jacksonville. Douglas served in a number of positions in state government before his election to Congress. These included terms as a state legislator, Illinois secretary of state, and an associate justice on the Illinois Supreme Court.

In 1842, Illinois voters elected Douglas to a seat in the U.S. House of Representatives. Two years later, he won reelection, and in 1846, the Illinois State Legislature chose him to represent the state in the U.S. Senate. At this time, senators were not popularly elected; rather, the members of the majority party in a state's legislature named the state's senators. Running reelection in 1858, Douglas gained nationwide fame as he debated a little-known Illinois legislator, Abraham Lincoln.

As a senator, Douglas was at the center of some of the most critical and controversial decisions regarding the issue of slavery in the United States. He strongly supported the Compromise of 1850, which brought

and congregate in the well (the area at the front of the chamber). When they are ready to vote, senators catch the eye of the clerk and vote, sometimes by indicating thumbs up or thumbs down. Roll-call votes are supposed to last fifteen minutes, but some have dragged on for more than an hour.

- Just before the Senate finishes its work for the day, the Majority Leader seeks unanimous consent for the agenda for the next session–when the Senate will convene, which senators will be recognized for early speeches, and specific time agreements for consideration of legislation.

See also: Bicameralism; Bipartisanship; Calendars, Senate; Classes of Senators; Committees; Confirmation Power of the Senate; Continental Congresses; Elections, Senatorial; Filibuster; Gavel; House of Representatives; How a Bill Becomes Law; Joint Committees; Joint Session; President Pro Tempore; Senatorial Courtesy; Seniority System; Seventeenth Amendment (1913); Treaty Power; United States Constitution, Article I, Sections 1–7, 1789, in the **Primary Source Library;** United States Constitution, Article II, Sections 2, 3, and 4, 1789, in the **Primary Source Library.**

Further Reading

Baker, Ross K. *House and Senate.* New York: W.W. Norton, 2000.

Gould, Lewis L. *The Most Exclusive Club: A History of the Modern United States Senate.* New York: Basic, 2006.

A - Z

California into the Union as a free state, but specifically refused to prohibit slavery in the newly organized New Mexico Territory. The compromise also outlawed the slave trade in Washington, DC, although slavery itself remained legal there. It also provided for a strict law requiring citizens of all states to assist in capturing escaped slaves and returning them to their owners.

In 1854, Douglas again addressed the slavery issue by sponsoring the Kansas-Nebraska Act. This bill overturned previous laws that had prohibited slavery in newly organized territories. Instead, it allowed residents of such territories to decide for themselves whether to permit slavery. The act led to a great deal of violence between pro- and anti-slavery forces, particularly in the territory of Kansas.

Douglas's efforts to find a compromise between supporters and opponents of slavery eventually led to a split within the Democratic Party. In the late 1850s, Douglas blocked President James Buchanan's efforts to pass a federal slave code. The code would have permitted the expansion of slavery into the territories, even if the people there were opposed to slavery. When Douglas won the Democratic nomination for president in 1860, southern members of the party rebelled and nominated their own candidate, Vice President John C. Breckinridge. The divided Democrats lost the election to Republican Abraham Lincoln (1861–1865). By early 1861, eleven Southern states seceded from the Union, touching off the Civil War. Douglas, who had worked so hard to find common ground between North and South, died a few weeks later.

Senatorial Courtesy

Custom by which the Senate refuses to confirm a presidential nominee within a particular state unless the nominee has been approved by the senators of the president's party from that state. Senatorial courtesy provides an incentive for the president to consult senators before making appointments to certain federal positions in the states.

A senator typically invoked the rule of courtesy by stating that the nominee was "personally obnoxious" to him. This might mean that the senator and the nominee were personal or political foes, or simply that the senator had another candidate for the post.

The tradition of senatorial courtesy declined in importance as positions once filled by patronage, or political favor, were brought into the civil service. It now primarily affects nominations of judges to federal district courts and certain other courts, U.S. attorneys, federal marshals, and other federal officials based locally.

Another aspect of senatorial courtesy, still widely observed, often enables a single senator to delay action on a nomination by placing a "hold" on it. While the number of nominations effectively controlled by senators in their home states has declined, the power to place a "hold" on a nomination to delay floor action has increased dramatically. Usually the leadership of a senator's party will honor the hold; to do otherwise would be self-defeating since a hold request usually carries the threat of a filibuster.

A senator who places a hold simply may be waiting for more information, or may want to be present when the nomination is brought to the floor. Also, the senator could be using the nominee as leverage on the administration or other senators. Holds on nominations, as well as on legislative matters, can be especially potent tools in the final days of a session of Congress when a delay of just a day or two can prove devastating. In the past, holds could be placed anonymously. In 1999, however, the Senate leadership announced that senators placing a hold on a matter would have to inform its sponsors and the committee with **jurisdiction** over it. The senator also would have to provide written notification to party leaders. The change made it easier for members to push for consideration of a stalled nomination or measure, without wasting time trying to discover who had placed the hold.

See also: Senate.

Senators

See Classes of Senators.

Seniority System

Congressional custom in which members who have served longer receive greater consideration for certain leadership positions and other privileges. The seniority system has its greatest impact within each political party for determining rank on committees. More senior members also enjoy access to the most desirable office space and the right to claim a limited number of suites in the Capitol itself for their personal use.

Seniority was at one time a much more important consideration than it is today. This began to change in the 1970s, as many senior members left Congress and were replaced by newer members who resented the domination of important positions by more senior members. Today, seniority is only one of many factors that determine who receives more influential posts in Congress.

There are three kinds of seniority in Congress:

- Seniority within the chamber among the entire House or Senate membership
- Seniority within a political party in the chamber
- Seniority on a committee

The second and third kinds are linked, because members are chosen for service on committees by the political parties and listed in order of seniority only with others from the same party. Members elected to a committee at the same time are then ranked in order of their full chamber seniority.

In the Senate, the most senior member of the majority party is elected automatically to the virtually powerless office of president pro tempore. The president pro tempore has the right to preside over the chamber in the absence of the president of the Senate (the vice president of the United States). This senator may wield substantial influence in another role because of seniority that would almost certainly also make the senator chair of a committee. The most important leadership positions in Congress–House Speaker and Majority Leader of the Senate–have never been filled on the basis of seniority.

Senate rank generally is determined according to the official date of the beginning of a member's service. When senators are sworn in on the same date, custom decrees that those with prior political experience are considered to have seniority over those who do not. Political experience includes previous Senate service, service as vice president, House service, service in the president's cabinet, and service as a governor. If all other factors are equal, senators are ranked by the population of their state in determining seniority.

In the House, being the most senior member carries no formal status. Like the Senate, rank in the House generally is determined by the official date of the beginning of a member's service, except when a representative is elected to fill a vacancy. In such cases, the date of election determines the rank. When members enter the

House on the same date, they are ranked in order of consecutive terms of House service. Any former members returning to the House are ranked above other freshmen, starting with those with the most previous terms of service. Experience as a senator or governor is disregarded.

See also: Committees.

Separation of Powers

The division of powers between different branches of government to ensure that no one branch exercises too much authority over the others. Separation of powers is one of the key features of U.S. government.

The most basic expression of separation of powers in the U.S. government is the existence of three branches of government with distinct areas of authority. By granting certain powers exclusively to one branch or another, the Founders ensured that all three branches would be vital to the workings of government. The Founders also provided for a system of checks and balances between branches. Under this system, any branch that tries too assume too much power can be checked by the actions of the others.

The Constitution gives the legislative branch a wide range of powers including the power to make laws, collect taxes, borrow and print money, regulate **commerce,** establish courts, raise and support armies and navies, declare war, and "make all laws necessary and proper to carry out powers granted Congress by the Constitution." The president, however, has the ability to **veto,** or reject laws passed by Congress. While Congress may raise armies and declare war, the president serves as commander-in-chief of the armed forces. The president also has the power to appoint a large number of government officials as well as all federal judges. The judiciary has no lawmaking power, but does have the authority to strike down laws it considers to be unconstitutional.

Separation of powers extends to the two houses of Congress as well. Both Houses must pass identical versions of a bill for it to become law. All **bills** intended to raise or spend money must originate in the House of Representatives. The Senate may accept or reject such bills, but it cannot **amend,** or formally change them in any way. The Senate, however, holds the power to approve or reject presidential appointees or treaties negotiated by the president. The House has no say in such matters.

One of the most important checks Congress has over the other branches is the power to **impeach,** or charge government officials with crimes while in office. This power is also divided between the two chambers. The House may bring impeachment charges against government officials, including judges and the president. If a majority of the House votes to impeach, the Senate holds a trial with senators sitting as jurors. If two-thirds of the senators present vote for conviction, the official is removed from office.

See also: Checks and Balances; Expressed Powers; Impeachment Power; Implied Powers; President and Congress; Supreme Court and Congress.

Sergeant at Arms

Officer in both the House and Senate who is responsible for enforcing rules and maintaining decorum, ensuring the security of buildings and visitors, and supervising the Capitol police. In addition, the House sergeant at arms is in charge of the mace, a traditional symbol of legislative power and authority. The House and Senate sergeants at arms also introduce the bearers of all messages, official guests, and members attending joint sessions; supervise doormen and **pages;** issue gallery passes; and perform a variety of custodial services.

The House sergeant at arms is responsible for overseeing the largest number of patronage jobs in the House. Patronage jobs are those obtained through political favors. The sergeant at arms supervises the officers of the press galleries, the doormen for the visitors' gallery and for the House chamber, the custodians, barbers, pages, and employees of the House document room, and employees of the folding room, which distributes newsletters, speeches, and other materials for representatives.

The sergeant at arms of the Senate supervises most of the patronage appointments in the Senate, including the Senate pages, doormen, elevator operators, custodians, officers of the Senate press galleries, and employees of the Senate post office. The Senate sergeant at arms also has the power to call for the arrest of absent senators and physically carry them into the Senate chamber. The most recent example of this occurred in 1988, when Capitol police forcibly brought Republican Senator Robert Packwood of Oregon into the chamber for debate on a campaign finance bill.

See also: Mace.

Sessions of Congress

Periods of time during which members of Congress meet to attend to legislative matters. The two-year period for which members of the House of Representatives are elected constitutes a Congress. The Constitution requires Congress to "assemble" at least once each year, which means that there are at least two sessions in each Congress.

Prior to **ratification,** or approval, of the Twentieth Amendment in 1933, the first, or "long," session of Congress began in December of odd-numbered years and lasted six months or so. The second, or "short" session, met from December to March of even-numbered years. This session thus did not begin until after the next election had already taken place.

This schedule led to a number of problems. Presidents, who took office on March 4, could make appointments and take other actions without consulting Congress until it met again the following December. Members often used delaying tactics during short sessions in order to block legislation that would expire when Congress **adjourned,** or suspended its activities, on March 3. Moreover, the Congresses that met in short session always included a substantial number of **lame-duck** members who had been defeated at the polls, yet were still able to influence the legislative outcome of the session.

The Twentieth Amendment established January 3 of the year following the election as the day on which the terms of senators and representatives would begin and end, and January 20

Sessions of Congress, 1967–2008

Session of Congress	Years in Session
90th	1967-1968
91st	1969-1970
92nd	1971-1972
93rd	1973-1974
94th	1975-1976
95th	1977-1978
96th	1979-1980
97th	1981-1982
98th	1983-1984
99th	1985-1986
100th	1987-1988
101st	1989-1990
102nd	1991-1992
103rd	1993-1994
104th	1995-1996
105th	1997-1998
106th	1999-2000
107th	2001-2002
108th	2003-2004
109th	2005-2006
110th	2007-2008

Sessions of Congress begin January of the odd-numbered year after the November election and last until January of the next odd-numbered year.

SPOTLIGHT

The Early Senate

In 1828–1829, this eyewitness description of the Senate in session in about 1796 was offered by William McKoy in a series of articles in Poulson's *American Daily Advertiser.*

> Among the Thirty Senators of that day there was observed constantly during the debate the most delightful silence, the most beautiful order, gravity, and personal dignity of manner. They all appeared every morning full-powdered and dressed, as age or fancy might suggest, in the richest material. The very atmosphere of the place seemed to inspire wisdom, mildness, and condescension. Should any of them so far forget for a moment as to be the cause of a protracted whisper while another was addressing the Vice President, three gentle taps with his silver pencilcase upon the table by Mr. Adams immediately restored everything to repose and the most respectful attention, presenting in their courtesy a most striking contrast to the independent loquacity of the Representatives below stairs, some few of whom persisted in wearing, while in their seats and during the debate, their ample cocked hats, placed "fore and aft" upon their heads.

as the day on which the president and vice president would take office. It also provided that Congress should meet annually on January 3 "unless they shall by law appoint a different day." The amendment was intended to permit Congress to extend its first session for as long as necessary and to complete the work of its second session before the next election, to avoid the problems with a **lame-duck** Congress. Today, each Congress has two regular sessions of equal length that begin in January of successive years.

The president may "on extraordinary occasions" call for a special session of one or both houses to achieve a political or legislative objective. For example, in 1997 President Bill Clinton (1993–2001) threatened to delay the adjournment of the first session of the 105th Congress by calling a special session to consider campaign finance reform legislation.

Adjournment *sine die* ("without a day") ends a session of Congress. Adjournment of the second session is the final action of a Congress and all legislation not passed by both houses expires. However, following adjournment there may still be some delay before legislation passed near the end of the session is presented to the president for action. Within a session, either house of Congress may adjourn for holiday observances or other brief periods of three days or less. In a typical week, for example, the Senate or House may meet through Thursday and then, by unanimous consent or by motion, convene on the following Monday. Neither house, however, may adjourn for more than three days without the consent of the other.

See also: Twentieth Amendment, 1933, in the **Primary Source Library.**

Seventeenth Amendment (1913)

Constitutional **amendment** that provided for popular election of members to the Senate. Prior to **ratification,** or approval of the amendment by the states in 1913, each state legislature chose the senators from that state.

Many of the delegates to the Constitutional Convention of 1787 were deeply suspicious of public opinion and felt it unwise to let the voters choose all of the members of Congress. As a result, the Constitution called for members of the House of Representatives to be popularly elected, but for state legislatures to choose the senators from their respective states. The delegates saw this as a way to ensure that the Senate would represent the broader interests of the nation and not be subject to narrow political pressures.

The Seventeenth Amendment is of particular interest because it clearly was forced on Congress–specifically on the Senate–by popular pressure. The change was a part of a movement in the late 1800s and early 1900s toward more democratic control of government. Being less immediately dependent on popular sentiment than the House, the Senate did not seek to reform itself. Only pressure from the public–expressed through the House of Representatives, the state governments, **special-interest groups,** petitions, and other means–persuaded the Senate that it must participate in its own reform.

Petitions from farmers' associations and other organizations, particularly in the West, and party **platforms** in state elections, pressed the issue until the national parties took it up. In 1901, Oregon adopted a plan under which voters could express their preferences for senator, but this was not legally binding. When the Oregon Legislature ignored the popular preference in its next election of a senator, voters passed an initiative to allow candidates for the legislature to indicate whether they would vote for the Senate candidate with the highest popular vote total. This "Oregon system" proved effective and was adopted in other states in modified forms. By December 1910, it was estimated that fourteen of the thirty senators about to be named by state legislatures had already been designated by popular vote.

In 1901, some legislatures began calling for a convention to amend the Constitution. A resolution was finally brought to the Senate floor in 1911, but its backers failed to gain the two-thirds support required. In a special session later that year, the House passed a different version of the resolution. The Senate this time approved its original resolution. On May 13, 1912, the House agreed with the Senate version, and by April 1913, three-fourths of the states had **ratified** the Seventeenth Amendment.

See also: Amending the Constitution; Elections, Senatorial; Senate; Seventeenth Amendment, 1913, in the **Primary Source Library.**

Sherman, Roger

See Connecticut Compromise.

Speaker of the House of Representatives

The presiding officer and leader of the majority party in the House of Representatives. The Speaker is widely regarded as the most powerful figure in Congress. Since 1947, the Speaker has also been second in line, after the vice president, to succeed the president.

Powers and Duties

The Speaker holds a variety of powers as the presiding officer of the House. The Speaker must recognize members before they may speak in the chamber and may call on any members, thus exerting control over floor debate. The Speaker also rules on points of order and is responsible for maintaining order in the House.

Speakers of the House, 1899–2008

Congress		Speaker
56th	(1899–1901)	David B. Henderson, R-Iowa
57th	(1901–1903)	Henderson
58th	(1903–1905)	Joseph G. Cannon, R-Ill.
59th	(1905–1907)	Cannon
60th	(1907–1909)	Cannon
61st	(1909–1911)	Cannon
62nd	(1911–1913)	James B. "Champ" Clark, D-Mo.
63rd	(1913–1915)	Clark
64th	(1915–1917)	Clark
65th	(1917–1919)	Clark
66th	(1919–1921)	Frederick H. Gillett, R-Mass.
67th	(1921–1923)	Gillett
68th	(1923–1925)	Gillett
69th	(1925–1927)	Nicholas Longworth, R-Ohio
70th	(1927–1929)	Longworth
71st	(1929–1931)	Longworth
72nd	(1931–1933)	John Nance Garner, D-Texas
73rd	(1933–1934)	Henry T. Rainey, D-Ill.[a]
74th	(1935–1936) (1936–1937)	Joseph W. Byrns, D-Tenn. William B. Bankhead, D-Ala.
75th	(1937–1939)	Bankhead
76th	(1939–1940) (1940–1941)	Bankhead Sam Rayburn, D-Texas
77th	(1941–1943)	Rayburn
78th	(1943–1945)	Rayburn
79th	(1945–1947)	Rayburn
80th	(1947–1949)	Joseph W. Martin Jr., R-Mass.
81st	(1949–1951)	Rayburn
82nd	(1951–1953)	Rayburn
83rd	(1953–1955)	Martin

(continued on next page)

Speakers of the House, 1899–2008, *continued*

Congress		Speaker
84th	(1955–1957)	Rayburn
85th	(1957–1959)	Rayburn
86th	(1959–1961)	Rayburn
87th	(1961) (1962–1963)	Rayburn John W. McCormack, D-Mass.
88th	(1963–1965)	McCormack
89th	(1965–1967)	McCormack
90th	(1967–1969)	McCormack
91st	(1969–1971)	McCormack
92nd	(1971–1973)	Carl Albert, D-Okla.
93rd	(1973–1975)	Albert
94th	(1975–1977)	Albert
95th	(1977–1979)	Thomas P. O'Neill Jr., D-Mass.
96th	(1979–1981)	O'Neill
97th	(1981–1983)	O'Neill
98th	(1983–1985)	O'Neill
99th	(1985–1987)	O'Neill
100th	(1987–1989)	Jim Wright, D-Texas
101st	(1989) (1989–1991)	Wright[b] Thomas S. Foley, D-Wash.
102nd	(1991–1993)	Foley
103rd	(1993–1995)	Foley
104th	(1995–1997)	Newt Gingrich, R-Ga.
105th	(1997–1999)	Gingrich
106th	(1999–2001)	J. Dennis Hastert, R-Ill.
107th	(2001–2003)	Hastert
108th	(2003–2005)	Hastert
109th	(2005–2007)	Hastert
110th	(2007–2009)	Nancy Pelosi, D-Ca.

Key to abbreviations: D—Democrat; R—Republican.

Notes: a. Rainey died in 1934, but was not replaced until the next Congress. b. Wright resigned and was succeeded by Foley on June 6, 1989.

Sources: *1999–2000 Congressional Directory, 106th Congress* (Washington, D.C.: Government Printing Office, 1999); *CQ Weekly*, selected issues.

The Speaker of the House is always a member of the majority party in the House of Representatives.

Sam Rayburn was one of the most respected Speakers of the House in the twentieth century. He served several terms as Speaker in the 1940s and 1950s. (Associated Press)

The Speaker may choose another member of the House to act as Speaker pro tempore ("for the time being") to preside over the House. In some instances, the entire House may meet as a single committee, known as the Committee of the Whole. On these occasions, the Speaker names a member to preside as chair.

The Speaker has great influence over the committee process. The Speaker selects nine of the thirteen members of the powerful Rules Committee, which exercises significant control over which **bills** come to the floor for debate. The Speaker appoints all members of special, or select, committees and conference committees, which resolve differences between versions of the same bill passed by both houses. The Speaker also determines which committee will consider each bill. Although the Speaker may vote like any other member, the Speaker usually votes only on very important matters or in cases where his or her vote decides the outcome of a debate.

Other duties of the Speaker include presiding over joint sessions of Congress, where both houses meet together, and overseeing officers of the House. These officers include the Sergeant at Arms, the Clerk, the Chief Administrative Officer, and the House Chaplain. The Speaker also has the power to appoint the House Historian, the General Counsel, and the House Inspector General.

History

The Framers of the Constitution were silent on the role they intended the Speaker to play. Some historians have suggested that this absence of any discussion indicated that the Framers thought the Speaker would act as both presiding officer and political leader. The duties of the first Speaker, Frederick A. C. Muhlenberg of Pennsylvania, were to preside at House sessions, preserve decorum and order, announce the results votes, appoint select committees of not more than three members, and vote in cases of a tie.

Early Speakers of the House wielded little real authority. Henry Clay, who took over the office in 1811, was the first truly powerful Speaker. No Speaker enjoyed as much influence as Clay until 1890, when Republican Thomas Brackett Reed of Maine used his authority to ensure that the minority could no longer block the legislative actions of a unified majority. "Czar" Reed was soon followed by Republican Joseph G. Cannon of Illinois, who served as Speaker from 1903 to 1911. Cannon's iron control over the House led to a revolt against him in 1910. Ultimately, the Speaker's powers as presiding officer were limited by House rules.

Cannon's tyrannical rule and the rebellion against it had a lasting effect on the office and the individuals who have held it. Power in the House became concentrated in the hands of the committee chairs until the mid-1970s. At that time, reforms restored many of the Speaker's powers, yet every powerful Speaker since Cannon has achieved influence chiefly through personal prestige, persuasion, and bargaining.

In the modern era, a Speaker must take care to ensure that his or her actions have the continued support of a majority of the party.

Decision Makers

Nancy Pelosi (1940-)

Representative Nancy Pelosi (D-CA) made history in January 2007—becoming the first woman Speaker of the House. Pelosi began her congressional career in 1987, representing California's Eighth District—which includes San Francisco. In 2002, her Democratic colleagues elected her House Minority Leader. She thus became the first woman to lead a major political party. As Speaker, Pelosi ranks second in the line of presidential succession, after the vice president.

Born in 1940, in Baltimore, Maryland, Pelosi grew up in a political family. Her father, Thomas D'Alesandro, Jr., served five terms in the United States Congress before becoming mayor of Baltimore. Her brother, Thomas D'Alesandro III, also served as the city's mayor. Pelosi attended Trinity College (now Trinity Washington University) and graduated in 1962. While in college, she met Paul Frank Pelosi, whom she married in 1963. The couple moved to San Francisco in 1969.

Pelosi began working her way through Democratic politics in the city and was elected the party chair for northern California in 1977. In 1987, after her youngest child became a high school senior, Pelosi decided to run for public office. Since her first electoral win in 1987, she has been reelected ten times—often winning more than 75 percent of her district's vote.

Upon being elected Speaker of the House, Pelosi said,

> I accept this gavel in the spirit of partnership, not partisanship, and look forward to working with you on behalf of the American people. In this House, we may belong to different parties, but we serve one country.

Democrat Jim Wright pushed his leadership close to the limits of its powers and caused resentment by acting without consulting other party members. Those actions, coupled with Wright's aggressive and sometimes abrasive style, left him politically vulnerable when a challenge to his personal ethics arose. The crisis eventually forced Wright to resign both the speakership and his House seat in 1989.

Republican Newt Gingrich, who took over after Wright's resignation, was the most powerful speaker since Cannon. He overcame political difficulties and personal ethics problems because he enjoyed support from a united party and from colleagues who valued strong leadership. When Gingrich's leadership no longer produced the desired results, the party replaced him in favor of a different approach. When Democrats regained control of the House in 2006, they chose California's Nancy Pelosi as the first female Speaker of the House.

See also: House of Representatives; Mace; Party Whips; Women in Congress.

Further Reading

Bentley, Judith. *Speaker of the House.* London: Franklin Watts, 1994.

Gutman, Howard. *America's Leaders–The Speaker of the House.* Chicago: Blackbirch, 2003.

Spoils System

Political practice in which the winning party in an election awards its supporters with government jobs rather than filling posts with the most qualified applicants. The term comes from the saying "To the victor belong the spoils."

The spoils system in the United States first arose in a limited form during the presidential administration of Thomas Jefferson (1801–1809). When Jefferson took office in 1801, he found himself surrounded by members of the opposing Federalist Party appointed by Washington and John Adams (1791–1801). Jefferson replaced enough of the Federalists with Democratic-Republicans to ensure, he said, a more even distribution of power between the parties.

The system became more fully developed during the administrations of James Monroe (1816–1825) and John Quincy Adams (1825–1829). At that time, members of the Senate increasingly insisted on control of federal appointments in their states. The Four Years Law of 1820, which provided fixed, four-year terms for many federal officers who previously had served at the pleasure of the president, greatly increased the number of such appointments available. Although it was intended to ensure the accountability of presidential appointees, the law soon became a tool to award patronage, or political favors.

While both Monroe and Adams renominated officers whose terms had expired, President Andrew Jackson (1829–1837) used the Four Years law to find jobs for his supporters. According to one historian, Jackson was "the first to articulate, legitimize, and translate the spoils system into the American experience." The spoils system led to power struggles, since Jackson had a House controlled by his own Democratic Party and a Senate in the hands of the opposition Whigs. Although Jackson was in constant conflict with the Senate over appointments, he was so popular that relatively few of his appointees were rejected.

The spoils system reached its peak from 1837 to 1877, when all presidents came under intense pressure to make patronage appointments. Abraham Lincoln (1861–1865) made masterful use of the appointment power to hold the divided **factions** of his party together and to advance his legislative goals. Early in his administration, he devoted much of his time to patronage. Most officers subject to presidential appointment had been removed after the 1860 election, and Lincoln tried to distribute these offices among his various supporters. Only for major posts was a high standard of qualification considered essential.

The assassination of President James Garfield (1881) by a disappointed office seeker in 1881 provided momentum for an end to the spoils system. The Pendleton Act of 1883 required office seekers to pass written tests to demonstrate their fitness for the jobs they sought. This led to the rise of a professional civil service and spelled the end of the spoils system.

See also: Patronage.

Supreme Court and Congress

The highest court in the United States and its relationship with Congress. The Supreme Court defines the limits of congressional authority, while Congress confirms the president's appointments to the Court, sets its **jurisdiction,** or area of authority, pays its **bills,** and holds the power to remove its justices. Through the power of judicial review, the Court may strike down acts of Congress that it thinks violate the Constitution.

Constitutional Basis

The Constitution describes the Supreme Court's powers in Article III with a minimum of detail and never specifically mentions the power of

A–Z

judicial review. Article III does state that "the judicial Power of the United States" extends to "all cases . . . arising under this Constitution, the Laws of the United States, and Treaties made, or which shall be made, under their Authority." In addition, the so-called supremacy clause states that the Constitution, laws, and treaties "shall be the supreme Law of the Land; and the Judges in every State shall be bound thereby, any Thing in the Constitution or Laws of any State to the Contrary notwithstanding."

Despite the vagueness of the wording in the Constitution, it seems clear that the Founders intended the judiciary to have the power to review acts of Congress. The Constitutional Convention even considered but rejected a proposal that the Supreme Court share with the president the power to **veto,** or reject, acts of Congress. The delegates, however, were cautious about giving the judiciary too much power.

Judiciary Act of 1789

After the states **ratified,** or formally approved, the Constitution, the First Congress promptly passed the Judiciary Act of 1789. This act established a federal system of courts, and determined and set the number of the Supreme Court justices at six. It also granted the Supreme Court authority to hear and decide appeals from state courts in cases in which:

1. A state court declared a federal law or treaty invalid,
2. A state law was applied instead of a federal law dealing with the same situation,
3. A state denied a person's claim to a right or privilege under a federal statute, treaty, or the Constitution.

The Supreme Court thus assumed the role of deciding constitutional questions in state matters. The Court made its first ruling in such a case in 1793, when two South Carolinians sued the state of Georgia for an unpaid debt. Georgia argued that the Supreme Court had no authority to hear the case, but the Court ruled in *Chisholm v. Georgia* that the suit was proper and that Georgia owed the money.

The decision shocked and angered many observers, who saw it as an intrusion by the federal government into state affairs. The decision was never enforced, and Congress quickly moved to protect the states from lawsuits filed in federal court. It proposed what was to become the Eleventh Amendment, which prohibits a resident of one state from suing another state in a federal court without that state's consent.

Marbury v. Madison *(1803)*

The principle of judicial review received its first major test in the case of *Marbury v. Madison.* The case involved President John Adams' (1797–1801) appointment of several judges two days before he was to leave office in 1801. By law, the new appointees could not take office until the secretary of state delivered their commissions, or written appointments. The outgoing secretary of state, however, was unable to deliver all of the commissions before his term of office expired. President Thomas Jefferson (1801–1809) ordered the new secretary of state, James Madison, not to deliver the commissions, thus denying judgeships to some of Adams' appointees.

Three of those appointees, including a man named William Marbury, sent a petition to the Supreme Court asking that it force Madison to deliver the commissions. Marbury filed his petition directly in the Supreme Court, so the Court needed to have original **jurisdiction** over the case in order to have the power to hear it. Marbury claimed that the Judiciary Act of 1789 granted the Supreme Court original jurisdiction for such petitions. The Court disagreed, ruling that the section of the Judiciary Act of 1789 that authorized the Court to issue such a writ was unconstitutional, and thus invalid. Marbury never received his commission, and Congress did not mount a challenge to judicial review.

Application of Judicial Review

The Court used the power to invalidate laws passed by Congress only twice before the Civil War (1861–1865), but much more frequently since then. Sometimes it uses judicial review to protect the powers of the states; other times, to protect the economic rights or civil liberties of individuals. The Court has also used its power of judicial review, however, to support

Senate Action on Nominations, 1949–2008

Congress	Received	Confirmed	Withdrawn	Rejected[a]	Unconfirmed[b]
81st (1949–1951)	87,266	86,562	45	6	653
82nd (1951–1953)	46,920	46,504	45	2	369
83rd (1953–1955)	69,458	68,563	43	0	852
84th (1955–1957)	84,173	82,694	38	3	1,438
85th (1957–1959)	104,193	103,311	54	0	828
86th (1959–1961)	91,476	89,900	30	1	1,545
87th (1961–1963)	102,849	100,741	1,279	0	829
88th (1963–1965)	122,190	120,201	36	0	1,953
89th (1965–1967)	123,019	120,865	173	0	1,981
90th (1967–1969)	120,231	118,231	34	0	1,966
91st (1969–1971)	134,464	133,797	487	2	178
92nd (1971–1973)	117,053	114,909	11	0	2,133
93rd (1973–1975)	134,384	131,254	15	0	3,115
94th (1975–1977)	135,302	131,378	21	0	3,903
95th (1977–1979)	137,509	124,730	66	0	12,713
96th (1979–1981)	156,141	154,665	18	0	1,458
97th (1981–1983)	186,264	184,856	55	0	1,353
98th (1983–1985)	97,893	97,262	4	0	627
99th (1985–1987)	99,614	95,811	16	0	3,787
100th (1987–1989)	94,687	88,721	23	1	5,942
101st (1989–1991)	96,130	88,078	48	1	8,003
102nd (1991–1993)	76,628	75,802	24	0	802
103rd (1993–1995)	79,956	76,122	1,080	0	2,754
104th (1995–1997)	82,214	73,711	22	0	8,481
105th (1997–1999)	46,290	45,878	40	0	372
106th (1999–2001)	45,802	44,980	25	0	797
107th (2001–2003)	49,615	48,724	79	0	812

(continued on next page)

Senate Action on Nominations, 1949–2008, *continued*

Congress	Received	Confirmed	Withdrawn	Rejected[a]	Unconfirmed[b]
108th (2003–2005)	52,420	48,627	39	0	4,177
109th (2005–2006)	55,841	53,820	38	0	1,983
110th (2007–2008)	Information Not Yet Available				

***Notes:* a. Category includes only those nominations rejected outright by a vote of the Senate. Most nominations that fail to win approval of the Senate are unfavorably reported by committees and never reach the Senate floor, having been withdrawn. In some cases, the full Senate may vote to recommit a nomination to committee, in effect killing it. b. Nominations must be returned to the president unless confirmed or rejected during the session in which they are made. If the Senate adjourns or recesses for more than thirty days within a session, all pending nominations must be returned. See Senate Rule XXI.**

Sources:* 71st to 80th Congresses: Floyd M. Riddick, *The United States Congress: Organization and Procedures;* 81st to 109th Congresses: "Résumé of Congressional Activity," *Congressional Record.

The Senate receives thousands of nominations each session, and the vast majority of them are approved. In general, nominations to the federal court system are examined closely.

A - Z

and strengthen the powers of Congress. Under Chief Justice John Marshall, the Court gave Congress broad powers to enact laws "necessary and proper" to fulfill its Constitutional obligations. It also protected Congress's power to regulate interstate **commerce** against interference by the states. The Court has generally avoided interfering with Congress's power to tax and spend, regulate its own affairs, or conduct investigations.

Appointments and Impeachment

The Court's power of judicial review is balanced by Congress's role in appointing and removing judges from office. While the president also plays a key role in judicial appointments, the executive branch has no power to remove judges once they have taken office.

Judicial Appointments

The Senate's "advice and consent" power gives Congress a role in the selection and confirmation of Supreme Court justices. Two-thirds of the members of the Senate present and voting must approve the appointment for a nominee to join the Court. Although Congress has only limited influence over a president's choice of a Supreme Court nominee, the Senate has taken its power to confirm appointees very seriously. Of the 150 nominations to the court, 28 have failed to win confirmation—some, because of **partisan** politics; others, because of legal philosophy; and at least two, because of questions about their qualifications. Even though the president gets to make a new selection, the Senate's rejection of a nominee can have significant effect. After Robert Bork was defeated for confirmation in 1987, President Ronald Reagan (1981–1989) turned to a somewhat less **conservative** judge, Anthony M. Kennedy, who won confirmation unanimously.

Partisan politics motivated most of the Senate's rejections of Supreme Court nominees before 1900. George Washington's (1789–1797) selection of John Rutledge to be chief justice in 1795 was defeated because of Rutledge's criticism of the Jay Treaty with England. On the eve of the Civil War (1861–1865), the Senate defeated President James Buchanan's (1857–1861) nomination of Jeremiah S. Black because his views on slavery were unacceptable to northern Republicans. After the Civil War, the Senate defeated Ulysses S. Grant's (1869–1877) choice of Ebenezer R. Hoar because Hoar had supported **civil service reform** and opposed the **impeachment** of President Andrew Johnson (1865–1869).

Legal philosophy became a more important factor in the Senate's consideration of Supreme Court nominees in the twentieth century. Four of the six unsuccessful nominees in the 1900s failed in part because of the Senate's disagreement with the nominees' views on legal issues.

JUSTICE FOR ALL

Court Packing

When Franklin D. Roosevelt (1933–1945) was inaugurated as president in 1933, the country was in the depths of the Great Depression, with nearly a quarter of the workforce unemployed. In order to stimulate the economy and reduce the jobless rolls, Roosevelt enacted a wide-ranging set of social programs called the New Deal. These included large-scale public works programs to provide jobs and the establishment of the modern Social Security system.

Roosevelt's programs were popular among most average Americans, who needed work and the hope of some financial and social stability. However, many groups were strongly opposed to the New Deal. Roosevelt's political opponents labeled the New Deal programs as a form of socialism and criticized the notion of direct and intensive government involvement with the nation's economic system. Eventually, Roosevelt's opponents began to challenge the New Deal in court, and the U.S. Supreme Court declared many of these government programs unconstitutional.

Frustrated with the court's attempts to block the New Deal, Roosevelt introduced a bill to Congress in 1937 called the Judiciary Reorganization Bill. The bill would allow the president to appoint an extra Supreme Court justice for every current justice over the age of 70 years and six months. If passed by Congress, the bill would have allowed Roosevelt to name six additional judges to the court. Placing his own nominees on the court would have given Roosevelt the votes needed to ensure his New Deal programs received the court's approval.

In the end, Congress refused to go along with Roosevelt's plan. Even members of his own Democratic Party felt that the president was overstepping his authority by trying to add extra judges to the court. Although his attempt to "pack" the court failed, it did send a message to Roosevelt's opponents on the court. The court upheld the next piece of New Deal legislation it considered, and soon after, one of Roosevelt's most vocal opponents on the court, Justice Willis Van Devanter, retired. Roosevelt replaced him with a judge more favorable to the president's views and thereafter met little judicial opposition to his New Deal programs.

Successful nominees have also encountered close questioning and in some cases forceful opposition because of their legal philosophies. In addition, the Senate has given greater scrutiny to nominees' records in public life.

Two of the Court's members in the 1990s—Chief Justice William H. Rehnquist and Justice Clarence Thomas—were narrowly confirmed after charges of improper conduct. Rehnquist was charged, among other things, with seeking to discourage African Americans from voting while he was a Republican campaign worker in Arizona. Thomas underwent a stormy confirmation hearing in 1991 over charges of sexual harassment of a former aide.

Impeachment

Congress also wields the power to **impeach** justices–to charge them with crimes and misdemeanors while in office. As with presidential impeachments, charges must first be filed in the House of Representatives. If a majority of House members vote for impeachment, a trial is held in the Senate. If two-thirds of the Senate votes for conviction on any charge, the justice is removed from the Court.

Only one justice, Samuel Chase, has ever been impeached. He was acquitted of charges of injudicious behavior in a politically charged Senate trial in 1805. Two other justices have faced serious attempts at impeachment. Abe Fortas resigned in 1969, while some House members were considering an impeachment inquiry into charges of financial misconduct. William O. Douglas was the subject of two House impeachment investigations, in 1953 and 1970, but both ended with no charges. In addition, Chief Justice Earl Warren faced scattered calls for his impeachment during the 1950s and 1960s, but the House never opened a formal inquiry.

See also: Checks and Balances; Constitution of the United States; Impeachment Power; Separation of Powers.

Further Reading

McGuire, Kevin T. *Understanding the U.S. Supreme Court.* New York: McGraw-Hill, 2001.

Toobin, Jeffrey. *The Nine: Inside the Secret World of the Supreme Court.* New York: Doubleday, 2007.

Teapot Dome Scandal

Popular name for a political scandal that occurred during the administration of President Warren G. Harding (1921–1923). An enduring legacy of Harding's presidency, Teapot Dome became a familiar code name for scandal in government. The Teapot Dome scandal involved the secret leasing of naval oil reserve lands to private companies by members of the Harding administration. After the disclosures of a long congressional investigation, Albert B. Fall, Harding's secretary of the interior, went to prison for accepting bribes to lease the government-owned oil reserves. Teapot Dome was only the most famous of several shady activities going on in Washington at that time. Taken together, these activities left a stain of corruption on the Harding administration.

The name Teapot Dome comes from a sandstone rock formation, somewhat resembling a teapot, that rises above the sagebrush plains of north-central Wyoming. Deep below this sandstone rock outcropping is a reservoir of oil that nature had formed vaguely in the shape of a dome. This underground oil and the land above it made up a tiny portion of the vast federal land holdings in the West. In 1915, President Woodrow Wilson (1913–1921) assigned control of Teapot Dome to the Navy Department as a reserve source of fuel for American warships. Two other oil fields, Elk Hills and Buena Vista in California, had also been selected to serve as fuel reserves. However, none had to be tapped during World War I (1917–1918) because the nation's petroleum supply turned out to be greater than expected.

In May 1921, Harding transferred supervision over the naval oil reserve lands to the U.S. Department of the Interior. Early the next year, the Interior Department, in quiet deals arranged by Secretary Fall, leased the Elk Hills reserve in California to Edward L. Doheny of the Pan-American Petroleum and Transport Company and the Teapot Dome reserve in Wyoming to Harry F. Sinclair's Mammoth Oil Company.

When Congress learned of the leases, pressure mounted for a congressional investigation of the transactions. President Harding was a Republican and tight Republican control of the House of Representatives blocked action in that chamber of Congress. However, Democrats and a number of Republicans in the Senate succeeded in passing a resolution that authorized the Senate Committee on Public Lands and Surveys to investigate the matter of leases of naval oil reserve lands. The committee was headed by a series of Republican chairs, but a Democrat on the panel, Thomas J. Walsh of Montana, took charge of the inquiry.

When the hearings opened on October 25, 1923, they concentrated at first on the legality of the two leases. Then Walsh received information that Secretary Fall had accepted bribes from both Doheny and Sinclair to arrange the leases. Doheny had given Fall at least $100,000, and Sinclair had given the interior secretary at least $300,000. Meanwhile, Fall resigned his cabinet post and protested that he had received only gifts and loans. He was later convicted of accepting a bribe from Doheny in connection with the Elk Hills lease. However, in a separate trial, Doheny was acquitted on charges of making the bribe. After Fall exhausted his court appeals, he entered prison in June 1931 and served eleven months.

Responding to a request from Congress, President Harding initiated court action to cancel the oil leases. The courts did so and overturned the executive order under which Harding transferred **jurisdiction** over the oil reserves from the Navy Department to the Interior Department.

VIEWPOINTS

Who Says a Watched Pot Never Boils?

A Senate investigating committee uncovered much of the evidence in the Teapot Dome Scandal of the 1920s. The scandal shattered the administration of President Warren G. Harding and shook the public's faith in government. (Library of Congress)

Acting on information from the Teapot Dome inquiry, the Senate on March 4, 1924, created a Select Committee to Investigate the Justice Department, which had appeared reluctant to investigate and prosecute the scandal. Calvin Coolidge (1923–1929), who had become president in 1923 after Harding's death, demanded the resignation of Attorney General Harry M. Daugherty. Daugherty, who had been Harding's campaign manager in the 1920 presidential election, was prosecuted for conspiracy to defraud the government, although at two trials the juries failed to reach a verdict.

Harry Sinclair of Mammoth Oil went to jail twice, first for three months for contempt of Congress over his refusal to answer questions and then for six months for contempt of court for attempting to bribe a juror at his trial on bribery charges arising from the Teapot Dome investigation. He was ultimately acquitted of those charges. Although the reputation of the Harding administration was ruined, the scandal had little long-term effect on his Republican Party.

Television Coverage of Congress

The televised broadcast of congressional proceedings. Congress for years resisted live televised coverage of its proceedings, fearful that cameras would prompt grandstanding or erode the dignity of its operations. Members, however, have found that television has proven to be a good way to gain public exposure and to follow floor action from their offices.

History

Broadcast coverage of floor proceedings had been proposed as early as 1944. It was not until 1977, however, that the House took its first steps in that direction. In that year, it held a ninety-day experiment with closed-circuit black-and-white telecasts. In March 1979, the Cable Satellite Public Affairs Network (C-SPAN), a private, nonprofit cable station, was launched with the express purpose of televising Congress. Tennessee representative Albert Gore, Jr., who had led the campaign for televising floor action, delivered the chamber's first televised speech. In 1986, Gore, by then a senator, teamed with Senate Minority Leader Robert Byrd, to win passage of a resolution permitting televised Senate proceedings. On June 2, 1986, the Senate premiered on a second C-SPAN channel.

The Senate had a long tradition of permitting television and radio coverage of its committee hearings, but the House did not permit broadcast coverage of such hearings until 1970. Even then, the House rules imposed severe restrictions on broadcasters. Public interest in the Judiciary Committee's 1974 televised broadcasts of **impeachment** proceedings against President Richard M. Nixon (1969–1974), however, did much to make other House committees more receptive to the presence of TV cameras.

Committee hearings are open to cameras from accredited news organizations, but each chamber keeps close control over broadcasts of floor action. Cameras are owned by Congress and operated by congressional staff. Although the recordings are not edited, the coverage provides only a limited view of floor action, usually focusing on the member who is speaking. Senators speak from their desks; representatives go to one of two lecterns in the House well or use the tables on either side of the central aisle. When votes are in progress, the cameras show the full chamber, with information about the vote superimposed on the screen.

Since May 1984, House cameras began to slowly pan the room during votes and special orders, a period at the end of a daily session when members may speak on various topics. In most cases, the coverage revealed a mostly empty chamber. When the Republicans took control of the House in 1995, procedures for panning the chamber changed. The camera would focus on individual members talking on benches in the chamber or reading the newspaper. After protests from members, Speaker Newt Gingrich ordered a halt to such close-in shots of members who are not directly participating in the business on the floor.

Impact

Television's effect on the legislative process remains difficult to evaluate. There have been widespread complaints from members about the increasing partisanship and "meanness" in debate. Some observers blame live coverage for encouraging use of floor speeches to produce sound bites—short, snappy quotes—for the evening news. Critics also charge that the presence of cameras leads to lengthier speeches and encourages members to offer amendments merely to appeal to their constituents back home. In the House, use of one-minute speeches for this purpose has become widespread, with outside interest groups sending suggested remarks for members to recite. A House rule prohibits use of the televised proceedings for political purposes, but it is enforceable only against sitting members.

In addition to affecting the issues that legislators take up, media coverage has changed the way that legislators do business. Perhaps the most obvious change is the expanding role of television advertising in political campaigns. Given the expense involved, lawmakers must spend ever-increasing amounts of time raising money.

Television coverage has had other effects as well. Members cannot now easily take stands on issues that differ greatly from those of their constituents. Television coverage also may lead members to oversimplify issues or to focus only on problems and solutions that are easy to understand. Televising Congress has also created more of an incentive for lawmakers to use the floor to appeal to voters or to generate support for certain causes. Television also seems to be spurring an ever-growing feeling of cynicism about Congress. "Congress started [televising its proceedings] under the premise that to know us is to love us," one member said, but, "The data shows that familiarity breeds contempt."

See also: Media and Congress.

Further Reading

Arnold, R. Douglas. *Congress, the Press, and Political Accountability.* Princeton, NJ: Princeton University Press, 2004.

Ranney, Austin. *Channels of Power: The Impact of Television on American Politics.* New York: Basic, 1985.

Terms and Sessions

The two-year period for which members of the House of Representatives are elected constitutes a term of Congress. Under the Twentieth Amendment to the Constitution, **ratified** in 1933, this period begins at noon on January 3 of an odd-numbered year, following the election of representatives the previous November, and ends at noon on January 3 of the next odd-numbered year. Congresses are numbered consecutively. The Congress that convened in January 2009 was the 111th in a series that began in 1789.

Before 1935, the term of a Congress began on March 4 of the odd-numbered year following the election and coincided with the inauguration of the president (also changed by the Twentieth Amendment to January 20 beginning in 1937), but Congress often did not actually convene until the first Monday in December.

Under the Constitution, Congress is required to "assemble" at least once each year. The Twentieth Amendment provides that these annual meetings shall begin on January 3 unless Congress "shall by law appoint a different day," which it frequently does. For example, before the first session of the 105th Congress **adjourned,** it passed a law, later signed by the president, to reconvene for the second session on January 27, 1998. Each Congress, therefore, has two regular sessions beginning in January of successive years.

The Legislative Reorganization Act of 1970 stipulates that unless Congress provides otherwise the Senate and House "shall adjourn *sine die* not later than July 31 of each year" or, in nonelection years, take at least a thirty-day recess in August. The provision is not applicable if "a state of war exists pursuant to a declaration of war by the Congress." Congress routinely dispenses with this restriction by passing a concurrent resolution. In practice, the annual sessions may run the entire year.

Adjournment *sine die* (literally, without a day) ends a session of Congress. Adjournment of the second session is the final action of a Congress and all legislation not passed by both houses expires. However, following adjournment there may still be some delay before legislation that has passed near the end of the session is enrolled and formally presented to the president. Members frequently include in the adjournment resolution language to authorize their leaders to call them back into session if circumstances require it. This occurred in 1998 when the House returned to consider **impeachment** charges against President Bill Clinton (1993–2001).

The president may "on extraordinary occasions" convene one or both houses in special session, or threaten to do so to achieve a political or legislative objective. For example, in 1997 President Clinton threatened to delay the adjournment of the first session of the 105th Congress by calling a special session to consider campaign finance reform legislation. The Senate quickly took up the major legislation but the proposal succumbed to a filibuster.

Within a session, either house of Congress may adjourn for holiday observances or other brief periods of three days or less. In a typical week, for example, the Senate or House may meet through Thursday and then, by unanimous consent or by motion, convene on the following Monday. By constitutional directive, neither house may adjourn for more than three days without the consent of the other, which they give through passage of a concurrent resolution.

The third session of the 76th Congress was the longest session in history; it lasted 366 days, from January 3, 1940, to January 3, 1941. Four other sessions have lasted 365 days: the first session of the 77th Congress (1941–1942), the second session of the 81st Congress (1950–1951), the first session of the 102nd Congress (1991–1992), and the first session of the 104th Congress (1995–1996).

See also: Twentieth Amendment, 1933, in the **Primary Source Library.**

Thirteen Colonies, Settling of the

The English-founded thirteen colonies that hugged the Atlantic seaboard and eventually became the independent United States. The government of each colony was rooted in the British parliamentary tradition. Although many of the colonies became royal colonies, they each maintained a governor and a legislature. Thus, colonial leaders carried a tradition of democratic government with them as they worked to establish the governmental structure of the United States.

Virginia

The Virginia Company of London, a joint-stock company with a charter from King James I (r. 1603–1625), founded the first permanent English settlement in America at Jamestown in 1607. After severe setbacks, the company found tobacco to be a thriving crop and profitable export and began to attract new settlers with "head rights" to fifty acres of land. The colony also imported slaves. The Virginia Company was dissolved in 1624, when Virginia became a royal colony. Its population had reached 15,000 by 1648.

Massachusetts

A small band of Pilgrims founded Plymouth in 1620. Few others came until 1630, when John Winthrop and other Puritan organizers of the Massachusetts Bay Company arrived with 1,000 colonists to settle Boston and nearby towns. The Bay Colony, which had attained a population of 16,000 by 1643, remained a self-governing Puritan **commonwealth** until its charter was annulled in 1684. In 1691, Massachusetts became a royal colony, incorporating Plymouth and Maine as well.

New Hampshire

Various groups of Puritans and Anglicans began a number of settlements between 1623 and 1640 on land granted to John Mason by King Charles I. Massachusetts annexed these settlements briefly, and border disputes between the two colonies continued even after New Hampshire became a royal colony in 1679. The governor of Massachusetts served also as governor of New Hampshire from 1699 to 1741.

New York

The Dutch West Indies Company founded New Netherland with posts at Albany (1624) and Manhattan (1626). Confined largely to the Hudson River Valley, the colony was seized by the English in 1664 and renamed New York as part of a grant by King Charles II (r. 1660–1685) to his brother, the Duke of York, of all land between the Connecticut and Delaware rivers. The duke attempted to run the colony without an assembly until 1683; as King James II (r. 1685–1688), he made it a royal colony in 1685.

Delaware

The town of Lewes, on the shore of Delaware Bay, was settled by the Dutch in 1631. They were followed by Swedish settlers, who called it New Sweden, until overcome by Dutch forces in 1655. The area was conquered by the English in 1664 and was included in the grant to the Duke of York, who sold it to William Penn in 1682. Known as the "Lower Counties," Delaware had its own assembly after 1704 but had the same proprietary governor as Pennsylvania until 1776.

Maryland

In 1632, King Charles I (r. 1625–1649) gave a proprietary charter to Maryland (originally a part of Virginia) to Sir George Calvert, who wanted a feudal domain for his family that would serve also as a refuge for English Catholics. Settlement began at St. Mary's in 1634. Protestants soon outnumbered Catholics, leading to continuous friction between settlers and the proprietor. Maryland became a royal colony in 1692, but was restored to the Calvert family in 1715.

Connecticut

Thomas Hooker led a group of Puritans from the Massachusetts Bay Colony to found Hartford in 1636. About the same time, other groups of Puritans settled Saybrook and New Haven. Modeled along the theocratic lines of Massachusetts, these and other settlements were joined when Connecticut in 1662 obtained from Charles II (r, 1660–1685) its own charter as a self-governing colony. The colony retained that status until 1776.

Rhode Island

Providence was founded in 1636 by Roger Williams, a strong believer in religious freedom who had been banished from Massachusetts for opposing the rule of Governor John Winthrop and the Puritans. The area drew other freethinkers and nonconformists, and in 1644, the settlements federated as Rhode Island and Providence Plantations. They obtained a royal charter of their own in 1663 and remained a self-governing colony until the Revolution.

New Jersey

In 1665, the Duke of York gave the land between the Hudson and Delaware rivers to Lord John Berkeley and Sir George Carteret (a former governor of the Isle of Jersey), who named the area New Jersey. The two proprietors later sold East and West Jersey separately, and although the two were reunited as a royal colony in 1702, confusion of land titles continued to plague New Jersey. The colony had the same governor as New York until 1738.

Carolinas

King Charles II gave proprietary title to all land between Virginia and Florida in 1663 to the Carolina proprietors, a group of promoters led by Sir John Colleton and the Earl of Shaftesbury. Charleston was founded in 1670 by settlers from England and Barbados. Later, French Huguenots and Scots came to settle. South Carolina became a plantation colony like Virginia. North Carolina became an area of small farms. The two became royal colonies in 1729.

Pennsylvania

William Penn, a Quaker convert, received proprietary title to Pennsylvania from the Duke of York in 1681. Penn attracted settlers from Europe as well as England with promises of political and religious liberty and the offer of land on generous terms. German Mennonites were among the first groups to come, settling Germantown in 1683. Pennsylvania prospered under Penn's tolerant rule, and it remained a proprietary colony until the American Revolution.

Georgia

General James Oglethorpe and other English **philanthropists** envisioned the territory known as Georgia as a refuge for debtors. They founded Savannah in 1733, and, in the next eight years, brought over about 1,800 colonists. Many of these settlers moved on to South Carolina, however, and Georgia had a total population of little more than 2,000 residents when it became a royal colony in 1752.

Further Reading

January, Brendan. *The Thirteen Colonies.* NY: Children's Press, 2001.

Sakuri, Gail. *The Thirteen Colonies.* NY: Children's Press, 2000.

Treaty Power

Constitutional authority granted to the Senate to advise the president on making treaties with foreign nations and to approve or reject treaties negotiated by the president. Technically speaking, the Senate does not have the power to **ratify,** or formally approve, treaties. However, the Constitution states that the president can ratify treaties only with the approval of two-thirds of the senators present and voting.

Procedures

Once the president sends a treaty to the Senate, it stays in that chamber until it is approved or rejected, or until the president requests its return and the Senate agrees to withdraw it. The Senate also may take the initiative to return a treaty to the president. The president may refuse to submit a treaty, may withdraw it after submitting it, or may refuse to ratify it even after the Senate has given its consent.

Reporting and Voting

The Senate Foreign Relations Committee has **jurisdiction,** or legal authority, over all treaties. The committee considers a treaty in much the same way it considers proposed legislation. It may hold open or closed hearings and may recommend Senate approval or rejection, with or without modifications. Committee decisions require a majority vote of the members present. No measure or recommendation discussed in committee can be **reported,** or sent to the full chamber for debate, unless a majority of the committee's members are physically present at the committee meeting.

Treaties reported by the Foreign Relations Committee are considered by the full Senate. Until 1929, many treaty debates happened in closed sessions to preserve the cloak of secrecy. By the late nineteenth century, however, there were increasing demands to open treaty debates to the public. On June 18, 1929, the Senate amended its rules to provide that all Senate business, including action on treaties, was to be conducted in open session. If a majority of the members agreed, however, the Senate could still hold a closed session to consider particularly sensitive matters.

Most issues during debate over a treaty are decided by majority vote. However, a motion to give advice and consent to the treaty, and a motion for indefinite postponement, must be approved by a two-thirds vote. A separate roll call vote normally is taken on each treaty. When it considers a large number of similar treaties, or a variety of non-controversial treaties, the

VIEWPOINTS

A 1920 political cartoon shows the United States Senate as a Democratic-Republican hybrid animal—part donkey and part elephant—unwilling to enter the ark of peace. The Senate refused to ratify the Treaty of Versailles as written, and President Woodrow Wilson (1913–1921) refused to compromise with the Senate. (The Granger Collection, New York)

Treaties Killed by Senate

Date of Vote	Country	Vote (Yea-Nay)	Subject
March 9, 1825	Colombia	0–40	Suppression of African Slave Trade
June 11, 1836	Switzerland	14–23	Personal and Property Rights
June 8, 1844	Texas	16–35	Annexation
June 15, 1844	German Zollverein	26–18	Reciprocity
May 31, 1860	Mexico	18–27	Transit and Commercial Rights
June 27, 1860	Spain	26–17	Cuban Claims Commission
April 13, 1869	Great Britain	1–54	Arbitration of Claims
June 1, 1870	Hawaii	20–19	Reciprocity
June 30, 1870	Dominican Republic	28–28	Annexation
Jan. 29, 1885	Nicaragua	32–23	Interoceanic Canal
April 20, 1886	Mexico	32–26	Mining Claims
Aug. 21, 1888	Great Britain	27–30	Fishing Rights
Feb. 1, 1889	Great Britain	15–38	Extradition
May 5, 1897	Great Britain	43–26	Arbitration
March 19, 1920	Multilateral	49–35	Treaty of Versailles
Jan. 18, 1927	Turkey	50–34	Commercial Rights
March 14, 1934	Canada	46–42	St. Lawrence Seaway
Jan. 29, 1935	Multilateral	52–36	World Court
May 26, 1960	Multilateral	49–30	Law of the Sea Convention
March 8, 1983	Multilateral	50–42	Montreal Aviation Protocol
Oct. 13, 1999	Multilateral	48–51	Comprehensive Nuclear Test Ban

Source: Compiled by Senate Historical Office from W. Stull Holt, *Treaties Defeated by the Senate* (Baltimore: Johns Hopkins University Press, 1933) and from *Senate Executive Journal*.

A two-thirds majority is required for Senate consent to the ratification of treaties. In many cases, treaties were blocked in committee or withdrawn before ever coming to a vote in the Senate.

Senate often considers the treaties as a group, taking a single vote on **resolutions** covering all of the treaties.

Amending Treaties

The Constitution sets forth no procedures for, or restrictions on, amending treaties. From the beginning, however, the Senate has claimed authority to modify treaties after the completion of negotiations. Critics have questioned the wisdom of the Senate practice of amending treaties, but on two occasions, the Supreme Court has upheld this power.

If the president and the other parties to the treaty accept an amendment, it changes the treaty for all parties. The Senate may place

SPOTLIGHT

The Kyoto Protocol

Finalized in December 1997, the Kyoto Protocol is an international treaty that lays out guidelines for actions to reduce greenhouse gases that scientists say contribute to global climate change. As of early 2008, the heads of state of 175 nations, including the United States, had signed the protocol. The United States Senate, however, has not **ratified,** or formally approved the treaty. As a result, the United States does not consider itself bound by the terms of the pact. The situation surrounding the Kyoto Protocol highlights a central aspect of the U.S. system of government. That is, even though the president may sign a treaty, it does not have the force of law unless two-thirds of the Senate votes to approve it.

The Kyoto Protocol was controversial in the United States before it had even been finished. Several months prior to finalization of the treaty, the Senate passed a resolution by a vote of 95—0 that stated the U.S. should not sign the agreement. Senators were displeased with the fact that the treaty set definite deadlines and specific goals for reducing greenhouse gas emissions in industrialized nations, but not for developing nations. Because the U.S. is the world's leading producer of greenhouse gases, the Senate felt that this was unfair and that it unjustly penalized industrialized nations.

The administration of President Bill Clinton (1993–2001) supported the treaty, and on November 12, 1998, Vice President Al Gore signed the protocol. Senate spokespersons, however, stated that the chamber would not act on it until the treaty outlined more specific goals for the reduction of greenhouse gases by developing nations. Realizing that it could not win the two-thirds vote needed for ratification, the Clinton administration never submitted the treaty for ratification.

Clinton's successor, George W. Bush (2001–2009), also refused to submit the treaty to the Senate. Bush, unlike Clinton, opposed the treaty, particularly because it exempted China from the emissions goals set for industrialized countries. Under the protocol, China is treated in many ways like a developing nation, even though it boasts one of the world's most rapidly growing economies and is the world's second-largest producer of the greenhouse gas carbon monoxide. The Bush administration also argues that meeting the treaty's targets would be so costly that it would hurt the U.S. economy.

Although the Senate opposes the Kyoto Protocol, many U.S. cities and states approve of its goals. Several states, including California and New York, have enacted their own programs to limit greenhouse gas emissions. Since 2006, officials in more than 600 cities have signed the U.S. Mayors Climate Protection Agreement, pledging to reduce greenhouse gas emissions, such as those contained in the Kyoto Protocol.

Decision Makers

The House and the Treaty Power

The Constitutional Convention of 1787 deprived the House of a share in the treaty-making power, thus relegating the House to a position subordinate to the Senate in treaty affairs. However, through its normal legislative powers, most especially the power of the purse, the House can at times exercise considerable—although indirect—influence over treaty matters. Often, this comes at the stage where legislation is needed to implement a treaty. The House also becomes an equal partner with the Senate when an international agreement is submitted as legislation requiring simple majorities in both chambers instead of as a treaty requiring a two-thirds majority in the Senate.

In the administration of George Washington (1789–1797), when the Senate agreed to a treaty with the dey [leader] of Algiers for release of American captives, "provided the expenses do not exceed $40,000," President Washington announced that he would wait to conclude negotiations until the money had been **appropriated** by Congress. The Senate objected, urging that the money be taken from the Treasury or raised by borrowing. As reported in *Jefferson's Writings,* the senators feared that "to consult the representatives on one occasion would give them a handle always to claim it." The House in 1792 then passed a bill appropriating a stated sum to cover the expenses involved, and the Senate consented to ratification of a treaty specifying the sum appropriated.

In considering **appropriations** for the Jay Treaty, the House called for all documents in the case. Washington refused this request on the grounds that "the assent of the House of Representatives is not necessary to the validity of a treaty." The House made the necessary appropriation in 1796 after a long debate, but at the same time it adopted a resolution that said, "it is the constitutional right and duty of the House of Representatives in all such cases to deliberate on the expediency or inexpediency of carrying such treaty into effect and to determine and act thereon as in their judgment may be most conducive to the public good."

Submission of commercial and **reciprocity treaties** has led to repeated assertions of authority by the House, frequently with support from the Senate. The reciprocity treaty with Great Britain in 1854 made its effectiveness dependent upon passage of the laws necessary to put it into operation. In 1883, the Senate amended a reciprocity convention with Mexico to provide that it should not come into force until the legislation called for had been passed by Congress, and the treaty never took effect because the House never acted on the implementing legislation.

(continued on next page)

In at least one case, House opposition prevented ratification of a treaty that would have required Congress to approve an appropriation. Shortly before the original treaty for the purchase of the Danish West Indies was submitted in 1867, the House resolved that "in the present financial condition of the country, any further purchases of territory were inexpedient, and this House will hold itself under no obligation to vote money for any such purpose unless there is greater necessity than now exists." In the debate, it was said that this resolution was intended to serve notice on the king of Denmark that "this House will not pay for that purchase." When the treaty was sent to the Senate, no action was taken. When the islands finally were acquired 50 years later, the price had risen from $7.5 to $25 million.

Attempts in the House to influence the treaty process have continued in modern times. In 1979, the House's appropriations powers gave that chamber an important voice in shaping legislation to implement the Panama Canal treaties. Angered that they had had no role in approving the treaties in 1978, many House members insisted on legislation giving Congress more control over canal operations than President Jimmy Carter (1977–1981) had been willing to grant.

Neither the Senate nor the House were called on to approve major trade agreements concluded in the early 1990s—the 1992 North American Free Trade Agreement (NAFTA) and the 1994 General Agreement on Tariffs and Trade (GATT). Nevertheless, both houses played important roles in approving the laws that put GATT into effect.

what is called a reservation on a treaty, which limits only the treaty obligations of the United States. In some cases, the reservation may be so significant that the other treaty parties may file similar reservations or refuse to ratify the treaty. The Senate may add "understandings," which are statements intended to clarify the legal effect of a treaty without necessarily changing it. It also may attach "declarations," which state U.S. policy in regards to a treaty or indicate how the U.S. intends to implement the treaty.

Questions and Controversies

Article II, Section 2, of the Constitution declares:

> He (the president) shall have Power, by and with the Advice and Consent of the Senate, to make Treaties, provided two-thirds of the Senators present concur.

However, the treaty clause is unclear on some points. For example, it does not specify either the Senate procedure for advising the president or when in the treaty-making process the Senate can exercise its advice function. In the early years of the nation, the executive branch sought to incorporate Senate advice into the process of treaty negotiations. As international relations became more complicated, presidents largely abandoned the practice of obtaining Senate advice.

Through the years, Senate action on treaties has repeatedly led to controversy. Generally, the dispute has centered on rival claims of the president and the Senate over the treaty power.

On the vast majority of treaties submitted to it, the Senate has adopted a simple resolution of consent to **ratification.** The importance of some of the rejected treaties, however, has prompted criticism of the Senate's treaty-making role and the two-thirds requirement for approval. In addition, there is a growing tendency to modify U.S. foreign relations through treaties made with several foreign states at once. It can be very difficult to persuade all the parties to accept a treaty after the Senate has amended it.

See also: Foreign Policy Powers; President and Congress; Senate; United States Constitution, Article II, Sections 2, 3, and 4, 1789, in the **Primary Source Library.**

Two-Thirds Rule

Rule that requires two-thirds of the members of a chamber of Congress to agree in order to make certain decisions. In each chamber of Congress a majority of the members must be present to make up a **quorum,** the minimum number needed to do business. In some situations, however, the Framers of the Constitution felt that something greater than a majority was essential to a balanced design of government.

The Constitution calls for a two-thirds requirement in six instances. No one may be convicted after **impeachment,** nor can a treaty be made, without the agreement of two-thirds of the senators "present". Neither chamber may expel a member without "the concurrence of two-thirds." A bill can be enacted over the president's **veto** by the votes of two-thirds of each chamber. Congress may propose amendments to the Constitution "whenever two-thirds of both Houses shall deem it necessary." Finally, if the House is called upon to decide the result of a presidential election, a quorum must "consist of a Member or Members from two-thirds of the States."

Delegate to the Constitutional Convention also considered but rejected proposals to require the consent of two-thirds of both houses to admit new states and to enact laws to regulate foreign **commerce.** They also considered permitting Congress to enact export taxes if two-thirds vote of both houses agreed. In the end, it prohibited such taxes altogether.

When trying impeachments and approving treaties, two-thirds of the members present and voting must reach agreement, rather than with two-thirds of the entire membership. In cases involving vetoes, expulsion of members, and constitutional amendments, it seems that the decision was meant to lie with two-thirds of the entire membership, including those members not present or voting. However, this is never clarified in the Constitution. Over time, Congress has established the custom that two-thirds of members "present" and voting was sufficient in those cases. The Supreme Court agreed with this interpretation in cases decided in the early twentieth century.

See also: Amending the Constitution; Exclusion of Members of Congress; Impeachment Power; Treaty Power; Vetoes and Veto Overrides.

★ ★ ★ U-V ★ ★ ★

Unicameralism

See Bicameralism.

Vetoes and Veto Overrides

The president's power to reject legislation passed by Congress, and Congress's power to pass legislation in spite of a presidential veto. Any bill Congress passes must go to the president, who must either sign it or **veto** it-send it back to Congress with objections. Congress can use its override of a veto and pass the legislation anyway if enough members in each house vote to do so.

The president may exercise either a regular veto or a "pocket veto." A pocket veto occurs when the president refuses to act on a bill until Congress **adjourns,** or temporarily suspends its activities. At that time, the bill is automatically killed. To override a veto requires the approval of two-thirds of members present and voting in each chamber.

Early History

Early American presidents saw the veto as a tool to be used rarely and only to prevent Congress from assuming powers the Constitution grants to other branches of government. Of the first six presidents, George Washington (1789-1797) vetoed only two **bills;** John Adams (1797-1801) and Thomas Jefferson 1801-1809) vetoed none; James Madison (1809-1817) and James Monroe (1817-1825) vetoed eight bills between them; and John Quincy Adams (1825-1829) also did not veto a single bill. In all but one case, presidents vetoed only bills they felt were unconstitutional, not merely those they opposed politically.

The concept of the veto changed dramatically under Andrew Jackson (1829-1837), who vetoed twelve bills—more than all six of his predecessors put together—mostly because he opposed their purpose. Jackson, who used the pocket veto for the first time, believed the president could reject any bill that he felt was harmful to the nation. His most noteworthy veto was of a bill to create a new charter, or founding document, for the **Bank of the United States.** The Bank's first charter had expired several years earlier. Jackson felt that the Bank existed solely to serve the interests of large business, and not those of the general public. According to one historian, Jackson's veto was "a landmark in the evolution of the presidency. For the first time in American history, a veto message was used as an instrument of party warfare . . . Though addressed to Congress, the veto message was an appeal to the nation."

In 1867, Congress overrode President Andrew Johnson's (1865-1869) veto of a bill to protect the rights of freed slaves. This marked the first override of a presidential veto on a major issue. It was only the first of several bills passed over Johnson's veto. Among others was the Tenure of Office Act, which prohibited the president from removing appointed officials from office until the Senate had confirmed their successors. When Johnson refused to abide by the provisions of the act, the House began **impeachment** proceedings against him.

Vetoes rose during the late nineteenth and early twentieth centuries. Grover Cleveland (1885-1889, 1893-1897), for example, vetoed 584 bills during two terms of office in the 1880s and 1890s. Franklin Roosevelt (1933-1945) broke Cleveland's record by vetoing 635 bills between 1933 and 1944. Roosevelt's

Vetoes and Veto Overrides

Public and Private Bills				
President	Total vetoes	Regular vetoes	Pocket vetoes	Vetoes overridden
Washington	2	2	0	0
J. Adams	0	0	0	0
Jefferson	0	0	0	0
Madison	7	5	2	0
Monroe	1	1	0	0
J.Q. Adams	0	0	0	0
Jackson	12	5	7	0
Van Buren	1	0	1	0
W.H. Harrison	0	0	0	0
Tyler	10	6	4	1
Polk	3	2	1	0
Taylor	0	0	0	0
Fillmore	0	0	0	0
Pierce	9	9	0	5
Buchanan	7	4	3	0
Lincoln	7	2	5	0
A. Johnson	29	21	8	15
Grant	93	45	48	4
Hayes	13	12	1	1
Garfield	0	0	0	0
Arthur	12	4	8	1
Cleveland (1st term)	414	304	110	2
B. Harrison	44	19	25	1
Cleveland (2nd term)	170	42	128	5
McKinley	42	6	36	0
T. Roosevelt	82	42	40	1
Taft	39	30	9	1
Wilson	44	33	11	6

(continued on next page)

Vetoes and Veto Overrides, *continued*

Public and Private Bills				
President	Total vetoes	Regular vetoes	Pocket vetoes	Vetoes overridden
Harding	6	5	1	0
Coolidge	50	20	30	4
Hoover	37	21	16	3
F.D. Roosevelt	635	372	263	9
Truman	250	180	70	12
Eisenhower	181	73	108	2
Kennedy	21	12	9	0
Johnson	30	16	14	0
Nixon	43	26	17	7
Ford	66	48	18	12
Carter	31	13	18	2
Reagan	78	39	39	9
G.H.W. Bush	44	29	15	1
Clinton	37	36	1	2
G.W. Bush	12	12	0	4
Total	2,562	1,496	1,066	110

Sources: *Presidential Vetoes, 1989–2004,* compiled by the Senate Library under the direction of Martha S. Pope, secretary, and Gregory Harness, librarian (Government Printing Office, 1994); and Congressional Quarterly.

Since 1789, presidents have vetoed more than 2,500 bills passed by Congress. Franklin D. Roosevelt vetoed the most bills during his 12 years in office.

immediate successors Harry S. Truman (1945-1953) and Dwight D. Eisenhower (1953-1961) continued to make extensive use of the veto, but presidents John F. Kennedy (1961-1963) and Lyndon B. Johnson (1963-1969) seldom had to use the veto or threaten it. They were activist presidents whose main interest lay in getting their programs through a Congress controlled by their own party. Like Eisenhower, Republican presidents Richard M. Nixon (1969-1974) and Gerald R. Ford (1974-1977) used the veto and its threat to prevent enactment of Democratic programs in the late 1960s and 1970s.

Recent History

Ronald Reagan (1981-1989) frequently threatened vetoes, but failed to follow through on many of these threats. He vetoed seventy-one bills, almost half using the pocket veto. George H. W. Bush, (1989-1993) on the other hand, used vetoes and veto threats to great effect. Like other recent Republican presidents, he faced a Democratic-controlled Congress. Bush issued around 60 veto threats per year, often not to kill legislation but to stimulate serious bargaining with Congress.

Bill Clinton (1993-2001) did not veto a bill from the Democratic-controlled Congress in the first two years of his first term. This changed drastically after Republicans took over both houses of Congress in 1995. Over the course of that year, Clinton vetoed ten spending bills proposed by Republicans to reduce the size of government and balance the budget. Clinton used vetoes and the threat of vetoes to counteract what he branded the "extremism" of the new congressional leaders. George W. Bush (2001–2009), like Reagan, has issued many veto threats, but vetoed few bills.

See also: How a Bill Becomes Law; Impeachment Power; President and Congress; Two-Thirds Rule.

Vice President

Executive branch officer who is first in line to succeed the president of the United States in case of disability or death. The vice president also serves as President of the Senate, a largely ceremonial position that presides over meetings of that chamber. In this role, the vice president may cast a vote only in case of a tie.

The Constitution originally provided that the candidate who received the second-highest total of electoral votes during presidential balloting would become vice-president. The rise of competitive political parties, however, led to problems with the original method of electing the vice president. In 1796, Federalist John Adams (1797–1801) won the presidency while his main opponent, Anti-Federalist Thomas Jefferson, became vice-president. In 1800, Thomas Jefferson (1801–1809) and Aaron Burr finished in a tie for president with 73 electoral votes apiece. The election became the first to be decided by the House of Representatives. After a week of deadlock, the House finally chose Jefferson as president with his foe, Burr, as vice president. In 1804 the states **ratified,** or approved, the Twelfth Amendment, which requires presidential electors to name separate choices for president and vice president.

As President of the Senate, the vice president's main function is to recognize senators.

John C. Calhoun served as vice president under John Quincy Adams and during Andrew Jackson's first term. He resigned the vice presidency in 1832, however, to take a seat in the United States Senate. (Library of Congress)

This is rarely a significant duty since Senate rules usually require the presiding officer to recognize the senator who requests recognition. The presiding officer also decides points of order, enforces decorum, administers oaths, and appoints members to special committees. The presiding officer also has the power to appoint senators to conference committees. These committees are composed of members from both chambers and meet to settle differences between **bills** passed in the House and Senate. Usually, however, the senator leading the debate on the bill in question recommends members for committee posts. The presiding officer typically accepts these recommendations.

There are several reasons that the Senate has not given the vice president any real power as presiding officer: The vice president is not chosen by the Senate; the vice president may not be a member of the majority party in the chamber; and, the vice president may not support the

Senate Votes Cast by Vice Presidents

Period	Vice President	Votes Cast	Period	Vice President	Votes Cast
1789–1797	John Adams	29	1901	Theodore Roosevelt	0
1797–1801	Thomas Jefferson	3	1905–1909	Charles W. Fairbanks	0
1801–1805	Aaron Burr	3	1909–1912	James S. Sherman	4
1805–1812	George Clinton	12	1913–1921	Thomas R. Marshall	8
1813–1814	Elbridge Gerry	6	1921–1923	Calvin Coolidge	0
1817–1825	Daniel D. Tompkins	3	1925–1929	Charles G. Dawes	2
1825–1832	John C. Calhoun	28	1929–1933	Charles Curtis	3
1833–1837	Martin Van Buren	4	1933–1941	John N. Garner	3
1837–1841	Richard M. Johnson	17	1941–1945	Henry A. Wallace	4
1841	John Tyler	0	1945	Harry S. Truman	1
1845–1849	George M. Dallas	19	1949–1953	Alben W. Barkley	8
1849–1850	Millard Fillmore	3	1953–1961	Richard M. Nixon	8
1853	William R. King	0	1961–1963	Lyndon B. Johnson	0
1857–1861	John C. Breckinridge	9	1965–1969	Hubert H. Humphrey	4
1861–1865	Hannibal Hamlin	7	1969–1973	Spiro T. Agnew	2
1865	Andrew Johnson	0	1973–1974	Gerald R. Ford	0
1869–1873	Schuyler Colfax	17	1974–1977	Nelson A. Rockefeller	0
1873–1875	Henry Wilson	1	1977–1981	Walter F. Mondale	1
1877–1881	William A. Wheeler	6	1981–1989	George Bush	7
1881	Chester A. Arthur	3	1989–1993	Dan Quayle	0
1885	Thomas A. Hendricks	0	1993–2001	Al Gore	4
1889–1893	Levi P. Morton	4	2001–2008	Dick Cheney	8
1893–1897	Adlai E. Stevenson	2	Total		244
1897–1899	Garret A. Hobart	1			

Source: Congressional Research Service, Library of Congress.

According to the Constitution, the vice president is able to cast a ballot to break a tie in the Senate. The first vice president, John Adams, cast the most-tie-breaking votes.

aims of the majority. John Adams established a **precedent,** a case that establishes a rule or guideline, by making little effort to guide the Senate. Most vice presidents preside only upon ceremonial occasions or when a close vote on a bill or amendment of interest to the administration is likely to occur.

A few vice presidents have attempted to use their position as presiding officer to achieve a **partisan** purpose. For example, John C.

Decision Makers

Vice President As Tie Breaker

From the beginning of the American republic, the executive branch has put to good use the constitutional authority granted the vice president to vote in the Senate in the event of a tie. Through 2008, vice presidents had cast votes on more than two hundred occasions. John Adams cast the first roll call vote by a vice president in 1789. His "no" vote, however, had no practical effect, because, by Senate rules, a bill is defeated in case of a tie vote. The vote was one of twenty-nine that Adams cast as vice president. Only John C. Calhoun, who cast twenty-eight votes as vice president, comes close to Adams's record.

The most active tie-breaking vice presidents in recent years have been Dick Cheney and George H. W. Bush. Most of the votes Bush cast in the 1980s were aimed at saving controversial weapons systems backed by the Reagan administration (1981–1989). Cheney's tie-breaking votes came mostly on tax and budget legislation favored by the administration of George W. Bush (2001–2009).

Calhoun, vice president to John Quincy Adams, was hostile to the Adams administration. He took advantage of an 1823 rule change in the House to place supporters of Andrew Jackson—Adams's main political rival—on key committees.

As president of the Senate, the vice president is in a good position to **lobby,** or apply political persuasion, on senators to support the president's programs. Vice President Al Gore wielded a good deal of influence during the administration of Bill Clinton (1993–2001). He exercised significant power over federal appointments and several key areas of government policy, most notably on government reorganization, technology, and the environment. Dick Cheney, who served as vice president under George W. Bush (2001–2009), assumed even greater authority and responsibilities. Cheney was a central figure in the Bush administration and was regarded by many observers to be the administration's key decision maker, particularly in the areas of foreign and military policy.

See also: President Pro Tempore.

Further Reading

Waldrup, Carole Chandler. *Vice Presidents: Biographies of the 45 Men Who Have Held the Second Highest Office in the United States.* Jefferson, NC: McFarland, 2006.

Virginia Plan

Proposal made during the Constitutional Convention of 1787 which established the basic structure of the federal government. Opposition to several aspects of the Virginia Plan produced a competing proposal called the New Jersey Plan. In the end, the delegates to the convention reached a compromise that established the current form of government in the United States.

The delegates who proposed the Virginia Plan favored a strong federal government and envisioned a more limited role for the people in choosing their leaders. Their plan called for a

A–Z

Decision Makers

Edmund Randolph (1753–1813)

Edmund Randolph, an early American statesman from Virginia, is best known as the author of the Virginia Plan, one of the competing proposals for the structure of the federal government presented at the Constitutional Convention of 1787. He later served as the first attorney general of the United States.

Randolph came from a prominent Virginia family that was active in colonial politics. When the Revolutionary War broke out in 1775, Randolph's father returned to Great Britain, while Edmund remained in America and joined the rebels. During the war, he served as an aide to General George Washington and as a member of the Continental Congress.

In 1787, the Virginia legislature selected Randolph as a delegate to the Constitution Convention that was charged with amending the Articles of Confederation. His Virginia Plan, which called for both houses of Congress to be chosen based on population, was unpopular with smaller states. In the end, the delegates agreed to a compromise plan to which Randolph raised several objections. Randolph never signed the final draft of the Constitution, although he later urged the states to ratify it.

In 1789, George Washington named Randolph the nation's first attorney general. He remained in that position until 1793, when he took over as secretary of state after Thomas Jefferson resigned the post. Two years later, Randolph also resigned after being accused of revealing government information to French diplomats.

bicameral, or two-house Congress–one house to be elected by the people and the other by members of the first; house. It also called for a single "National Executive," or president, to be chosen by the Legislature; and a national judiciary. Congress would have power to legislate in all cases where the states were "incompetent" or would interrupt "the harmony of the United States." It could also "negate" state laws it felt were unconstitutional. Under the Virginia Plan, each state received a number of seats in both houses of Congress in proportion to their wealth or their white population.

Some members from smaller states were alarmed by the larger states' insistence on proportional representation in both houses of Congress. Under one formula, the three most populous states–Virginia, Pennsylvania, and Massachusetts–would have received almost half of the seats in each house. To delegate Luther Martin of Maryland, such a plan meant "a system of slavery which bound hand and foot ten states of the Union and placed them at the mercy of the other three."

New Jersey's William Paterson and others drafted an alternative to the Virginia Plan. The New Jersey Plan, presented June 15, proposed a **unicameral,** or single-house legislature in which each state had the same number of seats, regardless of population. Instead of a single president, the plan featured a plural executive, chosen by Congress, as well as a federal judiciary. It proposed that treaties and acts of Congress "shall be the supreme law" and authorized

The Virginia Plan

Branches	Three - legislative, executive, and judicial. The legislature was more powerful, as it chose people to serve in the executive and judicial branches.
Legislature	Two houses (bicameral). The House of Representatives was elected by the people and the Senate was elected by the state legislatures. Both were represented proportionally.
Other Powers	The legislature could regulate interstate trade, strike down laws deemed unconstitutional and use armed forces to enforce laws.

The Virginia Plan provided for a strong central government with the separate branches and a bicameral legislature.

the executive branch to "call forth the power of the Confederated States" to enforce the laws if necessary. The states would retain a great deal of their **sovereignty,** or political independence.

The delegates eventually agreed to a modified version of the Virginia Plan. Known as the "Great Compromise," it retained the bicameral legislature contained in the Virginia Plan. Each state would receive a number of seats in the lower house, or House of Representatives, based on population. In the upper house, or Senate, however, each state would have two seats, regardless of population. The compromise also provided for a census every ten years to determine changes in population that might affect each state's representation in the House. The House was given the power to originate money **bills** that the Senate could either accept or reject, but not change in any way.

See also: Bicameralism; House of Representatives; Reapportionment; Redistricting; Senate.

Voice Votes

See Congressional Voting Methods.

Voting Methods of Congress

See Congressional Voting Methods.

Voting Rights Act (1965)

Legislation that outlawed the use of **literacy tests** as a qualification for voter registration. The law also called for the federal government to register voters in areas in which fewer than half of the eligible minority voters were registered.

Historical Background

In 1870, the Fifteenth Amendment to the U.S. Constitution prohibited voting rights discrimination on the basis of race, color, or previous condition of slavery. Nevertheless, Southern states found many other means to deny the vote to African Americans. Three of the most widely used methods were literacy tests, **poll taxes,** and so-called **grandfather clauses.** The first two methods took advantage of the poorer educational and employment opportunities available to blacks in the South to deny them the vote. Grandfather clauses provided exceptions to literacy tests and poll taxes for all persons allowed to vote before the Civil War, as well as their descendants. This allowed many poor, **illiterate** whites to vote who could not pass the literacy test or afford to pay a poll tax.

Civil rights groups struggled for many years to fight these practices and ensure blacks the right to vote, but they made little progress until Congress passed the Civil Rights Act of 1964. This prompted a major drive among civil rights leaders to secure voting rights for African Americans. On March 7, 1965, about 600 individuals marched out of Selma, Alabama along U.S. Highway 80. They hoped to walk to the state capitol building in Montgomery to protest the state's violation of black voting rights. After going only a short distance, however, they were attacked by

African Americans and their supporters march in favor of the Voting Rights Act of 1965, one of the most sweeping examples of civil rights legislation ever passed by Congress. The law assured minorities across the nation of their right to vote. (Library of Congress)

state troopers and sherrif's deputies using clubs and tear gas. Two days later, the Reverend Martin Luther King, Jr. led a second march to the site of the attack.

In the wake of these events, President Lyndon Johnson (1963–1969) called on Congress to pass a strong voting rights bill. The administration drafted such a bill and sent it to Congress on March 17, 1965. The Senate passed the bill on May 11, and the House approved it two months later. On August 6, 1965, President Johnson signed the bill into law.

Pre-Clearance Controversy

One aspect of the law that has caused a great deal of controversy is the practice of pre-clearance. The act requires the Department of Justice to review any attempt to change "any voting qualification or prerequisite to voting, or standard, practice, or procedure with respect to voting" in so-called "covered jurisdictions." Covered jurisdictions are ones in which fewer than half of voting-age citizens were registered in 1964. This includes nine states (Alabama, Alaska, Arizona, Georgia, Louisiana, Mississippi, South Carolina, Texas, and most of Virginia) and a number of counties, most of which are in the South. A number of towns in Michigan and New Hampshire are also included.

Under the act's provisions, these states and counties must submit any proposed changes in voter registration requirements to the Department of Justice. The changes may only be enacted with the approval of the Department of Justice. The states and counties affected by this provision of the act consider the law to be unfair and claim that discriminatory voting practices ended long ago. They feel they are being punished for a situation that no longer exists. Despite these objections, a recent review showed a steady decline in the number of proposed voting requirement changes rejected by the Department of Justice. The study found that the Department of Justice rejected less than one-tenth of one percent of all requests submitted between 1996 and 2006.

The act allows a covered **jurisdiction** to "bail out" or receive an exemption if approved by the Department of Justice. To do so, the jurisdiction must demonstrate that it did not practice voting discrimination for 10 years prior to the request to "bail out." It must also show that it has taken positive steps to improve minority voting opportunities. Congress has also allowed individual counties in a covered state to "bail out" separately, even if the state as a whole has not.

See also: Civil Rights Act (1964).

Further Reading

Garrow, David J. *Protest at Selma: Martin Luther King, Jr. and the Voting Rights Act of 1965.* New Haven, CT: Yale University Press, 1980.

War Powers

Constitutional authority granted to Congress and the president to declare war and undertake military operations. The splitting of war powers between Congress and the president has caused repeated controversy and debate involving rival claims by the executive and legislative branches.

Constitutional Basis

Article II, Section 2 of the Constitution provides: "The President shall be Commander in Chief of the Army and Navy of the United States, and of the Militia of the several States, when called into the actual Service of the United States." However, Article I, Section 8, states:

> The Congress shall have Power . . . To declare War, grant Letters of Marque and Reprisal, and make Rules concerning Captures on Land and Water; To raise and support Armies . . . ; To provide and maintain a Navy; To make Rules for the Government and Regulation of the land and naval Forces; To provide for calling forth the Militia to execute the Laws of the Union, suppress Insurrections and repel Invasions; To provide for organizing, arming, and disciplining the Militia, and for governing such Part of them as may be employed in the Service of the United States, reserving to the States respectively, the Appointment of the Officers, and the Authority of training the Militia according to the discipline prescribed by Congress.

At the time the American Constitution was framed, the executive branch wielded war-making power in all other countries. Some delegates to the Constitutional Convention of 1787 favored this practice; others did not think a single person could be trusted with such power. The committee in charge of drafting the Constitution gave to Congress the power to "to declare war." This left the president free to repel sudden attacks, but not to commence war without congressional approval. However, the debate over the division of war powers between the executive and legislative branches was far from settled with the signing of the Constitution.

Use of War Powers

Estimates of the number of instances in which the United States has used its armed forces abroad vary, but a 1999 Library of Congress study listed a total of 277 instances over two centuries. The engagements ranged from dispatching a few soldiers to protect American lives and property abroad to deploying of hundreds of thousands in Korea (1950–1953) and Vietnam (1964–1975) and millions in World War II (1941–1945).

Congress, however, has formally declared war in only five conflicts: the War of 1812, the Mexican War (1846–1848), the Spanish-American War (1890), World War I (1917–1918), and World War II. There have been no formal declarations of war since World War II, although U.S. combat troops were involved in wars in Korea, Vietnam, and the Persian Gulf (1991 and 2003–).

Declared Wars

Early presidents made little use of their war powers. In 1798, during an undeclared naval war with France, President John Adams (1797–1801) went so far as to give the title of commander in chief to George Washington. Three years later President Jefferson (1801–1809) forbade the Navy to attack North African pirates on the ground that Congress had not declared war.

Declared Wars
War of 1812
War with Mexico, 1846
War with Spain, 1898
World War I, 1917
World War II, 1941

The United States Congress has declared war only five times in the nation's history.

Congress's first declaration of war came in 1812. Although few Americans were enthusiastic about the prospects of war with Great Britain, Congress approved a declaration of war. However, President James Madison's (1809–1817) attempt to raise volunteers for an invasion of Canada stalled because some members of Congress felt that doing so would be unconstitutional.

The war with Mexico was also very unpopular among large numbers of Americans, particularly in the North. In 1845, the Democratic-controlled Congress voted to **annex** Texas–make it part of the United States. A year later, American and Mexican troops clashed in territory claimed by both sides and Congress declared war against Mexico. In the 1846, elections, however, the opposition Whig Party took control of the Senate. They attempted unsuccessfully to compel President James Polk (1845–1849) to end the war, or at least supply Congress with information on the objectives of the war and proposed peace terms with Mexico. Ultimately, neither the opposition of a considerable section of the population, nor the efforts of certain members of Congress hampered the administration's war effort.

The Spanish-American War (1898) and World War I (1917–1918) saw little struggle between the branches over war powers. The former was too brief and popular with the public to lead to much second-guessing. In the latter, the U.S. joined the conflict after three years of maintaining a strict policy of neutrality and only after repeated German provocations. Recognizing the complexity of modern technological warfare, Congress voted President Woodrow Wilson (1913–1921) extensive powers to conduct the war as he saw fit.

The last time Congress formally declared war was in response to the Japanese attack on Pearl Harbor in December 1941. Once again, the U.S. attempted to remain neutral while much of the world was at war. After the Japanese attack, however, public opinion swung strongly in favor or war with little dissent or controversy. As in World War I, Congress gave the president expanded powers to deal with the task of managing a global conflict.

Undeclared Wars

In each conflict since World War II (1941–1945), the president, not Congress, has taken the lead in committing U.S. troops. President Harry Truman (1945–1953) ordered American forces to aid South Korea when it was invaded by North Korea in June 1950. He never did ask Congress for a declaration of war, and he waited until six months after the start of hostilities to proclaim the existence of a national emergency. Congress signaled its approval of Truman's action by consistently approving funds to continue the war.

U.S. military aid to Vietnam was initiated by the Truman administration, and by 1964, there were about fifteen thousand U.S. advisers in Vietnam. Critics in Congress called for a total U.S. withdrawal as early as March of that year. However, on August 2 and August 4, 1964, North Vietnamese ships reportedly attacked American destroyers patrolling the Gulf of Tonkin. President Lyndon B. Johnson (1963–1969) responded by ordering an air strike on Hanoi's naval base. On August 7, both chambers of Congress adopted a resolution "to take all necessary measures to repel any armed attack against the forces of the United States and to prevent further aggression."

As opposition to the war grew, some lawmakers argued that the resolution did not commit the United States to massive participation in the war. Supporters of the war disagreed and maintained that, in "limited wars" such as Vietnam, a formal declaration of war was "inappropriate." On December 31, 1970, Congress approved legislation that repealed the Gulf of Tonkin Resolution. This had little effect on

In 1917, President Woodrow Wilson addressed Congress and asked for a declaration of war against Germany. Congress overwhelmingly approved on April 6. (Library of Congress)

presidential control over the war, as both Johnson and his successor, Richard Nixon (1969–1974), continued to increase the size and scope of the U.S. commitment.

The War Powers Resolution

Frustrated with its lack of influence on American military commitments abroad, in 1973 Congress passed legislation designed to limit the president's power to over U.S. forces abroad without congressional approval. Known as the War Powers Resolution, it stated that the president could commit U.S. forces in only three cases:

1. When Congress has declared war,
2. In case of an attack on the United States, its territories, or its armed forces, or
3. In any situation where the law gives the president specific authority to commit troops.

It required the president to consult with Congress before introducing U.S. forces into hostilities and to report any such commitment to Congress within forty-eight hours. The president was required to terminate any troop commitment within sixty to ninety days unless Congress specifically approved its continuation, or if Congress was unable to meet because of an attack on the United States.

President Nixon **vetoed,** or rejected, the resolution, saying it would impose dangerous and unconstitutional restrictions on presidential authority. Congress, however, overrode his veto and passed the resolution without Nixon's signature.

The War Powers Resolution was controversial when it was adopted and it has remained so. Presidents have refused to invoke the law—or even concede its constitutionality—while Congress has been reluctant to challenge the president directly.

Decision Makers

Congress vs. the Vietnam War

Beginning in 1970, the United States Congress passed a series of amendments and **resolutions** expressing its opposition to the way the administration of President Richard M. Nixon (1969–1974) was conducting the Vietnam War. These actions began in response to Nixon's deployment of U.S. troops and military advisers in Cambodia. Congress opposed what they saw as a widening of the war to neighboring countries. By 1973, however, the rift between the legislative and executive branches led Congress to seek to limit the president's power to send armed forces into battle.

In December 1970, Congress passed the Cooper-Church Amendment, which cut off funding to maintain U.S. ground troops in Cambodia and limited the amount of assistance the U.S. air force was allowed to provide for Cambodian troops. A year later, Congress voted to **repeal** the 1964 Gulf of Tonkin Resolution, which had provided the justification for sending U.S. troops into Vietnam. Nixon opposed both of these measures but did not **veto,** or reject, them. He knew that the provisions had enough support that Congress would override his veto and pass them anyway.

By 1973, popular opposition to the war had become widespread and pressure was mounting to end the conflict. In June of that year, Congress passed the Case-Church Amendment prohibiting further U.S. military involvement in Southeast Asia without congressional approval. Once again, President Nixon was forced to accept the legislation, which passed with majorities large enough to override a presidential veto.

The War Powers Resolution of 1973 marked the culmination of Congress's challenge to the president's authority to make war. The resolution states that the president must receive congressional approval before sending troops into action unless American forces troops are already under attack or serious threat of attack. While the constitutionality of the resolution is a matter of debate, Congress has cited the resolution both to oppose and to authorize U.S. involvement in several overseas conflicts since the 1990s.

Recent Developments

The War Powers Resolution has done little to restrain U.S. presidents from using force without explicit congressional approval. Most of the presidents who have served since passage of the resolution have deployed troops on their own authority, only later receiving official approval from Congress. These deployments often triggered clashes with Congress over the scope of the president's authority.

The most recent clash over the president's war powers involved the Authorization for Use of Military Force Against Iraq Resolution of 2002. This resolution gave President George W. Bush (2001–2009) the authority to use military force to "defend the national security of the

United States against the continuing threat posed by Iraq; and enforce all relevant United Nations Security Council Resolutions regarding Iraq." President Bush cited the resolution as authority for the subsequent U.S. invasion of Iraq in 2003.

Congressional opponents of the war argued that the invasion was unauthorized because Iraq posed no credible threat to the United States. Some legislators who voted in favor of the resolution at the time later argued they did not mean for it to be a blank check to invade Iraq. They asserted that they meant only to give the president the power to use force if necessary to protect national security.

See also: Checks and Balances; Foreign Policy Powers; 📖 Henry Clay in Support of the War of 1812, in the **Primary Source Library;** Iraq War Resolution (2002); 📖 Letter to President Bush Urging Him to End the War in Iraq, 2007, in the **Primary Source Library;** Power to Raise an Army; President and Congress; 📖 U.S. Declaration of War on Japan, 1941, in the **Primary Source Library;** 📖 U.S. Declaration of War on Germany, 1941, in the **Primary Source Library;** War Powers Resolution (1973).

Further Reading

Fisher, Louis. *Presidential War Power.* Lawrence: University of Kansas Press, 2004.

Irons, Peter. *War Powers; How the Imperial Presidency Hijacked the Constitution.* New York: Metropolitan, 2005.

War Powers Resolution (1973)

Legislation passed by Congress in 1973 which requires the president to seek congressional approval before committing U.S. forces to military action. The measure resulted from Congress's growing frustration with its inability to influence American military involvement in Indochina and elsewhere overseas. The War Powers resolution is a source of continuing debate concerning Congress's power to affect U.S. foreign policy.

History

On April 30, 1970, President Richard Nixon (1969–1974) surprised Congress by announcing that American forces had invaded Cambodia. Nixon had not consulted Congress about the invasion, and Congress reacted quickly. The House and Senate finally agreed on a compromise bill in 1973.

The final version of the resolution stated that the president could commit U.S. forces to hostilities or imminent hostilities only after Congress declared war, except in a few special cases. These included a national emergency created by an attack on the United States, its territories, or its armed forces; or situations specifically addressed by existing laws. The resolution required the president to consult with Congress "in every possible instance" before introducing U.S. forces into hostilities.

As Chairman of the Joint Chiefs of Staff of the United States armed forces and later as secretary of state, Colin Powell opposed the provisions of the War Powers Resolution. (AP Photo, Stephen Chernin)

The president was also required to notify Congress within forty-eight hours of committing forces to combat.

The resolution called for an end to troop commitments within sixty to ninety days unless Congress specifically permitted them to continue, or unless Congress was unable to meet because of an attack on the United States. It also permitted Congress to pass a concurrent resolution ordering the president to withdraw troops involved in an undeclared or unauthorized war. A concurrent **resolution** is a motion passed by both houses and used to override actions of the executive branch. Since it is not signed the by president, it cannot be **vetoed,** or rejected by the president, and sent back to Congress. In 1983, the Supreme Court declared the use of concurrent resolutions in this manner to be unconstitutional.

Nixon vetoed the resolution, declaring that it would impose restrictions on the authority of the president that would be "both unconstitutional and dangerous to the best interests of our nation." He argued that many of the act's provisions were unconstitutional. Nevertheless, a commanding majority of both houses supported the resolution. The House overrode the veto by a vote of 284–135, and the Senate completed the process with a 75–18 vote.

Constitutional Issues

Article 2 of the Constitution gives Congress the power to raise armies and declare war, but makes the president commander-in-chief of the armed forces. This has led to debate over whether the president or Congress has the authority to send troops into battle. Presidents historically have argued that, as commander-in-chief, the president must have the ability to respond quickly to attacks against the nation. Members of Congress have countered that having the ability to commit troops allows the president to become involved in hostilities without a declaration of war by Congress.

The War Powers Resolution was controversial when it was adopted and it has remained so. Presidents have refused to observe the law, or even to accept its constitutionality. For its part, Congress has been reluctant to challenge

War Powers Provisions

The 1973 War Powers Resolution:

- Stated that the president could commit U.S. armed forces to hostilities or situations where hostilities might be imminent only pursuant to a declaration of war, specific statutory authorization, or a national emergency created by an attack upon the United States, its territories or possessions, or its armed forces.
- Urged the president "in every possible instance" to consult with Congress before committing U.S. forces to hostilities or to situations where hostilities might be imminent, and to consult Congress regularly after such a commitment.
- Required the president to report in writing within forty-eight hours to the Speaker of the House and president pro tempore of the Senate when, in the absence of a declaration of war, U.S. forces were introduced: into hostilities or into situations where hostilities might be imminent; into foreign territory while equipped for combat, except for deployments related solely to supply, replacement, repair, or training of such forces; in numbers that substantially enlarged U.S. forces equipped for combat already located in a foreign country. Required supplementary reports at least every six months while the forces continued to be engaged in such hostilities or situation.
- Authorized the Speaker of the House and the president pro tempore of the Senate to ask the president to convene Congress, if it was not in session, to consider the president's report.
- Required the termination of a troop commitment within sixty days after the president's initial report was submitted, unless Congress declared war, specifically authorized continuation of the commitment, or was physically unable to convene as a result of an armed attack upon the United States; allowed the sixty-day period to be extended for up to thirty days if the president determined and certified to Congress that unavoidable military necessity respecting the safety of U.S. forces required their continued use in bringing about a prompt disengagement.
- Allowed Congress at any time U.S. forces were engaged in hostilities without a declaration of war or specific congressional authorization to pass a concurrent resolution directing the president to disengage such troops. (This use of a concurrent resolution, which does not require the signature of the president, became constitutionally suspect in 1983 when the Supreme Court in *Immigration and Naturalization Service v. Chadha* declared the so-called legislative veto unconstitutional.)
- Set up congressional procedures for consideration of any resolution or bill introduced pursuant to the provisions of the War Powers Resolution.
- Provided that if any provision of the War Powers Resolution was declared invalid, the remainder of the resolution would not be affected.

Passed during the Vietnam era, the War Powers Resolution places specific restrictions on the power of the president to send American troops into harm's way.

the president directly. Presidents have argued that the concurrent resolution provision is unconstitutional, as is the provision that forces the president to withdraw troops if Congress refuses to approve the troop commitment. They claim that this violates the "presentment clause," which states that every bill passed by Congress must be presented to the president before it becomes law. Presidents also have argued that the resolution allows Congress to interfere with the president's ability to carry out the president's constitutional duties as chief executive and commander-in-chief.

Views of members of Congress vary. A 1996 Congressional Research Service report noted opinions ranging from those who find it quite valuable to those who argue for it to be repealed. Although it has few fierce defenders, Congress turned back serious efforts to **repeal** it in 1988 and 1995. In the 1995 debate, Illinois Senator Henry J. Hyde called the resolution "a useless anachronism" and said that Congress could still stop a military operation in its tracks by exerting its power of the purse. Senator Lee H. Hamilton of Indiana disagreed: "The power of the purse is not equivalent to Congress sharing the critical . . . decision, up front, about whether to send troops at all." He went on to say that the power of the purse was usually exercised after the fact, at which point it was very difficult to cut off funding.

See also: Foreign Policy Powers; Power to Raise an Army; President and Congress; War Powers; War Powers Resolution, 1973, in the **Primary Source Library.**

VIEWPOINTS

The Supreme Court in July 1974 rejected President Richard M. Nixon's claim of executive privilege concerning the release of audiotapes made in the Oval Office. The Court ruled unanimously that the tape recordings had to be turned over to Congress. (Guernsey Le Pelley © 1974 *The Christian Science Monitor* [www.csmonitor.com]. All rights reserved.)

Watergate Hearings

Political scandal that moved President Richard M. Nixon (1969–1974) to resign, becoming the only sitting president ever forced out of office. Nixon and several of his top aides were tied to illegal activities that included violations of campaign finance laws and ordering burglars to break into the offices of Nixon's political foes.

Background

On June 17, 1972, District of Columbia police arrested five men who had broken into Democratic National Committee (DNC) offices in a Washington apartment-office complex called the Watergate. One of the men was James W. McCord Jr., director of security for the Committee for the Re-Election of the President. When the 93rd Congress met in January 1973, the Senate promptly created a committee to investigate rumors and charges related to the break-in.

On January 30, McCord and another Nixon aide, G. Gordon Liddy, pleaded guilty to the crime and were convicted. The trial judge, John J. Sirica, told the defendants that they could get lighter sentences if they told what they knew about the break-in. The defendants remained silent, and the White House denied any knowledge about or responsibility for the break-in. Many Washington officials, however, doubted that the president was being truthful. A grand jury was assembled to seek information to determine if criminal charges should be filed against anyone else in the matter.

On March 23, Judge Sirica stunned the court by reading a letter from McCord saying that he and the other defendants had been under political pressure not to identify others who were also involved in the break-in. A few weeks later, former White House aide Alexander Butterfield told the Watergate Committee that the president routinely taped conversations in his office. This set off a struggle between congressional investigators, who wanted to gain control of the tapes, and the White House, which wanted to keep the tapes secret. Several witnesses who testified before the Watergate Committee, including former White House counsel John Dean, claimed that Nixon was directly involved in ordering the break-in.

Members of the Senate Watergate Committee listen to witness Robert Odle (standing, foreground) as he testifies. (AP Photo, File)

Struggle for the Tapes

Nixon at first refused to obey a **subpoena**—an order issued by a court or Congress—to produce the tapes. Nixon claimed executive privilege, the right to resist subpoenas or search warrants for information the president feels must remain confidential. He argued that the taped conversations were "privileged communication." For him to provide the information would be "constitutionally inappropriate" and a violation of the separation of powers between the branches of government.

On August 29, Judge Sirica ruled that the president should surrender the tapes so that a special prosecutor for the government could review them. Later, however, Sirica ruled against the Watergate Committee's request for the same tapes. He said he had no authority to hand them over. On January 25, 1974, U.S. District Court Judge Gerhard A. Gesell ordered Nixon to respond to a subpoena for five tapes. Two weeks later, Nixon sent Gesell a letter saying that disclosure of the tapes "would not be in the public interest." Gesell refused to force the White House to turn over the tapes to the Senate, which unsuccessfully appealed Gesell's ruling.

Meanwhile, the House Judiciary Committee had begun an **impeachment** inquiry against Nixon. It, too, issued subpoenas for tapes and documents. Again, Nixon and his lawyers refused to comply. However, the day before the deadline set by the Judiciary Committee subpoena, Nixon announced that he would release written transcripts of forty-six tapes the next day. The committee was not satisfied. It voted May 1 to inform the president that "you have failed to comply with the committee's subpoena." The case eventually went to the Supreme Court.

Nixon's lawyer argued that the Constitution recognizes the president's claim of executive privilege as part of the doctrine of separation of powers between the branches of government. The Supreme Court disagreed, stating that the public's interest in enforcing criminal laws outweighed the president's claim of executive privilege. Within a week, the Judiciary Committee adopted three articles of impeachment, among them one citing Nixon for contempt of Congress for failing to comply with the panel's subpoenas.

On August 2, the president made public the transcripts of some of the tapes. They showed his participation in a cover-up after the Watergate break-in. They also revealed that he approved using the Central Intelligence Agency (CIA) to block an FBI investigation of the Watergate scandal. Those revelations led directly to his resignation on August 9. Nixon was spared criminal prosecution when he received a pardon from his successor, President Gerald R. Ford (1974–1977), on September 8, 1974. However, nearly twenty members of his 1972 reelection campaign, including several close associates, drew prison sentences for their criminal activities.

See also: Congressional Investigations; President and Congress.

Further Reading

Emery, Fred. *Watergate.* New York: Touchstone, 1995.

Woodward, Bob, and Carl Bernstein. *All the President's Men.* New York: Simon and Schuster, 1974.

Whip

See Party Whips.

Whitewater Investigations

Name given to congressional investigations into several matters involving President Bill Clinton (1993–2001) and First Lady Hillary Rodham Clinton. These investigations revolved around a real estate development company named Whitewater founded by the Clintons and some business partners in the 1980s. The company eventually folded, causing the failure of Madison Guaranty Savings and Loan, a bank that had invested money in the project.

The Investigations

During the 1992 presidential campaign, the *New York Times* reported that the Clintons' business partners in Whitewater were charged with fraud after Madison Guaranty folded. The Clintons never faced similar charges. In November 1993, however, a former Arkansas judge named David Hale claimed that Clinton, while governor of Arkansas, had pressured him to give an illegal loan to one of Clinton's business partners.

In July 1994, the House and Senate Banking committees held separate hearings to determine if any officials in the Clinton administration tried to interfere with government investigations into Whitewater. The hearings uncovered details of a number of improper contacts that led two top treasury officials to resign their posts. In a final report, Senate Banking Committee Democrats said that the Clintons violated no laws or ethical standards as a result of the contacts between White House aides and treasury officials.

When the Republicans gained control of Congress in 1995, they launched fresh inquiries into the Whitewater affair. The Senate created a special committee to handle the probe, while the House gave the task to its Banking Committee. The Senate hearings started with an inquiry into the death of Deputy White House Counsel Vincent W. Foster Jr., who had handled legal work for the Clintons related to Whitewater. After Foster's death, a number of documents apparently were removed from his office. The panel heard occasionally conflicting accounts about how White House aides searched for and handled Foster's papers immediately after his death. The committee also ordered the White House to release notes from meetings in which administration aides had discussed Whitewater. After at first refusing to release the notes, the White House turned them over in December 1995. In 1996, the special committee turned its attention to events in Arkansas during Clinton's term as governor. Among other issues, it focused on the legal work Hillary Rodham Clinton did for Madison Guaranty at that time.

Conflicting Conclusions

In their final report, committee Republicans portrayed a Clinton administration that feared the legal and political fallout from investigations into Whitewaters. The report said that the administration used the power of the executive branch to undermine the probes into the failure of Madison Guaranty. The Republicans said the White House's misuse of power was clearly evident in the hours and days following Foster's suicide. White House officials mishandled documents in Foster's office and thwarted law enforcement authorities in their investigation of Foster's death, the report said.

The report also claimed that Mrs. Clinton ordered the destruction of records related to her representation of Madison Guaranty at the same time federal regulators were investigating the savings and loan. However, Republicans stopped short of charging her with criminal behavior. In their questioning of Mrs. Clinton's actions, Republicans also pointed out the discovery in August 1995 of missing billing records from the Rose Law Firm in the White House private quarters. The Republicans contended that she likely placed the records in the White House book room.

The Democrats on the committee issued a dissenting report, which drew sharply different conclusions. They said Clinton did not misuse his office as either president or governor of Arkansas. The Democrats expressed surprise at the Republican "venom" directed toward Mrs. Clinton. They concluded that the White House did not interfere with ongoing investigations into Whitewater and related matters by government agencies. The evidence presented to the committee showed no unethical or unlawful conduct by any White House official in the days after Foster's suicide, Democrats said. As for the billing records, Democrats pointed out that the documents supported Mrs. Clinton's claim that she did only minor work for Madison Guaranty.

The Whitewater investigations reflected the bitter **partisan** divisions between the Republican-led Congress and the Clinton administration. Republicans repeatedly pressed for investigations into the personal and professional conduct of President Clinton and members of his administration. These efforts led the House to **impeach** Clinton in 1998 for providing false testimony concerning his involvement in an extramarital affair. The Senate acquitted the president, who remained popular with the American public despite the political turmoil surrounding him.

See also: Congressional Investigations; President and Congress.

Women in Congress

Participation by women as members of the Senate and House of Representatives. Women served in Congress before they even earned the right to vote in national elections. Nevertheless, women today still remained underrepresented in the national legislature.

The number of women in Congress has increased since the end of the twentieth century, but the percentage of women in Congress does not come close to representing their percentage in the general population. (Roger L. Wollenberg, UPI, Landov)

A – Z

History

The first woman to serve in Congress was Jeannette Rankin of Montana, elected to the House in 1917. Her state gave women the right to vote before the Nineteenth Amendment to the Constitution **enfranchising** women was **ratified,** or approved, in 1920. The first woman to serve in the Senate was Rebecca L. Felton, appointed October 1, 1922, to fill the Senate vacancy created by the death of Thomas E. Watson. Felton, a Georgia Democrat, took the oath of office on November 21. The next day she yielded her seat to Walter F. George, who had meanwhile been elected to fill the vacancy.

In many places, political parties often ran a deceased officeholder's widow for his vacant seat in the hope of receiving a sympathy vote. Sometimes a widow filled the office by brief appointment until the governor or party leaders could agree on a candidate. This so-called "widow's mandate" marked the beginning of political careers for some women. Edith Nourse Rogers, a Massachusetts Republican, entered the House after her husband died in 1925, and remained there until her death in 1960. Margaret Chase Smith filled her late husband's House seat in 1940 and went on to serve four terms in the Senate, from 1949 to 1973. Hattie W. Caraway, an Arkansas Democrat, was appointed to her late husband's Senate seat in 1931. Arkansas voters returned her to Congress in 1932 and 1938. As women became more active in politics at all levels, however, the congressional tradition of the widow's mandate weakened.

Marriages have also linked members of Congress. Emily Taft Douglas of Illinois was elected to the House in 1944, four years before her husband, Senator Paul H. Douglas. In 1976, Kansas Representative Martha Keys married her House colleague Andrew Jacobs of Indiana. This was the first ever marriage between members of Congress. In 1994, Representative Susan Molinari wed her New York state colleague, Representative Bill Paxon.

Molinari earned another distinction as one of the few women in Congress who were daughters of representatives. She won the seat held by her father, Guy Molinari, who left the House to become Staten Island borough president.

Women in Congress, 1947–2009

Congress	Senate	House
80th (1947-1949)	1	7
81st (1949-1951)	1	9
82nd (1951-1953)	1	10
83rd (1953-1955)	1	12
84th (1955-1957)	1	17
85th (1957-1959)	1	15
86th (1959-1961)	1	17
87th (1961-1963)	2	18
88th (1963-1965)	2	12
89th (1965-1967)	2	11
90th (1967-1969)	1	10
91st (1969-1971)	1	10
92nd (1971-1973)	1	13
93rd (1973-1975)	1	16
94th (1975-1977)	0	17
95th (1977-1979)	2	18
96th (1979-1981)	1	16
97th (1981-1983)	2	19
98th (1983-1985)	2	22
99th (1985-1987)	2	22
100th (1987-1989)	2	23
101st (1989-1991)	2	28
102nd (1991-1993)	3	29
103rd (1993-1995)	7	48
104th (1995-1997)	8	48
105th (1997-1999)	9	51
106th (1999-2001)	9	56
107th (2001-2003)	13	61
108th (2003-2005)	14	60
109th (2005-2007)	14	67
110th (2007-2009)	16	71

***Note:* House totals exclude non-voting delegates.**

Since 1947, the number of women in Congress has increased slowly, with the greatest gains in the last 20 years.

Decision Makers

Hillary Rodham Clinton (1947–)

Hillary Rodham Clinton, a Democratic Senator from New York, is the first former First Lady to serve as a member of Congress. Her husband, Bill Clinton, served two terms as President of the United States, from 1993–2001. In November 2000, Hillary Clinton won election to the Senate and was reelected in 2006.

Clinton played an active role in President Clinton's administration. In 1994, she headed an attempt, ultimately unsuccessful, to establish a universal government healthcare program. She later successfully promoted programs including the State Children's Heath Insurance Program, or S-CHIP. She was a center of attention during the Clinton impeachment hearings and became the only First Lady to be **subpoenaed,** or summoned to testify, by a grand jury.

Clinton's 2000 senatorial election made her the first woman to represent New York in the Senate. Six years later, she handily won reelection, receiving more than two-thirds of the votes cast. In January 2007, she announced her candidacy for the Democratic presidential nomination in 2008. In a closely fought campaign, Clinton competed with Illinois Senator Barack Obama. On January 8, 2008, she became the first woman to win a presidential primary, with a surprise victory in New Hampshire. Throughout the campaign for the Democratic nomination, the two leading candidates—Clinton and Obama—remained in very close contention. After the last primaries in June 2008, however, Clinton threw her support to Obama.

California Democrat Lucille Roybal-Allard won the House seat formerly held by her father, Edward R. Roybal. California Democrat Nancy Pelosi, who entered the House since 1987, was the daughter of Thomas J. D'Alesandro Jr., a House member from 1939 to 1947.

Growing Numbers and Power

The number of women in Congress rose slowly, even after women received the vote in 1920. The first notable increase came in 1928, when nine women were elected to the House. The number had scarcely more than doubled by 1961, when nineteen women served in Congress. After that, women's membership declined slightly and did not regain the 1961 level until 1975. Another drop followed until 1981, when female membership reached twenty for the first time.

The number of women elected to full Senate terms increased dramatically in the 1990s. Before 1987, only six women ever won election to full Senate terms. In 1992, Carol Moseley-Braun of Illinois became the first African American woman elected to the Senate. By 1999, the nine women serving in the Senate were all elected to full terms, and two states–California and Maine–were represented in the Senate solely by women. Democrats Barbara Boxer and Dianne Feinstein were both elected to the Senate from California in 1992; and Republicans Olympia J. Snowe and Susan Collins were elected from Maine in 1994 and 1996, respectively.

The 110th Congress, which opened in January 2007, included 86 women—70 in the House of Representatives and 16 in the Senate. Although these numbers represented historic highs in both chambers, women are still drastically underrepresented in proportion to their numbers in the population. More than half of all Americans are women, yet women make up just 16 percent of the membership in both the House and Senate.

Until recently, women have also found it difficult to move to the top committee and party leadership positions in Congress. Mae Ella Nolan, a California Republican who served from 1923 to 1925, was the first woman to chair a congressional committee. She headed the House Committee on Expenditures in the Post Office Department. In 1995, Nancy Kassebaum of Kansas became the first woman to chair a major Senate committee, Labor and Human Resources. In 2007, Democrat Nancy Pelosi of California made history by becoming the first female Speaker of the House, perhaps the most powerful leadership position in either chamber.

See also: Speaker of the House of Representatives.

Further Reading

Davidson, Roger H., Oleszek, Walter, and Frances E. Lee. *Congress and Its Members.* Eleventh edition. Washington, DC: CQ Press, 2007.

Pollack, Jill S. *Women on the Hill: A History of Women in Congress.* London: Franklin Watts, 1996.

Zone Whips

Another name for regional **whips,** the lowest level of the Democratic leadership structure. Party leaders in the 435-member House of Representatives need layers of assistant leaders to help them ride herd on their members. Regional whips keep in touch with party members from a particular area of the country. Regional whips at one time were known only as zone whips. Later they came to be called regional whips, but the older term is still used along with other names.

Whips are elected by their party caucuses. They are assisted by other party members variously called deputy whips, assistant whips, and at-large whips, as well as regional or zone whips. They play a key role in advising the leadership on how their colleagues intend to vote on the floor of the House and in seeing that their colleagues actually show up to cast their votes.

United States Constitution, Article I, Sections 1–7, 1789

The overall structure of the* bicameral *United States Congress is described in Article I, Sections 1–7, of the United States Constitution. The bicameral legislature is a result of the Connecticut Compromise introduced by Roger Sherman.

United States Constitution, Article I, Sections 1–7

Section 1 - The Legislature
All legislative Powers herein granted shall be vested in a Congress of the United States, which shall consist of a Senate and House of Representatives.

Section 2 - The House
The House of Representatives shall be composed of Members chosen every second Year by the People of the several States, and the Electors in each State shall have the Qualifications requisite for Electors of the most numerous Branch of the State Legislature.

No Person shall be a Representative who shall not have attained to the Age of twenty five Years, and been seven Years a Citizen of the United States, and who shall not, when elected, be an Inhabitant of that State in which he shall be chosen.

(Representatives and direct Taxes shall be apportioned among the several States which may be included within this Union, according to their respective Numbers, which shall be determined by adding to the whole Number of free Persons, including those bound to Service for a Term of Years, and excluding Indians not taxed, three fifths of all other Persons.)

The previous sentence in parentheses was modified by the 14th Amendment, Section 2.

The actual Enumeration shall be made within three Years after the first Meeting of the Congress of the United States, and within every subsequent Term of ten Years, in such Manner as they shall by Law direct. The Number of Representatives shall not exceed one for every thirty Thousand, but each State shall have at Least one Representative; and until such enumeration shall be made, the State of New Hampshire shall be entitled to chuse three, Massachusetts eight, Rhode Island and Providence Plantations one, Connecticut five, New York six, New Jersey four, Pennsylvania eight, Delaware one, Maryland six, Virginia ten, North Carolina five, South Carolina five and Georgia three.

When vacancies happen in the Representation from any State, the Executive Authority thereof shall issue Writs of Election to fill such Vacancies.

The House of Representatives shall chuse their Speaker and other Officers; and shall have the sole Power of Impeachment.

Section 3 - The Senate
The Senate of the United States shall be composed of two Senators from each State, *(chosen by the Legislature thereof,)*

The preceding words in parentheses were superseded by the 17th Amendment, Section 1.

for six Years; and each Senator shall have one Vote.

Immediately after they shall be assembled in Consequence of the first Election, they shall be divided as equally as may be into three Classes. The Seats of the Senators of the first Class shall be vacated at the Expiration of the second Year, of the second Class at the Expiration of the fourth Year, and of the third Class at the Expiration of the sixth Year, so that one third may be chosen every second Year; *(and if Vacancies happen by Resignation, or otherwise, during the Recess of the Legislature of any State, the Executive thereof may make temporary Appointments until the next Meeting of the Legislature, which shall then fill such Vacancies.)*

The preceding words in parentheses were superseded by the 17th Amendment, Section 2.

No person shall be a Senator who shall not have attained to the Age of thirty Years, and been nine Years a Citizen of the United States, and who shall not, when elected, be an Inhabitant of that State for which he shall be chosen.

The Vice President of the United States shall be President of the Senate, but shall have no Vote, unless they be equally divided.

The Senate shall chuse their other Officers, and also a President pro tempore, in the absence of the Vice President, or when he shall exercise the Office of President of the United States.

The Senate shall have the sole Power to try all Impeachments. When sitting for that Purpose, they shall be on Oath or Affirmation. When the President of the United States is tried, the Chief Justice shall preside: And no Person shall be convicted without the Concurrence of two thirds of the Members present.

Judgment in Cases of Impeachment shall not extend further than to removal from Office, and disqualification to hold and enjoy any Office of honor, Trust or Profit under the United States: but the Party convicted shall nevertheless be liable and subject to Indictment, Trial, Judgment and Punishment, according to Law.

Section 4 - Elections, Meetings
The Times, Places and Manner of holding Elections for Senators and Representatives, shall be prescribed in each State by the Legislature thereof; but the Congress may at any time by Law make or alter such Regulations, except as to the Place of Chusing Senators.

The Congress shall assemble at least once in every Year, and such Meeting shall *(be on the first Monday in December,)*

The preceding words in parentheses were superseded by the 20th Amendment, Section 2.

unless they shall by Law appoint a different Day.

Section 5 - Membership, Rules, Journals, Adjournment
Each House shall be the Judge of the Elections, Returns and Qualifications of its own Members, and a Majority of each shall constitute a Quorum to do Business; but a smaller number may adjourn from day to day, and may be authorized to compel the Attendance of absent Members, in such Manner, and under such Penalties as each House may provide.

Each House may determine the Rules of its Proceedings, punish its Members for disorderly Behavior, and, with the Concurrence of two-thirds, expel a Member.

Each House shall keep a Journal of its Proceedings, and from time to time publish the same, excepting such Parts as may in their Judgment require Secrecy; and the Yeas and Nays of the Members of either House on any question shall, at the Desire of one fifth of those Present, be entered on the Journal.

Neither House, during the Session of Congress, shall, without the Consent of the other, adjourn for more than three days, nor to any other Place than that in which the two Houses shall be sitting.

Section 6 - Compensation
(The Senators and Representatives shall receive a Compensation for their Services, to be ascertained by Law, and paid out of the Treasury of the United States.)

The preceding words in parentheses were modified by the 27th Amendment.

They shall in all Cases, except Treason, Felony and Breach of the Peace, be privileged from Arrest during their Attendance at the Session of their respective Houses, and in going to and returning from the same; and for any Speech or Debate in either House, they shall not be questioned in any other Place.

No Senator or Representative shall, during the Time for which he was elected, be appointed to any civil Office under the Authority of the United States which shall have been created, or the Emoluments whereof shall have been increased during such time; and no Person holding any Office under the United States, shall be a Member of either House during his Continuance in Office.

Section 7 - Revenue Bills, Legislative Process, Presidential Veto
All bills for raising Revenue shall originate in the House of Representatives; but the Senate may propose or concur with Amendments as on other Bills.

Every Bill which shall have passed the House of Representatives and the Senate, shall, before it become a Law, be presented to the President of the United States; If he approve he shall sign it, but if not he shall return it, with his Objections to that House in which it shall have originated, who shall enter the Objections at large on their Journal, and proceed to reconsider it. If after such Reconsideration two thirds of that House shall agree to pass the Bill, it shall be sent, together with the Objections, to the other House, by which it shall likewise be reconsidered, and if approved by two thirds of that House, it shall become a Law. But in all such Cases the Votes of both Houses shall be determined by Yeas and Nays, and the Names of the Persons voting for and against the Bill shall be entered on the Journal of each House respectively. If any Bill shall not be returned by the President within ten Days (Sundays excepted) after it shall have been presented to him, the Same shall be a Law, in like Manner as if he had signed it, unless the Congress by their Adjournment prevent its Return, in which Case it shall not be a Law.

Every Order, Resolution, or Vote to which the Concurrence of the Senate and House of Representatives may be necessary (except on a question of Adjournment) shall be presented to the President of the United States; and before the Same shall take Effect, shall be approved by him, or being disapproved by him, shall be repassed by two thirds of the Senate and House of Representatives, according to the Rules and Limitations prescribed in the Case of a Bill.

See also: House of Representatives in **Congress A to Z;** Senate in **Congress A to Z.**

United States Constitution, Article I, Section 8, 1789

Article I, Section 8, of the United States Constitution lists the powers of Congress. The last clause, often called the "necessary and proper clause," has been interpreted to give Congress far-reaching authority in areas as varied as interstate commerce and segregation.

United States Constitution, Article I, Section 8

The Congress shall have Power To lay and collect Taxes, Duties, Imposts and Excises, to pay the Debts and provide for the common Defence and general Welfare of the United States; but all Duties, Imposts and Excises shall be uniform throughout the United States;

To borrow money on the credit of the United States;

To regulate Commerce with foreign Nations, and among the several States, and with the Indian Tribes;

To establish an uniform Rule of Naturalization, and uniform Laws on the subject of Bankruptcies throughout the United States;

To coin Money, regulate the Value thereof, and of foreign Coin, and fix the Standard of Weights and Measures;

To provide for the Punishment of counterfeiting the Securities and current Coin of the United States;

To establish Post Offices and Post Roads;

To promote the Progress of Science and useful Arts, by securing for limited Times to Authors and Inventors the exclusive Right to their respective Writings and Discoveries;

To constitute Tribunals inferior to the supreme Court;

To define and punish Piracies and Felonies committed on the high Seas, and Offenses against the Law of Nations;

To declare War, grant Letters of Marque and Reprisal, and make Rules concerning Captures on Land and Water;

To raise and support Armies, but no Appropriation of Money to that Use shall be for a longer Term than two Years;

To provide and maintain a Navy;

To make Rules for the Government and Regulation of the land and naval Forces;

To provide for calling forth the Militia to execute the Laws of the Union, suppress Insurrections and repel Invasions;

To provide for organizing, arming, and disciplining the Militia, and for governing such Part of them as may be employed in the Service of the United States, reserving to the States respectively, the Appointment of the Officers, and the Authority of training the Militia according to the discipline prescribed by Congress;

To exercise exclusive Legislation in all Cases whatsoever, over such District (not exceeding ten Miles square) as may, by Cession of particular States, and the acceptance of Congress, become the Seat of the Government of the United States, and to exercise like Authority over all Places purchased by the Consent of the Legislature of the State in which the Same shall be, for the Erection of Forts, Magazines, Arsenals, dock-Yards, and other needful Buildings; And

To make all Laws which shall be necessary and proper for carrying into Execution the foregoing Powers, and all other Powers vested by this Constitution in the Government of the United States, or in any Department or Officer thereof.

See also: Constitution of the United States in **Congress A to Z;** Expressed Powers in **Congress A to Z;** Implied Powers in **Congress A to Z.**

United States Constitution, Article II, Sections 2, 3, and 4, 1789

Article II, Sections 2, 3, and 4, of the United States Constitution, outlines the key powers of the presidency and the checks and balances between the executive and legislative branches. Section 2 requires the Senate to ratify treaties; Section 4 gives Congress the power to impeach the president and other officials of the executive branch.

Article II, Sections 2, 3, and 4

Section 2 - Civilian Power over Military, Cabinet, Pardon Power, Appointments

The President shall be Commander in Chief of the Army and Navy of the United States, and of the Militia of the several States, when called into the actual Service of the United States; he may require the Opinion, in writing, of the principal Officer in each of the executive Departments, upon any subject relating to the Duties of their respective Offices, and he shall have Power to Grant Reprieves and Pardons for Offenses against the United States, except in Cases of Impeachment.

He shall have Power, by and with the Advice and Consent of the Senate, to make Treaties, provided two thirds of the Senators present concur; and he shall nominate, and by and with the Advice and Consent of the Senate, shall appoint Ambassadors, other public Ministers and Consuls, Judges of the supreme Court, and all other Officers of the United States, whose Appointments are not herein otherwise provided for, and which shall be established by Law: but the Congress may by Law vest the Appointment of such inferior Officers, as they think proper, in the President alone, in the Courts of Law, or in the Heads of Departments.

The President shall have Power to fill up all Vacancies that may happen during the Recess of the Senate, by granting Commissions which shall expire at the End of their next Session.

Section 3 - State of the Union, Convening Congress

He shall from time to time give to the Congress Information of the State of the Union, and recommend to their Consideration such Measures as he shall judge necessary and expedient; he may, on extraordinary Occasions, convene both Houses, or either of them, and in Case of Disagreement between them, with Respect to the Time of Adjournment, he may adjourn them to such Time as he shall think proper; he shall receive Ambassadors and other public Ministers; he shall take Care that the Laws be faithfully executed, and shall Commission all the Officers of the United States.

Section 4 - Disqualification

The President, Vice President and all civil Officers of the United States, shall be removed from Office on Impeachment for, and Conviction of, Treason, Bribery, or other high Crimes and Misdemeanors.

See also: House of Representatives in **Congress A to Z;** Senate in **Congress A to Z;** Treaty Power in **Congress A to Z.**

South Carolina Electoral Vote Document, 1789

The electors from South Carolina signed this document in 1789. It certified their vote for George Washington to be the country's first president.

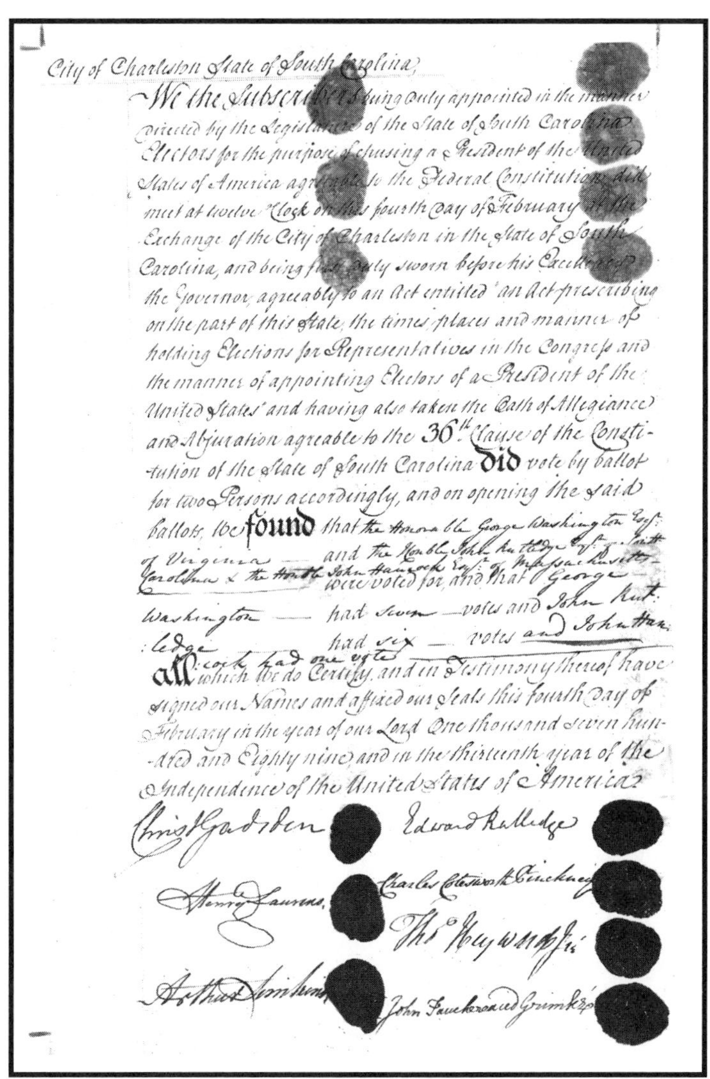

City of Charleston State of South Carolina

We the Subscribers being duly appointed in the manner directed by the Legislature of the State of South Carolina Electors for the purpose of chusing a President of the United States of America agreeable to the Federal Constitution did meet at twelve o'Clock on this fourth day of February at the Exchange of the City of Charleston in the State of South Carolina, and being first duly sworn before his Excellency the Governor agreeably to an Act entitled 'an Act prescribing on the part of this State the times places and manner of holding Elections for Representatives in the Congress and the manner of appointing Electors of a President of the United States' and having also taken the Oath of Allegiance and Abjuration agreeable to the 36th Clause of the Constitution of the State of South Carolina did vote by ballot for two Persons accordingly, and on opening the said ballots we found that the Honorable George Washington Esqr. of Virginia — and the Honble. John Rutledge Esqr. of South Carolina & the Honble. John Hancock Esqr. of Massachusetts were voted for, and that George Washington — had seven — votes and John Rutledge had six — votes and John Hancock had one vote all which we do Certify, and in Testimony thereof have signed our Names and affixed our Seals this fourth day of February in the year of our Lord One thousand seven hundred and Eighty nine, and in the thirteenth year of the Independence of the United States of America

Christ. Gadsden — Edward Rutledge

Henry Laurens — Charles Cotesworth Pinckney

Thos. Heyward Junr.

Arthur Simkins — John Faucheraud Grimké

Twelfth Amendment, 1804

The Twelfth Amendment was proposed as a direct result of a flaw in the Constitution's original process for electing the president and vice president. Because electors did not indicate their choices for the offices, the candidate with the most electoral votes became president and the runner up became vice president. This situation led to a tie electoral vote in the election of 1800.

Twelfth Amendment

Twelfth Amendment - Choosing the President, Vice-President

The Electors shall meet in their respective states, and vote by ballot for President and Vice-President, one of whom, at least, shall not be an inhabitant of the same state with themselves; they shall name in their ballots the person voted for as President, and in distinct ballots the person voted for as Vice-President, and they shall make distinct lists of all persons voted for as President, and of all persons voted for as Vice-President and of the number of votes for each, which lists they shall sign and certify, and transmit sealed to the seat of the government of the United States, directed to the President of the Senate;

The President of the Senate shall, in the presence of the Senate and House of Representatives, open all the certificates and the votes shall then be counted;

The person having the greatest Number of votes for President, shall be the President, if such number be a majority of the whole number of Electors appointed; and if no person have such majority, then from the persons having the highest numbers not exceeding three on the list of those voted for as President, the House of Representatives shall choose immediately, by ballot, the President. But in choosing the President, the votes shall be taken by states, the representation from each state having one vote; a quorum for this purpose shall consist of a member or members from two-thirds of the states, and a majority of all the states shall be necessary to a choice. And if the House of Representatives shall not choose a President whenever the right of choice shall devolve upon them, before the fourth day of March next following, then the Vice-President shall act as President, as in the case of the death or other constitutional disability of the President.

The person having the greatest number of votes as Vice-President, shall be the Vice-President, if such number be a majority of the whole number of Electors appointed, and if no person have a majority, then from the two highest numbers on the list, the Senate shall choose the Vice-President; a quorum for the purpose shall consist of two-thirds of the whole number of Senators, and a majority of the whole number shall be necessary to a choice. But no person constitutionally ineligible to the office of President shall be eligible to that of Vice-President of the United States.

See also: Amending the Constitution in **Congress A to Z;** Constitution of the United States in **Congress A to Z;** Constitutional Amendments Affecting the Presidency in **Congress A to Z;** Power to Select the President in **Congress A to Z.**

Henry Clay in Support of the War of 1812

In 1811, Kentuckian Henry Clay resigned his Senate seat and was elected without opposition to the House of Representatives. There, his colleagues elected him Speaker of the House.

Since the end of the American Revolution in 1783, the British had stirred up Native American resistance in the Northwest and interfered with the nation's foreign trade. Perhaps worst of all, Britain stopped American ships at sea and impressed, or kidnapped, sailors they claimed were British seamen. Many Americans, outraged at British actions, called for war; they became known as War Hawks. Clay, the leader of the War Hawks, favored war with Great Britain as a matter of national pride. With war imminent, Clay explained why he believed the nation should declare war on Great Britain.

Henry Clay in Support of the War of 1812

. . . [I]f the reports which we now hear are true, that with England all hope of honorable accommodation is at an end, and that with France our negotiations are in a fowardness encouraging expectations of a favorable result, where is the motive for longer delay? The final step ought to be taken; and that step is WAR. By what course of measures we have reached the present crisis, is not now a question for freemen and patriots to discuss. It exists; and it is by open and manly war only that we can get through it with honor and advantage to the country. Our wrongs have been great; our cause is just; and if we are decided and firm, success is inevitable.

Let war therefore be forthwith proclaimed against England. With her there can be no motive for delay. Any further discussion, any new attempt at negotiation, would be as fruitless as it would be dishonorable. With France we shall still be at liberty to pursue the course which circumstances may require. . . .

But it is said that we are not prepared for war, and ought therefore not to declare it. This is an idle objection, which can have weight with the timid and [cowardly] only. The fact is otherwise. Our preparations are adequate to every essential object. . . .

But our coast and seaport towns are exposed and may be annoyed. Even this danger, which exists in a certain degree, has been much exaggerated. No land force can be brought to bear against them, because Great Britain has none to spare for such a service; and without a land force, no great impression can be made. Ships of war cannot approach near the coast, except at the entrance of our great bays and rivers. They cannot annoy the sea coast generally by their cannon; and if detachments of marines should be sent on shore, they may be repelled by the militia where they land. . . .

The great question on which the United States have to decide, is, whether they will relinquish the ground which they now hold, or maintain it with the firmness and vigor becoming freemen. That the sense of the nation favors the latter course, is proved by a series of important and solemn facts, which speak a language not to be misunderstood. From the first attack by Great Britain on our neutral rights in 1805, to the present day, these facts have been multiplied, yearly, by the acts of Congress, by the proceedings of the state legislatures, and by the voice of the people. Let not the Representatives of the People, therefore, in either branch of the government, disappoint their reasonable wishes and just expectations.

The pretensions of Great Britain, so unjustly set up, and pertinaciously maintained, by her orders in council, not to enumerate other wrongs, particularly the impressment of our seamen, arrogate to her the complete dominion of the sea, and the exclusion of every flag from it, which does not sail under her license, and on the conditions which she imposes. These pretensions involve no local interest, nor are they of a transient nature. In their operation they violate the rights, and wound deeply the best interests, of the whole American people. If we yield to them, at this time, the cause may be considered as abandoned. There will be no rallying point hereafter. Future attempts to retaliate the wrongs of foreign powers and to vindicate our most sacred rights, will be in vain. . . .

See also: War Powers in **Congress A to Z.**

Gibbons v. Ogden, 1824

In* Gibbons v. Ogden, *1824, the United States Supreme Court clearly ruled that Congress has the authority, under the commerce clause of the Constitution, to regulate interstate commerce.

Gibbons v. Ogden

The acts of the Legislature of the State of New-York, granting to Robert R. Livingston and Robert Fulton the exclusive navigation of all the waters within the jurisdiction of that State, with boats moved by fire or steam, for a term of years, are repugnant to that clause of the constitution of the United States, which authorizes Congress to regulate commerce, so far as the said acts prohibit vessels licensed, according to the laws of the United States, for carrying on the coasting trade, from navigating the said waters by means of fire or steam. . . .

Aaron Ogden filed his bill in the Court of Chancery of that State, against Thomas Gibbons, setting forth the several acts of the Legislature thereof, enacted for the purpose of securing to Robert R. Livingston and Robert Fulton, the exclusive navigation of all the waters within the jurisdiction of that State, with boats moved by fire or steam, for a term of years which has not yet expired; . . .

The bill stated an assignment from Livingston and Fulton to one John R. Livingston, and from him to the complainant, Ogden, of the right to navigate the waters between Elizabethtown, and other places in New-Jersey, and the city of New-York; and that Gibbons, the defendant below, was in possession of two steam boats, called the Stoudinger and the Bellona, which were actually employed in running between New-York and Elizabethtown, in violation of the exclusive privilege conferred on the complainant, and praying an injunction to restrain the said Gibbons from using the said boats, or any other propelled by fire or steam, in navigating the waters within the territory of New-York. The injunction having been awarded, the answer of Gibbons was filed; in which he stated, that the boats employed by him were duly enrolled and licensed, to be employed in carrying on the coasting trade . . . . And the defendant insisted on his right, in virtue of such licenses, to navigate the waters between Elizabethtown and the city of New-York, the said acts of the Legislature of the State of New-York to the contrary notwithstanding. . . .

Principles of interpretation.

The power of regulating commerce extends to the regulation of navigation.

The power to regulate commerce extends to every species of commercial intercourse between the United States and foreign nations, and among the several States. It does not stop at the external boundary of a State.

But it does not extend to a commerce which is completely internal.

The power to regulate commerce is general, and has no limitations but such as are prescribed in the constitution itself.

The power to regulate commerce, so far as it extends, is exclusively vested in Congress, and no part of it can be exercised by a State.

State inspection laws, health laws, and laws for regulating the internal commerce of a State, and those which respect turnpike roads, ferries, &c. are not within the power granted to Congress.

The laws of N. Y. granting to R.R.L. and R. F. the exclusive right of navigating the waters of that State with steam boats, are in collision with the acts of Congress regulating the coasting trade, which being made in pursuance of the constitution, are supreme, and the State laws must yield to that supremacy, even though enacted in pursuance of powers acknowledged to remain in the States.

A license under the acts of Congress for regulating the coasting trade, gives a permission to carry on that trade.

The license is not merely intended to confer the national character.

The power of regulating commerce extends to navigation carried on by vessels exclusively employed in transporting passengers.

The power of regulating commerce extends to vessels propelled by steam or fire, as well as to those navigated by the instrumentality of wind and sails.

Mr. Webster, for the appellant, admitted, that there was a very respectable weight of authority in favour of the decision, which was sought to be reversed.

The laws in question, he knew, had been deliberately re-enacted by the Legislature of New-York; and they had also received the sanction, at different times, of all her judicial tribunals, than which there were few, if any, in the country, more justly entitled to respect and deference. The disposition of the Court would be, undoubtedly, to support, if it could, laws so passed and so sanctioned. He admitted, therefore, that it was justly expected of him that he should make out a clear case; and unless he did so, he did not hope for a reversal. It should be remembered, however, that the whole of this branch of power, as exercised by this Court, was a power of revision. The question must be decided by the State Courts, and decided in a particular manner, before it could be brought here at all. Such decisions alone gave the Court jurisdiction; and therefore, while they are to be respected as the judgments of learned Judges, they are yet in the condition of all decisions from which the law allows an appeal.

See also: Commerce Clause in **Congress A to Z;** *Gibbons v. Ogden* (1824) in **Congress A to Z.**

House Procedure for the Election of John Quincy Adams, 1825

The following rules were used in deciding the presidential election of 1824. On February 9, 1825, John Quincy Adams (1825–1829) was elected in accordance with these rules. They provide a precedent for future elections of a president, although the House can change the rules.

House Procedure for the Election of John Quincy Adams

1. In the event of its appearing, on opening all the certificates, and counting the votes given by the electors of the several States for President, that no person has a majority of the votes of the whole number of electors appointed, the same shall be entered on the Journals of this House.

2. The roll of the House shall then be called by States; and, on its appearing that a Member or Members from two-thirds of the States are present the House shall immediately proceed, by ballot, to choose a President from the persons having the highest numbers, not exceeding three, on the list of those voted for as President; and, in case neither of those persons shall receive the votes of a majority of all the States on the first ballot, the House shall continue to ballot for a President, without interruption . . . until a President be chosen.

3. The doors of the Hall shall be closed during the balloting, except against the Members of the Senate, stenographers, and the officers of the House.

4. From the commencement of the balloting until an election is made no proposition to adjourn shall be received, unless on the motion of one State, seconded by another State, and the question shall be decided by States. The same rule shall be observed in regard to any motion to change the usual hour for the meeting of the House.

5. In balloting the following mode shall be observed, to wit: The Representatives of each State shall be arranged and seated together, beginning with the seats at the right hand of the Speaker's chair, with the Members from the State of Maine; thence, proceeding with the Members from the States, in the order the States are usually named for receiving petitions . . . until all are seated.

A ballot box shall be provided for each State.

The Representatives of each State shall, in the first instance, ballot among themselves, in order to ascertain the vote of their State; and they may, if necessary, appoint tellers of their ballots.

After the vote of each State is ascertained, duplicates thereof shall be made out; and in case any one of the persons from whom the choice is to be made shall receive a majority of the votes given, on any one balloting by the Representatives of a State, the name of that person shall be written on each of the duplicates; and in case the votes so given shall be divided so that neither of said persons shall have a majority of the whole number of votes given by such State, on any one balloting, then the word "divided" shall be written on each duplicate.

After the delegation from each State shall have ascertained the vote of their State, the Clerk shall name the States in the order they are usually named for receiving petitions; and as the name of each is called the Sergeant-at-Arms shall present to the delegation of each two ballot boxes, in each of which shall be deposited, by some Representative of the State, one of the duplicates made as aforesaid of the vote of said State, in the presence and subject to the examination of all the Members from said State then present; and where there is more than one Representative from a State, the duplicates shall not both be deposited by the same person.

When the votes of the States are thus all taken in, the Sergeant-at-Arms shall carry one of said ballot boxes to one table and the other to a separate and distinct table. One person from each State represented in the balloting shall be appointed by the Representatives to tell off said ballots; but [if they] fail to appoint a teller, the Speaker shall appoint.

The said tellers shall divide themselves into two sets, as nearly equal in number as can be, and one of the said sets of tellers shall proceed to count the votes in one of said boxes, and the other set the votes in the other box.

When the votes are counted by the different sets of tellers, the result shall be reported to the House; and if the reports agree, the same shall be accepted as the true votes of the States; but if the reports disagree, the States shall proceed, in the same manner as before, to a new ballot.

6. All questions arising after the balloting commences, requiring the decision of the House, which shall be decided by the House, voting per capita, to be incidental to the power of choosing a President, shall be decided by States without debate; and in case of an equal division of the votes of States, the question shall be lost.

7. When either of the persons from whom the choice is to be made shall have received a majority of all the States, the Speaker shall declare the same, and that person is elected President of the United States.

8. The result shall be immediately communicated to the Senate by message, and a committee of three persons shall be appointed to inform the President of the United States and the President-elect of said election.

See also: Adams, John Quincy (1767–1848) in **Congress A to Z;** Power to Select the President in **Congress A to Z.**

Resolution Annexing Texas to the United States, 1845

In the election campaign of 1844, Democrat James K. Polk (1845–1849) called for the annexation of the Republic of Texas. After Polk's electoral victory, Congress acted to annex the ten-year old republic. Early in 1845, a joint resolution for annexation passed both houses of the U. S. Congress–even before Polk's inauguration. It was signed by outgoing President John Tyler (1841–1845) on March 1, 1845, subject to acceptance by the Republic of Texas. Texas quickly accepted the resolution.

Resolution Annexing Texas to the United States

Resolved by the Senate and House of Representatives of the United States in Congress assembled, That Congress doth consent the territory properly included within, and rightfully belonging to the Republic of Texas, may be erected into a new State, to be called the State of Texas, with a republican form of government, to be adopted by the people of said republic, by deputies in convention assembled, with the consent of the existing government, in order that the same may be admitted as one of the States of this Union.

2. And be it further resolved, That the foregoing consent of Congress is given upon the following conditions, and with the following guarantees, to wit:

First, Said State to be formed, subject to the adjustment by this government of all questions of boundary that may arise with other governments; and the constitution therof, with the proper evidence of its adoption by the people of said Republic of Texas, shall be transmitted to the President of the United States, to be laid before Congress for its final action, on or before the first day of January, one thousand eight hundred and forty-six.

Second, Said State, when admitted into the Union, after ceding to the United States, all public edifices, fortifications, barracks, ports and harbors, navy and navy-yards, docks, magazines, arms, armaments, and all other property and means pertaining to the public defence belonging to the said Republic of Texas, shall retain all the public funds, debts, taxes, and dues of every kind, which may belong to or be due and owning to said Republic of Texas; and shall also retain all the vacant and unappropriated lands lying within its limits, to be applied to the payment of the debts and liabilities of said Republic of Texas, and the residue of said lands, after discharging said debts and liabilities, to be disposed of as State may direct; but in no event are said debts and liabilities to become a charge upon the Government of the United States.

Third, New States, of convenient size, not exceeding four in number, in addition to said State of Texas, and having sufficient population, may hereafter, by the consent of the said State, be formed out of the territory thereof, which shall be entitled to admission under the provisions of the federal constitution. And as such States as may be formed out of that portion of said territory lying south of thirty-six degrees thirty minutes north latitude, commonly known as the Missouri compromise line, shall be admitted to the Union with or without slavery, as the people of each State asking permission may desire. And in such State or States as shall be formed north of said Missouri compromise line, slavery, or involuntary servitude, (except for crime) shall be prohibited.

3. And be it further resolved, That if the President of the United States shall in his judgement and discretion deem it most advisable, instead of proceeding to submit the foregoing resolution of the Republic of Texas, as an overture on the part of the United States for admission, to negotiate with the Republic; then,

Be it Resolved, That a State, to be formed out of the present Republic of Texas, with suitable extant and boundaries, and with two representatives in Congress, until the next appointment of representation, shall be admitted into the Union, by virtue of this act, on an equal footing with the existing States as soon as the terms and conditions of such admission, and the cession of the remaining Texian territory to the United States be agreed upon by the Governments of Texas and the United States: And that the sum of one hundred thousand dollars be, and the same is hereby, appropriated to defray the expenses of missions and negotiations, to agree upon the terms of said admission and cession, either by treaty to be submitted to the Senate, or by articles to be submitted to the two houses of Congress, as the President may direct.

See also: New States, Admission of in **Congress A to Z.**

Article of Impeachment Against Andrew Johnson, 1868

Andrew Johnson (1865–1869) was the first United States president to be impeached by the House of Representatives. After a tense Senate trial, Johnson was acquitted by one vote.

Article of Impeachment Against Andrew Johnson

ARTICLE I.

That said Andrew Johnson, President of the United States, on the 21st day of February, in the year of our Lord, 1868, at Washington, in the District of Columbia, unmindful of the high duties of his office, of his oath of office, and of the requirement of the Constitution that he should take care that the laws be faithfully executed, did unlawfully and in violation of the Constitution and laws of the United States issue and order in writing for the removal of Edwin M. Stanton from the office of Secretary for the Department of War, said Edwin M. Stanton having been theretofore duly appointed and commissioned, by and with the advice and consent of the Senate of the United States, as such Secretary, and said Andrew Johnson, President of the United States, on the 12th day of August, in the year of our Lord 1867, and during the recess of said Senate, having been suspended by his order Edwin M. Stanton from said office, and within twenty days after the first day of the next meeting of said Senate, that is to say, on the 12th day of December, in the year last aforesaid, having reported to said Senate such suspension, with the evidence and reasons for his action in the case and the name of the person designated to perform the duties of such office temporarily until the next meeting of the Senate, and said Senate thereafterward, on the 13th day of January, in the year of our Lord 1868, having duly considered the evidence and reasons reported by said Andrew Johnson for said suspension, and having been refused to concur in said suspension, whereby and by force of the provisions of an act entitled "An act regulating the tenure of certain civil offices," passed March 2, 1867, said Edwin M. Stanton did forthwith resume the functions of his office, whereof the said Andrew Johnson had then and there due notice, and said Edwin Stanton, by reason of the premises, on said 21st day of February, being lawfully entitled to hold said office of Secretary for the Department of War, which said order for the removal of said Edwin M. Stanton is, in substance, as follows, that is to say:

EXECUTIVE MANSION,

WASHINGTON, DC, *February* 21, 1868

SIR: By virtue of the power and authority vested in me, as President by the Constitution and laws of the United States, you are hereby removed from the office of Secretary for the Department of War, and your functions as such will terminate upon receipt of their communication. You will transfer to Brevet Major-General L. Thomas, Adjutant-General of the Army, who has this day been authorized and empowered to act as Secretary of War ad interim, all books, paper and other public property now in your custody and charge.

Respectfully yours, ANDREW JOHNSON.

Hon. E. M. Stanton, Secretary of War

Which order was unlawfully issued, and with intent then are there to violate the act entitled "An act regulating the tenure of certain civil office," passed March 2, 1867; and, with the further intent contrary to the provisions of said act, and in violation thereof, and contrary to the provisions of the Constitution of the United States, and without the advice and consent of the Senate of the United States, the said Senate then and there being in session, to remove said Edwin M. Stanton from the office of Secretary for the Department of War, the said Edwin M. Stanton being then and there Secretary of War, and being then and there in the due and lawful execution of the duties of said office, whereby said Andrew Johnson, President of the United States, did then and there commit, and was guilty of a high misdemeanor in office.

See also: Articles of Impeachment against Richard M. Nixon, 1974; Articles of Impeachment against William Jefferson Clinton, 1998; Impeachment Power in **Congress A to Z.**

Congressional Government, 1885

In 1885, Woodrow Wilson, then a graduate student at Johns Hopkins University, wrote a book titled* Congressional Government, *in which he criticized the committee system, run by powerful committee chairs, as fundamentally undemocratic. He came to this conclusion during a time in the nation's history when Congress, rather than the presidency, dominated the national government.

Congressional Government

Congress always makes what haste it can to legislate. It is the prime object of its rules to expedite law-making. Its customs are fruits of its characteristic diligence in enactment. Be the matters small or great, frivolous or grave, which busy it, its aim is to have laws always a-making. Its temper is strenuously legislative. That it cannot regulate all the questions to which its attention is weekly invited is its misfortune, not its fault; is due to the human limitation of its faculties, not to any narrow circumscription of its desires. If its committee machinery is inadequate to the task of bringing to action more than one out of every hundred of the bills introduced, it is not because the quick clearance of the docket is not the motive of its organic life. If legislation, therefore, were the only or the chief object for which it should live, it would not be possible to withhold admiration from those clever hurrying rules and those inexorable customs which seek to facilitate it. Nothing but a doubt as to whether or not Congress should confine itself to law-making can challenge with a question the utility of its organization as a facile statute-devising machine.

Wilson notes that legislators should look at the whole picture.

The political philosopher of these days of self-government has, however, something more than a doubt with which to gainsay the usefulness of a sovereign representative body which confines itself to legislation to the exclusion of all other functions. Buckle declared, indeed, that the chief use and value of legislation nowadays lay in its opportunity and power to remedy the mistakes of the legislation of the past; that it was beneficent only when it carried healing in its wings; that repeal was more blessed than enactment. And it is certainly true that the greater part of the labor of legislation consists in carrying the loads recklessly or bravely shouldered in times gone by, when the animal which is now a bull was only a calf, and in completing, if they may be completed, the tasks once undertaken in the shape of unambitious schemes which at the outset looked innocent enough. Having got his foot into it, the legislator finds it difficult, if not impossible, to get it out again. "The modern industrial organization, including banks, corporations, joint-stock companies, financial devices, national debts, paper currency, national systems of taxation, is largely the creation of legislation (not in its historical origin, but in the mode of its existence and in its authority), and is largely regulated by legislation. Capital is the breath of life to this organization, and every day, as the organization becomes more complex and delicate, the folly of assailing capital or credit becomes greater. At the same time it is evident that the task of the legislator to embrace in his view the whole system, to adjust his rules so that the play of the civil institutions shall not alter the play of the economic forces, requires more training and more acumen. Furthermore, the greater the complication and delicacy of the industrial system, the greater the chances for cupidity when backed by craft, and the task of the legislator to meet and defeat the attempts of this cupidity is one of constantly increasing difficulty."

Legislation unquestionably generates legislation. Every statute may be said to have a long lineage of statutes behind it; and whether that lineage be honorable or of ill repute is as much as question as to each individual statute as it can be with regard to the ancestry of each individual legislator. Every statute in its turn has a numerous progeny, and only time and opportunity can decide whether its offspring will bring it honor or shame. Once begin the dance of legislation, and you must struggle through its mazes as best you can to its breathless end, —if any end there be.

Lawmaking requires the full attention of Congress.

It is not surprising, therefore, that the enacting, revising, tinkering, repealing of laws should engross the attention and engage the entire energy of such a body as Congress. It is, however, easy to see how it might be better employed; or, at least, how it might add others to this overshadowing function, to the infinite advantage of the government. Quite as important as legislation is vigilant oversight of administration; and even more important than legislation is the instruction and guidance in political affairs which the people might receive from a body which kept all national concerns suffused in a broad daylight of discussion. There is no similar legislature in existence which is so shut up to the one business of law-making as is our Congress. As I have said, it in a way superintends administration by the exercise of semi-judicial powers of investigation, whose limitations and insufficiency are manifest. But other national legislatures command administration and verify their name of "parliaments" by talking official acts into notoriety. Our extraconstitutional party conventions, short-lived and poor in power as they are, constitute our only machinery for that sort of control of the executive which consists in the award of personal rewards and punishments. This is the cardinal fact which differentiates Congress from the Chamber of Deputies and from Parliament, and which puts it beyond the reach of those eminently useful functions whose exercise would so raise it in usefulness and in dignity.

An effective representative body, gifted with the power to rule, ought, it would seem not only to speak the will of the nation, which Congress does, but also to lead it to its conclusions, to utter the voice of its opinions, and to serve as its eyes in superintending all matters of government,—which Congress does not do. The discussions which take place in Congress are aimed at random. They now and again strike rather sharply the tender spots in this, that, or the other measure; but, as I have said, no two measures consciously join in purpose or agree in character, and so debate must wander as widely as the subjects of debate. Since there is little coherency about the legislation agreed upon, there can be little coherency about the debates. There is no one policy to be attacked or defended, but only a score or two of separate bills. To attend to such discussions is uninteresting; to be instructed by them is impossible. There is some scandal and discomfort, but infinite advantage, in having every affair of administration subjected to the test of constant examination on the part of the assembly which represents the nation. The chief use of such inquisition is, not the direction of those affairs in a way with which the country will be satisfied (though that itself is of course all-important), but the enlightenment of the people, which is always its sure consequence. Very few men are unequal to a danger which they see and understand; all men quail before a threatening which is dark and unintelligible, and suspect what is done behind the screen. If the people could have, through Congress, daily knowledge of all the more important transactions of the governmental offices, an insight into all that now so often shaken, would, I think, be very soon established. Because dishonesty *can* lurk under the privacies now vouchsafed our administrative agents, much that is upright and pure suffers unjust suspicion. Discoveries of guilt in a bureau cloud with doubts the trustworthiness of a department. As nothing is open enough for the quick and easy detection of peculation or fraud, so nothing is open enough for the due vindication and acknowledgment of honesty. The isolation and privacy which shield the one from discovery cheat the other of reward.

Inquisitiveness is never so forward, enterprising, and irrepressible as in a popular assembly which is given leave to ask questions and is afforded ready and abundant means of getting its questions answered. No cross-examination is more searching than that to which a minister of the Crown is subjected by the all-curious Commons. "Sir Robert Peel once asked to have a number of questions carefully written down which they asked him one day in succession in the House of Commons. They seemed a list of everything that could occur in the British empire or to the brain of a member of parliament." If one considered only the wear and tear upon ministers of state, which the plague of constant interrogation must inflict, he could wish that their lives, if useful, might be spared this blight of unending explanation; but no one can overestimate the immense advantage of a facility so unlimited for knowing all that is going on in the places where authority lives. The conscience of every member of the representative body is at the service of the nation. All that he feels bound to know he can find out; and what he finds out goes to the ears of the country. The questions is his, the answer the nation's. And the inquisitiveness of such bodies as congress is the best conceivable source of information. Congress is the only body which has the proper motive to act effectively upon the knowledge which the inquiries secure. The Press is merely curious or merely partisan. The people are scattered and unorganized. But Congress is, as it were, the corporate people, the mouthpiece of its will. It is a sovereign delegation which could as questions with dignity, because with authority and with power to act.

According to Wilson, Congress is the major force governing the nation.

Congress is fast becoming the governing body of the nation, and yet the only power which it possesses in perfection is the power which is but a part of government, the power of legislation. Legislation is but the oil of government. It is that which lubricates its channels and speeds its wheels; that which lessens the friction and so eases the movement. Or perhaps I shall be admitted to have hit upon a closer and apter analogy if I say that legislation is like a foreman set over forces of government. It issues the orders which others obey. It directs, it admonishes, but it does not do the actual heavy work of governing. A good foreman does, it is true, himself take a hand in the work which he guides; and so I suppose our legislation must be likened to a poor foreman, because it stands altogether apart from that work which it is set to see well done. Members of congress ought not to be censured too severely, however, when they fail to check evil courses on the part of the executive. They have been denied the means of doing so promptly and with effect. Whatever intention may have controlled the compromises of constitution-making in 1787, their result was to give us, not government by discussion, which is the only tolerable sort of government for a people which tries to do its own governing, but only *legislation* by discussion, which is no more than a small part of government by discussion. What is quite as indispensable as the debate of all matters f administration. It is even more important to know how the house is being built than to know how the plans of the architect were conceived and how his specifications were calculated. It is better to have skillful work—stout walls, reliable arches, unbending rafters, and windows sure to "expel the winter's flaw"—than a drawing on paper which is the admiration of all the practical artists in the country. The discipline of an army depends quite as much upon the temper of the troops as upon the orders of the day.

It is the proper duty of a representative body to look diligently into every affair of government and to talk much about what it sees. It is meant to be the eyes and the voice, and to embody the wisdom and will of its constituents. Unless Congress have and use every means of acquainting itself with the government, the country must be helpless to learn how it is being served; and unless Congress both scrutinize these things and sift them by every form of discussion, the country must remain in embarrassing, crippling ignorance of the very affairs which it is most important that it should understand and direct. The informing function of Congress should be even to its legislative function. The argument is not only that discussed and interrogated administration is the only pure and efficient administration, but, more than that, that the only really self-governing people is that people which discusses and interrogates its administration. The talk on the part of Congress which we sometimes justly condemn is the profitless squabble of words over frivolous bills or selfish party issues. It would be hard to conceive of there being too much talk about the practical concerns and processes of government. Such talk it is which, when earnestly and purposefully conducted, clears the public mind and shapes the demands of public opinion.

Seventeenth Amendment, 1913

Proposed by Congress in 1912 and ratified by the necessary 36 states in 1913, the Seventeenth Amendment allowed for the popular election of United States senators, just as members of the House of Representatives are elected. Under the original provisions of Article I, Section 3, of the Constitution, senators were appointed by each state's legislature.

Seventeenth Amendment

Clause 1. The Senate of the United States shall be composed of two Senators from each State, elected by the people thereof, for six years; and each Senator shall have one vote. The electors in each State shall have the qualifications requisite for electors of the most numerous branch of the State legislatures.

Clause 2. When vacancies happen in the representation of any State in the Senate, the executive authority of each State shall issue writs of election to fill such vacancies: Provided That the legislature of any State may empower the executive thereof to make temporary appointments until the people fill the vacancies by election as the legislature may direct.

Clause 3. This amendment shall not be so construed as to affect the election or term of any Senator chosen before it becomes valid as part of the Constitution.

POINT/COUNTERPOINT

Should the Seventeenth Amendment Be Repealed?

The Seventeenth Amendment, which provides for the direct, popular election of United States senators, was designed to make the government more democratic. However, some citizens believe that the amendment upset the balance of power between the states and the federal government.

United States Senate Web site

After the Civil War, problems in senatorial elections by the state legislatures multiplied. In one case in the late 1860s, the election of Senator John Stockton of New Jersey was contested on the grounds that he had been elected by a plurality rather than a majority in the state legislature. Stockton based his defense on the observation that not all states elected their senators in the same way, and presented a report that illustrated the inconsistency in state elections of senators. In response, Congress passed a law in 1866 regulating how and when senators were elected in each state. This was the first change in the process of senatorial elections created by the Founders. The law helped but did not entirely solve the problem, and deadlocks in some legislatures continued to cause long vacancies in some Senate seats. . . .

The impetus for reform began as early as 1826, when direct election of senators was first proposed. In the 1870s, voters sent a petition to the House of Representatives for a popular election. From 1893 to 1902, momentum increased considerably. Each year during that period, a constitutional amendment to elect senators by popular vote was proposed in Congress, but the Senate fiercely resisted change, despite the frequent vacancies and disputed election results. In the mid-1890s, the Populist party incorporated the direct election of senators into its party platform, although neither the Democrats nor the Republicans paid much notice at the time. In the early 1900s, one state initiated changes on its own. Oregon pioneered direct election and experimented with different measures over several years until it succeeded in 1907. Soon after, Nebraska followed suit and laid the foundation for other states to adopt measures reflecting the people's will. Senators who resisted reform had difficulty ignoring the growing support for direct election of senators. . . .

The Senate approved the resolution largely because of the senators who had been elected by state-initiated reforms, many of whom were serving their first term, and therefore may have been more willing to support direct election. After the Senate passed the amendment, which represented the culmination of decades of debate about the issue, the measure moved to the House of Representatives.

The House initially fared no better than the Senate in its early discussions of the proposed amendment. Much wrangling characterized the debates, but in the summer of 1912 the House finally passed the amendment and sent it to the states for ratification. The campaign for public support was aided by senators such as Borah and political scientist George H. Haynes, whose scholarly work on the Senate contributed greatly to passage of the amendment.

John MacMillan in *The Free Republic,* Oct 6, 2003

With respect to states' rights, it should be readily apparent to all that state governments cannot exert any meaningful influence or control over the federal government, judiciary, or any other federal institution.

Let us state the problem precisely. At the present time, there are no checks and balances available to the states over federal power or over Congress itself in any area. However, in the history of our country, it was not always this way. In the original design by the Framers of the U.S. Constitution, there was an effective check on Congress through the state legislatures' power to appoint (and remove) U.S. Senators. As such, the core of the problem with state's rights issues lies in the passage of the 17th Amendment which abrogated the state legislatures' right to appoint U.S. Senators in favor of popular election of those officials. This amendment created a fundamental structural problem which, irrespective of the political party in office, or the laws in effect at any one time, will result in excessive federal control in every area. It also results in a failure in the federalist structure, federal deficit spending, inappropriate federal mandates, and the evaporation of state influence over national policy . . . .

In my opinion, the 17th Amendment should be repealed. This would reinstate the states' linkage to the federal political process and would, thereby, have the effect of elevating the present status of the state legislatures from that of lobbyists, to that of a partner in the federal political process. The state legislatures would then have the ability to decentralize power when appropriate. It would give state legislatures direct influence over the selection of federal judges and the jurisdiction of the federal judiciary and much greater ability to modify federal court orders. This structure would allow the flow of power between the states and the federal government to ebb and flow as the needs of our federal republic change. The existing relationship, combined with the effect of the Supremacy Clause, is guaranteed to concentrate power into the hands of the federal government with little or no hope of return.

Document-Based Question

Why, according to the United States Senate web site, was the Seventeenth Amendment proposed and ratified? Why does John MacMillan believe the amendment upsets the balance of power between the federal government and the state governments?

Primary Source Library

Nineteenth Amendment, 1920

Women began demanding the right to vote as early as the 1848 Seneca Falls Convention, if not before. A proposed constitutional amendment was introduced into Congress in 1878, and every year after until 1919, when the amendment was approved by both houses of Congress. The Nineteenth Amendment was ratified by the states the following year.

Nineteenth Amendment

The right of citizens of the United States to vote shall not be denied or abridged by the United States or by any State on account of sex.

Congress shall have power to enforce this article by appropriate legislation.

Citizens Seek Changes in Volstead Act, 1932

The Volstead Act, or National Prohibition Act of 1919, enforced the Eighteenth Amendment banning the sale and use of intoxicating liquor. The law was unpopular in several parts of the United States, and, by the early 1930s, many people were calling for the law to be changed. The Twenty-first Amendment, ratified in 1933, repealed the Eighteenth Amendment and ended Prohibition.

Prohibition Repealed, 1933

The Eighteenth Amendment, 1919, launched the Prohibition Era by outlawing the manufacture and sale of liquor in the United States. Prohibition ended in 1933 after the Twenty-first Amendment repealed the Eighteenth Amendment. The Twenty-first Amendment is the only one that has been ratified by state conventions rather than by state legislatures.

Twentieth Amendment, 1933

The Twentieth Amendment,* ratified *in 1933, moved the beginning of congressional, presidential, and vice presidential terms from early March to the January following the November election.

Twentieth Amendment

1. The terms of the President and Vice President shall end at noon on the 20th day of January, and the terms of Senators and Representatives at noon on the 3d day of January, of the years in which such terms would have ended if this article had not been ratified; and the terms of their successors shall then begin.

2. The Congress shall assemble at least once in every year, and such meeting shall begin at noon on the 3d day of January, unless they shall by law appoint a different day.

3. If, at the time fixed for the beginning of the term of the President, the President elect shall have died, the Vice President elect shall become President. If a President shall not have been chosen before the time fixed for the beginning of his term, or if the President elect shall have failed to qualify, then the Vice President elect shall act as President until a President shall have qualified; and the Congress may by law provide for the case wherein neither a President elect nor a Vice President elect shall have qualified, declaring who shall then act as President, or the manner in which one who is to act shall be selected, and such person shall act accordingly until a President or Vice President shall have qualified.

4. The Congress may by law provide for the case of the death of any of the persons from whom the House of Representatives may choose a President whenever the right of choice shall have devolved upon them, and for the case of the death of any of the persons from whom the Senate may choose a Vice President whenever the right of choice shall have devolved upon them.

5. Sections 1 and 2 shall take effect on the 15th day of October following the ratification of this article.

6. This article shall be inoperative unless it shall have been ratified as an amendment to the Constitution by the legislatures of three-fourths of the several States within seven years from the date of its submission.

See also: Constitutional Amendments Affecting the Presidency in **Congress A to Z.**

U.S. Declaration of War on Japan, 1941

On December 8, 1941, the day after Japanese Imperial military forces launched a surprise attack on Pearl Harbor, Hawaii, President Franklin D. Roosevelt (1933–1945) went before Congress to ask for a declaration of war. Congress responded with this joint resolution.

U.S. Declaration of War on Japan

Joint Resolution Declaring that a state of war exists between the Imperial Government of Japan and the Government and the people of the United States and making provisions to prosecute the same.

Whereas the Imperial Government of Japan has committed unprovoked acts of war against the Government and the people of the United States of America: Therefore be it Resolved by the Senate and House of Representatives of the United States of American in Congress assembled, That the state of war between the United States and the Imperial Government of Japan which has thus been thrust upon the United States is hereby formally declared; and the President is hereby authorized and directed to employ the entire naval and military forces of the United States and the resources of the Government to carry on war against the Imperial Government of Japan; and, to bring the conflict to a successful termination, all of the resources of the country are hereby pledged by the Congress of the United States.

See also: War Powers in **Congress A to Z.**

U.S. Declaration of War on Germany, 1941

Germany declared war on the United States on December 11, 1941, four days after its ally Japan attacked the U.S. naval base at Pearl Harbor, Hawaii. Congress declared war on Germany later that same day.

U.S. Declaration of War on Germany

Joint Resolution Declaring that a state of war exists between the Government of Germany and the Government and the people of the United States and making provision to prosecute the same.

Whereas the Government of Germany has formally declared war against the Government and the people of the United States of America: Therefore be it

Resolved by the Senate and House of Representatives of the United States of America in Congress assembled, That the state of war between the United States and the

Government of Germany which has thus been thrust upon the United States is hereby formally declared; and the President is hereby authorized and directed to employ the entire naval and military forces of the United States and the resources of the Government to carry on war against the Government of Germany; and, to bring the conflict to a successful termination, all of the resources of the country are hereby pledged by the Congress of the United States.

See also: War Powers in **Congress A to Z.**

McCarthy Telegram to Truman, 1950

During World War II (1941–1945), the United States and the Soviet Union had been allies in the fight against the Axis Powers. After the war, however, many Americans, fueled by the accusations of Senator Joseph McCarthy of Wisconsin, feared that Communists were infiltrating the nation's government. McCarthy sent this telegram to President Harry S. Truman (1945–1953) in February 1950.

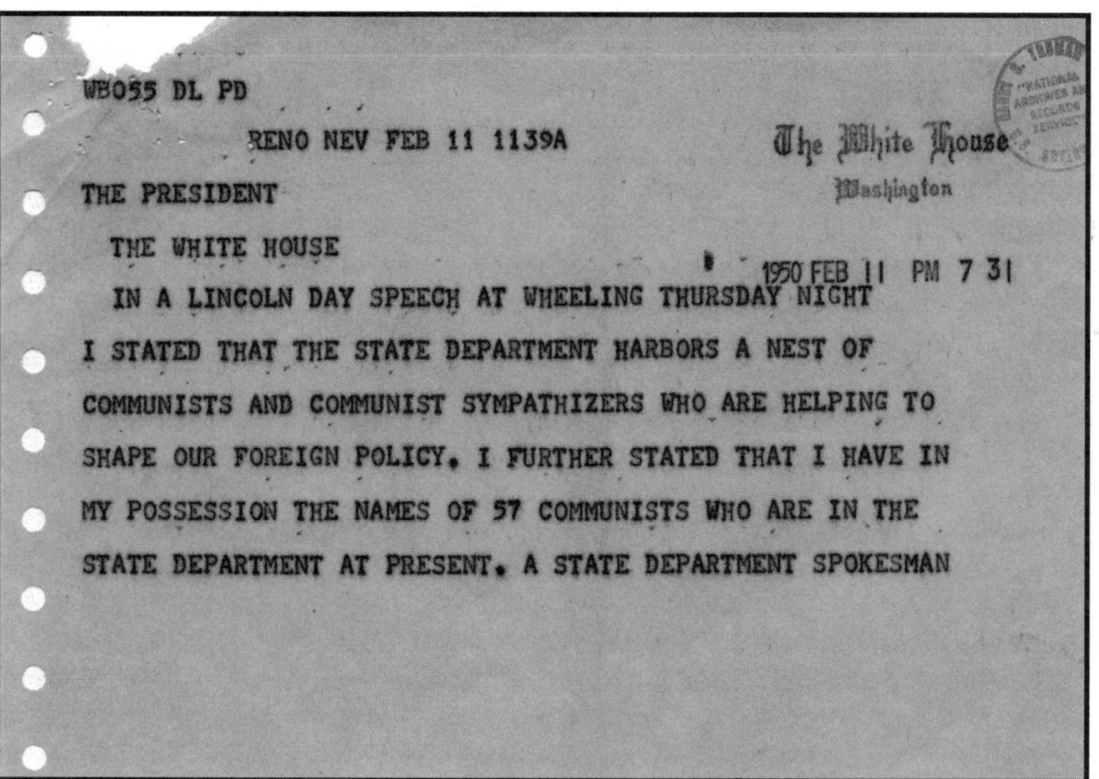

WBO55 DL PD

RENO NEV FEB 11 1139A

The White House
Washington

THE PRESIDENT

THE WHITE HOUSE

1950 FEB 11 PM 7 31

IN A LINCOLN DAY SPEECH AT WHEELING THURSDAY NIGHT I STATED THAT THE STATE DEPARTMENT HARBORS A NEST OF COMMUNISTS AND COMMUNIST SYMPATHIZERS WHO ARE HELPING TO SHAPE OUR FOREIGN POLICY. I FURTHER STATED THAT I HAVE IN MY POSSESSION THE NAMES OF 57 COMMUNISTS WHO ARE IN THE STATE DEPARTMENT AT PRESENT. A STATE DEPARTMENT SPOKESMAN

Censure of Senator Joseph McCarthy, 1954

In 1954, the Senate voted to censure Wisconsin Senator Joseph McCarthy because of his unwillingness to cooperate in investigations concerning allegations of communists in the federal government.

Censure of Senator Joseph McCarthy

Resolved, That the Senator from Wisconsin, Mr. McCarthy, failed to cooperate with the Subcommittee on Privileges and Elections of the Senate Committee on Rules and Administration in clearing up matters referred to that subcommittee which concerned his conduct as a Senator and affected the honor of the Senate and, instead, repeatedly abused the subcommittee and its members who were trying to carry out assigned duties, thereby obstructing the constitutional processes of the Senate, and that this conduct of the Senator from Wisconsin, Mr. McCarthy, is contrary to senatorial traditions and is hereby condemned.

Sec 2. The Senator from Wisconsin, Mr. McCarthy, in writing to the chairman of the Select Committee to Study Censure Charges (Mr. Watkins) after the Select Committee had issued its report and before the report was presented to the Senate charging three members of the Select Committee with "deliberate deception" and "fraud" for failure to disqualify themselves; in stating to the press on November 4, 1954, that the special Senate session that was to begin November 8, 1954, was a "lynch-party"; in repeatedly describing this special Senate session as a "lynch bee" in a nationwide television and radio show on November 7, 1954; in stating to the public press on November 13, 1954, that the chairman of the Select Committee (Mr. Watkins) was guilty of "the most unusual, most cowardly things I've ever heard of" and stating further: "I expected he would be afraid to answer the questions, but didn't think he'd be stupid enough to make a public statement"; and in characterizing the said committee as the "unwitting handmaiden," "involuntary agent" and "attorneys-in-fact" of the Communist Party and in charging that the said committee in writing its report "imitated Communist methods – that it distorted, misrepresented, and omitted in its effort to manufacture a plausible rationalization" in support of its recommendations to the Senate, which characterizations and charges were contained in a statement released to the press and inserted in the Congressional Record of November 10, 1954, acted contrary to senatorial ethics and tended to bring the Senate into dishonor and disrepute, to obstruct the constitutional processes of the Senate, and to impair its dignity; and such conduct is hereby condemned.

Twenty-fifth Amendment, 1967

The Twenty-fifth amendment was proposed in the aftermath of the assassination of President John F. Kennedy (1961–1963) in November 1963. For the first time, the sitting president was given the authority to fill an opening in the vice presidency. That provision of the amendment was first used in 1973, when President Richard M. Nixon (1969–1974) nominated, and Congress approved, Gerald R. Ford (1973–1974) to replace Vice President Spiro Agnew, who had resigned.

Twenty-fifth Amendment

1. In case of the removal of the President from office or of his death or resignation, the Vice President shall become President.

2. Whenever there is a vacancy in the office of the Vice President, the President shall nominate a Vice President who shall take office upon confirmation by a majority vote of both Houses of Congress.

3. Whenever the President transmits to the President pro tempore of the Senate and the Speaker of the House of Representatives his written declaration that he is unable to discharge the powers and duties of his office, and until he transmits to them a written declaration to the contrary, such powers and duties shall be discharged by the Vice President as Acting President.

4. Whenever the Vice President and a majority of either the principal officers of the executive departments or of such other body as Congress may by law provide, transmit to the President pro tempore of the Senate and the Speaker of the House of Representatives their written declaration that the President is unable to discharge the powers and duties of his office, the Vice President shall immediately assume the powers and duties of the office as Acting President.

Thereafter, when the President transmits to the President pro tempore of the Senate and the Speaker of the House of Representatives his written declaration that no inability exists, he shall resume the powers and duties of his office unless the Vice President and a majority of either the principal officers of the executive department or of such other body as Congress may by law provide, transmit within four days to the President pro tempore of the Senate and the Speaker of the House of Representatives their written declaration that the President is unable to discharge the powers and duties of his office. Thereupon Congress shall decide the issue, assembling within forty eight hours for that purpose if not in session. If the Congress, within twenty one days after receipt of the latter written declaration, or, if Congress is not in session, within twenty one days after Congress is required to assemble, determines by two thirds vote of both Houses that the President is unable to discharge the powers and duties of his office, the Vice President shall continue to discharge the same as Acting President; otherwise, the President shall resume the powers and duties of his office.

See also: Constitutional Amendments Affecting the Presidency in **Congress A to Z.**

War Powers Resolution, 1973

Dissatisfaction with the progress of the Vietnam War caused Congress to pass a joint resolution to limit the power of the president to send American troops into battle. Although controversial, provisions of this resolution have been used by presidents to seek authorization to send the military to liberate Kuwait in 1991 and to Iraq in 2003.

War Powers Resolution

Public Law 93-148
93rd Congress, H. J. Res. 542
November 7, 1973

Joint Resolution

Concerning the war powers of Congress and the President.

Resolved by the Senate and the House of Representatives of the United States of America in Congress assembled,

SHORT TITLE

SECTION 1. This joint resolution may be cited as the "War Powers Resolution".

PURPOSE AND POLICY

SEC. 2. (a) It is the purpose of this joint resolution to fulfill the intent of the framers of the Constitution of the United States and insure that the collective judgement of both the Congress and the President will apply to the introduction of United States Armed Forces into hostilities, or into situations where imminent involvement in hostilities is clearly indicate by the circumstances, and to the continued use of such forces in hostilities or in such situations.

(b) Under article I, section 8, of the Constitution, it is specifically provided that the Congress shall have the power to make all laws necessary and proper for carrying into execution, not only its own powers but also all other powers vested by the Constitution in the Government of the United States, or in any department or officer thereof.

(c) The constitutional powers of the President as Commander-in-Chief to introduce United States Armed Forces into hostilities, or into situations where imminent involvement in hostilities is clearly indicated by the circumstances, are exercised only pursuant to (1) a declaration of war, (2) specific statutory authorization, or (3) a national emergency created by attack upon the United States, its territories or possessions, or its armed forces.

CONSULTATION

SEC. 3. The President in every possible instance shall consult with Congress before introducing United States Armed Forces into hostilities or into situation where imminent involvement in hostilities is clearly indicated by the circumstances, and after every such introduction shall consult regularly with the Congress until United States

Armed Forces are no longer engaged in hostilities or have been removed from such situations.

REPORTING

SEC. 4. (a) In the absence of a declaration of war, in any case in which United States Armed Forces are introduced–

(1) into hostilities or into situations where imminent involvement in hostilities is clearly indicated by the circumstances;

(2) into the territory, airspace or waters of a foreign nation, while equipped for combat, except for deployments which relate solely to supply, replacement, repair, or training of such forces; or

(3) in numbers which substantially enlarge United States Armed Forces equipped for combat already located in a foreign nation; the president shall submit within 48 hours to the Speaker of the House of Representatives and to the President pro tempore of the Senate a report, in writing, setting forth–

(A) the circumstances necessitating the introduction of United States Armed Forces;

(B) the constitutional and legislative authority under which such introduction took place; and

(C) the estimated scope and duration of the hostilities or involvement.

(b) The President shall provide such other information as the Congress may request in the fulfillment of its constitutional responsibilities with respect to committing the Nation to war and to the use of United States Armed Forces abroad

(c) Whenever United States Armed Forces are introduced into hostilities or into any situation described in subsection (a) of this section, the President shall, so long as such armed forces continue to be engaged in such hostilities or situation, report to the Congress periodically on the status of such hostilities or situation as well as on the scope and duration of such hostilities or situation, but in no event shall he report to the Congress less often than once every six months.

CONGRESSIONAL ACTION

SEC. 5. (a) Each report submitted pursuant to section 4(a)(1) shall be transmitted to the Speaker of the House of Representatives and to the President pro tempore of the Senate on the same calendar day. Each report so transmitted shall be referred to the Committee on Foreign Affairs of the House of Representatives and to the Committee on Foreign Relations of the Senate for appropriate action. If, when the report is transmitted, the Congress has adjourned sine die or has adjourned for any period in excess of three calendar days, the Speaker of the House of Representatives and the President pro tempore of the Senate, if they deem it advisable (or if petitioned by at least 30 percent of the membership of their respective Houses) shall jointly request the President to convene Congress in order that it may consider the report and take appropriate action pursuant to this section.

(b) Within sixty calendar days after a report is submitted or is required to be submitted pursuant to section 4(a)(1), whichever is earlier, the President shall terminate any use of United States Armed Forces with respect to which such report was submitted (or required to be submitted), unless the Congress (1) has declared war or has enacted a specific authorization for such use of United States Armed Forces, (2) has extended by law such sixty-day period, or (3) is physically unable to meet as a result of an armed attack upon the United States. Such sixty-day period shall be extended for not more than an additional thirty days if the President determines and certifies to the Congress in writing that unavoidable military necessity respecting the safety of United States Armed Forces requires the continued use of such armed forces in the course of bringing about a prompt removal of such forces.

(c) Notwithstanding subsection (b), at any time that United States Armed Forces are engaged in hostilities outside the territory of the United States, its possessions and territories without a declaration of war or specific statutory authorization, such forces shall be removed by the President if the Congress so directs by concurrent resolution.

CONGRESSIONAL PRIORITY PROCEDURES FOR JOINT RESOLUTION OR BILL

SEC. 6. (a) Any joint resolution or bill introduced pursuant to section 5(b) at least thirty calendar days before the expiration of the sixty-day period specified in such section shall be referred to the Committee on Foreign Affairs of the House of Representatives or the Committee on Foreign Relations of the Senate, as the case may be, and such committee shall report one such joint resolution or bill, together with its recommendations, not later than twenty-four calendar days before the expiration of the sixty-day period specified in such section, unless such House shall otherwise determine by the yeas and nays.

(b) Any joint resolution or bill so reported shall become the pending business of the House in question (in the case of the Senate the time for debate shall be equally divided between the proponents and the opponents), and shall be voted on within three calendar days thereafter, unless such House shall otherwise determine by yeas and nays.

(c) Such a joint resolution or bill passed by one House shall be referred to the committee of the other House named in subsection (a) and shall be reported out not later than fourteen calendar days before the expiration of the sixty-day period specified in section 5(b). The joint resolution or bill so reported shall become the pending business of the House in question and shall be voted on within three calendar days after it has been reported, unless such House shall otherwise determine by yeas and nays.

(d) In the case of any disagreement between the two Houses of Congress with respect to a joint resolution or bill passed by both Houses, conferees shall be promptly appointed and the committee of conference shall make and file a report with respect to such resolution or bill not later than four calendar days before the expiration of the sixty-day period specified in section 5(b). In the event the conferees are unable to agree within 48 hours, they shall report back to their respective Houses in disagreement. Notwithstanding any rule in either House concerning the printing of conference reports in the Record or concerning any delay in the consideration of such reports, such report shall be acted on by both Houses not later than the expiration of such sixty-day period.

CONGRESSIONAL PRIORITY PROCEDURES FOR CONCURRENT RESOLUTION

SEC. 7. (a) Any concurrent resolution introduced pursuant to section 5(b) at least thirty calendar days before the expiration of the sixty-day period specified in such section shall be referred to the Committee on Foreign Affairs of the House of Representatives or the Committee on Foreign Relations of the Senate, as the case may be, and one such concurrent resolution shall be reported out by such committee together with its recommendations within fifteen calendar days, unless such House shall otherwise determine by the yeas and nays.

(b) Any concurrent resolution so reported shall become the pending business of the House in question (in the case of the Senate the time for debate shall be equally divided between the proponents and the opponents), and shall be voted on within three calendar days thereafter, unless such House shall otherwise determine by yeas and nays.

(c) Such a concurrent resolution passed by one House shall be referred to the committee of the other House named in subsection (a) and shall be reported out by such committee together with its recommendations within fifteen calendar days and shall thereupon become the pending business of such House and shall be voted on within three calendar days after it has been reported, unless such House shall otherwise determine by yeas and nays.

(d) In the case of any disagreement between the two Houses of Congress with respect to a concurrent resolution passed by both Houses, conferees shall be promptly appointed and the committee of conference shall make and file a report with respect to such concurrent resolution within six calendar days after the legislation is referred to the committee of conference.

Notwithstanding any rule in either House concerning the printing of conference reports in the Record or concerning any delay in the consideration of such reports, such report shall be acted on by both Houses not later than six calendar days after the conference report is filed. In the event the conferees are unable to agree within 48 hours, they shall report back to their respective Houses in disagreement.

INTERPRETATION OF JOINT RESOLUTION

SEC. 8. (a) Authority to introduce United States Armed Forces into hostilities or into situations wherein involvement in hostilities is clearly indicated by the circumstances shall not be inferred—

(1) from any provision of law (whether or not in effect before the date of the enactment of this joint resolution), including any provision contained in any appropriation Act, unless such provision specifically authorizes the introduction of United States Armed Forces into hostilities or into such situations and stating that it is intended to constitute specific statutory authorization within the meaning of this joint resolution; or

(2) from any treaty heretofore or hereafter ratified unless such treaty is implemented by legislation specifically authorizing the introduction of United States Armed Forces into hostilities or into such situations and stating that it is intended to constitute specific statutory authorization within the meaning of this joint resolution.

(b) Nothing in this joint resolution shall be construed to require any further specific statutory authorization to permit members of United States Armed Forces to participate jointly with members of the armed forces of one or more foreign countries in the headquarters operations of high-level military commands which were established prior to the date of enactment of this joint resolution and pursuant to the United Nations Charter or any treaty ratified by the United States prior to such date.

(c) For purposes of this joint resolution, the term "introduction of United States Armed Forces" includes the assignment of member of such armed forces to command, coordinate, participate in the movement of, or accompany the regular or irregular military forces of any foreign country or government when such military forces are engaged, or there exists an imminent threat that such forces will become engaged, in hostilities.

(d) Nothing in this joint resolution—

(1) is intended to alter the constitutional authority of the Congress or of the President, or the provision of existing treaties; or (2) shall be construed as granting any authority to the President with respect to the introduction of United States Armed Forces into hostilities or into situations wherein involvement in hostilities is clearly indicated by the circumstances which authority he would not have had in the absence of this joint resolution.

SEPARABILITY CLAUSE

SEC. 9. If any provision of this joint resolution or the application thereof to any person or circumstance is held invalid, the remainder of the joint resolution and the application of such provision to any other person or circumstance shall not be affected thereby.

EFFECTIVE DATE

SEC. 10. This joint resolution shall take effect on the date of its enactment.

See also: War Powers Resolution (1973) in **Congress A to Z.**

Articles of Impeachment Against Richard M. Nixon, 1974

On July 27, 1974, the House Judiciary Committee approved the first of three articles of impeachment charging Republican President Richard Nixon (1969–1974) with obstruction of justice. Six of the committee's 17 Republicans joined all 21 Democrats in voting for the article. The committee approved its second article, charging Nixon with abuse of power, on the following Monday. The third and final article, Contempt of Congress, was approved the next day. The president was eventually forced to resign.

Articles of Impeachment Against Richard M. Nixon

RESOLVED, That Richard M. Nixon, President of the United States, is impeached for high crimes and misdemeanors, and that the following articles of impeachment to be exhibited to the Senate:

ARTICLES OF IMPEACHMENT EXHIBITED BY THE HOUSE OF REPRESENTATIVES OF THE UNITED STATES OF AMERICA IN THE NAME OF ITSELF AND OF ALL OF THE PEOPLE OF THE UNITED STATES OF AMERICA, AGAINST RICHARD M. NIXON, PRESIDENT OF THE UNITED STATES OF AMERICA, IN MAINTENANCE AND SUPPORT OF ITS IMPEACHMENT AGAINST HIM FOR HIGH CRIMES AND MISDEMEANORS.

Article 1: Obstruction of Justice.

In his conduct of the office of the President of the United States, Richard M. Nixon, in violation of his constitutional oath faithfully to execute the office of President of the United States and, to the best of his ability, preserve, protect, and defend the Constitution of the United States, and in violation of his constitutional duty to take care that the laws be faithfully executed, has prevented, obstructed, and impeded the administration of justice, in that: On June 17, 1972, and prior thereto, agents of the Committee for the Re-Election of the President committed unlawful entry of the headquarters of the Democratic National Committee in Washington, District of Columbia, for the purpose of securing political intelligence. Subsequent thereto, Richard M. Nixon, using the powers of his high office, engaged personally and through his subordinates and agents in a course of conduct or plan designed to delay, impede and obstruct investigations of such unlawful entry; to cover up, conceal and protect those responsible and to conceal the existence and scope of other unlawful covert activities. The means used to implement this course of conduct or plan have included one or more of the following:

(1) Making or causing to be made false or misleading statements to lawfully authorized investigative officers and employees of the United States.

(2) Withholding relevant and material evidence or information from lawfully authorized investigative officers and employees of the United States.

(3) Approving, condoning, acquiescing in, and counseling witnesses with respect to the giving of false or misleading statements to lawfully authorized investigative officers

and employes of the United States and false or misleading testimony in duly instituted judicial and congressional proceedings.

(4) Interfering or endeavoring to interfere with the conduct of investigations by the Department of Justice of the United States, the Federal Bureau of Investigation, the office of Watergate Special Prosecution Force and congressional committees.

(5) Approving, condoning, and acquiescing in, the surreptitious payments of substantial sums of money for the purpose of obtaining the silence or influencing the testimony of witnesses, potential witnesses or individuals who participated in such unlawful entry and other illegal activities.

(6) Endeavoring to misuse the Central Intelligence Agency, an agency of the United States.

(7) Disseminating information received from officers of the Department of Justice of the United States to subjects of investigations conducted by lawfully authorized investigative officers and employes of the United States for the purpose of aiding and assisting such subjects in their attempts to avoid criminal liability.

(8) Making false or misleading public statements for the purpose of deceiving the people of the United States into believing that a thorough and complete investigation has been conducted with respect to allegation of misconduct on the part of personnel of the Executive Branch of the United States and personnel of the Committee for the Re-Election of the President, and that there was no involvement of such personnel in such misconduct; or

(9) Endeavoring to cause prospective defendants, and individuals duly tried and convicted, to expect favored treatment and consideration in return for their silence or false testimony, or rewarding individuals for their silence or false testimony.

In all of this, Richard M. Nixon has acted in a manner contrary to his trust as President and subversive of constitutional government, to the great prejudice of the cause of law and justice and to the manifest injury of the people of the United States.

Wherefore Richard M. Nixon, by such conduct, warrants impeachment and trial, and removal from office.

Article 2: Abuse of Power.

Using the powers of the office of President of the United States, Richard M. Nixon, in violation of his constitutional oath faithfully to execute the office of President of the United States and, to the best of his ability, preserve, protect, and defend the Constitution of the United States, and in disregard of his constitutional duty to take care that the laws be faithfully executed, has repeatedly engaged in conduct violating the constitutional rights of citizens, imparting the due and proper administration of justice and the conduct of lawful inquiries, or contravening the laws governing agencies of the executive branch and the purposes of these agencies.

This conduct has included one or more of the following:

(1) He has, acting personally and through his subordinated and agents, endeavored to obtain from the Internal Revenue Service, in violation of the constitutional rights of

citizens, confidential information contained in income tax returns for purposes not authorized by law, and to cause, in violation of the constitutional rights of citizens, income tax audits or other income tax investigation to be initiated or conducted in a discriminatory manner.

(2) He misused the Federal Bureau of Investigation, the Secret Service, and other executive personnel, in violation or disregard of the constitutional rights of citizens, by directing or authorizing such agencies or personnel to conduct or continue electronic surveillance or other investigations for purposes unrelated to national security, the enforcement of laws, or any other lawful function of his office; he did direct, authorize, or permit the use of information obtained thereby for purposes unrelated to national security, the enforcement of laws, or any other lawful function of his office; and he did direct the concealment of certain records made by the Federal Bureau of Investigation of electronic surveillance.

(3) He has, acting personally and through his subordinates and agents, in violation or disregard of the constitutional rights of citizens, authorized and permitted to be maintained a secret investigative unit within the office of the President, financed in part with money derived from campaign contributions to him, which unlawfully utilized the resources of the Central Intelligence Agency, engaged in covert and unlawful activities, and attempted to prejudice the constitutional right of an accused to a fair trial.

(4) He has failed to take care that the laws were faithfully executed by failing to act when he knew or had reason to know that his close subordinates endeavored to impede and frustrate lawful inquiries by duly constituted executive; judicial and legislative entities concerning the unlawful entry into the headquarters of the Democratic National Committee, and the cover-up thereof, and concerning other unlawful activities including those relating to the confirmation of Richard Kleindienst as attorney general of the United States, the electronic surveillance of private citizens, the break-in into the office of Dr. Lewis Fielding, and the campaign financing practices of the Committee to Re-elect the President.

(5) In disregard of the rule of law: he knowingly misused the executive power by interfering with agencies of the executive branch: including the Federal Bureau of Investigation, the Criminal Division and the Office of Watergate Special Prosecution Force of the Department of Justice, in violation of his duty to take care that the laws by faithfully executed.

In all of this, Richard M. Nixon has acted in a manner contrary to his trust as President and subversive of constitutional government, to the great prejudice of the cause of law and justice and to the manifest injury of the people of the United States.

Wherefore Richard M. Nixon, by such conduct, warrants impeachment and trial, and removal from office.

Article 3: Contempt of Congress.

In his conduct of the office of President of the United States, Richard M. Nixon, contrary to his oath faithfully to execute the office of the President of the United States, and to the best of his ability preserve, protect and defend the Constitution of the United States, and in violation of his constitutional duty to take care that the laws be faithfully executed, had failed without lawful cause or excuse, to produce papers and things as directed by duly authorized subpoenas issued by the Committee on the Judiciary of the House of Representatives, on April 11, 1974, May 15, 1974, May 30, 1974, and June 24, 1974, and willfully disobeyed such subpoenas. The subpoenaed papers and things were deemed necessary by the Committee in order to resolve by direct evidence fundamental, factual questions relating to Presidential direction, knowledge or approval of actions demonstrated by other evidence to be substantial grounds for impeachment of the President. In refusing to produce these papers and things, Richard M. Nixon, substituting his judgement as to what materials were necessary for the inquiry, interposed the powers of the Presidency against the lawful subpoenas of the House of Representatives, thereby assuming to himself functions and judgments necessary to the exercise of the sole power of impeachment vested by Constitution in the House of Representatives.

In all this, Richard M. Nixon has acted in a manner contrary to his trust as President and subversive of constitutional government, to the great prejudice of the cause of law and justice, and to the manifest injury of the people of the United States.

Wherefore, Richard M. Nixon, by such conduct, warrants impeachment and trial and removal from office.

See also: Article of Impeachment Against Andrew Johnson, 1868; Articles of Impeachment Against William Jefferson Clinton, 1998; Impeachment Power in **Congress A to Z.**

Articles of Impeachment Against William Jefferson Clinton, 1998

On December 19, 1998, the House of Representatives impeached President William Jefferson Clinton (1993–2001). The House charged Clinton with "high crimes and misdemeanors" for lying under oath and obstructing justice by attempting to cover up an inappropriate relationship with a White House intern. The Republican-led House voted largely along party lines to approve two of the four proposed articles of impeachment. However, President Clinton was acquitted of all charges.

Articles of Impeachment Against William Jefferson Clinton

Resolved, that William Jefferson Clinton, President of the United States, is impeached for high crimes and misdemeanors, and that the following articles of impeachment be exhibited to the United States Senate:

Articles of impeachment exhibited by the House of Representatives of the United States of America in the name of itself and of the people of the United States of

America, against William Jefferson Clinton, President of the United States of America, in maintenance and support of its impeachment against him for high crimes and misdemeanors.

Article I

In his conduct while President of the United States, William Jefferson Clinton, in violation of his constitutional oath faithfully to execute the office of President of the United States and, to the best of his ability, preserve, protect, and defend the Constitution of the United States, and in violation of his constitutional duty to take care that the laws be faithfully executed, has willfully corrupted and manipulated the judicial process of the United States for his personal gain and exoneration, impeding the administration of justice, in that:

On August 17, 1998, William Jefferson Clinton swore to tell the truth, the whole truth, and nothing but the truth before a Federal grand jury of the United States. Contrary to that oath, William Jefferson Clinton willfully provided perjurious, false and misleading testimony to the grand jury concerning one or more of the following: (1) the nature and details of his relationship with a subordinate Government employee; (2) prior perjurious, false and misleading testi mony he gave in a Federal civil rights action brought against him; (3) prior false and misleading statements he allowed his attorney to make to a Federal judge in that civil rights action; and (4) his corrupt efforts to influence the testimony of witnesses and to impede the discovery of evidence in that civil rights action.

In doing this, William Jefferson Clinton has undermined the integrity of his office, has brought disrepute on the Presidency, has betrayed his trust as President, and has acted in a manner subversive of the rule of law and justice, to the manifest injury of the people of the United States.

Wherefore, William Jefferson Clinton, by such conduct, warrants impeachment and trial, and removal from office and disqualification to hold and enjoy any office of honor, trust or profit under the United States.

Article II

In his conduct while President of the United States, William Jefferson Clinton, in violation of his constitutional oath faithfully to execute the office of President of the United States and, to the best of his ability, preserve, protect, and defend the Constitution of the United States, and in violation of his constitutional duty to take care that the laws be faithfully executed, has willfully corrupted and manipulated the judicial process of the United States for his personal gain and exoneration, impeding the administration of justice, in that:

(1) On December 23, 1997, William Jefferson Clinton, in sworn answers to written questions asked as part of a Federal civil rights action brought against him, willfully provided perjurious, false and misleading testimony in response to questions deemed relevant by a Federal judge concerning conduct and proposed conduct with subordinate employees.

(2) On January 17, 1998, William Jefferson Clinton swore under oath to tell the truth, the whole truth, and nothing but the truth in a deposition given as part of a Federal civil rights action brought against him. Contrary to that oath, William Jefferson Clinton willfully provided perjurious, false and misleading testimony in response to questions deemed relevant by a Federal judge concerning the nature and details of his relationship with a subordinate Government employee, his knowledge of that employee's involvement and participation in the civil rights action brought against him, and his corrupt efforts to influence the testimony of that employee.

In all of this, William Jefferson Clinton has undermined the integrity of his office, has brought disrepute on the Presidency, has betrayed his trust as President, and has acted in a manner subversive of the rule of law and justice, to the manifest injury of the people of the United States.

Wherefore, William Jefferson Clinton, by such conduct, warrants impeachment and trial, and removal from office and disqualification to hold and enjoy any office of honor, trust or profit under the United States.

Article III

In his conduct while President of the United States, William Jefferson Clinton, in violation of his constitutional oath faithfully to execute the office of President of the United States and, to the best of his ability, preserve, protect, and defend the Constitution of the United States, and in violation of his constitutional duty to take care that the laws be faithfully executed, has prevented, obstructed, and impeded the administration of justice, and has to that end engaged personally, and through his subordinates and agents, in a course of conduct or scheme designed to delay, impede, cover up, and conceal the existence of evidence and testimony related to a Federal civil rights action brought against him in a duly instituted judicial proceeding.

The means used to implement this course of conduct or scheme included one or more of the following acts:

(1) On or about December 17, 1997, William Jefferson Clinton corruptly encouraged a witness in a Federal civil rights action brought against him to execute a sworn affidavit in that proceeding that he knew to be perjurious, false and misleading.

(2) On or about December 17, 1997, William Jefferson Clinton corruptly encouraged a witness in a Federal civil rights action brought against him to give perjurious, false and misleading testimony if and when called to testify personally in that proceeding.

(3) On or about December 28, 1997, William Jefferson Clinton corruptly engaged in, encouraged, or supported a scheme to conceal evidence that had been subpoenaed in a Federal civil rights action brought against him.

(4) Beginning on or about December 7, 1997, and continuing through and including January 14, 1998, William Jefferson Clinton intensified and succeeded in an effort to secure job assistance to a witness in a Federal civil rights action brought against him in order to corruptly prevent the truthful testimony of that witness in that proceeding at a time when the truthful testimony of that witness would have been harmful to him.

(5) On January 17, 1998, at his deposition in a Federal civil rights action brought against him, William Jefferson Clinton corruptly allowed his attorney to make false and misleading statements to a Federal judge characterizing an affidavit, in order to prevent questioning deemed relevant by the judge. Such false and misleading statements were subsequently acknowledged by his attorney in a communication to that judge.

(6) On or about January 18 and January 20–21, 1998, William Jefferson Clinton related a false and misleading account of events relevant to a Federal civil rights action brought against him to a potential witness in that proceeding, in order to corruptly influence the testimony of that witness.

(7) On or about January 21, 23 and 26, 1998, William Jefferson Clinton made false and misleading statements to potential witnesses in a Federal grand jury proceeding in order to corruptly influence the testimony of those witnesses. The false and misleading statements made by William Jefferson Clinton were repeated by the witnesses to the grand jury, causing the grand jury to receive false and misleading information.

In all of this, William Jefferson Clinton has undermined the integrity of his office, has brought disrepute on the Presidency, has betrayed his trust as President, and has acted in a manner subversive of the rule of law and justice, to the manifest injury of the people of the United States.

Wherefore, William Jefferson Clinton, by such conduct, warrants impeachment and trial, and removal from office and disqualification to hold and enjoy any office of honor, trust or profit under the United States.

Article IV

Using the powers and influence of the office of President of the United States, William Jefferson Clinton, in violation of his constitutional oath faithfully to execute the office of President of the United States and, to the best of his ability, preserve, protect, and defend the Constitution of the United States, and in disregard of his constitutional duty to take care that the laws be faithfully executed, has engaged in conduct that resulted in misuse and abuse of his high office, impaired the due and proper administration of justice and the conduct of lawful inquiries, and contravened the authority of the legislative branch and the truth-seeking purpose of a coordinate investigative proceeding in that, as President, William Jefferson Clinton, refused and failed to respond to certain written requests for admission and willfully made perjurious, false and misleading sworn statements in response to certain written requests for admission propounded to him as part of the impeachment inquiry authorized by the House of Representatives of the Congress of the United States.

William Jefferson Clinton, in refusing and failing to respond, and in making perjurious, false and misleading statements, assumed to himself functions and judgments necessary to the exercise of the sole power of impeachment vested by the Constitution in the House of Representatives and exhibited contempt for the inquiry.

In doing this, William Jefferson Clinton has undermined the integrity of his office, has brought disrepute on the Presidency, has betrayed his trust as President, and has acted in a manner subversive of the rule of law and justice, to the manifest injury of the people of the United States.

Wherefore, William Jefferson Clinton, by such conduct, warrants impeachment and trial, and removal from office and disqualification to hold and enjoy any office of honor, trust or profit under the United States.

See also: Article of Impeachment Against Andrew Johnson, 1868; Articles of Impeachment Against Richard M. Nixon, 1974; Impeachment Power in **Congress A to Z.**

Letter to President Bush Urging Him to End the War in Iraq, 2007

Soon after assuming control of both Houses of Congress in January 2007, the Democratic leadership sent a letter to President George W. Bush asking him to begin ending the war in Iraq and opposing his plan to send even more American troops to the country.

Letter to President Bush

January 5, 2007

President George W. Bush
The White House
Washington, DC 20500

Dear Mr. President:

The start of the new Congress brings us opportunities to work together on the critical issues confronting our country. No issue is more important than finding an end to the war in Iraq. December was the deadliest month of the war in over two years, pushing U.S. fatality figures over the 3,000 mark.

The American people demonstrated in the November elections that they don't believe your current Iraq policy will lead to success and that we need a change in direction for the sake of our troops and the Iraqi people. We understand that you are completing your post-election consultations on Iraq and are preparing to make a major address on your Iraq strategy to the American people next week.

Clearly this address presents you with another opportunity to make a long overdue course correction. Despite the fact that our troops have been pushed to the breaking point and, in many cases, have already served multiple tours in Iraq, news reports suggest that you believe the solution to the civil war in Iraq is to require additional sacrifices from our troops and are therefore prepared to proceed with a substantial U.S. troop increase.

Surging forces is a strategy that you have already tried and that has already failed. Like many current and former military leaders, we believe that trying again would be a serious mistake. They, like us, believe there is no purely military solution in Iraq. There is only a political solution. Adding more combat troops will only endanger more Americans and stretch our military to the breaking point for no strategic gain.

And it would undermine our efforts to get the Iraqis to take responsibility for their own future. We are well past the point of more troops for Iraq . . . .

Rather than deploy additional forces to Iraq, we believe the way forward is to begin the phased redeployment of our forces in the next four to six months, while shifting the principal mission of our forces there from combat to training, logistics, force protection and counter-terror. A renewed diplomatic strategy, both within the region and beyond, is also required to help the Iraqis agree to a sustainable political settlement. In short, it is time to begin to move our forces out of Iraq and make the Iraqi political leadership aware that our commitment is not open ended, that we cannot resolve their sectarian problems, and that only they can find the political resolution required to stabilize Iraq.

Our troops and the American people have already sacrificed a great deal for the future of Iraq. After nearly four years of combat, tens of thousands of U.S. casualties, and over $300 billion dollars, it is time to bring the war to a close. We, therefore, strongly encourage you to reject any plans that call for our getting our troops any deeper into Iraq. We want to do everything we can to help Iraq succeed in the future but, like many of our senior military leaders, we do not believe that adding more U.S. combat troops contributes to success.

We appreciate you taking these views into consideration.

Senate Majority Leader Harry Reid

Speaker Nancy Pelosi

See also: War Powers in **Congress A to Z.**

Nancy Pelosi, Speaker of the House, 2007

In January 2007, Representative Nancy Pelosi became the first woman Speaker of the House. This poster commemorates a historic first by placing an image of the new Speaker in a classic World War II poster that reminded women that their strength was needed in the war effort.

Researching With Primary and Secondary Sources

A primary source is first-hand information or data. A primary source has not been subject to analysis by someone else. Typical primary sources–such as the Twelfth Amendment, the U.S. Declaration of War Against Germany, and the 1974 Articles of Impeachment Against Richard Nixon–are eyewitness accounts of an event, letters, diary entries, photographs, and documents. In the Primary Source Library, Part Three of this volume, there is a variety of primary sources, especially useful when researching how the U.S. government was formed and how it runs.

In contrast, a secondary source is information that has been reviewed and analyzed by someone else. For example, historian David McCullough's biography of the second U.S. president John Adams is a secondary source. The author (McCullough) has reviewed and analyzed a variety of primary and secondary sources to present a biography of his subject (Adams). Most magazine articles, books, and Internet sources are secondary sources.

Developing Research Questions

When you are assigned a report and select a topic for research, it is important to begin with a clear sense of direction. Ask yourself several questions that will help you limit your topic. For example, for a report on the process of filibustering, you will likely be able to find hundreds of primary and secondary sources. However, to help narrow the topic, ask yourself the following questions:

- What is a filibuster?
- How did this legislative action come about?
- Who can exercise this power?
- Under what circumstances would a member of Congress call for a filibuster?
- When has this power been used in the past?
- Was the tactic successful?
- How has this power been exercised recently?
- What was the impact of the threat to call a filibuster on modern politics?

With answers to these questions, you will have the focus you need to begin further research.

Identifying Sources of Information

You likely will begin looking for information in your school or local library. You can also locate other sources of information within your community, such as local government sources, newspaper offices, historical societies, and museums. All of these sources can provide valuable information. However, you must determine if the information will be useful to your research topic. Evaluate and decide on the usefulness of the source. Useful sources should have the following characteristics:

- **Pertinent and appropriate** Is the information related to your topic? Skim the book, and check the table of contents and the index.
- **Trustworthy and dependable** Is the source objective? Does it seem accurate? What sources did the author of the book or article use?
- **Current and recent** How old is the source? Is the information out-of-date? Keep in mind that historical documents such as the U.S. Constitution and topics such as the election of 1800 are researched and evaluated by political scientists and historians. Be sure that some of your sources are current analyses.
- **Typical and representative** Be certain to find balanced or unbiased sources. If you are writing about a controversial topic, such as the Iraq War Resolution, be sure to use sources that represent both sides of the issue.

Planning and Organizing

As you gather various primary and secondary sources, you begin to develop a plan for your report. This might include a preliminary outline with headings and subheadings that will help you organize your resources and report. With this plan you can decide what information to include in your notes.

Thorough notetaking is essential; you will want to document all the information you have gathered for your report. Following are useful tips for taking notes:

- Use ruled index cards.
- Use a separate card for each item of information.
- Use a separate card for each source.

Use the following techniques to record information:

- **Quote** Copy the information exactly as it appears in the source. Use quotation marks to indicate a direct quote.
- **Paraphrase** Rewrite the information in your own words.
- **Summarize** Condense the information, noting essential material and key ideas.

Documenting Sources for the Bibliography

On index cards, keep a record of the books, newspaper or magazine articles, Internet sites, and other sources you have consulted. As you locate useful sources, record the publishing data on your index cards, so you can easily find the information later. This data will be essential for compiling the bibliography at the end of your report.

Citing Sources

All writers must identify the sources of the words, facts, and thoughts that they find in other works. Noting your sources allows your reader to check those sources and determine how reliable or important a particular piece of information is.

What You Should Document

- Someone's exact words
- A close paraphrase of another's ideas or several ideas
- Information on the topic which is not found in most books on the subject or which is not generally known

What You Do Not Have To Document

- Simple definition, commonly used sayings, or famous quotations
- Information that is common knowledge or that is easily found in most sources

Author and Publication Information

Author information should always appear at the beginning of your citation, with the author's last name first.

- For books with two authors, reverse only the first author's name, followed by a comma and the second author's name.
- If no author is noted, list the editor; if no editor is identified, start with the title of the work.
- Should you use more than one work by the same author, you do not need to list the author information each time. Use three hyphens followed by a period to begin the line.
- The name of the work (underlined) appears next, followed by a period.

Publication information follows the author and title of the work. You also may need to include the editor's name, volume or edition number, and a series name.

Citing On-line Sources

When citing on-line sources, you likely will not be able to include all the information in the list that follows. Many on-line sources do not provide all this information. Therefore, provide as much information as possible.

- Author or editor of the source
- Title of a book (underlined)
- Title of an article, short work, or poem (in quotation marks)
- Publication information for any print version of the source
- Title of the database, scholarly project, periodical, or professional site (underlined)
- Version number of the source or journal; volume number, issue number, or other identifier
- Date of the electronic version or last update

Using the Primary Source Library in this Volume

In Part Three of this volume, you will find a wealth of primary sources useful for various research topics. In chronological order, important source documents appear that are related to the establishment, development, and daily functioning of the U.S. Congress. To help you find out about the powers of impeachment, for example, the following primary sources would be useful:

- United States Constitution, Article I, Sections 1–7, 1789
- Article of Impeachment Against Andrew Johnson, 1868
- Articles of Impeachment Against Richard M. Nixon, 1974
- Articles of Impeachment Against William Jefferson Clinton, 1998

For more information about doing research with authoritative sources, consult your local librarian, teacher, or one of numerous available publications.

Glossary

abstaining Refraining from something by choice, for example, choosing not to vote

adjourn To suspend until a later stated time

adjourned Delayed until a later time or indefinitely

aliens Those belonging or owing allegiance to another country or government

amend To make something better by changing or modifying it

amendment A change to the Constitution

anarchist One who believes in the doctrine that all forms of government are oppressive and should be abolished

annex To append, attach, or absorb

appropriate To set aside something, such as funds, for a specific use

appropriations Resources or funds set aside for a particular use

apportion To divide and assign according to a plan

apportionment The proportional distribution of the number of members of the U.S. House of Representatives on the basis of the population of each state

aristocratic Of or belonging to the upper classes or nobility

autonomy Condition of self-government or independence

balance of power Equality of power which prevents one party from forcing its will or interests onto others

Bank of the United States One of the two official national banks of the United States. The First Bank of the United States existed from 1791 to 1811; the Second Bank of the United States existed from 1816 until 1836, when its federal charter expired; President Andrew Jackson almost destroyed the bank when he ordered the Department of Treasury to stop depositing the nation's money into the bank

bicameral Consisting of a two-house legislature

bill of attainder A law that establishes guilt and punishes people without a trial

bills Proposed laws

bipartisan Involving members of two political parties

bloc A group united to promote a common interest

bosses Powerful political party leaders

ceded Yielded or granted

civil service reform The changing of the administrative service of the government, exclusive of the armed forces

commerce Exchange of goods, ideas, or opinions

commonwealth A nation or state governed by the people

conservative Someone who believes that the role of the government should be very limited and that individuals should be responsible for their own well-being

counterfeits Fake coins or currency

disenfranchised Deprived of the right to vote

Emancipation Proclamation The formal document delivered by President Abraham Lincoln which announced that slaves in rebel territory were free and became effective on January 1, 1863

embargo A country's banning of the export and import of goods to and from another country

enfranchising Granting the right to vote

engrossed Prepared as the formal or official copy of a document or bill

entitlement programs Sources of necessary government expenses

ex post facto After the fact; making criminal acts that were legal when they were committed

faction A group of people with a united interest

felonies Serious crimes such as murder, kidnapping, extortion, and arson

fiscal discipline A financial policy that emphasizes only necessary spending

franchise The right to vote

free trade Trade based on the unrestricted international exchange of goods

gerrymandering The division of a geographical area into voting districts to give an advantage to one party in elections

grandfather clauses Provisions that make exemptions in the law for a certain group based on previous conditions

habeas corpus (writ of) One of a variety of formal legal documents that may be issued to bring a party before a court or judge; serves to release the party from unlawful restraint

ideology A set of doctrines or beliefs that form the basis of a political, economic, or other societal system

illiterate Unable to read or write

impeach To formally accuse a public official of misconduct while in office

impeachment The formal accusation of misconduct in office against a public official

implied powers The powers of Congress which are not specifically spelled out in the United States Constitution, but are deemed necessary to carry out the expressed, or specific, powers of Congress

impound To refuse to spend funds appropriated by Congress

incumbent Politician running for the office that she or he is currently holding

injunction A court order prohibiting a party from a specific course of action

interrogator An examiner who questions formally or officially

jurisdiction The right and power of a court to interpret and apply the law

lame-duck A politician who, at the end of his or her current term, will be succeeded either due to choice or to term limits

liberal In the modern era, someone who believes the national government should be active in helping individuals and communities promote health, education, justice, and equal opportunity

literacy tests Exams given to determine how well-educated an individual is

lobby A group of persons engaged in trying to influence legislators or other public officials in favor of a specific cause

lobbying Trying to influence public officials on behalf of or against proposed legislation

lobbyist A person representing an interest group

majority-minority districts Legislative districts created specifically to include a majority of a minority group in order to increase the possibility that a member of that minority group will be elected from that district

mercenaries Individuals paid to perform services, often military in nature, for foreigners

natural rights Those rights with which all individuals are born

nullified To have made something of no consequence or value

pages Persons employed to run errands, carry messages, maintain schedules, and act as guides in the U.S. Congress or other legislature

partisan Devoted to or biased in favor of a party

philanthropist One who practices goodwill to others

platform A political party's statement of principles, beliefs, and positions on important issues

plurality The largest share (as of votes)
poll taxes Money paid in order to vote
Populist era The late 1800s in the United States and the time when a third political party, known as the Populist Party, organized and claimed to represent the goals of the common people
precedent An established course of action in a given situation
primary election An election in which qualified voters nominate or express a preference for a particular candidate or group of candidates for political office
progressive Wanting social, economic, and governmental reforms, especially in the late 1800s and early 1900s
prohibition Forbidding the production, transportation, sale, and consumption of alcoholic beverages
quorum A specific number of an organization's members required to conduct business
quorum calls Summoning of absent members to chambers for a vote
Radical Republicans Members of the Republican party who advocated extreme measures to bring about change in the South during and after the Civil War (1861–1865)
ratification A formal approval or confirmation (of an amendment or treaty)
ratified Approved
reciprocity treaty An agreement between two nations which establishes equal rights and privileges, as in trading rights or tariffs
Reconstruction The period in United States history when the former Confederate States were brought back into the Union, lasting from about 1865 until 1877
repeal To annul by legislative authority
reported Official recording of an account
republic A form of government in which the people rule through elected representatives
republican Relating to a republic
resolutions Statements of issues that are relevant to only one house of Congress and are passed only by the house to which they apply
secession The act of leaving or withdrawing from a nation or other political entity or organization
secessionist One who joins a secession or maintains that secession is a right
seniority The state of being older or higher in rank than others
soft money Political donations made to avoid federal campaign laws, such as a donation of money to a political organization rather than directly to a candidate
sovereignty Complete independence and self-government
special interest groups Organized individuals seeking to influence legislative or government policy to further often narrowly defined interests
subpoena A writ summoning a person to court to give testimony
subsidies Aid the government gives to businesses; usually financial aid
suffrage The right to vote
suffragist A person who advocates the extension of suffrage
tariff Tax on imported goods
unicameral Consisting of a one-house legislature
urban That which constitutes a city
veto Rejection of a bill
whip Assistant to the party floor leader
zealots Fanatically committed people

Selected Bibliography

Aaseng, Nathan. *Famous Trials–The Impeachment of Bill Clinton.* Farmington Hills, MI: Lucent, 1999.

Aikman, Lonnelle. *We, the People: The Story of the United States Capitol.* Fifteenth edition. Washington, DC: United States Capitol Historical Society, 2002.

Amar, Akhil R. *The Bill of Rights: Creation and Reconstruction.* New Haven: Yale University Press, 1998.

Architect of the Capitol. http://www.aoc.gov/.

Arnold, R. Douglas. *Congress, the Press, and Political Accountability.* Princeton, NJ: Princeton University Press, 2004.

Baker, Ross K. *House and Senate.* Third edition. New York: Norton, 2000.

Barbash, Fred. *The Founding: A Dramatic Account of the Writing of the Constitution.* New York: Linden Press/Simon and Schuster, 1987.

Benedict, Michael Les. *The Impeachment and Trial of Andrew Johnson.* New York: W.W. Norton, 1999.

Bentley, Judith. *Speaker of the House.* London: Franklin Watts, 1994.

Bickford, Charlene Bangs, and Kenneth R. Bowling. *Birth of the Nation: The First Federal Congress, 1789–1791.* Washington, DC: First Federal Congress Project, George Washington University; New York: Second Circuit Committee on the Bicentennial of the United States Constitution, 1989.

Bisnow, Mark. *In the Shadow of the Dome: Chronicles of a Capitol Hill Aide.* New York: Morrow, 1990.

Brown, Glenn. *Glenn Brown's History of the United States Capitol.* Washington, DC: United States Congress, 2007.

Browne, William P. *Groups, Interests, and U.S. Public Policy.* Washington, DC: Georgetown University Press, 1998.

Busch, Andrew E. *Horses in Midstream: U.S. Midterm Elections and Their Consequences.* Pittsburgh, PA: University of Pittsburgh Press, 1999.

Butler, Anne M. and Wendy Wolff. *United States Senate: Election, Expulsion and Censure Cases, 1973–1990.* Collingdale, PA: Diane, 1998.

Chong, Dennis. *Collective Action and the Civil Rights Movement.* Chicago: University of Chicago Press, 1991.

Cigler, Allan J, and Burdett A. Loomis (editors). *Interest Group Politics.* Seventh edition. Washington, DC: CQ Press, 2006.

Cogliano, Frank. *Revolutionary America, 1763–1815: A Political History.* London: Routledge, 1999.

Cohen, Daniel. *Joseph McCarthy: The Misuse of Political Power.* Millbrook, 1996.

Cole, John Y. *Jefferson's Legacy: A Brief History of the Library of Congress.* Washington, DC: U.S. Government Printing Office, 1993.

Collier, Christopher, and James Lincoln Collier. *Decision in Philadelphia: The Constitutional Convention of 1787.* New York: Ballantine, 1986.

Congressional Quarterly. *Congressional Pay and Perquisites: History, Facts, and Controversy.* Washington, DC: CQ Press, 1992.

Crabb, Cecil V., Jr., and Pat M. Holt. *Invitation to Struggle: Congress, the President, and Foreign Policy.* Fourth edition. Washington, DC: CQ Press, 1992.

Davidson, Roger H., Walter Oleszek, and Frances E. Lee. *Congress and Its Members.*

Eleventh edition. Washington, DC: CQ Press, 2007.

Deering, Christopher J., and Steven S. Smith. *Committees in Congress.* Third edition. Washington, DC: CQ Press, 1997.

deKieffer, Donald E. *The Citizen's Guide to Lobbying Congress.* Chicago: Chicago Review, 2007.

Dodd, Lawrence C., and Bruce I. Oppenheimer, eds. *Congress Reconsidered.* Eighth edition. Washington, DC: CQ Press, 2004.

Donovan, Sandy. *Making Laws: A Look at How a Bill Becomes Law.* Minneapolis, MN: Lerner, 2003.

Drew, Elizabeth. *The Corruption of American Politics: What Went Wrong and Why.* New York: Birch Lane, 1999.

Duvall, Jill. *Congressional Committees.* London: Franklin Watts, 1997.

Emery, Fred. *Watergate.* New York: Touchstone, 1995.

Enciso, Carmen E., and Tracy North. *Hispanic Americans in Congress, 1822–1995.* Darby, PA: Diane, 1996.

Federal Register. http://www.archives.gov/federal-register/the-federal-register/about.html.

Feinberg, Barbara. *Articles of Confederation.* Minneapolis, MN: Lerner, 2002.

Fenno, Richard F. Jr. *Home Style: House Members in Their Districts.* Boston: Little, Brown, 2002.

Fox, Harrison W., Jr., and Susan Webb Hammond. *Congressional Staffs: The Invisible Force in American Lawmaking.* New York: Free Press, 1979.

Fritz, Sara, and Dwight Morris. *Gold-Plated Politics: Running for Congress in the 1990s.* Washington, DC: CQ Press, 1992.

Gammon, C.L. *The Continental Congress: America's Forgotten Government.* Frederick, MD: PublishAmerica, 2005.

Garrow, David J.. *Protest at Selma: Martin Luther King, Jr. and the Voting Rights Act of 1965.* New Haven, CT: Yale University Press, 1980.

Goodrum, Charles A., and Helen W. Dalrymple. *Treasures of the Library of Congress.* New York: Abrams, 1991.

Government Printing Office. http://www.gpo.gov/.

Green, Nancy L., and Francois Weil, eds. *Citizenship and Those Who Leave: The Politics of Emigration and Expatriation.* Eagan, MN: Thomson West, 2007.

Gutman, Howard. *America's Leaders–The Speaker of the House.* Chicago: Blackbirch, 2003.

Hamilton, James. *The Power to Probe: A Study of Congressional Investigations.* New York: Vintage Books, 1977.

Hasday, Judy L. *The Civil Rights Act of 1964: An End to Racial Segregation.* London: Chelsea House, 2007.

Herrnson, Paul S. *Congressional Elections: Campaigning at Home and in Washington.* Fifth edition. Washington, DC: CQ Press, 2007.

Hewson, Martha S. *The Electoral College.* New York: Chelsea House, 2002.

James Madison, *Notes of Debates in the Federal Convention of 1787* (Athens: Ohio University Press, 1966), 30.

Katz, William L. *Constitutional Amendments.* New York: Franklin Watts, 1974.

Kelly, Alfred H., Winfred A. Harbison, and Herman Belz. *The American Constitution: Its Origins and Development.* Seventh edition. New York: Norton, 1991.

Kimmel. Barbara, and Alan M. Lubiner. *Citizenship Made Simple: An Easy-to-Read Guide to the U.S. Citizenship Process.* Dallas: Next Decade, 2006.

Koestler-Grack, Rachel A. *The House of Representatives.* London: Chelsea House, 2007.

Krasno, Johnathan S. *Challengers, Competition, and Reelection: Comparing Senate and House Elections.* New Haven, CT: Yale University Press, 1997.

Levy, Peter B. *The Civil Rights Movement.* Westport, CT: Greenwood, 1998.

Library of Congress. http://www.loc.gov/index.html.

Mackaman, Frank H., editor. *Understanding Congressional Leadership.* Washington, DC: CQ Press, 1981.

Madison, James, Alexander Hamilton, and John Jay (authors), and Clinton Rossiter (editor). *The Federalist Papers.* New York: Signet Classics, 2003.

Mann, Thomas E., and Norman J. Ornstein. *The Broken Branch: How Congress Is Failing America and How to Get It Back On Track.* New York: Oxford University Press, 2006.

Mayhew, David R. *Divided We Govern: Party Control, Lawmaking, and Investigations, 1946–2002.* New Haven, CT: Yale University Press, 2005.

Melder, Keith E. *City of Magnificent Intentions: A History of Washington, District of Columbia.* Silver Spring, MD: Intac, 1997.

Monmonier, Mark. *Bushmanders and Bullwinkles: How Politicians Manipulate Electronic Maps and Census Data to Win Elections.* Chicago: University of Chicago Press, 2001.

National Archives and Record Administration. http://www.archives.gov/.

Newman, John J. *American Naturalization Processes and Procedures: 1790–1985.* Indianapolis: Indiana Historical Society, 1985.

Newman, Roger K., ed. *The Constitution and Its Amendments.* New York: Macmillan, 1999.

Nichols, John. *The Genius of Impeachment: The Founders' Cure for Royalism.* New York: New Press, 2006.

Nugent, Margaret L., and John R. Johannes. *Money, Elections, and Democracy: Reforming Congressional Campaign Finance.* Boulder: Westview, 1990.

Office of the Clerk, United States House of Representatives. http://clerk.house.gov/art_history/house_history/.

Onuf, Peter S., ed. *Ratifying, Amending, and Interpreting the Constitution.* New York: Garland, 1991.

Orfield, Lester B. *Amending the Federal Constitution.* New York: Da Capo, 1971.

Peterson, Paul E., ed. *The President, the Congress, and the Making of Foreign Policy.* Norman: University of Oklahoma Press, 1994.

Pollack, Jill S. *Women on the Hill: A History of Women in Congress.* London: Franklin Watts, 1996.

Powledge, Fred. *Free at Last? The Civil Rights Movement and the People Who Made It.* Little, Brown, 1991.

Pritchett, C. Herman. *The American Constitution.* Third edition. New York: McGraw-Hill, 1977.

Ranney, Austin. *Channels of Power: The Impact of Television on American Politics.* New York: Basic Books, 1985.

Rebman, Renee C. *The Articles of Confederation.* Compass Point, 2006.

Remini, Robert V. *The House: The History of the House of Representatives.* New York: HarperCollins, 2007.

Richards, Leonard L. *The Life and Times of Congressman John Quincy Adams.* New York: Oxford University Press, 1988.

Rosenthal, Alan. *The Third House: Lobbyists and Lobbying in the States.* Washington, DC: CQ Press, 2001.

Sachs, Richard C. *The President Pro Tempore of the Senate: History and Authority of the Office.* New York: Nova Science, 2003.

Sandak, Cass R. *Congressional Committees.* Minneapolis: Lerner, 1997.

Schulman, Bruce J., and Julian Zelizer (eds.) *Rightward Bound: Making America Conservative in the 1970s.* Cambridge, MA: Harvard University Press, 2008.

Schwab, Larry M. *The Impact of Congressional Reapportionment and Redistricting.* Lanham, MD: University Press of America, 1988.

Senate Historical Office. http://www.senate.gov/artandhistory/history/common/generic/Senate_Historical_Office.htm.

Sherrow, Victoria. *Joseph McCarthy and the Cold War.* Woodbridge, CT: Blackbirch, 2001.

Thomas (Library of Congress). http://thomas.loc.gov/.

United States Government Manual.http://www.archives.gov/federal-register/publications/government-manual.html.

United States House of Representatives. http://www.house.gov/.

United States Senate. http://www.senate.gov/.

U.S. Congress. *The Capitol: A Pictorial History.* Ninth edition. Washington, DC: Government Printing Office, 1988.

Vigil, Maurilio E. *Hispanics in Congress.* Lanham, MD: University Press of America, 1996.

Vose, Clement E. *Constitutional Change: Amendment Politics and Supreme Court Litigation since 1900.* Lexington, MA: Lexington, 1972.

Waldman, Stephen. *The Bill: How Legislation Really Becomes Law.* New York: Penguin, 1996.

Waldrup, Carole Chandler. *Vice Presidents: Biographies of the 45 Men Who Have Held the Second Highest Office in the United States.* Jefferson, NC: McFarland, 2006.

Watkins, Arthur V. *Enough Rope: The Story of the Censure of Senator Joe McCarthy.* Englewood Cliffs, NJ: Prentice-Hall, 1969.

Welborn, Angie. *House Contested Election Cases: 1933–2000.* New York: Novinka, 2003.

Wheelan. Joseph. *Mr. Adams Last Crusade: John Quincy Adams' Extraordinary Post-presidential Life in Congress.* Washington, DC: PublicAffairs. 2008.

Wicker, Tom. *Shooting Star: The Brief Arc of Joe McCarthy.* Orlando, FL: Harcourt 2006.

Wolpe, Bruce C., and Bertram J. Levine, *Lobbying Congress: How the System Works.* Second edition. Washington, DC: CQ Press, 1996.

Woodward, Bob and Carl Bernstein. *All the President's Men.* New York: Simon and Schuster, 1974.

Wright, James. *You and Your Congressman.* Revised edition. New York: Capricorn, 1976.

General Index

Note: Page numbers in ***bold italic*** type indicate main encyclopedia entries. Page numbers in *italic* type indicate illustrations, figures, tables, or maps. Page numbers in **bold** type refer to terms that are highlighted in **bold** in the text and also defined in the Glossary.

C

D

E

F

M

N

R

S